Harmony of the Law
Volume III
By John Calvin

Devoted Publishing

Ingersoll, Ontario, Canada 2018

Harmony of the Law - Volume III
By John Calvin (1509-1564)
This Edition Edited by Anthony Uyl
Commentaries on the Four Last Books of Moses Arranged in the Form of a Harmony
Translated from the Original Latin, and Compared with the French Edition, with Annotations, etc.
By the Rev. Charles William Bingham, M.A.,
Rector of Melcombe-Horsey, Dorset, and Formerly Fellow of New College, Oxford

What kind of philosophies do you have?
Let us know!

Visit our webpage: www.devotedpublishing.com
Contact us at: devotedpub@hotmail.com
Visit our shop on Facebook: Devoted Publishing

Published in Ingersoll, Ontario, Canada 2018.

For bulk educational rates, please contact us at the above email address.

ISBN: 978-1-77356-291-9

Table of Contents

THE SECOND TABLE OF THE LAW - THE FIRST COMMANDMENT OF WHICH IS THE FIFTH OF THE LAW

The Fifth Commandment - EXODUS 20

Exodus 20:12

12. Honor thy father and thy mother; that thy days may be long upon the land which the Lord thy God giveth thee.

12. Honora patrem tuum et matrem tuam-- ut prorogentur dies tui super terram quam Jehova Deus tuus dat tibi.

ITS REPETITION DEUTERONOMY 5

Deuteronomy 5:16

16. Honor thy father and thy mother, as the Lord thy God hath commanded thee; that thy days may be prolonged, and that it may go well with thee, in the land which the Lord thy God giveth thee.

16. Honora patrem tuum et matrem tuam, quemadmodum praecepit tibi Jehova, Deus tuus: ut prorogentur dies tui et ut bene sit tibi super terram quam Jehova Deus tuus dat tibi.

I am not ignorant that the Tables of the Law are usually divided in a different manner; [1] for those, who make only one of the first two Commandments, are obliged finally to mangle the last. Thus the prohibition of God to covet either our neighbor's wife or his house, is foolishly separated into two parts, whereas it is quite clear that only one thing is treated of, as we gather from the words of Paul, who quotes them as a single Commandment. (Romans 7:7.) There is, however, no need of a lengthened discussion here, since the fact itself explains how one error has grown out of another; for, when they had improperly hidden the Second Commandment under the First, and consequently did not find the right number, they were forced to divide into two parts what was one and indivisible. A frivolous reason is assigned by Augustine why they comprised the First Table in three commandments, viz., that believers might learn to worship God in the Trinity, and thus to adore one God in three persons. By inconsiderately trifling with such subtleties, they have exposed God's law to the mockeries of the ungodly. Josephus [2] indeed rightly enumerates the Commandments themselves in their proper order, but improperly attributes five Commandments to each Table; as if God had had regard to arithmetic rather than to instruct His people separately in the duties of charity, after having laid down for them the rules of piety. For up to this point the rule of rightly serving God has been delivered, i.e., the First Table embraces a summary of piety; and now the Law will begin to show how men ought to live with each other, otherwise one Table would have been enough, nor would God have divided his Law without a purpose. But whereas piety [3] and justice comprise the perfect rule for the direction of our lives, it was necessary to distinguish these two parts, that the people might understand the object of the Law, of which we shall again speak hereafter.

Exodus 20:12. Honor thy father Although charity (as being "the bond of perfectness," Colossians 3:14) contains the sum of the Second Table, still, mutual obligation does not prevent either parents or others, who are in authority, from retaining their proper position. Nay, human society cannot be maintained in its integrity, unless children modestly submit themselves to their parents, and unless those, who are set over others by God's ordinance, are even reverently honored. But inasmuch as the reverence which children pay to their parents is accounted a sort of piety, some have therefore foolishly placed this precept in the First Table. Nor are they supported in this by Paul, though he does not enumerate this Commandment, where he collects the sum of the Second Table, (Romans 13:9;) for he does this designedly, because he is there expressly teaching that obedience is to be paid to the authority of kings and magistrates. Christ, however, puts an end to the whole controversy, where, among the precepts of the Second Table, He enumerates this, that children should honor their parents. (Matthew 19:19.)

The name of the mothers is expressly introduced, lest their sex should render them contemptible to their male children.

It will be now well to ascertain what is the force of the word "honor," not as to its grammatical meaning, (for כבד, cabad, is nothing else but to pay due honor to God, and to men who are in authority,) but as to its essential signification. Surely, since God would not have His servants comply with external ceremonies only, it cannot be doubted but that all the duties of piety towards parents are here comprised, to which children are laid under obligation by natural reason itself; and these may be reduced to three heads, i e., that they should regard them with reverence; that they should obediently comply with their commands, and allow themselves to be governed by them; and that they should endeavor to repay what they owe to them, and thus heartily devote to them themselves and their services. Since, therefore, the name of Father is a sacred one, and is transferred to men by the peculiar goodness of God, the dishonoring of parents redounds to the dishonor of God Himself, nor can any one despise his father without being guilty of an offense against God, (sacrilegium.) If any should object that there are many ungodly and wicked fathers whom their children cannot regard with honor without destroying the distinction between good and evil, the reply is easy, that the perpetual law of nature is not subverted by the sins of men; and therefore, however unworthy of honor a father may be, that he still retains, inasmuch as he is a father, his right over his children, provided it does not in anywise derogate from the judgment of God; for it is too absurd to think of absolving under any pretext the sins which are condemned by His Law; nay, it would be a base profanation to misuse the name of father for the covering of sins. In condemning, therefore, the vices of a father, a truly pious son will subscribe to God's Law; and still, whatsoever he may be, will acknowledge that he is to be honored, as being the father given him by God.

Obedience comes next, which is also circumscribed by certain limits. Paul is a faithful interpreter of this Commandment, where he bids "children obey their parents." (Ephesians 6:1; Colossians 3:20.) Honor, therefore, comprises subjection; so that he who shakes off the yoke of his father, and does not allow himself to be governed by his authority, is justly said to despise his father; and it will more clearly appear from other passages, that those who are not obedient to their parents are deemed to despise them. Still, the power of a father is so limited as that God, on whom all relationships depend, should have the rule over fathers as well as children; for parents govern their children only under the supreme authority of God. Paul, therefore, does not simply exhort children to obey their parents, but adds the restriction, "in the Lord;" whereby he indicates that, if a father enjoins anything unrighteous, obedience is freely to be denied him. Immoderate strictness, moroseness, and even cruelty must be born, so long as a mortal man, by wickedly demanding what is not lawful, does not endeavor to rob God of His right. In a word, the Law so subjects children to their parents, as that God's right may remain uninfringed. An objection here arises in the shape of this question: It may sometimes happen that a son may hold the office of a magistrate, but that the father may be a private person, and that thus the son cannot discharge his private duty without violating public order. The point is easily solved: that all things may be so tempered by their mutual moderation as that, whilst the father submits himself to the government of his son, [4] yet he may not be at all defrauded of his honor, and that the son, although his superior in power, may still modestly reverence his father.

The third head of honor is, that children should take care of their parents, and be ready and diligent in all their duties towards them. This kind of piety the Greeks call ἀντιπελαργία, [5] because storks supply food to their parents when they are feeble and worn out with old age, and are thus our instructors in gratitude. Hence the barbarity of those is all the more base and detestable, who either grudge or neglect to relieve the poverty of their parents, and to aid their necessities.

Now, although the parental name ought, by its own sweetness, sufficiently to attract children to ready submission, still a promise is added as a stimulus, in order that they may more cheerfully bestir themselves to pay the honor which is enjoined upon them. Paul, therefore, that children may be more willing to obey their parents, reminds us that this "is the first commandment with promise," (Ephesians 6:2;) for although a promise is annexed to the Second Commandment, yet it is not a special one, as we perceive this to be. The reward, that the days of children who have behaved themselves piously to their parents shall be prolonged, aptly corresponds with the observance of the commandment, since in this manner God gives us a proof of His favor in this life, when we have been grateful to those to whom we are indebted for it; whilst it is by no means just that they should greatly prolong their life who despise those progenitors by whom they have been brought into it. Here the question arises, since this earthly life is exposed to so many cares, and pains, and troubles, how can God account its prolongation to be a blessing? But whereas all cares spring from the curse of God, it is manifest that they are accidental; and thus, if life be regarded in itself, it does not cease to be a proof of God's favor. Besides, all this multitude of miseries does not destroy the chief blessing of life, viz., that men are created and preserved unto the hope of a happy immortality; for God now manifests Himself to them as a Father, that hereafter they may enjoy His eternal inheritance. The knowledge of this, like a lighted lamp, causes God's grace to shine forth in the midst of darkness. Whence it follows, that those had not tasted the main thing in life, [6] who have said that the best thing was not to be born, and the next best thing to be cut off as soon as possible; whereas God rather so exercises men by various afflictions, as that it should be good for them nevertheless to be created in His image, and to be accounted His children. A clearer explanation also is added in Deuteronomy, not only that they should live, but that it may go well with them; so that not only is length of life promised them, but other accessories also. And in fact, many who have been ungrateful and unkind to their parents only prolong their life as a punishment, whilst the reward of their inhuman conduct is repaid them by their children and descendants. But inasmuch as long life is not vouchsafed to all who have discharged the duties of piety towards their parents, it must be remembered that, with respect to temporal rewards, an infallible law is by no means laid down; and still, where God works variously and unequally, His promises are not made void, because a better compensation is secured in heaven for believers, who have been deprived on earth of transitory blessings. Truly experience in all ages has shown that God has not in vain promised long life to all who have faithfully discharged the duties of true piety towards their parents. Still, from the principle already stated, it is to be understood that this Commandment extends further than the words imply; and this we infer from the following sound argument, viz., that otherwise God's Law would be imperfect, and would not instruct us in the perfect rule of a just and holy life.

The natural sense itself dictates to us that we should obey rulers. If servants obey not their masters, the society of the human race is subverted altogether. It is not, therefore, the least essential part of righteousness [7] that the people should willingly submit themselves to the command of magistrates, and that servants should obey their masters; and, consequently, it would be very absurd if it were omitted in the Law of God. In this commandment, then, as in the others, God by synecdoche embraces, under a specific rule, a general principle, viz., that lawful commands should obtain due reverence from us. But that all things should not be distinctly expressed, first of all brevity itself readily accounts for; and, besides, another reason is to be noticed, i.e. that God designedly used a homely style in addressing a rude people, because He saw its expediency. If He had said generally, that all superiors were to be obeyed, since, pride is natural to all, it would not have been easy to incline the greater part of men to pay submission to a few. Nay, since subjection is naturally disagreeable, many would have kicked against it. God, therefore, propounds a specific kind of subjection, which it would have been gross barbarism to refuse, that thus, their ferocity being gradually subdued, He might accustom men to bear the yoke. Hence the exhortations are derived, that people should "honor the king;" that "every soul should be subject unto the higher powers;" that "servants should obey their masters, even the froward and morose." (Proverbs 24:21; 1 Peter 2:13; Romans 13:1; Ephesians 6:5; 1 Peter 2:14, 18.)

The Exposition of the Commandment - Leviticus 19

Leviticus 19:3

3. Ye shall fear every man his mother and his father.

3. Unusquisque patrem suum et matrem suam timeat.

Since this passage unquestionably relates to the explanation of the Fifth Commandment, it confirms what I have before shown, that the honor which God-commands to be paid to parents, does not consist in reverence only, but also embraces obedience. For the reverence which He now prescribes will render children submissive and compliant. Now, then, we more clearly understand how parents are to be honored, when God exhorts their children to beware of offending them; for this is, in a word, the true manifestation of filial piety, calmly to bear the yoke of subjection, and to prove by acts a sincere desire to obey.

The Supplements of the Fifth Commandment - Exodus 21

Exodus 21:15, 17

15. And he that smiteth his father or his mother shall be surely put to death.

15. Qui percusserit patrem suum aut matrem, morte moriatur.

17. And he that curseth his father or his mother shall surely be put to death.

17. Qui maledixerit patri suo vel matri suae, morte moriatur.

Leviticus 20

Leviticus 20:9

9. For every one that curseth his father or his mother shall be surely put to death: he hath cursed his father or his mother; his blood shall be upon him.

9. Qui maledixerit patri suo aut matri suae morte moriatur: qui patri suo et matri suae maledixit, sanguis ejus super eum.

The commandment is now sanctioned by the denunciation of capital punishment for its violation, yet not so as to comprehend all who have in any respect sinned against their parents, but sufficient to show that the rights of parents are sacred, and not to be violated without the greatest criminality. We know that parricides [8] as being the most detestable of all men, were formerly sewn up in a leathern sack and cast into the water; but God proceeds further, when He commands all those to be exterminated who have laid violent hands on their parents [9] or addressed them in abusive language. For to smite does not only mean to kill, but refers to any violence, although no wound may have been inflicted. If, then, any one had struck his father or mother with his fist, or with a stick, the punishment of such an act of madness was the same as for murder. And, assuredly, it is an abominable and monstrous thing for a son not to hesitate to assault those from whom he has received his life; nor can it be but that impunity accorded to so foul a crime must straightway produce cruel barbarism. The second law avenges not only violence done to parents, but also, abusive words, which soon proceed to grosser insults and atrocious contempt. Still, if any one should have lightly let drop some slight reproach, as is often the case ill a quarrel, this severe punishment was not to be inflicted upon such, all inconsiderate piece of impertinence: and the word קלל, kalal, from which the participle used by Moses is derived, not only means to reproach, but also to curse, as well as to esteem lightly, and to despise. Whilst, therefore, not every insult, whereby the reverence due to parents was violated, received the punishment of death, still God would have that impious pride, which would subvert the first principles of nature, held in abhorrence. But, inasmuch as it might seem hard that a word, [10] however unworthy of a dutiful son, should be the cause of death; this objection is met, by what is added by God in Leviticus, "his blood shall be upon him, because he hath cursed his father or mother:" as if He would put a stop to what men might otherwise presume to allege in mitigation of the severity of the punishment.

Deuteronomy 21

Deuteronomy 21:18-21

18. If a man have a stubborn and rebellious son, which will not obey the voice of his father, or the voice of his mother, and that, when they have chastened him, will not hearken unto them;

18. Quum quis habuerit filium perversum et rebellem, non obedientem voci patris sui et matris suae, et castigaverint illum, nec paruerit illis:

19. Then shall his father and his mother lay hold on him, and bring him out unto the elders of his city, and unto the gate of his place:

19. Tum apprehendent cum pater eius et mater eius, educentque ad seniores urbis suae et portam loci sui:

20. And they shall say unto the elders of his city, This our son is stubborn and rebellious, he will not obey our voice; he is a glutton and a drunkard.

20. Dicentque senioribus urbis, Filius iste noster perversus et rebellis est, non obediens voci nostrae, epulo est ac comessator.

21. And all the men of his city shall stone him with stones, that he die: so shalt thou put evil away from among you; and all Israel shall hear, and fear.

21. Tunc lapidabunt eum omnes homines urbis suae lapidibus, et morietur: atque ita auferes malum e medio tui, universusque Israel audiet, et timebit.

18. **If a man have a stubborn.** What God had previously adverted to in two clauses, tie now embraces in a general law, for it cannot be doubted but that by rebellious children all are designated who are abusive or insulting to their father and mother. For if it be a capital crime to be disobedient to parents, much more is it to strike, or beat them, and to assail them with reproachful words. In sum, Moses declares that those are deserving of death who are of such a stubborn

and intractable disposition as to reject the authority of their father and mother, and to hold them in contempt. Whence also we infer what it is to honor our father and mother, for the punishment is only denounced for the transgression of the Commandment. When, therefore, the law delivers over to death all who contumaciously rebel against the discipline of their parents, it follows that they have refused them their due honor. An admirable means, however, of moderating the severity of the law is introduced, when God requires the case to be decided on the evidence of the father and mother; and commands that it should be publicly heard, so that none may be condemned at the will of private individuals. By the Roman law the power of life and death over his children [11] was given to the father, because it was not probable that fathers would be carried away by such senseless inhumanity as to deal cruelly with their own bowels; but, since sometimes fathers are found who are not unlike wild beasts, and examples show us that many, blinded by hate or avarice, have not spared their own children, this concession of the Roman law is justly to be repudiated. I allow, indeed, that those who desired to inflict punishment on their children called their friends into council; but, whereas, the walls of a private dwelling conceal many disgraceful things, God imposed a much better restraint on parents when He did not suffer them to go further than to lay the information and to give their testimony. For, although he would have credit given to their testimony, still, when the children were brought to the tribunal of the judges, a legal trim undoubtedly ensued; and this form of proceeding is prescribed, viz., that the father and mother should bring their son and make their complaint before the judges of his incorrigible stubbornness. It is true that the sentence is immediately subjoined; yet we must infer, nevertheless, that the judges pronounced it before the criminal was stoned, else it would have been ridiculous that they should sit there like cyphers. The very mention of a trial, therefore, implies that the son was heard in his defense, so as to clear himself of the crime, if he was not guilty of it: for, suppose the moroseness of the father and mother were notorious; or that the father accused the son by the instigation of a stepmother; or that any unworthy spite were discovered; or that the father and mother had conspired to destroy their son in a fit of passion: the defense of the cause is, therefore, implied in the adverb then, [12] for it would have been more than absurd that the son should be condemned without being heard. Especially, when he was to be stoned by the whole people, it was necessary that he should be first convicted; and on this ground he was brought forth publicly, that he might be allowed to plead his cause. But although those were condemned who were addicted to other vices also, yet Moses expressly mentions gluttons and drunkards, to show that, although no capital crime were alleged, still, dissolute profligacy was sufficient, if the son could not be corrected by his parents; for it is plain that those are in a desperate state who have so east away submissiveness and shame as to receive no profit from the admonitions of their parents. From the end of the verse we gather what was the twofold object of the punishment -- that the earth should be purged of the sins whereby it was in a manner, polluted, and that the death of him who had transgressed might be an example to all.

Exodus 22

Exodus 22:28
28. Thou shalt not revile the gods, nor curse the ruler of thy people.
28. Diis non detrahes, et principi populi tui non maledices.

Deuteronomy 20

Deuteronomy 20:9
9. And it shall be, when the officers have made an end of speaking unto the people, that they shall make captains of the armies to lead the people.

9. Quum finem fecerint praefecti militares loquendi ad populum, constituent principes turmarum in capite populi.

Exodus 22:28. Thou shalt not revile the gods. These four passages confirm what I have said, that in the: Fifth Commandment are comprised, by synecdoche all superiors in authority.: For it was not the design of God to add to the Two Tables, as if something better and more perfect had afterwards come into His mind; which it is sinful to suppose. He was therefore content with the rule once laid down, although He afterwards spoke in a more explanatory manner. But the precepts here given would be unconnected with the Law, if they were not an adjunct, and therefore a part, of the Fifth Commandment.

First of all, He commands that we should think and speak reverently of judges, and others, who exercise the office of magistrate: nor is it to be questioned, that, in the ordinary idiom of the Hebrew language, He repeats the same thing twice over; and consequently that the same persons are called "gods," and "rulers of the people." The name of God is, figuratively indeed, but most reasonably, applied to magistrates, upon whom, as the ministers of His authority, He has inscribed a mark of His glory. For, as we have seen that honor is due to fathers, because God has associated them with Himself in the possession of the name, so also here His own dignity is claimed for judges, in order that the people may reverence them, because they are God's representatives, as His lieutenants, and vicars. And so Christ, the surest expositor, explains it, when He quotes the passage from Psalm 82:6, "I have said, Ye are gods, and all of you are children of the Most High," (John 10:34,) viz., "that they are called gods, unto whom the word of God came," which is to be understood not of the general instruction addressed to all God's children, but of the special command to rule.

It is a signal exaltation of magistrates, that God should not only count them in the place of parents, but present them to us dignified by His own name; whence also it clearly appears that they are not to be obeyed only from fear of punishment, "but also for conscience sake," (Romans 13:5,) and to be reverently honored, lest God should be despised in them. If any should object, that it would be wrong to praise the vices of those whom we perceive to abuse their power; the answer is easy, that although judges are to be borne with even if they be not the best, [13] still that the honor with which they are invested, is not a covering for vice. Nor does God command us to applaud their faults, but that the people should rather deplore them in silent sorrow, than raise disturbances in a licentious and seditious spirit, and so subvert political government.

Leviticus 19

Leviticus 19:32

32. Thou shalt rise up before the hoary head, and honor the face of the old man, and fear thy God: I am the Lord.

32. Ante canitiem assurge, et honora faciem senis, metueque Deum tuum: ego Jehova.

32. Thou shalt rise up before the hoary head. God teaches us that some sparks of His majesty shine forth in old men, whereby they approach to the honor of parents. It is not my purpose to gather quotations from profane authors in reference to the honor due to the old; let it suffice that what God here commands is dictated by nature itself. This appeared at Athens, [14] when an old man had come into the theater, and found no place among his fellow-citizens; but, when at length he was admitted with honor by the Spartan ambassador, (because old age is greatly reverenced among the Lacedemonians,) applause was raised on all sides; and then the Lacedemonian exclaimed, that "the Athenians knew what was right, but would not do it." It was surely manifested by this universal consent of the people that it is a natural law in the hearts of all to reverence and honor old men. Many old men, indeed, either by their levity, or lewdness, or sloth, subvert their own dignity; yet, although gray hairs may not always be accompanied by courteous wisdom, still, in itself, age is venerable, according to God's command.

Deuteronomy 16

Deuteronomy 16:18

18. Judges and officers shalt thou make thee in all thy gates, which the Lord thy God giveth thee, throughout thy tribes: and they shall judge the people with just judgment.

18. Judices et praefectos constitues tibi intra omnes portas tuas quas Jehova Deus tuus dabit tibi per tribus tuas, qui judicent populum judicio justitiae, hoc est recto.

18. Judges and officers shalt thou make. I have placed this passage among the Supplements of the Fifth Commandment, for, if it pleases God that judges should be appointed for ruling the people, it follows that their laws and edicts should be obeyed; and thus the parental authority extends also to them. But, in order that the people may more readily submit themselves to judges, God reminds them that the human race could not otherwise be preserved. Public utility, therefore, renders the authority of magistrates pleasant and agreeable, though it would else be hateful. But, although it be not conceded to all to elect their judges, because God honored His chosen people with this prerogative, still he here recommends in general a regular government, since He signifies that human society cannot hold together unless the lawful rulers have authority to

execute justice. Whether, then, magistrates are appointed by the suffrages of the people, or imposed in any other way, let us learn that they are the necessary ministers of God, to confine all men under the yoke of the laws. The latter passage, which I have annexed from Deuteronomy 7, refers to the same thing, viz., that even in war discipline is necessary, lest all things should be thrown into confusion. Now, if it pleases God that certain superior officers should have the command, it follows that they must be obeyed; for it would be ridiculous to appoint governors, if it were lawful to despise them with impunity. When, therefore, God sets military commanders over the people, He enforces the duty of humble submission.

Footnotes:

1. See Becon's Catechism, part 3, (Parker Society's edition,) p. 60, et seq. See also Bullinger's Decades, (Parker Society,) vol. 1, p. 212; and Hooper's Early Writings, (Parker Society,) pages 349-351; and Calvin's Institutes, lib. 2. cap. 8, Section 12. It appears that this error may be traced to Augustine, (Quaest. in Exodus 71, and Ep. ad. Jan. 119,) who, without omitting the Second Commandment, divided the precepts of the First Table into three, on the supposition that their number was allusive to the Trinity. He, however, contradicts himself elsewhere, (Quaest. Vet. et Novi Test., lib. 1:7;) but Peter Lomb. adopts his erroneous division, and separates the Tenth Commandment into two parts. (Lib. 3, Distinct. 37 and 40.)

2. See Jewish Antiq., book 3. chap. 5. Section 5. In sect. 8 it is added: "When he had said this he showed them two tables, with the ten commandments engraven upon them, five upon each table; and the writing was by the hand of God."

3. "La piete que nous devons a Dieu, et l'equite que nous devons a nos prochains;" the piety which we owe to God, and the equity which we owe to our neighbors. -- Fr.

4. There is a delightful illustration of this point, which will

occur to many, related in More's Life of Sir Thomas More, ch. 6. Section 5, -- "Now it was a comfortable thing for ante man to behold how two great rooms of Westminster-hall were taken up, one with the son, the other with the father, which hath as yet never been heard of before or since, the son to be Lord Chancellor, and the father, Sir John More, to be one of the ancientest Judges of the King's Bench, if not the eldest of all; for now he was near 90 year old. Yea, what a grateful spectacle was it, to see the son ask the father's blessing every day upon his knees, before he sat in his own seat, a thing expressing rare humility, exemplar obedience, and submissive piety."

5. "Let us consider what is meant by the Gentiles' ἀντιπελαργεῖν, which is to requite one good turn with another; and especially to nourish and cherish them, by whom thou thyself in thy youth was brought up and tendered. There is among the Gentiles a law extant, worthy to be called the mistress of piety, whereby it is enacted that the children should either nourish their parents or else lie fast lettered in prison. This law many men do carelessly neglect, which the stork alone, among all living creatures, doth keep most precisely. For other

creatures do hard, and scarcely know or look upon their parents, if peradventure they need their aid to nourish them; whereas the stork doth mutually nourish them, being stricken in age, and bear them on her shoulders, when for feebleness they cannot fly." -- Bullinger's Second Decade, Serm. 5, Parker Society's edit., vol. 1, p. 272. See also Hooper's Early Writings, Parker Society's edit., p. 359. "Follow the nature of the cicone, that in her youth nourisheth the old days of her parents." -- Plin., lib. 10 cap. 23, Nat. Hist. The Fr. concludes the sentence thus: "et ainsi nous sont comme maistresses pour nous apprendre a recognoistre le bien que nous avons receu de ceux qui nous ont mis au monde et elevez;" and so are, as it were, our mistresses to teach us to repay the benefits of those who have brought us into the world and reared us.

6. This famous sentiment of antiquity is found in the Elegies of Theognis, some 500 years B.C., -- Pa>ntwn me<n mh< fu~nai ejpicqoni>oisin a]riston, Mhd j ejsidei~n aujgav ojxe>ov hjeli>v. Fu>nta d j o[pwv w]kiva pu>lav aji`>daw perh~sai Kai< kei+sqai pollh<n gh~n ejpamhsa>menon. -- 425-428. It is also reported by Plutarch, in his Παραμυθητικὸς προς Απολλώνιον, by whom, as well as by Cicero, it is called the reply of Silenus to Midas, -- "Affertur etiam de Sileno fabella quaedam: qui cum a Mida captus esset, hoc ei muneris pro sua missione dedisse scribitur: docuisse regem, non nasci homini longe optimum esse; proximum autem, quamprimum mori." -- Tusc Quaest. 1:48. "Ex quo intelligi licet, non nasci longe optimum

esse, nec in hos scopulos incidere vitae; proximum autem, si natus sis, quamprimum mori, et tanquam ex incendio effugere fortunae. Sileni quae fertur fabula, etc." -- Consolatio. Lactantius refers to the latter passage, De falsa sapientia, Section 19. "Hinc nata est inepta illa sententia, etc."

7. "Pars justiciae non postrema." -- Lat. "Une partie de la justice, qui nous devons tous garder;" a part of righteousness which we ought all to observe. -- Fr.

8. By the Roman law parricides were sewn up in a leathern sack with a dog, a cock, a viper, and a monkey, and east into the sea, or the nearest river. -- Vide Cicero pro Rose. Amer., 2:25, 26.

9. "Ceux qui auront outrage pere ou mere, soit de faict, soit de parole;" those who shall have outraged father or mother either by act or word. -- Fr.

10. "Une injure verbale;" a verbal injury. -- Fr.

11. "A father among the Romans had the power of life and death over his children. He could not only expose them when infants, but, even when his children were grown up, he might imprison, scourge, send them bound to work in the country, and also put them to death by any punishment he pleased, if they deserved it. Sall. Cat., 39.; Liv., 2:41; 8:7; Dionys., 8:79." -- Adam's Rom. Antiq.

12. The particle v sometimes has this force, but is here translated in A V and

13. "Encore qu'ils ne sont pas tels qu'ils devroyent;" even though they be not what they should. -- Fr.

14. Cicero, de Senectute, 18; and Val. Max., lib. 4:5.

The Sixth Commandment - Exodus 20

Exodus 20:13

13. Thou shalt not kill.

13. Non occides.

THE REPETITION OF THE SAME COMMANDMENT - Deuteronomy 5

Deuteronomy 5:17

17. Thou shalt not kill.

17. Non occides.

The sum of this Commandment is, that we should not unjustly do violence to any one. In order, however, that God may the better restrain us from all injury of others, He propounds one particular form of it, from which men's natural sense is abhorrent; for we all detest murder, so as to recoil from those whose hands are polluted with blood, as if they carried contagion with them. Undoubtedly God would have the remains of His image, which still shine forth in men, to continue in some estimation, so that all might feel that every homicide is an offense against Him, (sacrilegium.) He does not, indeed, here express the reason, whereby He elsewhere deters men from murder, i e., by asserting that thus His image is violated, (Genesis 9:6;) yet, however precisely and authoritatively He may speak as a Legislator, He would still have us consider, what might naturally occur to everybody's mind, such as the statement of Isaiah 58:7, that man is our "own flesh." In order, then, that believers may more diligently beware of inflicting injuries, He condemns a crime, which all spontaneously confess to be insufferable. It will, however, more clearly appear hereafter, that under the word kill is included by synecdoche all violence, smiting, and aggression. Besides, another principle is also to be remembered, that in negative precepts, as they are called, the opposite affirmation is also to be understood; else it would not be by any means consistent, that a person would satisfy God's Law by merely abstaining from doing injury to others. Suppose, for example, that one of a cowardly disposition, and not daring to assail even a child, should not move a finger to injure his neighbors, would he therefore have discharged the duties of humanity as regards the Sixth Commandment? Nay, natural common sense demands more than that we should abstain from wrongdoing. And, not to say more on this point, it will plainly appear from the summary of the Second Table, that God not only forbids us to be murderers, but also prescribes that every one should study faithfully to defend the life of his neighbor, and practically to declare that it is dear to him; for in that summary no mere negative phrase is used, but the words expressly set forth that our neighbors are to be loved. It is unquestionable, then, that of those whom God there commands to be loved, He here commends the lives to our care. There are, consequently, two parts in the Commandment, -- first, that we should not vex, or oppress, or be at enmity with any; and, secondly, that we should not only live at peace with men, without exciting quarrels, but also should aid, as far as we can, the miserable who are unjustly oppressed, and should endeavor to resist the wicked, lest they should injure men as they list. Christ, therefore, in expounding the genuine sense of the Law, not only pronounces those transgressors who have committed murder, but also that

"he shall be in danger of the judgment who is angry with his brother without a cause; and whosoever shall say to his brother, Raca, shall be in danger of the council; but whosoever shall say, Thou fool, shall be in danger of hell-fire." (Matthew 5:22.)

For He does not there, as some have ignorantly supposed, frame t~ new law, as if to east blame upon His Father; but shows the folly and perversity of those interpreters of the Law who only insist on the external appearance, and husk of things, as is vulgarly said; since the doctrine of God must rather be estimated from a due consideration of. His nature. Before earthly judges, if a man have carried a weapon for the purpose of killing a man, he is found guilty of violence; and God, who is a spiritual Lawgiver, goes even further. With Him, therefore, anger is accounted murder; yea, inasmuch as He pierces even to the most secret feelings, He holds even concealed hatred to be murder; for so we must understand John's words, "Whosoever hateth his brother is a murderer," (1 John 3:15;) i.e., hatred conceived in the heart is sufficient for his condemnation, although it may not openly appear.

The Exposition of the Commandment - Leviticus 19

Leviticus 19:17

17. Thou shalt not hate thy brother in thine heart.
17. Ne oderis fratrem tuum in corde tuo.

I doubt not but that this part of the verse should be taken separately, nor do I approve of the introduction of the adversative particle but, by which translators [15] connect it with what follows. We know that we are not always to trust to the division of verses; and, since it is clear that whatever precepts we meet with in the writings of Moses for the regulation of our lives depend on the Decalogue, this sentence sufficiently proves that murder was forbidden, not only in order that none should slay his brother by his]land, or by a weapon, but also that he should not indulge in wrong-doing, by cherishing in himself hatred and ill-will. Hence the statement of Paul is confirmed, that "the Law is spiritual," (Romans 7:14;) and their folly is refuted who pretend that Moses was an earthly lawgiver to the Jews, like Lycurgus or Solon, since he thus penetrates even to the secret affections. It is also probable that John derived from this passage his saying, "He that hateth his brother is a murderer," (1 John

3:15;) for the word heart is here used emphatically; since, although no outward signs of hatred may appear, yet the internal feeling is accounted murder before God.

Leviticus 19

Leviticus 19:18

18. Thou shalt not avenge, nor bear any grudge against the children of thy people; but thou shalt love thy neighbor as thyself: I am the Lord.

18. Ne ulciscaris te, neque serves odium contra filios populi tui: sed diliges proximum tuum sicut teipsum: ego Jehova.

Hence it clearly appears that God had a further object than that men should not kill each other, for He not only restrains their hands, but requires their hearts to be pure from all hatred. For, since the desire of vengeance is the fountain and cause of enmities, it follows that under the word kill is condensed whatever is opposed to brotherly love. And this is confirmed by the antithesis, that none should hate his brother, but rather love him as himself. We need, then, seek for no other expositor of the Commandment but God Himself, who pronounces those to be guilty of murder who are affected with any malevolence, and not only those who, when offended, desire to return evil for evil, but those who do not sincerely love their neighbors, even when with justice they deem them to be their enemies. Wherefore, in order that God may absolve us from spiritual murder, let us learn to purify our hearts from all desire of vengeance, and, laying aside hatred, to cultivate fraternal affection with all men.

Although the latter part of the verse embraces the sum of the whole Second Table, yet, because love is contrasted with vengeance, I have not thought fit to separate things which are so properly connected with each other, especially when one depends on the other. The precept is indeed only given with reference to the children of Abraham, because the crime of vengeance would be more atrocious between those who were bound together by fraternal rights; yet it is not to be doubted but that God generally condemns the vice. In the schools [16] this sentence was grossly corrupted; for, since the rule (as they say) is superior to what is regulated by it. they have invented a preposterous precept, that every one should love himself first, and then his neighbors; of which subject I will treat more fully elsewhere. The word נטר, natar, meaning to guard, when used without any addition, is equivalent to bearing an injury in mind; as we also say in French: "garder une injure." [17]

Leviticus 19

Leviticus 19:14

14. Thou shalt not curse the deaf, nor put a stumblingblock before the blind, but shalt fear thy God: I am the Lord.

14. Surdo non maledices, et coram caeco non pones offendiculum, sed timebis a Deo tuo: ego Jehova.

Since the Law comprehends under the word murder, all the wrongs whereby men are unjustly injured, that cruelty was especially to be condemned by which those wretched persons are afflicted, whose calamity ought rather to conciliate our compassion. For, if any particle of humanity exists in us, when we meet a blind man we shall be solicitous lest he should stumble or fall, and, if he goes astray, we shall stretch out our hands to him and try to bring him back into the way; we shall also spare the deaf, for to insult them is no less absurd or barbarous than to assail stones with reproaches. It is, therefore, gross brutality to increase the ills of those whom our natural sense impels us to relieve, and who are already troubled more than enough. Let us, then, learn from these words, that the weaker people are, the more secure ought they to be from all oppression or injury, and that, when we attack the defenseless, the crime of cruelty is greatly aggravated, whilst any insult against the calamitous is altogether intolerable to God.

The Ceremonial Supplements of the Sixth Commandment - Deuteronomy 21

Deuteronomy 21:1-9

1. If one be found slain in the land which the Lord thy God giveth thee to possess it, lying in the field, and it be not known who hath slain him;

1. Quum inventum fuerit cadaver hominis occisi in terra quam Jehova Deus tuus dabit tibi ut possideas eam, prostratum in agro, nec cognitum fuerit quis percusserit eum:

2. Then thy elders and thy judges shall come forth, and they shall measure unto the cities which are round about him that is slain.

2. Tunc egredientur seniores tui, et judices tui, et metientur usque ad civitates quae sunt in circuitibus cadaveris hominis illius occisi.

3. And it shall be, that the city which is next unto the slain man, even the elders of that city shall take an heifer, which hath not been wrought with, and which hath not drawn in the yoke;

3. Et seniores urbis, propinquioris urbis illi cadaveri occiso, capient vitulam de armento qua nemo usus fuerit, et quae non traxerit jugum.

4. And the elders of that city shall bring down the heifer unto a rough valley, which is neither card nor sown, and shall strike off the heifer's neck there in the valley:

4. Et adducent seniores ejus urbis vitulam ad vallem asperare, quae nunquam fuerit arata, neque seminata, et praecident cervicem vitulae illic in valle.

5. And the priests, the sons of Levi, shall come near; (for them the Lord thy God hath chosen to minister unto him, and to bless in the name of the Lord;) and by their word shall every controversy and every stroke be tried

5. Et accedent sacerdotes filii Levi (eos enim elegit Jehova Deus tuus ut ministrent ipsi, et ad benedicendum in nomine Jehovae: et juxta quorum sermonem erit omnis lis atque omnis plaga.)

6. And all the elders of that city, that are next unto the slain man, shall wash their hands over the heifer that is beheaded in the valley:

6. Et omnes seniores ejus urbis ubi accesserint ad cadaver hominis occisi, lavabunt manus suas super vitulam percussam in valle.

7. And they shall answer and say, Our hands have not shed this blood, neither have our eyes seen it.

7. Et testificabuntur, ac dicent, Manus nostrae non effuderunt sanguinem istum, neque oculi nostri viderunt.

8. Be merciful, O Lord, unto thy people Israel, whom thou hast redeemed, and lay not innocent blood unto thy people of Israel's charge. And the blood shall be forgiven them.

8. Expia populum tuum Israel quem redemisti Jehova, et ne imputes sanguinem innocentem in medio populi tui Israel: et expiabitur ab eis sanguis.

9. So shalt thou put away the guilt of innocent blood from among you, when thou shalt do that which is right in the sight of the Lord.

9. Tu autem auferes sanguinem innocentem e medio tui, quum feceris quod rectum est in oculis Jehovae.

1. If one be found slain in the land. This Supplement: is of a mixed character, relating partly to the civil, and partly to the criminal law. We are informed by it how precious to God is the life of man; for, if a murder had been committed by some unknown person, He requires an expiation to be made, whereby the neighboring cities should purge themselves from the pollution of the crime. Whence it appears that the earth is so polluted by human blood, that those who encourage murder by impunity, implicate themselves in the guilt. The question here is as to a secret crime, the guilt of which attaches to the neighboring cities, until, by the institution of a diligent inquiry, they can testify that the author is not discovered; how much less excusable, then, will they be, if they allow a murderer to escape with impunity? The rite prescribed is, that the elders of the nearest city should take a heifer which had not drawn in a yoke, and bring it into a stony and barren valley, cut off its neck with the assistance of the priests, wash their hands, and bear witness that their hands as well as their eyes are pure, as not being cognizant of the criminal. God chose a heifer that had not born a yoke, in order that the satisfaction made by innocent blood might be represented in a more lively manner; whilst it was to be killed in a desert place, that the pollution might be removed from the cultivated lands. For, if the blood of the heifer had been shed in the middle of the market-place of the city, or in any inhabited spot, the familiarity with the sight of blood would have hardened their minds in inhumanity. For the purpose, therefore, of awakening horror, it was drawn out into a solitary and uncultivated spot, that they might be thus accustomed to detest cruelty. But although, properly speaking, this was not a sacrifice which could be offered nowhere except in the sanctuary, still it nearly approached to the nature of a sacrifice, because the Levites were in attendance, and a solemn deprecation was made; nevertheless, they were not only employed as ministers of the altar, but also as judges, for their office is expressed in the words, that they were "chosen to minister to God, to bless the people, and to pronounce sentence as to every stroke."

6. And all the elders of that city. The washing of their hands had the effect of stirring them up the more, so that they should not inconsiderately protest in that solemn rite that they were pure and guiltless; for it was just as if they had presented the corpse of the dead mall before God, and had stood themselves opposite to it to purge away the crime. At the same time, also, they ask for

pardon, because it might have been through their carelessness that the man was smitten; and again, since, by the sacrilege of Achan alone the whole people were contaminated, it was to be feared lest the vengeance of God should extend more widely on account of the offense committed. And thus they were again taught how greatly God abominates murders, when the people pray that they may be pardoned for the crime of another, as if, by the very looking upon it, they had contracted guilt. God at length declares that He will not impute it to them, when they have duly performed this rite of expiation; not because the heifer was the price of satisfaction to propitiate God, but because in this way they humbly reconciled themselves to Him, and shut the door against murders for the time to come. On this account it is said -- "Thou shalt put away the blood from among you;" for if the murder be passed over without observation, there remains a blot upon the people, and the earth itself, in a manner, stinks before God.

Deuteronomy 12

Deuteronomy 12:15, 16, 20-25

15. Notwithstanding thou mayest kill and eat flesh in all thy gates, whatsoever thy soul lusteth after, according to the blessing of the Lord thy God which he hath given thee: the unclean and the clean may eat thereof, as of the roe-buck, and as of the hart.

15. Pro omni desiderio animae tuae mactabis, et comedes carnes secundum benedictionem Jehovae Dei tui, quam dederit tibi intra omnes portas tuas: immundus et mundus comedet eas, sicut capream et cervum.

16. Only ye shall not eat the blood; ye shall pour it upon the earth as water.

16. Tantummodo sanguinem non comedetis, super terram effundetis illum instar aquae.

20. When the Lord thy God shall enlarge thy border, as he hath promised thee, and thou shalt say, I will eat flesh, (because thy soul longeth to eat flesh,) thou mayest eat flesh, whatsoever thy soul lusteth after.

20. Quum dilataverit Jehova Deus tuus terminum tuum, quemadmodum loquutus est tibi, et dixeris, Comedam carnem, quod concupiscat anima tua vesci carnibus: juxta omne desiderium animae tuae comedes carnes.

21. If the place which the Lord thy God hath chosen to put his name there be too far from thee, then thou shalt kill of thy herd, and of thy flock, which the Lord hath given thee, as I have commanded thee, and thou shalt eat in thy gates whatsoever thy soul lusteth after.

21. Quum longinquus a te fuerit locus quem elegerit Jehova Deus tuus ut ponat nomen suum ibi, mactabis de bobus tuis et de pecudibus tuis quas dederit Jehova tibi: quemadmodum praecepi tibi, et vesceris in portis tuis secundum omne desiderium animae tuae.

22. Even as the roe-buck and the hart is eaten, so thou shalt eat them; the unclean and the clean shall eat of them alike.

22. Certe quemadmodum comeditur caprea et cervus, sic comedes illas: immundus pariter et mundus vescentur illis.

23. Only be sure that thou eat not the blood: for the blood is the life; and thou mayest not eat the life with the flesh.

23. Tantum roborare ut non comedas sanguinem: quia sanguis est anima, et non comedes animam una cum carne.

24. Thou shalt not eat it; thou shalt pour it upon the earth as water.

24. Non comedes illum, sed in terram effundes illum instar aquae.

25. Thou shalt not eat it; that it may go well with thee, and with thy children after thee, when thou shalt do that which is right in the sight of the Lord.

25. Non vesceris illo, ut bene sit tibi, et filiis tuis post te, quum feceris quod rectum est in oculis Jehovae.

Leviticus 7

Leviticus 7:26-27

26. Moreover, ye shall eat no manner of blood, whether it be of fowl or of beast, in any of your dwellings.

26. Nullum sanguinem comedetis in cunctis habitationibus vestris, tam de avibus quam de jumentis.

27. Whatsoever soul it be that eateth any manner of blood, even that soul shall be cut off from his people.

27. Omnis anima quae comederit ullum sanguinem, excidetur anima illa e populis suis.

Leviticus 19

Leviticus 19:26

26. Ye shall not eat anything with the blood.

26. Non comedetis cum sanguine.

Deuteronomy 12:15. Notwithstanding thou mayest kill. What precedes I have introduced in its proper place, viz., that they should not kill the sacrifices anywhere but in the sanctuary, of which there was only one in Judea. Here the permission to eat meat is given, provided that they do not offer the animals to God, but eat of them as of wild beasts. By way of example, two kinds are mentioned, the roe-buck and the hart, of which no offering was made. They are, therefore, freely allowed to eat meat wheresoever they pleased, with this exception, that they should not taste the blood; for, although this was observed by their forefathers before the giving of the Law, God ratifies it anew when He would gather a peculiar people to Himself. We know that immediately after the deluge, Noah and his posterity were commanded to abstain from blood; but, inasmuch as the greater part of mankind soon degenerated, it is probable that all nations neglected God's command, and permitted to themselves a universal license on this point; and it is even questionable whether this observance, which was everywhere fallen into desuetude, prevailed among the family of Shem. Certainly it may be conjectured from the renewed promulgation of the law, that it was altogether obsolete; at any rate, God would have His chosen people distinguished by this mark of separation from heathen nations.

The reason of the prohibition which is now mentioned had already been declared, [18] viz., because the blood is the seat of life. But although it, was allowable to kill an animal for food, yet, was it a useful restraint to prevent inhumanity, that they should not touch the blood; for if they abstained from the blood of beasts, much more necessary was it to spare human blood. After God, therefore, has forbidden blood to be eaten, He immediately proceeds to speak of men themselves: "Whose sheddeth man's blood, by man shall his blood be shed: for in the image of God made he man." [19] (Genesis 9:4-6.) Hence I have deemed it appropriate to annex all the passages in which God commands the people to abstain from blood, to the Sixth Commandment. In itself, indeed, the eating of blood was a thing of no great importance: since, therefore, God so often inculcates a point of so little weight, it may be inferred that the law has some further object. To this may be added the severity of the punishment, for surely it was not a crime worthy of death to taste the blood of some little bird; and hence, also, it is manifested that the prohibition had another meaning, viz., that cruelty might be abhorred. And the words of Moses show that the eating of blood is not forbidden because it infected man with its uncleanness, but that they might account the life of man to be precious; for it is said, "the blood is the life," which, in the opinion of Augustine, [20] is equivalent to its being "the sign of life;" but Moses rather means that animal life is contained in the blood. Wherefore, blood, which represents the life, was not interdicted without reason, nor was it only sinful to eat the blood by itself, but also together with the flesh, as is expressly declared both in Deuteronomy and in the last passage from Leviticus.

23. Only be [21] sure that thou eat not. It is not without cause that he earnestly exhorts them to inflexible firmness, because it was both a matter trifling in appearance, and its observation troublesome, whilst it was easy to decline from it on account of the universal example of the Gentiles. For if they considered within themselves that it contributed not to holiness that they should not touch blood, hence a snare to indulgence might easily have arisen.

Leviticus 17

Leviticus 17:10-14

10. And whatsoever man there be of the house of Israel, or of the strangers that sojourn among you, that eateth any manner of blood; I will even set my face against that soul that eateth blood, and will cut him off from among his people.

10. Quicunque e domo Israel, et e peregrinis qui peregrinantur in medio eorum, comederit ullum sanguinem, ponam faciem meam in animam quae comederit sanguinem, et excidam eam e medio populi sui.

11. For the life of the flesh is in the blood; and I have given it to you upon the altar, to make an atonement for your souls: for it is the blood that maketh an atonement for the soul.

11. Quia anima carnis in sanguine est: ego autem dedi illum vobis super altare ad expiandum animus vestras, quia sanguis animam expiabit.

12. Therefore I said unto the children of Israel, No soul of you shall eat blood, neither shall any stranger that sojourneth among you eat blood.

12. Ideo dixi filiis Israel, Nulla anima ex vobis comedet sanguinem, et peregrinus qui pregrinatur in medio vestri non comedet sanguinem.

13. And whatsoever man there be of the children of Israel, or of the strangers that sojourn among you, which hunteth and catcheth any beast or fowl that may be eaten; he shall even pour out the blood thereof, and cover it with dust.

13. Et quicunque e filiis Israel, et e peregrinis qui peregrinantur in medio eorum, venatus fuerit venationem bestiae vel avis quae comeditur, effundet sanguinem ejus et cooperiet pulvere.

14. For it is the life of all flesh; the blood of it is for the life thereof: therefore I said unto the children of Israel, Ye shall eat the blood of no manner of flesh: for the life of all flesh is the blood thereof; whosoever eateth it shall be cut off.

14. Quia anima cujusque carnis, sanguis ejus est in anima: dixique filiis Israel, Sanguinem cujuscunque carnis non comedetis, quia anima cujusque carnis est sanguis ejus: quicunque comederit illum, excidetur.

10. And whatsoever make there be of the house of Israel. God here not only condemns to death whosoever shall have polluted themselves by eating of blood, but declares that He will Himself take vengeance on them, though they may escape from the hands of the judges; for He not only prescribes to the judges what it is right for them to do, but asserts for Himself the office of inflicting the punishment. For, if we consider the intention of the Law, is there anything to surprise us in this; for although it be not consistent that the blood of a brute should be compensated for by the death of a man, still we must remember that this mode of instruction [22] was necessary for a rude people, lest they should speedily lapse into barbarism. But, lest they should complain that no use remained for the blood, He reminds them that since it was given for atonement, they would be very ungrateful if they were not content with so great a blessing; and surely, since it was the price they were to pay for appeasing God, this was an employment of it far to be preferred to food. If, then, they desired to exchange into ordinary food the blood, which was destined to the altar for the reconciliation of God, Moses indirectly reproves their ingratitude; for when God took away the right of eating it, He left them something better, which should have abundantly satisfied them. But we have elsewhere [23] seen in what manner blood atones for souls, i e., in a sacramental manner, upon which it must be observed that what properly belongs to Christ is thus transferred by metonomy to figures and symbols, yet in such a way that the similitude should neither be empty nor inefficacious; for in so far as the fathers apprehended Christ in the external sacrifices, atonement was truly exhibited in them. In this passage also, I do not understand "the strangers" to be all such visitors as may have journeyed amongst them on matters of business, but those who had devoted themselves to the worship of God; for many foreigners, abandoning their superstitions, were circumcised, and it behooved that such as these should be expressly laid under the bonds of the Law, lest, if it had not referred to them, they should have withdrawn themselves from obeying it. This point must, therefore, be briefly adverted to, lest we should suppose that heathen sojourners were prohibited from the eating of blood, whereas they were allowed to buy for food [24] even flesh that had been torn by beasts.

Since, however, the Patriarchs before the Law had abstained from blood, and its prohibition had no reference to the First Table or the legal service, hence it came to pass that when the Apostles abrogated the ceremonial law, they did not dare to allow immediately the free eating of blood, lest great scandal should arise from this new and unwonted thing. (Acts 15:20.) Wherefore, lest so trifling a matter should cause deadly schisms in the Churches, they commanded the Gentiles not to eat of blood; adding as the reason, that those who were accustomed to read the writings of Moses, would be disturbed at this innovation; yet this was only observed for a short period, as we gather from Paul. [25] It was, not without superstition and misplaced zeal;. retained by some even to the days of Tertullian.

The Political Supplements of the Sixth Commandment - Leviticus 24

Leviticus 24:17, 19-22

17. And he that killeth any man shall surely be put to death.

17. Qui percusserit animam hominis, morte moriatur.

19. And if a man cause a blemish in his neighbor; as he hath done, so shall it be done to him;

19. Vir qui intulerit maculam proximo suo, secundum quod fecit sic fiat ei.

20. Breach for breach, eye for eye, tooth for tooth as he hath caused a blemish in a man, so shall it be done to him wain

20. Fracturam pro fractura, oculum pro oculo, dentem pro dente: sicut intulerit maculam hominis, sic inferetur ei.

21. And he that killeth a beast, he shall restore it; and he that killeth a man, he shall be put to death.

21. Qui percusserit animal reddet illud: qui vero percusserit hominem, moriatur.

22. Ye shall have one manner of law, as well for the stranger, as for one of your own country: for I am the Lord your God.

22. Judicium unum erit vobis, sicut peregrinus sic et indigena erit: quia ego Jehova Deus vester.

17. And he that killeth any man. We now proceed to the confirmation of the Sixth Commandment afforded by the Judicial Law; and first, the punishment of death is awarded to murderers. To "smite the life" [26] is equivalent to wounding mortally, so that death ensues, as Moses more clearly explains himself in Exodus. But although he speaks briefly, like a legislator, there is no doubt but that he would have those whom he adjudges to die put to death by the sentence of the judges; the manner of executing the punishment we shall see in its proper place. Now although God did not carry out to absolute perfection the laws which He enacted, yet in their principle He desired that a clear and unreserved approval of His Commandments should appear. And this was the reason why I commenced with this passage, because it directly corresponds with the Sixth Commandment. [27]

19. And if man cause a blemish in his neighbor, he now also subjects to punishment those who shall have mutilated the body of their neighbor by blows; and this was necessary, because otherwise every very great villain, who might be accomplished in the art of inflicting injury, would have broken his brother's leg or arm, and then would not only have laughed at the poor man himself, but also at God and His Law. If, therefore, a person had injured a

member of another, the law of retaliation is enacted, which has also been in use among other nations. [28] But God thus distinctly prescribes when and how the injury was to be retaliated, that the law might not be open at all to the foolish cavils with which Favorinus attacks the law of the Twelve Tables in Gellius. And certainly the words of the Decemvirs were too obscure, "Si membrum fregeris meum, ex pacto talio est." (If you have broken my limb; without agreement made, there must be retaliation.) But God does not command an eye to be plucked out for an eye, or a tooth for a tooth, till He has set forth that this was only to be the case if any one had knowingly and willfully inflicted the injury; thus, He does not bring to justice accidental blows, but only a premeditated crime. It is vain to object that the members of different persons can hardly be broken with exact. equality, for the intention of God was none other than that, being alarmed by the severity of the punishment, men should abstain from injuring others; and therefore these two things were connected together, If one killeth a man, let him die, and if one hath taken away a part of life, let him suffer a similar privation. And the same is the tendency of the distinction, that the loss of an animal may be repaid, but that if a man be killed, there could be no just compensation made by money.

22. Ye shall have one manner of law. That the people of Israel, with their usual arrogance, might not suppose the race of Abraham only to be privileged, the Law is extended also to foreigners; and thus God shows that the whole body of the human race are under His care, so that He would not have those that are farthest off exposed to the licentious violence of the ungodly. In other points tie provided special privileges for His elect people; but here, because He created all men without exception after His own image, He takes them under His care and protection, so that none might injure them with impunity.

Exodus 21

Exodus 21:12-14, 18-32

12. He that smiteth a man, so that he die, shall be surely put to death.

12. Qui percusserit virum ad mortem, morte moriatur.

13. And if a man lie not in wait, but God deliver him into his hand; then I will appoint thee a place whither he shall flee.

13. At qui non insidiatus fuerit ei, sed tradiderit illum Deus in manus ejus, tunc dabo locum ad quem fugiet.

14. But if a man come presumptuously upon his neighbor, to slay him with guile; thou shalt take him from mine altar, that he may die.

14. Sin vero insultando se extulerit quispiam in proximum suum, ut occidat eum malitiose, ab altari meo tolles eum ut moriatur.

18. And if men strive together, and one smite another with a stone, or with his fist, and he die not, but keepeth his bed;

18. Quod si rixati fuerint aliqui, et percusserit alter proximum suum lapide vel pugno, nec mortuus fuerit, sed jacuerit in lecto:

19. If he rise again, and walk abroad upon his staff, then shall he that smote him be quit: only he shall pay for the loss of his time, and shall cause him to be thoroughly healed.

19. Si surrexerit, et ambulaverit foris super baculum suum, tunc innocens erit qui percussit, tantum cessationem ejus pensabit: et medendo medicandum curabit

20. And if a man smite his servant or his maid, with a rod, and he die under his hand; he shall be surely punished.

20. Quum percusserit quispiam servum suum vel ancillam suam baculo, et mortuus fuerit sub manu ejus, vindicando vindicabitur.

21. Notwithstanding, if he continue a day or two, he shall not be punished: for he is his money.

21. Veruntamen si per diem vel duos dies steterit, non vindicabitur, quia pecunia ejus est.

22. If men strive, and hurt a woman with child, so that her fruit depart. from her, and yet no mischief follow: he shall be surely punished, according as the woman's husband will lay upon him; and he shall pay as the judges determine

22. Quum autem rixati fuerint viri, et percusserint mulierem praegnantem ut egrediatur foetus ejus, nec tamen sequatur mors, puniendo punietur quemadmodum imposuerit ei maritus mulieris, et solvet apud judices.

23. And if any mischief follow, then thou shalt give life for life,

23. Quod si mors fuerit, tunc dabis animam pro anima,

24. Eye for eye, tooth for tooth, hand for hand, foot for foot,

24. Oculum pro oculo, dentem pro dente, manum pro manu, pedem pro pede,

25. Burning for burning, wound for wound, stripe for stripe.

25. Adustionem pro adustione, vulnus pro vulnere, livorem pro livore.

26. And if a man smite the eye of his servant, or the eye of his maid, that it perish; he shall let him go free for his eye's sake.

26. Quum autem percusserit quispiam oculum servi sui, vel oculum ancillae suae, et corruperit eum, liberum dimittet eum pro oculo ejus.

27. And if he smite out his manservant's tooth, or his maid-servant's tooth; he shall let him go free for his tooth's sake.

27. Quod si dentem servi sui, vel dentem ancillae suae excusserit: liberum dimittet eum pro dente ejus.

28. If an ox gore a man or a woman, that they die: then the ox shall be surely stoned, and his flesh shall not be eaten; but the owner of the ox shall be quit.

28. Si cornu petierit bos virum aut mulierem ut moriatur, lapidando lapidabitur bos, neque comedetur caro ejus: dominus autem bovis erit innocens.

29. But if the ox were wont to push with his horn in time past, and it hath been testified to his owner, and he hath not kept him in, but that he hath killed a man or a woman; the ox shall be stoned, and his owner also shall be put to death.

29. Quod si bos cornupeta fuerit ab heri et nudiustertius, et contestatio facta fuerit domino ejus, nec custodierit eum, occidendo autem occiderit virum vel mulierem, bos lapidabitur, et dominus quoque ejus morietur.

30. If there be laid on him a sum of money, then he shall give, for the ransom of his life, whatsoever is laid upon him.

30. Si pretium redemptionis impositum fuerit ei, tunc dabit redemptionem animae suae quantum impositum fuerit ei.

31. Whether he have gored a son, or have gored a daughter, according to this judgment shall it be done unto him.

31. Sive filium cornu petierit, sive filiam, secundum judicium hoc fiet ei.

32. If the ox shall push a manservant, or maid-servant; he shall give unto their master thirty shekels of silver, and the ox shall he stoned.

32. Si servum bos cornu petierit, vel ancillam, argenti triginta siclos dabit domino ejus, et bos the lapidabitur.

12. He that smiteth a man, so that he die. This passage, as I have said, more clearly explains the details, and first makes a distinction between voluntary and accidental homicide; for, if a stone or an axe (Deuteronomy 19:5.) may have slipped from a man unintentionally, and struck anybody, He would not have it accounted a capital crime. And for this purpose the cities of refuge were given, of which brief mention is here made, and whose rights will be presently more fully spoken of, and where also the mode of distinguishing between design and ignorance will be laid down. But it must be remarked, that Moses declares that accidental homicide, as it is commonly called, does not happen by chance or accident, but according to the will of God, as if He himself led out the person, who is killed, to death. By whatever kind of death, therefore, men are taken away, it is certain that we live or die only at His pleasure; and surely, if not even a sparrow can fall to the ground except by His will, (Matthew 10:29,) it would be very absurd that men created in His image should be abandoned to the blind impulses of fortune. Wherefore it must be concluded, as Scripture elsewhere teaches, that the term of each man's life is appointed, [29] with which another passage corresponds,

"Thou turnest man to destruction, and savest, Return, ye children of men." (Psalm 90:3.)

It is true, indeed, that whatever has no apparent cause or necessity seems to us to be fortuitous; and thus, whatever, according to nature, might happen otherwise we call accidents, (contingentia;) yet in the meantime it must be remembered, that what might else incline either way is governed by God's secret counsel, so that nothing is done without His arrangement and decree. In this way we do not suppose a fate [30] such as the Stoics invented; for it is a different tiling to say that things which of themselves incline to various and doubtful events, are directed by the hand of God whithersoever He will, and to say that necessity governs them in accordance with the perpetual complication of causes, [31] and that this happens with God's connivance; nay, nothing can be more opposite than that God should be drawn and carried away by a fatal motive power, or that He tempers all things as He sees fit.

There is no reason to follow the Jews here in philosophizing more deeply, that none are delivered to death but those in whom God finds cause for it. It is indeed certain, that with God there always exists the best reason for His acts; but it is wrong to elicit from thence that those who by tits guidance meet with death must be guilty of some offense. Nor even if God should take away an innocent man, would it bc lawful to murmur against Him; as if His justice were naught, because it is concealed from us, and indeed incomprehensible.

14. But if a man come presumptuously upon his neighbor. He expresses the same thing in different ways; for although there is a wide difference between

slaying a man presumptuously [32] and with guile, yet Moses applies them both to a willful murder; for by guile he means a wicked disposition to injure, and by the word presumptuous he designates a violent assault, when a man in hate wantonly falls upon another. And surely truculence, and violence, and all cruelty is presumptuous, (superba;) for unless a man despised his brother, he would not assail him as an enemy.

Lest by overlooking murders they should defile the land, God commands that murderers should be torn away even from His altar, whereby He signifies that they are as unworthy of divine as of human aid. For, although the sanctity of the altar might afford an asylum for the protection of those who had transgressed through imprudence, or. error, yet it would have been wrong that impunity for crimes should have been derived from hence; because the sanctuary would have been thus converted into a den of thieves, and religion would have been subjected to gross profanation. Wherefore, although criminals embracing the altar should implore God's aid, the Law commands them to be torn away from thence to punishment, because it would have been disgraceful to abuse God's sacred name as affording license for sin. Hence it appears how great was the folly of old in supposing that churches were honored when they were made asylums for the encouragement of evil deeds. This, indeed, was derived from the ordinary custom of the heathen; but it was a foolish imitation thus to mix up God with idols in a spurious worship; although in this respect the Gentiles served their idols more purely and virtuously than the Christians [33] served God; for they refused the right of asylum to the sacrilegious and impure, so that the temple of the Samothracians was no secure hiding-place even to Perseus, [34] the king of Macedon. Livy records the following words, as having been spoken by a heathen, -- "Since, at the commencement of all our sacrifices, those whose hands are not pure are enjoined to retire, will ye suffer your sanctuaries to be contaminated by the blood-stained person of a robber?" Let us, then, be ashamed of polluting our temples under the pretext of reverence for them.

18. And if men strive together. The punishment here enacted for wounds and blows is so slight, that it might have served as a provocative to the mischievousness of the ill-disposed. Since the Law of the Twelve Tables only inflicted a fine of twenty-five asses upon a man who had beaten another unjustly, there was a certain Lucius Veratius, [35] who, in mere wanton sport, did not hesitate to box the ears of any one he met, and then to command one of his slaves to pay the amount of the fine, so that it was at length thought better that the law should fall into desuetude, than to suffer it to be thus ridiculously abused. The same thing might easily happen among the Jews, since a person, who had so beaten his neighbor as that he should lie in bed, only had to pay what the unhappy man had expended on his cure. For who would not willingly enjoy the pleasure of knocking down his enemies on this condition, of providing for their subsistence whilst they lay in bed? But we must remember the declaration of Christ, that on account of the perverse nature of the Jews, many things were allowed them "because of the hardness of their hearts," (Matthew 19:8, and Mark 10:5,) amongst which this indulgent provision is to be reckoned. Still God seems to have dealt more leniently with the man who had struck the blow, that He might also chastise the other, who, though of inferior strength, had rashly engaged in the conflict; for both were to be alike punished for the violence unjustly inflicted. Equal lenity seems, therefore, to

have been shown to both, since compensation is only made to the person struck for his private loss. [36] But the fact, that God did not carry out the political laws to their perfection, shows that by this leniency He wished to reprove the people's perverseness, which could not even bear to obey so mild a law. Whenever, therefore, God seems to pardon too easily: and with too much clemency, let us recollect that He designedly deviated from the more perfect rule, because He, had to do with an intractable people.

20. And if a man smite his servant. Although in civil matters there was a wide distinction between slaves and free-men, still, that God may show how dear and precious men's lives are to Him, He has no respect to persons with regard to murder; but avenges the death of a slave and a free-man in the same way, if he should die immediately of his wound. Indeed, it was a proof of gross barbarism amongst the Romans and other nations, to give to masters the power of life and death; for men are bound together by a more sacred tie, than that it should be permitted to a master to kill with impunity his wretched slave; nor are some men so set over others, as that they should exercise tyranny, or robbery, neither does reason permit that any private individual should usurp to himself the power of the sword. But, although unjust cruelty was not prohibited, as it should have been, by the laws of Rome, yet they [37] confessed that slaves should be used like hired servants. The exception, which immediately follows, does not seem very consistent, for, if the slave should die after some time, the penalty of murder is remitted; whereas it would often be preferable to die at once of a single wound, than to perish by a lingering illness; and it might happen that the slave should be so bruised and maimed by blows, as to die some time afterwards. In this ease, the cruelty of the master would be surely greater than if he had committed the murder under the impulse of burning anger: wherefore the enactment appears to be a very unjust one. But it must be remarked, that the murder of those slaves, who had been obliged to take to their bed from their wounds, was not unpunished. Whence we gather, that it was not allowable for cruel and truculent masters to wound their slaves severely; and this is what the words expressly imply, for the smiter is only exempted from punishment when he shall have so restrained himself as that the marks of his cruelty should not appear. For that the slaves should "stand for one or two days," [38] is equivalent to saying, that they were perfect and sound in all their members; but if a wound had been inflicted, or there was any mutilation, the smiter was guilty of murder. None, therefore, is absolved but he who only meant to chastise his slave; and where no injury appears, it is probable that there was no intention to kill him. Whilst, then, this law prohibits bloodthirsty assaults, it by no means gives greater license to murder. The reason, which is added, must be restricted to the private loss; because a murderer would never be absolved on the pretext that he had purchased his slave with money, since the life of a man cannot be so estimated.

22. If men strive, and hurt a woman. This passage at first sight is ambiguous, for if the word death [39] only applies to the pregnant woman, it would not have been a capital crime to put an end to the foetus, which would be a great absurdity; for the foetus, though enclosed in the womb of its mother, is already a human being, (homo,) and it is almost a monstrous crime to rob it of the life which it has not yet begun to enjoy. If it seems more horrible to kill a man in his own house than in a field, because a man's house is his place of most secure refuge, it ought surely to be deemed more atrocious to destroy a foetus

in the womb before it has come to light. On these grounds I am led to conclude, without hesitation, that the words, "if death should follow," must be applied to the foetus as well as to the mother. Besides, it would be by no means reasonable that a father should sell for a set sum the life of his son or daughter. Wherefore this, in my opinion, is the meaning of the law, that it would be a crime punishable with death, not only when the mother died from the effects of the abortion, but also if the infant should be killed; whether it should die from the wound abortively, or soon after its birth. But, since it could not fail but that premature confinement would weaken both the mother and her offspring, the husband is allowed to demand before the judges a money-payment, at their discretion, in compensation for his loss; for although God's command is only that the money should be paid before the judges, [40] still He thus appoints them to settle the amount as arbitrators, if the husband should chance to be too exorbitant. We plainly perceive, by the repetition of the lex talionis, that a just proportion is to be observed, and that the amount of punishment is to be equally regulated, whether as to a tooth, or an eye, or life itself, so that the compensation should correspond with the injury done; and therefore (what is first said of the life [41]) is correctly applied also to the several parts, so that he who has plucked out his brother's eye, or cut off his hand, or broken his leg, should lose his own eye, or hand, or leg. In fine, for the purpose of preventing all violence, a compensation is to be paid in proportion to the injury. But although God commands punishment to be inflicted on the guilty, still, if a man be injured, he ought not to seek for vengeance; for God does not contradict Himself, who so often exhorts His children not only to endure injuries patiently, but even to overcome evil with good. The murderer is to be punished, or he who has maimed a member of his brother; but it is not therefore lawful, if you have unjustly suffered violence, to indulge in wrath or hatred, so as to render evil for evil. Since this error was rife among the Jews, our Lord refutes it, and teaches that the punishment, which is publicly awarded to the wrong-doer, is not subservient to every man's private passion, so that he who is offended should make haste to retaliate. (Matthew 5:38.) Nor indeed are these words addressed to them in order to inflame or excite the desire of vengeance, but all violence is restrained by the fear of punishment.

26. **And if a man smite the eye.** Since, in the sight of God, there is neither slave nor free-man, it is clear that he sins as greatly who smites a slave, as if he had struck a free-man. Still, a distinction is made as regards the civil law and human justice, especially if any one have inflicted a wound on his own slave. For here a tooth for a tooth, or an eye for an eye, is not required, but the superiority, which he has improperly abused, is taken from the master; and in compensation for the injury, liberty, which is almost half their life, is given to the male or female slave. Thus, in consideration that it was his slave, t. he master is treated more leniently, when the severity of the punishment is thus mitigated; whilst, in compensation for his dislocation or fracture, the slave receives what is more advantageous to him, viz., that, being set free, he should not be exposed to another's cruelty.

28. **If an ox gore a man.** Moses now descends even to the brute animals, so that, if they injured any one, by their punishment men may be more and more deterred from shedding blood. If, therefore, a goring ox have killed a man, he commands that it should be stoned, and that its carcass should be thrown away as abominable. Though censorious persons mock at this law, as if it were

childish to punish a wretched animal, in which there is no criminality, their insolence requires but a brief refutation. For, since oxen were created for man's good, so we need not wonder that their death, as well as their life, should be made to contribute to the public advantage. If, then, an ox that had killed a, man should be kept, men would undoubtedly grow hardened in cruelty by beholding it; and to eat its flesh, would be almost the same thing as eating the flesh of man. The cruelty of men, therefore, could not better be restrained, so that they should hold the murder of each other in abhorrence, than by thus avenging a man's death. In the second place, God proceeds further, condemning the master of the ox himself to death, if he had been previously admonished to beware; for such a warning takes away the pretext of ignorance; nor should the punishment seem to be severe for gross neglect, because to give free outlet to dangerous beasts is equivalent to compassing men's death. He who knowingly and willfully exposes the life of his brother to peril, is justly accounted his murderer. The exception which is finally added, at first sight contains a kind of contradiction, because it was forbidden by the Law to compound with a murderer for money. But inasmuch as a delinquency (delictum) differs from a crime, although it was unlawful to covenant with murderers for the remission of their punishment, still the judges were permitted on their hearing of the case, to mitigate it, if a man were excused by his unconsciousness or inadvertency. This, then, is a special exception, which permits the judges to distinguish between the nature of offenses; viz., that, if they discovered a man not to be worthy of death, they should still punish his negligence by a pecuniary fine.

31. Whether he have gored a son. I know not whether they are correct who refer this to age, as if any young persons of either sex were meant by the words son and daughter; but I do not reject this opinion. Still Moses seems to extend the law, as if, in case a butting ox had killed its owner's son, the father himself should be subject to the punishment, for not having taken more care of his children. It might, however, be doubted, whether it would be just to condemn to death a father already weighed down by the loss of his child; still it affords a useful example, that parents should not escape with impunity, if their sons or daughters should die by their fault.

32. If the ox shall push a man-servant. It is not unreasonable that the punishment for the death of a slave should now be set at less than for that of a free-man. As regarded the crime of voluntary murder, there was no distinction between slaves and masters; but in a case of mischance (delicto) the severity might in some degree be mitigated; especially when the stoning of the ox sufficiently availed for bringing murder into detestation. God, therefore, showed admirable moderation in condemning the negligence of the master to be punished by the payment of thirty shekels; whilst He proposed the ox as an example, and reminded all by its death, how very precious in His sight is human blood.

Deuteronomy 17

Deuteronomy 17:6

6. At the mouth of two witnesses, or three witnesses, shall he that is worthy of death be put to death; but at the mouth of one witness he shall not be put to death.

6. In ore duorum vel trium testium interficietur qui moriturus est, non interficietur in ore unius testis.

Deuteronomy 19

Deuteronomy 19:15

15. One witness shall not rise up against a man for any iniquity, or for any sin, in any sin that he sinneth: at the mouth of two witnesses, or at the mouth of three witnesses, shall the matter be established.

15. Non stabit testis unus contra quenquam in quacunque iniquitate, et in quoeunque peccato quod peccaverit: in ore duorum testium vel in ore trium testium stabit verbum.

As His severity in exacting punishment, where murder has been unquestionably committed, shows how highly God rates the life of men, so the qualification, which we find here, declares, that he takes equal care for the preservation of innocent blood. For, since too great credulity would often impel the judges to condemn the guiltless, He here applies a remedy to this evil, forbidding that the crime should be punished unless proved by sure testimony. Although He has naturally inscribed this law upon every heart, yet he would have it written down, that its observance amongst the Israelites might be more sacred; for nothing is more dangerous than to expose men's lives to the tongue of a single individual; but, where the consent of two or three is carefully weighed, any lurking falsehood is for the most part detected.

Lest, therefore, any one should be rashly condemned, and so innocence should be oppressed by any light conjectures, or insufficient accusations, or unjust prejudices, God here interferes, and does not allow any to be harshly dealt with, unless duly convicted.

Deuteronomy 22

Deuteronomy 22:8

8. When thou buildest a new house, then thou shalt make a battlement for thy roof, that thou bring not blood upon thine house, if any man fall from thence.

8. Si aedificaveris domum novam, facies tabulatum per circuitum in tecto tuo: nec pones sanguinem in domo tua, si quispiam ceciderit ex eo.

This precept also has reference to the preservation of human life. We know that the roofs of the Jewish houses were fiat, so that they might freely walk upon them. If there were no railings round them, a fall would have been fatal; and every house would have often been a house of mourning. God, therefore, commands the edge to be fortified with battlements, or railings, or other inclosure, and accompanies the injunction with a severe denunciation; for He declares that the houses would be defiled with blood, if any one should fall from an uninclosed roof. Now, if guile were thus contracted by mere incautiousness, it hence appears how greatly He abominates deliberate cruelty;

and, if it behooved everybody to be thus solicitous as to the lives of their brethren, it shows how criminal it is to injure them purposely and in enmity.

Deuteronomy 24

Deuteronomy 24:7

7. **If a man be found stealing any of his brethren of the children of Israel, and maketh merchandise of him, or selleth him; then that thief shall die: and thou shalt put evil away from among you.**

7. Si quis furatus fuerit animam e fratribus suis e filiis Israel, et vendiderit: morietur vir ille, et auferes malum e medio tui.

The same punishment is here deservedly denounced against man-stealers as against murderers; for, so wretched was the condition of slaves, that liberty was more than half of life; and hence to deprive a man of such a great blessing, was almost to destroy him. Besides, it is not man-stealing only which is here condemned, but the accompanying evils of cruelty and fraud, i.e., if he, who had stolen a man, had likewise sold him. Now, such a sale could hardly be made among the people themselves, without the crime being immediately detected; and nothing could be more hateful than that God's children should be alienated from the Church, and delivered over to heathen nations.

Deuteronomy 21

Deuteronomy 21:22, 23

22. **And if a man have committed a sin worthy of death, and he be to be put to death, and thou hang him on a tree;**

22. Quum fuerit in aliquo peccatum ad judicium mortis, et interficiendus fuerit, et suspenderis illum in ligno:

23. **His body shall not remain all night upon the tree, but thou shalt in any wise bury him that day; (for he that is hanged is accursed of God;) that thy land be not defiled, which the Lord thy God giveth thee for an inheritance.**

23. Non pernoctabit cadaver ejus in ligno, sed sepeliendo sepelies eodem die: quia maledictio est Dei qui suspenditur, et non contaminabis terram tuam quam Jehova Deus tuus dat tibi in haereditatem.

The object of this precept was to banish inhumanity and barbarism from the chosen people, and also to impress upon them horror even of a just execution. And surely the body of a man suspended on a cross is a sad and hideous spectacle; for the rights of sepulture are ordained for man, both as a pledge and symbol of the resurrection, and also to spare the eyes of the living, lest they should be defiled by the sight of so horrible a thing. Moses does not here speak generally, but only of those malefactors who are unworthy of the honor of burial; yet the public good is regarded in the burial even of such as these, lest men should grow accustomed to cruelty, and thus become more ready to commit murder. Moreover, that they may take more careful heed in this matter, he declares that the land would be defiled, if the corpse should be left hanging on the cross, since such inhumanity pollutes and disgraces the land. And this was more intolerable in Judea, which God had given as an inheritance to his elect people, that he might be there worshipped reverentially, and purely, every profanation being excluded. The man so hanged is called [42] "the curse of God," because this kind of punishment is detestable in itself. God, indeed, does not forbid criminals to be crucified, or hanged on a gallows, but rather gives His sanction to this mode of punishment; He only, by His own example, exhorts the Israelites to abhor all atrocity. Although, therefore, He does not disapprove of the punishment, He still says that lie abominates those that are hanged on a tree, that the scandal may be immediately removed; nor does He call them accursed, as if their salvation was to be despaired of, but because the hanging was a mark of His curse. This passage Paul applies to Christ, to teach us that He was made κατάρα (a curse) for us, that He might deliver us from the curse of the Law. (Galatians 3:13.) For, since all are guilty of transgression, and thus the whole race of mankind is implicated in the curse, there was no other mode of deliverance, except that Christ should substitute Himself in our place. Nor was God unmindful of His sentence, when He suffered His only-begot, tea Son to be crucified. Hence it follows that He submitted Himself to our condition, in order; that we might receive God's blessing; since He was

> *"made sin for us, that we might be made the righteousness of God in Him."* (2 Corinthians 5:21.)

Deuteronomy 25

Deuteronomy 25:1-3

1. If there be a controversy between men, and they come unto judgment, that the judges may judge them; then they shall justify the righteous, and condemn the wicked.

1. Si fuerit lis inter aliquos, et accesserint ad judicium, et judicaverint eos: justificaverintque justum, et impium condemnaverint:

2. And it shall be, if the wicked man be worthy to be beaten, that the judge shall cause him to lie down, and to be beaten before his face, according to his fault, by a certain number.

2. Si quidem caedendus fuerit impius, tunc prosternet eum judex, et caedere jubebit illum coram se secundum iniquitatem ejus ad numerum.

3. Forty stripes he may give him, and not exceed: lest, /f he should exceed, and beat him above these with many stripes, then thy brother should seem vile unto thee.

3. Quadraginta plagis caedere jubebit illum, non addet: ne forte si addat caedere eum ultra plagis multis, vilescat frater tuus in oculis tuis.

Inasmuch as moderation and humanity are here enjoined, it is a Supplement of the Sixth Commandment. The sum is, that, if any one is judicially condemned to be beaten with stripes, the chastisement should not be excessive. The question, however, is as to a punishment, which by lawyers is called a moderate correction, [43] and which ought to be such, as that the body torn by the whip should not be maimed or disfigured. Since, therefore, God has so far spared the guilty, as to repress even just severity, much more would He have regard paid to innocent blood; and since He prohibits the judge from using too great rigor, much less will He tolerate the violence of a private individual, if he shall employ it against his brother. But it was necessary that zeal should be thus restrained, because judges, in other respects not unjust, are often as severe against lesser offenses (delicta) as against crimes. An equal measure of punishment is not indeed prescribed, as if all were to be beaten alike; it is only prohibited that the judges should order more than forty stripes in all to be inflicted for an offense. Thus the culprits were beaten deliberately, and not in such an indiscriminate manner as when it was not requisite to count the stripes; besides, they were not so injured for the future as to be deprived of the use of any of their limbs. With the same intent God would have the judges themselves to be present, that by their authority they may prevent any excess: and the reason is added, lest "thy brother should seem vile unto thee," because he had been beaten immoderately. This may be explained in two ways, either, lest his body should be disfigured by the blows, and so he should be rendered unsightly; or, lest, being stained for ever with ignominy and disgrace, he should be discouraged in mind; for we know how grievous and bitter it is to be mocked and insulted. A third sense, [44] which some prefer, is too far-fetched, viz., lest he should die like some vile and contemptible beast; for God only provides that the wretched man should be improved by his chastisement, and not that he should grow callous from his infamy. As the Jews were always ostentatious of their zeal in trifling matters, they invented a childish precaution, in order that they might more strictly observe this law; for they were scrupulous in not proceeding to the fortieth stripe, but, by deducting one, they sought after an empty reputation for clemency, as if they were wiser than God Himself, and superior to Him in kindness. Into such folly do men fall, when they dare out of their own heads to invent anything in opposition to God's word! This superstition already prevailed in Paul's time, as we gather from his words, where he reports that "five times he received forty stripes save one." (2 Corinthians 11:24.)

Deuteronomy 24

Deuteronomy 24:16

16. The fathers shall not be put to death for the children, neither shall the children be put to death for the fathers: every man shall be put to death for his own sin.

16. Non interficientur patres pro filiis, neque filii interficientur pro patribus: quisque in peccato suo morietur.

Here also God manifests how great is His regard for human life, so that blood should not be shed indiscriminately, when he forbids that children should be involved in the punishment of their parents. Nor was this Law by any means supererogatory, because on account of one man's crime his whole race was often severely dealt with. It is not without cause, therefore, that God interposes for the protection of the innocent, and does not allow the punishment to travel further than where the crime exists. And surely our natural common sense dictates that it is an act of barbarous madness to put children to death out of hatred to their father. If any should object, what we have already seen, that God avenges "unto the third and fourth generation," the reply is easy, that He is a law unto Himself, and that He does not rush by a blind impulse to the exercise of vengeance, so as to confound the innocent with the reprobate, but that He so visits the iniquity of the fathers upon their children, as to temper extreme severity with the greatest equity. Moreover, He has not so bound Himself by an inflexible rule as not to be free, if it so pleases Him, to depart from the Law; as, for example, He commanded the whole race of Canaan to be rooted out, because the land would not be purged except by the extermination of their defilements; and, since they were all reprobate, the children, no less than their fathers, were doomed to just destruction. Nay, we read that, after Saul's death, his guilt was expiated by the death of his children, (2 Samuel 21;) still, by this special exception, the Supreme Lawgiver did not abrogate what He had commanded; but would have His own admirable wisdom acquiesced in, which is the fountain from whence all laws proceed.

Deuteronomy 20

Deuteronomy 20:10-18

10. When thou comest nigh unto a city to fight against it, then proclaim peace unto it.

10. Quum accesseris ad urbem ut expugnes illam, clamabis ad eam pacem.

11. And it shall be, if it make thee answer of peace, and open unto thee, then it shall be, that all the people that is found therein shall be tributaries unto thee, and they shall serve thee.

11. Et erit, si pacem responderit tibi, et aperuit tibi, universus populus qui fuerit repertus in ea, erunt tibi tributarii, servientque tibi.

12. And if it will make no peace with thee, but will make war against thee, then thou shalt besiege it:

12. Si vero pacem non fecerit tecum, sed faciet tecum praelium, obsederisque eam;

13. And when the Lord thy God hath delivered it into thine hands, thou shalt smite every male thereof with the edge of the sword:

13. Et dederit eam Jehova Deus tuus in manu tua: tunc percuties omnem masculum ejus acie gladii.

14. But the women, and the little ones, and the cattle, and all that is in the city, even all the spoil thereof, shalt thou take unto thyself: and thou shalt eat the spoil of thine enemies, which the Lord thy God hath given thee.

14. Tantum mulieres, et parvulos, et animalia, et quicquid fuerit in urbe, omnia spolia ejus praedaberis tibi: comedesque spolia inimicorum tuorum, quos dederit tibi Jehova Deus tuus.

15. Thus shalt thou do unto all the cities which are very far off from thee, which are not of the cities of these nations.

15. Sic facies omnibus urbibus longinquis a te valde, quae non sunt de urbibus gentium istarum.

16. But of the cities of these people, which the Lord thy God doth give thee. for an inheritance, thou shalt save alive nothing that breatheth.

16. Tantum de urbibus populorum istorum quos Jehova Deus tuus dat tibi in haereditatem, non vivificabis ullam animam:

17. But thou shalt utterly destroy them; namely, the Hittites, and the Amorites, the Canaanites, and the Perizzites, the Hivites, and the Jebusites, as the Lord thy God hath commanded thee:

17. Sed perdendo perdes eos, Hitthaeum, Amorrhaeum, Chananaeum et Perisaeum, Hivaeum, et Jebusaeum, quemadmodum praecepit tibi Jehova Deus tuus:

18. That they teach you not to do after all their abominations, which they have done unto their gods; so should ye sin against the Lord your God.

18. Ne doceant vos facere secundum abominationes suas quas faciunt diis suis: et peccetis in Jehovam Deum vestrum.

10. When thou goest forth to war. He now teaches that, even in lawful wars, cruelty is to be repressed, and bloodshed to be abstained from as much as possible. He therefore commands that, when they shall have come to take a city, they should first of all exhort its inhabitants to obtain peace by capitulating; and if they should do so, to keep them alive, and to be content with imposing a tribute on them. This principle of equity was naturally implanted in all nations; hence heralds took their rise, [45] nor did they commence a just war without a solemn proclamation. Besides, inasmuch as the word hostis (an enemy) formerly signified a foreigner (peregrinum,) the Romans mitigated by its mildness the sadness of the reality. On this ground they deemed that faith was to be kept with an enemy; and that sentiment of Cicero is worthy of praise, "that wars must not be undertaken except that we may live in unmolested peace."

But if God would have his people mindful of humanity in the very midst of the din of arms, we may hence infer how greatly displeasing to Him is human bloodshed. Even those whom He has armed with his authority, He would still have disposed to clemency, and He represses their ardor, lest they should stain with blood the swords given them by His permission. How, then, shall it be lawful for a private person to assume the sword for the purpose of killing his brother? We now understand the object of the instructions here given, and how appropriately they are connected with the Sixth Commandment.

12. And if he will make no peace. The permission here given seems to confer too great a license; for, since heathen writers [46] command even the conquered to be spared, and enjoin that those should be admitted to mercy who lay down their arms, and cast themselves on the good faith of the General, although the battering-ram may have actually made a breach in the wall, how does God, the Father of mercies, give His sanction to indiscriminate bloodshed? It has already been stated, that more was conceded to the Jews on account of their hardness of heart, than was justly lawful for them. Unquestionably, by the law of charity, even armed men should be spared, if, casting away the sword, they crave for mercy; at any rate it was not lawful to kill any but those who were taken in arms, and sword in hand. This permission, therefore, to slaughter, which is extended to all the males, is far distant from perfection. [47] But, although in their ferocity the Jews would have hardly suffered the perfection of equity to be prescribed to them, still God would at least restrain their excessive violence from proceeding to the extremity of cruelty. The question is as to

cities taken by force, where it sometimes happens that there is no distinction of sex or age regarded; this inhumanity is here mitigated, since they might not kill either women or children.

15. Thus shalt thou do unto all the cities. An exception is introduced, that the Jews should not apply the common laws of war to the Canaanitish nations, with respect to whose extermination the sentence had passed. [48] For God had not only armed the Jews to carry on war with them, but had appointed them to be the ministers and executioners of His vengeance. We have elsewhere explained that there were just causes why He would have their race and memory radically destroyed; especially since He had borne with them for four hundred years, whilst in their wicked obstinacy they had not ceased to grow worse and worse, from whence their desperate impiety was manifest. What had been said before is here, however, repeated, i e., that since that land was consecrated to God's service, its inhabitants were to be exterminated, who could do nothing but contaminate it; and therefore this would be profitable for the Israelites, lest by their wiles they should be attracted to false superstitions.

Deuteronomy 23

Deuteronomy 23:15, 16

15. Thou shalt not deliver unto his master the servant which is escaped from his master unto thee:

15. Non trades servum domino suo, qui se ad te eripuerit a domino suo.

16. He shall dwell with thee, even among you, in that place which he shall choose in one of thy gates, where it liketh him best: thou shalt not oppress him.

16. Tecum habitabit in medio tui, in loco quem elegerit in una urbium tuarum prout placuerit, nec vim inferes ei.

Although this Law has a tendency to humanity and kindness, it still does not appear to be altogether just. Since many masters oppressed their slaves with tyrannical arrogance, their wickedness rendered it necessary to afford some alleviation to the poor creatures. Thus slaves were permitted to take refuge in temples, and at Rome at the statues of the Caesars, so that if they proved themselves to have been treated with injustice and inhumanity, they might, when their case was proved, be transferred by sale to merciful masters. This, indeed, was endurable, but the refuge which is here granted to slaves defrauds their masters of their just right; since, without their case being heard, they have liberty given them to reside in the land of Canaan; thus, too, the law of nations is violated, since the land is opened to every fugitive. Besides, since runaway slaves are generally wicked and criminal, whatever place may be their asylum, it will be filled with many sources of infection. I know not whether there is sufficient foundation for the opinion of some who think that the slaves were exempted by privilege from their former servitude, [49] in order that they might give themselves up to God's service, and that thus true religion might be propagated. It certainly does not seem consistent that filth and refuse of every sort should be received into the Church, because, in the end, it would have been filled with all kinds of corruptions; and besides, it was by no means decorous that whatever crime had been elsewhere committed should be sheltered under

God's name. For, suppose a thief, or an adulterer, or a murderer, should leave his master, and seek for an asylum in the Holy Land, what else would it have been to receive and protect such guests, but to overthrow law and justice, and to set up a state of foul barbarism? I think, therefore, that more is to be understood than the words express, viz., that, if it should be found that the slaves had not fled in consequence of their own evil doings, but on account of the excessive cruelty of their masters, the people should not drive them away, which would have been tantamount to giving them up to butchery. And, in fact, it may be inferred that judicial proceedings were to be instituted, because a choice is given as to the city in which they prefer to dwell.

Religion, indeed, stood them in some stead, because those who sought a place and home in the land of Canaan, were obliged to dedicate themselves to God, and to be initiated in His worship; still, God would never have allowed His name to be profaned by the reception of wicked persons without discrimination. Wherefore, as I briefly slated before, God inculcates humanity upon His people, lest, by the extradition of fugitive slaves, they should be necessary to the cruelty of others; because their masters would have been their executioners; and, since lie forbids the people from ill-treating them, He implies, by these words, that He only so far provides for the safety of these wretched beings, as to allow them to defend their innocence in a court of justice; wherefore I have thought fit to place this law amongst the Supplements of the Sixth Commandment.

Deuteronomy 22

Deuteronomy 22:6, 7

6. If a bird's nest chance to be before thee in the way in any tree, or on the ground, whether they be young ones or eggs, and the dam sitting upon the young, or upon the eggs, thou shalt not take the dam with the young:

6. Quum occurrerit tibi nidus avium in via in quavis arbore, aut super terram ubi pulli vel ova, et mater cubet super pullos aut super ova: non accipies matrem cum filiis:

7. But thou shalt in any wise let the dam go, and take the young to thee; that it may be well with thee, and that thou mayest prolong thy days.

7. Sed dimittendo dimittes matrem, pullos autem capies tibi, ut bene sit tibi et producas dies.

Since by this precept God instructed His people in the, law of kindness, it is a Supplement to the Sixth Commandment. Regard was had, indeed, to the preservation of the breed; but, besides, when birds are sitting, as being very lean, it is certain that they are not wholesome food; still there is no question but that it was God's intention to accustom His people to study humanity. For, if there be one drop of compassion in us, it will never enter into our minds to kill an unhappy little bird, which so burns either with the desire of offspring, or with love towards its little ones, as to be heedless of its life, and to prefer endangering itself to the desertion of its eggs, or its brood. Wherefore, it is not to be doubted but that in this elementary lesson, God prohibited His people from savageness and cruelty.

Exodus 23

Exodus 23:5

5. If thou see the ass of him that hateth thee lying under his burden, and wouldest forbear to help him; thou shalt surely help with him.

5. Si videris asinum inimici tui decumbentem sub onere suo, et cessaveris ab auxiliando ei, auxiliaudo auxiliaberis cum eo.

Deuteronomy 22

Deuteronomy 22:4

4. Thou shalt not see thy brother's ass or his ox fall down by the way, and hide thyself from them; thou shalt surely help him to lift them up again.

4. Non videbis asinum fratris tui aut boves ejus jacentes in via, et abscondes te ab eis: erigendo eriges cum eo.

By this law also, God exhorts His people to exercise the duties of humanity towards brute animals, in order that they may be the more disposed to assist their brethren; for we must bear in memory what Paul teaches, where God commands oxen to be kindly treated, viz., that He does not care so much for them in this, as for mankind. (1 Corinthians 9:9.) God prescribes elsewhere, that if any should see the ox or ass of his brother, or even of his enemy, going astray, he should catch it, and restore it to its master, (Deuteronomy 22:1-3, and Exodus 23:4;) but here He had another intention, i.e., that believers should testify their forgiveness of their enemies, by being merciful to their animals. If it had been simply said, that our enemies were to be helped, and that we must contend with them by acts of kindness, to overcome their ill-will, all cruelty would have been sufficiently condemned; but when God commands us not only to succor our enemies, to point out their way to those who are straying, and to lift up those who are fallen, but would also have us exercise these kindnesses to their very beasts, He more emphatically and strongly expresses how very far removed from hatred and the desire of vengeance He desires His children to be. Wherefore we see that what Christ afterwards taught His disciples is taught also in the Law, that we should love our enemies. (Matthew 5:44.) Nor is it merely the desire of vengeance which is here restrained, but something more is required, viz., that believers should conquer the ill-will of their enemies by kindnesses: since to bring back a straying ox or ass is a proof of sincere affection. But, in these two passages, what relates to the Sixth Commandment is represented in a more striking manner, viz., that assistance should be rendered to an ox or an ass, weighed down by its burden. Interpreters [50] are not agreed as to the meaning of the words, and Jerome has departed most widely from them. But others, who desire to translate them more accurately, read them interrogatively, -- If thou shall see an animal fall under its burden, etc., wilt thou hesitate to help? The other sense seems more appropriate, -- If thou shall; have seen and have hesitated to help, still do thou help: for in this way God anticipates a person, if, perchance, impelled at first by hatred, he should dislike to help his enemy: and then commands him to correct his guilty thought. The meaning, therefore, will be, -- if the sight of thine enemy should delay thee from aiding his beast, lay aside thine ill-will, and unite thyself with him, that you may together be humane and merciful to the wretched animal. Thus an opportunity was given to enemies for their mutual reconciliation. There is another difficulty in the word [51], גזב, gnazab, which, although it means to leave, still, in my judgment, is used for to assist, or to give help: although it is not translated amiss, to let fro, or to loose: or, if it be preferred, to strengthen; in which sense it is sometimes found.

Numbers 35

Numbers 35:9-34

9. And the Lord spoke unto Moses, saying,

9. Et locutus est Jehova ad Mosen dicendo:

10. Speak unto the children of Israel, and say unto them, When ye be come over Jordan into the land of Canaan,

10. Alloquere filios Israel, et dicas eis, Quum transieritis Jordanem in terra Chanaan,

11. Then ye shall appoint you cities to be cities of refuge for you; that the slayer may flee thither, which killeth any person at unawares.

11. Constituetis vobis urbes: urbes autem refugii erunt vobis, quo fugiet homicida qui percusserit aliquem per errorem.

12. And they shall be unto you cities for refuge from the avenger; that the manslayer die not, until he stand before the congregation in judgment.

12. Et erunt vobis urbes illae in refugium a propinquo, et non morietur homicida, donec steterit ipse ante congregationem adjudicium.

13. And of these cities which ye shall give, six cities shall ye have for refuge.

13. Et ex urbibus quas dabitis, sex urbes refugii erunt vobis.

14. Ye shall give three cities on this side Jordan, and three cities shall ye give in the land of Canaan, which shall be cities of refuge.

14. Tres urbes dabitis citra Jordanem, et tres urbes dabitis in terra Chanaan: urbes refugii erunt.

15. These six cities shall be a refuge, both for the children of Israel, and for the stranger, and for the sojourner among them; that every one that killeth any person unawares may flee thither.

15. Filiis Israel, et peregrino, et incolae in medio eorum, erunt sex urbes illae refugium, ut fugiat illuc quicunque percusserit aliquem per errorem.

16. And if he smite him with an instrument of iron, so that lie die, he is a murderer: the murderer shall surely be put to death.

16. Si instrumento ferreo percusserit eum, et mortuus fuerit, homicida est: moriendo morietur homicida.

17. And if he smite him with throwing a stone, wherewith he may die, and he die, he is a murderer: the murderer shall surely be put to death.

17. Si vero lapide manus, quo moriatur, percusserit eum, et mortuus fuerit, homicida est: moriendo morietur homicida.

18. Or if he smite him with an hand-weapon of wood, wherewith he may die, and he die, he is a murderer: the murderer shall surely be put to death.

18. Aut instrumento ligneo manus, quo moriatur, percusserit eum, et mortuus fuerit, homicida est: moriendo morietur homicida.

19. The revenger of blood himself shall slay the murderer: when he meeteth him, he shall slay him.

19. Propinquus sanguinis ipse interficiet homicidam: quum ipse obviaverit illi, ipse interficiet eum.

20. But if he thrust him of hatred, or hurl at him by laying of wait, that he die;

20. Si per odium, inquam, impulerit eum, aut projecerit aliquid in eum per insidias, et mortuus fuerit.

21. Or in enmity smite him with his hand, that he die: he that smote him shall surely be put to death; for he is a murderer: the revenger of blood shall slay the murderer when he meeteth him.

21. Aut per inimicitiam percusserit eum manu sua, mortuusque fuerit: moriendo morietur percussor, homicida est: propinquus sanguinis interficiet homicidam quum ipse occurrerit illi.

22. But if he thrust him suddenly without enmity, or have cast upon him ally thing without laying of wait;

22. Si autem casu absque inimicitiis impulerit eum, vel projecerit in eum quodvis instrumentum absque insidiis.

23. Or with any stone, wherewith a man may die, seeing him not, and cast it upon him, that he die, and was not his enemy, neither sought his harm;

23. Aut quemvis lapidem quo moriatur quem prius non videbat, et cadere fecerit super illum, mortuusque fuerit, et ipse non erat inimicus, neque quaerebat malum ejus;

24. Then the congregation shall judge between the slayer and the revenger of blood according to these judgments:

24. Tunc judicabit congregatio inter percussorem et propinquum sanguinis secundum judicia ista.

25. And the congregation shall deliver the slayer out of the hand of the revenger of blood, and the congregation shall restore him to the city of his refuge, whither he was fled; and he shall abide in it unto the death of the high priest, which was anointed with the holy oil.

25. Et eruet congregatio homicidam e manu propinqui sanguinis, et reverti faciet eum congregatio ad urbem refugii sui ad quam confugerat: habitabitque in ea donec moriatur sacerdos magnus qui unctus est oleo sanctitatis.

26. But if the slayer shall at any time come without the border of the city of his refuge, whither he was fled;

26. Quod si egrediendo egressus fuerit homicida terminum urbis refugii sui ad quam confugerat:

27. And the revenger of blood find him without the borders of the city of his refuge, and the revenger of blood kill the slayer; he shall not be guilty of blood:

27. Et invenerit eum propinquus sanguinis extra terminum urbis refugii sui, atque occiderit propinquus ille homicidam: non erit obnoxius morti.

28. Because he should have remained in the city of his refuge until the death of the high priest: but after the death of the high priest the slayer shall return into the land of his possession.

28. In civitate enim refugii sui habitabit donec moriatur sacerdos magnus: posteaquam autem mortuus fuerit sacerdos magnus, revertetur homicida in terram possessionis suae.

29. So these things shall be for a statute of judgment unto you throughout your generations, in all your dwellings.

29. Et erunt ista vobis in statutum judicii per generationes vestras, in omnibus habitationibus vestris.

30. Whoso killeth any person, the murderer shall be put to death by the mouth of witnesses: but one witness shall not testify against any person to cause him to die.

30. Quicunque percusserit aliquem, ad verbum testium occidet homicidam: solus enim testis non testificabitur in animam ut moriatur.

31. Moreover, ye shall take no satisfaction for the life of a murderer, which is guilty of death; but he shall be surely put to death.

31. Neque accipietis pretium pro anima homicidae qui est sceleratus, ut moriatur: sed moriendo morietur.

32. And ye shall take no satisfaction for him that is fled to the city of his refuge, that he should come again to dwell in the land, until the death of the priest.

32. Sed nec accipietis pretium ut fugiat ad urbem refugii sui, ut revertatur habitare in ea terra donec moriatur sacerdos.

33. So ye shall not pollute the land wherein ye are; for blood it defileth the land: and the land cannot be cleansed of the blood that is shed therein, but by the blood of him that shed it.

33. Et non polluetis terram in qua fueritis, quia sanguis iste polluet terram: neque terra expiabitur propter sanguinem qui effusus est in ea nisi per sanguinem illius qui effudit illum.

34. Defile not therefore the land which ye shall inhabit, wherein I dwell: for I the Lord dwell among the children of Israel.

34. Ne ergo polluatis terram in qua habitatis, et in cujus medio ego habito: ego enim Jehova habito in medio filiorum Israel.

10. Speak unto the children of Israel God appointed the cities of refuge, not only to make distinction between sills of malice and error, but also lest innocent blood should be rashly shed. Thus far we have seen how severely He would have murder punished: but, inasmuch as it would have been by no means just that he, who had not willfully but accidentally killed his neighbor, should be hurried away to the same punishment, to which willful murderers were subjected, an exception is added here, in order that he might escape who had killed another ignorantly, and unintentionally. Although, as has been said, God had a, further object, viz., lest murder upon murder should be committed, and the land should thus be polluted. Let us now examine the details in order. Although at the outset He only mentions the cities on the other side of Jordan, still we gather from what follows, that six cities were chosen for this purpose, of which three were on this side Jordan. He would have them so situated, that every part of the country should have one of them in its neighborhood, lest the exile of the unhappy persons, who were guiltless, should be rendered more painful by the distance they would have to travel. We have already briefly pointed out [52] that these cities were to be in the portions of Levi, in order that the dignity of the priesthood might the better protect the exiles, and also,

because it was probable that there would be more prudence and serious feeling in the Levites, so that the refuge accorded to the innocent should not also shield the guilty.

16. And if he smite him with an instrument of iron. God appears to contradict Himself, when, a little further on, He absolves involuntary murderers, although they may have inflicted the wound with iron or with a stone; whilst here He absolutely declares that whosoever shall smite another with wood, or iron, or a stone, shall be guilty of death; but this is easily explained if we consider his meaning; for, after having pardoned the unintentional act (errori,) lest [53] any should misconstrue this as affording impunity for crime, He at once anticipates them, and again inculcates what has been said before. By the express mention of iron, wood, and stone, He more dearly explains that no voluntary murders are to be pardoned; else, as laws are wont to be evaded by various subtleties, they would have endeavored, perhaps, to limit what had been said respecting the punishment of murderers to one single species of murder, viz., when a person had been slain with a sword. It is not, then, without cause that God condemns to death every kind of murderer, whether he have committed the crime with a weapon (of iron,) or by throwing a stone, or with a dub; since it is sufficient for his condemnation that he had conceived the intention to do the evil act. It is well known that [54] by the Lex Cornelia, whosoever had carried a weapon with the intention of killing a man was guilty; and Martianus cites the reply of Adrian, -- He who has killed a man, if he did it not with the intention of killing him, may be absolved; and he who has not killed a man, but has wounded him with intention to kill him, is to be condemned as a murderer; as Paulus also teaches, that in the said Lex Cornelia, the evil intention (dolus) is taken for the deed. Another reply of Adrian is very true, That in crimes, the will and not the result must be regarded. Whence that saying of Ulpian, That there is no difference between the man who kills, and him who causes the death of another. Here, therefore, God had no other object than to cut off from murderers all handles for subterfuge, if they should be convicted of a wicked intention, especially when it resulted in an actual attempt; since there was no difference whether they had made use of a sword, or a mallet, or a stone.

19. The revenger [55] of blood himself. When God commanded that murderers should suffer death, He required that they should be condemned by the judges after due trial; but it seems to savor somewhat of barbarism, that he should now permit the relative of the dead man to take vengeance; for it is a very bad precedent to give the power of the sword to private individuals, and this too in their own cause. It; was indeed formerly permitted, as we shall see in its proper place, to put to death robbers by night, as also it was lawful for the husband, or the father, of a ravished woman to kill the adulterer caught in the fact; but it is absurd that the law should allow a person to avenge the death of his brother. But it is not to be supposed that this license was ever accorded by God, that a man might neglect the public authorities, and inflict punishment on his brothers murderer, wherever he should meet him; for this would have been to give the reins to sudden anger, so that blood would be added to blood. Wherefore it is probable that the danger of this is here denounced, rather than the gate opened to private vengeance; as if it had been said, that unless a provision were made for the innocent, the fury of those whose kindred had been slain, could hardly be restrained; not because it was lawful for them to render

violence for violence, but because they would not consider it a crime, and impunity would prove a stimulus even to them, if their just indignation should be pardoned. It must be understood, then, that when a man had been maliciously and willfully killed, a death inflicted by his relative in vengeance was not punished; because it was hard that a man should be capitally condemned as a criminal, who had only slain a murderer already exposed to capital punishment, under the impulse of that love towards his own blood, which is naturally implanted in all. This, however, was tolerated, and not approved of, because, as I have already said, punishments are to be inflicted by public judgment, and not by private will. But, since this indulgence was conceded on account of the people's hardness of heart, God here reminds them how needful it was to provide an asylum for the innocent, because all murderers would else have been indiscriminately attacked. In short, a comparison is made between the guilty and the innocent, for, unless a just distinction had been drawn, all alike would have been exposed to death. The murderer, he says, is worthy of death, if, perchance, he is met by the kinsman of the man murdered. A remedy is, therefore, to be provided, lest one who is not criminal should accidentally receive the same punishment. Hence, at length it is gathered that a distinction is made between one and the other, by a lawful trial. The mode of procedure is also prescribed, viz., that the congregation should acquit the man who has killed another unwittingly. But because there is some perplexity in the words, it must be observed, that as soon as a person had slain another, he immediately betook himself to the place of refuge, and there declared that he sought shelter. After this declaration, it was open for the relatives of the dead man to lay their accusation, and then, after both parties were heard, judgment was pronounced. Otherwise there is a manifest contradiction in the context, since it is presently added; they "shall restore him to the city of his refuge, whither he was fled," whence it appears that, after the exile had presented himself to state his case, and to clear himself, it was usual that a day should be appointed, upon which his accusers should come forward. The sum is, that the murderer should nowhere find refuge, except he were acquitted of his crime. This was an excellent precaution, lest the same punishment should be inflicted upon mischance and criminality, whilst [56] at the same time, by the temporary banishment it was testified how carefully bloodshed was to be avoided. God likewise spared the eyes of those whose brother had been killed, lest their grief should be kept alive by continually beholding (the person who had killed him; [57]) and this we gather from verse 26, where impunity is conceded to the relations, if they had caught and killed out of the boundaries of his refuge the man, whose duty it was to withdraw himself; not because the fury of their indignation was excused before God, but because it would else have been difficult to restrain the strong desire of vengeance proceeding from the feelings of human nature.

28. Because he should have remained in the city of his refuge. The period of banishment is prescribed, "until the death of the high-priest," because it would have been anything but humane that all hopes of restoration should have been cut off from the unhappy exile; and, when a new priest succeeded to reconcile the people to God, this renewal of grace was to propitiate all offenses. Wherefore it was not unreasonable that God should entirely restore those who were only punished for inadvertency.

30. Whoso killeth any person, He now returns to willful murderers, whom he will not have spared, but yet not given over to punishment unless convicted by legal proofs. Literally it is, Whoso smiteth a soul, at the mouth of witnesses he shall slay him that slayeth: and this sentence is obscure, from its brevity, unless a noun be supplied before the second verb; and this may be understood either of the judges or the accuser. In the substance, however, there is no ambiguity, viz., that no one should be condemned unless he be lawfully convicted. Moreover, He declares that one witness would be insufficient, inasmuch as it would be most unjust that a man's life should be at the mercy of a single tongue. I have already adduced a similar passage, [58] in which Moses gave instructions that no capital causes was to be decided except at the mouth of two or three witnesses: and, because such declarations are of general application, I have purposely assigned to them a separate place. Now again, in referring to the condemnation of murderers, he takes occasion to state that two witnesses are required, since nothing is more likely to occur than that the innocent should be overwhelmed by calumnies and perjury, if it depended on the testimony of any single individual. But, when two are brought forward, it may be discovered in many ways, as has been said, whether there is any falsehood; for, if examined separately, they will scarcely accord in all particulars. But, whilst sure proof is required, in order to the punishment of guilt, so, when the murder is proved, God sternly requires, and commands that it should not remain unpunished. He expressly forbids that the right of refuge should be purchasable, since it would else have been in danger of being a shield for many crimes. When, therefore, He forbids a satisfaction to be taken from any one, who would betake himself to a city of refuge, His object is, that no one should enjoy this benefit, until his innocence was fully established; lest the mercy, whereby the innocent were succored, should be open to bribery.

33. So ye shall not pollute the land. In this concluding sentence, He again reminds them that, unless they should exercise severe justice against murderers, they would be guilty of sin against God; because the land stained with human blood is polluted, and lying under His curse, until expiation has been made. Again, since God dwells in the land of Canaan, having chosen His abode among the children of Israel, his sanctity is also profaned. The sum is, that, in every respect, care should be taken lest the land, which is sacred to God, should be contaminated by bloodshed.

Deuteronomy 19

Deuteronomy 19:1-13

1. When the Lord thy God hath cut off the nations, whose land the Lord thy God giveth thee, and thou succeedest them, and dwellest in their cities, and in their houses;

1. Quum exciderit Jehova Deus tuus gentes quarum ipse Jehova Deus tuus dat tibi terram, et possederis eas, habitaverisque in urbibus earum et in domibus earum.

2. Thou shalt separate three cities for thee in the midst of thy land, which the Lord thy God giveth thee to possess it.

2. Tres urbes separabis tibi in medio terrae tuae quam Jehova Deus tuus dat tibi ut possideas eam.

3. Thou shalt prepare thee a way, and divide the coasts of thy land, which the Lord thy God giveth thee to inherit, into three parts, that every slayer may flee thither.

3. Praeparabis tibi itinera, et in tres partes divides terminum terrae tuae, quam in haereditatem daturus est tibi Jehova Deus tuus: eritque ut fugiat illuc omnis homicida.

4. And this is the case of the slayer which shall flee thither, that he may live: Whoso killeth his neighbor ignorantly, whom he hated not in time past;

4. Haec autem est res homicidae. qui fugiet illuc, et vivet: qui percusserit proximum suum ignoranter, neque oderat eam ab heri et nudiustertius.

5. As when a man goeth into the wood with his neighbor to hew wood, and his hand fetcheth a stroke with the axe to cut down the tree, and the head slippeth from the helve, and lighteth upon his neighbor, that he die; he shall flee unto one of those cities, and live:

5. Quicunque abierit cum proximo suo in silvam ad caedenda ligna, et impulsa fuerit manus ejus in securim ad caedendum lignum, elapsum autem fuerit ferrum e ligno, inveneritque proximum suum, et moriatur: is fugiet ad unam urbium istarum, et vivet:

6. Lest the avenger of the blood pursue the slayer, while his heart is hot, and overtake him, because the way is long, and slay him; whereas he was not worthy of death, inasmuch as he hated him not in time past.

6. Ne persequatur propinquus sanguinis homicidam illum, quum incaluerit cor ejus, et assequatur eum, quod longior fuerit via: et percutiat eum anima, quum tamen non sit reus mortis, quod non odisset eum ab heri et nudiustertius:

7. Wherefore I command thee, saying, Thou shalt separate three cities for thee.

7. Idcirco ego praecipio tibi, dicendo: Tres civitates separabis tibi.

8. And if the Lord thy God enlarge thy coast, as he hath sworn unto thy fathers, and give thee all the land which he promised to give unto thy fathers;

8. Quod si dilataverit Jehova Deus tuus terminum tuum quemadmodum juravit patribus tuis, et dederit tibi universam terram quam dixit patribus tuis se daturum:

9. If thou shalt keep all these commandments to do them, which I command thee this day, to love the Lord thy God, and to walk ever in his ways; then shalt thou add three cities more for thee, besides these three:

9. Quum custodieris omnia praecepta ista, ut facias ea quae ego praecipio tibi hodie, nempe ut diligas Jehovam Deum tuum, et ambules in viis ejus omnibus diebus: tunc addes tibi adhuc tres urbes ultra tres istas:

10. That innocent blood be not shed in thy land, which the Lord thy God giveth thee for an inheritance, and so blood be upon thee.

10. Ut non effundatur sanguis innocens in medio terrae tuae quam Jehova Deus tuus dat tibi in haereditatem, neve sint super to sanguines.

11. But if any man hate his neigh-hour, and lie in wait for him, and rise up against him, and smite him mortally that he die, and fleeth into one of these cities;

11. At quum fuerit quispiam qui oderit proximum suum, et insidiatus fuerit ei, insurrexeritque in eum, et percusserit eum anima, et mortuus fuerit, fugerit autem ad unam urbium istarum.

12. Then the elders of his city shall send and fetch him thence, and deliver him into the hand of the avenger of blood, that he may die.

12. Tunc mittent seniores urbis illius, et abstrahent eum inde, dabuntque eum in manu propinqui sanguinis, et morietur.

13. Thine eye shall not pity him: but thou shalt put away the guilt of innocent blood from Israel, that it may go well with thee.

13. Non parcet oculus tuus ei, et auferes sanguinem innocentem ex Israele, et bene erit tibi.

1. When the Lord thy God hath cut off the nations. Moses repeats the same precepts which we have just been considering, that, in regard to murders, the people should distinguish between inadvertency and crime. With this view, he assigns six cities, wherein those who have proved their innocence before the judges should rest in peace and concealment. In one word, however, he defines who is to be exempt from punishment, viz., he who has killed his neighbor ignorantly, as we have previously seen; and this is just, because the will is the sole source and cause of criminality, and therefore, where there is no malicious feeling, there is no crime. But, lest under the pretext of inadvertency those who are actually guilty should escape, a mark of distinction is added, i.e., that no hatred should have preceded; and of this an instance is given, if two friends should have gone out together into a wood, and, without any quarrel or wrangling, the head of the axe should slip out of the hand of one of them, and strike the other. God, therefore, justly commands that the motive of the crime should be investigated, and shows how it is to be ascertained, viz., if there had been any previous animosity, or if any contention should have arisen. For it is incredible that any one should be so wicked as gratuitously to rush into so abominable a sin. It must be observed, however, that there was no room for this conjecture, except in a doubtful matter; for if any should stab his neighbor with a drawn sword, or should hurl a dart into his bosom, the inquiry would be superfluous, because the guilty intention would be abundantly manifest.

Footnotes:

15. So in V. "Non oderis fratrem tuum in corde tuo, sed publice argue eum," etc.

16. Fr., "Les Theologiens de la Papaute." C. refers elsewhere to this scholastic maxim: "Nor is the argument worth a straw, That the thing regulated must always be inferior to the rule. The Lord did not make self-love the rule, as if love towards others was subordinate to it; but whereas, through natural pravity, the feeling of love usually rests on ourselves, He shows that it ought to diffuse itself in another direction -- that is, should be prepared to do good to our neighbor with no less alacrity, ardor, and solicitude, than to ourselves." -- Inst., book 2, 8, Section 54. "Again, when Moses commanded us to love our neighbors as ourselves, he did not intend to put the love of ourselves in the first place, so that a man may first love himself and then love his neighbors: as the sophists of the Sorbonne are wont to cavil, that the rule must always go before what it regulates." -- Harm. of the Evangelists, (C. Society's Trans.,) [2]vol. 3, p. 59.

17. Addition in Fr., "Et pourtant il faut suppleer ou injure

ou rancune; and, therefore, injury or grudge must be supplied.

18. See on Leviticus 3:17, [3]vol. 2, p. 335, whence, however, he refers to Genesis 9:4. C. Society's edition, [4]vol. 1, p. 293.

19. Lat. "Qui effuderit sanguinem hominis in homine;" he who shall have shed the blood of man in man. -- Vide C. in loco.

20. Quaest. in Leviticum, 57 Section 2. "Illud appellatur anima, quod significat animam." -- Edit. Benedict. tom. 3, p. 1 pag. 516.

21. Lat., "Roberare." Margin, A. V., "Heb., Be strong."

22. "Hanc paedagogiam." -- Lat. "Ceste doctrine puerile." -- Fr.

23. See on Exodus 12:21, ante [5]vol. 1 p. 221.

24. See on Deuteronomy 14:21, ante [6]vol. 2, p. 69.

25. There is no reference here in the Latin, but the Fr. is, "comme il se peut recueillir par ce que Sainct Paul en escrit aux Corinthiens;" as may be gathered from what St. Paul writes respecting it to the Corinthians. In C.'s Commentary on the Acts, 15:28, he says, "We know that this law was foredone by Paul, so soon as the tumult and contention was once ended, when he teacheth that nothing is unclean, (Romans 14:14,)and when he granteth liberty to eat all manner of meats, yea, even such as were sacrificed to idols. (1 Corinthians 10:25.)" -- C. Society's edit., [7]vol. 2, p. 79. Tertullian, Apol., cap. 9, speaks as follows; "Erubescat error vester Christianis, qui ne animalium quidem sanguinem in epulis esculentas habemus, qui propterea quoque suffocatis et morticinis abstinemus, ne quo modo sanguine contaminemur, vel intra viscera sepulto." See Bingham, book 17 ch. 5 sec. 20 "But on the other hand, because it was the custom of the Catholic Church, almost to the time of St. Austin, to abstain from eating of blood, in compliance with the rule given by the Apostles to the Gentile converts; therefore, by the most ancient laws of the Church, all clergymen were obliged to abstain from it under pain of degradation. This is evident from the Apostolical Canons, and those of Gangra, and the second Council of Orleans, and the Council of Trullo. But as this was looked upon by some only as a temporary injunction, so it appears from St. Austin that it was of no force in the African Church. (Contra Faust., lib. 32, c. 13.) He that would see more about it may consult Curcellaeus, who has written a large dissertation upon the subject."

26. See margin of A. V.

27. Lat., "quia praecepto respondet quasi ἀντίϛροφος."

28. This is the earliest account we have of the Lex Talionis, or law of like for like, which afterwards prevailed among the Greeks and Romans. Among the latter it constituted a part of the Twelve Tables, so famous in antiquity; but the punishment was afterwards changed to a pecuniary fine, to be levied at the discretion of the Praetor. It prevails less or more in most civilized countries, and is fully acted upon in the Canon Law in reference to all calumniators: "Clumniator, si in accusatione defecerit, talionem recipiat." Nothing, however, of this kind was left to private revenge; the magistrate awarded the punishment when the fact was proved. Otherwise the Lex Talionis would have utterly destroyed the peace of society, and have sowed the seeds of hatred, revenge, and all

uncharitableness." -- Adam Clarke on Exodus 21:24. The enactment of the Twelve Tables to this effect appears from Festus to have been the following: "Si merebrum rupsit, (ruperit,) ni cum eo pacit, (paciscetur,) talio est;" presenting a singular coincidence with the Mosaic provision. See Aul. Gell., lib. 20 c. 1, where the words are given somewhat differently, as in C.'s text. The objection of Favorinus is that it was impossible to be kept; for if the like were inflicted for the like, as one wound for another, they must take care that the like wound in every respect should be made, neither longer nor deeper; if it were, then a new retaliation must arise, and so ad infinitum.

29. No reference is here given, but it is probably to Job 14:5, -- "Thou hast appointed his bounds that he cannot pass."

30. "Une necessite fatale." -- Fr.

31. "Une necessite confuse selon des causes entortillees;" a confused necessity according to complicated causes. -- Fr.

32. "Superbire, et insidiari longe differunt." -- Lat. "Ruer sup quelqu'un par fierte et malice, et l'aguetter." -- Fr.

33. "Ceux qui se glorifioyent du titre de Chrestiente;" those who prided themselves in the name of Christians. -- Fr.

34. See Livy, lib. 45:5. The words quoted are from an address of a certain L. Atilius to the popular assembly of Samothracia.

35. Aul. Gellius. Noct. Attic., 20:1.

36. "Ainsi il semble bien que tous deux ont este supportez quant au delict public, quand il n'y a que le dommage particulier qui soit recompense;" thus it plainly appears that both were set free, as regarded the public offense, since it was only the private injury for which compensation was made. -- Fr.

37. "Les gens prudens;" their wise men. -- Fr.

38. A. V., "continue for a day or two." Ainsworth, in loco: "Heb., stand, which the Greek translateth live."

39. It will be seen that the word אסון in the text is translated by C., mors; in A V., mischief. "The Chaldee expounds it, (says Ainsworth,) no death; but it implieth less also than death, as the words following manifest. The Greek refers it to the child; translating, if it be not figured, (ἐξεικονισμένον,) i e., have not the shape and proportion."

40. The word determine is added by our translators. Ainsworth's literal rendering is, "and he shall give by the judges."

41. Added from Fr.

42. See margin, A. V.

43. "Ce que les jurisconsultes appellent une reprimande moyenne." -- Fr.

44. This exposition is attributed to Vatablus in Poole's Synopsis.

45. "Feciales." -- Lat. "Les herauts d'armes." -- Fr. "The Romans never carried on any war without solemnly proclaiming it. This was done by a set of priests called Feciales. When the Romans thought themselves injured by any nation, they sent one or more of these Feciales to demand redress, (ad res repetundas,) Liv. 4:30, 38:45. Varro, L.L. 4:15. Dionys. 2:72; and, if it was not immediately given, thirty-three days were granted to consider the matter, after which war might be justly declared. Then the. Feciaks again

went to their confines, and having thrown a bloody spear into them, formally declared war against that nation, Liv. 1:32." -- Adam's Romans Antiq. The references in the two following sentences are to Cicero, de Off. 1:12, and 11, and 13.

46. "Et cum iis, quos vi deviceris, consulendum est; tum 2, qui, armis positis, ad imperatorum fidem confugient, quamvis murum aries percusserit, recipiendi sunt." -- Cic, de Off. 1:11.

47. Addition in Fr., "et equite qui doit estre en tous enfans de Dieu;" and from the equity which ought to be in all God's children.

48. Addition in Fr., "et l'execution commise aux enfans d'Israel;" and its execution committed to the children of Israel.

49. "The Chaldee addeth, a servant of the peoples, i.e., of the Gentiles, who for the religion of God cometh from his master to the Church of Israel. This servant that fleeth to the land (of Israel) he is a righteous stranger, (that is, a proselyte come unto the faith and covenant of God,) saith Maimony." -- Ainsworth in loco.

50. Margin A V., Exodus 23:5, "Wilt thou cease to help him? or, and wouldest thou cease to leave thy business for him; thou shalt surely leave it to join with him." The Vulg. translation is, "Si videris asinum odientis te jacere sub onere, non pertransibis, sed sublevabis cum eo:" and this precisely accords with LXX., οὐ παρελεύσ⁷Y αὐτὸ

51. Exodus 23:5 עזב, in its primary and most usual sense, signifies to leave; but a thing may be left from dislike or weariness; hence it signifies (2) to forsake. On the other hand, it may be left, because it has been brought into

that state, in which it needs no further help or security; and hence (3) it sometimes signifies to complete a defense, as Nehem. 3:8; 4:2; to relieve from a difficulty, as in this place -- W. The whole of this criticism is omitted, not only in the French translation, but also in the Latin edition of 1563, pp. 390, 391.

52. See [8]vol. 2 p. 251, on Numbers 35:6.

53. "De peur que cela ne tirast trop longue queue, et que les criminels en fissent couverture d'impunite, il exprime notamment les facons de tuer plus communes, quand on y va de guet-a-pens. Ainsi en nommant les instrumens, qui sont destinez, ou qu'on applique a mal faire," etc.; for fear this should be carried too far, and that criminals should make it a ground for impunity, he expressly mentions the more ordinary kinds of deliberate murder. Thus, by naming the instruments, which are intended, or used for inflicting injuries, etc. -- Fr.

54. Vide Digest. 48, tit. 8. In legem Corneliam de Sicariis, et Veneficiis, 1 Section 3. "Divus Hadrianus rescripsit, eum, qui hominem occidit, si non occidendi animo hoc admisit, absolvi posse: et qui hominem non occidit, sed vulneravit ut occidat, pro homicida damnandum: et ex re constituendum hoc." -- Ibid., 11 "Ulpianus, lib. 8, ad legem Juliam, et Papiam. Nihil interest, occidat quis, an causam mortis praebeat." Vide item, Julii Pauli Recept. Sentent., lib. 5, tit. 23, Section 2. "Qui hominem occiderit, aliquando absolvitur. Et qui non occidit, in homicida damnatur. Consilium enim uniuscujusque, non factum puniendum est. Ideoque qui cum velit occidere, id casu aliquo

perpetrare non potuerit, ut homicida punietur. Et is, qui casu jactu teli hominem imprudenter occiderit, absolvitur."

55. "Propinquus sanguinis." -- Lat.

56. The Fr. gives a different turn to this sentence; "que pour obvier a un nouveau meurtre en bannissant pour un temps celuy, qui avoit tue quelqu'un par erreur;" as well as to prevent a fresh murder, by banishing, for a time, the person who had killed another unintentionally.

57. Added from Fr.

58. Deuteronomy 17:6. See ante, [9]p. 45.

The Seventh Commandment

Exodus 20

Exodus 20:14

14. Thou shalt not commit adultery.
14. Non committes adulterium.

THE REPETITION OF THE COMMANDMENT - Deuteronomy 5

Deuteronomy 5:18

18. Neither shalt thou commit adultery.
18. Non committes adulterium.

Although one kind of impurity is alone referred to, it is sufficiently plain, from the principle laid down, that believers are generally exhorted to chastity; for, if the Law be a perfect rule of holy living, it would be more than absurd to give a license for fornication, adultery alone being excepted. Furthermore, it is incontrovertible that God will by no means approve or excuse before this tribunal, what the common sense of mankind declares to be obscene; for, although lewdness has everywhere been rampant in every age, still the opinion could never be utterly extinguished, that fornication is a scandal and a sin. Unquestionably what Paul teaches has been prevalently received from the beginning, that a good life consists of three parts, soberness, righteousness, and godliness, (Titus 2:12;) and the soberness which he commands differs not from chastity. Besides, when Christ or the Apostles are treating of a perfect life, they always refer believers to the Law; for, as it had been said of old by Moses, "This is the way, walk ye in it;" [59] Christ confirms this,

"If thou wilt enter into life, keep the commandments," (Matthew 19:17;)

and Paul corroborates it, "He that loveth another hath fulfilled the Law," (Romans 13:8,) whilst they constantly pronounce a curse against all fornicators. It is not worth while to quote the particular passages in which they do so. Now, if Christ and the Apostles, who are the best interpreters of the Law, declare that God's Law is violated no less by fornication than by theft, we assuredly infer, that in this Commandment the whole genus is comprehended under a single species. Wherefore, those have done nothing but betray their disgraceful ignorance, who have sought to be praised for their acuteness on the score of their ridiculous subtlety, when they admitted that fornication is indeed condemned with sufficient clearness and frequency in the New Testament, but not in the Law. For, if they had reasoned justly, inasmuch as God is declared to have blessed marriage, it must at once be concluded, on the contrary, that the connection of male and female, except in marriage, is accursed. This is the argument of the author of the Epistle to the Hebrews, where he contrasts two opposite things;

> *"Marriage (he says) is honorable in all, and the bed undefiled; but whoremongers and adulterers God will judge."* (Hebrews 13:4.)

So also, when God forbids the priest to marry a harlot, (Leviticus 21:14,) the manifest impropriety of fornication is declared; and, if it was unlawful for the daughters of Israel to be harlots, (Deuteronomy 23:17,) the same reasoning applies necessarily to males. Nor has Hosea taken that reproof from anywhere else but the Law? "Whoredom and wine take away the heart." (Hosea 4:11.) Thus, when the Prophets metaphorically condemn the corruptions of their nation, they do not always use the same; word as Moses here does, נאף, naaph, but compare them to fornications, whereas, if fornication were lawful in itself, this metaphor would be altogether inappropriate. Hosea was commanded to take a harlot for a wife, (Hosea 1:2;) no mention is made of adultery, and still the shame and baseness of the people is thus condemned. Who, then, would say that fornication is free from sin, since God brands it with no ordinary mark of ignominy? But if any should pertinaciously contest this, let him accuse Paul of error, who bears witness that an example is set before us in the Law, that we should. not "commit fornication as some of them committed, and fell in one day three-and-twenty thousand." (Numbers 25:9; 1 Corinthians 10:8.) Surely, if they had not transgressed the Law, so horrible a vengeance would not have overwhelmed them. If any should object that the crime of idolatry was mixed up with it., still the declaration of Paul remains untouched, that God was the avenger of fornication in this infliction of punishment, which would not accord, unless it were a transgression of the Law. And in truth, where, as recorded by Luke, (Acts 15:20,) the Apostles in their decree prohibit fornication amongst the Gentiles, the reason is at the same time added, that "Moses is read in the synagogues." Now, if it were not a vice opposed to the Law, no offense would have hence arisen.

We have already explained why, under this word adultery, every impure lust was condemned. We know how unbridled was the licentiousness of the Gentiles; for, although God never suffered all shame to be extinguished together with their purity, still respect for what was right was in a manner stifled, so that they evaded the grossness of the sin by ribaldry and scurrilous jests. At any rate, the doctrine of Paul was by no means understood, that those who indulge in whoredom "sin against their own body." (1 Corinthians 6:18.)

Since, then, the minds of all men were stupified by indulgence, it was needful to arouse them by declaring the atrocity of the sin, that they might learn to beware of all pollution. Nor are unbridled lusts only here condemned, but God instructs His people to cherish modesty and chastity. The sum is, that those who desire to approve themselves to God, should be pure "from all filthiness of the flesh and spirit," (2 Corinthians 7:1;) nor can we doubt but that Paul in these words would interpret the law, as he elsewhere exhorts, *"that everyone should possess his vessel in sanctification and honor; not in the lust of concupiscence, even as the Gentiles which know not God."* (1 Thessalonians 4:4, 5.)

Leviticus 18

Leviticus 18:20

20. Moreover, thou shalt not lie carnally with thy neighbor's wife, to defile thyself with her.

20. Uxori proximi tui non dabis concubitum tuum in semine, ut polluaris cum ea.

The object of this passage is the same as that of the foregoing ones. For, whilst all fornication pollutes a man, there is grosser impurity in adultery, because the sanctity of marriage is violated, and by the commingling of seed a spurious and illegitimate offspring is derived. Wherefore, God has justly enumerated this crime amongst the abominations of the Gentiles, as may be more clearly seen from the exordium of the chapter from whence this passage is taken.

Supplements of the Seventh Commandment - Leviticus 18

Leviticus 18:22-30

22. Thou shalt not lie with mankind as with womankind: it is abomination.

22. Cure masculo ne concumbas concubitu mulieris: abominatio est.

23. Neither shalt thou lie with any beast, to defile thyself therewith; neither shall any woman stand before a beast to lie down thereto: it is confusion.

23. Cum animali non coibis ut polluaris cum eo: nec mulier prostituet se animali ut coeat cum eo: turpitudo est.

24. Defile not ye yourselves in any of these things: for in all these the nations are defiled which I cast out before you.

24. Ne polluamini in omnibus his: nam in his omnibus polluerunt se gentes quas ego ejiciam a facie vestra.

25. And the land is defiled: therefore I do visit the iniquity thereof upon it, and the land itself vomiteth out her inhabitants.

25. Polluta fuit terra, et visitavi iniquitatem ejus super eam, evomuitque terra habitatores suos.

26. Ye shall therefore keep my statutes and my judgments, and shall not commit any of these abominations; neither any of your own nation, nor any stranger that sojourneth among you;

26. Vos ergo custodite statuta mea, et judicia mea: et ne faciatis ex omnibus abominationibus istis, indigena, vel peregrinus qui peregrinatur in medio vestri.

27. (For all these abominations have the men of the land done which were before you, and the land is defiled;)

27. Omnes enim abominationes istas fecerunt homines terrae qui fuerunt ante vos, et polluta fuit terra.

28. That the land spur not you out also, when ye defile it, as it spewed out the nations that were before you.

28. Ne evomat vos terra quod contaminetis eam, quemadmodum evomuit gentem quae fuit ante vos.

29. For whosoever shall commit any of these abominations, even the souls that commit them shall be cut off from among their people.

29. Quisquis enim fecerit ex omnibus abominationibus istis, animae quae fecerint excidentur e medio populi sui.

30. Therefore shall ye keep mine ordinance, that ye commit not any one of these abominable customs, which were committed before you, and that ye defile not yourselves therein: I am the Lord your God.

30. Custodite custodias meas, nec facietis e statutis abominationum quae facta sunt ante vos, neque polluatis vos in illis: ego Jehova Deus vester.

Political Supplements [60] - Exodus 22

Exodus 22:19

19. Whosoever lieth with a beast shall surely be put to death.
19. Quisquis concubuerit cum animali, morte moriatur.

We learn from these passages that the people were not only prohibited from adultery, but also from all sins [61] which are repugnant to the modesty of nature itself. In order that all impurity may be the more detestable, He enumerates two species of unnatural lust, from whence it is evident that when men indulge themselves in this respect, they are carried away by an impulse, which is more than beastly, to defile themselves by shameful wickedness. The beasts are satisfied with natural connection; it is therefore a gross enormity that this distinction should be confounded by man endowed with reason; for what is the use of our judgment and intelligent faculties if it be not that greater self-restraint should exist in us than in the brute animals? It is plain, therefore, that they must be blinded in a horrible manner who so shamefully defile themselves, as Paul says. (Romans 1:28.) The madness of lust has, however, invented several monstrous vices, whose names it would be better to bury, if God had not chosen that these shameful monuments should exist, to inspire us with fear and horror. It has at length advanced to such excesses, that men created in God's image, both male and female, have had connection with brutes.

Leviticus 18:24. Defile not yourselves in any of these things. An old proverb [62] says, that good laws have sprung from evil habits; and God reminds us that for this reason He has been induced expressly to advert to these disgusting and wicked things; for the monstrosities which He mentions would have been concealed in eternal silence had not necessity compelled Him to bring them to light. But since the Canaanitish nations had advanced to such a pitch of licentiousness, that the prodigious sins, which else would have been better concealed, had been but too familiarly known from their wicked habits, God warns His people to beware of their fatal examples. First, when He says that these abominations prevailed amongst the Gentiles, He indicates that evil habits by no means avail as an excuse; nay, that public consent is in vain alleged in defense of vice. But the better to deter them from imitating them, He sets before their eyes the vengeance He is about to take. It is true, indeed, that the nations of Canaan were destroyed for other reasons, but it is not without cause that He sets forth this amongst the rest, for undoubtedly God was offended by such pollutions.

26. Ye shall therefore keep my statutes He here contrasts His Law with the abominations of the Gentiles. The exhibition of His severity, which He had referred to, might indeed have sufficed for the instruction of His people; but in order to influence them more strongly, He at the same time adduces the way pointed out to them in the Law, which would not suffer them to go astray, if only they refused not to follow God. For that the Gentiles, who were destitute of light, should have been drawn aside in every direction was not surprising; but whilst they thus proved their blindness, it behooved true believers, on the contrary, to testify that they were not children of darkness, but of light. And to this Paul seems to allude, when he exhorts believers not to walk, like the Gentiles, "in the vanity of their mind." (Ephesians 4:17.) On this account God not only commends to them His precepts and statutes, but also His ordinances (custodias,) because He had omitted nothing in the Law which would be useful for the direction of men's lives. The sum is, that unless they order themselves constantly by the doctrine which enlightens them, the same destruction awaited them also which was about to overwhelm the (Canaanitish) nations.

Leviticus 20

Leviticus 20:13, 15, 16

13. If a man also lie with mankind, as he lieth with a woman, both of them have committed an abomination: they shall surely be put to death; their blood shall be upon them.

13. Quicunque coierit cum masculo coitu mulieris, abominationem fecerunt ambo: morte morientur, sanguis eorum super eos.

15. And if a man lie with a beast, he shall surely be put to death; and ye shall slay the beast.

15. Si quis intulerit coitum suum in brutum, moriendo morietur, et jumentum occidetis.

16. And if a woman approach unto any beast, and lie down thereto, thou shalt kill the woman and the beast: they shall surely be put to death; their blood shall be upon them.

16. Si mulier accesserit ad unum animal ad coeundum cum eo, occides mulierem et animal, moriendo morientur, sanguis eorum super eos.

13. If a man also [63] God had hitherto taught what was right, in order to restrain the people from sin, not only from fear of punishment, but for conscience' sake. But whereas all do not voluntarily dispose themselves to obedience, the awards severe punishments to those wicked despisers in whom there is no effort to be religious. And it is astonishing that almost all the Gentiles have so sunk into stupid and brutal folly, that they have tolerated with little less than impunity unnatural crimes, detestable in their very name.

I admit that even the wickedest of them were ashamed to justify so gross a crime; but although it was practiced with impunity, it was a common reproach to make even against the very public tribunals, that it ought to be more severely punished than other crimes, which they did not spare.

Both of the offending parties were subjected to the same punishment, because it is a pollution which ought by no means to be borne. Nay, if a man or woman offend with a beast, in order that, all may the more abhor and beware of the unnatural crime, the penalty is extended even to the harmless animal; as we have before seen that a goring ox is condemned to death if it had killed a man. Hence we infer how greatly displeasing to God is this kind of crime, since its iniquity is confirmed by the death of guiltless animals.

Leviticus 19

Leviticus 19:29

29. Do not prostitute thy daughter, to cause her to be a whore; lest the land fall to whoredom, and the land become full of wickedness.

29. Non pollues filiam tuam prostituendo eam: neque scortetur terra, et impleatur ipsa scelere.

This passage more clearly proves that all unlicensed connections [64] were always unlawful in God's sight. It is a tame and forced interpretation to apply what is here said to spiritual fornication; and those also, who suppose that public stews only are forbidden, restrict the law too much, whereas God rather gives a general injunction that parents should preserve their daughters by means of a pure and chaste education. But even although we admit that nothing else is prohibited but that parents should be the panders of their daughters, still we gather from the word pollute [65] (for some render the word חלל, chalal, too tamely to make common) that they are contaminated by their whoredom, and the reason given abundantly confirms the fact, that all whoredom is hateful to God, "lest the land fall to whoredom, (He says,) and the land become full of wickedness." It is plain that adultery is not in question here; but God declares it to be criminal if a man and woman have connection out of wedlock. Consequently, the people are taught in the Seventh Commandment to beware of all unchastity.

Deuteronomy 23

Deuteronomy 23:17

17. There shall be no whore of the daughters of Israel, nor a sodomite of the sons of Israel.

17. Non erit meretrix e filiabus Israel, neque erit scortum masculum e filiis Israel.

This passage is akin to the foregoing; for in the first clause He forbids that girls should be prostituted. Some think that a whore is called in Hebrew קדשה, kedeshah, because she is exposed to, and prepared for sin; [66] but her pollution, the opposite of sanctity, seems rather to be expressed by antiphrasis. At any rate, a precept of chastity is given, that it should not be lawful for unmarried girls to have connection with men. In the second clause there is some ambiguity, "There shall be no קדש, kadesh, of the sons of Israel;" for in other passages it is clearly used for a catamite, or male harlot, but there is no reason why it should not be rendered a fornicator. In this sense the word seems to be used in the Book of Job: "The hypocrites shall die in youth, (or in the flower of their age,) and their life is among the קדשים, kedeshim," which is equivalent to their being infamous and shameful in life. (Job 36:14.) But if it be preferred to apply it to sodomy, all impurity is condemned by synecdoche

Leviticus 20 ⁶⁷

Leviticus 20:10

10. And the man that committeth adultery with another man's wife, even he that committeth adultery with his neighbor's wife, the adulterer and the adulteress shall surely be put to death.

10. Vir qui adulterium commiserit cum uxore alterius, qui adulterium commiserit cum uxore proximi sui moriendo morientur adulter et adultera.

Deuteronomy 22

Deuteronomy 22:22-27

22. If a man be found lying with a woman married to all husband, then they shall both of them die, both the man that lay with the woman, and the woman: so shalt thou put away evil from Israel.

22. Si quis deprehensus fuerit coiisse cum muliere conjugata marito, morientur etiam ambo ipsi, vir qui coierit cum muliere, et mulier ipsa: atque auferes malum ex Israele.

23. If a damsel that is a virgin he betrothed unto an husband, and a man find her in the city, and lie with her;

23. Quum fuerit puella virgo desponsata viro, et invenerit eam aliquis in urbe, coieritque cum ea:

24. Then ye shall bring them both out unto the gate of that city, and ye shall stone them with stones that they die; the damsel, because she cried not, being in the city; and the man, because he hath humbled his neighbor's wife: so thou shalt put away evil from among you.

24. Adducetis utrunque ad portam urbis ejus, et lapidabitis eos lapidibus, ac morientur: puellam quidem, quod non clamaverit in urbe: et virum, propterea quod affiixit uxorem proximi sui: atque ita auferes malum e medio tui.

25. But if a man find a betrothed damsel in the field, and the man force her, and lie with her: then the man only that lay with her shall die:

25. At si in agro invenerit vir puellam desponsatam, et apprehenderit eam vir ille, et coierit cum ea, morietur vir qui coierit cum ea solus.

26. But unto the damsel thou shalt do nothing; there is in the damsel no sin worthy of death: for as when a man riseth against his neighbor, and slayeth hint, even so is this matter:

26. Puellae vero non facies quicquam: non est puellae peccatum mortis: nam quemadmodum insurgit quis in proximum suum, et occidit eum anima, sic se habet res ista.

27. For he found her in the field, and the betrothed damsel cried, and there was none to save her.

27. In agro invenit eam, clamavit puella desponsata, et nemo adfuit qui servaret eam.

Deuteronomy 22:22. If a man be found lying with. A Political Supplement, whereby it appears how greatly God abominates adultery, since He denounces capital punishment against it. And assuredly, since marriage is a covenant consecrated by God, its profanation is in no wise tolerable; and conjugal faith should be held too sacred to be violated with impunity, whilst it is an act of horrible perfidiousness to snatch from a man's bosom the wife who is as his very life, or at any rate half of himself. Wherefore, also, the Prophet ignominiously compares adulterers to neighing horses, (Jeremiah 5:8;) for where such lasciviousness prevails, men degenerate, as it were, into beasts. Another reason is, however, here referred to; for, if a man had broken faith with his wife by having connection with a harlot, it was not a capital offense; but if any man, though a bachelor, had committed adultery with the wife of another, (he was to die, [68]) because both the husband is grossly injured, and the dishonor descends to the offspring, and all adulterine race is substituted in place of the legitimate one, whilst the inheritance is transferred to strangers, and thus bastards unlawfully possess themselves of the family name. This cause impelled the Gentiles, even before the Law, to punish adultery with severity, as clearly appears from the history of Judah and Tamar. (Genesis 38:14.) Nay, by the universal law of the Gentiles, the punishment of death was always awarded to adultery; wherefore it is all the baser and more shameful in Christians not to imitate at least the heathen. Adultery is punished no less severely by the Julian law [69] than by that of God; whilst those who boast themselves of the Christian name are so tender and remiss, that they visit this execrable offense with a very light reproof. And lest they should abrogate God's law without a pretext, they allege the example of Christ, who dismissed the woman taken in adultery, whereas she ought to have been stoned; just as He withdrew Himself into a mountain that He might not be made a king by the multitude. (John 8:11, and 6:15.) For if we consider what the office was which the Father delegated to His only-begotten Son, we shall not be surprised that He was content with the limits of His vocation, and did not discharge the duties of a Judge. But those who have been invested with the sword for the correction of crime, have absurdly imitated His example, and thus their relaxation of the penalty has flowed from gross ignorance.

Although the disloyalty of husband and wife are not punished alike by human tribunals, still, since they are under mutual obligation to each other, God will take vengeance on them both; and hence the declaration of Paul takes effect before the judgment-seat of God, Let not married persons defraud one another; for the wife hath not power of her own body, nor the husband of his. (1 Corinthians 7:4, 5.)

23. If a damsel that is a virgin be betrothed. The severity of the punishment is now extended further, and a betrothed woman is counted as a wife; and this for a very good reason, because she has plighted her troth, and it is a token of abandoned incontinency for the mind of a woman to be so alienated from the man to whom she is betrothed, as to prostitute her virginity to another's embraces. But since one who has been ravished is not criminal, a woman is

absolved if she be forced in a field, because it is probable that she yielded unwillingly, inasmuch as she was far from assistance. Although, however, the terms are accommodated to the comprehension of a rude people, it was the intention of God to distinguish force from consent. Thus if a girl had been forced in a retired part of a building, from whence her cries could not be heard, God would undoubtedly have her acquitted, provided she could prove her innocence by satisfactory testimony and conjecture.

Leviticus 19

Leviticus 19:20-22

20. And whosoever lieth carnally with a woman that is a bond-maid, betrothed to an husband, and not at all redeemed, nor freedom given her; she shall be scourged: they shall not be put to death, because she was not free.

20. Vir si coierit cum muliere coitu seminis quae fuerit ancilla desponsata viro, nec redimendo redempta fuerit, nec fuerit manumissa, vapulatio erit: non morientur, quia non est libertate donata.

21. And he shall bring his trespass-offering unto the Lord, unto the door of the tabernacle of the congregation, even a ram for a trespass-offering.

21. Adducet autem oblationem, pro delicto suo Jehovae ad ostium tabernaculi conventionis, arietem pro delicto.

22. And the priest shall make au atonement for him with the ram of the trespass-offering before the Lord, for his sin which he hath done; and the sin which he hath done shall be forgiven him.

22. Et expiabit eum sacerdos per arietem pro delicto coram Jehova, propter peccatum suum quod peccavit: et remittet ei peccatum suum quod peccavit.

Albeit in God's sight there is no difference between bond and free, yet their condition is diverse as regards courts of justice; [70] nor do the same evil consequences ensue from adultery with a bond-maid, (as with a free woman.)[71] Notwithstanding, therefore, that the crime is worthy of death, still, in consideration of the people's infirmity, the punishment is mitigated, so that, if a person shall have corrupted a betrothed bond-maid, both shall be scourged.[72] From hence we infer that, if a concubine, who had already cohabited with a man, were seduced, it was accounted a capital adultery. Lest it should be falsely held, from the lenity or indulgence of the law, that the offense was a trifling one, this error is at once anticipated by the addition of the expiation: for, if one already beaten with stripes still required reconciliation, it follows that the measure of the offense is not to be estimated by its penalty.

Exodus 21:7-11

7. And if a man sell his daughter to be a maid-servant, she shall not go out as the men-servants do.

7. Quum vendiderit quispiam filiam suam in ancillam, non egredietur quemadmodum egredi solent servi.

8. If she please not her master, who hath betrothed her to himself, then shall he let her be redeemed: to sell her unto a strange nation he shall have no power, seeing he hath dealt deceitfully with her.

8. Si displicuerit hero suo, nec sibi desponderit eam, redimendam curabit: populo alieno non habebit potestatem vendendi eam, quum spreverit eam.

9. And if he have betrothed her unto his son, he shall deal with her after the manner of daughters.

9. Quod si filio suo desponderit eam, secundum morem filiarum faciet ei.

10. If he take him another wife; her food, her raiment, and her duty of marriage, shall he not diminish.

10. Si aliam acceperit sibi, alimentum illius, operimentum illius, et constitutionem illius non diminuet.

11. And if he do not these three unto her, then shall she go out free without money.

11. Quod si tria haec non fecerit illi, egredietur gratis absque argento.

From this passage, as well as other similar ones, it plainly appears how many vices were of necessity tolerated in this people. It was altogether an act of barbarism that fathers should sell their children for the relief of their poverty, still it could not be corrected as might have been hoped. Again, the sanctity of the marriage-vow should have been greater than that it should be allowable for a master to repudiate his bond-maid, after he had betrothed her to himself as his wife; or, when he had betrothed her to his son, to make void that covenant, which is inviolable: for that principle ought ever to hold good -- "Those whom God hath joined together, let not man put asunder." (Matthew 19:6; Mark 10:9.) Yet liberty was accorded to the ancient people in all these particulars; only provision is here made that the poor girls should not suffer infamy and injury from their repudiation. But, although God is gracious in remitting the punishment, still He shows that chastity is pleasing to Him, as far as the people's hardness of heart permitted. First of all, He does not allow a master to seduce his purchased maid-servant, but if he wishes to enjoy her embraces, a marriage must take place; for although He does not set this out in express terms, still we may infer from what He condemns, that the contrary is what He approves. From whence, too, their notion is refuted who suppose that fornication was lawful under the Law. But the words must be more closely examined on account of their ambiguity. First, the sex is treated with consideration, that the condition of a female may be somewhat more favorable than that of a male; since, otherwise, their weakness would render young women subject to injury and shame. An explanation then follows, respecting which, however, interpreters differ; for some read the particle ⁷⁴, לא lo, which is properly negative, for לו, lo; and hence arise two opposite meanings -- If he hath, or hath not, betrothed her to himself. If it be preferred to take it affirmatively, the meaning of the precept will be: If a master shall repudiate his bond-maid, whom he has loved and destined to be his wife, he must give her her liberty; for although literally it is, "he shall cause her to be redeemed," yet; the context shows that the obligation of setting her free is laid upon him; nor is this contradicted by the fact that he is only deprived of the power of selling her to a strange people; since I do not understand this as applying to foreigners only, but to others of his own nation, since sometimes those of another tribe or family are called strangers. For, even though there were no marriage-compact, it was not otherwise lawful to sell slaves of the holy and elect people to foreigners. Besides, amongst the Israelites, slavery was only temporary. But, to pass by everything else, let it suffice to observe the absurdity that a master should hold his wife as a slave to be sold at pleasure, if their opinion is received who suppose that the words refer to repudiation after betrothal. [75] I myself rather approve of the other opinion, that, although the master shall not have aspired to matrimony with her, if her appearance displeases him so that he would be unwilling to have her as his wife, at least he must provide for her redemption; because her chastity would be in jeopardy if she remained with him unmarried; unless perhaps Moses may signify that, after she had been seduced, her master did not honor her with marriage. But the other view which I have just expressed is more simple; and a caution is given lest masters should seduce their maid-servants at their pleasure. Thus the word despise [76] does not refer to repudiation, but is opposed to beauty, or conjugal love.

The next case is, that if he should betroth her to his son, (he must give her a dowry, [77]) in which, also, her modesty and honor is consulted, lest she should be oppressed by the right of ownership, and become a harlot. In the third place, it is provided that, if she should be repudiated, her condition should not be disadvantageous. If, therefore, he would make her his daughter-in-law, and betroth her to his son, he is commanded to deal liberally with her; for "after the manner of daughters" is equivalent to giving her a dowry, or, at any rate, to treating her as if she were free. Finally, he adds that, if he should choose another wife for his son, he should not reject the former one, nor defraud her of her food and raiment, or of some third thing, concerning which translators are not well agreed. Some render it time, but I do not see what is the meaning of diminishing her time; others, duty of marriage, but this is too free a translation; others, more correctly, affliction, since the girl would be humiliated by her repudiation; still, to diminish affliction, is too harsh an expression for to compensate an injury. Let my readers, then, consider whether the word, ענתה, gnonathah, is not used for compact or agreement; for thus the context will run very well: If his son have married another wife, that the girl who has suffered ignominious rejection should obtain her rights as to food, and raiment, and her appointed dowry; otherwise, God commands that she should be set free gratuitously, in order that her liberty may compensate for the wrong she has received.

Exodus 22

Exodus 22:16, 17

16. And if a man entice a maid that is not betrothed, and lie with her; he shall surely endow her to be his wife.

16. Quum seduxerit quispiam virginem quae non est desponsata, et coierit cum ea, dotando dotabit sibi in uxorem.

17. If her father utterly refuse to give her unto him, he shall pay money according to the dowry of virgins.

17. Si renuendo renuerit pater ejus ei dare ipsam, pecuniam appendet secundum dotem virginum.

Hence, also, it is manifest that, although God remits the judicial penalty, fornication is displeasing to Him. As to the spiritual judgment of the conscience, there were expiations to propitiate Him; He here only has consideration for young females, lest, being deceived, and having lost their virginity, they should become prostitutes; and thus the land should be defiled by whoredom. The remedy is, that lie who has corrupted girl should be compelled to marry her, and also to give tie a dowry from his own property, lest, if he should afterwards cast her off, she should go away from her bed penniless. But, if the marriage should not please her father, the penalty imposed on her seducer is, that he should assign her a wedding portion.

Deuteronomy 24

Deuteronomy 24:5

5. When a man hath taken a new wife, he shall not go out to war, neither shall he be charged with any business; but he shall be free at home one year, and shall cheer up his wife which he hath taken.

5. Quum quis acceperit uxorem novam, non egredietur ad bellum, neque injungetur ei munus: immunis erit in domo sua anno uno, et delectabit uxorem suam quam accepit.

The immunity here given has for its object the awakening of that mutual love which may preserve the conjugal fidelity of husband and wife; for there is danger lest, if a husband departs from his wife immediately after marriage, the bride, before she has become thoroughly accustomed to him, should be too prone to fall in love with some one else. A similar danger affects the husband; for in war, and other expeditions, many things occur which tempt men to sin. God, therefore, would have the love of husband and wife fostered by their association for a whole year, that thus mutual confidence may be established between them, and they may afterwards continually beware of all incontinency.

But that God should permit a bride to enjoy herself with her husband, affords no trifling proof of His indulgence. Assuredly, it cannot be but that the lust of the flesh must affect the connection of husband and wife with some amount of sin; yet God not only pardons it, but covers it with the veil of holy matrimony, lest that which is sinful in itself should be so imputed; nay, He spontaneously allows them to enjoy themselves. With this injunction corresponds what Paul says,

"Let the husband render unto his wife due benevolence: and likewise also the wife unto the husband. Defraud ye not one the other, except it be with consent for a time, that ye may give yourselves to fasting and prayer." (1 Corinthians 7:3, 5.)

Numbers 5

Numbers 5:11-31

11. And the Lord spoke unto Moses, saying,

11. Loquutus est Jehova ad Mosen, dicendo:

12. Speak unto the children of Israel, and say unto them, If any man's wife go aside, and commit a trespass against him,

12. Alloquere filios Israel, et dicas illis, Quum diverterit uxor cujuspiam, et praevaricata fuerit praevaricatione:

13. And a man lie with her carnally, and it be hid from the eyes of her husband, and he kept close, and she be defiled, and there be no witness against her, neither she be taken with the manner;

13. Et coierit aliquis cum ea coitu seminis, absconditum autem fuerit ab oculis viri sui et delituerit, ipsaque polluta fuerit: testis vero non fuerit contra eam, neque ipsa fuerit deprehensa:

14. And the spirit of jealousy come upon him, and he be jealous of his wife, and she be defiled; or if the spirit of jealousy come upon him, and he be jealous of his wife, and she be not defiled:

14. Et transierit super eum spiritus zelotypiae, zelatusque fuerit uxorem suam, et ipsa polluta fuerit: vel transierit super eum spiritus zelotypiae, zelatusque fuerit uxorem suam, et ipsa non fuerit polluta:

15. Then shall the man bring his wife unto the priest, and he shall bring her offering for her, the tenth part of an ephah of barley meal; he shall pour no oil upon it, nor put frankincense thereon; for it is an offering of jealousy, an offering of memorial, bringing iniquity to remembrance.

15. Tunc adducet vir uxorem suam ad sacerdotem, et afferet obtationem ejus cum illa, nempe decimam partem epha farinae hordeaceae: non fundet super eam oleum, neque ponet super eam thus, quia oblatio zelotypiarum est, oblatio memoriae revocans in memoriam iniquitatem.

16. And the priest shall bring her near, and set her before the Lord.

16. Et appropinquare faciet eam sacerdos, statuetque eam coram Jehova.

17. And the priest shall take holy water in an earthen vessel; and of the dust that is in the floor of the tabernacle the priest shall take, and put it into the water.

17. Tolletque sacerdos aquam sanctum in vase testaceo, de pulvere quoque qui fuerit in pavimento tabernaculi tollet sacerdos, et mittet in aquam illam.

18. And the priest shall set the woman before the Lord, and uncover the woman's head, and put the offering of memorial in her hands, which is the jealousy-offering: and the priest shall have in his hand. the bitter water that causeth the curse.

18. Tum statuet sacerdos mulierem coram Jehova, et discooperiet caput illius mulieris, ponetque super manus ejus oblationem memoriae, quae oblatio zelotypiarum est: et in manum sacerdotis erunt aquae amarae maledictae.

19. And the priest shall charge her by an oath, and say unto the woman, If no man have lain with thee, and if thou hast not gone aside to uncleanness with another instead of thy husband, be thou free from this bitter water that causeth the curse:

19. Et adjurabit eam sacerdos, dicetque illi, Si non coierit quispiam tecum, et si non declinaveris ad immunditiam sub viro tuo, munda esto ab aquis istis amaris maledictis:

20. But if thou hast gone aside to another instead of thy husband, and if thou be defiled, and some man have lain with thee besides thine husband:

20. Si vero declinaveris sub viro tuo, et polluta fueris, dederitque aliquis in te semen suum praeter virum tuum:

21. Then the priest shall charge the woman with an oath of cursing; and the priest shall say unto the woman, The Lord make thee a curse and an oath among thy people, when the Lord doth make thy thigh to rot, and thy belly to swell:

21. (Adjurabit, inquam, mulierem illam sacerdos adjuratione maledictionis, et dicet mulieri,) Det te Jehova in maledictionem et adjurationem in medio populi tui, quum dederit Jehova femur tuum cadens, et uterum tuum tumescentem:

22. And this water that causeth the curse shall go into thy bowels, to make thy belly to swell, and thy thigh to rot. And the woman shall say, Amen, amen.

22. Ingredianturque aquae maledictae istae in interiora tua, ut tumescere faciant uterum, et cadere faciant femur. Et dicet mulier illa, Amen, amen.

23. And the priest shall write these curses in a book, and he shall blot them out with the bitter water:

23. Et scriber maledictiones istas sacerdos in libro, et delebit postea illas cum aquis amaris:

24. And he shall cause the woman to drink the bitter water that causeth the curse: and the water that causeth the curse shall enter into her, and become bitter.

24. Tum ad potandum dabit mulieri aquas amaras maledictas, et ingredientur in eam aquae maledictae, in amaras.

25. Then the priest shall take the jealousy-offering out of the woman's hand, and shall wave the offering before the Lord, and offer it upon the altar.

25. Postea capiet sacerdos e manu mulieris oblationem zelotypiarum, et elevabit illam coram Jehova, offeretque eam super altare.

26. And the priest shall take an handful of the offering, even the memorial thereof, and burn it upon the altar, and afterward shall cause the woman to drink the water.

26. Tollet etiam sacerdos pugillum plenum de oblatione memoriam ejus, adolebitque illud super altare, et postea ad potandum dabit mulieri aquas:

27. And when he hath made her to drink the water, then it shall come to pass, that if she be defiled, and have done trespass against her husband, that the water that causeth the curse shall enter into her, and become

bitter, and her belly shall swell, and her thigh shall rot: and the woman
shall be a curse among her people.

*27. Ad potandum, inquam, dabit ei aquas illas: et erit, si polluta fuerit,
praevaricataque fuerit praevaricatione in virum suum, tunc ingredientur in
illam aquae maledictae versae in amaritudinem, intumescetque uterus ejus, et
cadet femur ejus: et erit mulier illa in maledictionem in medio populi sui.*

**28. And if the woman be not defiled, but be clean; then she shall be
free, and shall conceive seed.**

*28. Quod si non fuerit polluta mulier, sed munda fuerit, munda erit,
seminabiturque semine.*

**29. This is the law of jealousies, when a wife goeth aside to another
instead of her husband, and is defiled;**

*29. Haec est lex zelotypiarum, quum diverterit mulier sub viro suo, et
polluta fuerit.*

**30. Or when the spirit of jealousy cometh upon him, and he be jealous
over his wife, and shall set the woman before the Lord, and the priest shall
execute upon her all this law.**

*30. Aut viri super quem transierit spiritus zelotypiae, et zelatus fuerit
uxorem suam, statueritque mulierem coram Jehova, ac fecerit ei sacerdos
secundum omnem legem hanc.*

**31. Then shall the man be guiltless from iniquity, and this woman shall
bear her iniquity.**

*31. Et innocens erit vir ille ab iniquitate, mulier vero illa portabit
iniquitatem suam.*

11. And the Lord spoke unto Moses. Although this ceremony appears to be
part of the legal services, still I have thought fit to postpone it to this place,
because it relates to the observance of the Seventh Commandment. The object
of it is, lest women, trusting that they would escape punishment, should
abandon themselves to unchastity, or lest jealousy should lead to dissension,
and, by alienating the mind of the husband from the wife, should loosen the ties
of pure affection, since thus the door would be open to many iniquities. By this
rite, therefore, God proclaims Himself the guardian and avenger of conjugal
fidelity; and hence it appears how acceptable a sacrifice in His sight is the
chastity of married women, of which He condescends to profess Himself the
guardian. It is, therefore, no trifling consolation to husbands, that God
undertakes the cognizance of the secret wrong, if, perchance, their wives have
dealt treacherously with them.

But it will be better to examine the details in order. When at the outset he
says, -- If a man's wife go aside, and her offense be concealed, an absurdity
appears to be implied; as if He would thus bring to judgment none but those
who should be convicted, whereas, if the fact were established, there would be
no use in the application of the test. But the condition, "if she commit a trespass
against him," does not signify that the woman's adultery should be discovered,
but refers to the opinion of her husband; and thus the words must be
paraphrased in this way: If any one should think that his wife has had
connection with another man, and he cannot otherwise be relieved from the
anxiety which oppresses him, let him appeal to God for that judgment, which is
beyond the reach of man. Still God [78] seems designedly to have expressed the
crime, lest husbands should heedlessly involve their innocent wives in disgrace.

We know that many are causelessly suspicious; and when jealousy has once taken possession of the mind, there is no room for moderation or equity. [79] Wherefore it would be inhuman to permit morose and unreasonable husbands to drag their wives to this horrible judgment of God on account of certain trifling suspicions. For, if the husband were cruel and ungodly, it would be like putting a sword into the hands of a madman, to give him such a power without any distinction. God, therefore, implies that the priest should carefully consider, so as not too easily to receive every complaint; although He afterwards more clearly expresses Himself in another part of the conditions, "if a man be jealous of his wife, and she be not defiled."

15. Then shall the man bring his wife to the priest. This offering is different from the rest, which have been heretofore mentioned, because it is a kind of adjuration, whereby the woman exposes herself to be accursed. Pure meal without frankincense or oil is therefore offered, since the rite [80] of expiation would not be in accordance with the curse. That the woman may be more afraid of perjuring herself, she is presented before God, with her head uncovered too, as if the priest would drag her from her lurking-place; for it seems incongruous that, as some suppose, the veil was removed from her head in token of her infamy, since thus she would have been condemned before her case was heard. She is, then, brought before God's face with her head bare, that she may be seriously alarmed; and then follows the mode of absolution or condemnation. The priest is commanded to take holy water in an earthen vessel, to throw in some dust from the floor, and then a book or scroll, on which were written the words of the curse, so that the blots should remain in the water, and so to give the cup to the woman. Some interpret the holy water to be that which was kept ill the brazen laver, to be always ready for the ablution of those engaged in duly offering sacrifices. Let my readers, however, consider whether he does not rather mean the water in which the ashes of the red heifer were sprinkled, and whereby solemn purifications were made, (Numbers 19:1,) as we have already seen. For thus the woman was admonished that, if she perjured herself, no further means of expiation remained. The dust collected from the floor was also a sign of detestation: in short, the whole proceedings were calculated to humble her, so that she might not double her offense by perjury. Besides, the priest is commanded to repeat the words of the curse, lest she should seek to escape by some subterfuge or other. The question, however, arises, why she should be compelled to imprecate evil upon herself rather than others were who were suspected of murder or other atrocious crimes? and I think it was for this reason, because no other offense can be so easily concealed. Lest, therefore, women should grow hardened from their cunning and evil arts, a remedy is provided against their various deceptions; and thus God shows that the marriage-bed is under His protection and safeguard. We must remember, too, that this was not a mere empty bugbear, inasmuch as God undoubtedly appeared as the open avenger of unfaithfulness, according to His declaration. Nor is the threat added in vain, that if the woman be a deceiver, she should be a curse among the people, because her belly should swell and her thigh dissolve; whilst, on the other hand, He does not promise in vain, that if she be innocent, she should not only be free, but prolific also; so that God's blessing would be the seal of her absolution. For this is the meaning of the expression, "she shall be sown with seed;" [81] as, on the contrary, it was said that her thigh [82] should dissolve when she wasted away with barrenness.

We infer, from the opposite effects of the same water, that by the outward symbol God wrought with His secret power as the occasion demanded.

Deuteronomy 22

Deuteronomy 22:13-21

13. If any man take a wife, and go in unto her, and hate her,

13. Quum acceperit quis uxorem, et ingressus fuerit ad eam, et odio habuerit eam,

14. And give occasions of speech against her, and bring up an evil name upon her, and say, I took this woman, and when I came to her I found her not a maid:

14. Et imposuerit ei occasiones verborum, et traduxerit eam, dicendo: Uxorem hanc accepi, et accessi ad eam, et non inveni in ea virginitatem:

15. Then shall the father of the damsel, and her mother, take and bring forth the tokens of the damsel's virginity unto the elders of the city in the gate:

15. Tunc accipiet pater puellae et mater ejus, et proferent signa virginitatis puellae eorum senioribus urbis ad portam.

16. And the damsel's father shall say unto the elders, I gave my daughter unto this man to wife, and he hateth her:

16. Dicetque pater puellae senioribus, Filiam meam dedi viro huic in uxorem, et odio habet eam.

17. And, lo, he hath given occasions of speech against her, saying, I found not thy daughter a maid; and yet these are the tokens of my daughter's virginity. And they shall spread the cloth before the elders of the city.

17. Et ecce, imposuit occasiones verborum, dicendo: Non inveni in filia tua virginitatem: Ecce autem signa virginitatis filiae meae. Et expandent vestimentum coram senioribus urbis:

18. And the elders of that city shall take that man and chastise him:

18. Tunc apprehendent seniores urbis virum, et castigabunt eum.

19. And they shall amerce him in an hundred shekels of silver, and give them unto the father of the damsel, because he hath brought up an evil name upon a virgin of Israel; and she shall be his wife: he may not put her away all his days.

19. Et mulctabunt eum centum argenteis, quos dabunt patri puellae, quoniam traduxit virginem Israelis: habebitque eam uxorem, nec poterit dimittere omnibus diebus suis.

20. But if this thing be true, and the tokens of virginity be not found for the damsel:

20. Quod si vera fuit accusatio ista, et non inventa fuerit virginitas in puella:

21. Then they shall bring out the damsel to the door of her father's house, and the men of her city shall stone her with stones that she die; because she hath wrought folly in Israel, to play the whore in her father's house: so shalt thou put evil away from among you.

21. Tunc educent puellam ad ostium domus patris sui, et lapidabunt eam homines urbis ejus lapidibus, donec moriatur: quia perpetravit nequitiam in Israele, fornicando in domo patris sui: et auferes malum e medio tui.

13. **If any man take a wife.** This passage also tends to the exaltation of chastity. God provides against both cases, lest a husband should unjustly bring reproach upon a chaste and innocent young woman, and lest a young woman, having been defiled, should escape punishment, if she pretended to be a virgin. A third object is also to be remarked, viz., that parents were thus admonished to be more careful in watching over their children. This is, indeed, an act of gross brutality, that a husband, wittingly and willingly, should seek a false pretext for divorcing his wife by bringing reproach and infamy upon her; but, since it does not infrequently happen that the libidinous become disgusted with their vices, and then endeavor to rid themselves of them in every way, it was needful to correct this evil, and to prescribe a method whereby the integrity of the woman should be safe from the calumnies of an ungodly and cruel husband; whilst it was also just to give relief to an honest man, lest he should be compelled to cherish in his bosom a harlot, by whom he had been deceived; for it is a very bitter thing to ingenuous minds silently to endure so great an ignominy. An admirable precaution is here laid down, i e., that if a woman were accused by her husband, it was in the power of her parents to produce the tokens of chastity which should acquit her; but if they did not, that the husband should not be obliged against his will to keep her in his house, after she had been defiled by another. It is plain from this passage, that the tokens of virginity were taken on a cloth, on the first night of marriage, as future proofs of chastity. It is also probable that the cloth was laid up before witnesses as a pledge, to be a sure defense for pure and modest young women; for it would have been giving too much scope to the parents if it had been believed simply on their evidence; but Moses speaks briefly as of a well-known custom.

18. **And the elders of that city shall take that man.** Calumny in this case received a threefold punishment; first, that he, who had invented the false accusation, should be beaten with stripes; secondly, that he should pay an hundred pieces of silver to the father of the girl; thirdly, that he should never be allowed to put her away; and tie reason is given, "because he hath brought up an evil name upon a virgin of Israel." God here shows Himself to be the protector of virgins, that young women may be the more encouraged to cultivate chastity. If any should object that it was a bad provision for the unhappy woman that she should be subjected for ever to tyrannical rule, I reply, that this was done because there was no means for her release; for although, as we shall presently see, men were permitted to obtain a divorce from their wives, still it was neither just nor right to overthrow God's earliest institution. Besides, it was necessary to obviate the trick of the husband who would have gloried in her divorce, as having gained what he desired.

20. **But if this thing be true.** If the punishment should seem to anybody to be somewhat too severe, let him reflect that no kind of fraud is more intolerable. A false sale of a field or a house shall be accounted a crime, as also the utterance of false money; and, therefore, she who abuses the sacred name of marriage for deception, and offers an unchaste body instead of a chaste one, much less deserves to be pardoned. The cause of severity, however, which is expressly mentioned, is much more extensive, i e., because she hath wrought

wickedness, or filthiness in Israel. The translation which some. give, folly, is poor; for although the word. is derived from נבל, nabal, it still means something more atrocious than folly; just as Simeon and Levi, in excuse for their slaughter of the Shechemites, call the defilement of their sister [83] נבלה, nebalah, that is, filthiness in Israel. (Genesis 34:7.) Whence it appears once more how greatly acceptable to God is chastity.

Deuteronomy 24

Deuteronomy 24:1-4

1. When a man hath taken a wife, and married her, and it come to pass that she find no favor in his eyes, because he hath found some uncleanness in her; then let him write her a bill of divorcement, and give it in her hand, and send her out of his house.

1. Si acceperit quis uxorem, et coierit cum ea, non autem invenerit gratiam in oculis ejus, eo quod invenerit in ea maculam aliquam, et seripserit ei libellum repudii, ac tradiderit in manum ejus, et emiserit e domo sua:

2. And when she is departed out of his house, she may go and be another man's wife

2. Illa vero egressa e domo ejus, abierit, et nupserit alteri viro:

3. And if the latter husband hate her, and write her a bill of divorcement, and giveth it in her hand, and sendeth her out of his house; or if the latter husband die, which took her to be his wife;

3. Vir deinde hic posterior oderit eam, et scripserit libellum divortii, tradideritque in manum ejus, et emiserit e domo sua, aut si vir iste posterior mortuus fuerit qui sumpserit eam sibi uxorem:

4. Her former husband, which sent her away, may not take her again to be his wife, after that she is defiled; for that is abomination before the Lord: and thou shalt not cause the land to sin, which the Lord thy God giveth thee. for an inheritance.

4. Non poterit maritus ejus prior, quia eam a se demisit, reverti, et ducere eam sibi uxorem, posteaquam polluta est: quia abominatio est coram facie Jehovae: et non inquinabis peccato terram quam Jehova Deus tuus tradet tibi in haereditatem.

Although what relates to divorce was granted in indulgence to the Jews, yet Christ pronounces that it was never in accordance with the Law, because it is directly repugnant to the first institution of God, from whence a perpetual and inviolable rule is to be sought. It is proverbially said that the laws of nature are indissoluble; and God has declared once for all, that the bond of union between husband and wife is closer than that of parent and child; wherefore, if a son cannot shake off the paternal yoke, no cause can permit the dissolution of the connection which a man has with his wife. Hence it appears how great was the perverseness of that nation, which could not be restrained from dissolving a most sacred and inviolable tie. Meanwhile the Jews improperly concluded from their impunity that that was lawful, which God did not punish because of the hardness of their hearts; whereas they ought rather to have considered, agreeably to the answer of Christ, that man is not at liberty to separate those whom God hath joined together. (Matthew 19:6.) Still, God chose to make a provision for women who were cruelly oppressed, and for whom it was better that they should at once be set free, than that they should groan beneath a cruel tyranny during their whole lives. Thus, in Malachi, divorce is preferred to polygamy, since it would be a more tolerable condition to be divorced than to bear with a harlot and a rival. (Malachi 2:14.) And undoubtedly the bill or scroll of divorce, whilst it cleared the woman from all disgrace, cast some reproach on the husband; for he who confesses that he puts away his wife, because she does not please him, brings himself under the accusation both of moroseness and inconstancy. For what gross levity and disgraceful inconstancy it shows, that a husband should be so offended with some imperfection or disease in his wife, as to east away from him half of himself! We see, then, that husbands were indirectly condemned by the writing of divorce, since they thus committed an injury against their wives who were chaste, and in other respects what they should be. On these grounds, God in Isaiah, in order that He might take away from the Jews all subject of complaint, bids them produce the bill of divorce, if He had given any to their mother, (Isaiah 1:1;) as much as to say, that His cause for rejecting them was just, because they had treacherously revolted to ungodliness.

Some interpreters do not read these three verses continuously, but suppose the sense to be complete at the end of the first, wherein the husband testifies that he divorces his wife for no offense, but because her beauty does not satisfy his lust. If, however, we give more close attention, we shall see that it is only one provision of the Law, viz., that when a man has divorced his wife, it is not lawful for him to marry her again if she have married another. The reason of the law is, that, by prostituting his wife, he would be, as far as in him lay, acting like a procurer. In this view, it is said that she was defiled, because he had contaminated her body, for the liberty which he gave her could not abolish the first institution of God, but rather, as Christ teaches, gave cause for adultery. (Matthew 5:31, and 19:9.) Thus, the Israelites were reminded that, although they divorced their wives with impunity, still this license was by no means excused before God.

Leviticus 18

Leviticus 18:19

19. Also thou shalt not approach unto a woman to uncover her nakedness as long as she is put apart for her uncleanness.

19. Ad mulierem in segregatione immunditiae suae non accedes, revelando turpitudinem ejus.

Leviticus 20

Leviticus 20:18

18. And if a man shall lie with a woman having her sickness, and shall uncover her nakedness, he hath discovered her fountain, and she hath uncovered the fountain of her blood: and both of them shall be cut off from among their people.

18. Quicunque dormierit cum meretrice aegra, et revelaverit turpitudinem ejus, fontem ejus discooperuerit, ipsa etiam revelaverit fontem sanguinis sui: succidentur ambo e medio populi sui.

Leviticus 20:18. And if a man shall lie [84] The enormity of the crime is seen by the severity of the punishment; and surely, when a man and woman abandon themselves to so disgraceful an act, it is plain that there are no remains of modesty in them. God, therefore, does not only regard the offense itself, but the brutal impulse of lust, whereby men are so carried away as to degenerate from the very feelings of nature. For what wickedness would he abstain from who yields to such impurity, that he breaks through an obstacle in his fury which restrains the brutes themselves? Let us not wonder, then, that God is a severe avenger of such obscenity.

This precept [85] has no other tendency than that believers should be kept far from all filthiness, and that chastity may flourish among them. It is indeed true that a woman, under these circumstances, is withheld from connection with a man by the very foulness of the disease, whilst there is also danger of contagion; but God rather chooses here to be an instructor in decency to His people, than to perform the office of a physician. It must be remembered, therefore, that men are warned against all indelicacy, which is abhorrent to the natural sense; and, by synecdoche, married persons are exhorted to restrain themselves from all immodest lasciviousness, and that the husband should enjoy his wife's embraces with delicacy and propriety.

Leviticus 18

Leviticus 18:1-4, 6-18

1. And the Lord spoke unto Moses, saying,

1. Loquutus est autem Jehova ad Mosen, dicendo:

2. Speak unto the children of Israel, and say unto them, I am the Lord your God.

2. Alloquere filios Israel et die eis, Ego Jehova Deus vester.

3. After the doings of the land of Egypt, wherein ye dwelt, shall ye not do; and after the doings of the land of Canaan, whither I bring you, shall ye not do; neither shall ye walk in their ordinances.

3. Secundum opus terrae Aegypti in qua habitastis, ne feceritis: neque secundum opus terrae Chanaan in quam ego introduco vos, feceritis: et in statutis eorum ne ambuletis.

4. Ye shall do my judgments, and keep mine ordinances, to walk therein: I am the Lord your God.

4. Judicia mea facite, et statuta mea observate, ut in ipsis ambuletis: ego Jehova Deus vester.

6. None of you shall approach to any that is near of kin to him, to uncover their nakedness: I am the Lord.

6. Nemo ad propinquam carnis suae accedat ad revelandam turpitudinem: ego Jehova.

7. The nakedness of thy father, or the nakedness of thy mother, shalt thou not uncover: she is thy mother; thou shalt not uncover her nakedness.

7. Turpitndinem patris tui et turpitudinem matris tuae non revelabis: mater tua est, non revelabis turpitudinem ejus:

8. The nakedness of thy father's wife shalt thou not uncover: it is thy father's nakedness.

8. Turpitudinem uxoris patris tui non revelabis: turpitudo patris tui est.

9. The nakedness of thy sister, the daughter of thy father, or daughter of thy mother, whether she be born at home, or born abroad, even their nakedness thou shalt not uncover.

9. Turpitudinem sororis tuae, filiae patris tui, aut filiae matris tuae, quae genita est domi vel genita est foris, non revelabis turpitudinem earum.

10. The nakedness of thy son's daughter, or of thy daughter's daughter, even their nakedness thou shalt not uncover: for theirs is thine own nakedness.

10. Turpitudinem filiae filii tui, vel filiae tuae non revelabis, quia turpitudo tua sunt.

11. The nakedness of thy father's wife's daughter, begotten of thy father, (she is thy sister,) thou shalt not uncover her nakedness.

11. Turpitudinem filiae uxoris partis tui, prolis patris tui, quae soror tua est, non revelabis.

12. Thou shalt not uncover the nakedness of thy father's sister: she is thy father's near kinswoman.

12. Turpitudinem sororis patris tui non revelabis: nam consanguinea patris tui est.

13. Thou shalt not uncover the nakedness of thy mother's sister: for she is thy mother's near kinswoman.

13. Turpitudinem sororis matris tuae non revelabis, nam consanguinea matris tuae est.

14. Thou shalt not uncover the nakedness of thy father's brother, thou shalt not approach to his wife: she is thine aunt.

14. Turpitudinem fratris patris tui non revelabis, ad uxorem ejus non accedes: nam uxor fratris patris tui est.

15. Thou shalt not uncover the nakedness of thy daughter-in-law: she is thy son's wife; thou shalt not uncover her nakedness.

15. Turpitudinem nurus tuae non revelabis: uxor filii tui est, non revelabis turpitudinem ejus.

16. Thou shalt not uncover the nakedness of thy brother's wife: it is thy brother's nakedness.

16. Turpitudinem uxoris fratris tui non revelabis, quia turpitudo fratris tui est.

17. Thou shalt not uncover the nakedness of a woman and her daughter, neither shalt thou take her son's daughter, or her daughter's daughter, to uncover her nakedness; for they are her near kinswomen: it is wickedness.

17. Turpitudinem mulieris et filiae ejus non revelabis: filiam filii ejus et filiam filiae ejus non accipies ad revelandam turpitudinem ejus: consanguineae sunt, scelus est.

18. Neither shalt thou take a wife to her sister, to vex her, to uncover her nakedness, besides the other in her life-time

18. Mulierem quoque cum sorore sua non accipies ad affligendum et revelandum turpitudinem ejus contra eam (vel, super eam) in vita sua.

1. **And the Lord spoke unto Moses.** I have not introduced this declaration amongst other similar ones, which had for their object the preparation of their minds for the reverent reception of the Law, because, whatever conformity there may be in the words themselves, in their substance there is a great difference; for they were general, whereas this is specially confined to a single point. For it was not God's intention here merely to exhort the people to the study of the Law, but the address respecting the keeping of His statutes is directed to the present cause, since He does not refer indifferently to all the statutes of Himself and of the Gentiles, but restricts Himself to the subject-matter, as it is called; and thus, by the statutes of the Gentiles, He means those corruptions whereby they had perverted His pure institution as to holy matrimony. First, however, tie forbids them from following the customs of the Egyptians, and then includes all the Canaanitish nations. For, since all the Orientals are libidinous, they never had any scruple in polluting themselves by incestuous marriages; whilst it is abundantly proved by history, how great were the excesses of the Egyptians [86] in this respect. A brother had no abhorrence against marrying his uterine sister, nor a paternal or maternal uncle his niece; in a word, they were so dead to. shame that they were carried away by their lusts to trample upon all the laws of nature. This is the reason why God here enumerates the kinds of incest of which the mention would else have been superfluous.

4. **Ye shall therefore keep my statutes and my judgments.** Because it is no less difficult to correct vices, to which men have been long accustomed, than to cure diseases of long standing, especially because people in general so pertinaciously cleave to bad examples, God adduces His statutes, in order to recall the people from the errors of their evil habits into the right way. For nothing is more absurd than for us to fix our minds on the actions of men, and not on God's word, in which is to be found the rule of a holy life. It is, therefore, just as if God would overthrow whatever had been received from long custom, and abolish the universal consent of the world by the authority of His doctrine. With this object He commands His Law to be regarded not once only, as we have already seen, lest the Israelites should abandon themselves to filthy lusts; but He diligently inculcates upon them, that they should turn away from all abuses, and keep themselves within the bounds and ordinances of His Law. And to this refers the expression, "I am the Lord your God;" containing a comparison between Himself and the heathen nations, between whom and His people He had interposed, as it were, a wall of partition.

6. **None of you shall approach to any that is near.** This name does not include all female relations; for cousin-ger-mans of the father's or mother's side are permitted to intermarry; but it must be restricted to the degrees, which He proceeds to enumerate, and is merely a brief preface, declaring that there are certain degrees of relationship which render marriages incestuous. We may, therefore, define these female relations of blood to be those which are spoken of immediately afterwards, viz., that a son should not marry his mother, nor a son-in-law his mother-in-law; nor a paternal or maternal uncle his niece, nor a grandfather his granddaughter, nor a brother his sister, nor a nephew his paternal or maternal aunt, or his uncle's wife, nor a father-in-law his daughter-in-law, nor a brother-in-law his brother's wife, nor a step-father his stepdaughter. The Roman laws accord with the rule prescribed by God, as if their authors had learnt from Moses what was decorous and agreeable to nature.

The phrase which God uses frequently "to uncover the turpitude," is intended to awaken abhorrence, in order that the Israelites may beware more diligently of all incest. The Hebrew word, indeed, ערוה, gnervah, signifies nakedness, therefore some translate it actively, "the nakedness of thy father," i e., the womb which thy father hath uncovered; but this meaning would not be suitable to the nakedness of thy daughter, or thy daughter-in-law, or thy sister. Consequently, there is no doubt but that Moses means to denote that it is a filthy and shameful thing.

We must remember, what I have already hinted, that not only are incestuous connections out of wedlock condemned, but that the degrees are pointed out, within which marriages are unlawful. It is true, indeed, that this was a part of the political constitution which God established for His ancient people; still, it must be borne in mind, that whatever is prescribed here is deduced from the source of rectitude itself, and from the natural feelings implanted in us by Him. Absurd is the cleverness which some persons but little versed in Scripture pretend to, [87] who assert that the Law being abrogated, the obligations under which Moses laid his countrymen are now dissolved; for it is to be inferred from the preface above expounded, that. the instruction here given is not, nor ought to be accounted, merely political. For, since their lusts had led astray all the neighboring nations into incest, God, in order to inculcate chastity amongst his people, says; "I am the Lord your God, ye shall therefore keep my statutes; walk not after the doings of the land of Egypt and of Canaan;" and then He adds what are the degrees of consanguinity and affinity within which the marriage of men and women is forbidden. If any again object that what has been disobeyed in many countries is not to be accounted the law of the Gentiles, the reply is easy, viz., that the barbarism, which prevailed in the East, does not nullify that chastity which is opposed to the abominations of the Gentiles; since what is natural cannot be abrogated by any consent or custom. In short, the prohibition of incests here set forth, is by no means of the number of those laws which are commonly abrogated according to the circumstances of time and place, since it flows from the fountain of nature itself, and is founded on the general principle of all laws, which is perpetual and inviolable. Certainly God declares that the custom which had prevailed amongst the heathen was displeasing to Him; and why is this, but because nature itself repudiates and abhors filthiness, although approved of by the consent (suffragiis) of men? Wherefore, when God would by this distinction separate His chosen people from heathen nations, we may assuredly conclude that the incests which He commands them to avoid are absolute pollutions. Paul, on a very trifling point, sets before our eyes the law of nature; for, when he teaches that it is shameful and indecorous for women to appear in public without veils, he desires them to consider, whether it would be decent for them to present themselves publicly with their heads shorn; and finally adds, that nature itself does not permit it. (1 Corinthians 11:14.) Wherefore, I do not see, that, under the pretext of its being a political Law, [88] the purity of nature is to be abolished, from whence arises the distinction between the statutes of God, and the abuses of the Gentiles. If this discipline were founded on the utility of a single people, or on the custom of a particular time, or on present necessity, or on any other circumstances, the laws deduced from it might be abrogated for new reasons, or their observance might be dispensed with in regard to particular persons, by special privilege; but since, in their enactment, the perpetual decency of nature was alone regarded, not even a dispensation of them would be permissible. It may indeed be decreed that it should be lawful and unpunished, since it is in the power of princes to remit penalties; yet no legislator can effect that a thing, which nature pronounces to be vicious, should not be vicious; and, if tyrannical arrogance dares to attempt it, the light of nature will presently shine forth and prevail. When, formerly, the Emperor Claudius had married his niece Agrippina, [89] for the purpose of averting the shame, he procured a Senatusconsultum, which licensed such marriages; yet no one was found to imitate his example, except one freedman. Hence, just and reasonable men will acknowledge that, even amongst heathen nations, this Law was accounted indissoluble, as if implanted and engraved on the hearts of men. On this ground Paul, more severely to reprove the incest of a step-son with his father's wife, says, that such an occurrence "is not so much as named among the Gentiles." (1 Corinthians 5:1.)

If it be objected that such marriages are not prohibited to us in the New Testament, I reply, that the marriage of a father with his daughter is not forbidden; nor is a mother prohibited from marrying her son; and shall it therefore be lawful for those, who are near of kin, to form promiscuous connections? [90] Although Paul expressly mentions only one kind of incest, yet he establishes its disgrace by adducing the example of the Gentiles, that at least we should be ashamed if more delicacy and chastity is seen amongst them. And:. in fact, another admonition of the same Paul is enough for me, who thus writes to the Philippians:

"Whatsoever things are true, whatsoever things are honest, whatsoever things are just, whatsoever things are pure, whatsoever things are lovely, whatsoever things are of good report; if there be any virtue, and if there be any praise, think on these things." (Philippians 4:8.)

As to those who ascend or descend ill a direct line, it, sufficiently appears that there is a monstrous indecency in the connection of father and daughter, or mother and son. A licentious poet, [91] being about to relate the frantic incest of Myrrha, says:

"Daughters and fathers, from my song retire, I sing of horror."

In the collateral line, the uncles on both sides represent the father, and the aunts the mother; and, consequently, connection with them is forbidden, inasmuch as it would be of somewhat similar impropriety. The same rule affects affinity; for the step-mother, or mother-in-law, is held to stand in the relation of mother; and the step-daughter, or daughter-in-law, in that of daughter; as also the wife of the paternal or maternal uncle is to be regarded in the relation of mother. And, although express mention may not be made of it here, we must form our judgment by analogy as to what is prohibited; -- the uncle on the father's or mother's side is not here forbidden to marry his niece; but, since the nephew is interdicted from marrying his paternal or maternal aunt, the mutual relation of the inferior to the superior degree must prevail. But if any should contend that there is a difference, the reason added by Moses refutes his objection, for it is said, "She is thy father's or thy mother's near kinswoman." Hence it follows, that a niece is guilty of incest if she marries her uncle on either side. As to brothers and sisters, God pronounces that marriage with a sister, although she be not uterine, is unlawful; for He forbids the uncovering of the turpitude of a sister, who is either the daughter of thy father or thy mother.

16. Thou shalt not uncover the nakedness of thy brother's wife. They are bad [92] interpreters who raise a controversy on this passage, and expound it, that a brother's wife must not be taken from his bed, or, if she be divorced, that manage with her would be unlawful whilst her husband was still alive; for it is incongruous to twist into different senses declarations which are made in the same place, and in the same words. God forbids the uncovering of the turpitude of the wife of a father, an uncle, and a son; and when He lays down the same rule respecting a brother's wife in the very same words, it is absurd to invent a different meaning for them. If, therefore, it be not lawful to marry the wife of a father, a son, an uncle, or a nephew, we must. hold precisely the same opinion with respect to a brother's wife, concerning whom an exactly similar law is enacted in the same passage and context. I am not, however, ignorant of the source from whence those, who think otherwise, have derived their mistake; for, whereas God gives a command in another place, that if a man shall have died without issue, his surviving brother shall take his widow to wife, in order that he may raise up of her seed to the departed, (Deuteronomy 25:5,) they have incorrectly and ignorantly restricted this to own-brothers, although God rather designates other degrees of relationship. It is a well-known Hebrew idiom, to embrace under the name of brother all near kinsmen in general; and the Latins also formerly so denominated cousins-german. [93] The law, then, now before us, respecting marriage with a deceased brother's wife, is only addressed to those relations who are not otherwise prohibited from such a marriage, since it was not God's purpose to prevent the loss of a deceased person's name by permitting those incestuous marriages, which tie had elsewhere condemned. Wherefore these two points agree perfectly well, that an own-brother was prohibited from marrying his brother's widow, whilst the next of kin were obliged to raise up seed for the dead, by the right of their relationship, wherever their marriage was otherwise permissible by the enactment's of the law. On this ground Boaz married Ruth, who had previously been married to his near kinsman; and it is abundantly clear from the history, that the law applied to all the near kinsmen. But if any still contend that own-brothers were included in the number of these, on the same grounds the daughter-in-law must be married by her father-in-law, and the nephew's wife by the uncle, and even the mother-in-law by the son-in-law, which it is an abomination to speak of. If any object that Er, Onan, and Shelah, the sons of Judah, were own-brothers, and still that Tamar married two of them, the difficulty is easily solved, viz., that Judah, following the common and received practice of the Gentiles, acted improperly in permitting it. It is plain enough, from the histories of all ages, that there were disgusting and shameless mixtures in the marriages of Oriental nations. By evil communications, then, as is ever the case, Judah was led into giving the same wife to his second son as had before been married to the eldest. And, in fact, God expressly says that this offense was rife among the Gentiles, where tie condemns incestuous connections. This, therefore, I still hold to be unquestionable, that, by the law of Moses, marriage with the widow of an own-brother is forbidden.

18. Neither shalt thou take a wife to her sister. By this passage certain froward persons pretend that it is permitted, if a man has lost his wife, to marry

her own sister, because the restriction is added, not to take the one in the lifetime of the other. From whence they infer, that it is not forbidden that she should succeed in the place of the deceased. But they ought to have considered the intention of the legislator from his own express words, for mention is made not only of incest and filthiness, but of the jealousy and quarrels, which arise from hence. If it had merely been said, "Thou shalt not uncover her turpitude," there would have been some color to their pretext, that the husband being a widower, he would be free to marry his wife's sister; but, when a different object for the law is expressly stated, i e., lest she, who was legally married, should be troubled by quarrels and contentions, it is plain that the license for polygamy is restricted by this exception, in order that the Israelites should be contented with one evil, and, at least, should not expose two sisters to hostile contention with each other. The condition of the first wife was already painful enough, when she was compelled to put up with a rival and a concubine; but it was more intolerable to be constantly quarrelling with her near relative. The name of sister is not, therefore, restricted, I think, to actual sisters, but other relations are included in it, whose marriages would not otherwise have been incestuous. In a word, it is not incest which is condemned, so much as the cruelty of a husband, if he chose to contract a further marriage with the near kinswoman of his wife. Nor can we come to any other conclusion from the words of Moses; for if the turpitude of a brother is uncovered when his brother marries his widow, no less is the turpitude of a sister uncovered when her sister marries her husband after her decease. But hence we plainly see the diabolical arrogance of the Pope, who, by inventing new degrees of kindred, would be wiser than God; whilst he also betrays his cunning, because from this kind of sport he made himself a fat game-bag.

Since from long custom it is established that cousins-german should not marry, we must beware of giving scandal lest too unbridled a liberty should expose the Gospel to much reproach; and we must bear in mind Paul's admonition, to abstain even from things lawful when they are not expedient. (1 Corinthians 10:23.)

Deuteronomy 22

Deuteronomy 22:30

30. A man shall not take his father's wife, nor discover his father's skirt.

30. Non accipiet quisquam uxorem patris sui, neque discooperiet oram patris sui.

30. A man shall not take his father's wife. Since Moses does not here refer to any other kinds of incest, but speaks only of that with a step-mother, it is probable that, what he had more fully set forth before he here briefly recalled to the minds of the Israelites under a single head. At any rate, the prohibition of one offense does not open the gate to other abominations. The expression which he adds, "nor discover his father's skirt," is as much as to say, that the father is exposed to shame when the step-son has; no regard to decency, and goes in to his step-mother. Perhaps he alludes to the sin of Ham, who betrayed his ungodliness by exposing the shame of his father. (Genesis 9:22.)

These Supplements are Judicial [94] – Leviticus 20

Leviticus 20:11, 12, 14, 17, 19-24

11. And the man that lieth with his father's wife hath uncovered his father's nakedness: both of them shall surely be put to death; their blood shall be upon them.

11. Quicunque concubuerit cum uxore patris sui, turpitudinem patris sui revelavit: moriendo morientur ambo, sanguis eorum super eos.

12. And if a man lie with his daughter-in-law, both of them shall surely be put to death: they have wrought confusion; their blood shall be upon them.

12. Vir qui coierit cum nuru sua, moriendo morientur ambo: flagitium admiserunt, sanguis eorum super eos.

14. And if a man take a wife and her mother, it is wickedness: they shall be burnt with fire, both he and they; that there be no wickedness among you.

14. Qui acceperit mulierem et matrem ejus, scelus est: igni comburent illum et illas, ne sit scelus in medio vestri.

17. And if a man shall take his sister, his father's daughter, or his mother's daughter, and see her nakedness, and she see his nakedness; it is a wicked thing; and they shall be cut off ill the sight of their people: he hath uncovered his sister's nakedness; he shall bear his iniquity.

17. Quisquis acceperit sororem suam filiam patris sui, vel filiam matris suae, et viderit turpitudinem ejus, ipsaque viderit turpitudinem illius, foeditas est: propterea succindentur ambo coram oculis populi sui: turpitudinem sororis suae revelavit, iniquitatem suam feret.

19. And thou shalt not uncover the nakedness of thy mother's sister, nor of thy father's sister; for he uncovereth his near kin: they shall bear their iniquity.

19. Turpitudinem sororis matris tuae et sororis patris tui, non discooperies: quia propinquam suam nudavit, iniquitatem suam portabunt.

20. And if a man shall lie with his uncle's wife, he hath uncovered his uncle's nakedness: they shall bear their sin; they shall die childless.

20. Quisquis dormierit cum uxore fratris patris sui, turpitudinem fratris patris sui revelavit, iniquitatem suam portabunt, orbati morientur.

21. And if a man shall take his brother's wife, it is an unclean thing; he hath uncovered his brother's nakedness: they shall be childless.

21. Qui acceperit uxorem fratris sui, opprobrium est, turpitudinem fratris sui revelavit, orbati erunt.

22. Ye shall therefore keep all my statutes, and all my judgments, and do them; that the land, whither I bring you to dwell therein, spew you not out.

22. Custodite itaque omnia statuta mea, et omnia judicia, et facite ea, ut non evomat vos terra in quam ego introduco vos ut illic habitetis.

23. And ye shall not walk in the manners of the nations which I cast out before you: for they committed all these things, and therefore I abhorred them.

23. Neque ambuletis in statutis gentis quam ego ejiciam a facie vestra: omnia enim ista fecerunt, et detestatus sum eas.

24. But I have said unto you, Ye shall inherit their land, and I will give it unto you to possess it, a land that floweth with milk and honey: I am the Lord your God, which have separated you from other people.

24. Vobis autem dixi, Possidebitis terram eorum, quam ego daturus sum vobis ut haereditate eam possideatis terram fluentem lacte et melle: ego Jehova Deus vester qui separavi vos a populis.

Nothing new occurs here, for the object of Moses was, by the enactment of penalties, to sanction the instruction lately given. By previously condemning incestuous marriages, he would cite the Israelites before God, in order that their consciences might abhor the crime, although he gave them nothing to fear from earthly judges; whereas now he alarms them by the dread of punishment, in case any should indulge themselves with too great security. He does not chastise the incestuous with rods, as if they were only guilty of a light offense; but he pronounces it to be a capital crime, if any had sinned against the law of nature; and first he condemns the step-mother and step-son to death, if they should have had connection with each other; he then makes the same decree with reference to the father-in-law and daughter-in-law; and, thirdly, the step-father and step-daughter. But when, if a man cohabits at the same time with a mother and her daughter, he extends the punishment to the mother also, it must be understood, provided she also consents to the abominable medley; for, if a man, against the mother's will, seduces her daughter, and the mother is unable to resist it if she would, she is free from guilt. The same punishment is awarded to brother and sister, and nephew and aunt, and it is extended also to affinity; if any should cohabit with the wife of his uncle or his brother. We have elsewhere explained the meaning of the expression, "their blood shall be upon them;" i.e., that the cause of their death is to be imputed to none but the gross criminals themselves, lest their judges, under the cloak of humanity, should shrink from being severe, since it often happens that those who do not sufficiently weigh the atrocity of the evil, are led away by an empty show of clemency. [95] Moreover, Moses indirectly hints that if the guilty be pardoned, vengeance will be thus provoked against the whole people, since iniquity is fostered by impunity, until it bursts out like a deluge. The penalty of childlessness corresponds with the crime, for it is just that those should be exterminated in barrenness from the world, who have endeavored to corrupt the holy race of Abraham with their adulterous seed.

22. Ye shall therefore keep all my statutes He now warns the Israelites, for the third time, not to imitate the Gentiles, and exhorts them to keep themselves within the limits of the Law. I have already pointed out that this was not done without reason, since otherwise they might have easily fallen away into the approval of their evil habits. Moreover, lest they should shake off God's yoke, after He has said that the nations of Canaan were destroyed on account of similar abominations, He adds, that they were made the inheritors of the land on condition that they should separate themselves from heathen nations.

A Political Supplement - Deuteronomy 25 ⁹⁶

Deuteronomy 25:11, 12

11. When men strive together one with another, and the wife of the one draweth near for to deliver her husband out of the hand of him that smiteth him, and putteth forth her hand, and taketh him by the secrets;

11. Quum rixati fuerunt viri simul alter cum altero, et accesserit uxor unius ut eruat maritum suum e manu percutientis eum, et immiserit manum suam, apprehenderitque pudenda ejus:

12. Then thou shalt cut off her hand, thine eye shall not pity her

12. Tunc abscindes manum illius, nec oculus tuus parcet.

This Law is apparently harsh, but its severity skews how very pleasing to God is modesty, whilst, on the other hand, He abominates indecency; for, if in the heat of a quarrel, when the agitation of the mind is an excuse for excesses, it was a crime thus heavily punished, for a woman to take hold of the private parts of a man who was not her husband, much less would God have her lasciviousness pardoned, if a woman were impelled by lust to do anything of the sort. Neither can we doubt but that the judges, in punishing obscenity, were bound to argue from the less to the greater. A threat is also added, lest the severity of the punishment should influence their minds to be tender and remiss ill inflicting it. It was indeed inexcusable effrontery, willfully to assail that part of the body, from the sight and touch of which all chaste women naturally recoil.

Deuteronomy 22

Deuteronomy 22:12, 5

12. Thou shalt make thee fringes upon the four quarters of thy vesture, wherewith thou coverest thyself

12. Fimbrias facies tibi in quatuor oris operimenti tui quo operies te.

5. The woman shall not wear that which pertaineth unto a man, neither shall a man put on a woman's garment: for all that do so are abomination unto the Lord thy God.

5. Mulier non feret arma viri, nec induet vir muliebre vestimentum: quia abominatio Jehovae Dei tui est quicunque haec facit

12. This also was a part of, or accessory to, chastity, to have regard to modesty in dress; for since the thighs were then without covering, a door was thus opened to many improprieties, if the upper garments were not closed, and many, as if by accident, would have abused this, if it had been allowed, as an incentive to licentiousness; for we see that many rush into such excesses of lasciviousness, as to glory in their shame. God, therefore, would have the flaps of their gowns thus drawn together by ties or latchets, that not even by chance could those parts be uncovered, which cannot be decently or modestly looked upon. But if divine provisions were made even with respect to their garments, so that the elect people should cultivate decency, and diligently guard against everything immodest, it is abundantly clear that not only were adulteries

condemned, but whatever is repugnant to purity and chastity. This passage is improperly referred to the fringes which were sewed to their garments to renew the recollection of the Law, since decency and delicacy are here alone regarded.

5. This decree also commends modesty in general, and in it God anticipates the danger, lest women should harden themselves into forgetfulness of modesty, or men should degenerate into effeminacy unworthy of their nature. Garments are not in themselves of so much importance; but as it is disgraceful for men to become effeminate, and also for women to affect manliness in their dress and gestures, propriety and modesty are prescribed, not only for decency's sake, but lest one kind of liberty should at length lead to something worse. The words of the heathen poet are very true: [97]

"What shame can she, who wears a helmet, show, Her sex deserting?"

Wherefore, decency in the fashion of the clothes is an excellent preservative of modesty.

Footnotes:

59. The quotation is not from the writings of Moses, but an accommodation from Isaiah 30:21.

60. Omitted in Fr.

61. "Toutes dissolutions vilenes." -- Fr.

62. See [10]vol. 2, p. 281, and [11]note.

63. The Supplements of the Seventh Commandment are differently divided in the Fr. There is no such heading as "Judicial Supplements," and this passage, as well as several others, is removed into a separate class, headed "Political Supplements."

64. "Toute compagnie d'homme et de femme hors le mariage." -- Fr.

65. Margin A. V., "profane."

66. The Hebrew verb קדש has the double signification of sanctum esse and praeparare, (Taylor's Concordance,) though only, it would appear, to prepare by sanctifying.

67. These passages are also considered in the Fr. subsequently to some that follow.

68. Added from Fr.

69. See Plin., Ep. 6:13.

70. "Quant aux jugemens terreins, et humains." -- Fr.

71. Added from Fr.

72. C.'s Latin version and Commentary agree here with the margin of, A. V. rather than the text, "she shall be scourged;" margin, "there shall be a scourging." Dathe's translation is "vapulabunt ambo," and his note, "sic Vulgatus recte, sequitur enim pluralis non moriantur. Cf. Michaelis in J. M. P. V., p. 50."

73. This passage also taken further on in Fr.

74. The Hebrew text has לא, not, but with a mark of doubt as to the genuineness of the reading, and the Masoretic note directs the substitution of לו, to him C. follows S. M. in adhering to the text, whilst our A. V. and the LXX. reject not, in accordance with the Masora. -- W

75. This sentence is omitted in Ft., and the following substituted: "Ce mot doncques ou il est dit, Qu'il ne la pourra vendre a des estrangers, est entrelasse, pour monstrer, qu'il n'y eust eu nulle raison qu'il vendist celle qu'il a

abusee de vaine esperance;" this sentence, then, in which it is said that he may not sell her to strangers, is inserted to show that there was no reason why he should sell her whom he has abused with vain hopes.

76. A. V., "If she please not." Margin, "Heb., Be evil in the eyes of, etc."

77. Added from Fr., in which there is much verbal difference here.

78. "Toutefois il semble bien que Dieu ait poisee le cas, qu'une femme fust chargee de presomption vehemente;" still it fully appears that God has supposed the case, that the woman should be charged upon strong presumption. -- Fr.

79. "Nous savons qu'il y a beaucoup de gens ombrageux, qui concoyvent des fantasies a la volee;" we know that there are many suspicious persons who hastily take fancies into their heads. -- Fr.

80. "Litandi ritus." -- Lat. "La facon d'obtenir grace devant Dieu, et se reconcilier." -- Fr.

81. A. V., "and shall conceive seed." "Heb., shall be sown with seed; which the Chaldee expoundeth, shall prove with child." -- Ainsworth.

82. "Thy thigh to fall. Heb., thy thigh falling; in Greek, thy thigh fallen; in Chaldee, thy thigh dissolved. -- Ibid. "Something similar to the disease called prolapsus uteri." -- Adam Clarke.

83. "Folly, that which is contrary to sound reason, wickedness." -- Simon's Heb. Lex. -- W. Taylor, in his Concordance, says, "Folly, rather vice:, villany, or what can be supposed in bad morals to be answerable to sapless, withered flowers, leaves, or fruit.

Genesis 34:7; Joshua 7:15; Judges 19:23, 24."

84. This passage considered further on in Fr., under the head of "Political Supplements."

85. This commentary is, in Fr., appended to Leviticus 18:19, and included previously under the General Supplements of the Commandment.

86. "A very objectionable custom, which is not only noticed by Diodorus, but is fully authenticated by the sculptures both of Upper and Lower Egypt, existed among them from the earliest times, the origin and policy of which it is not easy to explain -- the marriage of brother and sister, which Diodorus supposes to have been owing to, and sanctioned by, that of His and Osiris; but as this was purely an allegorical fable, and these ideal personages never lived on earth, his conjecture is of little weight; nor does any ancient writer offer a satisfactory explanation of so strange a custom." -- Wilkinson's Popular Account of the Ancient Egyptians, 2:224.

87. Thus, the third Canon of the 24th Session of the Council of Trent declares; "Si quis dixerit, eos tantum consanguinitatis et affinitatis gradus, qui Levitico exprimentur, posse impedire matrimonium, et dirimere contractum: nec posse Ecclesiam in nonnullis illorum dispensare, aut constituere, ut plures impediant, et dirimant, anathema sit." "Atqui plane certum est, (says Lorinus, in loco,) praecepta de gradibus in isto capite contenta, cum non sint omnia pure moralia, et naturalia, sed quaedam positiva, et judicialia, per se non obligare Christianos, et idcirco posse per Ecclesiam in quibusdam dispensari."

88. "Sous couverture que la Loy de Moyse a cesse" -- Fr. Under the pretext that the Law of Moses has ceased.

89. "Nec Claudius ultra expectato, obvium apud forum praebet se gratantibus; senatumque ingressus decretum postulat, quo justae inter patruos, fratrumque filias nuptiae etiam in posterum statuerentur.' Neque tamen repertus est, nisi unus talis matrimonii cupitor, T. Alladius Severus, eques Romanus, quem plerique Agrippinae gratia impulsum ferebant." -- Tacitus Ann., Lib. 12:7.

90. "Leur sera il pourtant licite de se mesler confusement ensemble comme bestes?" shall it therefore be lawful to them to mix together confusedly like beasts?

91. Ovid. Metam., 10:300. "Dira canam: procul hinc natae, procul este parentes."

92. In Willet this exposition is attributed to Radulph., Blesensis, and Borrhaus.

93. Thus Augustine (De Civit. Dei. 15:16. Section 2,) says, -- "quod fiebat cum consobrina, pene cum sorore fieri videbatur: quia et ipsi inter se propter tam propinquam consanguinitatem fratres vocantur, et pene germani sunt."

94. Omitted in the French; and the ensuing verses considered under the "Political Supplements" of the Commandment.

95. "Sont ployables, et faciles a pardoner;" are pliable and easily disposed to pardon. -- Fr.

96. Considered in Fr., under the General Supplements.

97. The quotation is from Juvenal, Sat. 6:252: "Quem praestare potest mulier galeata pudorem, Quae fugit a sexu." The Fr. translation is forcible: "qu'une femme, qui contrefait le gendarme, et fuit son sexe, ne gardera nulle honte."

The Eighth Commandment - Exodus 20

Exodus 20:15

15. Thou shalt not steal.

15. Non furaberis.

THE REPETITION OF THE SAME COMMANDMENT - Deuteronomy 5

Deuteronomy 5:19

19. Neither shalt thou steal.

19. Non furaberis.

Since charity is the end of the Law, we must seek the definition of theft from thence. This, then, is the rule of charity, that every one's rights should be safely preserved, and that none should do to another what he would not have done to himself. It follows, therefore, that not only are those thieves who secretly steal the property of others, but those also who seek for gain from the loss of others, accumulate wealth by unlawful practices, and are more devoted to their private advantage than to equity. Thus, rapine is comprehended under the head of theft, since there is no difference between a man's robbing his neighbor by fraud or force. But, in order that God may the better withhold His people from all fraudulent injustice, He uses the word theft, which all naturally abhor as disgraceful. For we know under how many coverings men bury their misdeeds; and not only so, but also how they convert them into praise by false pretexts. Craft and low cunning is called prudence; and he is spoken of as provident and circumspect who cleverly overreaches others, who takes in the simple, and insidiously oppresses the poor. Since, therefore, the world boasts of vices as if they were virtues, and thus all freely excuse themselves in sin, God wipes away all this gloss, when tie pronounces all unjust means of gain to be so many thefts. Nor let us be surprised that this decision should be given by the divine tribunal, when the philosophers deliver nearly the same doctrine.

We must bear in mind also, that an affirmative precept, as it is called, is connected with the prohibition; because, even if we abstain from all wrong-doing, we do not therefore satisfy God, who has laid mankind under mutual obligation to each other, that they may seek to benefit, care for, and succor their neighbors. Wherefore He undoubtedly inculcates liberality and kindness, and the other duties, whereby human society is maintained; and hence, in order that we may not be condemned as thieves by God, we must endeavor, as far as possible, that every one should safely keep what he possesses, and that our neighbor's advantage should be promoted no less than our own.

The Exposition of the Commandment - Leviticus 19

Leviticus 19:11, 13

11. Ye shall not steal, neither deal falsely, neither lie one to another.

11. Non furabimini et non negabiris, neque mentiemini quisque proximo suo.

13. Thou shalt not defraud thy neighbor, neither rob him: the of him that is hired shall not abide with thee all night until the morning.

13. Non opprimes proximum tuum, neque rapies: nec morabitur opus mercenarii apud to usque mane.

God here explains somewhat more clearly His mind and design, for He enumerates as thefts eases in which either deceit or violence is employed. The two words, which we have translated to deny, and to lie, signify also to deceive; as also to lie, or to frustrate hope. [98] There is no question, then, but that God would restrain His people from all craft, or deceit, that they may deal sincerely and honestly with each other; even as Paul wisely explains the meaning of the Holy Spirit, when he exhorts believers to

"put away lying, and to speak every man truth with his neighbor; for we are members one of another." (Ephesians 4:25.)

In the second passage, God commands men to demean themselves meekly and temperately with their neighbors, so as to abstain from all unjust oppression. The meaning which Jerome [99] and others after him, have given to the word עשק gnashak, to calumniate, is incorrect altogether; for it is everywhere used for to oppress, despoil, rob, or lay hands on the goods of another. It is clear, therefore, that as Moses had previously provided against frauds, he now prohibits the iniquity of extorting from our neighbor what we have no right to. Still, violence, or open rapine, is better expressed by the other word גזל gezal; and these [100] two words are, ill my opinion, as it were, genus and species. After he had forbidden, therefore, that they should in any way oppress their brethren and possess themselves of their goods, he at the same time adds, that they should not use violence in despoiling them unjustly. Finally, he points out one mode of unjust oppression, when a person, who has hired himself as a laborer, is defrauded of his wages, and not only if he be sent away without payment, his wages being denied him, but if payment be deferred to the morrow. For we know that hirelings generally live from hand to mouth, and therefore, if there be ever so little delay, they must go without food. Consequently, if a rich man keeps a poor and wretched individual, whose labor he has abused, in suspense, he deprives him as it were of life, in depriving him of his daily food. The sum is, that humanity is so to be cultivated that none should be oppressed, or suffer loss from default of payment.

Deuteronomy 24

Deuteronomy 24:14, 15

14. Thou shalt not oppress an hired servant that is poor and needy, whether he be of thy brethren, or of thy strangers that are in thy land within thy gates:

14. Non opprimes mercenarium pauperem et egenum e fratribus tuis, et ex peregrinis tuis qui sunt in terra tua, intra portas tuas.

15. At his day thou shalt give him his hire, neither shall the sun go down upon it; for he is poor, and setteth his heart upon it: lest he cry against thee unto the Lord, and it be sin unto thee.

15. Die suo reddes mercedem ejus, neque occumbet super eam sol: quia pauper est, et ea sustentat animam suam: ne clamet contra te ad Jehovam, et sit in te peccatum.

14. Thou shalt not oppress an hired servant. This precept is akin to the foregoing. Moses pronounces that he who has hired a poor person for wages oppresses him unless he gives him immediate recompense for his labor; since the two admonitions, "thou shalt; not; oppress," and "thou shalt give him his hire," are to be read in connection with each other. Hence it follows, that if a hireling suffers from want because we do not pay him what he has earned, we are by our very delay alone convicted of unrighteousness. The reason is now more clearly expressed, viz., because he sustains his life by his daily labors. [101] Although, however, this provision only refers to the poor, lest they should suffer hunger from the negligence or pride of the rich, still humanity in general is enforced, lest, whilst the poor labor for our profit, we should arrogantly abuse them as if they were our slaves, or should be too illiberal and stingy towards them, since nothing can be more disgraceful than that, when they are in our service, they should not at least have enough to live upon frugally. Finally, Moses admonishes us that this tyranny on the part of the rich shall not be unpunished, if they do not supply their workmen with the means of subsistence, even although no account shall be rendered of it before the tribunals of men. Hence we infer that this law is not political, but altogether spiritual, and binding on our consciences before the judgment-seat of God; for although the poor man may not sue us at law, Moses teaches us that it is sufficient for him to appeal to the faithfulness of God. Wherefore, although the earthly judge may absolve us a hundred times over, let us not therefore think that we have escaped; since God will always require of us from heaven, whatever may have been unjustly excused us on earth. The question, however, here arises, whether, if he who has been oppressed should not cry out, the criminality will cease in consequence of his silence; for the words of Moses seem to imply this, when he says, that the rich will be guilty, if the poor cry unto God and make complaint of their wrongs. The reply' is easy, that Moses had no other intention than to over-. throw the vain confidence of the despisers, whereby they arc, stimulated to greater audacity in sin, and are hardened in iniquity. He says, therefore, that although, as far as men are concerned, they may allow us to pillage and rob, still a more awful judgment is to be dreaded; for God hears the complaints of the poor, who find no protector or avenger on earth. And surely, the more patiently he who is despoiled shall bear his wrong, the more ready will God be

to undertake his cause; nor is there any louder cry to Him than patient endurance. If, however, any should object that the cry here spoken of is at variance with Christ's command, that we should pray for our enemies, we answer at once, that God does not always approve of the prayers which He nevertheless answers. The imprecation of Jotham, the son of Gideon, took effect upon the Shechemites, (Judges 9:20,) although it was plainly the offspring of immoderate anger. Besides, it sometimes happens that the miserable, although they endure their injuries with pious meekness, still cease not to lay their sorrows and their groans in the bosom of God. Nor is this a slight consolation for the poor, that if no one on earth relieves them because their condition is low and abject, still God will hereafter take cognizance of their cause.

Deuteronomy 25

Deuteronomy 25:4

4. Thou shalt not muzzle the ox when he treadeth out the corn
4. Non obligabis os bovi trituranti.

4. Thou shalt not muzzle the ox. This passage, indeed, properly belongs to the Supplements of the Commandment, but, since it is a confirmation of the foregoing decree, it seemed fit to connect them; especially because its faithful expositor, Paul, declares, that God had no other design in delivering it than that the laborer should not be defrauded of his just hire, (1 Corinthians 9:10;) for, when he is speaking of the maintenance to be afforded to the ministers of the Gospel, he adduces it. in proof of his case. And, lest any should object that there is a difference between oxen and men, he adds, that God does not care for oxen, but that it was said for the sake of those that labor. Meanwhile, we must bear in mind, that men are so instructed in equity, that they are bound to exercise it even towards the brute animals; for well does Solomon magnify the injustice, whereby our neighbor is injured, by the comparison; "A righteous man regardeth the life of his beast." (Proverbs 12:10.) The sum is, that we should freely and voluntarily pay what is right, and that every one should be strict with himself as to the performance of his duty; for, if we are bound to supply subsistence to brute animals, much less must we wait for men to be importunate with us, in order that they may obtain their due.

Exodus 22

Exodus 22:21-24

21. Thou shalt neither vex a stranger, nor oppress him: for ye were strangers in the land of Egypt.
21. Peregrinum non opprimes, neque spoliabis: quia peregrini fuistis in terra AEgypti.
22. Ye shalt not afflict any widow, or fatherless child.
22. Nullam viduam nec pupillum affligetis.
23. If thou afflict them in any wise, and the, and cry at all unto me, I will surely hear their cry:

23. Si affligendo afflixeritis eum, certe si clamando clamaverit ad me, audiendo audiam clamorem ejus:

24. And my wrath shall wax hot, and I will kill you with the sword; and your wives shall be widows, and your children fatherless.

24. Irasceturque furor meus, et occidam vos gladio, eruntque uxores vestrae viduae, et filii vestri pupilli.

Leviticus 19

Leviticus 19:33, 34

33. And if a stranger sojourn with thee in your land, ye shall not vex him.

33. Si peregrinatus tecum fuerit peregrinus in terra vestra, non opprimetis illum.

34. But the stranger that dwelleth with you shall be unto you as one horn among you, and thou shalt love him as thyself; for ye were strangers in the land of Egypt: I am the Lord your God.

34. Tanquam indigena ex vobis, erit vobis peregrinus qui peregrinatur apud vos, et diliges eum sicut teipsum: quia peregrini fuistis in terra: ego Jehova Deus vester.

Leviticus 19:33. And if a stranger sojourn with thee in your land. Before I pass on to the other iniquities, I have thought fit to introduce this precept, wherein the people are commanded to cultivate equity towards all without exception. Fob if no mention had been made of strangers, the Israelites would have thought that, provided they had not injured any one of their own nation, they had fully discharged their duty; but, when God recommends guests and sojourners to them, just as if they had been their own kindred, they thence understand that equity is to be cultivated constantly and towards all men. Nor is it without cause that God interposes Himself and His protection, lest injury should be done to strangers; for since they have no one who would submit to ill-will in their defense, they are more exposed to the violence and various oppressions of the ungodly, than as if they were under the shelter of domestic securities. The same rule is to be observed towards widows and orphans; a woman, on account of the weakness of her sex, is exposed to many evils, unless she dwells under the shadow of a husband; and many plot against orphans, as if they were their prey, because they have none to advise them. Since, then, they are thus destitute of human aid, God interposes to assist them; and, if they are unjustly oppressed, He declares that He will be their avenger. In the first passage He includes widows and orphans together with strangers; in the latter He enumerates strangers only; yet the substance is the same, viz., that all those who are destitute and deprived of earthly succor, are under the guardianship and protection of God, and preserved by His hand; and thus the audacity of those is restrained, who trust that they may commit any wickedness with impunity, provided no earthly being resists them. No iniquity, indeed, will be left unavenged by God, but there is a special reason why He declares that strangers, widows, and orphans are taken under His care; inasmuch as the more flagrant the evil is, the greater need there is of an effectual remedy. He recommends strangers to them on this ground, that the people, who had themselves been sojourners in Egypt, being mindful of their ancient condition, ought to deal more kindly to strangers; for although they were at last oppressed by cruel tyranny, still they were bound to consider their entrance there, viz., that poverty and hunger had driven their forefathers thither, and that they had been received hospitably, when they were in need of aid from others. When He threatens, that if the afflicted widows and orphans cry unto Him, their cry shall be heard, He does not mean that He will not interfere, if they endure their wrongs in silence; but He speaks in accordance with the ordinary practice, that those who find no consolation elsewhere, are wont to appeal to Him. Meanwhile, let us be sure that although those who are injured abstain from complaining, yet God does not by any means forget His office, so as to overlook their wrongs. Nay, there is nothing which incites Him more to inflict punishment on the ungodly, than the endurance of His servants.

The nature of the punishment is also expressed; those who have afflicted widows and orphans shall perish by the sword, so that their own widows and orphans may be exposed to the audacity, violence, and knavery of the ungodly. Moreover, it must be observed that, in the second passage, they are commanded to love strangers and foreigners as themselves. Hence it appears that the name of neighbor is not confined to our kindred, or such other persons with whom we are nearly connected, but extends to the whole human race; as Christ shows in the person of the Samaritan, who had compassion on an unknown man, and performed towards him the duties of humanity neglected by a Jew, and even a Levite. (Luke 10:30.)

Deuteronomy 10

Deuteronomy 10:17-19

17. ...God,...regardeth not persons, nor taketh reward.

17. Deus non accipit personam, neque recipit munus.

18. He doth execute the judgment of the fatherless and widow, and loveth the stranger, in giving him food and raiment.

18. Faciens judicium pupillo et viduae, diligens peregrinum, dando et panem et vestimentum.

19. Love ye therefore the stranger; for ye were strangers in the land of Egypt

19. Diligite igitur peregrinum, quia peregrini fuistis in terra, AEgypti.

He confirms the foregoing decree by a reference to the nature of God Himself; for the vile and abject condition of those with whom we have to do, causes us to injure them the more wantonly, because they seem to be altogether deserted. But God declares that their unhappy lot is no [102] obstacle to His administering succor to them; inasmuch as He has no regard to persons. By the word person is meant either splendor, or obscurity, and outward appearance, as it is commonly called, as we gather from many passages. In short, God distinguishes Himself from men, who are carried away by outward appearance, to hold the rich in honor, and the poor in contempt; to favor the beautiful or the eloquent, and to despise the unseemly. Προσωποληψία is, therefore, an unjust judgment, which diverts us from the cause itself, when our minds are prejudiced by what ought not to be taken into account. Therefore Christ teaches us that a judgement is righteous, which is not founded upon the appearance, (John 7:23;) since truth and justice never prevail, except when we attend to the case itself. It follows that the contemptible are not afflicted with impunity, for although they may be destitute of human aid, God, who sitteth on high, "hath respect unto the lowly." (Psalm 138:6.) As regards strangers, God proves that he cares for them, because He is gracious in preserving them and clothing them; and then a special reason is again adduced, that the Israelites, when they were formerly sojourners in Egypt, had need of the compassion of others.

Leviticus 19

Leviticus 19:35, 36

35. Ye shall do no unrighteousness in judgment, in mete-yard, in weight, or in measure.

35. Non facietis iniquitatem in judicio, in dimensione, in pondere et mensura.

36. Just balances, just weights, a just ephah, and a just bin, shall ye have: I am the Lord your God, which brought you out of the land of Egypt.

36. Statera justa, pondera justa, epha justum, et hin justum erit vobis.

Deuteronomy 25

Deuteronomy 25:13-16

13. Thou shalt not have in thy bag divers weights, a great and a small.

13. Non erit tibi in sacculo tuo pondus et pondus, majus et minus:

14. Thou shalt not have in thine house divers measures, a great and a small.

14. Non erit tibi in domo tua modius et modius, major et minor.

15. But thou shalt have a perfect and just weight, a perfect and just measure shalt thou have: that thy days may be lengthened in the land which the Lord thy God giveth thee.

15. Pondus perfectum et justum erit tibi, modius perfectus et justus erit tibi, ut proroges dies tuos super terram quam Jehova Deus tuus dat tibi.

16. For all that do such things, and all that do unrighteously, are an abomination unto the Lord thy God.

16. Quia abominatio Jehovae Dei tui est quicunque facit haec, omnis faciens iniquitatem.

Leviticus 19:35 Ye shall do no unrighteousness in judgment. If you take the word judgment in its strict sense, this will be a special precept, that judges should faithfully do justice to all, and not subvert just causes from favor or ill-will. But since the word משפט, mishpat, often means rectitude, it will not be unsuitable to suppose that all iniquities contrary to integrity are generally condemned; and that he afterwards proceeds to particular cases, which he adverts to elsewhere, where he enumerates the most injurious thefts of all, and such as involve the grossest violation of public justice. For the corruption which tends to the subversion of judgments, or, by undermining rectitude, vitiates all contracts, leaves nothing in security; whilst deception in weights and measures destroys and sweeps away all legitimate modes of dealing. Now, if the laws of buying and selling are corrupted, human society is in a manner dissolved; so that he who cheats by false weights and measures, differs little from him who utters false coin: and consequently one, who, whether as a buyer or seller, has falsified the standard measures of wine or corn, or anything else, is accounted criminal. [103] By the laws of Rome, [104] he is condemned to a fine of double the amount; and by a decree of Adrian, he is to be banished to an island. It is not, therefore, without reason that Solomon reiterates this decree, that he may fix it the deeper in the hearts of all. (Proverbs 20:10, 23.) But although this pestilent sin is by no means to be endured, but to be severely punished, still God, even if legal punishments be not inflicted, summons men's consciences before His tribunal, and this he does both by promises and threats. A just weight (He says) and a just measure shall prolong a man's life; but he who has been guilty of deception in them, is an abomination before me. Length of life, indeed, has only a figurative connection with just weights and measures: but, because the avaricious, in their pursuit of dishonest gain, are too devoted to this transitory life, God, in order to withhold His people from this blind and impetuous covetousness, promises them long life, if they keep themselves from fraud and all knavish dealings. We perceive from the conclusion, that, not in this respect only, but in all our affairs, those trickeries are condemned, by which our neighbors are defrauded. For, after God has said that He abominates "all that do such things," He adds immediately by way of explanation, "all that do unrighteously." We see, then, that He sets Himself against all evil and illicit arts of gain.

Deuteronomy 19

Deuteronomy 19:14

14. Thou shalt not remove thy neighbor's land-mark, which they of old time have set in thine inheritance, which thou shalt inherit in the land that the Lord thy God giveth thee to possess it.

14. Non transferes terminum proximi tui quem finierint majores in haereditate tua, quam haereditate accipies in terra quam Jehova Deus tuus dat tibi ut possideas eam.

A kind of theft is here condemned which is severely punished by the laws of Rome; [105] for that every one's property may be secure, it is necessary that the land-marks set up for the division of fields should remain untouched, as if they were sacred. He who fraudulently removes a landmark is already convicted by this very act, because he disturbs the lawful owner in his quiet possession of the land; [106] whilst he who advances further the boundaries of his own land to his neighbor's loss, doubles the crime by the deceptive concealment of his theft. Whence also we gather that not only are those thieves, who actually carry away their neighbor's property, who take his money out of his chest, or who pillage his cellars and granaries, but also those who unjustly possess themselves of his land.

Exodus 22:26, 27
26. If thou at all take thy neighbor's raiment to pledge, thou shalt deliver it unto him by that the sun goeth down:

26. Si in pignus acceperis vestimentum proximi tui, antequam occubuerit sol restitues illud ei.

27. For that is his covering only; it is his raiment for his skin: wherein shall he sleep? and it shall come to pass, when he crieth unto me, that I will hear; for I am gracious.

27. Quia ipsum solum est operimentum ejus, illud vestimentum ejus est cuti suae in quo dormiat, et erit quum clamaverit ad me, tunc exaudiam: sum enim misericors.

Deuteronomy 24

Deuteronomy 24:6, 10-13, 17, 18
6. No man shall take the nether or the upper millstone to pledge: for he taketh a man's life to pledge.

6. Non accipiet quisquam pro pignore metam et catillum, quia animam ipse acciperet pro pignore.

10. When thou dost lend thy brother any thing, thou shalt not go into his house to fetch his pledge.

10. Quum mutuabis proximo tuo aliquid mutuum, non ingredieris domum ejus ut capias pignus ejus.

11. Thou shalt stand abroad, and the man to whom thou dost lend shall bring out the pledge abroad unto thee.

11. Foris subsistes, et vir cui mutuabis afferet ad te pignus foras.

12. And if the man be poor, thou shalt not sleep with his pledge.

12. Quod si vir pauper fuerit, non dormies cum pignore ejus.

13. In any case thou shalt deliver him the pledge again when the sun goeth down, that he may sleep in his own raiment, and bless thee: and it shall be righteousness unto thee before the Lord thy God.

13. Restituendo ei restitues pignus dum sol occumbit: ut dormiat in vestimento suo, et benedicat tibi: eritque tibi in justitiam coram Jehova Deo tuo.

17. Thou shalt not pervert the judgment of the stranger, nor of the fatherless, nor take a widow's raiment to pledge:

17. Non pervertes judicium pupilli et peregrini, non capies in pignus vestimentum viduae.

18. But thou shalt remember that thou wast a bond-man in Egypt, and the Lord thy God redeemed thee thence: therefore I command thee to do this thing.

18. Recordare quod servus fueris in AEgypto, et redemerit te Jehova Deus tuus inde: idcirco praecipio tibi ut hoc facias.

Deuteronomy 24:6 No man shall take the nether. God now enforces another principle of equity in relation to loans, (not to be too strict [107]) in requiring pledges, whereby the poor are often exceedingly distressed. In the first place, He prohibits the taking of anything in pledge which is necessary to the poor for the support of existence; for by the words which I have translated meta and catillus, i e., the upper and nether millstone, He designates by synecdoche all other instruments, which workmen cannot do without in earning their daily bread. As if any one should forcibly deprive a husbandman of his plough, or his spade, or harrow, or other tools, or should empty a shoemaker's, or potter's, or other person's shop, who could not exercise his trade when deprived of its implements; and this is sufficiently clear from the context, where it is said, "He taketh a man's life to pledge," together with his millstones. He, then, is as cruel, whosoever takes in pledge what supports a poor man's life, as if he should take away bread from a starving man, and thus his life itself, which, as it is sustained by labor, so, when its means of subsistence are cut off, is, as it were, itself destroyed.

10. When thou dost lend thy brother anything He provides against another iniquity in reclaiming a pledge, viz., that the creditor should ransack the house and furniture of his brother, in order to pick out the pledge at his pleasure. For, if this option were given to the avaricious rich, they would be satisfied with no moderation, but would seize upon all that was best, as if making an assault on the very entrails of the poor: in a word, they would ransack men's houses, or at any rate, whilst they contemptuously refused this or that, they would fill the wretched with rebuke and shame. God, therefore, will have no pledge reclaimed, except what the debtor of his own accord, and at his own convenience, shall bring out of his house, lie even proceeds further, that the creditor shall not take back any pledge which he knows to be necessary for the poor: for example, if he should pledge the bed on which he sleeps, or his counterpane, or cloak, or mantle. For it is not just that lie should be stripped, so as to suffer from cold, or to be deprived of other aids, the use of which he could not forego without loss or inconvenience. A promise, therefore, is added, that this act of humanity will be pleasing to God, when the poor shall sleep in the garment which is restored to him. He speaks even more distinctly, and says: The poor will bless thee, and it shall be accounted to thee for righteousness. For God indicates that He hears the prayers of the poor and needy, lest the rich man should think the bounty thrown away which lie confers upon a lowly individual. We must, indeed, be more than iron-hearted, unless we are disposed to such liberality as this, when we understand that, although the poor have not the means of repaying us in this world, still they have the power of recompensing us before God, i e., by obtaining grace for us through their prayers. An implied threat is also conveyed, that if the poor man should sleep inconveniently, or catch cold through our fault, God. will hear his groans, so that our cruelty will not be unpunished. But if the poor man, upon whom we have had compassion, should be ungrateful, yet, even though he is silent, our kindness will cry out to God; whilst, on the other hand, our tyrannical harshness will suffice to provoke God's vengeance, although he who has been treated unkindly should patiently swallow his wrong. To be unto righteousness [108] is equivalent to being approved by God, or being an acceptable act; for since the keeping of the Law is true righteousness, this praise is extended to particular acts of obedience. Although it must be observed that this righteousness fails and vanishes, unless we universally fulfill whatever God enjoins. It is, indeed, a part of righteousness to restore a poor man's pledge; but if a mall be only

beneficent in this respect., whilst in other matters he robs his brethren; or if, whilst free from avarice, he exercises violence, is given to lust or gluttony, the particular righteousness, although pleasing in itself to God, will not come into account. In fact, we must hold fast the axiom, that no work is accounted righteous before God, unless il, proceeds from a man of purity and integrity; whereas there is none such to be found. Consequently, no works are imputed unto righteousness, except because God deigns to bestow His gratuitous favor on believers. In itself, indeed, it would be true, that whatever act of obedience to God we perform, it is accounted for righteousness, i e., if the whole course of our life corresponded to it, whereas no work proceeds from us which is not corrupted by some defect. Thus, we must fly to God's mercy, in order that, being reconciled to us, He may also accept our work.

What he had previously prescribed respecting the poor, lie afterwards applies to widows alone, yet so as to recommend all poor persons to us under their name; and this we gather both from the beginning of the verse (17,) in which lie instructs them to deal fairly and justly with strangers and orphans, and also from the reason which is added, viz., that they should reflect that they were bondmen in the land of Egypt; for their condition there did not suffer them proudly to insult the miserable; and it is natural that he should be the more affected with the ills of others who has experienced the same. Since, then, this reason is a general one, it is evident also that the precept is general, that we should be humane towards all that are in want.

Leviticus 25

Leviticus 25:35-38

35. And if thy brother be waxen poor, and fallen in decay with thee, then thou shalt relieve him; yea, though he be a stranger, or a sojourner: that he may live with thee.

35. Si attenuatus fuerit frater tuus, et vacillaverit manus ejus apud te, fulcies illum (vel, apprehendes ut sustineas): peregrinum et advenam: et vivet tecum.

36. Take thou no usury of him, or increase: but fear thy God; that thy brother may live with thee.

36. Non accipies usuram ab eo et augmentum: sed timebis Deum tuum: vivetque frater apud te.

37. Thou shalt not give him thy money upon usury, nor lend him thy victuals for increase.

37. Pecuniam tuam non dabis ei ad usuram, nec cum augmento dabis escam tuam.

38. I am the Lord your God, which brought you forth out of the land of Egypt, to give you the land of Canaan, and to be your God.

38. Ego Jehova Deus vester qui eduxi vos de terra AEgypti, ut darem vobis terram Chanann, ac essem vobis in Deum.

Deuteronomy 23

Deuteronomy 23:19, 20

19. Thou shalt not lend upon usury to thy brother; usury of money, usury of victuals, usury of any thing that is lent upon usury.

19. Non foenerabis fratri tuo foenus pecuniae, foenus cibi, foenus cujuscunque rei in qua foenus exercetur.

20. Unto a stranger thou mayest lend upon usury, but unto thy brother thou shalt not lend. upon usury; that the Lord thy God may bless thee in all that thou settest thine hand to in the land whither thou goest to possess it.

20. Extraneo foenerabis, ac fratri tuo non foenerabis: ut benedicat tibi Jehova Deus tuus in omni applicatione manus tuae super terram ad quam ingrederis, ut possideas eam.

From these passages we learn that it is not enough to refrain from taking the goods of another, unless we also constantly exercise humanity and mercy in the relief of the poor. Heathen authors also saw this, although not with sufficient clearness, (when they declared [109]) that, since all men are born for the sake of each other, human society is not properly maintained, except by an interchange of good offices. Wherefore, that we may not defraud our neighbors, and so be accounted thieves in God's sight, let us learn, according to our several means, to be kind to those who need our help; for liberality is a part of righteousness, so that he must be deservedly held to be unrighteous who does not relieve the necessities of his brethren when he can. This is the tendency of Solomon's exhortation, that

"we should drink waters out of our own cistern, [110] and that our fountains should be dispersed abroad amongst our neighbors," (Proverbs 5:15, 16;)

for, after he has enjoined us each to be contented with what is our own, without seeking to enrich ourselves by the loss of others, he adds that those who have abundance do not enjoy their possessions as they ought, unless they communicate them to the poor for the relief of their poverty. For this is the reason, as Solomon tells us elsewhere, why "the rich and the poor meet together; and the Lord is the maker of them all." (Proverbs 22:2.)

Exodus 22

Exodus 22:25

25. If thou lend money to any of my people that is poor by thee, thou shalt not be to him as an usurer, neither shalt thou lay upon him usury.

25. Si pecuniam mutuam dederis populo, meo pauperi qui est tecum, non eris ei sicut usurarius: non imponetis ei usuram.

25. If thou lend money to any of my people Humanity ought to be very greatly regarded in the matter of loans, especially when a person, being reduced to extremities, implores a rich man's compassion; for this is, in. point of fact,

the genuine trial of our charity, when, in accordance with Christ's precept, we lend to those of whom we expect no return. (Luke 6:35.) The question here is not as to usury, as some have falsely thought, [111] as if he commanded us to lend gratuitously, and without any hope of gain; but, since in lending, private advantage is most generally sought, and therefore we neglect the poor; and only lend our money to the rich, from whom we expect some compensation, Christ reminds us that, if we seek to acquire the favor of the rich, we afford in this way no proof of our charity or mercy; and hence lie proposes another sort of liberality, which is plainly gratuitous, in giving assistance to the poor, not only because our loan is a perilous one, but because they cannot make a return in kind.

Before descending to speak of loans, God here adverts to poverty and distress, (Leviticus 25:35,) whereby men's minds may be disposed to compassion. If any one be afflicted with poverty, he commands us to relieve his necessity. He makes use, however, of a metaphor, [112] that he who is tottering should be strengthened, as if by catching hold of his hand. What follows about the stranger and sojourner extends and amplifies, in my opinion, the previous sentence; as if it were said that, since humanity is not to be denied even to strangers, much more is assistance to be given to their brethren. For, when it pleased God that strangers should be permitted to inhabit the land, they were to be kindly treated [113] according to the rights of hospitality; for to allow them to live is to make their condition just and tolerable. And thus God indirectly implies, that such unhappy persons are expelled and driven away, so as not to live, if they are oppressed by unjust burdens. This, then, is the sum of the first sentence, that the rich, who has the ability, should uplift the poor man who is failing, by his assistance, or should strengthen the tottering.

A precept is added as to lending without interest, which, although it is a political law, still depends on the rule of charity; inasmuch as it can scarcely happen but that the poor should be entirely drained by the exaction of interest, and that their blood should be almost sucked away. Nor had God any other object in view, except that mutual and brotherly affection should prevail amongst the Israelites. It is plain that this was a part of the Jewish polity, because it was lawful to lend at interest to the Gentiles, which distinction the spiritual law does not admit. The judicial law, however, which God prescribed to His ancient people, is only so far abrogated as that what charity dictates should remain, i.e., that our brethren, who need our assistance, are not to be treated harshly. Moreover, since the wall of partition, which formerly separated Jew and Gentile, is now broken down, our condition is now different; and consequently we must spare all without exception, both as regards taking interest, and any other mode of extortion; and equity is to be observed even towards strangers. "The household of faith." indeed, holds the first rank, since Paul commands us specially to do good to them, (Galatians 6:10;) still the common society of the human race demands that we should not seek to grow rich by the loss of others.

As touching the political law, no wonder that God should have permitted His people to receive interest, from the Gentiles, since otherwise a just reciprocity would not have been preserved, without which one party must needs be injured. God commands His people not to practice usury, and still lays the Jews alone, and not foreign nations, under the obligation of this law. In order, therefore, that equality (ratio analogica) might be preserved, He accords [114] the same liberty to His people which the Gentiles would assume for themselves; for this is the only intercourse that can be endured, when the condition of both parties is similar and equal. For when Plato [115] asserts that usurers are not to be tolerated in a well-ordered republic, lie does not go further than to enjoin, that its citizens should abstain from that base and. dishonest traffic between each other.

The question now is, whether usury is evil in itself; and surely that which heathens even have detested appears to be by no means lawful to the children of God. We know that the name of usurer has everywhere and always been infamous and detested. Thus Cato, [116] desiring to commend agriculture, says that thieves were formerly condemned to a fine of double, and usurers quadruple; from which he infers, that the latter were deemed the worst. And when asked what he thought of usury, he replied, "What do I think of killing a man?" whereby he wished to show, that it was as improper to make money by usury as to commit murder. This was the swing of one private individual, yet it is derived from the opinions of almost all nations and persons. And assuredly from this cause great tumults often arose at Rome, and fatal contentions were awakened between the common people and the rich; since it can hardly be but that usurers suck men's blood like leeches. But if we come to an accurate decision as to the thing itself, our determination must be derived from nowhere else than the universal rule of justice, and especially from the declaration of Christ, on which hang the law and the prophets, -- Do not unto others what ye would not have done to thyself. (Matthew 7:12.) For crafty men are for ever inventing some little subterfuge or other to deceive God. Thus, when all men detested the word foenus, another was substituted, which might avoid unpopularity under an honest pretext; for they called it usury, as being a compensation for the loss a man had incurred by losing the use of his money. But [117] there is no description of foenus to which this specious name may not be extended; for whosoever has any ready money, and is about to lend it, he will allege that it would be profitable to himself if he were to purchase [118] something with it, and that at every moment opportunities of gain are presenting themselves. Thus there will be always ground for his seeking compensation, since no creditor could ever lend money without loss to himself. Thus usury, [119] since the word is equivalent to foenus, is but a covering for an odious practice, as if such glosses would deliver us in God's judgment, where nothing but absolute integrity can avail for our defense. There was almost a similar mode of subterfuge among the Israelites. The name נשך, neschec, which is derived from biting, sounded badly; since then no one chose to be likened to a hungry dog, who fed himself by biting others, some escape from the reproach was sought; and they called whatever gain they received beyond the capital, תרבית, therbith, as being an increase. But God, in order to prevent such deception, unites the two words, (Leviticus 25:36,) and condemns the increase as well as the biting. For, where He complains of their unjust modes of spoiling and thieving in Ezekiel, [120] and uses both words as He does here by Moses, there is no doubt but that He designedly cuts off their empty excuses. (Ezekiel 18:13.) Lest any, therefore, should reply, that although he derived advantage from his money, he was not on that account guilty of usury, God at once removes this pretense, and condemns in general any addition to the principal. Assuredly both passages clearly show that those who invent new words in excuse of evil, do nothing but vainly trifle. I have, then, admonished men that the fact itself is simply to be considered, that all unjust gains are ever displeasing to God, whatever color we endeavor to give to it. But if we would form an equitable judgment, reason does not suffer us to admit that all usury is to be condemned without exception. If the debtor have protracted the time by false pretences to the loss and inconvenience of his creditor, will it be consistent that he should reap advantage from his bad faith and broken promises? Certainly no one, I think, will deny that usury ought to be paid to the creditor in addition to the principal, to compensate his loss. [121] If any rich and monied man, wishing to buy a piece of land, should borrow some part of the sum required of another, may not he who lends the money receive some part of the revenues of the farm until the principal shall be repaid? Many such cases daily occur in which, as far as equity is concerned, usury is no worse than purchase. Nor will that subtle argument [122] of Aristotle avail, that usury is unnatural, because money is barren and does not beget money; for such a cheat as I have spoken of, might make much profit by trading with another man's money, and the purchaser of the farm might in the meantime reap and gather his vintage. But those who think differently, may object, that we must abide by God's judgment, when He generally prohibits all usury to His people. I reply, that the question is only as to the poor, and consequently, if we have to do with the rich, that usury is freely permitted; because the Lawgiver, in alluding to one thing, seems not to condemn another, concerning which He is silent. If again they object that usurers are absolutely condemned by David and Ezekiel, (Psalm 15:5; Ezekiel 18:13,) I think that their declarations ought to be judged of by the rule of charity; and therefore that only those unjust exactions are condemned whereby the creditor, losing' sight of equity, burdens and oppresses his debtor. I should, indeed, be unwilling to take usury under my patronage, and I wish the name itself were banished from the world; but I do not dare to pronounce upon so important a point more than God's words convey. It is abundantly clear that the ancient people were prohibited from usury, but we must needs confess that this was a part of their political constitution. Hence it follows, that usury is not now unlawful, except in so far as it contravenes equity and brotherly union. Let each one, then, place himself before God's judgment-seat, and not do to his neighbor what he would not have done to himself, from whence a sure and infallible decision may be come to. To exercise the trade of usury, since heathen writers accounted it amongst disgraceful and base modes of gain, is much less tolerable among the children of God; but in what cases, and how far it may be lawful to receive usury upon loans, the law of equity will better prescribe than any lengthened discussions.

Let us now examine the words. In the first place, where we have translated the words, "Thou shalt not be to him as a usurer," [123] there is some ambiguity in the Hebrew word נשך, nashac, for it is sometimes used generally for to lend, without any ill meaning; but here it is undoubtedly applied to a usurer, who bites the poor; as also in Psalm 109:11, "Let the usurer catch all that he hath."[124] The sum is, that the poor are to be liberally aided, and not to be oppressed by harsh exactions: and therefore immediately afterwards it is added, "neither shalt thou lay upon him usury." When again He repeats, "And if thy brother be waxen poor," etc., we see that reference is everywhere made to the poor; because, although sometimes those who possess large properties are ruined by usury, (as Cicero says that certain luxurious and prodigal persons ill his days contended against usury with the fruits of their farms, because their creditors swallowed up the whole produce; [125]) still the poor alone, who had been compelled to borrow by want, and not by luxury, were worthy of compassion.

The third passage, however, admirably explains the meaning of God, since it extends usury to corn and wine, and all other articles. For many contracts were invented by artful men, whereby they pillaged the needy without ignominy or disgrace: and now-a-days no rapacity is more cruel than that which imposes a payment upon debtors, without any mention of usury; for instance, if a poor man should ask the loan of six measures of wheat, the creditor will require seven to be repaid; or if the same thing should happen as regards wine. This profit will not be called usury, because no money will pass; but God, indirectly casting ridicule upon their craftiness, shows that this plague of usury[126] extends itself to various things, and to almost all sorts of traffic; whence it clearly appears that nothing else is prescribed to the Israelites, but that they should humanely assist each other. But, since cupidity blinds men, and carries them, aside to dishonest dealings, God sets His blessing in opposition to all such iniquitous arts, whereby they hawk, as it were, for gain; and commands them to look for riches rather to Him the author of all good things, than to hunt for them by rapine and fraud.

Deuteronomy 22

Deuteronomy 22:1-3

1. Thou shalt not see thy brother's ox or his sheep go astray, and hide thyself from them: thou shalt in any case bring them again unto thy brother.

1. Non videbis bovem fratris tui aut pecudem errantes, et abscondes te ab eis: reducendo reduces ad fratrem tuum.

2. And if thy brother be not nigh unto thee, or if thou know him not; then thou shalt bring it unto thine own house, and it shall be with thee until thy brother seek after it, and thou shalt restore it to him again.

2. Etiam si non fuerit frater tuus propinquus tibi, neque noveris eum, colliges tamen illos in domum tuam, et erunt tecum donec requirat frater tuus ut restituas ei.

3. In like manner shalt thou do with his ass, and so shalt thou do with his raiment; and with all lost thing of thy brother's, which he hath lost, and thou hast found, shalt thou do likewise: thou mayest not hide thyself.

3. Sic facies de asino ejus, sic facies de vestimento ejus, sic facies de omni re amissa fratris tui quae perierit ab ipso: si inveneris eam, non occultabis te.

Exodus 23

Exodus 23:4

4. If thou meet thine enemy's ox or his ass going astray, thou shalt surely bring it back to him again.

4. Si occurreris bovi inimici tui, et asino ejus erranti, reducendo reduces ad illum.

Exodus 23:4. If thou meet thine enemy's ox. From these two passages it is very clear that he who abstains from evil doing, is not therefore guiltless before God, unless he also studies to do good. For our brethren's advantage ought to be so far our care, that we should be disposed mutually to aid each other as far as our means and opportunities permit. This instruction is greatly needed; because, whilst everybody is more attentive to his own advantage than he ought to be, he is willing to hold back from the assistance of others. But God brings him in guilty of theft who has injured his neighbors by his negligence; and justly, because it depended only upon him that the thing should be safe, which he knowingly and willfully suffered to perish. This duty, too, is extended even to enemies; wherefore our inhumanity is the more inexcusable, if we have not helped our friends. The sum therefore is, that believers should be kind, [127] that they may imitate their heavenly Father; and should not only bestow their labor upon the good, who are worthy of it, but should treat the unworthy also with kindness: and since many might invent means of subterfuge, God anticipates them, and commands that the beast of a person unknown should be kept until reclaimed by its owner; and lays down the same rule as to all things that may be lost.

Numbers 5

Numbers 5:5-7

5. And the Lord spoke unto Moses, saying,

5. Loquutus est Jehova ad Mosen, dicendo:

6. Speak unto the children of Israel, when a man or woman shall commit any sin that men commit, to do a trespass against the Lord, and that person be guilty;

6. Alloquere filios Israel, Vir sive mulier quum fecerint ex omnibus peccatis hominum, transgrediendo transgressione in Jehovam, et deliquerit anima illa:

7. Then they shall confess their sin which they have done: and he shall recompense his trespass with the principal thereof, and add unto it the fifth part thereof, and give it unto him against whom he hath trespassed.

7. Fatebuntur peccatum suum quod fecerunt: et restituet delictum suum in solidum, et quintam ejus partem superaddet, dabitque ei in quem peccaverit.

5. And the Lord spoke unto Moses. Although at the outset He seems to include all trespasses, yet we gather from the context that the precept only refers to things stolen or fraudulently withheld, that he, who is conscious of his guilt, should make reparation. It must be observed, however, that the law relates to more secret thefts, which are not usually brought to justice: and on this account it is said, "If they have committed any sin after the manner of men, they must not seek for subterfuge from ordinary use and custom." Although, therefore, they may have many companions, God declares that this will not avail for their excuse; and consequently commands them voluntarily to restore what they have fraudulently or wrongfully appropriated. He will treat hereafter of the punishment of theft; He now only prescribes that, although no one shall bring the guilty parties to justice, and their crime may not be discovered, still they should diligently examine their consciences, and themselves ingenuously

declare the secret transgression; and also make compensation for the loss
conferred, since, without restitution, their confession would be but illusory. I
now pass over what Moses adds, that, if no heir exists to whom the stolen
goods may be restored, they should offer it to the priest, because I have already
expounded it: except that we gather frost thence, that a contamination is
contracted by fraud and rapine, which is never purged unless the house is well
cleared of the ill-gotten gain. But this offering was treated of amongst the laws
of the priests: [128] now, with respect to the restitution, we must consider that the
fifth part was superadded, not so much in order that he, who had suffered the
loss, should be enriched, as that all should diligently beware of every offense,
which they hear not only to be useless to themselves, but also to be productive
of loss. Besides, when a man has been robbed, it is often of more consequence
than this additional fifth part, that he should have been deprived of the use of
his property.

Exodus 23

Exodus 23:8

**8. And thou shalt take no gift: for the gift blindeth the wise, and
perverteth the words of the righteous.**

*8. Ne accipias munus: quia munus excaecat videntes, et pervertit verba
justorum.*

Leviticus 19

Leviticus 19:15

**15. Ye shall do no unrighteousness in judgment; thou shalt not respect
the person of the poor, nor honor the person of the mighty: but in
righteousness shalt thou judge thy neighbor.**

*15. Non facies iniquitatem in judicio, non suscipies faciem pauperis, neque
honorabis causam magni: in justitia judicabis proximum tuum.*

Exodus 23:8 And thou shalt take no gift. This kind of theft is the worst of
all, when judges are corrupted either by bribes, or by affection, and thus ruin
the fortunes which they ought to protect: for, since their tribunal is as it were
sacred asylum, to which those who are unjustly oppressed may fly, nothing can
be more unseemly than that they should there fall amongst robbers. [129] Judges
are appointed to repress all wrongs and offenses; if therefore they show favor to
the wicked, they are harborers of thieves; than which there is no more deadly
pest. And besides, since their authority excludes every other remedy, they are
themselves like rob-hers with arms in their hands. The greater, therefore, their
power of injury is, and the greater the damage committed by their unjust
sentences, the more diligently are they to be warned to beware of iniquity; and
thus it was necessary to keep them in the path of duty by special instructions,
lest they should conceal and encourage thievery by their patronage. Now, as
avarice is the root of all evils, when it thus lays hold of the minds of judges, no
integrity can continue to exist. But, since all utterly condemn this vice, even
though they may be entirely under its influence, God speaks of it the more

plainly and popularly, enjoining that judges should withhold their hands from every gift: for there is no more fatal poison for the extinction of all uprightness, than when a judge suffers himself to be cajoled by gifts. Let those who accept gifts allege as much as they please that they still maintain their integrity, the fact itself clearly shows that they are venal, and seek their own pecuniary advantage when they are thus attracted by gain. Formerly it was enough to render judges infamous that they were called nummarii, (moneyers.) [130] But it is superfluous to treat any further of this matter, since God cuts off all handles for subterfuge in a single sentence: "for gifts (He says) blind the eyes of him that seeth, and pervert the judgment of the righteous." If, then, we acquiesce in His decision, there is no light of intelligence so bright but that gifts extinguish it, nor any probity so great but that they undermine it; in fact, gifts infect a sound mind before they soil the hand; I mean those which a person receives in reference to the judgment of a cause; for there is no question here as to those gifts of mutual kindness which men reciprocate with each other. Thus, in the passage from Deuteronomy 16, before God speaks of gifts, He forbids that justice should be wrested., or men's persons respected: whence we gather, that only those snares are condemned which are set to curry favor. It must be observed on the passage from Leviticus, that to judge in righteousness is contrasted with respecting the person: and consequently, as soon as the judge turns away his eyes ever so little from the cause itself, he forgets equity. Moreover, to wrest judgment is equivalent to doing iniquity in judgment; but since injustice is not always openly manifested, but rather disguised by various artifices, after God in Leviticus has condemned corrupt and unjust judgments, He uses this word to wrest (inclinandi), in Deuteronomy, in order to dissipate all vain pretexts.

Deuteronomy 16

Deuteronomy 16:19, 20

19. Thou shalt not wrest judgment; thou shalt not respect persons, neither take a gift: for a gift doth blind the eyes of the wise, and pervert the words of the righteous.

19. Non inflectes judicium, non agnosces personam, neque capies munus: quia munus excaecat oculos sapientum, et pervertit verba justorum.

20. That which is altogether just shalt thou follow, that thou mayest live, and inherit the land which the Lord thy God giveth thee.

20. Justitiam, justitiam sequeris, ut vivas, et possideas terram quam Jehova Deus tuus dat tibi.

20. *That which is altogether just* [131] By an emphatic repetition God inculcates that judges should study equity with inflexible constancy; nor is this done without cause, for nothing is more likely to happen than that men's minds should be clouded by favor or hatred. Besides there are so many quibbles whereby justice is perverted, that, unless judges are very cautious in watching against deception, they will often find themselves ensnared.

Exodus 23

Exodus 23:3, 6

3. Neither shalt thou countenance a poor man in his cause.
3. Pauperem non honorabis ex sua causa.
6. Thou shalt not wrest the judgment of thy poor in his cause.
6. Non inflectes judicium pauperis tui in lite ejus.

6. Thou shalt not wrest the judgment of thy poor. Since laws are enacted to repress the vices which are of frequent occurrence, no wonder that God should put forward the case of the poor, to whom it often happens that they fail though their causes are good, both because they are without interest and are exposed to injury through the contempt in which they are held, and also because they cannot contend with the rich in incurring expense. Justly, then, is provision made for their inferiority, lest the iniquity of judges should rob them of the little they possess. But the other point here referred to might appear superfluous, viz., that judges should not favor the poor, which very rarely takes place. It would also be incongruous that what God elsewhere prescribes and praises should here be reprehended. I reply, that rectitude is so greatly pleasing to God, that the judge would in no wise be excusable, under whatever pretext he might decline from it ever so little, and that this is the intention of this precept. For, although the poor is for the most part tyrannically oppressed, still ambition will sometimes impel a judge to misplaced compassion, so that he is liberal at another's expense. And this temptation is all the more dangerous, because injustice is done under the cloak of virtue. For, if a judge only directs his attention to the poverty of the litigant, a foolish fear will at the same time insinuate itself lest his sentence should ruin the man whom he would wish to save; thus he will award to the one what belongs to the other. Sometimes the temerity, audacity, and obstinacy of the poor in commencing and prosecuting suits is greater than that of the rich; and when they despair of their cause, they are sure to have recourse to tears and lamentations, by which they deceive incautious judges, who, forgetful of the cause itself, only consider how their misery and want is to be relieved. Besides, too, whilst they think little of the rich man's loss, because he can easily bear it, they make no scruple of declining from equity in favor of the poor. But hence it better appears how greatly God is offended by the oppression of the poor, when He will not have even them befriended to the injury of the rich.

Political Supplements to the eighth Commandment - Exodus 22

Exodus 22:1-4

1. If a man shall steal an ox, or a sheep, and kill it, or sell it; he shall restore five oxen for an ox, and four sheep for a sheep.
1. Quum furatus fuerit quis bovem aut pecudem, et jugulaverit, aut vendiderit, quinque boves reddet pro illo bove, et quatuor pecudes pro pecude illa:

2. If a thief be found breaking up, and be smitten that he die, there shall no blood be shed for him.

2. (Si in effossione inventus fuerit fur, et percussus fuerit, et inde mortuus, non erit ei in sanguinem.

3. If the sun be risen upon him, there shall be blood shed for him; for he should make full restitution: if he have nothing, then he shall be sold for his theft.

3. Si ortus fuerit sol super eum, erit ei in sanguinem:) reddendo reddet: si non sit ei, vendetar propter furtum suum.

4. If the theft be certainly found in his hand alive, whether it be ox, or ass, or sheep, he shall restore double.

4. Si deprehendatur in manu ejus furtum a bove usque ad asinum, usque ad pecudem: viva duo reddet.

Thus far God has proclaimed Himself the avenger of iniquities, and, citing thieves before His tribunal, has threatened them with eternal death. Now follow the civil laws, the principle of which is not so exact and perfect; since in their enactment God has relaxed His just severity in consideration of the people's hardness of heart.

What God formerly delivered to His people the heathen legislators afterwards borrowed. Draco, indeed, was more severe, but his extreme rigor became obsolete by the silent consent of the people of Athens; and the Decemvirs borrowed from Solon part of their law, which they published in the ten tables, although there were some variations in the distinction of the double or quadruple restitution, and in process of time other alterations were afterwards made. But if all things be duly considered, it will be found that both Solon and the Decemvirs have made a change for the worse, wherever they have varied from the law of God. First of all, no distinction [132] is here made, such as the Roman laws decree, between manifest thieves and those that are not manifest; for by them the thief not manifest is condemned to a double amend, and the manifest to quadruple; and he is called a manifest thief who is caught before he has carried what he has stolen to the place of its destination. I suppose that the awarders of the punishment had this point in view, that the wickedness of that person was the more egregious who was so greedily and anxiously set on his prey as not to be afraid of disgrace; and undoubtedly he who has no fear of shame is more audacious ill sin. But, on the contrary, God condemns to a double amend those upon whom the stolen goods were found; and to quadruple, those who had killed or sold it; and deservedly so, because greater obstinacy in crime betrays itself where the theft is turned to profit, nor is there any hope of repentance; and thus by this further process the crime of dishonesty is doubled. It might be that, immediately after the offense, the thief should be alarmed; but he who had dared to kill the stolen animal or to sell it, is altogether hardened in his sin. Besides, the more difficult its investigation is, the greater is the punishment which a misdemeanor deserves. Meanwhile, it is to be remembered, that the pecuniary fine imposed upon thieves did not free them from guilt; for, as Marcellus says, [133] not even the president of a province can bring it to pass, that infamy should not pursue a man condemned of theft; and there was no need of establishing by law that in which all by nature are agreed. Thus, when God punished thieves by a fine, He left them still marked by infamy. I know not whether they [134] assign the true cause why he who had stolen an ox is fined to a larger amount than he who had stolen a goat, or sheep, or other cattle, who say that the loss of the owner is taken into account to whom the labor of the ox is especially useful in agriculture; for what is said as to an ox I extend to cows and the whole herd. Those seem to come nearer to the truth who say the audacity of the thief is punished who, when he stole the larger animal, did not fear being observed by witnesses; yet it seems to me more likely that the different sentence depended on the price of the article; for assuredly it is more reasonable that he who has done the most harm should be exposed to the greater punishment.

2. If a thief be found breaking up. This clause is to be taken separately, and is inserted by way of parenthesis; for, after having decreed the punishment, God adds in connection, "he should make full restitution; if he have nothing, then he should be sold for his theft;" and this exception as to the thief in the night is introduced parenthetically. But although the details are not expressed with sufficient distinctness, still the intention of God is by no means ambiguous, viz., that if a thief should be killed in the dark, his slayer should be unpunished; for he can then hardly be distinguished from a robber, especially when he proceeds with violence; because he cannot enter another man's house by night without either digging through a wall or breaking down a door. The Twelve Tables [135] differ slightly from this; for they permit the killing of a thief by night, and also by day if he should defend himself with a weapon. But, since God had sufficiently repressed by other laws murders and violent assaults, He is silent here respecting robbers who use the sword in their attempts at plunder. He therefore justly condemns to death those who have avenged by murder a theft in open day.

3. He should make full restitution. These words, as I have said, are connected with the first verse, since here the execution of the punishment is only enjoined; as if God forbade thieves to be spared, but that they should pay either twofold or quadruple, or even quintuple, according to the measure of their crime. But, if they were unable to pay, He commands them to be sold as slaves, which also was the custom at Rome. Whence the saying of Cato, [136] "that private thieves lived in bonds and fetters, but public ones in gold and purple." And since this condition was a harsh one, a caution is expressly given, that they were not to be absolved on the score of their poverty. If any one should ask whether it was lawful for the owner of the thing stolen to recover double or quadruple its value, I answer, that what God awards, a man has the best of rights to; meanwhile, in equity men were bound to take care that they did not grow rich at the expense of others, but rather were they to apply whatever they gained to pious and holy uses.

Exodus 22

Exodus 22:5-15

5. If a man shall cause a field or vineyard to be eaten, and shall put in his beast, and shall feed in another man's field; of the best of his own field, and of the best of his own vineyard, shall he make restitution.

5. Si depasci fecerit quispiam agrum aut vitem, et immiserit jumentum suum ut depasceretur agrum alterius: bonum agri ejus et bonum vineae ejus restituet.

6. If fire break out, and catch in thorns, so that the stacks of corn, or the standing corn, or the field, be consumed therewith; he that kindled the fire shall surely make restitution.

6. Quum egressus fuerit ignis, et invenerit spinas: absumptusque fuerit acervus, vel seges, vel ager, reddendo redder qui ignem accendit, rem combustam.

7. If a man shall deliver unto his neighbor money or stuff to keep, and it be stolen out of the man's house; if the thief be found, let him pay double.

7. Quum dederit quispiam proximo suo argentum, vel vasa ad custodiendum, et furto ablatum fuerit e domo viri illius: si inventus fuerit fur, reddet duplum.

8. If the thief be not found, then the master of the house shall be brought unto the judges, to see whether he have put his hand unto his neighbor's goods.

8. Si non inventus fuerit fur, tunc applicabitur dominus domus ad judices, annon miserit manum suam in substantiam proximi sui.

9. For all manner of trespass, whether it be for ox, for ass, for sheep, for raiment, or for any manner of lost thing, which another challengeth to be his, the cause of both parties shall come before the judges; and whom the judges shall condemn, he shall pay double unto his neighbor.

9. Super omni causa praevaricationis, super bove, super asino, super pecude, super vestimento, super omni re amissa: quum dixerit quispiam hoc esse, usque ad judices veniet causa utriusque: et quem damnaverint judices, is reddat duplum proximo suo.

10. If a man deliver unto his neighbor an ass, or an ox, or a sheep, or any beast, to keep, and it die, or be hurt, or driven away, no man seeing it:

10. Si dederit quispiam proximo suo asinum, vel bovem, vel pecudem, aut quodcunque animal ad custodiendum, et mortuum fuerit, aut contractum, aut ab hostibus captum nemine vidente.

11. Then shall an oath of the Lord be between them both, that he hath not put his hand unto his neighbor's goods; and the owner of it shall accept thereof, and he shall not make it good.

11. Juramentum Jehovae erit inter utrumque, annon miserit manum suam in substantiam proximi sui, et juramentum suscipiet dominus ejus, et non reddet.

12. And if it be stolen from him, he shall make restitution unto the owner thereof.

12. Quod si furto ablatum fuerit ei, reddet domino ejus.

13. If it be torn in pieces, then let him bring it for witness, and he shall not make good that which was torn.

13. Si vero rapiendo raptum fuerit, adducet ei testem: raptum non reddet.

14. And if a man borrow ought of his neighbor, and it be hurt, or die, the owner thereof being not with it; he shall surely make it good.

14. Si commodato acceperit quispiam a proximo suo, et confractum fuerit aut mortuum domino ejus absente, reddendo reddet.

15. But if the owner thereof be with it, he shall not make it good: if it be an hired thing, it came for his hire.

15. Si dominus ejus fuerit cum eo, non reddet: si conductum fuerit, veniens pro mercede sua.

9. For all manner of trespass. An action for theft is here permitted, but with a fine attached if any should rashly accuse his neighbor; for else it might be doubted when or for what reasons the restitution of double or quadruple was to be required. He therefore permits that if any one suspects another of theft, he should summon that person to plead his cause; and if he should prove his case, that he should recover double the thing lost; but if the judges should pronounce that he had brought his action groundlessly, that he, on the contrary, should pay the penalty of his false accusation. For such an action as this is not altogether a civil one, but carries with it the stain of infamy, and thus it would be unjust that a man should be injured by false suspicions whom the judges acquit of crime. The word used here for judges is אלהים, elohim, which properly means gods, as being of the plural number; it is, however often used for God. [137] It is transferred to judges for the purpose of dignifying their office; because in it they represent the person of God, in whose hand alone is all dominion and power. Therefore Christ says they were called gods, because to them "the word of God came," (John 10:34,) i.e., that they should preside in His name, and be set over others, on which subject we treated under the Fifth Commandment.

5. If a man shall cause a field or vineyard to be eaten. This kind of fraud is justly ranked among thefts; viz., if any man shall have put in his beast to feed in another's field or vineyard. For if a person have made improper use of his servant to steal by him, he himself is deemed guilty of the offense, even although he may have touched nothing with his own hand; nor does he less do wrong who has given occasion of injury by means of a brute. Still, God restricts the punishment to a compensation of double the amount, because it cannot be certainly established that the master of the animal desired to effect the damage fraudulently and designedly; yet He requires the loss to be made up at the highest estimate of its value; [138] for thus I interpret "the goodness of his field and his vineyard," that the place having been examined, a liberal restitution shall be awarded to its owner, according to the utmost it would have probably produced in its greatest state of fertility.

6. If fire break out and catch in thorns. This injury is somewhat different from the foregoing, for he who kindles the fire is commanded to make good the damage done by him, although there may have been no willful intention to do harm. For the incendiary who had maliciously destroyed either a cornfield or a vineyard was to be far more severely punished; here, however, mere carelessness is punished. Although no mention is made either of house or barn, still the law includes all similar cases requiring compensation from him who had kindled a fire even in an open field. But it seems that such a person would be blameless, because he could not. foresee that the fire would ignite the thorns; yet, in order that every one should take as much care of the property of another as of his own, God commands him to suffer the penalty of his heedless or stupid negligence.

7. If a man shall deliver unto his neighbor money. It is here determined under what circumstances an action for theft would lie in case of a deposit, viz., if an inanimate thing, as a garment or furniture, be given ill charge, and the person with whom it is deposited should allege that it is stolen, God commands that, if the thief be discovered, he should pay double; but, if not, that an oath should be required of the man who declares that the thing has been stolen from him. But, if it be an animal that was given in charge, a somewhat different provision is made, viz., that if it have been violently carried away, or torn by

beasts, the person with whom it was deposited should be free; but if it had been stolen, that he should make restitution. In order to understand the principle of this law, we must observe that depositaries are not to be compelled to do more than faith. fully preserve the thing entrusted to them; just as a prudent and careful father of a family is attentive to the preservation of his property. When they have acquitted themselves diligently in this respect, it would be unjust to require more, of them; otherwise, when they undertake the burden of this gratuitous office, their generosity would be an injury to themselves. But, since it is not so easy to steal an animal from the stall, or from the hands of the shepherd, the negligence of the shepherd betrays itself in the loss of the beast,[139] supposing no violence to have been used. Justice, then, is done in both cases, i e., that the depository shall not make good a vessel, or money, or a garment, because this would be in a manner to put him in the place of the thief; but that if the animal be stolen he shall pay its price, unless he can cleat' himself of carelessness. If any should think that too great indulgence is shown to the depositary, when God would have the dispute terminated by his oath; the reply is easy, that we do not entrust anything to be kept by another, unless we are persuaded of his honesty. Whoever, then, has chosen a guardian for his property, has borne witness to his own prejudice that he is a good and trustworthy man; and consequently, it would be absurd that he should soon afterwards be involved in all accusation of theft without proof. Wherefore it was reasonable that God would have the owner of the lost goods acquiesce in the oath of him. whom he has considered to be his faithful friend. Besides, a man is altogether acquitted who clears himself by calling God to witness his innocence, unless any sinister suspicion is alleged against him, and provided he excuses himself on probable evidence.

10. If a man deliver unto his neighbor an ass. Since in the passage from whence I have taken these four verses, mention is made of a deposit, and Moses is professedly providing against frauds, and robberies, and thefts, I have thought it well to place them under this head. It has indeed some relation to the Third Commandment, because it shows the lawful use of an oath, viz., that in matters of concealment men should have recourse to the witness of God, and that, by the interposition of His sacred name, an end should be put to their strife. But, while the authority attributed to oaths depends on the reverence due to God, at the same time faith and piety are enforced in them, [140] so that all things should correspond. I have, however, considered the main point, i e., how controversies as to things concealed should be brought to an end for the advancement of peace and equity. He would therefore have the depositary acquitted, if he swears that the animal entrusted to him is lost (either by death or violence, [141]) although lie should produce no witness of the matter, since it would be unjust that he should bear the blame, unless fraud, or some more palpable offense, have been committed by him. At the conclusion, then, it is said, "the owner of it shall accept" the oath, which is equivalent to saying, that lie shall be compelled to acquiesce, and shall give no more trouble about it. The expression, "an oath of the Lord shall be between them both," is a remarkable one, whereby the obligation and sanctity of an oath are enforced, whilst Moses reminds us that God is the author of this sacred mode of attestation, and presides over it as its judge and avenger.

Moses now lays down the law as to a borrowed animal, if it die, or be mutilated, or injured. There is, however, a wide distinction between a thing borrowed and a thing deposited, for he who lends confers a favor; and therefore, when a man borrows a thing, he binds himself to restore it in safety, as far as in him lies. A distinction, however, is made, if the owner himself of the animal be an eye-witness of the death or fracture, he shall bear the loss; but if the animal should die or be injured in his absence, its value is awarded to him. His presence is tantamount to this, as if it were said, if he shall have seen with his own eyes that the injury did not occur by the fault of him to whom he lent it, then he shall give him no trouble about it. For instance, if you have lent me a horse, and take the journey with me, although anything untoward should happen -- supposing you are assured that it did not occur by my temerity, or negligence, or bad management, I am free, and exempt from loss.

What is here laid down as to a borrowed animal must be applied also to all other things borrowed.

Leviticus 24

Leviticus 24:18, 21

18. And he that killeth a beast shall make it good; beast for beast.
18. Qui percusserit animam animalis, restituet illud: animam pro anima.
21. And he that killeth a beast, he shall restore it; and he that killeth a man, he shall be put to death.
21. Qui percusserit animal, reddet illud.

God here prescribes, that whosoever has inflicted a loss upon another shall make satisfaction for it, although he may not have turned it to his own profit; for in respect to a theft, its profit is not to be considered, but the intention to injure, or other cause of guilt; for it might happen that he who has killed another's ox should not deliberately desire to do him an injury, but in a fit of passion, or from unpremeditated impulse, should nevertheless have inflicted loss upon him. In whatever way, therefore, a man should have committed an offense, whereby another is made poorer, he is commanded to make good the loss. Whence it is clear, that whosoever do not so restrain themselves as to care for a neighbor's advantage as much as for their own, are accounted guilty of theft before God. The object, however, of the law is, that no one should suffer loss by us, which will be the case if we have regard to the good of our brethren.

Exodus 21

Exodus 21:33-36

33. And if a man shall open a pit, or if a man shall dig a pit, and not cover it, and an ox or an ass fall therein;
33. Quum aperuerit quis cisternam, vel foderit quis cisternam, et non cooperuerit eam: cecideritque illuc bos vel asinus:
34. The owner of the pit shall make it good, and give money unto the owner of them; and the dead beast shall be his.
34. Dominns cisternae reddet pecuniam, et restituet domino ejus: et quod mortuum est, erit illius.

35. And if one man's ox hurt another's, that he die; then they shall sell the live ox, and divide the money of it; and the dead ox also they shall divide.

35. Si percusserit bos alicujus bovem proximi sui, mortuusque fuerit, tunc vendet bovem vivum, et partientur pretium ejus: mortuum quoque partientur.

36. Or if it be known that the ox hath used to push in time past, and his owner hath not kept him in; he shall surely pay ox for ox; and the dead shall be his own.

36. Quod si notum fuerit bovem esse cornupetam ab heri et nudiustertius, et non custodierit eum dominus ejus, reddendo reddet bovem pro bove, et mortuus erit illius.

33. And if a man shall open a pit He enumerates still more cases of damage inflicted, in which restitution is to be demanded of the person who gave occasion for the occurrence. First, it is said, If a man shall open a pit, or cistern, and not cover it, and an animal shall fall into it, he is bound to pay its value; and justly, since his carelessness approaches to actual guilt. Here, again, we see how God would have all men to be anxious for their neighbor's advantage; yet, inasmuch as there was no fraud or malice in the case, he is permitted, after paying its price, to appropriate the carcass to himself. But, if one man's ox should be killed by another's, a most just appointment is made, viz., that, if it happened unexpectedly, and by sudden accident, they should divide the dead ox between them, and, having sold the other, each should take half the price; but if the ox was a savage one, that its owner should undergo a greater penalty by paying its full price; because he ought to have anticipated the mischief, and thus was scarcely so kind as he should have been, giving occasion to the injury.

Deuteronomy 23

Deuteronomy 23:24, 25

24. When thou comest into thy neighbor's vineyard, then thou mayest eat grapes thy fill at thine own pleasure; but thou shalt not put any in thy vessel.

24. Quum ingressus fueris vineam proximi tui, comedes uvas pro desiderio tuo ad satietatem tuam: at in vase tuo non pones.

25. When thou comest into the standing corn of thy neighbor, then thou mayest pluck the ears with thine hand; but thou shalt not move a sickle unto thy neighbor's standing corn.

25. Quum ingressus fueris segetem proximi tui, decerpes spicas manu tua: at falcem non attolles in segetem proximi tui.

Since God here concedes a great indulgence to the poor, some restrict it to the laborers in the harvest and vintage, [142] as if He permitted them to pluck the ears of corn and grapes with their hands for food alone, and not to carry away. I have no doubt, however, that it refers to all persons, and that no greater license is given than humanity demands. For we must not strain the words too precisely, but look to the intention of the Lawgiver. God forbids men to introduce a sickle into the harvest of another; now, if a man should pluck with his hands as many ears of corn as he could carry on his shoulders, or lay upon a horse, could he excuse himself by the puerile explanation that he had not used a sickle? But, if common sense itself repudiates such gross impudence, it is plain that the Law has another object, viz., that no one should touch even an ear of another man's harvest, except for present use, which occurred to Christ's disciples, when they were compelled by hunger to rub the ears of corn in their hands, lest they should faint by the way. (Matthew 12:1.) The same view must be taken as to grapes. If any man deliberately breaks into another's vineyard and gorges himself there, whatever excuse he may make, he will be accounted a thief. Wherefore, there is no doubt but that this Law permits hungry travelers to refresh themselves by eating grapes, when they have not enough of other food. But although the liberty of eating to their fill is granted, still it was not. allowable oil this pretext to gorge themselves. Besides, vineyards were enclosed with hedges and guarded; whence it appears that the grapes were not exposed to every glutton. This, then, is the sum, that it is not accounted a theft, if a traveler, in order to relieve his hunger, should stretch forth his hand to the hanging fruit, [143] until he should arrive at his resting-place where he may buy bread and wine.

Leviticus 19

Leviticus 19:9, 10

9. **And when ye reap the harvest of your land, thou shalt not wholly reap the corners of thy field, neither shalt thou gather the gleanings of thy harvest.**

9. Quum messueritis messem regionis vestrae, non finies metere angulum agri tui, et collectionem messis tuae non colliges.

10. **And thou shalt not glean thy vineyard, neither shalt thou gather every grape of thy vineyard; thou shalt leave them for the poor and stranger: I am the Lord your God.**

10. Et vineam tuam non racemabis, neque grana vineae tuae colliges: pauperi et peregrino relinques ea: ego Jehova Deus vester.

Leviticus 23

Leviticus 23:22

22. **And when ye reap the harvest of your land, thou shalt not make clean riddance of the corners of thy field when thou reapest, neither shalt thou gather any gleaning of thy harvest; thou shalt leave them unto the poor, and to the stranger: I am the Lord your God.**

22. Quum metetis messem regionis vestrae, non absolves usque ad angulum agri tui: nec collectionem messis tuae colliges: pauperi et peregrino relinques eam: Ego Jehova Deus vester.

Deuteronomy 24

Deuteronomy 24:19-22

19. When thou cuttest down thine harvest in thy field, and hast forgot a sheaf in the field, then shalt not go again to fetch it: it shall be for the stranger, for the fatherless, and for the widow; that the Lord thy God may bless thee in all the work of thine hands.

19. Quum messueris messem in agro tuo, et oblitus fueris manipulum in agro, non reverteris ad eum tollendum: peregrino, pupillo, et viduae erit: ut benedicat tibi Jehova Deus tuus in omni opere manuum tuarum.

20. When then beatest thine olive-tree, thou shalt not go over the boughs again: it shall be for the stranger, for the fatherless, and for the widow.

20. Quum excusseris olivam tuam, non scrutaberis ramos post te: peregrino, pupillo, et viduae erit.

21. When thou gatherest the grapes of thy vineyard, thou shalt not glean it afterward: it shall be for the stranger, for the fatherless, and for the widow.

21. Quum vindemiabis vineam tuam, non colliges racemos post te: peregrino, pupillo, et viduae erunt.

22. And thou shalt remember that thou wast a bond-man in the land of Egypt: therefore I command thee to do this thing.

22. Memento quod servus fueris in terra AEgypti: idcirco praecipio tibi ut hoc facias.

God here inculcates liberality upon the possessors of land, when their fruits are gathered: for, when His bounty is exercised before our eyes, it invites us to imitate Him; and it is a sign of ingratitude, unkindly and maliciously, to withhold what we derive from His blessing. God does not indeed require that those who have abundance should so profusely give away their produce, as to despoil themselves by enriching others; and, in fact, Paul prescribes this as the measure of our alms, that their relief of the poor should not bring into distress the rich themselves, who kindly distribute. (2 Corinthians 8:13.) God, therefore, permits every one to reap his corn, to gather his vintage, and to enjoy his abundance; provided the rich, content with their own vintage and harvest, do not grudge the poor the gleaning of the grapes and corn. Not that He absolutely assigns to the poor whatever remains, so that they may seize it as their own; but that some small portion may flow gratuitously to them from the munificence of the rich. He mentions indeed by name the orphans, and widows, and strangers, yet undoubtedly He designates all the poor and needy, who have no fields of their own to sow or reap; for it will sometimes occur that orphans are by no means in want, but rather that they have the means of being liberal themselves; nor are widows and strangers always hungry; but I have explained elsewhere why these three classes are mentioned.

Deuteronomy 15

Deuteronomy 15:1-11

1. At the end of every seven years thou shalt make a release.

1. Septimo quoque anno facies remissionem.

2. And this is the manner of the release: Every creditor that lendeth ought unto his neighbor shall release it; he shall not exact it of his neighbor, or of his brother; because it is called the Lord's release.

2. Haec autem est ratio remissionis, ut remittat omnis qui mutuum dederit manu sua, id quod mutuum dederit amico suo: non reposcet ab amico suo, aut a fratre suo, quia proclamata est remissio Jehovae.

3. Of a foreigner thou mayest exact it again: but that which is thine with thy brother thine hand shall release;

3. Ab alienigena reposces, aut quod fuerit tibi apud fratrem tuum, remittet manus tua:

4. Save when there shall be no poor among you; for the Lord shall greatly bless thee in the land which the Lord thy God giveth thee for an inheritance to possess it:

4. Nisi quia non sit (vel, prorsus certe non erit) in te mendicus: quia benedicendo benedicet tibi Jehova in terra quam ipse Deus tuus dat tibi in haereditatem ut possideas eam.

5. Only if thou carefully hearken unto the voice of the Lord thy God, to observe to do all these commandments which I command thee this day.

5. Sed ita duntaxat, si obediendo obedieris voci Jehovae Dei tui, ita ut custodias faciendo omne praeceptum istud quod ego praecipio tibi hodie.

6. For the Lord thy God blesseth thee, as he promised thee: and thou shalt lend unto many nations, but thou shalt not borrow; and thou shalt reign over many nations, but they shall not reign over thee.

6. Nam Jehova Deus tuus benedixit tibi, quemadmodum dixit tibi: tum mutuo accepto pignore dabis gentibus multis, tu autem non accipies mutuo: et dominaberis gentibus multis, at tibi non dominabuntur.

7. If there be among you a poor man of one of thy brethren within any of thy gates, in thy land which the Lord thy God giveth thee, thou shalt not harden thine heart, nor shut thine hand from thy poor brother;

7. Si fuerit apud te mendicus quispiam e fratribus tuis, in una e portis tuis, in terra tua quam Jehova Deus tuus dat tibi: non indurabis cor tuum, neque claudes manum tuam a fratre tuo mendico.

8. But thou shalt open thine hand wide unto him, and shalt surely lend him sufficient for his need, in that which he wanteth.

8. Sed aperiendo aperies illi manum tuam, et mutuando mutuabis ei ad sufficientiam usque, id quo indiguerit.

9. Beware that there be not a thought in thy wicked heart, saying, The seventh year, the year of release, is at hand; and thine eye be evil against thy poor brother, and thou givest him naught, and he cry unto the Lord against thee, and it be sin unto thee.

9. Cave tibi ne sit quidpiam in corde tuo impium, dicendo, Propinquus est annus septimus, annus remissionis: et malignus sit oculus tuus in fratrem tuum mendicum, ita ut non des ei: clamet autem contra te ad Jehovam, et erit in te peccatum.

10. Thou shalt surely give him, and thine heart shall not be grieved when thou givest unto him: because for this thing the Lord thy God shall bless thee in all thy works, and in all that thou puttest thine hand unto.

10. Dando dabis ei, neque malignum erit cor tuum quum dederis ei: quia hujus rei gratia benedicet tibi Jehova Deus tuus in omnibus operibus tuis, et in omni expensione manuum tuarum.

11. For the poor shall never cease out of the land: therefore I command thee, saying, Thou shalt open thine hand wide unto thy brother, to thy poor, and to thy needy, in thy land.

11. Non enim deerit mendicus de medio terrae: idcirco praecipio tibi dicendo, Aperiendo aperies manum tuam fratri tuo, id est pauperi tuo et mendico tuo in terra tua.

1. At the end of every seven years. A special act of humanity towards each other is here prescribed to the Jews, that every seven years, brother should remit to brother whatever was owed him. But, although we are not bound by this law at present, and it would not be even expedient that it should be in use, still the object to which it tended ought still to be maintained, i e., that we should not be too rigid in exacting our debts, especially if we have to do with the needy, who are bowed down by the burden of poverty. The condition of the ancient people, as I have said, was different. They derived their origin from a single race; the land of Canaan was their common inheritance; fraternal association was to be mutually sustained among them, just as if they were one family: and, inasmuch as God had once enfranchised them, the best plan for preserving' their liberty for ever was to maintain a condition of mediocrity, lest a few persons of immense wealth should oppress the general body. Since, therefore, the rich, if they had been permitted constantly to increase in wealth, would have tyrannized over the rest, God put by this law a restraint on immoderate power. Moreover, when rest was given to the land, and men reposed from its cultivation, it was just that the whole people, for whose sake the Sabbath was instituted, should enjoy some relaxation. Still the remission here spoken of was, in my opinion, merely temporary. Some, indeed, suppose that all debts were then entirely cancelled; [144] as if the Sabbatical year destroyed all debtor and creditor accounts; but this is refuted by the context, for when the Sabbatical year is at hand, God commands them to lend freely, whereas the contract would have been ridiculous, unless it had been lawful to seek repayment in due time. Surely, if no payment had ever followed, it would have been required simply to give: for what would the empty form of lending have availed if the money advanced was never to be returned to its owner? But God required all suits to cease for that year, so that no one should trouble his debtor: and, because in that year of freedom and immunity there was no hope of receiving back the money, God provides against the objection, and forbids them to be niggardly, although the delay might produce some inconvenience. First of all, therefore, He commands them to make a remission in the seventh year, i e., to abstain from exacting their debts, and to concede to the poor, as well as to the land, a truce, or vacation. On which ground Isaiah reproves the Jews for observing the Sabbath amiss, when they exact [145] their debts, and "fast for strife and debate." (Isaiah 58:3, 4.) The form of remission is added, That no one should vex his neighbor in the year in which the release of God is proclaimed.

3. Of a foreigner thou mayest exact it. An exception follows, that it should be lawful to sue foreigners, and to compel them to pay; and this for a very good reason, because it was by no means just that despisers of the Law should enjoy the Sabbatical benefit, especially when God had conferred the privilege on His elect people alone. What follows in the next verse, "Unless because there shall be no beggar," interpreters twist into various senses. Some translate it, Nevertheless (veruntamen,) let there be no beggar among thee; as if it were a prohibition, that they should not suffer their poor brethren to be overwhelmed with poverty, without assisting them; and, lest they should object that, if they should be so liberal in giving, they would soon exhaust themselves, God anticipates them, and bids them rely upon his blessing. Others, however, understand it as a promise, and connect it thus, That there should be no beggar among them, if only they keep the Law, since then God would bless them. Nor would this meaning be very unsuitable. What they mean who expound it, Insomuch that there should be no beggar with thee, I know not. Let my readers, however, consider whether [146] אפס כי, ephes ci, is not better rendered "unless because," (nisi quod:) and then this clause would be read parenthetically, as if it were said, Whenever there shall be any poor among your brethren, an opportunity of doing them good is presented to you. Therefore the poverty of your brethren is to be relieved by you, in order that God may bless you. But, that the sentence may be clearer, I take the two words, אפס כי, ephes ci, exclusively, as if it were, On no account let there be a beggar: or, howsoever it may be, suffer not that by your fault there should be any beggar amongst you; for He would put an end to all vain excuses, and, as necessity arose, would have them disposed to give assistance, lest the poor should sink under the pressure of want and distress, tie does not, therefore, mean generally all poor persons, but only those in extreme indigence; such as the Prophet Amos complains are "sold for a pair of shoes." (Amos 2:6.) In order, then, that they may more cheerfully assist their distresses, He promises that His blessing shall be productive of greater abundance. And from hence Paul seems to have derived his exhortation to the Corinthians:

"He which soweth bountifully, shall reap also bountifully. God is able to make all grace abound toward you; that ye, always having all sufficiency in all things, may abound to every good work.: Now he that ministereth seed to the sower, shall both minister bread for your food, and multiply your seed sown, and increase the fruits of your righteousness, that, being enriched in every thing, you may abound unto all bountifulness." (2 Corinthians 9:6-11.)

In short, God would have them without carefulness, since He will abundantly recompense them with His blessing, if they have diminished their own stores by liberality to the poor.

6. For the Lord thy God blesseth thee. He confirms the foregoing declaration, but ascends from the particular to the general; for, after having taught that they might expect from God's blessing much more than they have bestowed on the poor, he now recalls their attention to the Covenant itself, as much as to say, that whatever they have is derived from that original fountain of God's grace, when He made them inheritors of the land of Canaan. God reminds them also that He then promised them abundant produce; and thus indicates that, if they were mean and niggardly, they would cause the land to be

barren. When He says that they should lend to all nations, he speaks by way of amplification; and also in the next clause, that they should reign over the Gentiles; whence it follows, that if there were any in want among them, it would arise from the wickedness and depravity, of the people themselves.

7. If there be among you a poor man The same word אביון, ebyon, is used, which we have seen just above, verse 4; nor is there any contradiction when He commands them to relieve beggars, whom He had before forbidden to exist among His people; for the object of the prohibition was, that if any were reduced to beggary, they should not be cast out and forsaken. Now, however, He explains the mode of preventing this, viz., that the hands of the rich should be open to assist them. In order to incline them to compassion, he again reminds them of their common brotherhood, and sets before them, as its token and pledge, the land in which by God's goodness they dwell together. Again, that they may be willing and prompt in their humanity, He forbids them to harden their heart, thereby signifying that avarice is always cruel. Finally, He applies this instruction to the year of release, viz., that they should straightway relieve their poor brethren towards the beginning of that year, just as if they would receive back in a few days the money which the poor man would retain to its end.

11. For the poor shall never cease out of the land. The notion [147] of those is far fetched who suppose that there would be always poor men among them, because they would not keep the law, and consequently the land would be barren on account of their unrighteousness. I admit that this is true; but God does not here ascribe it to their sins that there would always be some beggars among them, but only reminds them that there would never be wanting matter for their generosity, because He would prove what was in their hearts by setting the poor before them. For, (as I have observed above,) this is why the rich and poor meet together, and the Lord is maker of them all; because otherwise the duties of charity would not be observed unless they put them into exercise by assisting each other. Wherefore God, to stir up the inactivity of the rich, declares that lie prescribes nothing but what continual necessity will require.

Exodus 21

Exodus 21:1-6

1. Now these are the judgments which thou shalt set before them.
1. Haec sunt judicia quae propones eis.
2. If thou buy an Hebrew servant, six years he shall serve; and in the seventh he shall go out free for nothing.
2. Si emeris servum Hebraeum, sex annis serviet: septimo egredietur gratis.
3. If he came in by himself, he shall go out by himself; if he were married, then his wife shall go out with him.
3. Si cum corpore suo ingressus fuerit, cum corpore suo egredietur: si maritus mulieris erat, egredietur et uxor ejus cum ipso.
4. If his master have given him a wife, and she have born him sons or daughters; the wife and her children shall be her master's, and he shall go out by himself.

4. Si herus ejus dederit ei uxorem, et pepererit ei filios, vel filias, uxor et filii ejus erunt heri sui: ipse vero egredietur cum corpore suo.

5. And if the servant shall plainly say, I love my master, my wife, and my children; I will not go out free:

5. Quod si dicendo dixerit servus, Diligo herum meum, et uxorem meam, et filios meos, non egredietur liber:

6. Then his master shall bring him unto the judges; he shall also bring him to the door, or unto the doorpost: and his master shall bore his ear through with an awl; and he shall serve him for ever.

6. Tunc adducet eum herus ejus ad judices, et applicabit eum ad ostium, vel ad postem, perforabitque herus ejus aurem ejus subula, et serviet ei in saeculum.

1. Now these are the judgments. Both passages contain the same appointment, viz., that as to the Hebrews slavery must end at the seventh year; for God would have the children of Abraham, although obliged to sell themselves, to differ from heathen and ordinary slaves. Their enfranchisement is, therefore, enjoined, but with an exception, which Moses expresses in the first passage but omits in the latter, i e., that if the slave had married a bond-woman, and had begotten children, they should remain with the master, and that he should alone be free. Whence it appears how hard was the condition of slaves, since it could not be mitigated without an unnatural exception (sine prodigio;) for nothing could be more opposed to nature than that a husband, forsaking his wife and children, should remove himself elsewhere. But the tie of slavery could only be loosed by divorce, that is to say, by this impious violation of marriage. There was then gross barbarity in this severance, whereby a man was disunited from half of himself and his own bowels. Yet there was no remedy for it; for if the wife and children had been set free, it would have been a spoliation of their lawful master to take them with him, not only because the woman was his slave, but because he had incurred expense in the bringing up of the young children. The sanctity of marriage therefore gave way in this case to private right; and this defect is to be reckoned amongst the others which God tolerated on account of the people's hardness of heart, because it could hardly be remedied; yet, if any one were withheld by chaste affection, and unwilling to abandon his wife and offspring, an alternative is presented, viz., that he should give himself up also to perpetual slavery. The form of this is more clearly pointed out in Exodus than in Deuteronomy; for, in the latter, it is only said that the master, in order to assert his perpetual right to the slave, should bore his ear; whereas in Exodus the circumstance is added, that a public process should first take place; for, if each private individual had been his own judge in this matter, the rich men's houses would have been like slaughterhouses to put their wretched slaves to the torment in. [148] We read in Jeremiah, (34:11,) that this law fell into contempt, and that the Jews, contrary to all law and justice, retained perpetual dominion over their slaves; nay, that when they were severely reprimanded under King Zedekiah, and liberty was anew proclaimed, the wretched men were immediately dragged back to their yoke of tyranny, as if they had been set free in mockery. Care was therefore to be taken lest, by secret tortures, they should compel the unwilling to continue as their slaves; and the provision against this evil was an open confession of their desire before the judges; whilst the boring of the ear was a kind of stigma

upon them. For the Orientals were accustomed to brand slaves, or fugitives, or criminals, or those who were in any wise suspected; and although God did not choose to have this mark of ignominy imprinted on the foreheads of his people, yet, if any one voluntarily consented to endure perpetual slavery, He willed that he should bear this token of his servitude upon his ear. Still we must remember that even this slavery, although it is said to endure for ever, was brought to a close at the jubilee, because then the condition of the land and people was altogether renewed.

Deuteronomy 15

Deuteronomy 15:12-18

12. And if thy brother, an Hebrew man, or an Hebrew woman, be sold unto thee, and serve thee six years, then in the seventh year thou shalt let him go free from thee.

12. Si venditus fuerit tibi frater tuus Hebraeus, vel Hebraea, et servierit tibi sex annis: anno septimo dimittes eum liberum a te.

13. And when thou sendest him out free from thee, thou shalt not let him go away empty:

13. Et quum dimittes eum liberum a te, non dimittes eum vacuum.

14. Thou shalt furnish him liberally out of thy flock, and out of thy floor, and out of thy wine-press: of that wherewith the Lord thy God hath blessed thee thou shalt give unto him.

14. Onerando onerabis eum, de pecudibus tuis, et de area tua, et de torculari tuo: in quibus benedixit tibi Jehova Deus tuus, dabis ei.

15. And thou shalt remember that thou wast a bond-man in the land of Egypt, and the Lord thy God redeemed thee: therefore I command thee this thing today.

15. Et recordaberis quod servus fuisti in terra AEgypti, et redemerit te Jehova Deus tuus: idcirco ego praecipio tibi hoc hodie.

16. And it shall be, if he say unto thee, I will not go away from thee; (because he loveth thee and thine house, because he is well with thee;)

16. Quod si dixerit tibi, Non egrediar a te: propterea quod diligat te et domum tuam, et quod bene sit ei tecum:

17. Then thou shalt take an awl, and thrust it through his ear unto the door, and he shall be thy servant for ever: and also unto thy maidservant thou shalt do likewise.

17. Tunc accipies subulam, et adiges in aurem ejus in porta: eritque tibi servus in saeculum: sic etiam ancillae tuae facies.

18. It shall not seem hard unto thee when thou sendest him away free from thee; for he hath been worth a double hired servant to thee, in serving thee six years: and the Lord thy God shall bless thee in all that thou doest.

18. Non sit durum in oculis tuis quum dimittes eum liberum a te, quia duplo secundum mercedem mercenarii servivit tibi sex annis: et benedicet tibi Jehova in omnibus quae facies.

13. And when thou sendest him out free from thee. Here not only is the enfranchisement of slaves enjoined, but an exhortation to liberality is also added, viz., that they should not send away their slaves without their hire; for this is not a civil enactment for the purpose of extorting from the avaricious more than they were willing to give. The rule of Paul here applies:

"Every man according as he purposeth in his heart, so let him give; not grudgingly or of necessity: for God loveth a cheerful giver." (2 Corinthians 9:7.)

But, since the Hebrew slaves were brethren, God would not allow them to be placed in a worse condition than hirelings. That He commands them to be furnished out of the wine-press, and floor, and flock, does not mean that they were to be enriched, or that a large provision should be assigned to them, but He justly lays a constraint on the rich, whose varied abundance supplied them with the means of liberality; as if He would show them from whence they received their gratuitous gifts, which were at the same time a just compensation for the labors of their slaves.

18. It shall not seem hard unto thee. I have lately observed how difficult and inconvenient to the Jews was the observance of this law; wherefore it is not without reason that God reproves their mean and niggardly pride, if they enfranchised their slaves grudgingly. And, indeed, He first urges them to obey on the score of justice, and then from the hope of remuneration. For He reminds them that for six years the slave had earned double the wages of a hireling, either because his life was more laborious, inasmuch as heavier tasks are required from slaves than from free-men, who are paid for their work; or because he had completed twice as long a period as hirelings were wont to be engaged for. For the Jewish (commentators) [149] infer from this passage, that three years was the term prescribed for hired servants; and thus they suppose the six years were counted. But since this is a mere conjecture, I know not whether my opinion is not more suitable, that for six years their labors had been twice as profitable as would have been those of a free-man who is not under the compulsion of a slave.

Leviticus 25

Leviticus 25:39-55

39. And if thy brother that dwelleth by thee be waxen poor, and be sold unto thee; thou shalt not compel him to serve as a bond-servant:

39. Si attenuatus fuerit frater tuus apud te, ita ut vendat se tibi, non uteris opera ejus tanquam servi opera.

40. But as an hired servant, and as a sojourner, he shall be with thee, and shall serve thee unto the year of jubilee:

40. Tanquam mercenarius, tanquam colonus erit tecum: usque ad annum Jubilaei serviet tibi.

41. And then shall he depart from thee, both he and his children with him, and shall return unto his own family, and unto the possession of his fathers shall he return.

41. Egredietur autem a te ipse, et liberi ejus cum eo, ac revertetur ad familiam suam, et ad possessionem patrum suorum revertetur.

42. For they are my servants, which I brought forth out of the land of Egypt: they shall not be sold as bond-men.

42. Sunt enim servi mei quos eduxi e terra AEgypti: non vendentur venditione servili.

43. Thou shalt not rule over him with rigor, but shalt fear thy God.

43. Non dominaberis illis dure sed timebis a Deo tuo.

44. Both thy bond-men and thy bond-maids, which thou shalt have, shall be of the heathen that are round about you; of them shall ye buy bond-men and bond-maids.

44. Servus autem tuus et ancilla tua qui erunt tibi, de gentibus erunt quae sunt in circuitu vestro, ex iis emetis servum et ancillam.

45. Moreover, of the children of the strangers that do sojourn among you, of them shall ye buy, and of their families that are with you, which they begat in your land; and they shall be your possession:

45. Et etiam de filiis incolarum qui versantur apud vos, emetis: et de familia eorum qui apud vos sunt, quos procreaverunt in terra vestra: eruntque vobis in possessionem.

46. And ye shalt take them as an inheritance for your children after you, to inherit them for a possession; they shall be your bond-men for ever: but over your brethren the children of Israel, ye shall not rule one over another with rigor.

46. Et jure haereditario possidebitis eos pro filiis vestris post vos, ad possidendum possessionem: in perpetuum utemini opera, eorum: fratribus autem vestris filiis Israel quisque fratri suo non dominabitur dure.

47. And if a sojourner or stranger wax rich by thee, and thy brother that dwelleth by him wax poor, and sell himself unto the stranger or sojourner by thee, or to the stock of the stranger's family:

47. Si autem apprehenderint manus peregrini et advenae qui est apud te, et attenuatus fuerit frater tuus qui apud illum versatur, seque vendiderit peregrino et advenae qui est apud te, vel stirpi familiae peregrini:

48. After that he is sold he may be redeemed again; one of his brethren may redeem him:

48. Postquam vendiderit se, redemptio erit ei: unus e fratribus ejus redimet eum:

49. Either his uncle, or his uncle's son, may redeem him, or any that is nigh of kin unto him of his family may redeem him; or, if he be able, he may redeem himself.

49. Aut patruus ejus, aut filius patrui ejus redimet eum, aut propinquus carnis ejus e familia ejus redimet eum: aut si apprehenderit manus ejus, tunc redimet seipsum.

50. And he shall reckon with him that bought him, from the year that he was sold to him, unto the year of jubilee: and the price of his sale shall be according unto the number of years, according to the time of an hired servant shall it be with him.

50. Et supputabit cum eo qui emit ipsum, ab anno quo se vendidit illi, usque ad annum Jubilaei, aestimabiturque pecunia venditionis ejus secundum numerum annorum: et secundum dies mercenarii fiet cum eo.

51. If there be yet many years behind, according unto them he shall give again the price of his redemption out of the money that he was bought for.

51. Si adhuc multi fuerint anni, secundum eos restituet redemptionem suam de argento venditionis suae.

52. And if there remain but few years unto the year of jubilee, then he shall count with him, and according unto his years shall he give him again the price of his redemption.

52. Quod si parum reliquum sit ex annis usque ad annum Jubilaei, tunc supputabit cum eo: et secundum annos suos restituet redemptionem suam.

53. And as a yearly hired servant shall he be with him: and the other shall not rule with rigor over him in thy sight.

53. Tanquam mercenarius annuus erit cum illo: non dominabitur ei dure in oculis tuis.

54. And if he be not redeemed in these years, then he shall go out in the year of jubilee, both he, and his children with him.

54. Si non se redemerit in illis, egredietur in anno Jubilaei ipse et filii ejus:

55. For unto me the children of Israel are servants; they are my servants, whom I brought forth out of the land of Egypt: I am the Lord your God.

55. Quia mihi sunt filii Israel servi, servi mei sunt quos eduxi e terra AEgypti: ego Jehova Deus vester.

39. And if thy brother. He now proceeds further, i e., that one who has bought his brother should treat him with humanity, and not otherwise than a hired servant. We have seen, indeed, just above, that the labor of a slave is estimated at twice as much, because the humanity of his master will never go so far as to indulge or spare his slave as if he were a hireling. It is not, therefore, without reason that God puts a restraint upon that rule, which experience shows to have been often tyrannical. Still He prescribes no more than heathen philosophers did, [150] viz., that masters should treat their slaves like hired servants. And this principle of justice ought to prevail towards all without exception; but since it was difficult to prescribe the same rule respecting strangers as respecting their brethren, a special law is enacted, that at least they should observe moderation towards their brethren, with whom they had a common inheritance and condition. First:. therefore, it is provided as to Hebrew slaves that they should not be treated harshly and contemptuously like captives (mancipia;) and then that their slavery should come to an end in the year of jubilee. But here the question arises, since their liberty was before accorded to them in the, seventh year, why it is now postponed to the fiftieth? Some get over the difficulty by supposing that [151] if the jubilee occurred during the six years, they must then be set free, although they had not completed the whole term; but this is too forced a conjecture. The view that most approves itself to me is, that the word יבל, yobel, is extended to mean every seventh year, or, at any rate, that moderation towards those slaves is specially prescribed who were most exposed to violence and other injurious treatment. For they would not have dared to oppress at pleasure their slaves, who were soon afterwards to be free; but those who, by having their ears bored, had subjected themselves to the longer period of slavery, would have been more outrageously harassed, unless God had interposed. And this opinion I freely adopt, that although their slavery

lasted to the jubilee, yet flint their masters were to treat them with moderation and humanity. This too is confirmed by what immediately follows, where it is enjoined that the children should be set free with their fathers, which did not take place in the seventh year.

42. For they are my servants. God here declares that His own right is invaded when those, whom He claims as His property, are taken into subjection by another; for He says that He acquired the people as His own when He redeemed them from Egypt. Whence He infers that His right is violated if any should usurp perpetual dominion over a Hebrew. If any object that this is of equal force, when they only serve for a time, I reply, that though God might have justly asserted His sole ownership, yet He was satisfied with this symbol of it; and therefore that He suffered by indulgence that they should be enslaved for a fixed period, provided some trace of His deliverance of them should remain. In a word, He simply chose to apply this preventative lest slavery should altogether extinguish the recollection of His grace, although He allowed it to be thus smothered as it were. Lest, therefore, cruel masters should trust that their tyranny would be exercised with impunity, Moses reminds them that they had to do with God, who will at length appear as its avenger. Although the political laws of Moses are not now in operation, still the analogy is to be preserved, lest the condition of those who have been redeemed by Christ's blood should be worse amongst us, than that of old of tits ancient people. To whom Paul's exhortation refers:

"Ye masters, forbear threatening your slaves, knowing that both your and their Master is in heaven." [152] (Ephesians 6:9.)

44. Both thy bond-men, and thy bond-maids. What God here permits as regards strangers was everywhere customary among the Gentiles, viz., that their power over their slaves should exist not only until their death, but should continue in perpetual succession to their children; for this is the force of the expression, "ye shall possess them for your children," that the right of ownership should pass to their heir's also; nor is there a distinction made only as to perpetuity, [153] but also as to the mode of their treatment. For we must observe the antithesis, "ye shall make use of their service, but over his brother no man shall rule with rigor;" [154] whence it appears that a restraint was imposed upon them lest they should imperiously rule the children of Abraham, and not leave them half their liberty in comparison with the Gentiles. Not that a tyrannical or cruel exercise of power oyer strangers was allowed, but that God would have the race of Abraham, whose liberator lie was, exempted by certain privileges from the common lot.

47. And if a sojourner or a stranger. A caution is here introduced as to the Israelites who had enslaved themselves to strangers. But by strangers understand only those who inhabited the land of Canaan; for, if any one]lad been carried away into other countries, God would have enacted this law as to their redemption in vain. A power, therefore, of redeeming the slave is granted to his relatives, or, if he had himself obtained sufficient to pay his price, the same permission is accorded to himself. The mode and the form of this are then expressed: that a calculation of the time which remained before the jubilee should be made, and the period which had already elapsed should be subtracted from the sum, viz., if he had been sold for fifty shekels he should only pay ten

shekels in the fortieth year, because only a fifth part of the time remained. But
if none of his family aided him, and the unhappy man's hope of redemption was
frustrated, He commands that he should be set free in the jubilee year, in which
a general enfranchisement took place as regarded the children of Abraham. The
object of the law was, that none of those whom God had adopted, should be
alienated from their race, and thus should depart from the true worship of God
Himself. The whole of this is comprehended in the last verse, where God
declares that the children of Abraham were His property, inasmuch as He had
led them forth from the land of Egypt, and, on the other hand, that He is their
peculiar God. For, whilst it was just that they should enjoy His blessing, so also
it behooved that they should be kept sound in His pure and undivided worship;
whereas, if they had been the slaves of Gentiles, not only would the elect
people have been diminished in numbers, but circumcision would have been
corrupted and a door opened to impious perversions. Yet God so mitigates His
law as to lay no unjust burden upon sojourners, since He concedes more to
them, with respect to Hebrew slaves, than to the natives of the land; for if they
had sold themselves to their brethren, they went forth free in the seventh year,
whilst their slavery under sojourners was extended to the fiftieth year. This
exception only was introduced that the stranger who had bought slaves should
enfranchise them on the payment of their value. Since God had previously
promised to His people a large and manifold abundance of all good things, the
poverty here adverted to could only occur from the curse of God; [155] we see,
therefore, that of His incomparable loving-kindness He stretches forth His hand
to the transgressors of His law; and, whilst He chastises them with poverty, still
looks upon them, unworthy as they are, and provides a remedy for the ills
which their own guilt had brought upon them.

Leviticus 25

Leviticus 25:23-34

23. The land shall not be sold for ever: for the land is mine; for ye are strangers and sojourners with me.

23. Terra autem non vendetur absolute, quia mea est terra: vos enim peregrini, et advenae estis apud me.

24. And in all the land of your possession ye shall grant a redemption for the land.

24. In universa autem terra possessionis vestrae redemptionem dabitis terrae.

25. If thy brother be waxen poor, and hath sold away some of his possession, and if any of his kin come to redeem it, then shall he redeem that which his brother sold.

25. Quum attenuatus fuerit frater tuus, et vendiderit de possessione sua: tunc veniet redemptor ejus propinquus ipsi: et redimet venditionem fratris sui.

26. And if the man have none to redeem it, and himself be able to redeem it;

26. Et, si non fuerit viro redemptor, sed apprehenderit manus ejus, et invenerit quod sufficit ad ejus redemptionem;

27. Then let him count the years of the sale thereof, and restore the overplus unto the man to whom he sold it, that he may return unto his possession.

27. Tunc supputabit annos venditionis suae, et restituet quod superest viro cui vendidit, et revertetur ad possessionem suam.

28. But if he be not able to restore it to him, then that which is sold shall remain in the hand of him that hath bought it until the year of jubilee: and in the jubilee it shall go out, and he shall return unto his possession.

28. Si vero non invenerit manus ejus quod sufficiat ad reddendum illi, tum erit venditio ejus in manu ejus, qui emit illum, usque ad annum Jubilaei: at egredietur in Jubilaeo, reverteturque ad possessionem suam.

29. And if a man sell a dwelling-house in a walled city, then he may redeem it within a whole year after it is sold: within a full year may he redeem it.

29. Vir autem quum vendiderit domum habitationis in urbe murata, erit redemptio ejus donec compleatur annus venditionis ejus: anno uno erit redemptio ejus.

30. And if it be not redeemed within the space of a full year, then the house that is in the walled city shall be established for ever to him that bought it, throughout his generations: it shall not go out in the jubilee.

30. Quod si non redimatur donec impleatur illi annus integer, remanebit domus quae fuerit in civitate cui est murus, absolute ementi illam in generationibus ejus: non egredietur in Jubilaeo.

31. But the houses of the villages, which have no walls round about them, shall be counted as the fields of the country; they may be redeemed, and they shall go out in the jubilee.

31. Domus autem villarum quibus non est murus in circuitu, secundum agrum terrae aestimabitur, redemptio erit ei, et in Jubilaeo egredietur.

32. Notwithstanding the cities of the Levites, and the houses of the cities of their possession, may the Levites redeem at any time.

32. Urbium autem Levitarum, et domorum urbium possessionis eorum, redemptio perpetua erit Levitis.

33. And if a man purchase of the Levites, then the house that was sold, and the city of his possession, shall go out in the year of jubilee: for the houses of the cities of the Levites are their possession among the children of Israel.

33. Qui autem emerit a Levitis, egredietur venditio domus, et urbis possessionis ejus in Jubilaeo, quia domus urbium Levitatum est possessio eorum in medio filiorum Israel.

34. But the field of the suburbs of their cities may not be sold; for it is their perpetual possession.

34. Ager autem suburbii urbium eorum non vendetur, quia possessio perpetua est illis.

23. The land shall not be sold for ever. Since the reason for this law was peculiar to the children of Abraham, its provisions can hardly be applied to other nations; for so equal a partition of the land was made under Joshua, that the inheritance was distributed amongst the several tribes and families; nay, in order that each man's possession should be more sacred, the land had been

divided by lot, as if God by His own hand located them in their separate stations. In fact, that allotment was, as it were, an inviolable decree of God Himself, whereby the memory of the covenant should be maintained, by which the inheritance of the land had been promised to Abraham and his posterity; and thus the land of Canaan was an earnest, or symbol, or mirror, of the adoption on which their salvation was founded. Wherefore it is not to be wondered at that God was unwilling that this inestimable benefit should ever be lost; and, lest this should be the case, like a provident father of a family, He laid a restraint on His children, to prevent them from being too prodigal; for, when a man has any suspicions of his heir, he forbids him to alienate the patrimony he leaves him. Such, therefore, was the condition of the ancient people; yet it cannot be indiscriminately transferred to other nations who have had no common inheritance given them. Some vestige of it appears in the right of redemption; [156] but, because that depends on the consent of the parties, and is also a special mode of contract, it has nothing to do with the law of Moses, which entirely restored both men and lands, (in the year of jubilee, [157]) That God should call the land of Canaan His, is, as it were, to assert His direct Lordship [158] (dominium,) as they call it, over it; as He immediately afterwards more clearly expresses His meaning, where He says that the children of Israel sojourn in it as His guests. [159] For although their condition was the best in which just and perpetual owners can be placed, still, as respected God, they were but His tenants (coloni,) only living there at His will. In fine, God claims the freehold (fundum) for Himself, lest the recollection of tits having granted it to them should ever escape them.

24. *And in all the land of your possession.* Before the jubilee came, He permits not only the relations to redeem land sold by a poor man, but the seller also, if no other redeemer interposed. The same power was also given to relations amongst other nations, though with a different object, viz., the preservation of the family name; still, the seller was never allowed to redeem, unless a special clause to that effect was contained in the contract. But God desired that the lands should be retained by their legal possessor, in order that the people might deviate as little as possible from the division made by Joshua. Meanwhile, He had in view the private advantage of individuals; but in the perpetual succession to the land He considered Himself rather than men, in order that the recollection of His kindness should never be lost. Finally, He orders all lands to return in the year of jubilee to their original owners; and all sales to be cancelled, as if, in the fiftieth year, he renewed the lot for the division of the land.

29. *And if a man sell a dwelling-house.* He here distinguishes houses from lands, providing that the power of redemption should not extend beyond a year; and also, that the purchase should hold good even in the jubilee. A second distinction, however, is also added between different kinds of houses, viz., that houses in towns might be altogether alienated, whilst the condition of those in the country should be the same as that of the lands themselves, as being annexed so as to form part of them. As regarded houses fix towns, because they were sometimes burdensome to their owners, it was an advantage that they might pass into the hands of the rich who were competent to bear the expenses of building. Besides, a house does not supply daily food like a field, and it is more tolerable to be without a house than a field, in which you may work, and from the cultivation of which you may support yourself and family. But it was

necessary to except houses in the country, because they were appendages to the land; for what use would there be in harvesting the fruits, if you had no place to store them in? Nay, what would it profit to possess a farm which you could not cultivate? for how could oxen plough without any stalls in its vicinity? Since, then, lands without farm-buildings or cottages are almost useless, and they cannot be conveniently separated, justly did God appoint that, in the year of Jubilee, every rural possession should revert to its former owner.

32. Notwithstanding the cities of the Levites. Another exception, that the Levites should recover the houses they had sold, either by the right of redemption, or gratuitously in the year of jubilee. And this is not only appointed out of favor to them, but because it concerned the whole people, that they should be posted like sentries in the place which God had assigned to them. As to the suburbs, or the lands destined for the support of their cattle, God forbids their alienation, because thus they would have forsaken their proper station and removed elsewhere; whereas it was of importance to the whole people that such a dispersion should not occur.

Deuteronomy 20

Deuteronomy 20:19, 20

19. When thou shalt besiege a city a long time, in making war against it to take it, thou shalt not destroy the trees thereof by forcing an axe against them: for thou mayest eat of them, and thou shalt not cut them down, (for the tree of the field is man's life,) to employ them in the siege:

19. Si obsederis urbem, diebus multis pugnando adversus eam, ut capias eam, non disperdes arbores ejus, impellendo in eas securim: quia ex illarum fructibus vesceris, propterea ipsas non succides: (quia an homo arbor agri ut ingrediatur a facie tua in munitionem?)

20. Only the trees which thou knowest that they be not trees for meat, thou shalt destroy and cut them down; and thou shalt build bulwarks against the city that maketh war with thee, until it be subdued.

20. Veruntamen arbores quas noveris non esse fructiferas, disperdes, et succides: et aedificabis munitionem adversus urbem illam quae tecum dimicat, donec descendat ipsa.

19. When thou shalt besiege a city a long time. I have not hesitated to annex this precept to the Eighth Commandment, for when God lays a restraint on the liberty of inflicting injuries in the very heat of war, with respect to felling trees, much more did He desire His people to abstain from all mischievous acts in time of peace. The sum is, that although the laws of war opened the gate to plunder and rapine, still they were to beware, as much as possible, lest the land being desolated, it should be barren for the future; in short, that the booty was so to be taken from the enemy, as that the advantage of the human race should still be considered, and that posterity might still be nourished by the trees which do not quickly arrive at the age of fruit-bearing. He commands them to spare fruit-trees, first of all, for this reason, because they supply food to all men; and thus the blessing of God is manifested in them. He then adds, as a second reason, that trees are exposed to everybody, whereby He signifies that war should not be waged with them as with men. This passage is

indeed variously explained, but the sense which I have chosen accords very well and appears to be the right one. For, [160] although the letter h is demonstrative, according to the rules of grammar, and thus points out the enemy; yet, in my opinion, the sentence is to be taken interrogatively. But מצור, matzor, signifies rather a bulwark than a siege. God, therefore, indirectly reproves the stupidity and madness of men, who, when in arms, exert their strength against a tree which does not move from its place, but waits to meet them. Thus the open field is contrasted with the bulwark. Meanwhile, God permits ramparts and palisadoes, and other machines used in sieges, to be made of trees which do not bear fruit, and only provides that the tempest of war, which ought to be momentary, should not strip the land of its ornaments for many years. Still, there is no such strict rule laid down as that a fruit-tree may not be cut down if necessity demands it; but God restrains the Israelites from giving way to destruction and devastation under the impulse of anger and hatred, and in forgetfulness of the calls of humanity.

Deuteronomy 21

Deuteronomy 21:14-17

14. And it shall be, if thou have no delight in her, then thou shalt let her go whither she will; but thou shalt not sell her at all for money, thou shalt not make merchandise of her, because thou hast humbled her.

14. Si non placuerit tibi uxor captiva, dimittes eam pro desiderio suo: nec vendendo vendes eam pecunia, neque negotiaberis de ea, quod afflixeris eam.

15. If a man have two wives, one beloved, and another hated, and they have borne him children, both the beloved and the hated; and if the first-born son be her's that was hated:

15. Quum fuerint viroduae uxores, una dilecta et altera exosa, et pepererit ei filios dilecta et exosa, fuerit autem filius primogenitus exosae:

16. Then it shall be, when he maketh his sons to inherit that which he hath, that he may not make the son of the beloved first-born before the son of the hated, which is indeed the first-born:

16. Die quo haeredes instituet filios suos eorum quae habuerit, non poterit dare jus primogeniturae filio dilectae ante filium exosae primogenitum.

17. But he shall acknowledge the son of the hated for the first-born, by giving him a double portion of all that he hath: for he is the beginning of his strength; the right of the first-born is his.

17. Sed primogenitum filium exosae agnoscet, ut det ei mensuram duorum ex omnibus quae habuerit: ipse enim principium fortitudinis ejus, ipsius est jus primogeniturae.

14. And it shall be, if thou have no delight in her. I have been compelled to separate this sentence from the foregoing context which I have explained elsewhere; [161] for Moses there gave instructions how a captive woman was to be taken to wife if her beauty attracted a Jewish husband. That law then had reference to chastity and conjugal fidelity, and especially to the purity of God's worship; but now Moses prescribes that, if a man have dishonored a captive woman, he should not sell her, but let her go free, and by this satisfaction wipe out, or at any rate diminish, the injury. Hence we infer that this rule of justice

depends on the Eighth Commandment, Let none defraud another. This condition was at least tolerable for the captive; for, although chastity is a special treasure, yet liberty, which is justly called an inestimable blessing, was no trifling consolation to her. The penalty, then, of lust, was that the conqueror should lose his booty.

15. If a man have two wives. Inasmuch as it is here provided that a father should not unjustly transfer what belongs to one son to another, it is a part and supplement of the Eighth Commandment, the substance of which is, that every one's rights should be preserved to him. For, if the father substituted another son in the place of his first-born, it was unquestionably a kind of theft. But, since it rarely happens that a father unnaturally degrades his first-born from his precedence, if all are born of the same mother, God reminds us that He did not enact this law without cause; for, where polygamy was allowed, the mind of the husband was generally most inclined to the second wife; because, if he had loved the first with true affection, he would have been contented with her as the companion of his life and bed, and would not have thought of a second. When, therefore, the husband grew tired of his first wife, and desired a second, he might be coaxed by her blandishments to leave away from the children of his first marriage what naturally belonged to them. Hence, therefore, the necessity of the remedy whereby the father's power of altering the right of primogeniture is barred; for, although they might allege that they only gave what was their own, yet it was an act of ungodly arrogance to reject him whom God had deigned to honor. For he who arrogates such power to himself, or who assigns the birth-right to whom he will, almost arrogates to himself the ability to create. This right, as is stated in verse 17, was a double portion of the paternal inheritance. The reason which is added, is equivalent to saying, that the first-born is the principal honor and ornament of the father. Still, if there was a just cause for disinheriting the first-born, another successor might be substituted in his stead, as Jacob shewed in his case when he disinherited Reuben. (Genesis 49:4.) When it is said, "before the son of the hated," some expound it to mean "during his lifetime;" others retain the Hebrew phrase, "before his face." Their opinion, however, is probable, who take this particle comparatively, for "instead of her son." The wife is called hated, not that her husband is positively her enemy, but because he loves her least; for contempt is considered as hatred, and he is called an enemy who does not render conjugal benevolence.

Deuteronomy 20

Deuteronomy 20:5-8

5. And the officers shall speak unto the people, saying, What man is there that hath built a new house, and hath not dedicated it? let him go and return to his house, lest he die in the battle, and another man dedicate it.

5. *Quum bellandum erit, alloquentur praefecti populum, dicendo, Quis est vir qui aedificavit domum novam, et non dedicavit eam? abeat, et revertatur ad domum suam, ne forte moriatur in praelio, et alius dedicet eam.*

6. And what man is he that hath planted a vineyard, and hath not yet eaten of it? let him also go and return unto his house, lest he die in the battle, and another man eat of it.

6. Et quis est vir qui plantavit vineam, et non fecit eam communem? abeat et revertatur ad domum suam: ne forte moriatur in praelio, et alius communem eam faciat.

7. And what man is there that hath betrothed a wife, and hath not taken her? let him go and return unto his house, lest he die in the battle, and another man take her.

7. Et quis est vir qui despondit mulierem, et non accepit eam? abeat et revertatur domum suam ne forte moriatur in praelio, et alius eam accipiat.

8. And the officers shall speak further unto the people, and they shall say, What man is there that is fearful and faint-hearted? let him go and return unto his house, lest his brethren's heart faint as well as his heart.

8. Addent praefecti alloqui populum, dicendo, Quis est vir timidus et mollis corde? abeat, et revertatur domum suam, ne dissolvatur cor fratrum ejus, sicut cor illius.

5. And the officers shall speak unto the people. I have added the commencement, "quum bellandum erit," (when there shall be war,) that my readers may know what is the subject here discussed; for although the instruction given may seem somewhat remote from the prohibition of theft, still it accords well, and is closely connected with it. For by this indulgence God shews how just it is, that every one should enjoy peaceably what he possesses; because, if it be hard that men on account of war should be deprived of the use of their new house, or of the produce of their vineyard, how much more harsh and intolerable it will be to deprive men of their fortunes, or to drive them from the lands which they justly call their own! Since, therefore, it is expedient for the state that vineyards should be sown or planted, and that houses should be built, whilst men would not address themselves to these duties with sufficient alacrity, unless encouraged by the hope of enjoying them, God gives them the privilege of exemption from fighting, if they be owners of new houses which they have not yet inhabited. He makes also the same appointment as to possessors of vineyards, if they have not yet tasted of the fruit of their labor, and will not have men torn from their affianced wives until they have enjoyed their embraces. A different principle applies to a fourth class, because the faint-hearted and lazy are not deserving that God should have consideration for their cowardice, when they shun dangers to be incurred for the public welfare; but because it concerns the whole people that soldiers should go forth readily to war, God will not have more required from any one than he is disposed to bear. We now understand the substance of this passage, viz., that, when every man's right is asserted to enjoy what he possesses, it extends so far as that a man who has built a house should not be dragged unwillingly to war, until by dwelling in it he shall have received some advantage from the expenses incurred. To make a vineyard common, [162] or to profane it, is equivalent to applying the vintage to the common uses of life; for it was not lawful, as we saw under the First Commandment, [163] to gather its first-fruits, as if it were as yet uncircumcised; therefore the recompence for their industry and diligence is made when those who have planted vines are thus set free, until they have enjoyed some of their produce. As regards the betrothed, although it seems to have been an indulgence granted in honor of marriage, that they should return to the wives whom they had not yet enjoyed, yet it is probable that they were not torn away from the dearest of all possessions, in order that every man's property should be

maintained. Besides, if the hope of progeny were taken away, the inheritance would be thus transferred to others, which would have been tantamount to diverting it from its rightful owner. We have said that the lazy and timid were sent home, that the Israelites might learn that none were to be pressed beyond their ability; and this also depends upon that rule of equity[164] which dictates that we should abstain from all unjust oppression.

Deuteronomy 25

Deuteronomy 25:5-10

5. If brethren dwell together, and one of them die, and have no child, the wife of the dead shall not marry without unto a stranger: her husband's brother shall go in unto her, and take her to him to wife, and perform the duty of an husband's brother unto her.

5. Quum habitaverint fratres pariter, et mortuus fuerit unus ex ipsis, nec fuerit ei filius, non abnubet uxor mortui viro extraneo: cognatus ejus ingredietur ad eam, et capiet eam sibi in uxorem, et affinitatem contrahet cum ea.

6. And it shall be, that the first-born which she beareth shall succeed in the name of his brother which is dead, that his name be not put out of Israel.

6. Atque ita primogenitus quem peperit, surget nomine fratris ejus defuncti: ne deleat nomen ejus ex Israele.

7. And if the man like not to take his brother's wife, then let his brother's wife go up to the gate unto the elders, and say, My husband's brother refuseth to raise up unto his brother a name in Israel, he will not perform the duty of my husband's brother.

7. Quod si noluerit vir ille accipere affinem suam, tunc ascendet ipsa ad portam ad seniores, et dicet, Renuit affinis meus suscitare fratri suo nomen in Israele, nec vult affinitatem contrahere mecum.

8. Then the elders of his city shall call him, and speak unto him: and if he stand to it, and say, I like not to take her;

8. Tunc accersent illum seniores urbis illius, et loquentur cum eo: et ubi steterit, ac dixerit, Non placet accipere eam:

9. Then shall his brother's wife come unto him in the presence of the elders, and loose his shoe from off his foot, and spit in his face, and shall answer and say, So shall it be done unto that man that will not build up his brother's house.

9. Accedet postea cognata ejus ad ipsum in oculis seniorum, et solvet calceamentum ejus a pede ipsius, et spuet in faciem ejus: loqueturque, ac dicet, Sic fiet viro qui non aedificaverit domum fratris sui.

10. And his name shall be called in Israel, The house of him that hath his shoe loosed.

10. Et vocabitur nomen ejus in Israel, Domus discalceati.

5. **If brethren dwell together, and one of them die.** This law has some similarity with that which permits a betrothed person to return to the wife, whom he has not yet taken; since the object of both is to preserve to every man what he possesses, so that he may not be obliged to leave it to strangers, but

that he may have heirs begotten of his own body: for, when a son succeeds to the father, whom he represents, there seems to be hardly any change made. Hence, too, it is manifest how greatly pleasing to God it is that no one should be deprived of his property, since He makes a provision even for the dying, that what they could not resign to others without regret and annoyance, should be preserved to their offspring. Unless, therefore, his kinsman should obviate the dead man's childlessness, this inhumanity is accounted a kind of theft. For, since to be childless was a curse of God, it was a consolation in this condition to hope for a borrowed offspring, that the name might not be altogether extinct.

Since we now understand the intention of the law, we must also observe that the word brethren does not mean actual brothers, but cousins, and other kinsmen, whose marriage with the widows of their relative would not have been incestuous; otherwise God would contradict Himself. But these two things are quite compatible, that no one should uncover the nakedness of his brother, and yet that a widow should not marry out of her husband's family, until she had raised up seed to him from some relation. In fact, Boaz did not marry Ruth because he was the brother of her deceased husband, but only his near kinsman. If any should object that it is not probable that other kinsmen should dwell together, I reply that this passage is improperly supposed to refer to actual living together, as if they dwelt in the same house, but that the precept is merely addressed to relations, whose near residence rendered it convenient to take the widows to their own homes; for, if any lived far away, liberty was accorded to both to seek the fulfillment of the provision elsewhere. Surely it is not probable that God would have authorized an incestuous marriage, which He had before expressed His abomination of. Nor can it be doubted, as I have above stated, but that the like necessity was imposed upon the woman of offering herself to the kinsman of her former husband; and although there was harshness in this, still she seemed to owe this much to his memory, that she should willingly raise up seed to the deceased; yet, if any one think differently, I will not contend the point with him. If, however, she were not obliged to do so, it was absurd that she should voluntarily obtrude herself: nor was there any other reason why she should bring to trial the kinsman, from whom she had suffered a repulse, except that she might acquire the liberty of marrying into another family. Yet it is not probable that he was to be condemned to an ignominious punishment, without being admitted to make his defense, because sometimes just reasons for refusal might be alleged. This disgrace, therefore, was only a penalty for inhumanity or avarice. By giving up his shoe, he renounced his right of relationship, and gave it up to another: for, by behaving so unkindly towards the dead, he became unworthy of reaping any of the advantages of his relationship.

Footnotes:

98. A. V., "deal falsely, neither lie." Ainsworth, "neither falsely deny, nor deal falsely."

99. A. V., "Non facies calumniam proximo tuo, nec vi opprimes eum." "The first of these terms signifies to oppress by fraud; the second to oppress by violence. Against both these offenses, John the Baptist warned the soldiers who came to him; Luke 3:14." -- Bush from Ainsworth.

100. "Et a mon avis que le premier est comme genre, et le second comme espece;" and, in my opinion, that the first is, as it were,

genus, and the second species. -- Fr.

101. The expression on which C. founds this statement is translated by himself "ea (i.e., mercede) sustentat animam suam;" in our A. V., "setteth his heart upon it;" margin, "Heb., lifteth his soul unto it." Dathe has, "eam anhelat;" Ainsworth, "and unto it he lifteth up his soul," and his note is, "that is, hopeth for and desireth it for the maintenance of his life. So the Greek here translateth, he hath hope; and in. Jeremiah 22:27, and 44:14, the lifting up of the soul signifieth a desire; and the soul is often put for the life. Hereupon the Hebrews say, Whosoever withholdeth the hireling's wage, is as if he took away his soul (or life) from him" etc.

102. The Fr. gives a different turn to this: "Or Dieu declare que leur pourete et misere n'empechera point de les secourir: d'autant qu'ils ne amusent point a la personne;" Now, God declares, that their poverty and misery shall not prevent their being succored; so that they should not be interested by their person.

103. "Inter falsarios." -- Lat. "Pour faussaire." -- Fr.

104. Modest. 1. penult, ad legem Corn. de fals. -- C. This law is to be found in Digest. 48, tit. 11, De falsis, 32, "Si venditor mensuras publice probatas vini, frumenti, vel cujuslibet rei, aut emptor corruperit, dolove malo fraudem fecerit, quanti ea res est, ejus dupli condemnatur. Decretoque Divi Hadriani praeceptum est in insulam eos relegari, qui pondera, aut mensuras falsassent."

105. "In the digests there is a vague law, de termino moto, Digestor. Lib. 47. tit. 21, on which

Calmer remarks, that, though the Romans had no determined punishment for those who removed the ancient land-marks, yet, if slaves were found to have done it with an evil design, they were put to death; that persons of quality were sometimes exiled when found, guilty; and that others were sentenced to primary fines, or corporal punishment. -- Adam Clarke, in loco.

106. "Est desia assez convaincu par ce seul acte d'avoir voulu debouter le possesseur de son champ;" is already sufficiently convicted by this act alone of having wished to deprive the possessor of his land. -- Fr.

107. Added from Fr.

108. "It shall be righteousness unto thee," A V., and rightly, as it would appear, for, as Piscator (in Poole's Syn.) remarks, "ante צצע deficit praepositio."

109. Added from Fr. "Atque ita placet Stoicis, quae in terris gignuntur ad usum hominum omnia creari, homines autem hominum causa esse generatos, ut ipsi inter se aliis alii prodesse possent." -- Cic. de Off. 1:7.

110. It will be seen that these verses are abbreviated, and slightly paraphrased by C. His exposition of them, which is not the ordinary one, agrees with that of Junins in Poole's Syn.

111. See C. on Luke 6:35. Harmony of the Evang., [12]vol. 1 p. 302. -- (Calvin Soc. edit.,) together with the Editor's note.

112. Margin. A. V., "If his hand faileth, then thou shalt strengthen him." "When a man is so impoverished that he hath no means, they are commanded to strengthen him, as taking him by the hand; so the Lord is said to strengthen the right hand of Cyrus,

when he assisted him against his enemies, Isaiah 45:11, etc." -- Willet, in loco.

113. "Il a entendu qu'on les traittast humainement;" He implied that they should be treated with humanity. -- Fr.

114. "Il permet aux Juifs pareille liberte envers les nations estranges, que les Payens se donnoyent envers les Juifs; "He permits the Jews to have equal liberty with respect to foreign nations, with that which the heathen gave themselves with respect to the Jews. -- Fr.

115. Πολιτεία Γ. in fin.

116. "Furem dupli condenmari, foeneratorem quadrupli." Cato de R. Rust. in procem. "Ex quo genere comparationis illud est Catonis senis; a quo quum quaereretur, quid maxime in re familiari expediret, respondit, Bene pascere. Quid secundum? Satis bene pascere. Quid tertium? Male pascere. Quid quartum? orare. Et, cum ille, qui quaesierat, dixisset, Quid foenerari? Tum Cato, Quid hominem, inquit, occidere?" Cic. de Off. 2:24.

117. In Fr. the following sentence is here inserted: -- "Ce titre la doncques a este favorable: comme en nostre langage Francois le mot d'Usure sera assez en horreur, mais les interests ont la vogue sous nulle difficulte ni scrupule:" This title then was an euphemism, as in our French language, the word Usury will be sufficiently dreaded, whilst Interest is current without difficulty or scruple. Say. Econ. Polit. B. 2 Ch. 8 Section 1., tells us that, "L'interet...s'appelait, auparavant usure, et c'etait le mot propre, puisque l'interet est un prix, un loyer qu'on paie pour avoir la jouissance d'une valeur. Mais ce mot est devenu odieux; il ne reveille plus que l'idee d'un interet illegal, exorbitant, et on lui en a substitue un autre plus honnete et moins expressif selon la coutume."

118. "Terre ou marchandise." -- Fr.

119. "Ainsi, combien que ce nom d'Usure ait este favorable de soy du commencement, en la fin il a este diffame;" Thus, although this word Usury was of no ill meaning in its origin, in the end it has been abused. -- Fr.

120. See C. on Ezekiel 18:5-9, where the subject is more fully discussed. C. Soc. Edit. [13]vol. 2 p. 225, et seq. See also Mr. Myers's Dissertation, ibid., [14]p. 469.

121. Addition in Fr., "Je say qu'on nomme cela Interest, mais ce m'est tout un:" I know that they call this interest, but this is all the same to me.

122. Polit., lib. 1. cap. 10. "The enemies to interest in general, (says Blackstone,) make no distinction between that and usury, holding any m-crease of money to be indefensibly usurious. And this they ground, as well on the prohibition of it by the Law of Moses among the Jews, as also upon what is said to be laid down by Aristotle, that money is naturally barren, and to make it breed money is preposterous, and a perversion of the end of its institution, which was only to serve the purposes of exchange, and not of increase." The hypothetical form in which he attributes this dictum to Aristotle, he explains in a note to be, because "this passage hath been suspected to be spurious." -- Comment, on the Laws of England, b. 2. ch. 30 sec. 454.

123. C. here uses the word foenerator; whereas his translation is, it will be seen, usurarius.

124. A. V., "The extortioner."

125. "Neque id (quod stultissimum est) certare cum usuris fructibus praediorurn." Cic. Or. in Cat. 2da. 8, i.e., says Facciolati in voce certo, "tot usuris se onerare, ut praediorum fructus exaequent: qua ratione fructus cum usuris committuntur, et certant, et plerumque superantur, quia usurae quotannis certae sunt, fructus autem incerti." Fr., "Car combien que ceux qui possedent beaucoup soyent aucunefois epuisez, pource qu'ils ne sont que receveurs de ceux auxquels ils doyvent;" for, although those who possess much are often ruined, because they are only the receivers of their creditors, etc.

126. Foenebre malum." -- Lat. "Ceste vermine d'usure." -- Fr.

127. "Soyent pitoyables, et humains pour faire plaisir a chacun;" should be pitiful and humane, to show kindness to all. -- Fr.

128. See [15]vol. 2, p. 273, on Numbers 5:8.

129. "Il n'y a rien plus enorme, que d'en faire une caverne de brigans;" there is nothing more enormous than to make a den of robbers of it. -- Fr.

130. Fr. "Et de faict, ce titre la suffit entre les payens pour diffamer les juges, de les appeler argentiers;" and, in fact, this title sufficed among the heathen to bring their judges into disrepute, to call them argentiers. See Cic. Ep. in Att. 1:16, "Insectandis vero, exagitandisque nummariis judicibus." Item, Verr. 5:57, et pro Cluent., 36.

131. "Justitiam, justitiam." -- Lat. See Margin A. V., "Heb., Justice, justice."

132. The negative added from Fr. See A. Gell. 11:18.

133. "Il est dit en la loy;" it is said in the law. -- Fr.

134. This first opinion is "that (says Corn. a Lapide) of S. Thomas, 1:2. q. 105, art. 2. ad 9., after Strabo; God commands that a thief should restore five oxen for one, because the ox has five utilities; first, it is killed in sacrifice; secondly, its flesh is eaten; thirdly, it ploughs; fourthly, it gives milk; fifthly, it supplies leather; -- whilst a sheep only has four advantages; for, first, it is slain in sacrifice; secondly, its flesh is eaten; thirdly, it gives milk; fourthly, it gives wool." The second opinion is attributed to Junius by Willet, "oportet hunc furem audacem, et versutum esse."

135. This provision of the Twelve Tables is thus given by A. Gell. 11. ult., "Si nox furtum faxit, sim (si eum) quis occisit, jure caesus esto: si luci furtum faxit, sim aliquis endo (in) ipso furto capsit, verberator, illique, cui furtum factum escit (erit) addicitor, sed non nisi is, qui interemturus erat, quiritaret," i.e., shall have called out for assistance.

136. "Sed enim M. Cato in oratione quam de praeda militibus dividenda scripsit, vehementibus et illustribus verbis de impunitate peculatus atque licentia conqueritus. Ea verba, quoniam nobis impense placuerunt, adscripsimus: Fures (inquit) privatorum furtorum in nervo atque in compedibus aetatem agunt: fures autem publici in auto atque in purpura." -- A. Gell. 11 ult.

137. "Le Dieu vivant." -- Fr.

138. C.'s view of these words seems to be adopted by none of the commentators. They understand them more simply, that the restitution was to be made in kind, and of the best of the aggressor's produce. Whether we read with C. "bonum agri," or with others "de bono," or "de optimo," as Dathe and A. V., does not appear to affect this sense.

139. "Que la beste se soit esvanouye sans qu'il en ait rien sceu;" in that the beast has vanished without his knowing anything about it. -- Fr.

140. For these latter words, which I hardly understand, the following are substituted in Fr., "Cela touche quant et quant a son service et religion."

141. Added from Fr.

142. "The Chaldee translateth, when thou art hired; and of such do the Hebrews understand this Law, that laborers hired to work in a vineyard are to eat of the fruit thereof." -- Ainsworth. So also Vatablus from the Chaldee and Arabic, in Poole's Synopsis.

143. "Cueille des espis, ou des raisins pour sa necessite," should gather ears of corn or grapes for his necessary wants. -- Fr.

144. "The Hebrews (says Ainsworth) for the most part hold the remission to be perpetual." He, however, argues from the word שמטה, an intermission, and its use in that sense in Exodus 23:11, that C.'s interpretation is the correct one. So also Dathe, who quotes Jos. Meyer in his Treatise on the Festivals of the Jews, ch. 17 sec. 20; and Michaelis, in his Laws of Moses, P. 3. sec. 157.

145. A. V., "all your labors;" margin, "things wherewith ye grieve others; Heb., griefs;" C.'s own version, "omnes facultates vestras exigitis."

146. S. M., However. A. V., Save when; or, in its margin, To the end that. S.M. refers to Jewish expositors as saying, "The meaning is, Thou shalt not fear that this law may do you an injury; for, if you be such zealous observers of my precepts, I will so bless you, and make all things needful for you to increase, that there shall be no poor man amongst you, to whom you need give what is lent. And if there be any person needing your assistance, and ye, for my sake, forgive his debt, as I have commanded, the man who doth thus shall not lose what was owed him, but shall receive from me a more abundant blessing." The learned reader may find this expression further discussed in Noldii Concord. partic. Art., 509 of Annot and Vindic. -- W.

147. "I know that ye will not obey me with a perfect heart, and therefore my blessing shall be lessened towards you, and there shall be poor among you." Hebrew commentators quoted in Munster and Fagius. -- Poole's Syn.

148. "Pour tormenter, et gehener les poures serfs." -- Fr.

149. "The Chaldee, Vatablus, and other more recent commentators translate it, Since he has served thee for six years for double the wages of a hireling; which the Hebrews thus explain, that the wages of a slave of six years' standing are called double, because hirelings amongst the Hebrew's only engaged themselves for three years, whereas the slave served for sir years; therefore he served twice as long, and earned twice as much." -- Corn. a Lapide in loco.

150. Seneca de Benef. 3:22.
"Servus (ut placet Chrysippo)
perpetuus mercenarius est." See
also Sen. Epp. 6:47, in which the
following beautiful sentiment
occurs: "Haec tamen mei praecepti
summa est, Sic cum inferiore
vivas, quemadmodum tecum
superiorem velis vivere."

151. So the Hebrew doctors,
and Ainsworth, Caietan, and
Willet. Michaelis supposes that
servants were regularly restored to
freedom after six years' service,
(not on the Sabbatical year, but on
the seventh from the sale;) but
supposing them bought less than
six years before the jubilee, they
received their freedom on that
year. Laws of Moses, vol. 2 p. 176.
-- Brightwell.

152. See Margin of A. V.

153. "Or la diversite d'entre les
estrangers, et les enfans d'Israel
n'est pas seulement mis, etc.;" now
the diversity between strangers and
the children of Israel is not only
placed, etc. -- Fr.

154. See Margin of A.V. on
ver. 46. "His in perpetuum
tanquam servis utamini,
popularibus vero vestris Israelitis
ne severius imperetis." -- Dathe.

155. Addition in Fr., "Et d'un
juste chastiment de leurs pechez;"
and as a just chastisement of their
sins.

156] "Redemptio in Law, a
faculty or right of re-entering upon
lands, etc., that have been sold and
assigned, upon reimbursing the
purchase-money with legal costs.
Bargains wherein the faculty, or, as
some call it, the equity of
redemption is reserved, are only a
kind of pignorative contracts. A
certain time is limited, within
which the faculty, of redemption
shall be exercised; and beyond
which it shall not extend. --
Chambers's Encyclopaedia.

157. Added from Fr.

158. "La seigneurie directe
(qu'on appelle,) ou fonsiere." -- Fr.

159. Addition in Fr., "Ou
fermiers, ou grangiers."

160. S M. and the LXX. agree
in regarding h as interrogative
here, hence S M. renders the
clause, "Thinkest thou that the tree
of the field is man that he must
depart from thy face in the siege?"
and he quotes Rabbi Solomon as
giving a similar exposition. But he
also quotes Aben-Ezra as rendering
the clause in the same manner as
our A V. The word מצור admits of
either of the two interpretations
quoted by C. -- W Dathe's version
is, "for they (i.e. the trees) are
appointed by God for the use of
men," and he thinks that Moses
undoubtedly had in view the
precept in Genesis 1:29.

161. Vide [16]vol. 2, p. 70.

162. See margin of A.V., ver.
6.

163. See on Leviticus 19:23,
[17]vol. 2, p. 49.

164. "Et cela est de l'equite
commune, a laquelle se rapporte le
Huitieme Commandement;" and
this is a part of that common equity
to which the Eighth
Commandment has reference. --
Fr.

The Ninth Commandment – Exodus 20

Exodus 20:16

16. Thou shalt not bear false witness against thy neighbor.

16. Non dices adversus proximum tuum falsum testimonium (vel, non loqueris contra proximum tuum ut testis mendacii.)

Deuteronomy 5

Deuteronomy 5:20

20. Neither shalt thou bear false witness against thy neighbor.

20. Non dices in proximum tuum falsum testimonium.

God here makes a provision for every man's character and good name, lest any should be undeservedly weighed down by calumnies and false accusations. The same synecdoche exists here, which I have pointed out in the previous Commandments, for God comprises many things under a single head. With reference to the words, inasmuch as d, gned, properly means a witness, it may be literally translated, "Thou shalt not answer a false witness against thy neighbor," but then the particle as must be supplied. The Hebrews poorly translate it in the vocative case, Thou shalt not speak, O false witness, etc.[165] Although God seems only to prescribe that no one, for the purpose of injuring the innocent, should go into court, and publicly testify against him, yet it is plain that the faithful are prohibited from all false accusations, and not only such as are circulated in the streets, but those which are stirred in private houses and secret corners. For it would be absurd, when God has already shewn that men's fortunes are cared for by Him, that He should neglect their reputation, which is much more precious. In whatever way, therefore, we injure our neighbors by unjustly defaming them, we are accounted false witnesses before God. We must now pass on from the prohibitive to the affirmative precept: for it will not be enough for us to restrain our tongues from speaking evil, unless we are also kind and equitable towards our neighbors, and candid interpreters of their acts and words, and do not suffer them, as far as in us lies, to be burdened with false reproaches. Besides, God does not only forbid us to invent accusations against the innocent, but also to give currency to reproaches and sinister reports in malevolence or hatred. Such a person may perhaps deserve his ill-name, and we may truly lay such or such an accusation to his charge; but if the reproach be the ebullition of our anger, or the accusation proceed from ill-will, it will be vain for us to allege in excuse that we have advanced nothing but, what is true. For when Solomon says that "love covereth many sins;" whereas "hatred brings reproaches to light," [166] (Proverbs 10:12;) he signifies, as a faithful expositor of this precept, that we are only free from falsehood when the reputation of our neighbors suffers no damage from us; for, if the indulgence of evil-speaking violates charity, it is opposed to the Law of God. In short, we must conclude that by these words a restraint is laid on all virulence of language which tends to bring disgrace on our brethren; and on all petulance also, whereby their good name suffers injury; and on all detractions, which flow from malice, or envy, and rivalry, or any other improper feeling. We must also go further, and not be suspicious or too curious in observing the defects of others; for such eager inquisitiveness betrays malevolence, or at any rate an evil disposition. For, if love is not suspicious, he who condemns his neighbor either falsely, or upon trifling surmises, or who holds him in light esteem, is undoubtedly a transgressor of this Commandment. Consequently, we must close our ears against false and evil speaking; since he is just as injurious to his brother who eagerly listens to sinister reports respecting him, as he who exercises his tongue in maligning him. The necessity of this instruction let each man estimate by his own disposition; for scarcely one in a hundred will be found who will be as kind in sparing the character of others, as he himself desires to be pardoned for manifest vices; nay, slander is often praised under the pretext of zeal and conscientiousness. Hence it happens that this vice insinuates itself even among the saints, creeping in under the name of virtue. Moreover, the volubility of the tongue causes us to think it a light transgression to inflict a deadly and disgraceful wound on our brother, to whom, nevertheless, his good name is of more importance than his life. The sum is, that we should manifest our charity no less by candor, and by abstaining from slander, than by the performance of other duties.

The Exposition of the Commandment - Exodus 23

Exodus 23:1, 2, 7

1. Thou shalt not raise a false report: put not thine hand with the wicked to be an unrighteous witness.

1. Non suscipies vocem mendacii, neque adjicias manum tuam impio ut sis testis mendax.

2. Thou shalt not follow a multitude to do evil; neither shalt thou speak in a cause to decline after many to wrest judgment

2. Non eris post multos ad mala, neque respondebis in causa, ut declines post multos ad pervertendum.

7. Keep thee far from a false matter; and the innocent and righteous slay thou not: for I will not justify the wicked.

7. A sermone mendacii longe aberis: nec occides innocentem et justum: quia non justificabo impium.

1. Thou shalt not receive (margin) a false report. It might also be translated, Thou shalt not raise, or stir up: and, if this be preferred, God forbids us to invent calumnies; but, if we read, Thou shalt not receive, He will go further, i e., that none should cherish, or confirm the lie of another by his support of it. For it has been stated that sin may thus be committed in two ways: either when the wicked invent false accusations, or when other over-credulous persons eagerly associate themselves with them; and thus either sense would be very applicable, that the original authors are condemned, who raise a false

report, or those who help on their wickedness, and give it, as it were, their endorsement. But, since it immediately follows, "put not thine hand with" them, I willingly embrace the version, "Thou shalt not receive," in order that the two clauses may combine the better. Indeed Moses uses this word with great propriety, for a lie would soon come to nothing from its own emptiness, and fall to the ground, if it were not taken up and supported by the unrighteous consent of others. God, therefore, recalls His people from this wicked conspiracy, [167] lest by their assistance they should spread abroad false accusations; and calls those false witnesses who traduce their neighbors by lending their hand to the ungodly: because there is but little difference between raising a calumny and keeping it up.

If it be thought preferable to restrict the second verse to judges, it would be a Supplement to the Sixth Commandment as well as the Eighth, viz., that none should willingly give way to the unjust opinions of others, which might affect either the means or the life of an innocent person. But, inasmuch as the error of those who are too credulous is reproved by it, whence it arises that falsehood prevails, and calumniators throw what is clear into obscurity, it finds a fit place here. [168]

7. Keep thee far from a false matter. Since he seems to speak of perjury, which brings about the death of the innocent, some might perhaps prefer that this passage should be annexed to the Sixth Commandment; but this is easily solved; for Moses is expressly condemning false-witness, and at the same time instances one case of it, whereby it may appear how detestable a crime it is, viz., the slaying of a brother by calumny, because the false witness rather kills him with his tongue than the executioner with his sword. Although, therefore, it is a gross act of inhumanity to lie in general against one's brother, yet is its atrocity increased if he be put to death by perjury; because murder is thus combined with perfidy. A threat follows, whereby God summons false-witnesses before His tribunal, where they who have brought the good into peril by their falsehoods shall not escape with impunity.

Leviticus 19

Leviticus 19:16, 17

16. Thou shalt not go up and down as a tale-bearer among thy people; neither shalt thou stand against the blood of thy neighbor: I am the Lord.

16. Non incedes obtrectator in populis tuis, nec stabis contra sanguinem proximi tui: ego Jehova.

17. Thou shalt in any wise rebuke thy neighbor, and not suffer sin upon him.

17. Corripiendo corripies proximum tuum, neque excitabis super eum crimen.

16. Thou shalt not go up and down. The principle of the second clause is the same as that of the foregoing verse, for it is added to a general precept, whereby detraction is condemned: and much more ought we to be deterred from it, whilst we acknowledge that our tongue is thus armed cruelly to shed innocent blood. Some suppose that the word רכיל, racil, is metaphorically taken from merchants, because the tale-bearer or whisperer [169] is no less busy in

hunting for false reports, which he may afterwards circulate, than the merchant is diligently bent on buying and selling. Others think that there is a change of the letter g into k; and that thus the word is derived from the feet; because calumniators are always wandering about to hunt for grounds of detraction; and therefore is always joined with a verb which signifies to walk. I do not think, however, that it is always used in the same sense; for when Ezekiel reproves the Israelites, because there were always men called רכיל, racil, among them, to shed blood, [170] I understand men of fraud, or fraudulent persons, who plot against the good to procure their destruction. (Ezekiel 22:9.) Some also translate it spies. Meanwhile, I doubt not, but that Moses, in this passage, designates those vagabonds, who too eagerly run about hither and thither, and in their malignant inquisitiveness penetrate into everybody's secrets, to bring quiet people into trouble. In short, we are taught that they are accounted false witnesses before God, whosoever by the virulence of their tongue bring their brethren into danger and inconvenience.

17. Thou shalt in any wise rebuke thy neighbor. Because many, under the pretext of conscientiousness, are not only rigid censors of others, but also burst out in the open proclamation of their defects, Moses seeks to prevent this preposterous zeal, shewing how they may best restrain it, not by encouraging sin through their connivance or silence, whilst they are still far from evil-speaking. For those who labor under this disease of carping and vituperating, are wont to object that sins are nourished by silence, unless all are eager in reproving them; and hence their ardor in exclaiming against them and deriding them. But Moses points out a more useful remedy, that they should bring back wanderers into the way by private rebukes, and not by publishing their offenses. For whosoever triumphs in the infamy of his brother, precipitates his ruin as far as in him lies; whereas a well-regulated zeal consults the welfare of one who is ruining himself. Therefore we are commanded to rebuke the wandering, and not to regard our brethren as enemies. A similar course is prescribed by Christ, "If thy brother shall trespass against thee, go and tell him his fault between thee and him alone." (Matthew 18:15.) In fine, an immoderate love of fault-finding will always be found to be arrogant and cruel. The word נשא, nasa, undoubtedly means to publish what was concealed, and thus by exposure to drive to despair those who would else have been corrigible.

Supplement to the Ninth Commandment - Deuteronomy 19

Deuteronomy 19:16-21

16. If a false witness rise up against any man, to testify against him that which is wrong;

16. Quum steterit testis mendax contra aliquem, ut testificetur contra eum verbum perversum:

17. Then both the men, between whom the controversy is, shall stand before the Lord, before the priests and the judges which shall be in those days:

17. Tunc stabunt duo illi homines quibus est lis, coram Jehova, id est coram sacerdotibus et judicibus qui fuerint in diebus illis.

18. And the judges shall make diligent inquisition: and, behold, if the witness be a false witness, and hath testified falsely against his brother;

18. Et inquirent judices diligenter, et si testis ille est testis mendax, mendacium testificatus est contra fratrem suum:

19. Then shall ye do unto him as he had thought to have done unto his brother: so shalt thou put the evil away from among you.

19. Facietis ei, quemadmodum cogitavit facere fratri suo, et auferes malum e medio tui.

20. And those which remain shall hear, and fear, and shall henceforth commit no more any such evil among you.

20. Et qui remanserint, audient ac timebunt, nec addent facere ultra malum simile huic in medio tui.

21. And thine eye shall not pity; but life shall go for life, eye for eye, tooth for tooth, hand for hand, foot for foot.

21. Neque parcet oculus tuus: animam pro anima, oculum pro oculo, dentem pro dente, manum pro manu, pedem pro pede.

16. If a false witness rise up against any man. Because the fear of God does not so prevail in all men, as that they should voluntarily abstain from the love of slander, God here appoints the punishment to be inflicted for perjury: for political laws are enacted against the ungodly and disobedient, in order that those who despise God's judgment should be brought before the tribunal of men. Although perjury is not here ordained to be tried before the judges, unless there should be an accuser, who should complain that he had been unjustly injured by false-witness, still reason dictates, that if any man have been condemned to death by false-witnesses, the judges should not hesitate to make an official inquiry into the matter. Yet, inasmuch as men are generally disposed to assert their own innocence, God has deemed it sufficient to put the case, that if any complaint should be lodged, the judges should diligently investigate it, and if the crime be proved, should inflict the punishment of retaliation (talionis.) Whence it appears that false-witnesses and murderers stand in the same light before God. By commanding that the inquiry should be made not only by the judges, but also by the priests, as if God Himself were present, He shews that He requires unusual diligence to be used; because a secret crime is not easily detected without the most anxious care.

Footnotes:

165. Addition in Fr., "Or revenons a la substance."

166. "Hatred stirreth up strifes; but love covereth all sins." -- A.V. The latter clause, in C.'s quotation, is probably rather intended to be the necessary converse of the latter part of the proverb than a paraphrastic rendering of the first, which it does not appear that the words will bear.

167. "De s'accoupler avecques les malins et les menteurs pour diffamer le prochain;" of associating themselves with the malicious and with liars to defame their neighbor. -- Fr.

168. "Ceste sentence doit estre comprinse aussi bien sous les faux tesmoignages;" this declaration ought to be comprised under the head of false testimony. -- Fr.

169. "Delator aut susurro." -- Lat. "The original properly signifies a trader, a pedlar, and is here applied to one who travels up and down dealing in slanders and detractions, as a merchant does in wares, possessing himself of the secrets of individuals and families, and then blazing them abroad, usually with a false colouring as to motives and a distortion of facts." -- Bush. "Some explain רכיל as if רגיל, (the g being changed into k,) from רגל, to run about, to explore." -- Fagius, from the Hebrew Commentators, in Poole's Synopsis. "Non reperimus in S. Scriptura dictionem רכילות, quae non sit scripta lingua הליכה, i e., ambulationis." -- Sal. Jarchi in loco. See C. on Jeremiah 9:4, Cal. Soc. edit., [18]vol. 1, p. 464

170. "In thee are men that carry tales (margin, men of slanders) to shed blood." -- A.V.

Tenth Commandment - Exodus 20

Exodus 20:17

17. Thou shalt not covet thy neighbor's house, thou shalt not covet thy neighbor's wife, nor his man-servant, nor his maid-servant, nor his ox, nor his ass, nor any thing that is thy neighbor's.

17. Non concupisces domum proximi tui, non concupisces uxorem proximi tui, neque servum ejus, neque ancillam ejus, neque bovem ejus, neque asinum ejus, neque quicquam eorum quae sunt proximi tui.

ITS REPETITION - Deuteronomy 5

Deuteronomy 5:21

21. Neither shalt thou desire thy neighbor's wife, neither shalt thou covet thy neighbor's house, his field, or his man-servant, or his maid-servant, his ox, or his ass, or any thing that is thy neighbor's.

21. Neque concupisces uxorem proximi tui, neque concupisces domum proximi tui, agrum ejus, aut servum ejus, aut ancillam ejus, bovem ejus, aut asinum ejus: neque quicquam eorum quae sunt proximo tuo.

Exodus 20:17. Thou shalt not covet thy neighbor's wife. There is no question but that this Commandment extends also to those that have preceded it. God had already sufficiently forbidden us to set our hearts on the property of others, to attempt the seduction of their wives, or to seek for gain at another's loss and inconvenience. Now whilst He enumerates oxen and asses, and all other things as well as their wives and servants, it is very clear that His precept is directed to the same things, but in a different way, viz., in order to restrain all ungodly desires either of fornication or theft. The question, however, occurs, -- since it has been said before that, agreeably to the nature of the Lawgiver, the inward purity of the heart is everywhere required, and therefore, that under the head of adultery, not only are all filthy acts prohibited, but secret unchastity also; and under the head of theft, all unlawful appetite for gain, -- why does God now forbid in His people the lust for theft and fornication? For it seems to be a superfluous repetition which would be very absurd in ten short precepts, wherein God has embraced the whole rule of life, so that their very brevity might render it, easy, and the better attract their readers to learn them. Still, on the other hand, it must be remembered that, although it was God's design, by the whole Law, to arouse men's feelings to sincere obedience of it, yet such is their hypocrisy and indifference, that it was necessary to stimulate them more sharply, and to press them more closely, lest they should seek for subterfuges under pretense of the obscurity of the doctrine. For if they had only heard, Thou shalt not kill, nor commit fornication, nor steal, they might have supposed that their duty would have been fully performed by mere outward observance. It was not then in vain that God, after having treated of piety and justice, should give a separate admonition, that they were not only to abstain from evil doing, but also, that what He had previously commanded should be performed with the sincere affection of the heart. Hence Paul gathers from this Commandment, that the whole "Law is spiritual," (Romans 7:7 and 14,) because God, by His condemnation of lust, sufficiently shewed that He not only imposed obedience on our hands and feet, but also put restraint upon our minds, lest they should desire to do what is unlawful. Paul confesses, too, that whereas he before slept in easy self-deceit, he was awakened by this single word; for since he was blameless in the eyes of men, he was persuaded that he was righteous before God: He says that he was once alive, as if the Law were absent or dead, because, being puffed up with confidence in his righteousness, he expected salvation by his works; but, when he perceived what the Commandment, Thou shalt not covet, meant, the dead Law was raised as it were to life, and he died, i e., he was convinced he was a transgressor, and saw the sure curse overhanging him. Nor did he perceive himself to be guilty of one or two sins, but then, at length, he was shaken out of his torpor, when he recognized that all the evil desires, of which he was conscious, must be accounted for before God, whereas he had before been satisfied with the mere outward appearance of virtue. We now perceive, therefore, that there is nothing inappropriate in the general condemnation of concupiscence by a distinct commandment; for after God has broadly and popularly laid down rules for moral integrity, at length He ascends to the fountain itself, and at the same time points out with His finger, as it were, the root from which all evil and corrupt fruits spring forth. It must here be added that something more is expressed by the words coveting and wishing for, or desiring, than a desiderium formatum, as it is commonly called; for the flesh often tempts us to wish for this or that, so that the evil concupiscence betrays itself, although consent may not yet be added. Since, therefore, the sin [171] of the will had been already condemned, God now proceeds further, and puts a restraint upon evil desires before they prevail. [172] James points out these progressive steps, where he says that lust conceives before it begets sin; and then "sin, when it is finished, bringeth forth death," (James 1:15,) for the begetting of which he speaks, is not only in the external act but in the will itself, before it has assented to the temptation. I admit, indeed, that the corrupt thoughts which arise spontaneously, and so also vanish before they affect the mind, do not come into account before God; yet, although we do not actually acquiesce in the evil desire, still, if it affects us pleasantly, it is sufficient to render us guilty. In order that this may be understood better, all temptations are, as it were, so many fans; if they hurry us on into consent, the fire is lighted; but, if they only awaken the heart to corrupt desires, concupiscence betrays itself in these sparks, although it neither acquires its full warmth nor breaks forth into a flame. Concupiscence, therefore, is never without desire (affectu,) although the will may not altogether yield. Hence it appears what entire perfection of righteousness we must bring in order to satisfy the Law, since not only are we commanded not to will anything, except what is right and pleasing to God, but also that no impure desire should affect our hearts. Nor would Paul have laid such great stress upon this precept if the Law condemned no concupiscence except that which takes such hold on the mind of man as to exercise dominion over it; for the sin of the will must ever be condemned even by heathen philosophers, nay, and by earthly legislators also; but he says that the Law, by

resisting concupiscence, makes sin to "become exceeding sinful." (Romans
7:13.) Now, it is not credible that, at the time in which he confesses that he
knew not what concupiscence was, he was so senseless and stupid as to think
no harm of wishing to kill a man, or of being inclined through lust to commit
adultery with his brother's wife; but, if he was not unaware that the will to sin
was vicious, it follows that the concupiscence in which he saw no harm was
some more hidden disease. Hence, too, it is manifest under what delusion Satan
must have held all the Popish schools [173] through which echoes this axiom, that
concupiscence is no sin in the baptized, because it is a stimulus to the exercise
of virtue; as if Paul did not openly condemn concupiscence, which entraps us in
its snares, although we do not altogether assent to it.

Footnotes:

171. "Mala voluntas." -- Lat.
"Toutes mauvaises affections." --
Fr.

172. "Derant qu'ils ayent
gagne pour venir en propos
delibere;" before they have gone so far as to arrive at a deliberate
purpose. -- Fr.

173. See the first decree of the
Fifth Session of the Council of
Trent, together with C.'s remarks
amongst his Tracts. -- Calvin
Society edition, vol. 3, pp. 78-88.

The Sum of the Law - Deuteronomy 10

Deuteronomy 10:12, 13

12. And now, Israel, what doth the Lord thy God require of thee, but to fear the Lord thy God, to walk in all his ways, and to love him, and to serve the Lord thy God with all thy heart, and with all thy soul,

12. Nunc ergo Israel, quid Jehova Deus tuus petit a te, nisi ut timeas Jehovam Deum tuum, ut ambules in omnibus viis ejus, ut diligas eum, colasque Jehovam Deum tuum in toto corde tuo, et tota anima tua?

13. To keep the commandments of the Lord, and his statutes, which I command thee this day for thy good?

13. Custodiendo praecepta Jehovae, et statuta ejus, quae ego praecipio tibi hodie, ut bene sit tibi.

Deuteronomy 6

Deuteronomy 6:5

5. And thou shalt love the Lord thy God with all thine heart, and with all thy soul, and with all thy might.

5. Diliges Jehovam Deum tuum toto corde tuo, tota anima tua, et tota fortitudine tua.

Deuteronomy 10:12. And now, Israel, what doth the Lord thy God require? After having expounded each Commandment in its order, it now remains for us to see what is the sum of the contents of the Law, and what the aim and object of its instructions. For Paul elicits its true use, when he declares that its end is

"charity, out of a pure heart and of a good conscience, and of faith unfeigned," (1 Timothy 1:5,)

since even then it had its false interpreters, who, he says, had "turned aside unto vain jangling," when they swerved from that object. Now, as it is contained in two Tables, so also Moses reduces it to two heads, that we should love God with all our heart, and our neighbor as ourselves; for, although he does not unite the two in one passage, yet Christ, by whose Spirit he spoke, ought to suffice to explain to us his intention, (Matthew 22:37;) for, when He was asked what was the great Commandment of the Law, He replied that the first indeed was, that God should be loved, and the second like unto it, regarding the love of our neighbor; as if He had said, that the whole perfection of righteousness, which is set before us in the Law, consists of two parts, that we should serve God with true piety, and conduct ourselves innocently towards men according to the rule of charity. The same is the sense of Paul's words, for the faith, which is there called the source and origin of charity, comprehends in it the love of God. At any rate, the declaration of Christ stands sure, that nothing is required of us by the Law, but that we should love God, together with our neighbors. From hence a short and clear definition may be laid down, that nothing is required unto a good life except piety and justice. [174]

Paul, indeed, seems to add a third clause, when he says, that

"the grace of God hath appeared, teaching us that, denying ungodliness and worldly lusts, we should live soberly, righteously, and godly, in this present world," (Titus 2:11, 12;)

but this σωφροσύνη, (soberness,) is there added as the seasoning, so to speak, of a just and pious life; and assuredly no one will prove that he aims at holiness and integrity, unless by living chastely, honestly, and temperately. Thus, where the service of God is omitted, [175] and the doctrine of the Law confined to the love of our neighbor alone, it is not so much that religion is put out of sight [176] (sepelitur,) as that the proof of it is made to rest on serious self-examination; for since it is the way with hypocrites to cover themselves with ceremonies as with a mask of sanctity, whilst they are puffed up with pride, burn with avarice and rapacity, are full of envy and malice, breathe out threatenings and cruelty, and are abandoned to filthy lusts, Christ, in order to disperse these clouds of pretense, declares that the three chief points in the Law are "judgment, mercy," and fidelity, [177] (Matthew 23:23;) and elsewhere, discoursing of the righteousness of the Law, He makes no mention of the First Table. (Matthew 19:18.)

For the same reason, Paul calls charity the fulfillment of the Law, (Romans 13:8,) and elsewhere, "the bond of perfectness." (Colossians 3:14.) Still, nothing was further from their intention than to draw us away from the fear of God, that we might devote ourselves to our duties towards men, as I have already shown from another passage, where Christ, in summing up the Law, begins with the love of God. And Paul, where he teaches that we should be altogether perfect, if faith works in us by love, (Galatians 5:6,) does not omit the cause and principle of a good life. And thus are reconciled the passages which else might appear contradictory, via, that holiness is perfected in the fear of the Lord, when

"we cleanse ourselves from all filthiness of the flesh and spirit," (2 Corinthians 7:1;)

and

"all the law is fulfilled in one word, even in this, Thou shalt love thy neighbor as thyself," (Galatians 5:14;)

that is to say, because our piety cannot otherwise make itself clear by certain proof, unless we behave justly and harmlessly towards men. [178] Again, since "our goodness extendeth not to" God, so it is perceived what our mind is by our performance of the duties of the Second Table, as it is said in the Psalm, *"my goodness extendeth not to thee, but to the saints that are in the earth, in whom is all my delight,"* [179] (Psalm 16:2, 3;)

for how will any one boast, (as John says,) that he loves God, whom he does not see, if he loveth not his brother with whom he is familiarly united? (1 John 4:20.) Since, therefore, falsehood is thus detected, God exercises us in piety by mutual charity; and hence John concludes, that

"this Commandment have we from him, That he who loveth God love his brother also." (1 John 4:21.)

Before, however, I say any more of these two precepts, we must observe the end of the Law as it is described by Moses; "Now, Israel, what doth the Lord thy God require of thee, but to fear the Lord thy God, to walk in all his ways, and to love him, and to serve the Lord thy God with all thy heart and all thy soul?" For, although he further eulogizes the Law, because it prescribes nothing which nature does not itself dictate to be most certain and most just, and which experience itself does not shew us to be more profitable, or more desirable than anything else, still, at the same time, he reminds us what is the means by which it is to be kept. [180] Therefore he sets before us at the same time the fear and the love of God; for, inasmuch as God is the Lord, He justly desires to be feared in right of His dominion; and, inasmuch as He is our Father, He requires to be loved, as it is said in Malachi 1:6. Let us learn, therefore, if we would set ourselves about keeping the Law, that we must begin with the fear of God, which is hence called the "beginning of wisdom." (Psalm 111:10; Proverbs 1:7, and Proverbs 9:10.) But, since God has no pleasure in extorted and forced obedience, love is immediately added. And this deserves to be well weighed, that whereas there is nothing pleasanter than to love God, still it always occupies the first place in all His service. Surely he must be more than iron-hearted who is not attracted by such kindness; since, for no other cause, does He invite and exhort us to love Him, than because He loveth us; nay, He has already prevented us with His love, as is said in 1 John 4:10. Meanwhile, we may at the same time gather, that nothing is pleasing to God which is offered "grudgingly or of necessity; for God loveth a cheerful giver." (2 Corinthians 9:7.) It is true that Paul is there speaking of alms-giving; but this voluntary and hearty inclination to obey, such as we see in good and ingenuous children, who take delight in subjection to their parents, ought to be extended to all the actions of our lives. And assuredly the reverence which is paid to God flows from no other source than the tasting of His paternal love towards us, whereby we are drawn to love Him in return; as it is said in Psalm 130:4, "There is forgiveness with thee, that thou mayest be feared." Whenever, then, we hear what Scripture constantly inculcates; "O love ye Jehovah, [181] all ye his meek ones!" (Psalm 31:23.) let us remember that God shews Himself loving towards us, in order that we may willingly and with becoming cheerfulness acquiesce in what He commands.

The perfection which is here required shews with sufficient clearness how far we are from a thorough obedience to the Law. We are commanded to love God with all our heart, and soul, and strength. However much we strive, our efforts are weak and imperfect, unless the love of God has possession of all our senses, and all our desires and thoughts are altogether devoted to Him, whilst all our endeavors are also directed to Him alone. But every one is abundantly convinced by his own experience, in how many ways our minds are carried away to vanity; how many corrupt affections creep over us; how difficult it is for us to restrain and overcome the evil motions of our flesh. Surely the very best wrestler, with all his strivings, is hardly able to make advances in this spiritual warfare; and if it be a great attainment not to faint altogether, certainly none will dare to boast that he comes near the mark which is set before us in the Law. In short, whenever worldly snares and foolish appetites insinuate themselves upon us, we must so often feel that some part of our soul is empty of the love of God, since otherwise nothing repugnant to it would penetrate there. The word heart here, [182] as elsewhere, is not used for the seat of the affections, but for the intellect; and, therefore, it would have been superfluous to add διάνοιας, as the Evangelists have done, unless for the purpose of removing all ambiguity; but because this signification was not commonly in use among the Greeks, they have not hesitated to add a word of their own in explanation. Those, however, who are well acquainted with the teaching of Moses, are not ignorant that the word heart is equivalent to mind; for he elsewhere says, "The Lord hath not given you an heart to understand, [183] and eyes to see, unto this day," (Deuteronomy 29:4;) but the expression would have been obscure to the Greeks, as being unusual in their language. [184]

Leviticus 19

Leviticus 19:18

18. Thou shalt love thy neighbor as thyself.
18. Diliges proximum tuum sicut to ipsum.

18. Thou shalt love thy neighbor as thyself. What every man's mind ought to be towards his neighbor, could not be better expressed in many pages that in this one sentence. We are all of us not only inclined to love ourselves more than we should, but all our powers hurry us away in this direction; nay, φιλαυτία (self-love) blinds us so much as to be the parent of all iniquities. Since, therefore, whilst we are too much given to love ourselves, we forget and neglect our brethren, God could only bring us back to charity by plucking from our hearts that vicious passion which is born with us and dwells deeply in us; nor, again, could this be done except by transferring elsewhere the love which exists within us. On this point no less has the dishonesty betrayed itself than the ignorance and folly of those [185] who would have the love of ourselves come first: "The rule (say they) is superior to the thing regulated by it; and according to God's commandment, the charity which we should exercise towards others is formed upon the love of ourselves as its rule." As if it were God's purpose to stir up the fire which already burns too fiercely. Naturally, as I have said, we are blinded by our immoderate self-love; and God, in order to turn us away from this, has substituted our neighbors, whom we are to love no less than ourselves; nor will any one ever perform what Paul teaches us to be a part of charity, viz., that she "seeketh not her own," (1 Corinthians 13:5,) until he shall have renounced himself.

Not only those with whom we have some connection are called our neighbors, but all without exception; for the whole human race forms one body, of which all are members, and consequently should be bound together by mutual ties; for we must bear in mind that even those who are most alienated from us, should be cherished and aided even as our own flesh; since we have[186] seen elsewhere that sojourners and strangers are placed in the same category (with our relations; [187]) and Christ sufficiently confirms this in the case of the Samaritan. (Luke 10:30.)

Footnotes:

174. "Que la somme de bien vivre est d'honorer Dieu, et converser justement avec les hommes;" that the sum of a good life is to honor God, and to demean ourselves justly towards men. -- Fr.

175. "En d'aucuns passages;" in some passages. -- Fr.

176. "Ce n'est pas tant pour ensevelir la religion, et ce qui concerne la premiere table, que pour en rendre tesmoignage par fruits;" it is not so much to bury religion, and what concerns the first table, as to give testimony of it by its fruits. -- Fr.

177. Faith. -- A.V. "Faith (says C. Harm. of Evang., [19]vol. 3. 90,) is nothing else than strict integrity; not to attempt anything by cunning, or malice, or deceit, but to cultivate towards all that mutual sincerity which every man wishes to be pursued towards himself." See also Inst., book 2. ch. 8. sect. 52.

178. "Innoxie" -- Lat. "En bonne simplicite" -- Fr.

179. "Voluntas mea." -- Lat.

180. "Quel est le moyen de bien garder la Loi, quand on saura ou elle nous mene;" what is the means of properly keeping the Law, when we know whither it leads us. -- Fr.

181. "O love the Lord, all ye his saints." -- A.V. See C.'s version, Calvin Society's edition. "Misericordes ejus, i.e., quotquot sensistis bonitatem ejus." -- Vatablus in Poole's Synopsis.

182. The word לבב, lebab, the heart, is "extensively applied to the mind, and includeth the mind and every faculty, action, passion, disposition, and affection thereof, as thoughts, understanding, reasoning, memory, will, judgment, wisdom, counsel; desire, love, hatred, courage, fear, joy, sorrow, anger." -- Taylor's Concordance. See C. on Matthew 22:37, Mark 12:33, and Luke 10:27, in Harmony of Evangelists: (Calvin Society's translation,) [20]vol. 3, p. 58

183. "An heart to perceive." -- A.V.

184. The last sentence omitted in Fr.

185. "Les docteurs Papistes." -- Fr. See ante on Leviticus 19:18, [21]p. 23.

186. On Leviticus 19:33, ante [22]p. 118.

187. Added from Fr.

The Use of the Law

Inasmuch as in the Law the difference between good and evil is set forth, it is given for the regulation of the life of men, so that it may be justly called the rule of living well and righteously. This object of the Law is known to almost all men, because all confess without controversy that God here prescribes what is right, lest we should wander all our lifetime in uncertainty; for since His will is the perfect law of righteousness, it can alone direct us to the mark. The knowledge of good and evil is indeed imprinted by nature on men, whereby they are rendered inexcusable; nor has any amount of barbarism ever so extinguished this light as that no form of law should exist. But, since the main principle of righteousness is to obey God, it was by special privilege that He deposited with His elect people the rule of living aright as a pledge of His adoption. Hence the declarations which so often occur in the writings of Moses: I command thee to keep and to do, etc. But, since we are "carnal, sold under sin," (Romans 7:14,) we are so far from being able to fulfill the Law, which is spiritual, that all our imaginations are at enmity with its righteousness, as Paul teaches elsewhere. (Romans 7:7.) Those, therefore, who [188] content themselves with using it for instruction, do wrong in confining themselves to this one point, since no advantage can hence be derived from it, as long as we shall remain in our corrupt nature. Nay, as soon as the Law presents itself before us, the curse of God falls upon our heads, as if He smote us with a thunder-bolt from heaven. I will not heap together all the testimonies to this effect; let one peculiarly striking passage suffice:

"The law (says Paul) is holy, and the commandment holy and just and good: but sin, that it might appear sin, worketh death in me by that which is good." (Romans 7:12, 13.)

What he elsewhere says, that "the law worketh wrath," (Romans 4:15,) and that "it was added because of transgressions," (Galatians 3:19,) seems harsh indeed to profane persons, who only judge as philosophers; yet this is the theological use of the Law, for, by discovering our unrighteousness, it can bring nothing but death. Here, however, [189] rebellious questions arise, what use there could be in prescribing what we are unable to perform: why God should mock miserable men by imposing a burden whereby they are totally overwhelmed: how it is consistent that a law should be given for us to keep, and yet that we should be devoid of strength to do so: if we have not liberty to choose good or evil, why it should be brought in accusation against us that we yield to the sin to which we are naturally addicted? The enemies of God are very ingenious in amassing such calumnies, and eloquent in exaggerating them; but when they have disgorged all that their rabid dishonesty has dictated, their own conscience will always abundantly refute them; for they will be compelled to acknowledge that the Law is just, and that, when they transgress it by voluntary impulse, they are deservedly condemned. Let them, then, rave against God as they like, that

He unjustly imposes upon them a heavier burden than they are able to bear, their natural reason will retain them under the conviction, that whatever God commands to be done for Him is His due. We must now see where the blame lies, that they are unable to satisfy Him. Surely their efforts to relieve themselves from it will be vain, because conscience will again make itself felt on the opposite side, and will hold them fast in the bond of condemnation, from which there is no escape. But the whole of Scripture teaches that it arises from the corruption of our nature that all our affections are repugnant to the Law, and also that, on the other hand, the Law is against us; for Adam, being alienated from God the fountain of all righteousness, ruined himself and us; and hence it comes that not only our strength is insufficient to perform the service we owe to God, but that we are impelled by a blind and headlong impetus to shake off His yoke. From this Paul infers that we are "under the curse," because the Law pronounces all transgressors to be accursed. (Galatians 3:10.) For ridiculous will be the objection that it is in the power of every one's free-will not to transgress, because there is nothing to be found in us which is not corrupt; and, in fact, the stupidity of those is most shameless who suppose that nothing impossible is commanded, whereas in every trifle, not merely our weakness, but our ἀδυναμία (powerlessness) betrays itself. But, although Paul says that the Law [190] is deadly to us, (2 Corinthians 3:6,) yet he vindicates it from all objection, when he shews that this evil is accidental, and therefore must be imputed to ourselves. Let it therefore be established, that the Law was given not only for instruction, so that men might follow what they had learnt from it to be right, but also to convict them of their iniquity, that they might acknowledge themselves to be lost; as if they saw in a mirror their destruction through the just vengeance of God. Now this knowledge would by itself overwhelm all with horrible despair if they did not emerge from the deep abyss; for, since they are puffed up with vain confidence, and arrogate to themselves the merit of living righteously, it is necessary that they should be humbled; first of all, that, being condemned, they may learn to fly for refuge to God's mercy; and secondly, that being convinced of their infirmity, they may implore the aid of the Holy Spirit, which in their security they had before neglected. Hence it appears that it is expedient for them to be slain by the Law, and that the death which it inflicts is life-giving. And this occurs in two ways; for, first, being stripped of the false opinion of their righteousness, wherein they prided themselves, they begin to seek in Christ what they mistakenly supposed might be found in themselves, so as to please God by gratuitous reconciliation, whereas they had previously sought to propitiate Him by the merit of their works; secondly, they learn that they are not sufficient to perform a single tittle of the Law, unless, being regenerated by God's Spirit, they who were the slaves of sin live unto righteousness. And hence, in fine, the utility and fruit of the teaching of the Law proceeds; for, until we are renewed and God has given us hearts of flesh instead of hearts of stone, in vain are precepts dinned in our ears, since in our natural depravity we cordially reject them; but when He has engraved His law within our hearts, its outward instruction also profits us; for He so governs His children by the Spirit of reconciliation, as at the same time to will that they should be attentive and obedient to His voice. Still, because they are always far from attaining to perfect observance of it, they not only learn from it what is right, but also that they have need of His gratuitous mercy, that they may please

Him through indulgence and grace, although they are still conscious of much infirmity.

Further, because Paul seems to abrogate the Law, as if now-a-days it did not concern believers, we must now see how far this is the case. And, first, indeed, it is easy to perceive that he does not treat of the Law in the abstract, but sets it forth invested with those of its qualities, wherein it is opposed to the Gospel; for, inasmuch as his controversy was with those who interpreted it amiss, he could not help contrasting the Law with the Gospel, as if they were in opposition to each other: not that they were really so, if their respective doctrine be dexterously applied to its proper object, but because such a conflict arose from the absurd mixture, which the false apostles introduced. They asserted that men are justified by the works of the Law, and, if this were admitted, the righteousness of faith was destroyed, and the Gospel fell to the ground. They, moreover, restored the yoke imposed on the ancient people, as if no liberty had been obtained by the blood of Christ. In this discussion it was necessary for Paul to advert only to that which is peculiar to Moses, and distinct from Christ; for although Christ and Moses perfectly accord in the substance of their doctrine, still, when they are compared with each other, it is fitting to distinguish what is peculiar to each. In this respect Paul calls the Law "the letter," [191] because Moses had no other charge than to speak in the name of God, (2 Corinthians 3:6;) and this in itself is not only useless, but also deadly; for when the word resounds in the ears only, it produces nothing but condemnation. Besides, he considers the Law as connected with promises and threatenings. Whence it follows, that salvation can only be procured by it if its precepts be exactly fulfilled. Life is indeed promised in it, but only if whatever it commands be complied with; whilst, on the other hand, it denounces death against its transgressors, so that to have offended in the slightest point is enough to condemn and destroy a person; and thus it overwhelms all men with despair. Lastly, because the ceremonies by which God prepared His ancient people as by puerile and elementary instruction for the faith of the Gospel, [192] were annexed to the Law, Paul embraces those also in his comparison between the Law and the Gospel. Hence it follows that, in so far as Moses is distinguished from Christ, his ministration has ceased, although his embassy was identical with that which Christ afterwards discharged. As regards the ceremonies, we must consider that an end was put upon them by Christ's coming, in such a way as to establish their truth more firmly than as if they still remained in use: for we acknowledge that in them, as in a mirror, was formerly shewn to the Fathers, what is now displayed to us in its reality. Whence it appears that they are greatly mistaken who altogether reject as useless that instruction which we read in the writings of Moses; and that the squeamishness of those who despise it is also intolerable. [193] Let my readers seek in the Second Book of my Institutes, Chapter 7., what further tends to the explanation of this subject.

Footnotes:

188. "Ceux doncques qui ne cherchent en la Loy, sinon de savoir, comment on doit servir a Dieu, s'abusent, etc.;" those, therefore, who only search in the law to know how we ought to serve God, deceive themselves, etc. -- Fr.

189. "Or ici les esprits fantastiques s'escarmouchent en demandant." -- Fr.

190. "The letter killeth." -- A.V.

191. "By the term letter he means outward preaching, of such a kind as does not reach the heart; and, on the other hand, by spirit he means living doctrine, of such a nature as worketh effectually (1 Thessalonians 2:13) on the minds of men, through the grace of the Spirit. By the term letter, therefore, is meant literal preaching, that is, dead and ineffectual, perceived only by the ear. By the term spirit, on the other hand, is meant spiritual doctrine, that is, whatever is not merely uttered with the mouth, but effectually makes its way to the souls of men with a lively feeling." -- C. on 2 Corinthians 3:6, Cal. Soc. edit., [23]vol. 2, p. 172.

192. "Comme par un a, b, c, de petits enfans." -- Fr.

193. "Et que ceux, qui le meprisent comme superflu, sont aussi a condamner comme trop delicats;" and that those who despise it as superfluous are to be condemned as too fastidious. -- Fr.

Sanctions of the Law contained in the Promises and Threats

We now come to the conclusion of the Exposition of the Law, wherein we are to treat of the sanctions of it contained both in the promises and threats. For, although God might in His own right simply require what He pleased, yet such is His kindness to men, that He chose to entice them by promises to obey Him freely. Since, therefore, we are naturally attracted by the hope of reward, we are slow and lazy, until some fruit appears. Consequently God voluntarily promises, in order to arouse them from their sloth, that if men obey His Law, He will repay them. Nor is this an ordinary act of liberality that He prefers to agree with us for the payment of a recompense, rather than simply to command by His sovereignty. For we must bear in mind the declaration of Christ, that when we have fulfilled the whole Law, we still deserve nothing; since God claims for Himself our entire services. (Luke 17:10.) However we may strive, therefore, even beyond our strength, and devote ourselves entirely to keep the Law, still God lies under no obligation to us, except in so far as He has Himself voluntarily agreed, and made Himself our spontaneous debtor. And this has been pointed out even by the common theologians, that the reward of good works does not depend upon their dignity or merit, but upon His covenant. [194] Still, as we shall soon see, such promises would not avail us the least if God rewarded every one according to his works; but, because this defect is adventitious, God's great mercy nevertheless shines forth in the fact that he has deigned to encourage us to obedience by setting before us the hope of eternal life. And hence He reproves the ingratitude of the Israelites by Ezekiel 20:21; because they had despised His good commandments, of which it was said that "if a man do them, he should live in them."

We now perceive how the authority of the Law was confirmed by the promises; but because we are not only indolent but also refractory, He added on the other side threats which might inspire terror, both to subdue the obstinacy of the flesh and to correct the security in which we are too apt to indulge. It will be expedient now to treat of both.

Leviticus 18

Leviticus 18:5

5. Ye shall therefore keep my statutes and my judgments; which if a man do, he shall live in them: I am the Lord.

5. Custodite statuta mea, et judicia mea, quae homo si faciat, rivet in ipsis.

5. Ye shall therefore keep my statutes. Although Moses introduces this passage, where he exhorts the Israelites to cultivate chastity in respect to marriage, and not to fall into the incestuous pollutions of the Gentiles, yet, as it

is a remarkable one, and contains general instruction, from whence Paul derives his definition of the righteousness of the Law, (Romans 10:5,) it seems to me to come in very appropriately here, inasmuch as it sanctions and confirms the Law by the promise of reward. The hope of eternal life is, therefore, given to all who keep the Law; for those who expound the passage as referring to this earthly and transitory life are mistaken. [195] The cause of this error was, because they feared that thus the righteousness of faith might be subverted, and salvation grounded on the merit of works. But Scripture does not therefore deny that men are justified by works, because the Law itself is imperfect, or does not give instructions for perfect righteousness; but because the promise is made of none effect by our corruption and sin. Paul, therefore, as I have just said, when he teaches that righteousness is to be sought for in the grace of Christ by faith, (Romans 10:4,) proves his statement by this argument, that none is justified who has not fulfilled what the Law commands. Elsewhere also he reasons by contrast, where he contends that the Law does not accord with faith as regards the cause of justification, because the Law requires works for the attainment of salvation, whilst faith directs us to Christ, that we may be delivered from the curse of the Law. Foolishly, then, do some reject as an absurdity the statement, that if a man fulfills the Law he attains to righteousness; for the defect does not arise from the doctrine of the Law, but from the infirmity of men, as is plain from another testimony given by Paul. (Romans 8:3.) We must observe, however, that salvation is not to be expected from the Law unless its precepts be in every respect complied with; for life is not promised to one who shall have done this thing, or that thing, but, by the plural word, full obedience is required of us. The pratings of the Popish theologians about partial righteousness are frivolous and silly, since God embraces at once all the commandments; and who is there that can boast of having thoroughly fulfilled them? If, then, none was ever clear of transgression, or ever will be, although God by no means deceives us, yet the promise becomes ineffectual, because we do not perform our part of the agreement.

Deuteronomy 27

Deuteronomy 27:11-26

11. And Moses charged the people the same day, saying,

11. Praecepitque Moses populo eo die, dicendo:

12. These shall stand upon mount Gerizim to bless the people, when ye are come over Jordan; Simeon, and Levi, and Judah, and Issachar, and Joseph, and Benjamin.

12. Hi stabunt ad benedicendum populo super montem Garizim, quando transieris Jordanem, Simon, et Levi, et Juda, et Issachar, et Joseph, et Benjamin:

13. And these shall stand upon mount Ebal to curse; Reuben, Gad, and Ashur, and Zebulun, Dan, and Naphtali.

13. Isti vero stabunt ad maledictionem in monte Ebal, Ruben, Gad, et Aser, et Zebulon, Dan et Nephthali.

14. And the Levites shall speak, and say unto all the men of Israel with a loud voice,

14. Loquentur autem Levitae, ac dicent ad omnem virum Israel voce excelsa:

15. Cursed be the man that maketh any graven or molten image, an abomination unto the Lord, the work of the hands of the craftsman, and putteth it in a secret place: and all the people shall answer and say, Amen.

15. Maledictus vir ille qui fecerit sculptile, et conflatile, abominationem Jehovae, opus manuum artificis, et posuerit in abscondito: et respondebunt universus populus, ac dicent, Amen.

16. Cursed be he that setteth light by his father or his mother: and all the people shall say, Amen.

16. Maledictus qui vilipenderit patrem suum, aut matrem suam: et dicet universus populus, Amen.

17. Cursed be he that removeth his neighbor's land-mark: and all the people shall say, Amen.

17. Maledictus qui transfert terminum proximi sui, et dicet universus populus, Amen.

18. Cursed be he that maketh the blind to wander out of the way: and all the people shall say, Amen.

18. Maledictus qui aberrare facit caecum in via: et dicet universus populus, Amen.

19. Cursed be he that perverteth the judgment of the stranger, fatherless, and widow: and all the people shall say, Amen.

19. Maledictus qui pervertit judicium peregrini, pupilli, et viduae: et dicet universus populus, Amen.

20. Cursed be he that lieth with his father's wife; because he uncovereth his father's skirt: and all the people shall say, Amen.

20. Maledictus qui coierit cum uxore patris sui, quia discooperuit oram patris sui, et dicet universus populus, Amen.

21. Cursed be he that lieth with any manner of beast: and all the people shall say, Amen.

21. Maledictus qui coierit cum quovis animali, et dicet universus populus, Amen.

22. Cursed be he that lieth with his sister, the daughter of his father, or the daughter of his mother: and all the people shall say, Amen.

22. Maledictus qui coierit cum sorore sua, filia patris sui, vel filia matris suae, et dicet universus populus, Amen.

23. Cursed be he that lieth with his mother-in-law: and all the people shall say, Amen.

23. Maledictus qui coierit cum socru sua: et dicet universus populus, Amen.

24. Cursed be he that smiteth his neighbor secretly: and all the people shall say, Amen.

24. Maledictus qui percusscrit proximum suum abscondite: et dicet universus populus, Amen.

25. Cursed be he that taketh reward to slay an innocent person: and all the people shall say, Amen.

25. Maledictus qui acceperit munus, ut percutiat plaga animae sanguinem innocentem: et dicet universus populus, Amen.

26. Cursed be he that confirmeth not all the words of this law to do them: and all the people shall say, Amen.

26. Maledictus qui non stabilierit verba Legis istius faciendo illa: et dicet universus populus, Amen.

11. And Moses charged the people the same day. In order that both the promises and threats might have more efficacy in affecting the minds of all, God enjoined not only that they should be proclaimed in a solemn rite, but also that they should be approved by the people in a loud voice, and sealed, as it were, by their consent. It is elsewhere recorded that this was faithfully performed by Joshua. (Joshua 8:33.) Let it suffice to say at present that they were all summoned, and conducted before God to subscribe to them, so that henceforth all subterfuge might be put an end to. The tribes of Israel were divided into two parties, that they might stand opposite to each other, and that the blessings might sound forth from one side, and the curses from the other, [196] like ἀντίστροφοι. I confess I do not know why the descendants of Simeon, Levi, Judah, Issachar, Joseph, and Benjamin, were chosen by God to proclaim the blessings, rather than the others; [197] for there is no force in the opinion of the Hebrew writers that those who descended from free mothers were placed in the post of highest dignity: since the tribe of the first-born, Reuben, was united with some who sprang from the bond-maids; unless, perhaps, we may say that the descendants of Reuben were degraded into the second class as a mark of ignominy; but, since both the blessings and curses were offered in the name of the whole people, it is not a point of much importance. For, if this division [198] was made to bear witness to their common consent, it was equivalent to their all alike confessing that the transgressors of the Law were accursed, and those who kept it blessed; and consequently I am not very curious to know why, in their common office, God preferred some to the others. Moses will elsewhere relate that the tribes, which are here separated, were then united together. It would perhaps be a probable conjecture that God, who well knew what would hereafter be the inheritance of every tribe, placed them severally in that station which would correspond to their future allotment.

In order that the sanction might have more solemnity, God chose that the Levites should dictate the words as if He Himself spoke from heaven; for, since they were appointed to be the expounders of the Law, as it behooved them faithfully to repeat what God had dictated out of His own mouth, so they were heard with greater attention and reverence.

15. Cursed be the man that maketh any graven. Hence it appears that Moses is silent as to the half (of what he had spoken of before; [199]) for no mention is made of the blessings [200] which occupied before the first place. Perhaps the Spirit would indirectly rebuke the wickedness of the people, from whence it arose that He was not at liberty to proclaim the praises conveyed in the blessings; for, when they ought to have embraced cheerfully the reward promised to them, their ungodliness deprived them of this honor; and nothing remained but that they should submit themselves to the just punishment of their iniquities. Meanwhile, it cannot be doubted but that they were taught by the forms of cursing which we here read what course was to be observed in blessing. For, when God pronounces His condemnation of transgressors, we may hence infer that the hope of blessedness is laid up for His true servants, if any fulfill His law. Besides, in the list of curses here recorded, a synecdoche is to be observed, since no special curse is separately denounced against blasphemers, perjurers, Sabbath-breakers, slanderers, and adulterers. It is plain,

therefore, that some kinds of crime which were worthy of the greatest abomination, were selected, in order that the people might learn from hence that transgression against any particular of the Law would not be unpunished; for, by speaking of graven images, God undoubtedly defends His worship from all pollutions; and thus this curse extends to every breach of the First Table. Moreover, when He threatens to punish secret sins, we may readily infer that, although offenders might be hidden from earthly judges, and escape from their hands a hundred times, still God would be the avenger of His polluted worship. If any had put an idol in a secret place, or had smitten his neighbor secretly, he will not suffer the punishment which cannot be inflicted unless his crime be detected, and he is convicted of the offense; but, lest impunity should encourage any one to become obdurate in sin, the people are summoned before the heavenly tribunal of God, that they may be retained in the path of duty, not only by the fear of punishment, but for conscience-sake. Whence, again, it is clear that God did not only deliver a political Law, which should merely direct their outward morals, but one which would require true sincerity of heart.

16. *Cursed be he that setteth light by his father.* What follows refers to the Second Table of the Law; and, first, He pronounces those cursed who should be undutiful (impii) to their parents; for the word קלל, kalal, [201] which means to despise, as well as to curse, is put in opposition to the honor which, by the Fifth Commandment, is due to our father and mother. Then He mentions such thefts as generally escape the knowledge of men; as also, He only adverts to those acts of fornication which are anxiously concealed on account of their filthiness. To have connection with a beast, with one's mother-in-law, or step-mother, or sister, is so unnatural and detestable a crime, that it is generally concealed more carefully. But God admonishes us that, whatever modes of concealment the sinner shall adopt, they will profit him nothing, but that, when He shall at length ascend His judgment-seat, their shame shall be discovered. For the same reason he does not curse all murderers, but only such as have shed innocent blood for hire, which nefarious compact cannot easily be discovered so as to be punished by laws. [202]

26. *Cursed is he that confirmeth not.* Although it was God's purpose to summon the consciences of all men before Him, and, in order that they might not only fear human judgments, He designedly threatened them with the punishment of secret sins, yet the conclusion, which is now added, extends the same judgment to all iniquities of whatever kind. Nay, He briefly declares, that whosoever shall not perform what the Law requires, are accursed. From whence Paul rightly infers, that "as many as are of the works of the Law are under the curse." (Galatians 3:10.) For let the most perfect man come forward, and, although he may have striven ever so diligently to keep the Law, he will have at least offended in some point or other; since the declaration of James must be borne in mind, "Whosoever shall keep the whole law, and yet offend in one point, he is guilty of all;" for he that forbade murder and adultery, forbade theft also. (James 2:10, 11.) Paul indeed does not quote the very words of Moses, for he thus cites his testimony;

"Cursed is every one that continueth not in all things which are written in the book of the law to do them," (Galatians 3:10;)

but there is no difference in the sense, since all are here condemned without exception, who have not confirmed the Law of God, so as to fulfill to the uttermost whatever it contains. Whence if is clear that, in whatever respect the deficiency betrays itself, it brings men under the curse; and to this the Israelites are commanded to assent, so as to acknowledge that they were all without exception lost, since they were involved in the curse. And now-a-days, also, it is necessary that we should all to a man be struck with the same despair, in order that, embracing the grace of Christ, we should be delivered from this melancholy state of guilt; since he was made accursed for us, that He might redeem us from the curse of the Law. (Galatians 3:13.)

Deuteronomy 11

Deuteronomy 11:26-32

26. Behold, I set before you this day a blessing and a curse;

26. Vide, ego pono coram vobis hodie benedictionem et maledictionem:

27. A blessing, if ye obey the commandments of the Lord your God, which I command you this day:

27. Benedictionem, si obedieritis praeceptis Jehovae Dei vestri, quae ego praecipio vobis hodie:

28. And a curse, if ye will not obey the commandments of the Lord your God, but turn aside out of the way which I command you this day, to go after other gods, which ye have not known.

28. Maledictionem vero, si non obedieritis praeceptis Jehovae Dei vestri, sed recesseritis e via quam ego praecipio vobis hodie, ut ambuletis post deos alienos quos non novistis.

29. And it shall come to pass, when the Lord thy God hath brought thee in unto the land whither thou goest to possess it, that thou shalt put the blessing upon mount Gerizim, and the curse upon mount Ebal.

29. Quumque introduxerit te Jehova Deus tuus in terram quam tu ingrederis ut possideas eam, tunc dabis benedictionem super montem Garizim, et maledictionem super montem Ebal.

30. Are they not on the other side Jordan, by the way where the sun goeth down, in the land of the Canaanites, which dwell in the champaign over against Gilgal, beside the plains of Moreh?

30. Annon sunt trans Jordanem post viam ad occasum solis vergentem in terra Chananaei, qui habitant in planitie e regione Gilgal, juxta campestria Moreh?

31. For ye shall pass over Jordan, to go in to possess the land which the Lord your God giveth you, and ye shall possess it, and dwell therein.

31. Vos enim transituri estis Jordanem, ut pergatis ad possidendam terram quam Jehova Deus vester dat vobis, et haereditabitis eam, et habitabitis in ea.

32. And ye shall observe to do all the statutes and judgments which I set before you this day.

32. Custodite ergo ad faciendum omnia statuta, et judicia, quae ego pono ante faciem vestram hodie.

26. Behold, I set before you this day. He now embraces the two points at once, viz., that they would be blessed if they earnestly apply themselves to the keeping of the Law, and cursed, if they shake off its yoke and revel in their lusts. But, when he says that he here sets before them a blessing and a curse, it is as much as to declare, that he does not merely tell them what is right, but that the reward is prepared if they obey; and if not, that the punishment is also at hand. Thus we see, that the doctrine which he had hitherto delivered is sealed by hope and fear, since they would not lose their labor if they obeyed it, nor be unpunished if they rejected it. But, that they may learn surely to embrace the promises and to fear the threatenings, he repeats what we have met with before,[203] that God, who is both a faithful rewarder, and a severe judge, is the Author of the Law; yet at the same time he magnifies his own ministry, [204] since it behooved them to depend upon God, and to acquiesce in His commandments, in such a manner as still to submit themselves to His Prophet. For such is men's pride, that they desire to fly above the clouds to listen to God; whilst He would be heard in His servants, by whose mouth He speaks. Moses, therefore, would again enforce upon them this humility, when he states that he enjoins what God has commanded, as if to call himself the organ of the Holy Spirit.

29. And it shall come to pass, when the Lord. I have lately expounded a similar passage, which, although it is subsequent in the order observed by Moses, yet, inasmuch as it sets out the matter more clearly, I have not hesitated for perspicuity's sake to put first. I said that God's intention was, whilst appointing the Israelites to proclaim their own condemnation, to lay them under more solemn obligation to keep the Law. If He had Himself declared His will through the Levites only, they ought indeed to have been seriously affected, and to have listened with reverence both to the blessings and the curses; but when each of them testifies with his own mouth what the Levites dictated by God's command, the introduction of this assent, as a solemn ratification, [205] was more efficacious in awakening their zeal and attention. A more fitting season, however, for this protest was after they had entered the promised land than as if it had been made in the plain of Moab; for the sight of the land tended to its confirmation, as if they had been brought into court to make a covenant with God.

These [206] two mountains are situated opposite to each other, in such a manner that the two divisions of the people might easily stand to bless and to curse, so that they might in concert approve of the promises and threats of God.

30. Are they not on the other side of Jordan. Although the form of interrogation is common in Hebrew, yet in this place Moses affirms more vehemently than as if he had only stated directly that these mountains were in the land of Canaan; for he wishes to encourage them in the confidence of entering the promised inheritance; just as he adds immediately afterwards, "Ye shall pass over Jordan." For, although they had already experienced the miraculous power of God in the conquest of the Amorites, and in heir occupation of the land of Bashan, yet such was their incredulity, that it was necessary constantly to dissipate their fears, so that they might lay aside all hesitation, and boldly prepare to advance. Finally, he founds an exhortation upon this great goodness of God; for the actual enjoyment of the land ought to have stimulated them the more in the service of God, because they were made to inherit it for the purpose of keeping the Law.

Leviticus 26:3-13

3. If ye walk in my statutes, and keep my commandments, and do them;

3. Si in decretis meis ambulaveritis, et praecepta mea servaveritis, et feceritis ea:

4. Then I will give you rain in due season, and the land shall yield her increase, and the trees of the field shall yield their fruit.

4. Dabo pluvias vestras tempore suo, dabitque terra fructum suum, et arbores agrorum dabunt fructum suum.

5. And your thrashing shall reach unto the vintage, and the vintage shall reach unto the sowing-time; and ye shall eat your bread to the full, and dwell in your land safely.

5. Apprehendetque vobis tritura vindemiam, et vindemia apprehendet sementem: comedetisque panem vestrum ad saturitatem, et habitabitis confidenter in terra vestra.

6. And I will give peace in the land, and ye shall lie down, and none shall make you afraid; and I will rid evil beasts out of the land, neither shall the sword go through your land.

6. Dabo namque pacem in terra, et dormietis, neque erit exterrens: auferamque bestias malas e terra, et gladius non transibit per terram vestram.

7. And ye shall chase your enemies, and they shall fall before you by the sword.

7. Et persequemini inimicos vestros, cadentque coram vobis gladio.

8. And five of you shall chase an hundred, and an hundred of you shall put ten thousand to flight: and your enemies shall fall before you by the sword.

8. Persequentur quinque ex vobis centum, et centum ex vobis decem millia persequentur: et corruent inimici vestri coram vobis gladio.

9. For I will have respect unto you, and make you fruitful, and multiply you, and establish my covenant with you.

9. Vertam enim me ad vos, et crescere faciam vos, atque multiplicabo vos, stabiliamque pactum meum vobiscum.

10. And ye shall eat old store, and bring forth the old because of the new.

10. Et comedetis vetus inveteratum, et vetus propter novum educetis.

11. And I will set my tabernacle among you, and my soul shall not abhor you.

11. Et ponam tabernaculum in medio vestri, neque abominabitur vos anima mea.

12. And I will walk among you, and will be your God, and ye shall be my people.

12. Ambulabo autem in medio vestri, eroque vobis in Deum, et vos eritis mihi in populum.

13. I am the Lord your God, which brought you forth out of the land of Egypt, that ye should not be their bond-men; and I have broken the bands of your yoke, and made you go upright.

13. Ego Jehova Deus vester qui eduxi vos de terra Aegypti, ne essetis illis servi: et confregi lora jugi vestri, et incedere feci vos erecta facie.

ITS REPETITION

3. If ye walk in my statutes. We have now to deal with two remarkable passages, in which he professedly treats of the rewards which the servants of God may expect, and of the punishments which await the transgressors. I have indeed already observed, that whatever God promises us on the condition of our walking in His commandments would be ineffectual if He should be extreme in examining our works. Hence it arises that we must renounce all the compacts of the Law, if we desire to obtain favor with God. But since, however defective the works of believers may be, they are nevertheless pleasing to God through the intervention of pardon, hence also the efficacy of the promises depends, viz., when the strict condition of the law is moderated. Whilst, therefore, they reach forward and strive, reward is given to their efforts although imperfect, exactly as if they had fully discharged their duty; for, since their deficiencies are put out of sight by faith, God honors with the title of reward what He gratuitously bestows upon them. Consequently, "to walk in the commandments of God," is not precisely equivalent to performing whatever the Law demands; but in this expression is included the indulgence with which God regards His children and pardons their faults. The promise, therefore, is not without fruit as respects believers, whilst they endeavor to consecrate themselves to God, although they are still far from perfection; according to the teaching of the Prophet, "I will spare them as a man spareth his own son that serveth him," (Malachi 3:17;) as much as to say, that their obedience would not be acceptable to Him because it was deserving, but because He visits it with His paternal favor. Whence it appears how foolish is the pride of those who imagine that they make God their debtor, as if according to His agreement.

The restriction of the recompense, which is here mentioned, to this earthly and transitory life, is a part of the elementary instruction of the Law; for, just as the spiritual grace of God was represented to the ancient people by shadows and images, so also the same principle applied also both to rewards and punishments. Reconciliation with God was represented to them by the blood of cattle; there were various forms of expiation, but all outward and visible, because their substance had not yet appeared in Christ. For the same reason, therefore, because so clear and familiar an acquaintance with eternal life, and the final resurrection, had not yet been attained by the Fathers, as now shines forth in the Gospel, God for the most part shewed forth by external proofs that He was favorably disposed to His people or offended with them. Because now-a-days God does not openly take vengeance on sins as of old, fanatics infer that He has almost changed His nature; nay, on this pretense, the Manicheans [207] imagined that the God of Israel was different from ours. But this error springs from gross and disgraceful ignorance; for, by not distinguishing His different modes of dealing, they do not hesitate impiously to cut God Himself in two. The earth does not now cleave asunder to swallow up the rebellious: [208] God does not now thunder from heaven as against Sodom: He does not now send fire upon wicked cities as He did in the Israelitish camp: fiery serpents are not sent forth to inflict deadly bites: in a word, such manifest instances of punishment are not daily presented before our eyes to make God terrible to us;

and for this reason, because the voice of the Gospel sounds much more clearly in our ears, like the sound of a trumpet, whereby we are summoned to the heavenly tribunal of Christ. Let us then learn to tremble at that sentence, which banishes all the wicked from the kingdom of God. So, on the other hand, God does not appear, as of old, as the rewarder of His people by earthly blessings; and this because we "are dead, and our life is hid with Christ in God;" because it becomes us to be conformed to our Head, and through many tribulations to enter the kingdom of heaven. Thus, the greater are the adversities that oppress us, the more cheerfully it behooves us to lift up our heads, until Christ shall gather us into the fellowship of His glory, and to pursue the course of our calling for the hope which is set before us in heaven; in a word,

"denying ungodliness and worldly lusts, to live soberly, righteously, and godly in this present world, looking for that blessed hope, and the glorious appearing of the great God, and our Savior Jesus Christ." (Titus 2:12, 13.)

I admit, indeed, the truth of what Paul teaches, that "godliness" even now has "the promise of the life that now is, as well as of that which is to come," (1 Timothy 4:8;) and assuredly believers already taste on earth of that blessedness which they shall hereafter enjoy in its fullness. God also inflicts His judgments on the ungodly in order to remind us of the last judgment; but still the distinction to which I have adverted is obvious, that since God has opened to us the heavenly life in the Gospel, He now calls us directly to it, whereas He led the Fathers to it as it were by steps. For this reason Paul elsewhere teaches, that believers are afflicted in this world as

"a manifest token of the righteous judgment of God, that they may be counted worthy of the kingdom of God for which they also suffer, seeing it is a righteous thing with God to recompense," etc. (2 Thessalonians 1:5, 6.)

In short, let us no more wonder that the Israelites were only attracted and alarmed by temporal rewards and punishments, than that the land of Canaan was to them a symbol of their eternal inheritance, in which, nevertheless, they confessed themselves strangers and pilgrims; from whence the Apostle correctly concludes, that they desired a better country. (Genesis 47:9; Psalm 39:12; Hebrews 11:16.) And thus the wild absurdity of those is refuted, who suppose that the Fathers were contented with perishable felicity, as if God merely gorged them in a tavern. [209] Still the distinction which I have noted remains, that God manifested Himself more fully as a Father and Judge by temporal blessings and punishments than since the promulgation of the Gospel.

4. Then I will give you rain in due season. He might in one word have promised great abundance of food, but, that His grace may be more illustrious, the instruments are mentioned which He employs for its supply. He might give us bread as He formerly rained down manna from heaven; but in order that the signs of His paternal solicitude may be constantly before us, after the seed is sown, the earth requires rain from heaven; and thus the order of the seasons is so regulated that every day may renew the memory of God's bounty. For this reason rain is mentioned, and the increase of the fruits of the earth; and the continued succession of thrashing, the vintage, and sowing-time, indicates a very abundant supply of corn and wine. For, if the harvest be small, there will

not be much work to occupy the husbandman; and, if the vintage be light, hence also will arise an unsatisfactory period of leisure. But when God declares that from harvest to sowing-time they shall have constant employment, He bids them expect a fruitful year, as immediately follows, "ye shall eat your bread to the full." And since no prosperity can be gratifying without peace, He says that they shall be quiet and free from all disturbance. And this must be carefully observed that, so unpalatable are all God's blessings without the seasoning of tranquillity, nothing is more wretched than inquietude. The sum is, that for the true servants of God not only is there food laid up with Him, but also its peaceful and pleasant enjoyment, since it is in His power and will to drive far from them all annoyances. Still these two things do not seem altogether consistent with each other, that there shall be none to make them afraid, and that they shall subdue their enemies, so that [210] ten shall suffice to chase a hundred; for of what use would their military strength be if there were no enemies to trouble them? But if we may take the latter sentence disjunctively, there will be no absurdity, viz., if it should happen that war be brought against them, they should fight successfully. Still the easiest solution of this difficulty is, that it soon afterwards was necessary for them to contend with a great multitude of enemies, in order to obtain possession of the land. We gather from the accommodation by the Prophets of this peculiar blessing of a secure and tranquil life to the kingdom of Christ, that the promises, which from the nature of the Law were of none effect, are still useful for believers; for, when God has reconciled them to Himself, He also liberally bestows upon them what they have not deserved; and yet their obedience, such as it is, is also rewarded.

9. *For I will have respect unto you* [211] God is said to "turn Himself" to the people, whom He undertakes to cherish and preserve; just as also when He forsakes those who have alienated themselves from Him, He is said to be turned away from them. Hence the common exhortation in the Prophets, "Be ye turned to me, and I will be turned to you;" whereby God reminds us that He has not promised in vain what we here read. Therefore the eyes of the Lord are over the righteous, to confirm His covenant towards them by watching for their safety. Hence, too, we are also taught, that when we depart from God, His covenant is made void by our own fault; wherewith Jeremiah reproaches the Israelites. (Jeremiah 31:32.) In order, therefore, that God's covenant should remain firm and effectual, it is not only necessary that the Law should be engraven on our hearts, but also that He should add another grace, and not remember our iniquities. When He says, "Ye shall eat old store," He again magnifies their abundance; for, whereas scarcity compels us to make immediate use of the new fruits, so it is a great sign of abundance to bring forth old wheat from the granary, and old wine from the cellar. The continuance of His bounty is represented in the end of the verse, where He says that there shall be no place for the new fruits, unless they empty their store-houses; because [212] it might happen that, after a year of scarcity, all their storehouses should be empty, and there would be no new corn to succeed in place of the old.

11. *And I will set my tabernacle among you.* He alludes, indeed, to the visible sanctuary in which He was worshipped; still He would shew them that it should be effectually manifested, that He had not chosen His home amongst them in vain, inasmuch as He would exert His power by sure proofs to aid and preserve them. In a word, He signifies that the sanctuary would not be an empty sign of His presence, but that the reality should correspond with the sign; and

this He further confirms in the next verse, where He says that He would "walk among" them. For as yet they had not arrived at their place of rest, and therefore had need of Him as their Leader, in order that their journey might be prosperous. Although He does not say in express terms that they should be spiritually blessed, still there is no doubt but that He lifts their thoughts above the world when He promises that He would be their God; for this expression, "I will be your God," contains, as Christ interprets it, the hope of eternal immortality; because He is the fountain of life, and "not the God of the dead." (Matthew 22:32.) The true and solid felicity, then, is now promised, which was typically represented. For this reason David, although he greatly magnifies the earthly blessings of God, yet, by the conclusion which he adds, demonstrates that he did not stop short with them;

"God's mercy (he says) shall follow me all the days of my life, and I will dwell in the house of the Lord, to length of days." [213] (Psalm 23:6.)

And elsewhere, when he had said that they are happy, to whom God abundantly supplies all things (needful, [214]) presently adds, as if in explanation,

"Happy is that people, whose God is the Lord." (Psalm 144:15.)

Finally, He recalls to their recollection that He had been their Deliverer, that they may assuredly gather from what was past, that the flow of His grace would be continuous, if only they themselves do run the course unto which He had called them.

Deuteronomy 28

Deuteronomy 28:1-14
1. And it shall come to pass, if thou shalt hearken diligently unto the voice of the Lord thy God, to observe and to do all his commandments which I command thee this day, that the Lord thy God will set thee on high above all nations of the earth:

1. Et erit, si audiendo audieris vocem Jehovae Dei tui, ut custodias ad faciendum omnia praecepta ejus quae ego paecipio tibi hodie: tunc constituet to Jehova Deus tuus superiorem onmibus gentibus terrae.

2. And all these blessings shall come on thee, and overtake thee, if thou shalt hearken unto the voice of the Lord thy God.

2. Et venient super to omnes benedictiones istae, apprehendentque te, si modo obedieris voci Jehovae Dei tui.

3. Blessed shalt thou be in the city, and blessed shalt thou be in the field.

3. Benedictus eris in urbe ipsa, et benedictus eris in agro.

4. Blessed shall be the fruit of thy body, and the fruit of thy ground, and the fruit of thy cattle, the increase of thy kine, and the flocks of thy sheep.

4. Benedictus fructus ventris tui, et fructus terrae tuae, et fructus jumenti tui, foetus boum tuorum et greges ovium tuarum.

5. Blessed shall be thy basket and thy store.

5. Benedictum canistrum tuum, et conspersio tua.

6. Blessed shalt thou be when thou comest in, and blessed shalt thou be when thou goest out.

6. Benedictus eris in tuo ingressu, et benedictus eris in egressu tuo.

7. The Lord shall cause thine enemies that rise up against thee to be smitten before thy face: they shall come out against thee one way, and flee before thee seven ways.

7. Dabit Jehova hostes trios qui insurrexerint in te, percussos coram te, per viam unam egredientur ad te, et per septem vias fugient coram te.

8. The Lord shall command the blessing upon thee in thy storehouses, and in all that thou settest thine hand unto; and he shall bless thee in the land which the Lord thy God giveth thee.

8. Mandabit Jehova tecum benedictionem in horreis tuis, et in omni ad quod miseris manum tuam: et benedicet tibi in terra quam Jehova Deus tuus dat tibi.

9. The Lord shall establish thee an holy people unto himself, as he hath sworn unto thee, if thou shalt keep the commandments of the Lord thy God, and walk in his ways.

9. Statuet te Jehova sibi in populum sanctum, quemadmodum juravit tibi, quum custodieris praecepta Jehovae Dei tui, et ambulaveris in viis ejus.

10. And all people of the earth shall see that thou art called by the name of the Lord, and they shall be afraid of thee.

10. Tunc intelligent omnes populi quod nomen Jehovae invocatum sit super te, et timebunt sibi a te.

11. And the Lord shall make thee plenteous in goods, in the fruit of thy body, and in the fruit of thy cattle, and in the fruit of thy ground, in the land which the Lord sware unto thy fathers to give thee.

11. Et abundare faciet to Jehova in bonum fructu ventris tui, et fructu jumenti tui, et fructu terrae tuae, super terram quam juravit Jehova patribus tuis se daturum tibi.

12. The Lord shall open unto thee his good treasure, the heaven to give the rain unto thy land in his season, and to bless all the work of thine hand: and thou shalt lend unto many nations, and thou shalt not borrow.

12. Aperiet Jehova tibi thesaurum suum optimum, coelum, ut det pluviam terrae tuae in tempore suo, et benedicat omni operi marius tuae, et mutuabis gentibus multis, tu vero non accipies mutuum.

13. And the Lord shall make thee the head, and not the tail; and thou shalt be above only, and thou shalt not be beneath; if that thou hearken unto the commandments of the Lord thy God, which I command thee this day, to observe and to do them:

13. Ponetque te Jehova in caput, et non in candam, erisque duntaxat sursum, et non deorsum: quando obedieris praeceptis Jehovae Dei tui, quae ego praecipio tibi hodie ut custodias et facias.

14. And thou shalt not go aside from any of the words which I command thee this day, to the right hand or to the left, to go after other gods to serve them.

14. Neque recesseris ab omnibus verbis quae ego praecipio vobis hodie, ad dextram aut ad sinistram, eundo post deos alienos ut colatis eos.

1. And it shall come to pass, if thou shalt hearken. He teaches the same thing as before in different words; but the diversity of expression, as well as the repetition, tends to its confirmation. First, God says that He would deal with them so bountifully that they should excel all other nations; for this is the meaning of the words, that they should be illustrious above all the rest of the world on account of the special blessings of God. He afterwards enumerates the blessings which shall never depart from them, if they persevere in the service of God; and here it must be observed that they are reminded, not only in how many ways God is bountiful towards His servants, but also to how many necessities they are exposed, which require His direct and constant aid; for if we are blessed in the city and in the field, we can no more move a foot than stand still, except by His blessing. Such also is the tendency of the whole list, that a scarcity of all things impends over us at every moment, unless God should continually succor us by remedies sent down from heaven, and that every good thing can only come from that one source.

9. The Lord shall establish thee a holy people unto himself. This refers indeed to earthly blessings, as if Moses said, that by them would be manifested God's love towards His chosen people; still it rises higher, so that the Israelites, led on by degrees, should learn to embrace God alone, and to trust in Him according to the covenant which He had made with Abraham, "I am thy exceeding great reward." (Genesis 15:1.) For the children of Abraham were set apart and chosen to be a holy people, not only in order that, being well fed, and with a full belly, they should aspire to nothing but earthly things, but that they might be confidently assured that they would be blessed in death as well as life. Although their adoption was gratuitous, still, inasmuch as they were called unto purity, it is not without reason that God promises that what He had spoken should be sure, if by keeping the Law the Israelites themselves should continue in the covenant; as much as to say, that their sanctification [215] should be firm and perpetual if they walked in the commandments of the Law. When He adds that it should be manifest "to [216] all people of the earth that the name of God was called upon them," it is equivalent to saying, that it should be known that they were under God's defense and patronage, and that thus they should always be safe and secure in His protection.

12. The Lord shall open to thee his good treasure. He again repeats, that the goodness of God shines forth in many ways in the life of men, since He not only supplies the bread that they eat, but that the rain which descends from heaven waters the earth; and that thus He produces whatever is required for food from His plenteous store-house or treasure. Let us learn, therefore, both above and beneath, as well in the temperature of the atmosphere, in the quickening heat of the sun, in the rain, and in other means, as in the fertility of the earth, to contemplate the manifold riches which God brings forth from His treasures. And when He declares that He will bless the work of our hands, hence, too, let us learn that we can attain nothing by our industry and hardest labors, except in so far as God vouchsafes us good success; and that all our efforts without His secret blessing are mere useless fatigue. For the figure which Paul uses in reference to the spiritual culture of the Church, is taken from nature itself:

"Neither is he that planteth anything, neither he that watereth, but God that giveth the increase." (1 Corinthians 3:7.)

God would not, indeed, have [217] us lie idle, and therefore He requires the labor of our hands, but He would have the fruit of our labors attributed to Himself.

After having spoken of the whole Law, and forbidden that they should turn aside to the right or the left, He adverts to the principal point, i.e., that they should not revolt to strange gods. Wherefore, the sum comes to this, that, in order that God may continue to shew us the favor which He has begun towards us, we ought on our sides to be altogether submissive to His rule. This indeed He demands of us by His word, and enables us to perform it by the power of His Spirit; not, it is true, fully to do our duty, but to strive to reach the goal; and, whereas we are far from attaining perfection, His indulgence supplies what is wanting in us.

Here, however, a difficult question arises, -- If all prosperity proceeds from the peculiar blessing which God vouchsafes to His servants, whence is it that many of His despisers have children, easy and happy circumstances, abundance of the fruits of fire earth, enjoyment and luxury, honors and power? I answer, that the happy condition of life, which He assigns to His servants, does not prevent Him from diffusing His bounty promiscuously over the whole human race. He is truly called in Psalm 36:6, the preserver of "man and beast." It is said elsewhere, [218] that His mercy is extended over all His creatures, (Psalm 145:17;) and justly does Christ exalt His unbounded goodness, in that "He maketh his sun to rise on the evil and on the good." (Matthew 5:45.) But equally true is the exclamation of the Prophet;

"Oh, how great is thy goodness, which thou hast laid up for them that fear thee!" (Psalm 31:19.)

For since all without exception enjoy all the supports of life, God's goodness, which thus contends with the wickedness of men, shines forth universally even towards the ungodly, so that He does not cease to cherish and preserve those whom He has created, although they be unworthy. He therefore does good to the ungodly, because He is their Creator; besides, in order to keep the minds of believers in suspense in expectation of the final judgment, He now suffers many things to be confusedly mixed together, and hides His judgment in the darkness of night, as it were, or at least under clouds; whilst He also so tempers His patience towards the reprobate, as that, in this confusion of which I have spoken, some signs of His anger and favor are manifested. Thus, although the government of the world is not yet reduced to a perfect rule, still God shews by it that He is both the avenger of sins and the rewarder of righteousness, and some sparks are seen through the darkness; whilst the faithful, although they do not attain to the full enjoyment of the blessing promised them, nevertheless taste of it as far as is expedient. But to the ungodly, although they abound with all sorts of good things, not a single drop of God's goodness is dispensed; for unless a sense of God's paternal favor is awakened by His blessing, the blessing itself ceases to exist; nay, the more they gorge themselves, they attain to a deadly fatness; and God purposely lifts them up, that He may cast them down more heavily from their high estate. In a word, they are fed, as the Prophet says,[219] "unto the day of slaughter."

It must be concluded, therefore, that the blessings which God here promises to His servants are seasoned by Him with spiritual salt, lest they should be tasteless; whilst the reprobate, who are destitute of a sense of His grace, are also deprived altogether of all His blessings. There still, however, remains a difficulty, because the felicity here spoken of does not always, nor equally fall to the lot of God's servants; nay, even under the Law they were sharply tried by many troubles and adversities. I answer, that since none, not even the most holy, was ever a perfect keeper of the Law, since none was ever free from all transgression, it is no cause of surprise that they only partially enjoyed the promised blessings; inasmuch as they were not fit recipients (capaces) of their fullness; and, if it sometimes happens that they are chastised more severely than the ungodly, neither in this is there any absurdity, since God usually begins His judgment at His own house. (Isaiah 10:12; 1 Peter 4:17.) Still, even in this confusion we see what the Prophet teaches, that the righteous are never forsaken, (Psalm 37:25,) and that they are like green and fruitful olive-trees in the courts of the Lord, (Psalm 52:8,) whilst the ungodly, although for a season they may be exalted like cedars of Lebanon, yet are plucked up in a moment by the roots, so that no trace of them remains.

Deuteronomy 7

Deuteronomy 7:9-15

9. Know therefore that the Lord thy God, he is God, the faithful God, which keepeth covenant and mercy with them that love him, and keep his commandments, to a thousand generations;

9. Scias quod Jehova Deus tuus, est Deus, Deus fidelis, custodiens pactum et misericordiam diligentibus se, et custodientibus praecepta sua, usque ad mille generationes:

10. And repayeth them that hate him to their face, to destroy them: he will not be slack to him that hateth him, he will repay him to his face.

10. Et rependens odio habenti ipsum, in faciem ejus, ut perdat eum: neque tardabit, odio habenti ipsum, in faciem ejus rependet ei.

11. Thou shalt therefore keep the commandments, and the statutes, and the judgments, which I command thee this day, to do them.

11. Custodias ergo praecepta, et statuta, et judicia quae ego praecipio tibi hodie, ut ea facias.

12. Wherefore it shall come to pass, if ye hearken to these judgments, and keep and do them, that the Lord thy God shall keep unto thee the covenant and the mercy which he sware unto thy fathers.

12. Et erit, propterea quod audieritis judicia ista, et custodieritis, feceritisque ea: custodiet Jehova Deus tuus tibi pactum, et misericordiam de quo juravit patribus tuis.

13. And he will love thee, and bless thee, and multiply thee: he will also bless the fruit of thy womb, and the fruit of thy land, thy corn, and thy wine, and thine oil, the increase of thy kine, and the flocks of thy sheep, in the land which he sware unto thy fathers to give thee.

13. Diliget quoque te, et benedicet tibi, multiplicabitque te: benedicet namque fructui ventris tui, et fructui terrae tuae, frumento tuo, et musto tuo, et oleo tuo, foetui boum tuorum, et gregibus ovium tuarum, in terra quam juravit patribus tuis se daturum tibi.

14. Thou shalt be blessed above all people: there shall not be male or female barren among you, or among your cattle.

14. Benedictus eris prae cunctis populis: non erit in te infoecundus, neque infoecunda, neque in jumentis tuis.

15. And the Lord will take away from thee all sickness, and will put none of the evil diseases of Egypt, which thou knowest, upon thee; but will lay them upon all them that hate thee.

15. Auferetque a te Jehova omnem morbum, et onmes aegritudines Aegypti pessimas quas nosti: non ponet illas in te, sed ponet eas in omnibus qui te oderint.

9. Know therefore that the Lord thy God, he is God. The verb [220] might have been as properly translated in the future tense; and, if this be preferred, an experimental knowledge, as it is called, is referred to, as if he had said that God would practically manifest how faithful a rewarder He is of His servants. But if the other reading is rather approved, Moses exhorts the people to be assured that God sits in heaven as the Judge of men, so that they may be both alarmed by the fear of His vengeance, and also attracted by the hope of reward. This declaration, however, [221] was appended to the Second Commandment, and there expounded; for since it is comprehended in the Decalogue, it was not right to separate it from thence; but since it is now repeated in confirmation of the whole Law, it is fitly inserted in this place. It will not be amiss, nevertheless, slightly to advert to what I there more fully explained. The promise stands first, because God chooses rather to invite His people by kindness than to compel them to obedience from terror. The word mercy is coupled with the covenant, that we may know that the reward which believers must expect, does not depend on the merit of their works, since they have need of God's mercy. We may, however, thus resolve the phrase -- keeping the covenant of mercy -- or the covenant founded on mercy -- or the mercy which He covenanted.

When it is required of believers that they should love God before they keep His Commandments, we are thus taught that the source and cause of obedience is the love wherewith we embrace God as our Father. With respect to the "thousand generations," it is better that we should refer to the Second Commandment, because it is a point which cannot be hurried over in a few words.

10. And repayeth them that hate him. There is no mention here made of the vengeance "unto the third and fourth generation? [222]

Those who expound the passage that God confers kindnesses on the wicked, whilst they are living in this world, [223] that He may at length destroy them in final perdition, wrest the words too violently. Nor is the opinion of others probable, that God repays the wicked with the reward of hatred, in His face, or anger. I therefore interpret it to mean the face of those to whose disobedience God opposes Himself when He humbles their arrogance; for He alludes to their pride and audacity, because they do not hesitate to provoke God, as if He were without the courage or the power to contend with them. He declares, then, that their impudence and brazen front shall avail them nothing, but that He will cast down the impertinence of their countenance, and the insolence of their forehead; and signifies that they shall as certainly feel the judgment which they despise, as if He presented it before their eyes. He adds, moreover, that He will not deal towards the wicked with the clemency which he uses towards His children; for He so chastises them that His correction is always profitable for their salvation, whilst He denounces deadly punishment against the former; for although He seems to deal alike with both, when He inflicts temporal punishment, still, that which is but a medicine for believers, is to the reprobate a foretaste of their eternal destruction. What He says, however, as to taking vengeance without delay, does not seem to accord with other passages of Scripture, in which He declares Himself to be slow to anger, kind, and long-suffering. Besides, it seems also to be contradicted by experience, since He does not immediately hasten to inflict punishment, but proceeds slowly, so as to compensate by His severity for the slowness with which He acts. But we must remember what He says in Psalm 90:4, that a thousand years in His sight are but as a single day; and consequently, when we think that He delays, He is, in His infinite wisdom, hastening as much as is necessary. He seems, indeed, to take no notice for a time, that He may thus invite men to repent; but still He declares that He will not delay, but that He will come suddenly, like a whirlwind, to hasten His judgments, lest the ungodly should grow drowsy from their security. Let us, therefore, learn quietly and patiently to wait for the fit season of His vengeance.

12. *Wherefore it shall come to pass.* God appears so to act according to agreement, as to leave (His people) no hope of His favor, unless they perform their part of it; and undoubtedly this is the usual form of expression in the Law, in which the condition is inserted, that God will do good to His people if they have deserved it by their obedience. Still we must remember what we have elsewhere seen, that, after God has so covenanted with them, He Himself, in order that His promise may not be made of none effect, descends to the gratuitous promise of pardon, whereby He reconciles the unworthy to Himself. Thus the original covenant only avails to man's condemnation. But when salvation is offered to them gratuitously, their works at the same time become pleasing to God. Inasmuch, however, as the cause of reward is unconnected with men and their works, all calculation of merit is out of the question: still it is profitable to believers that a reward should be promised them if they walk in the commandments of God; since, in His inestimable liberality, He deals with them as if they did something to deserve it.

In conclusion, Moses enumerates some of the proofs of God's favor, such as fecundity, and an abundance of the fruits of the earth. It is questionable whether by what is added at the end respecting the diseases of Egypt, he means the boils which were generated by the scattered ashes, (Exodus 9:8,) or the lice which infested both man and beast, (Exodus 8:17,) or whether he extends them to those diseases which had prevailed long before the departure of the people. I am disposed to embrace the latter opinion; [224] for in Deuteronomy 28:27, after mentioning "the botch of Egypt," he adds "emerods, and the scab, and the itch:" it is, therefore, probable that the Egyptians were subject to various maladies, from which Moses declares that the people should be free by special privilege, if only they obeyed God's Law.

Deuteronomy 12

Deuteronomy 12:28

28. Observe and hear all these words which I command thee, that it may go well with thee, and with thy children after thee for ever, when thou does that which is good and right in the sight of the Lord thy God.

28. Custodi, et audi omnia verba ista quae ego praecipio tibi, ut bene sit tibi et fillis tuis post te usque in saeculum, quum feceris quod bonum est et rectum in oculis Jehovae Dei tui.

Here, again, God invites the obedience of the people by the promise of reward; not that the hope of reward at all avails in itself to arouse men, but because He would thus keep all under the conviction of their just condemnation: for how will it help them to answer that they are not sufficient to perform what God requires, when it appears that they are thus wretched through their own fault? But, as has been said before, it is profitable by indulgence to believers that the reward of obedience should be promised them when they have kept the Law, since their innumerable defects are not imputed to them. Still this doctrine remains sure, that if men devote themselves to the keeping of the Law, God, although He owes them nothing, will nevertheless faithfully reward them.

Leviticus 26

Leviticus 26:14-45

14. But if ye will not hearken unto me, and will not do all these commandments;

14. Si autem non audieritis me, neque feceritis omnia praecepta ista.

15. And if ye shall despise my statutes, or if your soul abhor my judgments, so that ye will not do all my commandments, but that ye break my covenant:

15. Et, si decreta mea spreveritis, et judicia mea abominata fuerit anima vestra, ita ut non faciatis omnia praecepta mea, et irritum faciatis pactum meum:

16. I also will do this unto you; I will even appoint over you terror, consumption, and the burning ague, that shall consume the eyes, and cause sorrow of heart: and ye shall sow your seed in vain; for your enemies shall eat it.

16. Etiam ego faciam hoc vobis: constituam super vos terrorem, tabem, et febrem, consumentia oculos, et dolore afficientia animam, seretisque frustra semen vestrum: nam comedent illud inimici vestri.

17. And I will set my face against you, and ye shall be slain before your enemies: they that hate you shall reign over you; and ye shall flee when none pursueth you.

17. Dabo praeterea iram meam in vos, et trademini coram inimicis vestris, dominabunturque vobis qui odio habent vos: fugietisque, nec erit persequens vos.

18. And if ye will not yet for all this hearken unto me, then I will punish you seven times more for your sins.

18. Quod si usque ad haec non audieritis me, addam corripere vos septuplo propter peccata vestra.

19. And I will break the pride of your power; and I will make your heaven as iron, and your earth as brass.

19. Conteramque superbiam fortitudinis vestrae, ac dabo coelum vestrum sicut ferrum, et terram vestram sicut aes.

20. And your strength shall be spent in vain: for your land shall not yield her increase, neither shall the trees of the land yield their fruits.

20. Et consumetur frustra fortitudo vestra, neque dabit terra vestra fructum suum, et arbores regionis non dabnut fructum suum.

21. And if ye walk contrary unto me, and will not hearken unto me; I will bring seven times more plagues upon you, according to your sins.

21. Si autem ambulaveritis mecum fortuito, et nolueritis audire me, addam super vos plagam septuplo secundum peccata vestra.

22. I will also send wild beasts among you, which shall rob you of your children, and destroy your cattle, and make you few in number; and your high-ways shall be desolate.

22. Immittamque in vos bestiam agri, et orbabit vos, et succidet jumentum vestrum, ac diminuet vos, et desolabuntur viae vestrae.

23. And if ye will not be reformed by me by these things, but will walk contrary unto me;

23. Quod si per haec non recipiatis doctrinam meam, sed ambulaveritis mecum fortuito:

24. Then will I also walk contrary unto you, and will punish you yet seven times for your sins.

24. Ambulabo etiam ego vobiscum fortuito, et percutiam vos quoque septuplo propter peccata vestra:

25. And I will bring a sword upon you, that shall avenge the quarrel of my covenant: and when ye are gathered together within your cities, I will send the pestilence among you; and ye shall be delivered into the hand of the enemy.

25. Atque inducam super vos gladium ultorem ultionis foederis: ubi congregati eritis ad urbes vestras, tunc mittam pestilentiam in medium vestri, ac trademini in manum inimici.

26. And when I have broken the staff of your bread, ten women shall bake your bread in one oven, and they shall deliver you your bread again by weight: and ye shall eat, and not be satisfied.

26. Dum confregero vobis baculum panis, coquent decem mulieres panem vestrum in clibano uno, reddentque panem vestrum in pondere: comedetis autem, et non saturabimini.

27. And if ye will not for all this hearken unto me, but walk contrary unto me;

27. Quod si in hoc non audieritis me, sed ambulaveritis mecum fortuito:

28. Then I will walk contrary unto you also in fury; and I, even I, will chastise you seven times for your sins.

28. Incedam vobiscum in ira fortuito, et corripiam vos etiam ego septuplo propter peccata vestra.

29. And ye shall eat the flesh of your sons, and the flesh of your daughters shall ye eat.

29. Comedetisque carnem filiorum vestrorum, et carnem filiarum vestrarum comedetis.

30. And I will destroy your high places, and cut down your images, and cast your carcases upon the carcases of your idols, and my soul shall abhor you.

30. Atque dissipabo excelsa vestra, et succidam imagines vestras: ponamque cadavera vestra super cadavera idolorum vestrorum, et abominabitur vos anima mea.

31. And I will make your cities waste, and bring your sanctuaries unto desolation, and I will not smell the savour of your sweet odorous.

31. Daboque urbes vestras in desolationem, ac desolabo sanetuaria vestra, neque odorabor odorem quietis vestrae.

32. And I will bring the land into desolation; and your enemies which dwell therein shall be astonished at it.

32. Desolabo, inquam, ego terram, ita ut obstupescant super eam inimici vestri qui habitabunt in ea.

33. And I will scatter you among the heathen, and will draw out a sword after you; and your land shall be desolate, and your cities waste.

33. Vos autem dispergam in gentes, et evaginabo post vos gladium: eritque terra vestra desolata, et urbes vestrae erunt destructae.

34. Then shall the land enjoy her sabbaths, as long as it lieth desolate, and ye be in your enemies' land; even then shall the land rest, and enjoy her sabbaths.

34. Tunc perficiet (vel, oblectabitur) terra sabbatha sua cunctis diebus quibus desdata fuerit: vos autem eritis in terra inimicorum vestrorum: tunc, inquam, requiescet terra, et perficiet sabbatha sua.

35. As long as it lieth desolate it shall rest; because it did not rest in your sabbaths, when ye dwelt upon it.

35. Omnibus diebus quibus desolata fuerit, requiescet: quia non requievit in sabbathis vestris, dum habitaretis in ea.

36. And upon them that are left alive of you I will send a faintness into their hearts in the lands of their enemies; and the sound of a shaken leaf shall chase them; and they shall flee, as fleeing from a sword; and they shall fall when none pursueth.

36. Qui autem remanserint ex vobis, inducam teneritudinem in cor eorum in terris inimicorum suorum, et persequetur eos sonus folii impulsi, et fugient fuga gladii, cadentque nemine persequente.

37. And they shall fall one upon another, as it were before a sword, when none pursueth: and ye shall have no power to stand before your enemies.

37. Impingent autem alter in alterum tanquam a facie gladii, nullo persequente: neque erit vobis resistentia coram inimicis vestris.

38. And ye shall perish among the heathen, and the land of your enemies shall eat you up.

38. Et peribitis inter Gentes, et absumet vos terra inimicorum vestrorum.

39. And they that are left of you shall pine away in their iniquity in your enemies' lands; and also in the iniquities of their fathers shall they pine away with them.

39. Et qui remanserint ex vobis, dissolventur propter iniquitatem suam in terris inimicorum vestrorum, atque etiam propter iniquitates patrum suorum, cum eis dissolventur.

40. If they shall confess their iniquity, and the iniquity of their fathers, with their trespass which they trespassed against me, and that also they have walked contrary unto me;

40. Donec confiteantur iniquitatem suam, et iniquitatem patrum suorum, juxta praevaricationem suam qua praevaricati sunt in me: et etiam quod ambulaverint mecum fortuito:

41. And that I also have walked contrary unto them, and have brought them into the land of their enemies; if then their uncircumcised hearts be humbled, and they then accept of the punishment of their iniquity:

41. Quod etiam ego ambulaverim cum illis fortuito, et induxerim eos in terram inimicorum suorum: tuncque humilietur cor eorum incircuncisum, ac propitient pro iniquitate sua.

42. Then will I remember my covenant with Jacob, and also my covenant with Isaac, and also my covenant with Abraham will I remember; and I will remember the land.

42. Tunc recordabor pacti mei cum Jacob, et etiam pacti mei cum Isaac, et insuper pacti mei cum Abraham recordabor, terrae quoque memor ero.

43. The land also shall be left of them, and shall enjoy her sabbaths, while she lieth desolate without them: and they shall accept of the punishment of their iniquity; because, even because they despised my judgments, and because their soul abhorred my statutes.

43. Terra interim deseretur ab eis, et perficiet sabbatha sua quae desolata est ab illis, et ipsi exsolvent mulctam suam, eo quod, inquam, judicia mea spreverint, et decreta mea abominata sit anima eorum.

44. And yet for all that, when they be in the land of their enemies, I will not cast them away, neither will I abhor them, to destroy them utterly, and to break my covenant with them: for I am the Lord their God.

44. Et tamen etiam hoc modo quum ipsi fuerint in terra inimicorum suorum, non reprobavi eos, neque abominatus sum eos, ut consumerem eos, irritum faciendo pactum meum cum eis: ego enim Jehova Deus eorum.

45. But I will for their sakes remember the covenant of their ancestors, whom I brought forth out of the land of Egypt in the sight of the heathen, that I might be their God: I am the Lord.

45. Sed recordabor propter eos pacti priorum, ego qui eduxi eos e terra Aegypti in oculis Gentium, ut essem illis in Deum: ego Jehova.

14. **But if ye will not hearken unto me.** Thus far a kind invitation has been set before the people in the shape of promises, in order that the observance of the Law might be rendered pleasant and agreeable; since, as we have already seen, our obedience is then only approved by God when we obey willingly. But, inasmuch as the sluggishness of our flesh has need of spurring, threatenings are also added to inspire terror, and at any rate to extort what ought to have been spontaneously performed. It may seem indeed that it may thus be inferred that threats are absurdly misplaced when applied to produce obedience to the Law, which ought to be voluntary; for he who is compelled by fear will never love God; and this is the main point in the Law. But what I have already shewn, will in some measure avail to solve this difficulty, viz., that the Law is

deadly to transgressors, because it holds them tight under that condemnation from which they would wish to be released by vain presumptions; whilst threats are also useful to the children of God for a different purpose, both that they may be prepared to fear God heartily before they are regenerate, and also that, after their regeneration, their corrupt affections may be daily subdued. For although they sincerely desire to devote themselves altogether to God, still they have to contend continually with the remainders of their flesh. Thus, then, although the direct object of threats is to alarm the reprobate, still they likewise apply to believers, for the purpose of stimulating their sluggishness, inasmuch as they are not yet thoroughly regenerate, but still burdened with the remainders of sin.

15. And if ye shall despise my statutes. This seems only to apply to ungodly and depraved apostates, who deliberately revolt from the service and worship of God: for if a person falls through infirmity, and offends from levity and inconsideration, he will not be said to have despised God's Law, or to have made void His covenant. And certainly it is probable that God designedly spoke of gross rebellion, which could not be extenuated under the pretense of error. Still it must be borne in mind that all transgressors, whether they have violated the Law in whole or in part, are brought under the curse. But God would remind His people betimes to what lengths those at last proceed who assume the liberty of sinning; and also from what source all transgressions arise. For, although every one who turns out of the right path into sin does not altogether repudiate or abominate the Law, yet all sins betray contempt of the Law, and tend to break the covenant of God. He justly, therefore, denounces them as covenant-breakers, and proud despisers, unless they obey His commandments: and, first, He threatens that He will destroy them with "terror, consumption," and other diseases; and then adds external calamities, such as scarcity of corn, violent invasions of enemies, and the plunder of their goods; of which it will be more convenient to speak more fully in expounding the passage in Deuteronomy.

18. And if ye will not yet for all this hearken. The gradation of punishments, which is here mentioned, shews that they are so tempered by God's kindness, that He only lightly chastises those whose stupidity or hardness of heart he has not yet proved; but when obstinacy in sin is superadded, the severity of the punishments is likewise increased; and justly so, because those who, being admonished, care not to repent, wage open war with God. Hence the more moderately He deals with us, the more attentive we ought to be to His corrections, in order that even the gentle strokes, which He in His kindness softens and tempers, may be enough. Paul says that hypocrites heap up to themselves a treasure of greater vengeance, if they take occasion from His forbearance to continue unmoved, (Romans 2:4, 5;) for those who do not repent, when admonished by light chastisements, are the less excusable. Wherefore let us give heed to that exhortation of David, that we "be not as the horse, or as the mule, which have no understanding, whose mouth must be held in with bit and bridle;" because "many sorrows shall be to the wicked." (Psalm 32:9, 10.) In sum, as soon as God has begun to put forth His hand to smite us, there is one remedy whereby He may be appeased, i e., teachableness. It would be more prudent of us to anticipate Him, and to return to Him of our own accord, though He should withhold punishment; but when we are smitten without profit, it is a sin of obstinate wickedness. He threatens, therefore, that

unless they repent when smitten with the ferule, He will use the rod to correct them. When He says, "I will punish you seven times more," He does not mean to define the number, but, according to the common phrase of Scripture, uses the number seven, by way of amplification. In the next verse He shews that there is a just cause for His becoming more severe, because they cannot be subdued except by violent means; for although the word [225], גאון geon, is not always used in a bad sense, still, in this passage, it signifies that they are disobedient, being puffed up to be proud by their power; for, as Moses says elsewhere, Israel "waxed fat, and kicked" against God, just as horses grow restive by being overfed. He therefore calls their obstinacy, wherein they became more hardened, although God spared them, "the pride of their power;" for prosperity begets security, in which stubborn men try their strength against the scourges of God.

21. And if ye walk. Translators give various renderings of the word [226],קרי keri. The Chaldee takes it to mean with hardness, as if it were their purpose to contend against God. Jerome renders it ex adverso mihi, (in opposition to me;) but, since the word signifies an accidental occurrence, or contingency, this sense has seemed to me much the most appropriate. To "walk at adventures" (fortuito) with God, therefore, is equivalent to passing by His judgments with their eyes shut; and even so to stupify themselves as to ascribe their adversities to fortune, and thus not to be humbled beneath His mighty hand; for hence arises unconquerable obstinacy, when the sinner imagines that whatever he suffers happens by chance. Therefore Jeremiah inveighs against the Jews in a severe reproof, because they supposed that evil and good did not proceed from the ordinance and decree of God, (Lamentations 3:38;) for hence is engendered brutal madness, so that wretched men rush with all their might to their own destruction. It will accord very well, then, that if men do not take heed to God's judgments, but rush onwards like furious beasts, His meeting with them will be, as it were, fortuitous, when He shall smite them indiscriminately, from right to left, high and low, as we say in French aller a tors et travers. This, therefore, the sinner at length obtains by his stupid obstinacy, that, overwhelmed by his manifold punishments, he sees no end to his troubles. Meanwhile there is no doubt but that Moses rebukes the iron obstinacy of the people, as David declares, that with the gentle God will be gentle, but that He will be stubborn, as it were, with the perverse. (Psalm 18:25, 26.) He finally points out the source of obstinacy, when the sinner is intoxicated by his stupidity into contempt for God, whilst he turns away from himself, as much as possible, the sense of His wrath. Let us learn, then, to withdraw our thoughts from vague speculations to the consideration of God's hand in all the punishments which He inflicts; because hence will arise acknowledgment of our guilt, which may lead to repentance. Else that will occur which Isaiah seems to have taken from this passage, that God's anger will never be turned away; but that, when we think that we are acquitted, His hand will be stretched out still. (Isaiah 9:12.)

25. And I will bring a sword upon you. There is no doubt but that He means the hostile swords of all the nations, whereby the Israelites were sorely afflicted; and teaches that whosoever should bring trouble and perplexity upon them were the just executioners of His vengeance; just as He constantly declares by the prophets that He was the Leader of the people's enemies, and that the Assyrians and Chaldeans both fought under Him. He calls the Assyrian His axe, and the rod of His anger which He wields in His hand, (Isaiah 10:15,

and 5;) and Nebuchadnezzar His hired soldier. He says that He will call the Egyptians with a hiss, and will arouse the Chaldeans by the sound of his trumpet. (Isaiah 7:20, 18, and elsewhere.) But since this point is sufficiently well known, there will be no occasion of further proofs. The sum is, that all wars are stirred by His command, and that the soldiers are armed at His will, and are strong in His strength. Hence it follows that He has innumerable forces by whose hand He may execute His vengeance whensoever He pleases. Afterwards, therefore, when the Israelites were harassed, and even cruelly oppressed by their enemies, God's truth was manifested in all those continual defeats; whilst, from His great severity, we may gather how gross was the perversity of their conduct.

26. And when I have broken the staff of your bread. By these words God implies, that although He should not punish them by the sterility of the land, still He was prepared with other means for destroying them by famine. We shall indeed see hereafter that, when God was wroth, the earth in a manner shut up her bowels so as to produce no food; and that the heaven also grew hard so as not to fertilize it with dew or rain. In a word, all unseasonableness of weather and infertility of soil is a sign of the curse of God; but now He goes further, viz., that although there should be no scarcity of food, still they should suffer from hunger, when He had taken away its nourishing qualities from their bread. This curse confirms the instruction which we have seen elsewhere, that man does not live by bread, but by [227] the command of God, just as if the efficacy contained in the bread proceeded out of His mouth. (Deuteronomy 8:3.) And assuredly an inanimate thing could not give rigor to our senses except by the secret ordinance of God. He employs a very appropriate comparison, calling the support of bread, whereby man's strength is refreshed, "the staff;" as we see the old and weak leaning on their sticks as they walk, when otherwise they would totter and fall. God says, then, that it is in His power to break this staff, so that their bread should only fill their stomachs without refreshing their strength. Ezekiel has borrowed from Moses this figure, which he makes use of in several places, (Ezekiel 4:16; 5:16; and 14:13,) although he there adverts to two sorts of punishment, like another Prophet, when He says, "Ye have sown much and bring in little; ye eat, but ye have not enough; ye drink, but ye are not filled with drink; ye clothe you, but there is none warm; and he that; earneth wages, earneth wages to put it into a bag with holes;" and again,

"Ye looked for much, and, lo, it came to little; and when ye brought it home, I did blow upon it;" (Haggai 1:6, 9;)

for he points out scarcity of food as one of God's scourges, and the inability to profit by their abundance, as another; and with this Micah also accords, for after he has said, "Thou shalt eat, but not be satisfied," he adds,

"Thou shalt sow, but thou shalt not reap; thou shalt tread the olives, but thou shalt not anoint thee with oil; and sweet wine, but shalt not drink wine." (Micah 6:14, 15.)

But Moses, in order that the curse may be more apparent, says that there shall be abundance of bread; and also that there shall be no deception practiced in kneading and baking it; for that two [228] women shall come to one oven together, who may mutually observe whether weight is duly given. He implies, therefore, that there shall be abundance in their hands, and yet, when they are filled, they shall not be satisfied.

29. And ye shall eat the flesh of your sons. This scourge is still more severe and terrible (than the others;) [229] yet we know that the Israelites were smitten with it more than once. This savage act would be incredible; but we gather from it how terrible it is to fall into the hands of God, when men, by adding crime to crime, cease not to provoke His wrath. Jeremiah [230] mentions this monstrous case among others: "The hands of the pitiful women have sodden their own children," and prepared them for food, (Lamentations 4:10;) and hence, not without cause, he mourns that this had not been done elsewhere, that women should devour the offspring which they themselves had brought up. (Lamentations 2:20.) And [231] the last siege of Jerusalem, which in the fullness of their crimes was, as it were, the final act of God's vengeance, reduced the wretched people who were then alive to such straits, that they commonly partook of this unholy food.

When He again declares that He "will cast their carcases upon those of their idols," He shews by the very nature of the punishment that their impiety would be manifest; for apostates take marvelous delight in their superstitions, until God openly appears as the avenger of His service. But that their idols should be cast into a common heap with the bones of the dead, was as if the finger of God pointed out His abomination of their false worship. And then, because their last resource was in sacrifices, He declares that they should be of no avail for atonement; for, in the expression, "savour of peace," [232] He embraces all the expiatory rites, by their confidence in which they were the more obstinate. Afterwards He threatens banishment as well as the desolation of the land; by which punishment He made it apparent that they were utterly renounced, as we shall again see a little further on.

34. Then shall the land enjoy her Sabbaths. In order that the observance of the Sabbath should be the more honored, God in a manner associated the land in it together with man; for whereas the land had rest every seventh year from sowing, and harvest, and all cultivation, He thus desired to stir up men more effectually to a greater reverence for the Sabbath. God now bitterly reproves the Israelites because they not only profane the Sabbath themselves, but do not even allow the land to enjoy its prescribed rest; for this repose of the seventh year did not hinder the land from continually groaning under a heavy burden as long as it nourished such ungodly inhabitants. He says, therefore, that the land was disturbed by ceaseless inquietude, and thus was deprived of its lawful Sabbaths, since it bore on its shoulders, as it were, and not without great distress, such impious despisers of God. Moreover, because the whole worship of God is sometimes included by synecdoche in the word Sabbath, (Jeremiah 17:21; Ezekiel 20:12,) He indirectly administers a sharp reproof to His people, because not only is He defrauded of His right by their impiety, but He cannot be duly honored in the Holy Land unless He expels them all from hence; as if He had said, that this was the only means that remained for the assertion of the honor due to His name, viz., that the land should be cleared of its inhabitants, and reduced to desolation; inasmuch as this extorted rest should be substituted in the room of the voluntary Sabbath.

39. And they that are left of you. This is another form of vengeance, that, although they may survive for a time, still they shall gradually pine away; and

this may be referred both to those who go into captivity, and to those who shall remain in the land. He had before threatened that they should be destroyed either by famine or sword; but now lest they should boast that they had escaped, if they had not perished by a violent death, He pronounces that they also should die a lingering death; and He also declares the manner of it, viz., that He will fill their hearts with trembling, so that they should fly when none pursued them, (as Solomon also says, Proverbs 28:1,) and fear at the sound of a falling leaf. Thus He signifies that the ungodly shall be no better off, although free from external troubles, because they are afflicted internally by hidden torments; for although their audacity may proceed even to madness, still it cannot be but that their evil conscience should smite them continually. Their forgetfulness of God may sometimes stupify them; nay, they may seek to shake off all feeling; but, after God has suffered them thus to become brutalized, He presently interrupts their lethargy, and hurries them on so that they are their own executioners. This passage shews us that, the more strait-hearted the wicked are in their contempt of God, the weaker they become, so as to tremble at their own shadow; and this condition is far more wretched than to be cut off at a single blow.

40. If they shall confess their iniquity. Although Moses has been discoursing of very severe and cruel punishments, still he declares that even in the midst of this awful severity God is to be appeased if only the people should repent, notwithstanding that they may have stripped themselves of all hope of pardon by their long-continued sins. For he does not address sinners in general, but those who by their obstinacy and brutal impetuosity have come nearer and nearer to the vengeance of God; and even these he encourages to a good hope, if only they be converted from their hearts. Let us be assured, then, that God's mercy is offered to the worst of men, who have been plunged by their guilt in the depths of despair, as though it reached even to hell itself. Whence, too, it follows, that all punishments are like spurs to rouse the inert and hesitating to repentance, whilst the sorer plagues are intended to break their hard hearts. Yet at the same time it must be observed that this favor is vouchsafed by special privilege to the Church of God; for Moses soon afterwards expressly assigns its cause, i e., that God will remember His covenant. Whence it is plain that God, out of regard to His gratuitous adoption, will be gracious to the unworthy whom He has elected; and whence also it comes to pass, that, provided we do not close the gate of hope against ourselves, God will still voluntarily come forward to reconcile us to Himself, if only we lay hold of the covenant from which we have fallen by our own guilt, like ship-wrecked sailors seizing a plank to carry them safe into port. But it will be well for us earnestly to examine the fruits of repentance which Moses here enumerates. In the first place stands confession, not such as is exacted under the Papacy, that wretched men should unburden themselves in the ear of a priest (sacrifici,) as if secretly disgorging their sins, but whereby they acknowledge themselves to be guilty before God. This confession stands contrasted both with the noisy complaints, and the subterfuges and evasions of the wicked. A memorable instance of it occurs in the case of David, who, when overwhelmed by the reproof of the Prophet Nathan, ingenuously confesses that he has sinned against God. (2 Samuel 12:13.) By the word "fathers" He magnifies the greatness of their sins, because for a long space of time they had not ceased to add sin to sin, as if the fathers had conspired with their children, and the children with their own

descendants; and, since God is a just avenger even to the third and fourth generation, it is not without reason that posterity is commanded humbly to pray that God would pardon the guilt contracted long ago. Hence also it is plainly seen how little the imitation of their fathers will avail to extenuate the faults of the children, since we perceive that it renders them less excusable, so far is God from admitting this silly plea. It is further added, that their confession should correspond with the greatness of their transgressions, and that it should not be trifling and perfunctory; for although hypocrites, when convicted, do not deny that they have sinned, still in confessing they extenuate their guilt, as if they were only guilty of venial offenses. God, therefore, would have the circumstances of their sins taken into account, and this also He prescribes with respect to their obstinacy, lest they should pretend that their punishments were not deservedly redoubled, because they had walked [233] at adventures with God.

Finally, in order to prove the reality of their conversion, all dissembling is excluded by the humbling of their hearts; for it is as if God would reject their prayers, until in sincere and heart-felt humility they should seek for pardon. This humiliation is contrasted with security as well as with contumacy and pride; and it is also compared with circumcision, where the heart is called uncircumcised before it is subdued and reduced to obedience. For, whereas circumcision was a mark of distinction between the people of God and heathen nations, it must needs have been also a sign of regeneration. [234] But since the Jews neglected the truth, and foolishly and improperly gloried only in the outward symbol, Moses, by reproving the uncircumcision of their hearts, refutes that empty boast. Thus, as Paul testifies, unless the Law be obeyed, literal circumcision is useless, and is made into uncircumcision. (Romans 2:25.) So Moses accuses the Israelites of unfaithfulness, because they profess to be God's holy people, whilst they cherish filthiness and uncleanness in their heart. The Prophets also often reproach them with being uncircumcised in heart, or in ears; and in this Stephen followed them. (Jeremiah 6:10; Ezekiel 44:7; Acts 7:51.)

Others elicit a very different meaning from the words [235] which we have translated, "let them atone (propitient) for their iniquity." The noun used is עָוֹן, gnevon, which means both iniquity and punishment; and the verb רָצָה, ratzah, which is to expiate, or to esteem grateful, or to appease. Some, therefore, explain it, they shall bear their punishment patiently, or esteem it pleasant; but it appears to me that Moses connects with repentance the desire of appeasing God, without which men are never really dissatisfied with themselves, or renounce their sins; and his allusion is to the sacrifices and legal ablutions, whereby they reconciled themselves to God. The sum is, that when they shall seriously endeavor to return to God's favor, He will be propitiated towards them on account of His covenant.

43. *The land also shall be left of them.* He again refers to the punishment of banishment, which is equivalent to their being disinherited; and at the same time repeats that the worship of God could not be restored in the Holy Land, until it should be purified from their defilements; yet immediately afterwards He moderates this severity, inasmuch as, when He seemed to deal with them most rigorously, He still will not utterly cast them off. The verbs He uses [236] are in the past tense, though they have reference to the future; as much as to say, even then "they shall feel that they are not rejected." He therefore stretches out His hand to them, as it were, in their miserable estate, to uplift them to

confidence, and commands them, although afflicted with the extremity of trouble, nevertheless to put their trust in His Covenant. Herein His marvelous and inestimable goodness is displayed, in still retaining as His own those who are alienated from Him: thus, it is said in Hosea, (2:23,) "I will say to them that are not my people, Thou art my people."

When He promises that He will remember His covenant "for their sakes," He does not mean for their merit, or because they have acquired such a favor for themselves; but for their profit or salvation, in that the recollection of the Covenant shall extend even to them. Their deliverance (from Egypt) is also added in confirmation of the Covenant, as though He had said that He would be the more disposed to forgive them, not only because He always perseveres in His faithfulness to His promises, but because He would maintain His goodness towards them, and carry it on even to the end. Thus we see He refers the cause of His mercy only to Himself.

Deuteronomy 28

Deuteronomy 28:15-68

15. But it shall come to pass, if thou wilt not hearken unto the voice of the Lord thy God, to observe to do all his commandments and his statutes, which I command thee this day, that all these curses shall come upon thee, and overtake thee.

15. Et erit, si non obedieris voci Jehovae Dei tui, ut custodias faciendo omnia praecepta ejus, et statuta ejus quae ego praecipio tibi hodie, venient super te onmes maledictiones istae, et apprehendent te.

16. Cursed shalt thou be in the city, and cursed shalt thou be in the field.

16. Maledictus eris in urbe, et maledictus in agro.

17. Cursed shall be thy basket and thy store.

17. Maledictum canistrum tuum, et conspersio tua.

18. Cursed shall be the fruit of thy body, and the fruit of thy land, the increase of thy kine, and the flocks of thy sheep.

18. Maledictus fructus ventris tui, et fructus terrae tuae, foetus boum tuorum, et greges ovium tuarum.

19. Cursed shalt thou be when thou comest in, and cursed shalt thou be when thou goest out.

19. Maledictus eris in ingressu, et maledictus in egressu.

20. The Lord shall send upon thee cursing, vexation, and rebuke, in all that thou settest thine hand unto for to do, until thou be destroyed, and until thou perish quickly; because of the wickedness of thy doings, whereby thou hast forsaken me.

20 Mittet Jehova in te maledictionem, contritionem, (vel, tumultum,) et perditionem, (vel, increpationem,) in omnibus ad quae applicueris manum tuam, et feceris: donec delearis, et pereas velociter, propter malitiam operum tuorum quibus dereliquisti me.

21. The Lord shall make the pestilence cleave unto thee, until he have consumed thee from off the land whither thou goest to possess it.

21. Adhaerere faciet Jehova tibi pestilentiam, donec consumat te de terra ad quam tu ingrederis ut possideas eam.

22. The Lord shall smite thee with a consumption, and with a fever, and with an inflammation, and with all extreme burning, and with the sword, and with blasting, and with mildew; and they shall pursue thee until thou perish.

22. Percutiet te Jehova phthisi, et febri, et ardore, et aestu, et gladio, et ariditate, et rubigine: et persequentur te donec pereas.

23. And thy heaven that is over thy head shall be brass, and the earth that is under thee shall be iron.

23. Eruntque coeli tui qui sunt supra caput tuam, aerei: et terra, quae est subter te, ferrea.

24. The Lord shall make the rain of thy land powder and dust: from heaven shall it come down upon thee, until thou be destroyed.

24. Dabit Jehova pluviam terrae tuae pulverem et cinerem: et e coelis descendet super te, donec disperdaris.

25. The Lord shall cause thee to be smitten before thine enemies: thou shalt go out one way against them, and flee seven ways before them; and shalt be removed into all the kingdoms of the earth.

25. Dabit te Jehova caesum coram inimicis tuis: per viam unam ingredieris ad illum, et per septem vias fugies coram eo: erisque in commotionem omnibus regnis terrae.

26. And thy carcase shall be meat unto all fowls of the air, and unto the beasts of the earth, and no man shall fray them away.

26. Erit praterea cadaver tuum esca omni volucri coeli et animali terrae, nec erit qui absterreat.

27. The Lord will smite thee with the botch of Egypt, and with the emerods, and with the scab, and with the itch, whereof thou canst not be healed.

27. Percutiet te Jehova ulcere Aegypti, et morbis ani, et scabie, et prurigine, quibus non possis curari.

28. The Lord shall smite thee with madness, and blindness, and astonishment of heart:

28. Percutiet te Jehova amentia et caecitate, et stupore cordis.

29. And thou shalt grope at noonday, as the blind gropeth in darkness, and thou shalt not prosper in thy ways; and thou shalt be only oppressed and spoiled evermore, and no man shall save thee

29. Palpabisque in meridie, quemadmodum palpat caecus in caligine, neque secundabis vias tuas: et eris tantummodo oppressus, et direptus omnibus diebus, nec erit servator.

30. Thou shalt betroth a wife, and another man shall lie with her: thou shalt build an house, and thou shalt not dwell therein: thou shalt plant a vineyard, and shalt not gather the grapes thereof.

30. Uxorem desponsabis, et vir alius dormiet cum ea: domum aedificabis, et non habitabis in ea: vineam plautabis, nec vindemiabis eam.

31. Thine ox shall be slain before thine eyes, and thou shalt not eat thereof: thine ass shall be violently taken away from before thy face, and shall not be restored to thee: thy sheep shall be given unto thine enemies, and thou shalt have none to rescue them

31. Bos tuus mactabitur in oculis tuis: et non comedes ex eo: asinus tuus rapietur a facie tua, nec revertetur ad te: pecudes tuae tradentur inimicis tuis, nec erit servatot.

32. Thy sons and thy daughters shall be given unto another people, and thine eyes shall look, and fail with longing for them all the day long; and there shall be no might in thine hand.

32. Filii tui et filiae tuae tradentur populo alteri, et oculi tui videbunt, ac deficient propter illos, tota die: nec erit fortitudo in manu tua.

33. The fruit of thy land, and all thy labors, shall a nation which thou knowest not eat up; and thou shalt be only oppressed and crushed alway:

33. Fructum terrae tuae, et omnem laborem tuum comedet populus quem non noveras: et eris tantummodo oppressus, et confractus omni tempore:

34. So that thou shalt be mad for the sight of thine eyes which thou shalt see.

34. Et obstupesces propter ea quae videbunt oculi tui.

35. The Lord shall smite thee in the knees, and in the legs, with a sore botch that cannot be healed, from the sole of thy foot unto the top of thy head.

35. Percutiet te Jehova ulcere pessimo in genibus et in coxis, ita ut non possis curari, a planta pedis tui usque ad verticem tuum.

36. The Lord shall bring thee, and thy king, which thou shalt set over thee, unto a nation which neither thou nor thy fathers have known; and there shalt thou serve other gods, wood and stone.

36. Abducet Jehova te et regem tuum quem constitues super te, ad gentem quam non nosti tu et patres tui: colesque ibi deos alienos, lignum et lapidem.

37. And thou shalt become an astonishment, a proverb, and a byword, among all nations whither the Lord shall lead thee.

37. Et eris in stuporem, et parabolam, et fabulam, omnibus populis ad quos deducet te Jehova.

38. Thou shalt carry much seed out into the field, and shalt gather but little in: for the locust shall consume it.

38. Semen multum educes ad agrum, et parum colliges: quia absumet illud locusta.

39. Thou shalt plant vineyards, and dress them, but shalt neither drink of the wine, nor gather the grapes: for the worms shall eat them.

39. Vineas plantabis, et coles: et vinum non bibes, neque colliges: quia devorabit illud vermis.

40. Thou shalt have olive-trees throughout all thy coasts, but thou shalt not anoint thyself with the oil: for thine olive shall cast his fruit

40. Olivae erunt tibi in omni termino tuo, at oleo non unges te, quia decidet oliva tua.

41. Thou shalt beget sons and daughters, but thou shalt not enjoy them: for they shall go into captivity.

41. Filios et filias generabis, et non erunt tibi: quia ibunt in captivitatem.

42. All thy trees, and fruit of thy land, shall the locust consume.

42. Omnem arborem tuam, et fructum terrae tuae absumet locusta.

43. The stranger that is within thee shall get up above thee very high, and thou shalt come down very low.

43. Peregrinus qui est in medio tui ascendet super to superne, superne: et tu descendes inferne, inferne.

44. He shall lend to thee, and thou shalt not lend to him: he shall be the head, and thou shalt be the tail.

44. Ipse mutuabit tibi, et tu non mutuabis ei: ipse erit in caput, et tu eris in caudam.

45. Moreover, all these curses shall come upon thee, and shall pursue thee, and overtake thee, till thou be destroyed; because thou hearkenedst not unto the voice of the Lord thy God, to keep his commandments and his statutes which he commanded thee.

45. Venient autem super te omnes maledictiones istae, teque persequentur, et apprehendent te, donec disperdaris: eo quod non obedieris voci Jehovae Dei tui, custodiendo praecepta ejus, et statuta ejus quae praecepit tibi.

46. And they shall be upon thee for a sign, and for a wonder, and upon thy seed for ever.

46. Et erunt in te in signum et in portentum, et in semine tuo usque in saeculum.

47. Because thou servedst not the Lord thy God with joyfulness, and with gladness of heart, for the abundance of all things;

47. Propterea quod non colueris Jehovam Deum tuum in laetitia, et in hilaritate cordis, propter abundantiam omnium rerum.

48. Therefore shalt thou serve thine enemies, which the Lord shall send against thee, in hunger, and in thirst, and in nakedness, and in want of all things: and he shall put a yoke of iron upon thy neck, until he have destroyed thee.

48. Et servies inimicis tuis quos immiserit Jehova contra te in fame, et siti, et nuditate, et penuria omnium rerum, ponetque jugum ferreum super collum tuum, donec disperdat te.

49. The Lord shall bring a nation against thee from far, from the end of the earth, as swift as the eagle flieth; a nation whose tongue thou shalt not understand;

49. Adducet Jehova adversum to gentem e longinquo, ab extremo terrae sicuti volat aquila, gentema cujus non intelliges linguam:

50. A nation of fierce countenance, which shall not regard the person of the old, nor shew favor to the young:

50. Gentem duram facie, quae non attollet faciem suam ad senem, nec puero parcet.

51. And he shall eat the fruit of thy cattle, and the fruit of thy land, until thou be destroyed: which also shall not leave thee either corn, wine, or oil, or the increase of thy kine, or flocks of thy sheep, until he have destroyed thee.

51. Et devorabit fructum jumenti tui, et fructum terrae tuae, donec disperdaris: non relinquet tibi frumentum, mustum, et oleum, foetus boum tuorum, nec greges ovium tuarum, donec perdat te.

52. And he shall besiege thee in all thy gates, until thy high and fenced walls come down, wherein thou trustedst, throughout all thy land; and he shall besiege thee in all thy gates, throughout all thy land, which the Lord thy God hath given thee.

52. Et obsidebit te in omnibus urbibus tuis, donec concidant muri tui excelsi et muniti, quibus tu confidis, in tota terra tua: obsidebit inquam te in omnibus urbibus tuis, in tota terra tua quam tibi dedit Jehova Deus tuus.

53. And thou shalt eat the fruit of thine own body, the flesh of thy sons and of thy daughters, which the Lord thy God hath given thee, in the siege, and in the straitness, wherewith thine enemies shall distress thee:

53. Et comedes fructum ventris tui, carnem filiorum tuorum et filiarum tuarum, quos dederit tibi Jehova Deus tuus, in obsidione, et coartatione qua coartabit te inimicus tuus.

54. So that the man that is tender among you, and very delicate, his eye shall be evil toward his brother, and toward the wife of his bosom, and toward the remnant of his children which he shall leave:

54. Viri teneri et delicati apud te valde, oculus invidebit fratri suo, et uxori sinus sui, et reliquis filiis suis, quos residuos fecerit,

55. So that he will not give to any of them of the flesh of his children whom he shall eat; because he hath nothing left him in the siege, and in the straitness, wherewith thine enemies shall distress thee in all thy gates.

55. Ne det illis de carne filiorum suorum quos comedet: eo quod nihil ei relictum fuerit in obsidione, et coartatione qua coartabit te inimicus tuus in omnibus urbibus tuis.

56. The tender and delicate woman among you, which would not adventure to set the sole of her foot upon the ground for delicateness and tenderness, her eye shall be evil toward the husband of her bosom, and toward her son, and toward her daughter,

56. Tenerae apud te et delicatae, quae non tentavit plantam pedis sui firmare super terram, prae deliciis et teneritudine, invidebit oculus viro sinus sui, filio et filiae suae.

57. And toward her young one that cometh out from between her feet, and toward her children which she shall bear: for she shall eat them for want of all things secretly in the siege and straitness, wherewith thine enemy shall distress thee in thy gates.

57. Dum secundinas suas quae egressae fuerint e pedibus suis, et filios suos quos pepererit, comedet clam prae egestate omnium rerum in obsidione, et coartatione qua coartabit te inimicus tuus in urbibus tuis.

58. If thou wilt not observe to do all the words of this law that are written in this book, that thou mayest fear this glorious and fearful name, The Lord thy God;

58. Nisi custodieris ut facias omnia verba Legis hujus quae scripta sunt in hoc libro, ad timendum nomen gloriosum istud et terribile, Jehovam Deum tuum:

59. Then the Lord will make thy plagues wonderful, and the plagues of thy seed, even great plagues, and of long continuance, and sore sicknesses, and of long continuance.

59. Admirabiles reddet Jehova plagas tuas, et plagas seminis tui, plagas magnas et certas, (vel, constantes,) et morbos malos et certos, (vel, constantes.)

60. Moreover, he will bring upon thee all the diseases of Egypt, which thou wast afraid of; and they shall cleave unto thee:

60. Convertesque in teomnes morbos Aegypti, a quibus timuisti tibi, et adhaerebunt tibi.

61. Also every sickness, and every plague, which is not written in the book of this law, them will the Lord bring upon thee, until thou be destroyed.

61. Omnem morbum, et omnem plagam quae non est scripta in libro Legis hujus, inducet Jehova super te, donec tu perdaris.

62. And ye shall be left few in number, whereas ye were as the stars of heaven for multitude; because thou wouldest not obey the voice of the Lord thy God.

62. Et relinquemini pauci numero pro eo quod eratis sicut stellae coeli in multitudinem: quia non obedisti voci Jehovae Dei tui.

63. And it shall come to pass, that, as the Lord rejoiced over you to do you good, and to multiply you; so the Lord will rejoice over you to destroy you, and to bring you to nought: and ye shall be plucked from off the land whither thou goest to possess it.

63. Et erit praeterea, quemadmodum laetatus est Jehova super vos benefaciendo vobis, et multiplicando vos: sic laetabitur Jehova super vos, perdendo et delendo vos: evelleminique e terra ad quam ingredimini ut possideatis eam.

64. And the Lord shall scatter thee among all people, from the one end of the earth even unto the other; and there thou shalt serve other gods, which neither thou nor thy fathers have known, even wood and stone.

64. Et disperget to Jehova in omnes populos, ab uno extremo terrae usque ad alterum extremum terrae, colesque ibi deos alienos quos non nosti tu, neque patres tui, lignum et lapidem.

65. And among these nations shalt thou find no ease, neither shall the sole of thy foot have rest: but the Lord shall give thee there a trembling heart, and failing of eyes, and sorrow of mind:

65. Neque in gentibus ipsis requiesces, neque erit requies plantae pedis tui: dabit item illic Jehova tibi cor pavidum, et defectum oculorum, et moerorem animi.

66. And thy life shall hang in doubt before thee; and thou shalt fear day and night, and shalt have none assurance of thy life:

66. Et erit vita tua suspensa tibi e regione, ac pavebis nocte et die, neque credes vitae tuae.

67. In the morning thou shalt say, Would God it were even! and at even thou shalt say, Would God it were morning! for the fear of thine heart wherewith thou shalt fear, and for the sight of thine eyes which thou shalt see.

67. Mane dices, Quis dabit vesperam? et in vespera dices, Quis dabit mane? prae pavore cordis tui quo pavebis, et prae visione oculorum tuorum quam videbis.

68. And the Lord shall bring thee into Egypt again with ships, by the way whereof I spake unto thee, Thou shalt see it no more again: and there ye shall be sold unto your enemies for bond-men and bond-women, and no man shall buy you

68. Reducetque te Jehova in Aegyptum navibus per viam de qua dixi tibi, Non addes adhuc ut videas illam: et vendetis vos illic inimicis vestris in servos et in ancillas: et non erit qui emat.

15. But it shall come to pass, if thou wilt not hearken. This list of curses is longer than the previous one which was proclaimed from Mount Sinai, undoubtedly because the Spirit of God foresaw that the sluggishness of the people had need of sharper stimulants. If they had been only moderately teachable, what they had already heard would have been even more than sufficient to alarm them; but now God redoubles His threatenings against them

in their inertness and forgetfulness, that they might not only be compelled to fear, but also aroused by constant reminding. For this reason, He declares that they should be "cursed in the city and in the field," i e., at home and abroad, in the house or out of the house; and again, that their food should be cursed in the seed and in the meal. Afterwards, He enumerates three kinds of fruit in which they should be cursed, viz., their own offspring, the produce of the soil, and the young of their animals; for all these Scripture embraces in the word fruit, as sufficiently appears from this passage.

19. Cursed shalt thou be when thou comest in. God here pronounces that all their undertakings should meet with ill success; for going out and coming in signifies their various actions, and the whole course of their life; and this is more clearly expressed in the next verse, where He denounces against them misfortune in all their affairs, in that God would confound and mar whatever they should undertake. The words [237] מהומה, mehumah, and מגערת, migegnereth, are indeed variously explained. Still the sum comes to this, that God would be against them, so as to discomfit and overthrow all their counsels and labors. Hence we are taught that all men's endeavors are useless and vain, unless they seek for success from God.

21. The Lord shall make the pestilence cleave unto thee. He now proceeds to diseases which are as it were the lictors of God; and finally, His executioners, if men pertinaciously continue in their ungodliness. He does not, therefore, merely declare that He will send the pestilence, but that He will cause it to cleave to them, and when it shall have once laid hold of them, that it shall be impossible to remove it. It might also be translated, The Lord shall cause that the pestilence should seize thee; but with the same meaning, viz., that the pestilence should be fixed, or glued (agglutinatam) upon them, until it should consume them in the Holy Land itself. He adds phthisis, or consumption, which disease emaciates the body, and gradually exhausts its juices. It is superfluous to speak particularly of the other diseases, only let us learn that, whilst the multitude of diseases is almost innumerable, they are all so many ministers (satellites) prepared to execute God's vengeance. It is true, indeed, that diseases are contracted in various ways, and especially by intemperance; still, this does not prevent God from smiting the transgressors of the Law with them, although no natural cause may be apparent. He adds war, which He designates by the name of "the sword," but of this curse He will soon speak more fully.

He then unfolds in more distinct detail what He had before adverted to with respect to the curse on the produce of the land. And, first, He names two blights of the corn, which destroy it just as it is ripening, and snatch the bread, as it were, out of men's mouths; for dryness [238] is not here used for all want of moisture in the soil, but for that emptying of the ears, which is caused by the east wind. Mildew occurs from the sudden heat of the sun, if it strikes upon the corn when moistened with cold dew. Now, although these evils arise from natural causes, still God, the Author of nature, in His supreme power, so controls the atmosphere, that its unwholesomeness is His undoubted scourge.[239]

23. And thy heaven that is over thy head. He enumerates other causes of barrenness, and especially drought. Often does God by the Prophets, desirous of giving a token of His favor towards the people, promise them the rain of autumn and of spring: the one immediately following the sowing, the other giving growth to the fruits before they begin to ripen; whilst in many passages He also threatens that it should be withheld. To this refers what He now says,

that the heavens shall be of brass, and the earth of iron, because neither shall the moisture descend from heaven to fertilize the earth, whilst the earth, bound up and hardened, shall have no juice or dampness in order to production. Whence we gather, that not even a drop of rain falls to the earth except distilled by God, and that whenever it rains, the earth is irrigated as if by His hand. It must, however, be observed, as we have seen before, that the land of Canaan was not like Egypt, which was watered by the care and industry of man, but fertilized by the bounty of heaven. Thus God, by the Prophet, marks the degrees which are worthy of observation, viz., that when He is reconciled to His people, He will "hear the heavens, and they shall hear the earth; and the earth shall hear the corn, and the wine, and the oil;" so that, finally, all these things shall hear starving men. [240] (Hosea 2:21, 22.)

It is not superfluous that He should expressly speak of the "heaven over our head," and the earth that is "under our feet," for He thus indicates that His weapons are prepared both above and below to execute His vengeance, so as to assail the people on all sides. Another Prophet confirms this, although only in a brief allusion:

"Therefore the heaven over you is stayed from dew, and the earth is stayed from her fruit; and I called for a drought," etc. (Haggai 1:10, 11.)

Another mode of expression is then used to make the same thing more sure, viz., that the rain should be turned into "powder and dust;" still this clause may be explained in two ways, either that the rain shall no more fertilize the ground than as if it were ashes; or that, instead of rain, dust should fall, as though God would dry up the rich soil by scattering ashes on it.

25. The Lord shall cause thee to be smitten before thine enemies. What He had briefly threatened in His mention of "the sword," He now more fully pursues, that they should be given up to the will of their enemies, so as to be indiscriminately slaughtered. We have previously seen that those who execute punishment on the transgressors of the Law, are stirred up and armed by the just judgment of God; Moses does not now touch on that point, but merely declares that the enemies of the people should be their conquerors, should cruelly entreat them and pursue them in their flight. Moreover, in order that God's judgment might be more conspicuous, He says, that when they have gone out to battle by one way, i e., with their army in regular order, they should return by seven ways, because, in the confusion of their flight, they should be dispersed in all directions. Hence we gather that the bravery of men is in God's power, so that He can make cowards of the boldest whenever He so pleases. And we must bear in mind what we shall see elsewhere, "How should one chase a thousand, and two put ten thousand to flight, except God had sold them and had shut them up" under their hand? (Deuteronomy 32:30.) And for this reason God calls Himself the God of hosts, in order that believers may live securely under His guardianship; whilst the wicked, and the despisers of the Law, should dread the slightest motion when He is wroth with them.

What follows, that they should be "for [241] a removing in all the kingdoms of the earth," some take to mean that they should be a laughing-stock; because we usually shake or move our heads by way of insult; but others explain it, that they should be wanderers and vagabonds in unknown places of exile. The first exposition is the one I prefer. In Ezekiel [242] (23:46,) it is used for a tumultuous rout; nor am I indisposed to understand it in this way, that whatever nations shall assail them, they should be shaken by their slightest attacks.

26. And thy carcase shall be meat. The punishment is here doubled by the disgrace which is added to death; for it is ignominious to be deprived of burial, and justly reckoned amongst the curses of God; whilst it is a sign of His paternal favor that we should be distinguished from the brutes, inasmuch as the rites of burial arouse us to the hope of resurrection and everlasting life. Wherefore, on the contrary, God deprives of burial those whom He curses. But as we have said that punishments affecting the body are common to the pious and the reprobate, so also we must think of being deprived of sepulture, since it sometimes happens that the reprobate are honorably buried, as Christ relates of the luxurious Dives, (Luke 16:22,) whilst the bodies of the pious are ignominiously cast a prey for birds and beasts; as the Prophet complains in Psalm 79:2. Still such an interchange does not prevent God from avenging the contempt of His Law by this mode of punishment, as by pestilence, famine, or sword.

27. The Lord will smite thee with the botch of Egypt. Whether you understand this passage of the extraordinary plagues which God inflicted on the Egyptians at the time of His people's deliverance, or of the ordinary diseases which had before prevailed among them, though the latter is more probable, still Moses signifies, that whilst the Egyptians were smitten with these plagues, God's people escaped them, in order that this distinction might more clearly represent His favor. For it could not happen naturally that in the same place the diseases, from which the Israelites were free, should afflict the Egyptians alone. God therefore threatens, that if they should despise His Law, He would deal with them as they had seen Him deal with heathen nations. And assuredly, since God then chose to multiply His people miraculously, it can be by no means doubted but that He wonderfully privileged them by the bestowment of health and rigor. It is doubtful whether by diseases of the fundament He signifies hemorrhoids or prolapsus, or some other secret disease, such as that which attacked the Philistines when they captured the ark of the covenant. (1 Samuel 5:6.) He subjoins other diseases, in which there appear special marks of God's wrath; for although they sometimes affect the children of God also, still I have shewn elsewhere that the same punishments are so dealt out to them respectively, that they widely differ from each other. When Job was smitten with terrible ulcers, so as to become corrupt, he seemed for a time to present the marks of a reprobate person; but what in that holy man was an exercise of patience, is in the transgressors of the Law the just reward of their crimes by the curse of God.

28. The Lord shall smite thee with madness and blindness. This punishment is very often referred to by the Prophets, when God is said to smite the wicked with a spirit [243] of giddiness and madness, to make them drunk with astonishment. Now, whatever God declares respecting this blindness or fury of mind, has a wide application; for hence it arises that the wicked rush willfully into vile lusts, shudder at no crime, are hurried headlong to destruction, are utterly deprived of discretion, throw away the remedies which are in their hands; and although [244] the carnal sense is not greatly disturbed by this form of vengeance, still it is much more severe and awful than any bodily disease. The Poets imagined that wicked men were agitated and terrified by the furies, because experience taught them that it was not without a secret impulse from

God that they became so senseless, when, their minds being affected, they were like beasts in the shape of men. Even heathens, then, perceived that when the wicked are given over to a reprobate mind, God thus manifests Himself as the just Avenger of their crimes. And so it is in all cases of "astonishment;" for it is plain that those who are thus stupified by their miseries, are prostrated by the hand of God.

30. *Thou shalt betroth a wife, and another man.* He here denounces that all they possessed should be rifled and plundered by their enemies. He, however, puts the most painful thing of all in the first place, viz., that they shall be despoiled of their wives, and magnifies the enormity of the evil, by saying, that not only shall the wife be torn from her husband's bosom, but that the betrothed virgin shall be defiled. The same denunciation is extended to their houses and vineyards. It is grievous indeed to see the fruit of our labors seized on by our enemies before we have been permitted to enjoy them; since the frustration of our hope does not slightly increase our pain. He then passes on to their flocks and their herds: then to their children, and in their case heightens the calamity, in that their sons and their daughters should be taken from them in their very sight, so that their eyes should fail with grief, and their hands, as if dead, should be unable to afford them assistance. For two reasons He says that the robbers, who shall strip them of everything, should be unknown to them; both because they might expect less consideration and kindness from strangers and barbarians than from neighbors; and also that the Jews might be alarmed by this threat, so as not to suppose that they only had to deal with neighboring nations; inasmuch as it was in God's power to fetch nations from afar. Finally, He adds that there shall be no end to their affliction, until the magnitude of their calamities [245] shall stupify them.

35. *The Lord shall smite thee in the knees.* Since death is common to the whole human race, they must needs also be all subject to disease; nor is it a matter of surprise that the whole posterity of Adam, which is infected with the taint of sin, should so be liable to many afflictions, which are the wages of sin. But, since the offenses of all are not alike, God also maintains a just proportion in the execution of His various punishments; thus, in this passage He does not speak only of common maladies, but of those whereby He openly shews His vengeance against the transgressors of the Law; of which sort are incurable diseases.

36. *The Lord shall bring thee, and thy king.* The fulfillment of this prophecy at length taught the Jews, though too late, that it was no empty threat, merely for the purpose of frightening them; and this also applies to the other predictions. For, on account of the great distance from them, the Jews would never have supposed that the Assyrians and Chaldeans were God's scourges, as they actually found them to be; because they placed no faith in the words of Moses. Much less credible was it to them that the king, whom they had appointed, should be dragged as a prisoner to distant countries. And surely this was a very sad and formidable punishment, since all their safety depended on the stability of their kingly government. Thus Jeremiah magnifies this evil above all others, that the Christ of God, who was the breath of the Church, and under whose shadow they hoped to be everywhere safe, should be taken. [246] (Lamentations 4:20.) And this was fulfilled in the case of Jeconiah, as well as in that of Jehoiachin and Zedekiah. Let us, therefore, learn not to measure God's judgments by our own reason, but to tremble at them, although they are

hidden from us. All aggravation of their captivity is also added, i e., that they should be oppressed by such tyranny as to be compelled to serve wood and stone. Dull and stupid as they were, still they ought to have retained their abomination of such gross wickedness. Hence it might be gathered that they would not be reduced to such a necessity except by the terrible vengeance of God. For although they had been attracted by the superstitions of the Gentiles, so as eagerly to run after them, still, after they were deprived of the worship of God, and had undergone the yoke of the wretched and ungodly servitude which was imposed on them, the foulness of idolatry must have been more fully understood. There is also an antithesis implied in these words, viz., that because they had refused to submit themselves to the true God, and to obey His Law, they should become the slaves of idols.

37. And thou shalt become an astonishment. The climax of their miseries is here added, that they should be so far from receiving consolation from men, that on every side their misery should meet with taunts and insults; for nothing more bitterly wounds the wretched than this indignity of being harassed by reproaches and sarcasms; and thus to be a laughing-stock and byword to all nations, is a dreadful infliction. Again, there is an implied antithesis between the ignominy to which God condemns His ungrateful people, and the extraordinary dignity with which He had honored them, so that they should be illustrious before the whole world. Hence the Prophets have often imitated this mode of expression; I will not quote the instances of it which everywhere occur.

38. Thou shalt carry much seed out into the field. He again makes mention of the scarcity of wine, of wheat, and all sorts of corn; but He assigns different causes for it. He proclaims that the harvest shall be scanty, notwithstanding an abundant sowing, because the locust shall consume the seed; that the vintage shall be poor, nay, almost nothing, because the worms shall devour the bunches; that the oil produced should be little, because the olives should wither on the trees and fall of themselves. Thus He admonishes them that He has at hand innumerable ministers (satellites) wherewith to destroy by famine the transgressors of His Law. Thus, whenever we see beetles, and locusts, and other insects attacking the fruits, we should remember that God, as it were, puts forth His arm to take away the food which He had given: thus Joel reminds us, that when the locust eats that which the palmer-worm hath left, and another insect that which the locust hath left, the curse of God is sufficiently conspicuous. [247] (Joel 1:4.) Philosophers discover the reason why more of these little creatures are generated in one year than another; but we must remember the teaching of Moses, that they never trouble us except by God's command. For if we were submissive to God, as we ought to be, such a prodigy would never happen as that vile and filthy insects should devour the fruits of the earth which He Himself has provided for the sustenance of His children.

43. The stranger that is within thee shall get up above thee. This also was no doubtful mark of God's wrath, that the sojourners who dwelt in the land of Canaan by sufferance should in a manner become its masters; for we know how those who are in debt are under the power of their creditors. In fact, what Solomon says is found to be true, that

"the rich ruleth over the poor, and the borrower is servant to the lender." (Proverbs 22:7.)

The Israelites, therefore, must have felt that God was contrary to them, when they were suppliants to their own guests, especially since He had promised that He would so enrich them that they should lend to others. This revolution of affairs, then, plainly convinced them of their iniquities. Meanwhile, it must be observed that poverty as well as wealth is in God's hands, and that whilst the latter is a proof of God's favour the former is reckoned amongst His curses; still, however, in such a manner that God often chastises His own children with want, or proves and exercises their patience without ceasing to be their Father, whilst he bestows abundance upon the reprobate, wherewith they may gorge themselves to their own destruction. God's blessing, however, shines forth in the elect, as far as it is expedient for them; nor is it said in vain in the Psalm, "Wealth and riches are in the house (of the just,") in order that he may lend and be bountiful. (Psalm 112:3.)

45. Moreover, all these curses shall come upon thee. He not only confirms what he has already said, but takes away all hope of alleviation, since God's scourges shall not cease until they have repented. He declares that all the curses shall come upon them; for although they are not always congregated into a single band, still it is true that God pays the wages of the transgressors of His Law with this multitude of miseries which Moses has recounted. By the word pursue, he takes away all hope of escape, whilst to overtake is equivalent to laying hold of them tenaciously, till, as it is further said, they be destroyed. The sum is, that the ungodly by their subterfuges only bring it to pass that they accumulate upon themselves heavier punishments, which will never cease to afflict them until they are destroyed by them. For this reason, he says that they shall be "for a sign and a wonder," i e., that they shall awaken astonishment in all men; for those who are but little moved by the common and ordinary judgments of God, are compelled, whether they will or no, to give attention to these prodigies. Thus, notable punishments, and such as are worthy of special observation, are "for a sign and a wonder."

Their ingratitude is also reproved as well as their contempt of the Law, because they served not God "with joyfulness and gladness of heart," when He had been so abundantly generous to them; for it is the fault of a corrupt and malignant nature, that it should not be possible to bring it to serve God joyfully, when He invites us by His liberality. But Moses takes it for granted that, since God will prevent the Israelites with His favor, before He proceeds to inflict punishments upon them, they will be guilty of this brutal sin, not to allow themselves to be liberally sustained by Him.

49. The Lord shall bring a nation against them from far. He enforces the same threatenings in different words, viz., that unknown and barbarous enemies should come, who shall attack them with great impetuosity and violence. And still further to aggravate their cruelty, He says that their language shall be a strange one; for, when there can be no oral communication, there is no room for entreaties, which sometimes awaken the most savage to mercy. But Jeremiah shews that this was fulfilled in the case of the Chaldeans;

"Lo, I will bring a nation upon you from far, O house of Israel; it is a mighty nation, a nation whose language thou howest not, neither understandest what they say." (Jeremiah 5:15.)

On the other hand, when Isaiah promises them deliverance, he mentions this among the chief of their blessings, that the Jews should "not see a fierce people," that they should not hear

"a people of deeper speech than they could perceive, of a stammering tongue [248] *that they could not understand."* (Isaiah 33:19.)

For, as I have elsewhere said, the Prophets were careful to take their form of expression from Moses, lest the Jews should, according to their custom, proudly despise the threats which God had interwoven with His Law.

Lest the distance of their countries should lull them into security, He says that they should be like eagles in swiftness, so as suddenly to overwhelm them, just as God often compares the ministers of His wrath to the whirlwind and the storm. Jeremiah has also imitated this similitude, where he declares that the slaughter which the Jews in their false imagination had supposed to be far away from them, should come suddenly upon them. (Jeremiah 4:13.)

Moses adds, that this nation shall be "strong of face, [249] which shall not regard the person of the old, nor shew favor to the young," whereby he signifies their extreme ferocity. I have already expounded what follows respecting their rapine and plunder.

52. And he shall besiege thee in thy gates. He overthrows every ground of false confidence. The number of their towns inspired them with courage, because they never would have supposed that their enemies would undergo so much fatigue as not to cease from fighting till they were all taken. He therefore includes all their towns, in reliance upon whose multitude they despised hostile aggression. He adds, that in vain they trust in their high and fortified walls, which will be either overthrown by military engines, or shall voluntarily surrender from the length of their besiegal; for the passage may be explained in both ways, either that the enemies shall overthrow and lay prostrate all their fortresses, or that by their perseverance they shall pass over the walls however high. It seems to me that the length of the siege as well as their valiant fighting is indicated. The repetition which follows magnifies the evil, viz., that they shall be thus sorely pressed in their own land given them by God; for the very associations of the place only increased the indignity.

53. And thou shalt eat the fruit of thine own body. This is one of those portents which was mentioned a little while ago; for it is an act of ferocity detestable and more than tragical, that fathers and mothers should eat their own offspring, so great love of which is naturally implanted in every heart, that parents often forget themselves in their anxiety for their children; and many have not hesitated to die to insure their safety. Nay, when the brute animals so carefully cherish their young, what can be more disgusting or abominable than that men should cease to care for their own blood? But this is the most monstrous of all atrocities, when fathers and mothers devour the offspring which they have procreated, and yet this threat by no means failed of its fulfillment, as we have elsewhere seen. We ought then to be the more alarmed when we see that God thus terribly punished the sins of those whom He had deigned to choose for His own. Still, it was not without very just cause that this wrath was so greatly kindled against the Jews who had left no kind of iniquity undone, so that their wickedness was altogether intolerable. Never, then, must it be forgotten that those of the household of the Church to whom God's truth is

revealed, are on that account the less excusable, because they knowingly and willfully provoke His wrath, whilst their continued perseverance in sin is altogether unworthy of pardon. The monstrous brutality of the act is heightened, when He says that men, in other respects tender and accustomed to delicacies, should be so savage through hunger that they shall refuse to give a share of this horrible food to their wives and surviving children; as also Jeremiah expressly says, the pitiful women shall be so maddened by hunger as to cook their own children. (Lamentations 4:10.) What follows as to the after-birth is still more horrible, for thus they call the membrane by which the foetus is covered in the womb, with all its excrements. That they should dress for food a filthy skin, the very look of which is disgusting, plainly demonstrates the awfulness of God's vengeance.

58. If thou wilt not observe to do all the words of this law. Inasmuch as even believers, although they are disposed to a willing obedience to the Law, and earnestly apply themselves to it, are still impeded and withheld by the infirmity of their flesh from fulfilling their duty, care and attention is here demanded of them; for "to observe (custodire) to do" is equivalent to giving sedulous and diligent heed. Now, God declares that, unless the Israelites thoroughly devote themselves to the keeping of the Law, vengeance is prepared for their neglect. It is indeed a harsh and severe threat whereby transgression in any respect is without remission; for perfect obedience is required by the words, "to do all the words that are written in the Law." But it is necessary that we should bear in mind what I have already shewn, that Moses was thus severe in his exactions, in order that the people, being convinced of their condemnation, should betake themselves to the mercy of God; for no one longs after Christ, unless he first abandons all confidence in his works, and rests all his hope of salvation in gratuitous pardon. The curse here recorded so awaits the transgressors of the Law, that, whilst God pardons His children, He at the same time sometimes chastises them, and executes upon the reprobate the vengeance they deserve. The fountain-head of obedience is indicated when it is said, "that thou mayest fear the Lord;" for all virtues are but smoke, which do not spring from the fear of God. Moreover, in order that their contempt may be without excuse, God's name is called "glorious and fearful;" for it is a mark of gross stupidity, when God's majesty and glory are openly set before us, not to be affected with becoming reverence so as to humble ourselves before Him. He, however, threatens something more terrible than before, when he says that the plagues shall be wonderful not only on the parents but on their children and descendants; instead of which some construe it, [250] He shall increase in a wonderful manner; and others, He shall separate; but this is too constrained and obscure. The word פלא, phela, signifies to be wonderful, or secret and hidden: thus, in my opinion, he means extraordinary and incredible modes of vengeance which shall surpass the comprehension of the human mind. He puts plagues and sicknesses in apposition with each other, as explaining by the latter of what nature the plagues shall be; unless, perhaps, it may be rather thought that the species is appended to the genus, which seems to be more probable. Further, he calls the plagues veritable, or faithful; either because they shall certainly occur, or because they shall continue to the end; for the Hebrew word [251], נאמנית neumanoth, is explained in both ways; and undoubtedly it sometimes signifies veracious, or what does not deceive, sometimes firm and stable, or perpetual;

and this sense appears to me to suit it best here, so that continued duration should be added to the greatness of the plagues.

He again mentions "the diseases of Egypt," not those which they had themselves suffered in Egypt, but those under which they had seen the Egyptians laboring. He says, therefore, that the severity of God against unbelievers, of which they had been spectators, should fall upon their own heads, if they should be followers of their ungodliness; for it was natural that they should tremble at the judgments of God, whereof they had been eye-witnesses; and not only so, but at which they had trembled for fear.

61. Also every sickness and every plague. This passage confirms what I have said about the plague and the sickness, for the sickness stands first as the species, and then the plague follows, which has a wider meaning, and comprehends all the curses in itself. Still, after he has enumerated so many forms of punishment, he declares that God is armed with yet other weapons to smite them; and assuredly as His blessings are endless and innumerable, so also His power is incomprehensible for avenging the contempt of His Law. Posterity has experienced, and we also even now partly perceive how true these threatenings were; for, as the obstinacy of men has burst forth and exalted itself more and more, so new and unheard of punishments have abounded from God, like a deluge.

62. And ye shall be left few in number. Since it had been promised to Abraham that his seed should be like the stars of heaven in multitude, it was a signal token of God's wrath that his posterity should be reduced [252] to so small a number; thus the comparison which is here made for the purpose of heightening their calamity, must not simply be referred to the "multitude" or great band, and the "fewness in number," but must be extended to the promise, the truth of which had been clearly manifested; so that, on the other hand, they might perceive that their former populousness could only have been put an end to, like waters dried up by the excessive heat of the sun, through the wrath of God.

63. And it shall come to pass, that as the Lord rejoiced over you. The wonderful and inestimable love of God towards His people is here set forth, via, that He had rejoiced in heaping blessings upon them; wherefore their depravity was all the more base and intolerable, in that God, though voluntarily disposed to be bountiful, was obliged by it to lay aside His affection for them. But although it is only by a metaphor that God is said to rejoice in destroying the wicked, yet it is not without good reason that this expression is applied to him; that we may know that He can no more fail to be the defender of His Law, and the Avenger of its contempt, than deny Himself. He complains, indeed, by Isaiah, (10:24) that He is unwillingly forced to punish the Jews; but these two things are quite consistent, that He rejoices in His just judgment, and at the same time is mindful of His clemency and indulgence, so that He would rather pardon, if the wickedness of men would allow Him. But this expression of Moses, that God receives consolation from punishing the wicked, constantly occurs in the Prophets.

64. And the Lord shall scatter thee among all people. At the end of the preceding verse, he had threatened them with banishment, which was far more painful to the people of Israel than to other nations. Inasmuch as affection for our country is natural to all, it is disagreeable to be away from it; but the condition of the Israelitish people was peculiar, for to them the inheritance of Canaan was promised them by God, and they could not be expelled from it

without being renounced by their heavenly Father. But he now proceeds a second and third step further; for he adds to banishment a miserable scattering, and to scattering, trembling and wanderings full of disquietude. For, if they had been expelled all together into any one corner of the world, their banishment would have been more tolerable from their very association with each other. Their calamity is, therefore, augmented when the storm of God's wrath scatters them hither and thither like chaff, so that they should be dispersed, and dwell in widely different countries. Another kind of servitude, which I have elsewhere noticed, is incidentally added, i e., that He would enslave them not only to men, but to idols also. The third step is their want of rest, for there was to be no fixed abode for them in their captivity; and this is far the most wretched state of all, to serve tyrannical conquerors as captives, and to have no certain master. Still it was a most just reward of the people's ingratitude, that they should nowhere find a fixed resting-place, because they had rejected the rest offered them by God, as we read in Isaiah (28:12.) He, however, extends the evil, bitter as it was in itself, still further, for they were not only to be compelled to wander in confusion, and immediately to pass onwards, but, wheresoever they should come, inward perturbation of mind was to follow them as their inseparable companion. Now, it is more sad to be agitated within with secret fear, than to be oppressed by external violence; for believers, although they too may be unsettled and tossed by many troublesome waves, still repose with tranquil minds on God; whilst the wicked, however they may desire to lull themselves in security, are nevertheless always without true peace; and if, for a while, they sink into lethargy, are still soon compelled to arouse themselves by God whether they will or not. Surely as the repose of a well-regulated mind is a signal mark of God's favor, so a constant and irremediable fear, such as is here referred to, is one of His terrible punishments.

Since the fear of spiritual punishments but lightly affects ungodly men, Moses magnifies in many words what the Israelites would else have carelessly passed over. Especially he points out what dreadful torments of anxiety would affect the wicked, when he says that their life should hang in suspense, as it were, before their eyes, so that they should fear day and night. An amusing device is related of Dionysius, [253] who commanded an exquisite supper, supplied with every delicacy, to be prepared for a courtly flatterer by whom his happiness had been lauded; he placed him in his own seat, so [254] that he might feast pleasantly, but ordered a sword to be suspended by a thread so as to overhang his head, insomuch that he who had pronounced the tyrant to be happy, when he saw that death was so near him every moment, did not dare to taste either of meat or drink. Dionysius, therefore, confessed, and not without shame to himself, that he and all other tyrants, whilst they are formidable to others, are tormented by perpetual fear. Now, this same disquietude is common to all the despisers of God; for the more wantonly they rage in forgetfulness of His fear, the more deservedly they dread their own shadow. Besides, when we look around us and see by how many forms of death our lives are beset, it cannot be but that innumerable anxieties should naturally possess us; how, then, can the wicked help being harassed by miserable and perplexing doubts when they perceive themselves to be shut out from the protection of God, and exposed to so many evils? Tranquillity of mind, therefore, can only arise from having God as our Keeper, and from resting under His protection.

By the words, "the sight of thine eyes," I have no doubt but that Moses designates those spectres [255] and bug-bears whereby death is set before the eyes of the reprobate.

68. And the Lord shall bring thee into Egypt again with ships. We know that the people were so driven about in the desert amidst divers perils, that they only escaped from it in safety by extraordinary miracles. It was therefore a thing most highly to be desired by their posterity, that they should never be carried back into those mighty depths. He who had once rescued them from those deaths might indeed often be their deliverer; but in order to make His blessing at that time more memorable, He had provided that they should never return into that wilderness. To bring them back into it again, was, then, in a manner to blot out the grace of redemption. If any object that it was impossible that the people should be conveyed in ships through dry places, the reply is easy, that since mention is made of the captivity, there is no absurdity in their being carried in ships and landed on the shore which [256] belongs to the plain of Moab, so as to finish their journey by wandering through the desert on foot.

Finally, he shews how melancholy their condition would be, since they would desire to sell themselves to their enemies, and would find none to buy them on account of their vileness.

Deuteronomy 4

Deuteronomy 4:25-31

25. When thou shalt beget children, and children's children, and ye shall have remained long in the land, and shall corrupt yourselves, and make a graven image, or the likeness of any thing, and shall do evil in the sight of the Lord thy God, to provoke him to anger;

25. Quum genueris filios et nepotes, et senueritis in terra illa, corruperitis autem vos, et feceritis sculptile, imaginem cujuscunque rei atque feceritis malum in oculis Jehovae Dei vestri, irritando illum,

26. I call heaven and earth to witness against you this day, that ye shall soon utterly perish from off the land whereunto ye go over Jordan to possess it; ye shall not prolong your days upon it, but shall utterly be destroyed.

26. Testor contra vos hodie coelum et terram, quod pereundo peribitis cito e terra ad quam pergendo transituri estis Jordanem, ut possideatis eam: non protrahetis dies in ea: quia disperdendo disperdemini.

27. And the Lord shall scatter you among the nations, and ye shall be left few in number among the heathen, whither the Lord shall lead you.

27. Ac disperget vos Jehova inter populos, et relinquemini homines pauci numero in gentibus ad quas deducet vos Jehova.

28. And there ye shall serve gods, the work of men's hands, wood and stone, which neither see, nor hear, nor eat, nor smell.

28. Servietisque ibi diis, operi manuum hominum, ligno et lapidi, quae non vident, nec audiunt, nec comedunt, nec odorantur.

29. But if from thence thou shalt seek the Lord thy God, thou shalt find him, if thou seek him with all thy heart, and with all thy soul.

29. Quod si requisieris inde Jehovam Deum tuum, tum invenies, si requisieris eum toto corde tuo, et tota anima tua.

30. When thou art in tribulation, and all these things are come upon thee, even in the latter days, if thou turn to the Lord thy God, and shalt be obedient unto his voice;

30. Quum fuerit tibi angustia, invenerintque te omnia ista, in novissimis diebus si reversus fueris ad Jehovam Deum tuum, et parueris voci ejus:

31. (For the Lord thy God is a merciful God;) he will not forsake thee, neither destroy thee, nor forget the covenant of thy fathers, which he sware unto them.

31. (Quia Deus misericors est Jehova Deus tuus) non derelinquet te, neque disperdet te, neque oblivisectur pacti patrum tuorum de quo juravit illis.

25. When thou shalt beget children, and children's children. Although at the outset he only adverts to idolatry, yet, inasmuch as he thence takes occasion to inveigh generally against the transgressors of the Law, and denounces punishment against them, I have thought it advisable to introduce this passage amongst the Sanctions (of the Law.) He had already strictly forbidden them to turn aside to idols; he now requires this instruction to be handed down to their grand-children and their whole race; as though he had said, that they must continue faithfully in the pure worship of God, not only lest they should deprive themselves of entering the land of Canaan, but also lest, after having long enjoyed quiet possession of it, they should be expelled from it. For long possession might have hardened their minds in security and arrogance, as if they had no change to fear. Lest, therefore, as time should pass away, they should trust that they were firmly established, and advance to greater license, he now reminds them that the punishment which he had already taught them to await themselves, would also be extended to their descendants; since it was no less easy for God to drive their [257] distant posterity from their quiet nest, than it would have been for Him to prevent their taking possession of it. But although he is treating of idols, still he addresses them on the subject of the curse, which overhangs all despisers of God. And, in order that the threat may affect them more deeply, he calls on "heaven and earth to witness;" as though he had said, that even things inanimate and without reason were in a manner conscious of the vengeance of God. Their opinion [258] is a poor one who think that angels and men are thus designated by a metonymy; for we shall see a little further on that the same form of expression is repeated. And when he says in his song, (Deuteronomy 32:1,) "Give ear, O ye heavens, and I will speak; and hear, O earth," it is to signify by hyperbole that his address is worthy of being listened to by all creatures. Thus Isaiah, the more to shame the Jews, who had become stupified in their folly, addresses his words to the heavens and earth. (Isaiah 1:2.)

When he calls heaven and earth to witness God's vengeance, it is as much as to say, that it will as clearly appear as the heaven and earth appear before our eyes; and after he has said that they shall perish, he also declares in what manner, viz., that God would scatter them hither and thither, and reduce them to a small number. What follows might seem absurd, inasmuch as it ought not to be reckoned among their punishments that they should serve idols among strangers, whereas they had already worshipped them of their own accord in their own land; but this difficulty is easily solved, and in two ways, either that banishment was a just reward to them in order that there they might indulge to their full these impure dispositions; and thus there will be an antithesis between the nations of the heathen and the Holy Land, as though God had said that He would not; suffer them to profane the latter by their superstitions; or else, that then, the veil being as it were removed, they should be ashamed when they should be compelled to serve dead idols. Nor can it be questioned but that then they were wounded in spirit by the same disgusting practices in which they had before taken pleasure; and I (See ante on Deuteronomy 28:36, [28]p. 254.) have stated elsewhere that I prefer this latter sense. Meanwhile, he reproaches them for their stupidity in adoring [259] dead images, formed of corruptible things, and the work of men's hands.

29. But if from thence thou shalt seek the Lord. In this passage also he exhorts and encourages them in the confidence of obtaining pardon, and thus anticipates them, so that they might not be overwhelmed with sorrow when smitten by God's hand; for despair awakens such rage in the wretched that they cannot submit themselves to God. He sets before them, then, another object in their punishments, that they may not cease to taste of God's goodness in the midst of their afflictions, whereby He invites them to repentance. For the sinner will never set about seeking God, unless he deems Him to be accessible to prayer. Moreover, he warns them to return truly and sincerely to a sound mind, because they will gain nothing by false profession. We know that nothing is more common than to make complaint to God whenever we are oppressed with troubles, but, when they are at all intermitted, immediately to return to our natural state. Sincere conversion is, therefore, prescribed; for "all the heart" is precisely equivalent to an upright heart, (integrum,) which is contrasted with a double or feigned one; and this must be noted, [260] lest a sense of our infirmity should disturb us; for, since it is not possible for men to give themselves wholly to God, the knowledge of their own inability is apt to induce listlessness; whereas, provided we do not deal deceitfully, it is declared that our penitence is approved by God.

30. When thou art in tribulation. He here shews the advantage of punishments, on the ground of their usefulness and profit; for what the Apostle says is confirmed by experience, that

"no chastening for the present seemeth to be joyous, but grievous; nevertheless afterward it yieldeth the peaceable fruit of righteousness to them that are exercised thereby." (Hebrews 12:11.)

Lest, therefore, they should be provoked to wrath by God's stripes, he reminds them of their usefulness to them, because they would never turn to God unless aided by this remedy. He tells them that, after they shall have been afflicted by the curses of God, if they sought after Him, they should find Him: and further, he gives them grounds for hope both in God's nature and in His covenant. He assures them that God will be willing to be appeased, because He is by nature merciful; but he adds another confirmation of this, which is more certain and familiar, viz., because God had adopted them by a perpetual covenant.

Deuteronomy 29

Deuteronomy 29:10-28

10. Ye stand this day all of you before the Lord your God; your captains of your tribes, your elders, and your officers, with all the men of Israel,

10. Vos adstatis hodie omnes vos eoram Jehova Deo vestro, principes vestri tribuum vestrarum, seniores vestri, et praefecti vestri, omnes viri Israel:

11. Your little ones, your wives, and thy stranger that is in thy camp, from the hewer of thy wood unto the drawer of thy water;

11. Parvuli vestri, uxores vestrae, et peregrini tui qui habitant in medio castrorum tuorum, a caesore lignorum tuorum usque ad haurientem aquas tuas:

12. That thou shouldest enter into covenant with the Lord thy God, and into his oath, which the Lord thy God maketh with thee this day;

12. Ut transeas in pactum Jehovae Dei tui, et in jusjurandum ejus quod Jehova Deus tuus pangit tecum hodie:

13. That he may establish thee today for a people unto himself, and that he may be unto thee a God, as he hath said unto thee, and as he hath sworn unto thy fathers, to Abraham, to Isaac, and to Jacob.

13. Ut statuat te hodie sibi in populum, et ipse sit tibi in Deum, quemadmodum loquutus est tibi, et quemadmodum juravit patribus tuis, Abraham, Isaac, et Jacob.

14. Neither with you only do I make this covenant and this oath;

14. Neque vobiscum solis pango pactum istud, et jusjurandum istud.

15. But with him that standeth here with us this day before the Lord our God, and also with him that is not here with us this day:

15. Sed cum eo qui est hic nobiscum stans hodie coram Jehova Deo nostro, et cum eo qui non est hic nobiscum hodie.

16. (For ye know how we have dwelt in the land of Egypt, and how we came through the nations which ye passed by;

16. Vos enim nostis quomodo habitavimus in terra Aegypti, et quomodo transivimus per medium gentium quas transistis:

17. And ye have seen their abominations, and their idols, wood and stone, silver and gold, which were among them:)

17. Et vidistis abominationes earum, et idola earum, lignum, et lapidem, argentum et aurum, quae sunt apud illas.

18. Lest there should be among you man, or woman, or family, or tribe, whose heart turneth away this day from the Lord our God, to go and serve the gods of these nations; lest there should be among you a root that beareth gall and wormwood;

18. Ne forte sit inter vos vir, aut mulier, aut familia, aut tribus, cujus cor avertat sese hodie a Jehova Deo vestro, et abeat ad colendum Deos gentium harum: ne forte sit in vobis radix fructificans venenum et absinthium.

19. And it come to pass, when he heareth the words of this curse, that he bless himself in his heart, saying, I shall have peace, though I walk in the imagination of mine heart, to add drunkenness to thirst:

19. Sitque quum ipse audierit verba maledictionis hujus, ut benedicat sibi in corde suo, dicendo, Pax erit mihi, etiamsi in cogitatione cordis mei ambulavero: ut addat ebriam sitienti.

20. The Lord will not spare him; but then the anger of the Lord and his jealousy shall smoke against that man, and all the curses that are written in this book shall lie upon him, and the Lord shall blot out his name from under heaven.

20. Non placebit Jehovae parcere illi, sed tunc fumabit furor Jehovae, et zelus ejus in eum virum: et recubabit in eo omnis maledictio quae scripta est in libro isto, et delebit Jehova nomen ejus de sub coelo.

21. And the Lord shall separate him unto evil out of all the tribes of Israel, according to all the curses of the covenant that are written in this book of the law.

21. Et separabit eum Jehova in malum ab universis tribubus Israelis, juxta omnes maledictiones pacti scripti in libro Legis hujus.

22. So that the generation to come of your children that shall rise up after you, and the stranger that shall come from a far land, shall say, when they see the plagues of that land, and the sicknesses which the Lord hath laid upon it;

22. Et dicet generatio postera, filii vestri qui surgent post vos, et alienigena qui veniet e terra longinqua, quum viderint plagas terrae hujus, et morbos quibus aegrotare fecerit Jehova in ea:

23. And that the whole land thereof is brimstone, and salt, and burning, that it is not sown, nor beareth, nor any grass groweth therein, like the overthrow of Sodom and Gomorrah, Admah and Zeboim, which the Lord overthrew in his anger, and in his wrath;

23. Sulphur, et sal, combustionem in toto solo ejus, ut non seratur, neque germinet, neque ascendat in ea ulla herba, ut in subversione Sodomiae, Gomorrhae, Admae, et Seboiim, quas subvertit Jehova in excandescentia sua et ira sua:

24. Even all nations shall say, Wherefore hath the Lord done thus unto this land? what meaneth the heat of this great anger?

24. Dicent, inquam, omnes gentes, Quare fecit sic Jehova terrae huic? quae est ira excandescentiae hujus magnae?

25. Then men shall say, Because they have forsaken the covenant of the Lord God of their fathers, which he made with them when he brought them forth out of the land of Egypt:

25. Et dicent, Eo quod dereliquerunt pactum Jehovae Dei patrum suorum, quod pepigit cum eis, quum educeret eos e terra Aegypti:

26. For they went and served other gods, and worshipped them, gods whom they knew not, and whom he had not given unto them:

26. Et abeuntes coluerunt deos alienos, incurvaveruntque se eis: deos, inquam, quos non noverant, et qui nihil impertiti fuerant illis:

27. And the anger of the Lord was kindled against this land, to bring upon it all the curses that are written in this book:

27. Et irata est excandescentia Jehovae in terram ipsam, ut induceret super eam omnem maledictionem scriptam in hoc libro:

28. And the Lord rooted them out of their land in anger, and in wrath, and in great indignation, and cast them into another land, as it is this day.

28. Extirpavitque eos Jehova e terra ipsorum in ira, et indignatione, et excandescentia magna, et projecit eos in terram aliam, sicut hodie.

10. Ye stand this day all of you before the Lord your God. Again does Moses, as God's appointed [261] representative, sanction the doctrine proclaimed by him by a solemn adjuration. With this design he says that the Israelites stood there not only to hear the voice of God, but to enter into covenant with Him, in order that they might apply themselves seriously, and with becoming reverence, to perform the promise they had given. Nor does he only address their chiefs, but, after having begun with the officers, the elders, and men, [262] he descends to the little children and the wives, in order that they might understand that their whole race, from the least to the greatest, were bound to keep the Law: nay, he adds all the strangers, who had devoted themselves to the service of the God of Israel, and states particularly that the very porters and lacqueys [263] were included in the covenant, in order that the minds of those, who derive their origin from the holy Patriarchs, should be more solemnly impressed. Moreover, in order that they may accept the covenant with greater reverence, he says that it was established with an oath. Now, if perjury between man and man is detestable, much less pardonable is it to belie that which you have promised God by his sacred name. Finally, he requires that the covenant should be reverenced, both on account of its advantages and its antiquity. Nothing was more advantageous for the Israelites than that they should be adopted by God as His people; this incomparable advantage, therefore, ought deservedly to render the covenant gratifying; and, besides the exceeding greatness of this blessing, God had prevented them by His grace many ages [264] before they were born.

It would have been, therefore, very disgraceful not to embrace eagerly and ardently so signal a pledge of his love. Nevertheless, the question here arises, how the little children could have passed into covenant, when they were not yet of a proper age to learn (its contents; [265]) the reply is easy, that, although they did not receive by faith the promised salvation, nor, on the other hand, renounce the flesh so as to dedicate themselves to God, still they were bound to God by the same obligations under which their parents laid themselves; for, since the grace was common to all, it was fitting that their consent to testify their gratitude should also be universal; so that when the children had come to age, they should more cheerfully endeavor after holiness, when they remembered that they had been already dedicated to God. For circumcision was a sign of their adoption from their mother's womb; and therefore, although they were not yet possessed of faith or understanding, God had a paternal power over them, because He had conferred upon them so great an honor. Thus, now-a-days, infants are initiated into the service of God, [266] whom they do not yet know, by baptism; because He marks them out as His own peculiar people, and claims them as His children when He ingrafts them into the body of Christ. Moses goes further, stating that their descendants were bound by the same covenant, as if already enthralled to God; and surely, since slavery passes on by inheritance, it ought not to appear absurd that the same right should be assigned to God which mortal men claim for themselves. What he says, then, is tantamount to reminding the Israelites that they covenanted with God in the name of their offspring, so as to devote both themselves and those belonging to them to His service.

16. For ye know how we have dwelt in the land of Egypt. We know how greatly men's minds are tickled by novelty; and this might occur to the Israelites when, upon entering the land of Canaan, they would see many forms of idolatry hitherto unknown, which would be so many snares to entangle them. Although, therefore, they were not as yet accustomed to such corruptions, he exhorts them to beware by former instances; for they were not ignorant that God had held in abomination the superstitions of Egypt, and also of other nations, which He had punished in terrible ways. Consequently Moses reminds them that there was no reason why the people should be carried away to imitate the rites of the Gentiles with which they were unacquainted, since they knew by extraordinary proofs that whatever imaginations had been invented by heathen nations were hateful to God. This argument, then, is drawn from experience, whereby the Israelites had been abundantly admonished, that they should hereafter beware of all delusions. But, when he passes from individual men and women to families and tribes, he indicates that those who are associated with others in sin, seek to excuse themselves in vain by their numbers; since a whole nation is as much to be condemned as a single person.

The conclusion of verse 18, "lest there should be among you a root," etc., seems to be tamely explained by some, [267] lest there should be venomous men, who should bring forth bitter fruits to God; for by the word root I rather understand the hidden principles of sins, which, unless they be prevented in good time, spring up with collected vigor and lift themselves on high; for indulgence in sin increases by concealment and connivance. And to this the author of the Epistle to the Hebrews seems to allude when he exhorts believers lest, through their negligence, "any root of bitterness, springing up, trouble them, and thereby many be defiled." (Hebrews 12:15.) As soon, therefore, as any one should endeavor to excite his brethren to worship false gods, God commands him to be plucked up, lest the poison should burst forth, and the bitter root should produce its natural fruits in the corruption of others. Wormwood [268] (absinthium) is here used, as often elsewhere, in a bad sense, on account of its unpleasant savour; unless perhaps it is some other herb, as is more probable.

19. And it come to pass when he heareth the words. He shews that it is not without reason that he has used so solemn and severe an adjuration; since nothing is more common than for men to flatter themselves, and by levity to evade the decision of God. He therefore repeats, that they are standing before God, who neither deceives, nor is deceived, nor even allows Himself to be thought lightly of; in order that they may tremble at His threats. Let the majesty of God, he says, be dreaded by you; so that none who despises Him, and wantons in his own lusts, should promise himself impunity. "To bless himself in his heart," is to hope in his secret imaginations that all will go well; as the hypocrites do, who, in their foolish self-adulation, applaud themselves deceitfully, lest they should hear God thundering. [269]

From this passage, therefore, let us learn that nothing is worse than to hope for peace, whilst we wage war with God; and to promise ourselves that He will let us alone, when we provoke Him by the impetuosity of our lusts.

The conclusion of the verse, "to add the drunken to the thirsty," is variously explained on account of its ambiguity. [270] I am ashamed to repeat the silly triflings of the Hebrew interpreters. To me it seems unquestionable that Moses, by a proverbial figure of speech, forbids us to excite the appetites of the flesh, already sufficiently heated, by new stimulants. As, therefore, they are said to add oil to the grate, who add more flames to a fire already lighted, [271] so they are said to add the drunken to the thirsty who seek provocatives of their audacity, in order to sin more freely; for lust in a man is like an insatiable dropsy; and if any one indulges in such intemperance, he adds the drunken to the thirsty, i e., the madness of his own folly to unrestrained desire. רויה, ravah, however, is, in my opinion, used actively, as elsewhere. In Psalm 23:5, it is said, "My cup רויה, revayah, runneth over;" and, in like manner, in Psalm 66:12, a well-watered land [272] is expressed by the same word, because it abundantly moistens the corn and grass. It is very appropriate that the desires of the flesh, that we burn with, should be compared to thirst; and the licentious impetuosity, which carries us away without reflection, to drunkenness; because the sinner stupifies himself into forgetfulness of the distinction between good and evil. And thence Paul calls those who are plunged in brutal forgetfulness of God and themselves, ἀπηλγηκότες (past feeling.) (Ephesians 4:19.)

20. The Lord will not spare him. Moses here teaches us that the obstinacy in which the wicked are willfully hardened, shuts against them the door of hope, so that they will find that God is not to be appeased. And assuredly it is the climax of all sins that a wretched man, who is abandoned to vice, should extinguish the light of his own reason, and destroy the image of God within him, so as to degenerate into a beast: and not only so, but also that he should dethrone God, as if He were not the Judge of the world. And this is the insult which they put upon Him who abandon themselves to sin in the confident expectation of impunity. [273] Thus, by Isaiah, God swears that this was an inexpiable crime, that, when He called them to baldness and to mourning, the Israelites encouraged each other to gladness; and, whilst feasting luxuriously, said in ridicule, "Tomorrow we shall die." (Isaiah 22:12, 13.) By the word, אבה, ahab, Moses altogether shuts out the grace of God. [274] Meanwhile he contrasts God's fixed purpose, -- that He will not be willing to pardon, -- with the depraved pleasures of those who take too much delight in their sins. Behold, then, what poor sinners gain by their proud contempt when they endeavor to cast off God's judgment together with His fear!

Further, in order the better to express that God will be irreconcilable to such great perversity, he declares that He will exterminate from the earth those who have so wantonly exulted in iniquity; and finally adds, that He will give them up to be accursed (in anathemata,) so that they shall no longer hold a place among the people of Israel. Now, it is a much more grievous thing to be cut off from the elect people, and to be set apart unto evil, as it is here said, than to be deprived of natural life.

22. So that the generation to come of your children. God enforces what we have already seen, that the punishments which He would inflict would be no ordinary ones, or such as should fall into contempt from their common use; but like portents, which should awaken astonishment among their posterity. For the question which is here put is such as refers to something extraordinary, and what is not easily comprehended. It is not, however, confined to the preceding clause, but refers to the whole list of curses; not as if each of them by itself had awakened such horror, but because, when heaped one upon another, they compelled all men to wonder, both on account of their number and their severity and duration, and thus were for a sign and a prodigy. For it everywhere occurs that men are afflicted with diseases, and barrenness for a single season is a common evil; but that sicknesses should cleave as it were to the marrow of a

whole people, and that the earth should be dried up as if it were burnt with sulphur, this is an awful spectacle, in which God's vengeance, which else would be incredible, manifestly appears; and therefore the cases of Sodom and Gomorrah are adduced, in whose destruction it might be seen what end awaits all the reprobate. [275] (Jude 7.) Now the Israelites always had their desolation before their eyes, from the time that they entered the land, in order that they might be warned by so terrible a judgment, and might tremble at it. It is also worthy of notice, that strangers are introduced making inquiry; in which words Moses signifies that this vengeance would be terrible even to heathen nations; and with this corresponds what we read in Jeremiah; "many nations shall pass by this city, and they shall say every man to his neighbor, Wherefore hath the Lord done thus unto this great city? Then they shall answer, Because they have forsaken the covenant of the Lord their God, and worshipped other gods, and served them." (Jeremiah 22:8, 9.) A similar divine menace is recorded in 1 Kings 9:8, 9; "And at this house," referring to the Temple brought to desolation, "every one that passeth by it shall be astonished and shall hiss; and they shall say, Why hath the Lord done thus to this house? And they shall answer, Because they forsook the Lord their God, and have taken hold upon other gods," etc. What we find further on is still more fearful; "Behold, I am bringing such evil upon Jerusalem and Judah, that whosoever heareth of it, both his ears shall tingle." (2 Kings 21:12.)

Moses amplifies the crime of their rebellion, when he says, that forsaking the God of their fathers, God their deliverer, God who had made a covenant with them, they had gone and served strange and unknown gods, from [276] whom they had received no benefits to induce them. For God had bound them to Himself for ever, both by His instruction [277] and the incomparable manifestation of His power; there could therefore be no pretense of ignorance, or mistake to excuse their defection from Him, and their prostitution of themselves to unknown idols.

In the meantime, let us learn from this passage anxiously to inquire who is the true God, and what is His will; because there is no true religion without knowledge; and again, if He convicted His ancient people of wicked ingratitude on account of their deliverance, that we also are now much more inexcusable, unless we constantly abide in the faith of our eternal Redeemer.

Deuteronomy 30

Deuteronomy 30:1-10, 15-20

1. And it shall come to pass, when all these things are come upon thee, the blessing and the curse, which I have set before thee, and thou shalt call them to mind among all the nations whither the Lord thy God hath driven thee,

1. Erit autem, quum evenerint tibi omnia verba haec, benedictio et maledictio quas proposui tibi, et reduxeris ad cor tuum in cunctis gentibus ad quas expulerit te Jehova Deus tuus:

2. And shalt return unto the Lord thy God, and shalt obey his voice, according to all that I command thee this day, thou and thy children, with all thine heart, and with all thy soul;

2. Et conversus fueris ad Jehovam Deum tuum, obedierisque voci ejus per omnia ut ego praecipio tibi hodie, tu et filii tui toto corde tuo, et tota anima tua:

3. That then the Lord thy God will turn thy captivity, and have compassion upon thee, and will return, and gather thee from all the nations whither the Lord thy God hath scattered thee.

3. Tunc reducet Jehova Deus tuus captivitatem tuam, et miserebitur tui: et conversus congregabit to de cunctis populis ad quos disperserit te Jehova Deus tuus.

4. If any of thine be driven out unto the outmost parts of heaven, from thence will the Lord thy God gather thee, and from thence will he fetch thee.

4. Si fuerit expulsus tuus in extremo coeli, illinc congregabit te Jehova Deus tuus, et illinc accipiet te:

5. And the Lord thy God will bring thee into the land which thy fathers possessed, and thou shalt possess it; and he will do thee good, and multiply thee above thy fathers.

5. Reducetque te Jehova Deus tuus ad terram quam possederant patres tui, ac possidebis eam: benefacietque tibi, et multiplicabit te magis quam patres tuos.

6. And the Lord thy God will circumcise thine heart, and the heart of thy seed, to love the Lord thy God with all thine heart, and with all thy soul, that thou mayest live.

6. Et circuncidet Jehova Deus tuus cor tuum, et cor seminis tui, ut diligas Jehovam Deum tuum toto corde tuo, et tota anima tua, propter vitam tuam.

7. And the Lord thy God will put all these curses upon thine enemies, and on them that hate thee, which persecuted thee.

7. Dabit autem Jehova Deus tuus omnes maledictiones istas super inimicos tuos, et super odio habentes te, et qui persequuti sunt te.

8. And thou shalt return, and obey the voice of the Lord, and do all his commandments, which I command thee this day.

8. Tu ergo revertaris, et obedias voci Jehovae, et fadas omnia praecepta ejus quae ego praecipio tibi hodie.

9. And the Lord thy God will make time plenteous in every work of thine hand, in the fruit of thy body, and in the fruit of thy cattle, and in the fruit of thy land, for good: for the Lord will again rejoice over thee for good, as he rejoiced over thy fathers;

9. Et abundare te faciat Jehova Deus tuus in omni opere manuum tuarum, in fructu ventris tui, et in fructu jumenti tui, et in fructu terrae tuae, in bonum: quoniam convertetur Jehova ut laetetur super te in bonum quemadmodum laetatus est super patres tuos:

10. If thou shalt hearken unto the voice of the Lord thy God, to keep his commandments and his statutes, which are written in this book of the law, and if thou turn unto the Lord thy God with all thine heart, and with all thy soul.

10. Si tamen obedieris voci Jehovae Dei tui, custodiendo praecepta ejus, et statuta ejus scripta in hoc libro Legis: quum conversus fueris ad Jehovam Deum tuum toto corde tuo, et tota anima tua.

15. See, I have set before thee this day life and good, and death and evil;

15. Vide, proposui tibi hodie vitam, et bonum, mortem et malum.

16. In that I command thee this day to love the Lord thy God, to walk in his ways, and to keep his commandments, and his statutes, and his judgments, that thou mayest live and multiply: and the Lord thy God shall bless thee in the land whither thou goest to possess it.

16. Quando ego praecipio tibi hodie ut diligas Jehovam Deum tuum, ut ambules in viis ejus, et custodias praecepta ejus et statuta ejus, et judicia ejus: ut vivas, et multipliceris, benedicatque tibi Jehova Deus tuus in terra ad quam ingrederis ut possideas eam.

17. But if thine heart turn away, so that thou wilt not hear, but shalt be drawn away, and worship other gods, and serve them;

17. Qued si averterit se cor tuum, et non audieris, et impulsus adoraveris Deos alienos, coluerisque eos:

18. I denounce unto you this day, that ye shall surely perish, and that ye shall not prolong your days upon the land whither thou passest over Jordan to go to possess it.

18. Denuntio vobis hodie, pereundo peribitis, non prorogabitis dies super terram ad quam transmisso Jordane pergis, ut possideas eam.

19. I call heaven and earth to record this day against you, that I have set before you life and death, blessing and cursing: therefore choose life, that both thou and thy seed may live;

19. Testor contra vos hodie coelum et terram, quod vitam et mortem proposui, benedictionem et maledictionem: deligas ergo vitam, ut vivas tu, et semen tuum.

20. That thou mayest love the Lord thy God, and that thou mayest obey his voice, and that thou mayest cleave unto him; (for he is thy life, and the length of thy days;) that thou mayest dwell in the land which the Lord sware unto thy fathers, to Abraham, to Isaac, and to Jacob, to give them.

20. Diligendo Jehovam Deum tuum, obediendo voci ejus, adhaerendo ei: ipse enim est vita tua, et longitudo dierum tuorum, ut habites super terram quam juravit Jehova patribus tuis, Abrahm, Isaac et Jacob se daturum illis.

1. And it shall come to pass, when all these things are come. He again confirms what we have elsewhere seen, that God never so severely afflicts His Church as not to be ready to return to mercy; nay, that by their punishments, however cruel in appearance, the afflicted, who were destroying themselves as if their hearts were bent upon it, are invited to repentance, so as to obtain pardon. Although, therefore, cause for despair is everywhere besetting them from the burning wrath of God, still he bids them take heart and be of good hope. Still, we must bear in mind what I have already shewn from the words of Moses, that reconciliation is not offered to all indiscriminately, but that this blessing exists by peculiar privilege in the Church alone; and this we gather also from the special promise, [278] I will visit their iniquities with the rod; nevertheless I will not take away my loving-kindness from them. Now, however, it must also be added, that this is not common to all who profess to be members of the Church, but only belongs [279] to the residue of the seed, and those whom Paul calls the remnant of grace, (Romans 11:5;) for it is no more profitable for the hypocrites, though they are mixed with believers, to be smitten with the scourges of God unto salvation, than it is for strangers.

Wherefore this promise is only addressed to a certain number, because it was always necessary that some people should remain as a residue, in order that God's covenant should stand firm and sure.

Still, Moses does not only enjoin the Israelites to profit by the corrections of God, but also to reflect upon His blessings whereby they might be led to serve Him with pleasure. For this comparison was of no slight avail in illustration of the judgments of God. [280] If the punishments alone had occupied their minds, their knowledge would have been but partial or more obscure; whereas, when on the one hand they considered that they had not served God in vain, and on the ether, that in forsaking Him they had fallen from the height of felicity into the deepest misery, it was easy for them to infer that whatever misfortunes they suffered were the fruit and reward of their ungodliness. Nor is it to be doubted but that, under the Law, God so adapted Himself to a tender and ignorant people, that the course of his blessings and curses was perfectly manifest; so that it was plainly shewn that they neither threw away their labor in keeping the Law, nor violated it with impunity. Often does He declare by the Prophets, that, as long as His children were obedient, He on His part would be their Father; that thence it might be more clearly perceived that the deterioration of their circumstances arose from His just indignation. Under this pretext, indeed, the wicked formerly endeavored to defend their superstitions; as, for instance, when in order to refute Jeremiah, they proudly boasted that it was well with them when they "burnt incense unto the frame of heaven;" [281] but such wanton depravity is admirably reproved by the Prophet, who shews that God had most manifestly avenged such pollutions by the destruction of their city and the fall of the Temple. (Jeremiah 44:17, 22.) The distinction, therefore, of which Moses now speaks, could not escape them, unless they willfully shut out the light. Moreover, because it rarely happens that men are wise in prosperity, he advises the Israelites to return to their senses, at any rate when sorely afflicted; for He addresses the exiles, who, disinherited by God, had no hope left; and promises them, that if, when banished to distant lands, they at length repented, God would be propitiated towards them. For "to [282] bring back to their heart" is equivalent to considering what before had been despised through contempt, or neglect, or stupidity, and buried as it were in voluntary oblivion. Still, lest they should presume on God's kindness, and only seek for pardon in a perfunctory manner, serious conversion is required, the results of which should appear in their life, since newness of life accompanies (genuine [283]) repentance. Nor does Moses speak only of the outward correction of the life, but demands sincere desires to obey, for we have elsewhere seen [284] that "all the heart" means with integrity of heart.

4. If any of thine be driven out. Since their dispersion into unknown countries might have altogether annihilated their hope of restoration, Moses anticipates this doubt, and teaches them that, although they might be driven out into the utmost regions of the earth, the infinite power of God sufficed to gather them from thence; as also it is said in Psalm 147:2,

"The Lord doth build up Jerusalem; he gathereth together the outcasts of Israel."

With this intent, the adverb "from thence" is twice repeated, lest they should imagine that the distance of place would be any impediment to the fulfillment of what God had promised.

We have seen elsewhere that it was not without reason that their dwelling in the land of Canaan was magnified as a peculiar blessing, because it behooved that, until the time of Christ's coming, the hope of an eternal inheritance should be cherished in their minds by an earthly and visible symbol.

6. And the Lord thy God will circumcise thine heart. This promise far surpasses all the others, and properly refers to the new Covenant, for thus it is interpreted by Jeremiah, who introduces God thus speaking, --

"Behold, the days come that I will make a new covenant with the house of Israel, and the house of Judah, not according to the covenant that I made with their fathers, which covenant they brake, but I will put my law in their inward parts, and write it in their hearts." (Jeremiah 31:31-33.)

Moses now declares the same thing in different words, that, lest the Israelites, according to their wonted instability, should fall back from time to time into new rebellions, a divine remedy was needed, i.e., that God should renew and mould their hearts. In short, he reminds them that this would be the chief advantage of their reconciliation, that God should endow them with the Spirit of regeneration. There is a metaphor in this word circumcise; for Moses alludes to the legal sign of consecration, whereby they were initiated into the service of God. The expression, therefore, is equivalent to his saying, God will create you spiritually to be new men, so that, cleansed from the filth of the flesh and the world, and separated from the unclean nations, you should serve Him in purity. Meanwhile, he shews that, whatever God offers us in the Sacraments, depends on the secret operation of His Spirit. Circumcision was then the Sacrament of repentance and renewal, as Baptism is now to us; but "the letter," as Paul calls it, (Romans 2:27,) was useless in itself, as also now many are baptized to no profit. So far, then, is God from resigning the grace of His Spirit to the Sacraments, that all their efficacy and utility is lodged in the Spirit alone.

Although Moses seems to make a division of the matter between men and God, so as to ascribe to them the beginning of repentance, and to make Him the author of perseverance (only, [285]) nevertheless this difficulty is easily solved; for according to the ordinary manner of Scripture, when he exhorts them to repentance, he is not teaching them that it is a gift of the Spirit, but simply reminding them of their duty. Meanwhile, the defenders of free-will foolishly conclude, that more is not required of men than they are able to perform; for in other places they are taught to ask of God whatever He enjoins. Thus, in this passage, Moses treats of the means of propitiating God, viz., by returning into the right way with an unfeigned heart; but, after he has testified that God will be gracious to them, he adds, that there is need of a better remedy, so that, being once restored by Him, they may be perpetual recipients of His grace. Still, it is not his intention to restrict the circumcision of the heart to the subsequent course of their lives, as if it depended on their own will and choice to circumcise themselves before God should work in them. And surely it is not at all more easy to rise when you have fallen, than to stand upright after God has set you up. I confess that perseverance is an excellent grace; but how shall the sinner, who is enthralled to Satan, free himself from those chains, unless God shall deliver him? Therefore, what Moses lays down as to the gift, of perseverance, applies no less to the commencement of conversion; but he only wishes to teach us that, although God should pardon our sins, that blessing would be but transient, unless He should keep us in subjection to His Law. And, in fact, He regenerates by His Spirit unto righteousness all those whose sins He pardons.

8. And thou shalt return [286] and obey the voice of the Lord. The copula which Moses here employs is equivalent to the illative particle; for he argues from their certainty of obtaining pardon, that they should not hesitate to return to God, nay, rather that they should set about it with a cheerful and ready mind; and then that they should constantly proceed in the course of obedience. But, when he now requires of the people the perseverance which he had just before declared to be given by God alone, we may at once infer that they deal foolishly who estimate the powers of man by the commands of God. Meanwhile, let us bear in mind this main point, that true conversion is proved by the constant tenor of the life; because we are redeemed, as Zecharias testifies, to this end that we should serve God, our Deliverer, "in holiness and righteousness all the days of our life." (Luke 1:74, 75.)

15. See, I have set before thee this day. A solemn injunction, similar to the foregoing ones, that the Israelites should consider how inestimable a blessing it was that God should have condescended to deposit His Law with them; and that if they did not receive it with reverence, the punishments for such foul ingratitude would be by no means light. For, in order to deprive them of the pretext of error, He separates them from the heathen nations, which through ignorance of the right way vacillated, as in uncertainty, between life and death. He says, therefore, that He has set before their eyes life, and that indeed connected with true and complete happiness; and likewise death with its consequences. Now, there is no one who, under the guidance of nature, would not seek for life and recoil from death; and thence Moses reproaches them with being more than senseless if they should plunge voluntarily into all miseries. Meanwhile, he signifies that he is not addressing to them mere idle menaces, but that his doctrine is armed with the power of God, so that whosoever should embrace it would find salvation in it, whilst none would despise it with impunity. The distribution of the two clauses then follows, viz., that the love of God and the keeping of His Law is prescribed that they may live; but if they turn away from it, their destruction is denounced. It is not, then, without reason that I have called the promises and threats the Sanctions of the Law, because, in order that its authority may be assured to us, it is necessary that both the recompence of obedience, and also the punishment of transgression, should be set before us. By the worship of other gods, he means every revolt from God, as I have observed already. He does not speak of their being "drawn away" to superstition as an excuse for their instability, but rather as an aggravation of their crime, inasmuch as they are carried away by their depraved desires, [287] and thus desert the truth of God when well acquainted with it.

19. I call heaven and earth to record this day against you. Though the verb is in the past tense, it indicates a present act. It is in order to deal with them with greater urgency that he calls heaven and earth to witness the vengeance of God. In these words he does not address men and angels, as some tamely expound it, but in amplification attributes sense to things inanimate. I pass this over briefly, because I have [288] treated it more fully before; as also what soon afterwards follows about life and death. For the Law, as respects its doctrine, contains in it life and death; for the reward of eternal life is not promised in it in

vain; but since no one is found worthy of the promised reward, Paul justly teaches that the Law ministers death. Still this is accidental, and proceeds not from any fault in the doctrine, but from the corruption of men. Nevertheless, it is asked how, if the corruption of our nature causes that the Law should engender nothing but death, Moses commands us to "choose life," which the sinner cannot attain to by it? Thence the Papists uplift their crests, both to extol free-will and to boast of merits; as if Moses did not also testify and proclaim the gratuitous mercy of God, and direct his disciples to Christ in order to seek salvation from Him. When, therefore, he speaks of keeping the Commandments, he does not exclude the two-fold grace of Christ, that believers, being regenerated by the Spirit, [289] should aspire to the obedience of righteousness, and at the same time should be reconciled freely to God through the forgiveness of their sins. And assuredly, since the same covenant is common to us and to the ancient people, it is not to be doubted but that they "chose life" who of old embraced the doctrine of Moses. At the same time, in so far as his legation was different from the Gospel, he rather insists on the office peculiarly entrusted to him, so that the distinction between Christ and himself might more clearly appear. This is the reason why he more sparingly touches upon justification by faith, whilst he enlarges fully on loving and serving God and fulfilling His Commandments.

Footnotes:

194. "Sur ceste paction, que Dieu en a faite;" but upon that agreement which God has made to give it. -- Fr. Bishop Davenant, after quoting William Archbishop of Paris, Aquinas, and Durandus, to the same effect, says, "To these may be added Scotus, Gregory, Occam, Gabriel, (Biel,) Alfonsus, and very many others of the better class of writers among the Romanists, who avowedly maintain that the works of the righteous, wrought by the assistance of grace, do not on that account acquire any intrinsic worthiness for life eternal; but that, as regards this reward, it depends entirely upon the gracious acceptance and promise of God." -- Disputatio de Justitia. Allport's Transl., vol. 2, p. 70.

195. "This some understand only of temporal life and prosperity in this world, Origen, Tostat. Oleaster, Vatablus; and make this to be the meaning, -- that, as the transgressors of the Law were to die, so they which kept it should preserve their life, Thom. Aquin. 1. 2. q. 100, a. 12; but I prefer rather Hesychius' judgment, -- Per quas oeterna vita hominibus datur," etc. -- Willet Hexapla, in loco. There appears to be unusual discrepancy on this point between the commentators, whether Romanist or Protestant. Bush and Holden apply it to temporal life. Bonar says, "If, as most think, we are to take, in this place, the words live in them,' as meaning eternal life to be got by them,' the scope of the passage is, that so excellent are God's laws, and every special minute detail of these laws, that if a man were to keep these always and perfectly, the very keeping would be eternal life to him. And the quotations in Romans 10:5, and Galatians 3:12, would seem to determine this to be the true and only sense here." C.'s view appears to be confirmed by our Lord's reply

in Matthew 19:17, referred to in Poole's Synopsis.

196. "Comme correspondantes." -- Fr. "It was also customary on some occasions to dance round the altars whilst they sung the sacred hymns, which consisted of three stanzas or parts; the first of which, called strophe, was sung in turning from east to west; the other, named antistrophe, in returning from west to east: then they stood before the altar and sung the epode, which was the last part of the song." -- Potter's Antiq. of Greece, Book II. chap. 4.

197. "The six nobler tribes answered amen to the blessings; the six more ignoble to the curses, viz., four who descended from the children of the hand-maids, i.e., Gad, Asher, Dan, and Naphtali, to whom Reuben is added, because he had defiled his father's bed incestuously; and Zebulun, because he was the youngest son of Leah. So Raban and Theod., q. 34." -- Corn. a Lapide, in loco.

198. "De six a six." -- Fr.

199. Added from Fr.

200. "Howbeit, though Moses appointed these to bless, yet he expresseth not the blessings; by such silence leading his prudent reader to look for them by another, which is Christ. John 1:17, Acts 3:26. For silence in the holy story often implieth great mysteries, as the Apostle (in Hebrews 7.) teacheth from the narration of Melchisedek, in Genesis 14." -- Ainsworth.

201. He assumes, what is scarcely tenable, that מקלה is derived from קלל rather than from קלה -- W

202. "Des hommes." -- Fr.

203. Added in Fr., "Plusieurs fois."

204. Added in Fr., "Disant que c'est luy qui commande apres Dieu;" saying that it is he who commands after God.

205. The Latin word used by C. is a legal one, ratihabitio, explained by Du Cange by "confirmatio, occurring more than once in the Digest, and in more modern writers." -- Adelung's Gloss. Man., in voce.

206. "Ebal and Gerizim are two closely adjoining mountains, separated by a narrow valley, about a furlong in breadth, in which stands the town of Naplous, the ancient Shechem. This beautiful valley, covered with olive woods and corn fields, has Mount Gerizim on the south, and Mount Ebal on the north. The two mountains are, according to Buckingham, nearly equal in altitude, neither of them exceeding seven or eight hundred feet above the level of the valley, but much more above the level of the sea, as the whole country here is considerably elevated." -- Illustrated Comment on Deuteronomy 27:4.

207. "Through him (Manes) Christianity was to be set free from all connection with Judaism." -- Neander's Church Hist., (Rose's Transl.,) vol. 2, p. 145. "The theological error which naturally and immediately flowed from these principles, (i.e., the principles of Dualism,) was the entire rejection of the authority of the Old Testament. In respect to this question, Manes was compelled by his adoption of the oriental philosophy to reject the theosophy of the Jews." -- Waddington's Hist. of the Church, vol. 1 p. 154.

208. "Comme Core, Dathan, et Abiram." -- Fr.

209. "This discussion, which would have been most useful at

any rate, has been rendered necessary by that monstrous miscreant Servetus, and some madmen of the sect of the Anabaptists, who think of the people of Israel as they would do of some herd of swine, absurdly imagining that the Lord gorged them with temporal blessings here, and gave them no hope of a blessed immortality." -- Institutes, B. 2. ch. 10. sect. 1. Cal. Soc. Trans., vol. 1, p. 501.

210. The oversight of ten for five here is scarcely worth noticing.

211. Literally, "I will turn myself to you."

212. This last sentence omitted in Fr.

213. See Margin A.V.

214. Added from Fr.

215. "Leur election." -- Fr.

216. "And all the people of the earth shall see that those are called by the name of the Lord." -- A.V. "And all peoples of the earth shall see that the name of Jehovah is called upon thee," i.e., "thou art called by his name." -- Ainsworth.

217. "Que nous demeurions assis, et lesjambes croissees comme des faineans;" that we should remain seated, with our legs crossed, like do-nothings. -- Fr.

218. See margin A.V., "Merciful, or bountiful in all his works."

219. No reference is here given in the original. The allusion might be to Jeremiah 12:3, or 51:40.

220. "Heb. And thou shalt know." -- Ainsworth. "Et scies." -- V.

221. See on Deuteronomy 5:9, 10, [24]vol. 2, p. 110, et seq.

222. Added in Fr., "Mais seulement que Dieu punira les delinquans;" but only that God will punish the transgressors.

223. The question is as to the word פניו, literally his or their face. The first explanation noticed by C., in their lifetime, is that of the Chaldee and Syriac versions, and also of the Hebrew Commentators; the second, in his anger, is attributed in Poole's Synopsis, amongst others, to S M. Dathe's translation is, "praesentissima pernicie;" and his note "mihi quidem videtur פנים dictum esse pro nomine reciproco ille, ipse, ut Exodus 33:15; Deuteronomy 4:37; 2 Samuel 17:11. Vide Noldius sub hac voce, num. 2. Latine non commode iisdem verbis exprimi potest. Igitur notionem, quae vocabulo Hebraeo subisse videtur, cum sequenti להאבידו conjunetim indicavi."

224. "Certain diseases, peculiar to Egypt, are meant; such as various diseases of the skin, as the scab, elephantiasis, plague, etc. Pliny, Nat. Hist., 26., calls Egypt the mother of such diseases. Even at the present day, there are in Egypt several peculiar diseases, especially ophthalmia, variolous diseases, and plague." -- Rosenmuller. Hengstenberg also, in his "Egypt and the Books of Moses," has an article on this subject, p. 454, confirmative of the above. He quotes Wagner as calling Egypt, in his Natural History of Man, "a great focus of the diseases in universal history."

225. "Applied to men, it signifies superior honor, virtue; excellency, lustre; or pride, arrogance, haughtiness." Taylor's Concordance, in voce, גאה

226. "Fortuito." -- Lat. A noun from קרה, to meet, to run against, to occur. It is not from S M. that C. has learnt what he here correctly

states, viz., that the Chaldee Paraphrast, or Onkelos in his Targum on the Pentateuch gives קשיו, hardness, as his interpretation of the word. -- W

227. "Mais de la parole sortant de la bouche de Dieu, comme s'il inspiroit au pain la faculte de nous sustenter;" but by the word proceeding out of the mouth of God, as if He inspired the bread with the power of supporting us. -- Fr.

228. C. is here at issue with the commentators in general. The usual view is that stated by Bush: "There shall be such a scarcity of bread that one ordinary oven shall answer for the baking of ten, that is a great many families; whereas in common circumstances one oven would serve (or rather be required) for one family." Dr. Kitto supposes that "ten families, represented by their females, clubbed their dough together, and the produce being no more than an ordinary supply for one family, it was baked in one oven instead of each family, as usual, making a separate baking. Afterwards the cakes thus baked were proportioned by weight to the respective contributors, so precious was the bread. This is implied in the words, shall deliver you your bread again by weight;' which shews that the bread was previously theirs, and had been baked for them, not that it was sold to them by weight."

229. Added from Fr.

230. "Jeremie recite que cest acte monstreux est advenu de son temps;" Jeremiah relates that this monstrous act occurred in his own times. -- Fr.

231. See Josephus' Jewish War, B. 7. c. 2.

232. "Savour of your sweet odours." -- A.V. "Odoris pacifici."

-- Lat. "D'odeur paisible, ou de repos." -- Fr.

233. "Fortuito." -- Lat. See ante on verse 21, [25]p. 234.

234. "Un Sacrament de regeneration." -- Fr.

235. "And they then accept the punishment of their iniqulty," verse 41,. -- A.V. Dathe appears to take C.'s view; "tunc luent peccatorum suorum culpam."

236. i.e., in verse 44, and are so translated in LXX., V., Chald., and Syriac, and also by Pagninus. See Poole's Synopsis, in loco.

237. מהומה, "Vexation." -- A V. "Bruising, trampling, destruction." -- Robertson, Clavis Pentateuchi. מגערת, "Rebuke." -- A V. "Reproach," from גער. -- W

238. "Ariditas." -- Lat. "Blasting." -- A.V.; "i.e., (says Ainsworth,) of corn and fruit with a dry wind, 2 Kings 19:26, for the original word signifieth dryness; and such was the east wind that blasted in those parts, Genesis 41:6. Therefore the Greek translateth it corruption with wind."

239. "Un certain signe de son ire;" a certain sign of His wrath. -- Fr.

240. See C. in loco. Calvin Society's edit., [26]vol. 1, p. 118.

241. See Margin, A.V. "In commotionem." -- Lat. The first exposition, approved by C., is that of S.M. and Malvenda, who refers to Psalm 21:8, and 44:15. See Poole's Synopsis in loco.

242. This reference is omitted altogether in Fr.

243. C gives no references here. It is probable that the passage, which he most had in his mind, was Isaiah 19:14, "The Lord hath mingled a perverse spirit;" in V., "Dominus miscuit in medio ejus spiritrum vertiginis, etc." His

own Commentary on these words is, "The expression is metaphorical, as if one were to mix wine in a cup, that the Lord thus intoxicates the wise men of this world so that they are stunned and amazed, and can neither think nor act aright." Calvin Soc. edit., [27]vol. 2, p. 64. He also might refer to Isaiah 51:17; Jeremiah 25:15; Psalm 60:3, etc.

244. "L'apprehension commune des hommes;" the ordinary apprehension of men. -- Fr.

245. Ver. 34. "Obstupesces." -- Lat. "Thou shalt be mad." -- A.V. The former is the rendering of Pagninus, the Samaritan text, and LXX.; the latter of Vatablus, Munster, Oleaster, Malvenda, and the Arabic Version. See Poole's Synopsis, in loco.

246. "The breath of our nostrils, the anointed of the Lord, was taken in their pits, of whom we said, Under his shadow we shall lie among the heathen." -- Lamentations 4:20.

247. "Que la main de Dieu est toute evidente;" that God's hand is quite evident. -- Fr.

248. "Cui lingua stridet absque intelligentia." -- Lat. "Lesquels grondent sans intelligence." -- Fr.

249. See margin, A.V.

250. So V. The translation, "He shall separate, or shall make distinct from all others, because they shall be greater and worse," is that of Oleaster, quoted in Poole's Synopsis.

251. Root אמן, amen; and here rendered by Taylor, fidoe, constantes

252. "A une pongnee de gens;" to a handful of people. -- Fr.

253. This well-known story of Dionysius of Syracuse and his courtier Damocles, is beautifully

told by Cicero. -- Tusc. Quoest. 5. 21.

254. "Pour reciter ceste felicite, qu'il avoit tant preschee;" to make a rehearsal of this felicity, which he had so greatly praised. -- Fr.

255. "Toutes illusions, fantasmes, et espouvantails, qui nous menacent de la mort;" all illusions, phantoms, and horrors, which threaten us with death. -- Fr.

256. There appears to be some oversight here. The Latin is "littus, quod planitiem Moah respicit;" and the Fr. sufficiently removes any difficulty which the latter word would present, by simply translating it "pour les jetter en la plaine de Moab;" i.e., to put them ashore on the plain of Moab. Now, the only shores of the plain of Moab would be formed by the Dead Sea, and this would, of course, be inapplicable in the circumstances referred to. The very impossibility of crossing the desert in ships, clearly proves that the word way must not be understood as indicating the line of route. Thus Holden paraphrases the words: "Thou shalt be taken there in ships, and not by the way in which I appeared and spake to thee;" and Dathe's translation is, "Navibus Jova vos deportari sinet in Aegyptum, quam terram nunquam a vobis revisendam dixerat." The wonderful fulfillment of the prophecy is thus well summed up by Dr. Kitto: "This was accomplished on several occasions. It is related both by Aristeas and Josephus, that in the time of Ptolemy Philadelphus, there were vast numbers of Hebrew slaves in Egypt, and that the king himself bought above 100,000 of them from their masters, and set them free. Egypt, indeed, was the great

slave-mart of ancient times; and several of the conquerors and oppressors of the Jews sent at least a portion of their captives thither to be sold. Titus had 90,000 captives after Jerusalem was taken. Those above seventeen years of age were sent to different parts of the Roman empire to labor on the public works, besides great numbers who perished in compulsory combats with wild beasts. Those under seventeen were doomed to be sold for slaves; but in such deep contempt and detestation was the nation held, that few were willing to buy them; and the Jews who remained at large, were too few and poor to be able to redeem their brethren. The market was also glutted with their numbers, so that they were sold at a mere nominal price, -- sometimes thirty for a small piece of money. Those who remained unpurchased were sent into confinement, where they perished by hundreds and by thousands together, from neglect and hunger. Egypt received a large proportion of these slaves, who were probably sent thither in ships, as the Romans had a fleet in the Mediterranean, and this was a much easier and safer way of transporting them than by land across the desert. The same things precisely took place on the final desolation of Israel by Hadrian, who may be said to have consummated their doom by decreeing, with the concurrence of the Roman Senate, that no Jew should ever, on pain of death, enter the land of his fathers." -- Illust. Comment. in loco.

257. "Abnepotes," -- Lat.; i.e., their grandchild's grandchildren.

258. "When he calls heaven and earth to witness, he calls all things which are in heaven and in earth, by metonomy; and especially angels and men, who are properly called witnesses. Thus Theodoret. So the Poet says: Vos aeterni ignes, and non violabile numen Tester; (Virg.Aen., 2. 154;) for the Platonists thought that the heavenly fires, i.e., the stars, were animated by their intelligences, or guardian angels, whom they worshipped as inferior gods." -- Corn. a Lapide in loco. De Lyra's note is, "i.e., every intellectual creature existing in heaven and earth, since none but an intellectual creature can properly bear witness."

259. "Des marmousets sans sens;" senseless puppets. -- Fr.

260. Addition in Fr., "car s'il avoit une pleine perfection requise;" for if entire perfection were here required.

261. "Stipulator." -- Lat. "Un notaire stipulant." -- Fr.

262. "Peres de famille." -- Fr.

263. "Calones, et lixas." -- Lat. "Les buscherons, porteurs de bagages, et gouiats;" the wood-carriers, baggage-porters, and soldiers'-boys. -- Fr.

264. "Quatre cens ans;" four hundred years. -- Fr.

265. Added from Fr.

266. "Luy sont consacrez par le baptesme, pour estre siens;" are consecrated to Him by baptism, to be His own. -- Fr.

267. Amongst others, De Lyra, whose gloss is, "Some one corrupted by idolatry, who should further corrupt others by his wicked persuasions." Dathe says, "It is a proverbial expression, and its meaning is: lest there should be any rebel against the primary law of worshipping one God, and he should think within himself the things which follow in the next verse."

268. "The word לענה certainly denotes an extremely disagreeable and bitter plant; and that it was wormwood is a well-supported and probable interpretation. We therefore give a cut of the Artemisia absinthium. It must be confessed, however, that the Scripture seems to attribute to the לענה stronger effects than the wormwood of Europe will produce. We may therefore understand that some more hurtful species is intended: unless, as suggested by Gesenius, in the strong passages which seem to call for such an explanation, the name of the plant is employed figuratively to express poison." -- Illust. Comment. on Proverbs 5:4

269. Addition in Fr., "par maniere de dire."

270. Lat., "Ut addat ebriam sitienti." A.V., "To add drunkenness to thirst;" Margin, "The drunken to the thirsty." So Ainsworth, "To add the drunken, to wit, the drunken soul to the thirsty, or the moist to the dry, meaning to add sin unto sin in abundance, as in Isaiah 30:1." Dathe follows Le Clerc, and explains it, "to add water to a thirsty soul;" and compares it to Isaiah 44:3, where, he says, the same metaphor is used, though in a good sense.

271. "Que ceux, qui augmentent le mal, mettent l'huile en la cheminee;" that those who augment an evil put oil into the chimney. -- Fr.

272. A.V., "a wealthy (margin, moist) place." See Cal. Soc. Comment. on Psalms, [29]vol. 2, p. 473.

273. "Car ceux qui sous ombre d'eschapper son jugement s'abandonnent a pecher, luy font ce dishonneur de le despouiller de son empire;" for those who abandon

themselves to sin under cover of escaping His judgment, do him this dishonor of despoiling him of his empire. -- Fr.

274. "Le verbe que nous avons translate condescendre, signifie venir a gre. Ainsi Moyse exclud toutes graces de Dieu;" the verb which we have translated condescend, (the Lord will not condescend to spare him,) signifies to consent. Thus Moses shuts out all the graces of God. -- Fr יאבה, acquiescet. -- Taylor.

275. Addition in Fr., "Comme Sainct Jude aussi declare, que la foudre dont elles ont este abysmees, est figure du feu eternal;" as St. Jude also declares, that the thunderbolt whereby they were destroyed, is a type of the eternal fire.

276. See margin, A.V. -- "Who had not given to them any portion," v, 26.

277. "Sa parole;" His word. -- Fr.

278. 2 Samuel 12:14, 15; Psalm 89:32, 33.

279. "Residuum semen." -- Lat. "La semence, que Dieu se reserve;" the seed which God reserves to Himself. -- Fr.

280. "A donner lustre a la gloire de Dieu;" to give lustre to the glory of God. -- Fr.

281. See margin, A.V., Jeremiah 44:17.

282. "Call them to mind." -- A.V. "And thou shalt cause them to return to thine heart, or reduce, bring again to thine heart, i.e., call to mind, consider seriously; so in Deuteronomy 4:39." -- Ainsworth.

283. Added from Fr.

284. See ante on Deuteronomy 4:29, [30]p. 271.

285. Added from Fr.

286. "Return thou therefore," etc. -- Lat.

287. Addition in Fr., "comme d'un tourbillon;" as by a whirlpool.

288. See ante on Deuteronomy 4:26, [31]p. 270.

289. "S'adonnent a observer la Loy, et pource qu'ils n'en peuvent venir a bout, qu'ils ne soyent toujours redevables, que leur fautes leurs soyent gratuitement pardonnees;" should devote themselves to the keeping of the Law; and because they could never attain its end, so as not to be always indebted to it, that their faults should be gratuitously pardoned. -- Fr.

Return to the History - Exodus 31

Exodus 31:1-11

1. And the Lord spake unto Moses, saying,

1. Loquutus est Jehova ad Mosen, dicendo:

2. See, I have called by name Bezaleel the son of Uri, the son of Hur, of the tribe of Judah:

2. Vide, vocavi ex nomine Besaleel filium Uri, filii Hur, e tribu Jehuda:

3. And I have filled him with the spirit of God, in wisdom, and in understanding, and in knowledge, and in all manner of workmanship,

3. Et replevi eum Spiritu Dei, sapientia et intelligentia, scientia et onmi arte,

4. To devise cunning works, to work in gold, and in silver, and in brass,

4. Ad excogitandum quicquid fabrefieri potest ex auro, et argento, et aere:

5. And in cutting of stones, to set them, and in carving of timber, to work in all manner of workmanship.

5. Et in arte gemmaria, ad replendum, et in arte lignaria, ut operetur in omni opere.

6. And I, behold, I have given with him Aholiab the son of Ahisamach, of the tribe of Dan: and in the hearts of all that are wise-hearted I have put wisdom, that they may make all that I have commanded thee;

6. Et ego ecce constitui cum eo Aholiab filium Ahisamach e tribu Dan, et in corde omnis sapientis corde, dedi sapientiam, ut faciant quaecunque praecepi tibi:

7. The tabernacle of the congregation, and the ark of the testimony, and the mercy-seat that is thereupon, and all the furniture of the tabernacle,

7. Tabernaculum Ecclesiae, et arcam testimonii, et propitiatorium quod est super eam, et omnia vasa tabernaculi,

8. And the table and his furniture, and the pure candlestick with all his furniture, and the altar of incense,

8. Et mensam et vasa ejus: et candelabrum mundum, et omnia vasa ejus, et altare suffimenti,

9. And the altar of burnt-offering with all his furniture, and the laver and his foot,

9. Et altare holocausti, et omnia vasa ejus, et concham et basin ejus,

10. And the clothes of service, and the holy garments for Aaron the priest, and the garments of his sons, to minister in the priest's office,

10. Et vestes ministerii, et vestes sanctitatis ipsi Aharon sacerdoti, et vestes filiorum ejus, ut sacerdotio fungantur.

11. And the anointing oil, and sweet incense for the holy place: according to all that I have commanded thee shall they do.

11. Et oleum unctionis, et suffimentum aromaticum pro sanctuario juxta onmia quae praecepi tibi facient.

2. See, I have called by name Bezaleel. In the remainder of this work we shall follow the course of the history to the end of Deuteronomy, where the death of Moses himself is recorded.

Although God had omitted nothing which related to the form of the tabernacle, but had accurately prescribed every thing that was to be done, still the actual difficulty of the work might have overwhelmed both Moses and the whole people with despair; for this was no ordinary work, or one on which the most skillful artificers might exercise their ingenuity, but a marvelous structure, the pattern of which had been shewn on the Mount, so that it might seem incredible that any mortals should be able by their art to compass what God had commanded. Besides, they had been entirely engaged in servile tasks in Egypt, such as would extinguish all intellectual vigor, and prevent them from aspiring to any liberal arts. Hence we gather that all, who obediently follow God's voice, are never destitute of His aid. In all our difficulties, then, let this prayer encourage us to proceed: [290] "Give what Thou commandest: and command what Thou wilt."

To "call by name," is equivalent to rendering eminent, so that Moses signifies that Bezaleel should be something extraordinary, as being endowed with a peculiar gift. Thus Cyrus is said in Isaiah 45:4, to be called by his name, because in the purpose of God he had been destined in a remarkable manner to execute such great things. Still, although the call of Bezaleel was special, because, as I have just said, God entrusted to him an unusual and by no means ordinary work, we gather that no one excels even in the most despised and humble handicraft, except in so far as God's Spirit works in him. For, although "there are diversities of gifts," still it is the same Spirit from whom they all flow, (1 Corinthians 12:4;) and also as God has seen fit to distribute and measure them out to every man. Nor is this only the case with respect to the spiritual gifts which follow regeneration, but in all the branches of knowledge which come into use in common life. It is, therefore, a false division, when ungodly men ascribe all the means of our support partly to nature and God's blessing, and partly to the industry of man, since man's industry itself is a blessing from God. The poets are more correct who acknowledge that all which is suggested by nature comes from God; that all the arts emanate from Him, and therefore ought to be accounted divine inventions. The utility of this doctrine is two-fold; first, that all things which have reference to the support and defense of life, whenever we meet with them, should excite our gratitude, and that whatever seems to be derived from man's ingenuity, should be regarded as proofs of God's paternal solicitude for us; and, secondly, that we should honor God as the Author of so many good things, since He sanctifies them for our use. Moses applies many epithets to the Spirit, because he is speaking of so remarkable a work; yet we must conclude, float whatever ability is possessed by any emanates from one only source, and is conferred by God. This is the only difference, that Bezaleel was endued with consummate excellence, whilst God makes distribution to others according to His pleasure.

6. And I, behold, I have given with him Aholiab. It is no matter of surprise that the principal workman should be chosen from the tribe of Judah; [291] why a

companion should be given him from the tribe of Dan can hardly be accounted for, unless its obscurity more highly illustrated the grace of God.

A kind of contradiction at first sight appears, when it is added immediately afterwards that God had put wisdom in the hearts of all that were wise-hearted; for, if they already excelled in intelligence, what was the object of this new inspiration? Hence it has been commonly supposed, that the special grace of God was only given in aid of that ability which we naturally possess. But rather are we taught by this passage that, when anything grows in us, and our endowments manifest themselves more conspicuously, our progress is only derived from the continued operation of the Spirit. God had already conferred acuteness and intelligence on the artificers in question; yet their dexterity was only, as it were, the seed; and He now promises that He will give them more than had previously appeared. I know that the words may be thus explained, -- Whosoever shall be fit and proper for the work, have therefore been endowed with intelligence, because God has inspired it by His secret influence; but the other exposition is more simple. What follows as to the various parts of the tabernacle has been already treated of elsewhere.

Exodus 35

Exodus 35:20-35

20. And all the congregation of the children of Israel departed from the presence of Moses.

20. Egressi sunt universus coetus filiorum Israel a facie Mosis,

21. And they came, every one whose heart stirred him up, and every one whom his spirit made willing, and they brought the Lord's offering to the work of the tabernacle of the congregation, and for all his service, and for the holy garments.

21. Veneruntque vir quem extulit cor suum, qui liberalis fuit spiritu suo: attuleruntque oblationem ad opus tabernaculi conventionis, et ad omne opus ejus, et ad vestes sanctitatis.

22. And they came, both men and women, as many as were willing-hearted, and brought bracelets, and ear-rings, and rings, and tablets, all jewels of gold: and every man that offered, offered an offering of gold unto the Lord.

22. Venerunt viri et mulieres, quicunque liberalis fuit corde, attulerunt fibulas, et inaures, et annulos, et armillas, quodlibet vas aureum, et omnis vir qui attulit levationem auri Jehovae.

23. And every man with whom was found blue, and purple, and scarlet, and fine linen, and goat's hair, and red skins of rams, and badgers' skins, brought them

23. Praeterea onmis vir apud quem inveniebatur hyacinthus, purpura, coccus, byssus, et pili caprarum, et pelles arietum rubricatae, et pelles taxorum, haec attulerunt.

24. Every one that did offer an offering of silver and brass, brought the Lord's offering: and every man with whom was found shittim-wood, for any work of the service, brought it

24. *Omnis tollens levationem argenti et aeris, obtulerunt levationem Jehovae: et omnis apud quem inveniebantur ligna sittim, pro universo opere ministerii attulerunt.*

25. And all the women that were wise-hearted did spin with their hands, and brought that which they had spun, both of blue, and of purple, and of scarlet, and of fine linen.

25. *Praeterea omnis mulier intelligenti corde, manibus suis neverunt, et attulerunt quod nendo operatae fuerant, hyaciuthum, purpuram, coccum et byssum.*

26. And all the women, whose hearts stirred them up in wisdom, spun goats' hair

26. *Omnes quoque mulieres quas excitavit cor ipsarum, intelligenter neverunt pilos caprinos.*

27. And the rulers brought onyx-stones, and stones to be set, for the ephod, and for the breastplate;

27. *Principes quoque attulerunt lapides onychinos, et gemmas inserendas in ephod et pectorali:*

28. And spice, and oil for the light, and for the anointing oil, and for the sweet incense.

28. *Aromata etiam et oleum pro luminari, et pro oleo unctionis, et pro incenso aromatico.*

29. The children of Israel brought a willing offering unto the Lord, every man and woman, whose heart made them willing to bring, for all manner of work which the Lord had commanded to be made by the hand of Moses.

29. *Omnis vir et mulier qui liberales fuerunt corde suo ad offerendum pro cuncto opere quod mandaverat Jehova fieri per manum Mosis, obtulerunt filii Israel donum voluntarium Jehovae.*

30. And Moses said unto the children of Israel, See, the Lord hath called by name Bezaleel the son of Uri, the son of Hur, of the tribe of Judah:

30. *Tunc ait Moses ad filios Israel, Videte, vocavit Jehova nomine Besaleel filium Uri, filii Hur, de tribu Juda:*

31. And he hath filled him with the spirit of God, in wisdom, in understanding, and in knowledge, and in all manner of workmanship;

31. *Et implevit cum Spiritu Dei, in sapientia et intelligentia, in scientia et omni artificio,*

32. And to devise curious works, to work in gold, and in silver, and in brass,

32. *Ad excogitandum ingeniosa opera, ut faciat in auro, argento et aere:*

33. And in the cutting of stones, to set them, and in carving of wood, to make any manner of cunning work.

33. *Et in artificio gemmarum; ut illas includat in artificio ligni, ut faciat quodcunque opus ingeniosum.*

34. And he hath put in his heart that he may teach, both he and Aholiab the son of Ahisamach, of the tribe of Dan.

34. *Et posuit in corde ejus ut doceat, ipse et Aholiab filius Ahisamach, e tribu Dan.*

35. Them hath he filled with wisdom of heart, to work all manner of work of the engraver, and of the cunning workman, and of the

embroiderer, in blue, and in purple, in scarlet, and in fine linen, and of the weaver, even of them that do any work, and of those that devise cunning work.

35. Replevit eos sapientia cordis, ut faciant omne opus artificis, et phrygionis, et acupictoris, ex hyacintho, et purpura, et vermiculo cocci, et bysso, et textura, facientes omne opus, et excogitantes inventiones.

20. And all the congregation of the children of Israel. There is no reason why any one should be surprised that the order of the narrative is changed, since it plainly appears from many passages that the order of time is not always observed by Moses. Thus he appears here to connect the fall of the people with the foregoing injunctions, both with respect to the building of the tabernacle, and the rest of the religious service of God. But I have shewn [292] upon good grounds that the tabernacle was built before the people fell into idolatry. Therefore Moses now supplies what had been before omitted, though I have followed the thread of the narrative in order to render it less difficult.

The sum of this relation is, that whatever was necessary for the building of the tabernacle was liberally contributed. It must be observed that they had departed from the presence of Moses: for we gather from this circumstance that, having severally retired to their tents, they had considered apart by themselves what they should give. Hence their liberality is deserving of greater praise, because it was premeditated; for it often happens that when a person has been bountiful from sudden impulse, he afterwards repents of it. When it is added that "they came, every one," it is a question whether he means that the minds of the whole people were prompt and cheerful in giving, or whether he indirectly rebukes the stinginess and sordidness of those who meanly neglected their duty. In whichever way we choose to take it, Moses repeats what we have seen before, that the offerings were not extorted by force or necessity, but that they proceeded from voluntary and cordial feelings. I thus construe the words, "They came, every one, as his heart stirred each of them up," as if he had said that they were not compelled by any law imposed upon them, but that every one was his own lawgiver, of his own good-will. This passage is absurdly twisted by the Papists in proof of free-will; as if men were incited by themselves to act rightly and well; for Moses, even while praising their spontaneous feelings, does not mean to exclude the grace of the Spirit, whereby alone our hearts are inclined to holy affections; but this stirring up is contrasted with the unwillingness by which ungodly men are withheld and restrained. Those, therefore, whom the Spirit rules, He does not drag unwillingly by a violent and extrinsic impulse, as it is called, but He so works within them upon their will, that believers stir up themselves, and they voluntarily follow His leadings. So that when it is added, "whose spirit was liberal in himself," [293] the commencement of well-doing is not ascribed to men, nor is even their concurrence praised, as if they co-operated apart from God, but only the internal impulse of their minds, and the sincerity of their desires·

22. And they came, both men and women. Express mention is made of the women, not only whose bounty, but whose labors, as it soon afterwards appears, God designed to make use of in the work of the sanctuary. Moses magnifies the fervor of their pious desires, because they did not spare their ornaments; of which people, and especially women, are generally so fond, that they would rather suffer cold, hunger, or thirst, than touch them. [294] It was,

therefore, a sign of no ordinary zeal to deprive themselves of their rings and bracelets, which many are so slow to part with, even when they are dying of hunger. Again, the contribution of those is praised who gave brass, iron, shittim-wood, and rams' skins; so that the poor might not doubt but that, although their ability might not be equal to their wishes, the offering, which they presented willingly in their poverty, was no less acceptable to God than when the rich man of his abundance gave what was a hundred times more valuable.

30. See, the Lord hath called by name Bezaleel. This was a great stimulus to encourage them, when they plainly saw that God presided over the work; a conspicuous proof of which was that new and extraordinary power wherewith Bezaleel and Aboliab were endued; for although they had before been noble and excellent artificers, still there is no doubt but that they were still further endowed with higher gifts, even to a miracle. Hence it is not without cause that he bids the people attend to this unexpected exertion of God's power; since it was exactly as if he had stretched forth His hand from heaven for the advancement of the work. For which reason also the tribe of each of them is referred to, because of the conspicuous excellency of the grace, the memory of which it was fitting to celebrate in all generations. Now, as God conferred this honor on the architects of the visible sanctuary, so He declares that their names shall be glorious in heaven, who, being furnished with the illustrious gifts of the Spirit, faithfully employ their labors in the building of His spiritual temple. (Daniel 12:3.)

By "the wisdom of heart," both in the men and women, which is so often mentioned here, understand activity of mind: for not only is the seat of the affections called the heart, but also the power and faculty of the intellect as it is called: thus in Deuteronomy 29:4, it is said, "Yet the Lord hath not given you a heart to understand." [295]

31. And he hath filled him with the spirit of God. He again magnifies at greater length the excellence of genius and ability, (which had been given to Bezaleel.) [296] For it was a remarkable instance of God's power, that, after the Israelites had been so contemptuously and oppressively enslaved, there should exist in their nation men still endowed with such talent. God is said to have "filled him with the Spirit of God," i e., with the Divine Spirit; in order that we may understand that these endowments were not natural to the man, nor even acquired by his own industry. For although even the gifts of nature proceed from the Spirit of God, who gives their intellect to all men no less than their life; still the distribution of peculiar gifts is conspicuous in a higher and different degree. Besides, God had regard to the exquisite nature of this work, so as to endow these artificers with wonderful and extraordinary ability. The faculty of teaching is also added, because two persons by themselves would never have completed so arduous a work in their whole life-time: and this capacity, too, was the gift of Divine grace; for else they would never have overcome the fatigue of instructing the ignorant, nor would have so speedily prepared such a great multitude of men for fashioning the various parts of the work with incredible symmetry.

Exodus 36

Exodus 36:1-38

1. Then wrought Bezaleel and Aholiab, and every wise-hearted man, in whom the Lord put wisdom and understanding, to know how to work all manner of work for the service of the sanctuary, according to all that the Lord had commanded.

1. Fecit ergo Beseleel et Aholiab, et omnis vir sapiens corde, quibus dederat Jebova sapientiam et intelligentiam, ut scirent facere omne opus ministerii sanctuarii, quaecunque praeceperat Jehova.

2. And Moses called Bezaleel and Aholiab, and every wise-hearted man, in whose heart the Lord had put wisdom, even every one whose heart stirred him up to come unto the work to do it:

2. Nam vocavit Moses Beseleel et Aholiab, omnemque virum sapientem corde, cujus cordi indiderat Jehova sapientiam, et omnem cujus cor excitaverat ipsum ut accederet ad opus ad faciendum illud.

3. And they received of Moses all the offering which the children of Israel had brought for the work of the service of the sanctuary, to make it withal. And they brought yet unto him free-offerings every morning.

3. Tuleruntque a facie Mosis omnem oblationem quam attulerant filii Israel ad opus ministerii sanctuarii: illi autem afferebant ad eum adhuc oblationem spontaneam quotidie.

4. And all the wise men, that wrought all the work of the sanctuary, came every man from his work which they made;

4. Venerunt itaque omnes sapientes qui faciebant omne opus sanctuarii, singuli ab opere quod faciebant:

5. And they spake unto Moses, saying, the people bring much more than enough for the service of the work which the Lord commanded to make.

5. Et loquuti sunt ad Mosen, dicendo: Plus affert populus afferendo quam opus sit ad ministerium pro opere faciendo quod praecepit Jehova fieri.

6. And Moses gave commandment, and they caused it to be proclaimed throughout the camp, saying, Let neither man nor woman make any more work for the offering of the sanctuary. So the people were restrained from bringing.

6. Praecepit ergo Moses ut proclamarent in castris, dicendo: Vir et mulier ne quid addant ultra ad oblationem sanctitatis. Itaque prohibitus est populus ab offerendo.

7. For the stuff they had was sufficient for all the work to make it, and too much.

7. Materia enim erat ad sufficientiam eis pro toto opere ad faciendum illud, et superabundabat.

8. And every wise-hearted man, among them that wrought the work of the tabernacle, made ten curtains of fine twined linen, and blue, and purple, and scarlet: with cherubims of cunning work made he them.

8. Et fecerunt omnis sapiens corde inter facientes opus, tabernaculum e decem cortinis, quae erant ex bysso retorta, et hyacintho, et purpura, et vermiculo cocci, ex Cherubin opere phrygionico fecit illas.

9. The length of one curtain was twenty and eight cubits, and the breadth of one curtain four cubits; the curtains were all of one size.

9. Longitudo cortinae unius erat octo et viginti cubitorum, et quatuor cubitorum latitudo cortinae unius, mensura erat omnibus cortinis.

10. And he coupled the five curtains one unto another; and the other five curtains he coupled one unto another.

10. Postea conjunxit quinque cortinas alteram cum altera, et quinque alias cortinas conjunxit alteram cum altera.

11. And he made loops of blue on the edge of one curtain, from the selvedge in the coupling; likewise he made in the uttermost side of another curtain, in the coupling of the second.

11. Fecit et laqueolos hyacinthinos in ora cortinae unius, in extremo in conjunctione: sic fecit in ora cortinae extrema in conjunctione secundae.

12. Fifty loops made he in one curtain, and fifty loops made he in the edge of the curtain which was in the coupling of the second: the loops held one curtain to another.

12. Quinquaginta laqueolos fecit; in cortina una, et quinquaginta laqueolos fecit in extremo cortinae secundae, quae erat in conjunctione secunda: oppositi erant laqueoli alter alteri.

13. And he made fifty taches of gold, and coupled the curtains one unto another with the taches: so it became one tabernacle.

13. Fecit et quinquaginta uncinos aureos, et conjunxit cortinas alteram cum altera uncinis, et ita factum est tabernaculum unum.

14. And he made curtains of goats' hair for the tent over the tabernacle: eleven curtains he made them.

14. Fecit insuper cortinas e caprarum pilis in tentorium super tabernaculum.

15. The length of one curtain was thirty cubits, and four cubits was the breadth of one curtain: the eleven curtains were of one size.

15. Longitudo cortinae unius triginta cubitorum, et quatuor cubitorum latitudo cortinae unius, mensura una erat undecim cortinis.

16. And he coupled five curtains by themselves, and six curtains by themselves.

16. Conjunxit quinque cortinas seorsum, et sex cortinas seorsum.

17. And he made fifty loops upon the uttermost edge of the curtain in the coupling, and fifty loops made he upon the edge of the curtain which coupleth the second.

17. Fecit etiam laqueolos quinquaginta in ora cortinae extrema, in conjunctione: quinquaginta item laqueolos fecit in ora cortinae, in conjunctione secunda.

18. And he made fifty taches of brass to couple the tent together, that it might be one.

18. Fecit praeterea uncinos aereos quinquaginta ad conjungendum tentorium, ut esset unum.

19. And he made a covering for the tent of rams' skins dyed red, and a covering of badgers' skins above that

19. Fecit insuper operimentum tentorio e pellibus arietum rubricatis, et operimentum e pellibus taxorum superne.

20. And he made boards for the tabernacle of shittim-wood, standing up.

20. *Fecit et tabulas tabernaculo e lignis sittim stantes.*

21. The length of a board was ten cubits, and the breadth of a board one cubit and a half.

21. *Decem cubitorum erat longitudo tabubae, cubiti vero et dimidii latitudo tabulae.*

22. One board had two tenons, equally distant one from another: thus did he make for all the boards of the tabernacle.

22. *Duo cardines erant tabulae uni instar scalarum gradus dispositi, alter e regione alterius: sic fecit omnibus tabulis tabernaculi.*

23. And he made boards for the tabernacle: twenty boards for the south side, southward.

23. *Fecit inquam tabulas tabernaculo, viginti tabulas ad latus, austri ad meridiem.*

24. And forty sockets of silver he made under the twenty boards: two sockets under one board for his two tenons, and two sockets under another board for his two tenons.

24. *Et quadraginta bases argenteas fecit sub viginti tabulis, duas bases sub tabula una pro duabus clastraturis ejus, et duas bases sub tabula altera pro duabus clastraturis ejus.*

25. And for the other side of the tabernacle, which is toward the north corner, he made twenty boards,

25. *In latere vero tabernaculi secundo, nempe in latere aquilonari, fecit viginti tabulas.*

26. And their forty sockets of silver: two sockets under one board, and two sockets under another board.

26. *Et quadraginta bases earum argenteas, duas bases sub tabula una, et duas bases sub tabula altera.*

27. And for the sides of the tabernacle westward he made six boards.

27. *In latere autem tabernaculi ad occidentem fecit sex tabalas.*

28. And two boards made he for the corners of the tabernacle in the two sides.

28. *Duas tabulas fecit angulis tabernaculi in duobus lateribus.*

29. And they were coupled beneath, and coupled together at the head thereof, to one ring: thus he did to both of them in both the corners.

29. *Et erant quasi gemellae inferne, et pariter quasi gemellae in summitate ejus, in circulum unum: sic fecit utrique in duobus angulis.*

30. And there were eight boards; and their sockets were sixteen sockets of silver, under every board two sockets.

30. *Fuerunt itaque octo tabulae, et bases earum argenteae sedecim, bases binae sub qualibet tabula.*

31. And he made bars of shittim-wood; five for the boards of the one side of the tabernacle,

31. *Fecit et vectes e lignis sittim, quinque pro tabulis unius lateris tabernaculi:*

32. And five bars for the boards of the other side of the tabernacle, and five bars for the boards of the tabernacle for the sides westward.

32. *Et quinque vectes pro tabulis alterius lateris tabernaculi, et quinque vectes pro tabulis lateris tabernaculi, in lateribus duobus ad occidentem.*

33. And he made the middle bar to shoot through the boards from the one end to the other.

33. Fecit item vectem medium, ut transiret per medium tabularum, ab extremo ad extremum.

34. And he overlaid the boards with gold, and made their rings of gold to be places for the bars, and overlaid the bars with gold.

34. Tabulas antem texit auro, et annulos earum fecit ex auro, per quos trajicerentur vectes: et texit vectes auro.

35. And he made a vail of blue, and purple, and scarlet, and fine twined linen: with cherubims made he it of cunning work.

35. Fecit etiam velum ex hyacintho, et purpura, et vermiculo cocci, et bysso retorta: opere phrygionico fecit illud, cum figuris cherubim.

36. And he made thereunto four pillars of shittim-wood, and overlaid them with gold; their hooks were of gold: and he cast for them four sockets of silver.

36. Et fecit illi quatuor columnas de lignis sittim, et texit eas auro: uncini autem earum erant aurei: et fudit eis quatuor bases argenteas.

37. And he made an hanging for the tabernacle-door of blue, and purple, and scarlet, and fine twined linen, of needle-work;

37. Fecit quoque velum ad ostium tabernaculi ex hyacintho, et purpura, et vermiculo cocci, et bysso retorta, opere phrygionico.

38. And the five pillars of it with their hooks; and he overlaid their chapiters and their fillets with gold: but their five sockets were of brass.

38. Et columnas ejus quinque, et uncinos earum: texitque capita earum, et fila ea cingentia auro, bases autem earum quinque aereas.

1. Then wrought Bezaleel and Aholiab. Although Moses might have seemed to be unnecessarily prolix in recording the injunctions which God gave respecting the building of the tabernacle, yet he repeats the same narrative here almost in the same words; and this he does with the best design, and for very good reasons. For it was of much importance that it might be seen by actual comparison how exactly the artificers had conformed everything to the pattern laid down by God: and this, not only in commendation of their obedience, but because it behooved that there should be nothing human in the structure; for although they might each of them have exerted themselves strenuously in the work, still it was not lawful for them to give the slightest scope to their own inventions; nay, this would have been a profanation of the sacred edifice, not to follow in every part what had been so carefully dictated to Moses. And this might avail as a restraint upon them in future times, so that they might not violate God's commands by any change or innovation. They did not indeed understand the reason of everything either in reference to number or measure; but it became them to be assured that God had commanded nothing without a purpose. Hence, also, their minds should have been elevated to the heavenly pattern, so as reverently to look up to the mysteries, obscure as they were, which it contained, until its full manifestation. This verbal repetition, then, reminds us how accurately the labor and art of men in the building corresponded with the command of God.

2. And Moses called Bezaleel and Aholiab. It is not without reason that Moses so often exalts the grace of God's Spirit in the ingenuity and artistic skill of the workmen. In the first place he speaks of them as skillful architects, and then, by way of correction, adds that they were furnished from above with such intelligence. Thus the absurdity of the Papists is refuted, who, in order to prove

free-will, think it sufficient to drag forward the passages in which rectitude of will is commended: whereas, even though men may will aright, it is foolish to infer that therefore they are possessed of free-will, unless it be proved that the will proceeds from themselves. Consequently, what follows in the text, -- that every one contributed either of his labor or his substance to the building of the tabernacle, according as their hearts stirred them up, -- does not so make men the authors of pious affections, as to defraud God of His praise. It is true that men understand -- are willing -- encourage themselves to holy endeavors; but the question is, from whence comes their intelligence, their will, and their zeal in well-doing? Scripture decides that they are the gifts of God and the Spirit: the Papists improperly arrogate them to themselves.

3. And they received of Moses all the offering. Here is set forth, first of all, the diligence and prudence both of Moses and the artificers, and secondly, their integrity. Their prudence is shewn in the distribution of the materials among them; their diligence in the quickness with which they commence the work, without waiting till they have enough for its completion; whilst they testify their extraordinary integrity when they voluntarily declare that enough has been given, and put a stop to the offerings, lest they should be more than they required. We know how few restrain themselves [297] when an opportunity is given of thieving without detection; and, even if there be no disposition to deceive, yet most people are tempted by ambition, greedily to long for more to pass through their hands than they need. We see, then, how God directed them all to undertake the work of the sanctuary, and impelled them to persevere in it by His Spirit. This grace, however, manifests itself most fully in the marvelous ardor of the people. They were not very rich, for they had had no treasures laid up for a long period; and the wealthiest among them had no more than what they had secretly conveyed away out of Egypt; whilst the building was sumptuous; and still they do not cease from contributing more than was necessary, until an edict forbade them. Such promptitude and liberality was worthy of no common praise; and hence it is more wonderful that they should soon afterwards neglect the true God in whose service they were thus zealous, and fall into foul idolatry. Let us learn from hence, that the pious zeal, which existed in them for a short time, emanated from the inspiration of the Holy Spirit; and further, that all our best feelings vanish, unless the gift of stedfastness be superadded.

What follows represents, as by a lively image, as we have said, how faithfully they executed whatever God had prescribed, so as not to vary from it even in the smallest thread.

Exodus 37

Exodus 37:1-29

1. **And Bezaleel made the ark of shittim-wood: two cubits and a half was the length of it, and a cubit and a half the breadth of it, and a cubit and a half the height of it.**

1. Fecit etiam Beseleel arcam e lignis sittim: duorum cubitorum et dimidii longitudo ejus: cubiti et dimidii latitudo ejus: cubiti quoque et dimidii altitudo ejus.

2. And he overlaid it with pure gold within and without, and made a crown of gold to it round about.

2. Et texit eam auro mundo intrinsecus, et extrinsecus: fecitque ei coronam auream in circuitu.

3. And he cast for it four rings of gold, to be set by the four corners of it; even two rings upon the one side of it, and two rings upon the other side of it.

3. Et fudit ei quatuor annulos aureos ad quatuor angulos ejus, duos videlicet annulos in latere ejus uno, et duos annulos in latere ejus altero.

4. And he made staves of shittim-wood, and overlaid them with gold.

4. Fecit et vectes e lignis sittim, et texit eos auro.

5. And he put the staves into the rings by the sides of the ark, to bear the ark.

5. Induxitque vectes in annulos in lateribus arcae ad portandum arcam.

6. And he made the mercy-seat of pure gold: two cubits and a half was the length thereof, and one cubit and a half the breadth thereof.

6. Fecit et propitiatorium ex auro mundo: duorum cubitorum et dimidii longitudo ejus, cubiti et dimidii latitudo ejus.

7. And he made two cherubims of gold, beaten out of one piece made he them, on the two ends of the mercy-seat;

7. Fecit quoque duos Cherubim ex auro, ductiles fecit eos in duabus extremitatibus propitiatorii.

8. One cherub on the end on this side, and another cherub on the other end on that side: out of the mercy-seat made he the cherubims on the two ends thereof.

8. Cherub unum ab extremo hinc, et cherub alterum ab extremo inde: ex propitiatorio fecit cherubim in duabus extremitatibus ejus.

9. And the cherubims spread out their wings on high, and covered with their wings over the mercy-seat, with their faces one to another; even to the mercy-seat-ward were the faces of the cherubims.

9. Cherubim autem extendebant alas sursum versus, tegentes alis suis propitiatorium et facies eorum altera ad alteram: ad propitiatorium facies Cherubim.

10. And he made the table of shittim-wood: two cubits was the length thereof, and a cubit the breadth thereof, and a cubit and a half the height thereof.

10. Fecit et mensam e liguis sittim: duorum cubitorum longitudo ejus, et cubiti latitudo ejus, cubiti autem et dimidii altitudo ejus.

11. And he overlaid it with pure gold, and made thereunto a crown of gold round about.

11. Et texit eam auro puro, fecitque ei coronam auream in circuitu.

12. Also he made thereunto a border of an handbreadth round about; and made a crown of gold for the border thereof round about.

12. Fecit quoque ei clausuram palmi per circuitum: et fecit coronam auream clausurae illi per circuitum.

13. And he cast for it four rings of gold, and put the rings upon the four corners that were in the four feet thereof.

13. Fudit ei etiam quatuor annulos aureos, quos posuit in quatuor angulis qui erant in quatuor pedibus ejus.

14. Over against the border were the rings, the places for the staves, to bear the table.

14. Contra clausuram illam erant annuli per quos traducerentur vectes ad portandam mensam.

15. And he made the staves of shittim-wood, and overlaid them with gold, to bear the table.

15. Fecit etiam vectes e lignis sittim, quos texit auro ad portandam mensam.

16. And he made the vessels which were upon the table, his dishes, and his spoons, and his bowls, and his covers to cover withal, of pure gold.

16. Et fecit vasa quae erant super mensam, scutellas ejus, et cochlearia ejus, et crateras ejus, et opercula quibus libabatur, ex auro mundo.

17. And he made the candlestick of pure gold: of beaten work made he the candlestick; his shaft, and his branch, his bowls, his knops, and his flowers, were of the same:

17. Fecit et candelabrum ex auro puro, ductile fecit candelabrum, hastile ejus, et calamus ejus, scyphi ejus, sphaerulae ejus, et flores ejus ex ipso erant.

18. And six branches going out of the sides thereof; three branches of the candlestick out of the one side thereof, and three branches of the candlestick out of the other side thereof:

18. Porro sex calami egrediebantur e lateribus ejus, tres calami candelabri ex latere ipsius uno, et tres calami candelabri ex latere ejus altero.

19. Three bowls made after the fashion of almonds in one branch, a knop and a flower; and three bowls made like almonds in another branch, a knop and a flower: so throughout the six branches going out of the candlestick.

19. Tres calices in speciem nucis amygdalinae deformati erant in calamo uno, sphaerula et flos: et tres calices in speciem nucis amygdalinae deformati in calamo altero, sphaerula et flos: sic sex calamis egredientibus e candelabro.

20. And in the candlestick were four bowls made like almonds, his knops and his flowers:

20. Et in candelabro erant quatuor calices in speciem nucis deformati, sphaerulae ejus, et flores ejus.

21. And a knop under two branches of the same, and a knop under two branches of the same, and a knop under two branches of the same, according to the six branches growing out of it.

21. Et erat sphaerula sub duobus calamis ex ipso, et sphaerula altera sub duobus calamis ex ipso, et sphaerula tertia sub duobus calamis ex ipso: sic sex calamis egredientibus ex ipso.

22. Their knops and their branches were of the same: all of it was one beaten work of pure gold.

22. Sphaerulae eorum et calami eorum ex ipso fuerunt: totum erat ductile unum ex auro puro.

23. And he made his seven lamps, and his snuffers, and his snuff-dishes, of pure gold.

23. Fecit et lucernas ejus septem, et forcipes ejus, et receptacula ipsius, ex auro puro.

24. Of a talent of pure gold made he it, and all the vessels thereof.

24. Et talento puri auri fecit ipsum, et omnia vasa ejus.

25. And he made the incense-altar of shittim-wood: the length of it was a cubit, and the breadth of it a cubit, (it was four-square,) and two cubits was the height of it; the horns thereof were of the same.

25. Fecit etiam altare incensi e lignis sittim: cubitus longitudo ejus: et cubitus latitudo ejus, quadratum: duo autem cubiti altitudo ejus: ex ipso erant cornua ejus.

26. And he overlaid it with pure gold, both the top of it, and the sides thereof round about, and the horns of it: also he made unto it a crown of gold round about.

26. Et texit illud auro puro, tectum ejus scilicet et parietes ejus in circuitu, et cornua ejus, fecitque ei coronam auream per circuitum.

27. And he made two rings of gold for it under the crown thereof, by the two corners of it, upon the two sides thereof, to be places for the staves to bear it withal.

27. Duos similiter annulos aureos fecit ei sub corona ejus in duobus angulis ejus, in duobus lateribus ejus, per quos trajicerentur vestes ad portandum illud ipsis.

28. And he made the staves of shittim-wood, and overlaid them with gold.

28. Et fecit vectes ipsos e lignis sittim, et texit eos auro.

29. And he made the holy anointing oil, and the pure incense of sweet spices, according to the work of the apothecary.

29. Fecit et oleum unctionis, sanctitatem, et suffimentum aromaticum purum, opere unguentarii.

If the repetition, which might appear to be superfluous in these chapters, should be wearisome to us, let us reflect on the intention of the Holy Spirit, who, in narrating the execution of the work, uses almost the identical words wherein He had previously set forth the commands of God, viz., that we may understand that Moses, and the artificers themselves, did not vary in the smallest point from the rule prescribed to them. God had commanded the Ark of the Covenant to be made, together with its cover; and Moses relates how it was completed, so that the artificers did not omit even its very minutest detail. He ordered a table to be made for the offering of bread, and not a single syllable is neglected. As to the candlestick there was the same scrupulous obedience, so that they did not alter it in any part. In the altar of incense there was no kind of dissimilarity between the command and the work; and, finally, the composition of the oil exactly corresponds with the command. There is no question, then, but that Moses commends obedience, as it is the foundation of true piety, and at the same time reminds us that there was no exercise of the imagination in the whole service of the tabernacle, because there is nothing more opposite to the purity of religion than to do anything which is not enjoined.

Exodus 38

Exodus 38:1-31

1. And he made the altar of burnt-offering of shittim-wood: five cubits was the length thereof, and five cubits the breadth thereof, (it was foursquare,) and three cubits the height thereof.

1. Fecit quoque altare holocausti e lignis sittim, quinque cubitorum latitudo ejus, et quinque cubitorum latitudo ejus, quadratum: et trium cubitorum altitudo ejus.

2. And he made the horns thereof on the four corners of it; the horns thereof were of the same: and he overlaid it with brass.

2. Et fecit cornua ejus in quatuor angulis ejus, ex ipso erant cornua ejus, et texit illud aere.

3. And he made all the vessels of the altar, the pots, and the shovels, and the basons, and the flesh-hooks, and the fire-pans: all the vessels thereof made he of brass.

3. Fecit insuper omnia vasa altaris, lebetes scilicet, et scopas, et crateras, et tridentes, et receptacula: omnia vasa ejus fecit aerea.

4. And he made for the altar a brasen grate of net-work, under the compass thereof, beneath unto the midst of it.

4. Fecit praeterea altari cribrum opere reticulato aeneum sub ambitu ejus inferne usque ad medium ejus.

5. And he cast four rings for the four ends of the grate of brass, to be places for the staves.

5. Fudit item quatuor annulos in quatuor extremitatibus cribro aeneo, in quos inducerentur vectes.

6. And he made the staves of shittim-wood, and overlaid them with brass.

6. Et fecit vectes e lignis sittim, quos texit aere.

7. And he put the staves into the rings on the sides of the altar, to bear it withal; he made the altar hollow with boards.

7. Introduxitque vectes ipsos in annulos illos per latera altaris ad ferendum illud illis: vacuum tabularum fecit illud.

8. And he made the laver of brass, and the foot of it of brass, of the looking-glasses of the women assembling, which assembled at the door of the tabernacle of the congregation.

8. Fecit similiter concham aeneam, et basim ejus aeneam ex speculis mulierum convenientium, quae conveniebant ad ostium tabernaeuli conventionis.

9. And he made the court: on the south side southward, the hangings of the court were of fine twined linen, an hundred cubits:

9. Fecit postremo atrium ad plagam austri ad meridiem: cortinae atrii e bysso retorta centum cubitorum.

10. Their pillars were twenty, and their brasen sockets twenty: the hooks of the pillars and their fillets were of silver.

10. Columnae earum viginti, et bases earum viginti ex aere: capitella columnarum, et fila eas cingentia, ex argento.

11. And for the north side the hangings were an hundred cubits, their pillars were twenty, and their sockets of brass twenty: the hooks of the pillars and their fillets of silver.

11. Et ad plagam aquilonis cortinae centum cubitorum: columnae earum viginti, et bases earum viginti ex aere: capitella columnarum, et fila eas cingentia, ex argento.

12. And for the west side were hangings of fifty cubits, their pillars ten, and their sockets ten: the hooks of the pillars and their fillets of silver.

12. Ad plagam vero occidentis cortinae quinquaginta cubitorum: columnae earum decem, et bases earum decem: capitella columnarum, et fila eas cingentia, ex argento.

13. And for the east side eastward, fifty cubits.

13. Et ad plagam orientis ad ortum cortinae quinquaginta cubitorum.

14. The hangings of the one side of the gate were fifteen cubits, their pillars three, and their sockets three.

14. Cortinae quindecim cubitorum erant in uno latere: columnae earum tres et bases earum tres.

15. And for the other side of the court-gate, on this hand and that hand, were hangings of fifteen cubits, their pillars three, and their sockets three.

15. Et in latere altero hinc et inde portae atrii, cortinae quindecim cubitorum: columnae earum tres, et bases earum tres.

16. All the hangings of the court round about were of fine twined linen:

16. Omnes cortinae atrii per circuitum erant ex bysso retorta.

17. And the sockets for the pillars were of brass; the hooks of the pillars and their fillets of silver; and the overlaying of their chapiters of silver: and all the pillars of the court were filled with silver.

17. Bases vero columnarum ex aere: capitella columnarum, et fila eas cingentia, ex argento: et operimenta capitellorum earum ex argento: ipsae etiam omnes columnae atrii cinctae erant argento.

18. And the hanging for the gate of the court was needle-work, of blue, and purple, and scarlet, and fine twined linen; and twenty cubits was the length, and the height in the breadth was five cubits, answerable to the hangings of the court.

18. Velum autem portae atrii opere phrygionis ex hyacintho, et purpura, et vermiculo cocci, et bysso retorta: cujus longitudo erat viginti cubitorum, altitudo vero in latitudine quinque cubitorum ad cortinas atrii.

19. And their pillars were four, and their sockets of brass four; their hooks of silver, and the overlaying of their chapiters and their fillets of silver.

19. Et columnae earum quatuor, basesque earum quatuar ex aere, uncini earum ex argento: et operimenta capitellorum earum, et fila eas cingentia, ex argento.

20. And all the pins of the tabernacle, and of the court round about, were of brass.

20. Omnes veto clavi tabernaculi et atrii in circuitu erant ex aere.

21. This is the sum of the tabernacle, even of the tabernacle of testimony, as it was counted, according to the commandment of Moses, for the service of the Levites, by the hand of Ithamar, son to Aaron the priest.

21. Ista sunt numerata tabernaculi, tabernaculi, inquam, testimonii, quae numerata sunt ad jussum Mosis, per manum Ithamar filii Aharon sacerdotis, in ministerium Levitarum.

22. And Bezaleel the son of Uri, the son of Hur, of the tribe of Judah, made all that the Lord commanded Moses.

22. Besaleel autem filius Uri filii Hur, de tribu Jehudah, fecit omnia illa quae praeceperat Jehova Mosi.

23. And with him was Aholiab, son of Ahisamach, of the tribe of Dan, an engraver, and a cunning workman, and an embroiderer in blue, and in purple, and in scarlet, and fine linen.

23. Et cum eo Aholiab filius Ahisamach, de tribu Dan, artifex, et acupictor et phrygio, in hyacintho, et purpura, et vermiculo cocci, et bysso.

24. All the gold that was occupied for the work, in all the work of the holy place, even the gold of the offering, was twenty and nine talents, and seven hundred and thirty shekels, after the shekel of the sanctuary.

24. Universum aurum insumptum in ipso opere, id est in toto opere sanctuarii (fuit autem aurum oblationis) fuit novem et viginti talentorum, et septingentorum triginta siclorum, secundum siclum sanctuarii.

25. And the silver of them that were numbered of the congregation was an hundred talents, and a thousand seven hundred and threescore and fifteen shekels, after the shekel of the sanctuary:

25. Et argentum numeratorum in coetu erat centum talenta et mille septingenti septuaginta quinque sicli, secundum siclum sanctuarii.

26. A bekah for every man, that is, half a shekel, after the shekel of the sanctuary, for every one that went to be numbered, from twenty years old and upward, for six hundred thousand, and three thousand, and five hundred and fifty men

26. Semissis in singula capita, id est dimidium sicli, secundum siclum sanctuarii omnibus transeuntibus ad numeratos, ab eo qui natus erat viginti annos et supra, in sexcentis tribus millibus quingentis et quinquaginta.

27. And of the hundred talents of silver were cast the sockets of the sanctuary, and the sockets of the vail; an hundred sockets of the hundred talents, a talent for a socket.

27. Fueruntque centum talenta argenti ad fundandas bases sanctuarii, et bases veli: centum bases ex centum talentis, talentum pro basi.

28. And of the thousand seven hundred seventy and five shekels he made hooks for the pillars, and overlaid their chapiters, and filleted them.

28. Et ex mille septingentis septuaginta quinque siclis fecit epistylia columnis, et texit capita ipsarum, et texit eas.

29. And the brass of the offering was seventy talents, and two thousand and four hundred shekels.

29. Aes autem oblationis fuit septuaginta talentorum, et duorum millium, et quadringentorum siclorum,

30. And therewith he made the sockets to the door of the tabernacle of the congregation, and the brasen altar, and the brasen grate for it, and all the vessels of the altar,

30. Et fecit ex eo bases ostii tabernaculi conventionis, et altare aereum, et cribrum ejus aereum, omniaque vasa altaris.

31. And the sockets of the court round about, and the sockets of the court-gate, and all the pins of the tabernacle, and all the pins of the court round about.

31. Et bases atrii per circuitum, et bases portae atrii, praeterea omnes palos tabernaculi, omnesque palos atrii per circuitum.

1. And he made the altar of burnt-offering. The purport of this chapter is the same as that of the last, except that the order of some parts of it is transposed, though not a word is changed. He begins with the altar of burnt-offering, which he states to have been made of the materials and the form prescribed by God, in order that the people might there offer with surer confidence their sacrifices for the expiation of sin, and for thanksgiving. One thing which had not been mentioned before, is here added respecting the laver of brass, or cauldron (concha,) from whence they took the water of sprinkling for expiation, viz., that this laver was ornamented with the mirrors of the women. Some explain this, [298] that the vessel was so bright that it might be easily discovered on every side whether there was any scandalous, or wanton, or indelicate act committed; for we know that impure and ungodly men sometimes conceal their iniquities under the cover of religion, even as it; is written that the women who frequented the tabernacle for religious exercises were defiled by the sons of Eli, the priests. (1 Samuel 2:22.) But there is another conjecture equally probable, that these mirrors were dedicated by holy women for the ornament of the Temple, and for sacred purposes; for, whereas women are only too much given to outward adornment and finery, they have been always very fond of mirrors, both for the purpose of painting their cheeks and arranging their hair, so that not a single hair should be out of place. Isaiah, therefore, (3:23,) enumerates mirrors amongst the luxuries [299] of the female world. Some, then, think that women, being devoted to God's service, laid aside this vanity, and consecrated their mirrors in testimony of their repentance. It might, however, have been that, amongst the other gifts before spoken of, they offered mirrors also, which were mounted as embossments in this brasen laver. Others suppose that they were carvings, by which the portraits of females were depicted, as if seen in mirrors. The simple notion is most approved by me, that they were votive offerings, wherewith pious women had desired to decorate the sanctuary, and that they had been applied to this use by the advice of the artificers; for he does not speak generally of all the women, but of those who warred or assembled by troops at the door of the tabernacle; for translators[300] variously explain this word צבא, tzaba, both in this passage and that from Samuel which I have just quoted. It is also applied to the Levites, who are said[301] "to war the warfare" of the sanctuary, whilst performing their appointed work. (Numbers 4:3; 8:24.) Indeed this metaphor is by no means unsuitable to watchings and long-continued prayers. The sum is, that the laver was cast of their materials, or, as I rather suppose, embossed with these mirrors, in order that it might be more splendid.

21. This is the sum of the tabernacle [302] As much as to say that this was the computation, or these the numbers; for he gives us to understand that not only was the tabernacle thus at once completed, but that its several parts were numerically distinguished, and consigned as it were to registers, [303] so as to be given in charge to the Levites, lest any part of it should be lost. For the reference here is not so much to the fabric, or the architecture of the tabernacle,

as to its perpetual conservation, viz., that Ithamar the priest deposited its several parts with the Levites, and this in accordance with the command of Moses.

22. And Bezaleel, the son of Uri. He again impresses upon us that the whole work was divine, both because Moses faithfully delivered the commands of God, and the artificers followed them with precise accuracy. At the same time, he counts up the whole sum of gold and silver, and shews us on what it was consumed. Hence we gather that every one honestly discharged his duty, and that no one was corrupted or drawn aside by covetousness so as to fall from his integrity. We are also informed from whence the amount of silver was obtained, viz., from the census of the people; for a tax of a common shekel, which was half a shekel of the sanctuary, was imposed on every head, as we[304] have already seen. Moses now shews that this entire sum was collected and paid without fraud, and so applied as that none should be lost.

Exodus 39

Exodus 39:1-43

1. And of the blue, and purple, and scarlet, they made clothes of service, to do service in the holy place, and made the holy garments for Aaron; as the Lord commanded Moses.

1. Ex hyacintho autem, et purpura, et vermiculo cocci fecerunt vestes ministerii ad ministrandum in sanctuario: fecerunt item vestes sanctitatis, quae erant Aharonis, quemadmodum praeceperat Jehova ipsi Mosi.

2. And he made the ephod of gold, blue, and purple, and scarlet, and fine twined linen.

2. Fecit et ephod ex auro, hyacintho, et purpura, et vermiculo cocci, et bysso retorta.

3. And they did beat the gold into thin plates, and cut it into wires, to work it in the blue, and in the purple, and in the scarlet, and in the fine linen, with cunning work.

3. Extenderuntque bracteas aureas, et inciderunt fila, ut texerent in medio hyacinthi, et in medio purpurae, et in medio vermiculi cocci, et in medio byssi, opere phrygionico.

4. They made shoulder-pieces for it, to couple it together: by the two edges was it coupled together.

4. Oras fecerunt ei copulantes sese, et in duabus extremitatibus ejus conjungebantur.

5. And the curious girdle of his ephod, that was upon it, was of the same, according to the work thereof, of gold, blue, and purple, and scarlet, and fine twined linen; as the Lord commanded Moses.

5. Et cingulum ephod quod erat super illud, ex ipso erat juxta opus suum, ex auro, hyacintho, et purpura, et vermiculo cocci, et bysso retorta, quemadmodum praeceperat Jehova Mosi.

6. And they wrought onyx-stones inclosed in ouches of gold, graven, as signets are graven, with the names of the children of Israel.

6. Et aptaverunt lapides onychinos circundatos palis aureis, sculptos sculpturis annuli cum nominibus filiorum Israel.

7. And he put them on the shoulders of the ephod, that they should be stones for a memorial to the children of Israel; as the Lord commanded Moses.

7. Posuitque illos in lateribus ephod, ut essent lapides memoriae filiis Israel, quemadmodum praeceperat Jehova Mosi.

8. And he made the breastplate of cunning work, like the work of the ephod; of gold, blue, and purple, and scarlet, and fine twined linen.

8. Fecit et pectorale opere phrygionis, sicut opus ephod, ex auro, hyacintho, et purpura, et vermiculo cocci, et bysso retorta.

9. It was four-square; they made the breastplate double: a span was the length thereof, and a span the breadth thereof, being doubled.

9. Quadratum erat, duplicatum fecerunt pectorale: palmus longitudo ejus, palmusque latitudo ejus: duplicatum.

10. And they set in it four rows of stones; the first row was a sardius, a topaz, and a carbuncle: this was the first row.

10. Impleverunt autem in eo quatuor ordines lapidum, ordo autem talis erat, sardius, topazius, et carbunculus, erat ordo primus.

11. And the second row, an emerald, a sapphire, and a diamond.

11. Ordo vero secundus, smaragdus, sapphirus, et jaspis.

12. And the third row, a ligure, an agate, and an amethyst.

12. Ordo praeterea tertius, lyncurius, achates, et amethystus.

13. And the fourth row, a beryl, an onyx, and a jasper: they were inclosed in ouches of gold in their inclosings.

13. Postremo quartus ordo, chrysolitus, onychinus, et beryllus circundati palis aureis in plenitudinibus suis.

14. And the stones were according to the names of the children of Israel, twelve, according to their names, like the engravings of a signet, every one with his name, according to the twelve tribes.

14. Porro lapides illi juxta nomina filiorum Israel erant, duodecim, juxta nomina eorum, sculpturae sigilli, quilibet juxta nomen suum, secundum duodecim tribus.

15. And they made upon the breastplate chains at the ends, of wreathen work of pure gold.

15. Fecerunt et super pectorale catenas terminationis opere plectili ex auro puro.

16. And they made two ouches of gold, and two gold rings, and put the two rings in the two ends of the breastplate.

16. Fecerunt etiam duas palas aureas, et duos annulos aureos: posueruntque duos illos annulos in duabus extremitatibus pectoralis.

17. And they put the two wreathen chains of gold in the two rings on the ends of the breastplate.

17. Et inseruerunt duas catenas aureas duobus illis annulis qui erant in extremitatibus pectoralis.

18. And the two ends of the two wreathen chains they fastened in the two ouches, and put them on the shoulder-pieces of the ephod, before it.

18. Duas autem extremitates duarum catenarum inseruerunt duabus illis palis, posueruntque eas in oris ephod a fronte ipsius.

19. And they made two rings of gold, and put them on the two ends of the breastplate, upon the border of it, which was on the side of the ephod inward.

*19. Fecerunt item duos annulos aureos, quos posuerunt in duabus
extremitatibus pectoralis, in ora ejus quae erat in latere ephod intrinsecus.*

20. And they made two other golden rings, and put them on the two
sides of the ephod underneath, toward the fore-part of it, over against the
other coupling thereof, above the curious girdle of the ephod.

*20. Fecerunt praeterea duos alios annulos aureos, quos posuerunt in
duabus oris ephod inferne, a fronte ipsius, e regione conjunctionis ejus, supra
balteum ephod.*

21. And they did bind the breastplate by his rings unto the rings of the
ephod with a lace of blue, that it might be above the curious girdle of the
ephod, and that the breastplate might not be loosed from the ephod; as the
Lord commanded Moses.

*21. Et ligaverunt pectorale ab annulis suis ad annulos ipsius ephod, filo
hyacinthino, ut esset supra balteum ipsius ephod, neque separaretur pectorale
ab ephod: quemadmodum praeceperat Jehova ipsi Mosi.*

22. And he made the robe of the ephod of woven work, all of blue.

22. Fecit insuper pallium ipsi ephod opere textoris, totum hyacinthinum.

23. And there was an hole in the midst of the robe, as the hole of
habergeon, with a band round about the hole, that it should not rend.

*23. Et foramen pallii in medio ejus, sicut foramen loricae labrum erat in
orificio ipsius per circuitum, ne frangeretur.*

24. And they made upon the hems of the robe pomegranates of blue,
and purple, and scarlet, and twined linen

*24. Feceruntque in fimbriis pallii malogranata ex hyacintho, et purpura, et
vermiculo cocci, et bysso retorta.*

25. And they made bells of pure gold, and put the bells between the
pomegranates, upon the hem of the robe, round about between the
pomegranates:

*25. Fecerunt et tintinnabula exauro puro, posueruntque tintinnabula illa in
medio malogranatorum, in fimbriis pallii per circuitum, in medio, inquam,
malogranatorum.*

26. A bell and a pomegranate, a bell and a pomegranate, round about
the hem of the robe to minister in; as the Lord commanded Moses.

*26. Tintinnabulum et malogranatum, tintinnabulum et malogranatum in
fimbriis pallii in circuitu, ad ministrandum, quemadmodum praeceperat et
Jehova ipsi Mosi.*

27. And they made coats of fine linen, of woven work, for Aaron, and
for his sons;

*27. Post haec fecerunt tunicas ex bysso opere textorio ipsi Aharon et filiis
ejus:*

28. And a mitre of fine linen, and goodly bonnets of fine linen, and
linen breeches of fine twined linen;

*28. Mitram quoque ex bysso, et decora galerorum ex bysso, et foeminalia
linee ex bysso retorta:*

29. And a girdle of fine twined linen, and blue, and purple, and scarlet,
of needle-work; as the Lord commanded Moses.

*29. Balteum praeterea ex bysso retorta, et hyacintho, ex purpura, et
vermiculo cocci, opere phrygionis, quemadmodum praeceperat Jehova ipsi
Mosi.*

30. And they made the plate of the holy crown of pure gold, and wrote upon it a writing, like to the engravings of a signet, Holiness to the Lord.

30. Fecerunt postremo laminam coronae sanctificationis ex auro, scripseruntque in ea scriptura caelaturarum annuli, Sanctitas ipsi Jehovae.

31. And they tied unto it a lace of blue, to fasten it on high upon the mitre; as the Lord commanded Moses.

31. Et inseruerunt in eam filum hyacinthinum, ut poneretur super tiaram superne, quemadmodum praeceperat Jehova Mosi.

32. Thus was all the work of the tabernacle of the tent of the congregation finished: and the children of Israel did according to all that the Lord commanded Moses, so did they.

32. Perfectum est igitur totum opus tabernaculi conventionis: et fecerunt filii Israel juxta omnia quae praeceperat Jehova ipsi Mosi, sic fecerunt.

33. And they brought the tabernacle unto Moses, the tent, and all his furniture, his taches, his boards, his bars, and his pillars, and his sockets;

33. Attuleruntque tabernaculum illud ad Mosen, tabernaculum et omnia vasa ejus, circulos ejus, tabulas ejus, vectes ejus, et columnas ejus, et bases ejus.

34. And the covering of rams' skins dyed red, and the covering of badgers' skins, and the vail of the covering;

34. Opertorium quoque ex pellibus arietum rubricatis, et opertorium ex pellibus taxorum, et velum operimenti.

35. The ark of the testimony, and the staves thereof, and the mercy-seat;

35. Arcam testimonii, et vectes ejus, et propitiatorium,

36. The table, and all the vessels thereof, and the shew-bread;

36. Mensam, omnia vasa ejus, et panem facierum,

37. The pure candlestick, with the lamps thereof, even with the lamps to be set in order, and all the vessels thereof, and the oil for light;

37. Candelabrum purum, lucernas inquam ordinationis, et omnia vasa ejus, et oleum luminaris,

38. And the golden altar, and the anointing oil, and the sweet incense, and the hanging for the tabernacle-door;

38. Et altare aureum, et oleum unctionis, et suffimentum aromaticum, et aulaeum pro ostio tabernaculi.

39. The brasen altar, and his grate of brass, his staves, and all his vessels; the laver and his foot;

39. Altare aereum, et cribrum ejus aereum, vectes ejus, et omnia vasa ejus, et concham, et basim ejus.

40. The hangings of the court, his pillars, and his sockets, and the hanging for the court-gate, his cords, and his pins, and all the vessels of the service of the tabernacle, for the tent of the congregation;

40. Cortinas atrii, et columnas ejus, et aulaeum pro porta atrii, et funes ejus, et palos ejus, et omnia vasa ministerii tabernaculi, tabernaculi conventionis.

41. The clothes of service to do service in the holy place; and the holy garments for Aaron the priest, and his sons' garments, to minister in the priest's office.

41. Vestes ministerii ad ministrandum in sanctuario, vestes sanctas ipsi Aharon sacerdoti, et vestes filiorum ejus, ad fungendum sacerdotio.

42. According to all that the Lord commanded Moses, so the children of Israel made all the work.

42. Juxta omnia quae praeceperat Jehova Mosi, sic fecerunt filii Israel universum opus.

43. And Moses did look upon all the work, and, behold, they had done it as the Lord had commanded, even so had they done it: and Moses blessed them.

43. Videns vero Moses universum opus, quod prorsus fecissent illud quemadmodum praeceperat Jehova, benedixit illis.

1. And of the blue, and purple, and scarlet. The description of the sacerdotal garments, which is repeated in this chapter, is more accurate than it would have been had he been speaking of some unimportant matter. And assuredly, since Christ was vividly represented in the person of the high priest, this was a most important part of the legal service. We have elsewhere set forth how far it was from being an empty pomp, as when the Popish sacrificers now-a-days, in order to acquire dignity, dazzle the eyes of the simple by the splendor of their vestments, and their magnificent paraphernalia; but that rather it was for the purpose of placing before men's eyes all that faith ought to consider in Jesus Christ. We have especially seen how great mysteries were contained in the mitre, which was Holiness to the Lord: and in the ephod, in which shone forth the light of truth and integrity of life, and in which were the symbols of the ten tribes, so that the priest bore the people itself upon his shoulders and before his breast, in such a manner that in the person of one all might be presented familiarly before God. For this reason he repeats seven times the clause, "as the Lord commanded Moses;" which certainly has the effect of awakening attention.

32. Thus was all the work of the tabernacle. A brief summary is now subjoined, whereby he indicates that in no part was there the least defect, and also declares that the children of Israel had so obeyed God's commands, that the work itself varied in no respect from its pattern. "The children of Israel," he says, "did according to all that the Lord commanded Moses, so did they;" whence we gather that no part of the building was impaired by any admixture. Afterwards it is added, that the tabernacle with its utensils and furniture was brought before Moses, and that all things were approved of by his judgment; for he is said to have "blessed them," because they had duly and faithfully obeyed God's command. This, however, was not a simple prayer, as of a private individual; but it was a promise of reward, such as might awaken confidence in the minds of the people, when they heard from the mouth ("D'un tel Prophete;" of such a Prophet. -- Fr.) of this excellent and unimpeachable witness that their labor was pleasing to God.

Exodus 24

Exodus 24:1-18

1. And he said unto Moses, Come up unto the Lord, thou, and Aaron, Nadab and Abihu, and seventy of the elders of Israel; and worship ye afar off.

1. Et dixit ad Mosen, Ascende ad Jehovam tu et Aharon, Nadab et Abihu, et septuaginta e senioribus Israel, et adorabitis procul.

2. And Moses alone shall come near the Lord; but they shall not come nigh, neither shall the people go up with him.

2. Solus autem Moses perveniet ad Jehovam: ipsi vero non pervenient, nec populus ascendet cum eo.

3. And Moses came and told the people all the words of the Lord, and all the judgments: and all the people answered with one voice, and said, All the words which the Lord hath said will we do.

3. Venit ergo Moses, et narravit populo omnia verba Jehovae, omniaque judicia, Et respondit totus populus una voce, ac dixerunt, Quaecunque verba loquutus est Jehova, faciemus.

4. And Moses wrote all the words of the Lord, and rose up early in the morning, and builded an altar under the hill, and twelve pillars, according to the twelve tribes of Israel.

4. (Seripserat autem Moses omnia verba Jehovae): surgensque mane aedificavit altare sub monte, et duodecim statuas secundum duodecim tribus Israel.

5. And he sent young men of the children of Israel, which offered burnt-offerings, and sacrificed peace-offerings of oxen unto the Lord.

5. Misitque juniores filiorum Israel, qui immolaverunt holocausta, et sacrificaverunt sacrificia prosperitatum ipsi Jehovae, vitulos.

6. And Moses took half of the blood, and put it in basins; and half of the blood he sprinkled on the altar.

6. Accepit Moses dimidium sanguinis, et posuit in crateribus: dimidium vero sanguinis sparsit super altare.

7. And he took the book of the covenant, and read in the audience of the people: and they said, All that the Lord hath said will we do, and be obedient.

7. Sumpsit deinde librum foederis, et legit in auribus populi: qui dixerunt, Quaecunque dixit Jehova, faciemus, et obediemus.

8. And Moses took the blood, and sprinkled it on the people, and said, Behold the blood of the covenant, which the Lord hath made with you concerning all these words.

8. Tulit quoque Moses sanguinem, et sparsit super populum, ac dixit, Ecce, sanguis foederis quod pepigit Jehova vobiscum super cunctis his sermonibus.

9. Then went up Moses and Aaron, Nadab and Abihu, and seventy of the elders of Israel;

9. Ascendit autem Moses, et Aharon, Nadab et Abihu, et septuaginta e senioribus Israel.

10. And they saw the God of Israel: and there was under his feet as it were a paved work of a sapphire-stone, and as it were the body of heaven in his clearness.

10. Et viderunt Deum Israel: et sub pedibus ejus erat tanquam opus tabulae sapphiri, et sicut species coeli serenitate.

11. And upon the nobles of the children of Israel he laid not his hand: also they saw God, and did eat and drink.

11. Et in principes filiorum Israel non extendit manum suam: et viderunt Deum, et comederunt, et biberunt.

12. And the Lord said unto Moses, Come up to me into the mount, and be there; and I will give thee tables of stone, and a law, and commandments which I have written; that thou mayest teach them.

12. Dixitque Jehova ad Mosen, Ascende ad me in montem, et esto ibi; daboque tibi duas tabulas lapideas, et Legem atque praeceptum, quae scripsi ad docendum eos.

13. And Moses rose up, and his minister Joshua; and Moses went up into the mount of God.

13. Surrexit itaque Moses et Jehosua minister ejus; et ascendit Moses in montem Dei.

14. And he said unto the elders, Tarry ye here for us, until we come again unto you: and, behold, Aaron and Hur are with you: if any man have any matters to do, let him come unto them.

14. Senioribusque dixit, Manete hic donec revertamur ad vos: et ecce, Aharon et Hur sunt vobiscum: quisquis habuerit causas, accedet ad eos.

15. And Moses went up into the mount, and a cloud covered the mount.

15. Tunc ascendit Moses in montem, et operuit nubes montem.

16. And the glory of the Lord abode upon mount Sinai, and the cloud covered it six days: and the seventh day he called unto Moses out of the midst of the cloud.

16. Habitavitque gloria Jehovae; super montem Sinai, et operuit eum nubes sex diebus: vocavitque ipsum Mosen die septimo e medio nubis.

17. And the sight of the glory of the Lord was like devouring fire on the top of the mount in the eyes of the children of Israel.

17. Et aspectus gloriae Jehovae erat tanquam ignis comburens in vertice montis, in oculis filiorum Israel.

18. And Moses went into the midst of the cloud, and gat him up into the mount: and Moses was in the mount forty days and forty nights.

18. Et ingressus est Moses in medium nubis, ascenditque in montem: et fuit Moses in monte quadraginta diebus, et quadraginta noctibus.

1. Come up unto the Lord, thou, and Aaron, Nadab and Abihu. Before Moses erected the tabernacle and consecrated it by a solemn ceremony, it was necessary for him to fetch the Tables of the Covenant, which were a pledge of God's favor; otherwise, if the ark had nothing in it, the sanctuary would have been in a manner empty. For this reason, he is commanded to go up into the mount, but not without a splendid train of companions, in order that an appropriate preparation might arouse their minds for a fit reception of this especial blessing. He is, therefore, commanded to take with him Aaron his brother, and Nadab and Abihu, together with seventy of the elders of the people. This was the number of witnesses selected to behold the glory of God. Before, however, they ascended the mount, a sacrifice was offered by the whole people, and the Book of the Law was read. Finally, Moses alone was received into the top of the mount, to bring from thence the Tables written by the hand of God.

Here, however, (See this subject [37]further discussed on Numbers 11:16, infra.) arises a question respecting the seventy elders; for we shall see elsewhere that the seventy were not chosen till the people had departed from Mount Sinai; whereas mention is made of them here, before the promulgation of the Law, which seems to be by no means consistent. But this difficulty is removed, if we allow, what we gather from this passage, that, even before they came to Mount Sinai, each tribe had appointed its governors (praefectos), who would make up this number, since there were six of every tribe; but that when Moses afterwards desired to be relieved of his burdens, part of the government was transferred [305] to these seventy persons, since this number was already sanctioned by custom and use. Certainly, since it is plainly stated that there were [306] seventy from the very first, it is probable that this number of coadjutors was given to Moses in order to make as little change as possible. For we know that, when a custom has obtained, men are very unwilling to depart from it. But it might have also been that the desire and intention of the Israelites was thus to celebrate the memory of their origin; for seventy persons had gone down into Egypt with Jacob, and, in less than two hundred and twenty years after they went there, their race had increased to six hundred thousand, besides women and children. It is not, therefore, contrary to probability that seventy persons were appointed to preside over the whole people, in order that so marvelous a blessing of God might continue to be testified in all ages, as if to trace the commencement of their race up to its very source.

2. And Moses alone shall come near the Lord. Three gradations are here marked. A station is prescribed for the people, from whence they may "worship afar off;" the elders and the priests are appointed to be the companions of Moses, to come closer, and thus to be witnesses to the people of all the things which we shall afterwards see to be shewn them; whilst, as they were separated from the multitude, so finally Moses alone was received up into the higher glory; for he was caught up on high in the covering of the cloud. This [307] distinction is marked in the words, "Moses alone shall come near...; but they shall not come nigh; neither shall the people go up." Some translators render the verbs in the past tense; but improperly, in my opinion; for Moses is not yet relating what was done, but only what God had commanded, as is plain from the next verse, wherein also the modesty and humility of the people is commended, because they received with reverence a command which was not in itself very agreeable or likely to be approved. For, such is the ambition of men, that it might have appeared insulting that they should be set afar off and prohibited from approaching the mountain, like strangers and heathens. It is, therefore, an evidence of their pious reverence, that they should submit to be placed at a distance, and should be contented with a position apparently less honorable. And Moses more clearly expresses their promptitude to obey, when he reports their words, that they would do all that he had declared to them from the mouth of God.

4. And Moses [308] wrote all the words of the Lord. This parenthesis is opportunely inserted; for we shall see a little further on that the book was read before the people; but, in order to awaken greater attention, before the reading he built an altar and offered victims in the sight of all the people. Moreover, it must be observed that statues [309] were erected near the altar according to the number of the tribes, that they might know that they were not kept afar off in token of rejection, but only that, conscious of their own unworthiness, they might humble themselves before God in fear and trembling; for, though they were removed to a considerable distance, still they were remembered before God, and thus He embraced them all, as it were, by means of these statues. What Moses, however, calls by this name, were not images bearing the shape

of a man, but heaps of stones, which might be as monuments representing the twelve tribes; that they might know that they were by no means excluded from the sanctity of the altar.

5. And he sent young men of the children of Israel. He either means that they were the sacrificial attendants (victimarios,) by whose hands the victims were killed, or that some were chosen who might be active and strong to drag the oxen to the altar. The tribe of Levi was not yet consecrated; whereas the word used for "offering," [310] is only applied to the priests, where a distinction is marked between the Levites and the rest of the people. The first meaning is, therefore, the most suitable.

We have stated elsewhere that the [311] sacrifices of prosperities were designed as acts of thanksgiving; and yet that they were not only expressions of gratitude, but also that prayers were mixed with them in supplication of good success. This offering, however, comprised in it a ratification of the Covenant, as appears immediately afterwards; for, in order to increase the sanctity and security of covenants, they have in all ages, and even [312] amongst heathen nations, been accompanied with sacrifices. To this end Moses, the victims being slain, pours half the blood upon the altar, and keeps half in basins to sprinkle the people, that by this [313] symbol the Covenant might be ratified, whereof he was the mediator and surety. Paul, in allusion to this custom, says, that he should rejoice, if he were "offered upon the sacrifice and service of their faith" whom he had gained for Christ, (Philippians 2:17;) and he uses the word σπένδεσθαι, which [314] is primarily applied to covenants. But the case of this sacrifice was peculiar; for God desired the Jews to be reminded of the one solid confirmation of the Covenant, which He made with them; as if He had openly shown that it would then only be ratified and effectual, when it should be sealed with blood. And this the Apostle (Hebrews 9:19) carefully takes into consideration, when he says, that after the Law had been declared, Moses "sprinkled both the book and all the people" with blood; for, although there is no express mention here made of the book, the Apostle does not unreasonably comprise it under the word "altar." He also alludes to another kind of sacrifice, treated of in Numbers 19:5, and therefore mentions "the scarlet-wool and hyssop." The sum is, that the blood was, as it were, the medium whereby the covenant was confirmed and established, since the altar, as the sacred seat of God, was bathed with half of it, and then the residue was sprinkled over the people. Hence we gather that the covenant of gratuitous adoption was made with the ancient people unto eternal salvation, since it was sealed with the blood of Christ in type and shadow. Now, if this doctrine hold good under the Law, much more must it occupy a place with us now; and hence, in order that God's promises may always maintain their power and certainty, let this sealing be constantly kept before us; and let us remember that the blood of Christ has therefore once been shed, that it might engrave upon our hearts the covenant whereby we are called to the hope of the kingdom of heaven. For this reason Christ in the Holy Supper commends His blood as the seal of the New Covenant; nay, whenever we take the sacred books into our hands, the blood of Christ, ought to occur to our minds, as if the whole [315] of its sacred instruction were written therewith; for it is obvious that Christ compares with the figure the truth which was manifested in Himself; to which also the admonition of the Apostle, which I have just quoted, refers.

We must now carefully observe the course of the proceeding. First, Moses states that he read the book before the people; and then adds that the people themselves embraced the covenant proposed to them. Finally, he relates that when the people had professed their obedience, he sprinkled the blood, not without adding his testimony, and that in a loud voice. The context here shews us the true and genuine nature of the Sacraments, together with their correct and proper use; for unless doctrine precede them to be a connecting link between God and man, they will be empty and delusive signs, however honorable may be the encomiums passed on them. But inasmuch as mutual consent is required in all compacts, so, when God invites His people to receive grace, He stipulates that they should give Him the obedience of faith, so as to answer, Amen. Thus nothing can be more preposterous than the invention of dumb sacraments: such as those childish charms which the Papists hawk about as sacraments, without the word of God; whilst, at the same time, it must be added that the word, which gives life to the Sacraments, is not an obscure whisper, like that magical incantation of the Papists, when they blow on the bread and the cup, and which they call the consecration; but it is a clear and distinct voice which is addressed to men, and avails to beget faith in them. Thus Moses here speaks aloud to the people, and reminds them that God enters into covenant with him.

Now, although the profession here recorded might seem to be derived from too great confidence, when the people declare that they will do whatsoever God commands, still it contains nothing amiss or reprehensible; inasmuch as the faithful among them promised nothing, except in reliance on the help of God: and gratuitous reconciliation, if they should sin, was included in it. This was not indeed the proper office of the Law, to incline men's hearts to the obedience of righteousness; as also under the Law there was no true and real expiation to wash away the guilt of sins; but the office of the Law was to lead men step by step to Christ, that they might seek of Him pardon and the Spirit of regeneration. It is, therefore, unquestionable that the elect of God embraced by faith the substance and truth of the shadows when they voluntarily offered themselves to keep the covenant of God.

9. Then went up Moses and Aaron, Nadab and Abihu. Thus it is that I connect the history: Moses, having finished reading the Law, and having sprinkled the blood, took with him the companions pointed out to him by God, and having left the people, went with these some way up the mountain. I have thought it well slightly to touch upon this, because some translators render the verb improperly in the pluperfect tense, as if he and the elders had already before [316] been separated from the people; but this is very absurd, for it was necessary for him to remain in the plain, in order to address the people.

There the glory of God was beheld more closely by the elders, that they might afterwards relate to the people what they had seen, and that thus the thing, being proved by competent witnesses, might obtain undoubted credit. For this reason he says, that "they saw the God of Israel," not in all His reality and greatness, but in accordance with the dispensation which He thought best, and which he accommodated to the capacity of man. The form of God is indeed nowhere described, but the pediment (basis) on which He stood was like a work of sapphire. [317] The word לבנת, libnath, some translate stone, others whiteness, others brick. Whichever sense it is preferred to take it in, but little affects the main point in the matter; for the color of a sapphire was presented to them, to elevate their minds by its brightness above the world; and therefore it is immediately added, that its appearance was as of the clear and serene sky. By this symbol they were reminded that the glory of God is above all heavens; and since in His very footstool there is such exquisite and surpassing beauty, something still more sublime must be thought of Himself, and such as would ravish all our senses with admiration. Thus the throne of God was shewn to Ezekiel "as the appearance of a sapphire-stone." (Ezekiel 1:26; 10:1.)

Finally, on the footstool Infinite Majesty appeared, such as to strike the elders with astonishment, so that they might humble themselves with greater reverence before the incomprehensible glory of God.

11. *And upon the nobles of the children of Israel.* These words, as it seems to me, are violently distorted by those [318] who expound them, that the elders were not made participators of the prophetic gift, or that the virtue of God did not extend to them; for these clauses are to be taken connectedly thus: although they saw God, His hand was not laid upon them but they ate and drank. Hence we may gather that God's paternal favor towards them is pointed out in that He spared them; for we must bear in mind what is said elsewhere, "There shall no man see my face and live." (Exodus 33:20.) Thus, amongst the ancients, this was a kind of proverbial expression: We shall die, because we have seen God. So Jacob, in commendation of God's grace, says, "I have seen God face to face, and my life is preserved." (Genesis 32:30.) For if the mountains melt at the sight of Him, what must needs happen to a mortal man, than whom there is nothing more frail or feeble? Herein, then, does God's incomparable lenity betray itself, when, in manifesting Himself to His elect, He does not altogether absorb and reduce them to nothing; especially when some special vision is presented to them. In sum, therefore, Moses shews us that it was a miracle that the rulers of Israel remained safe and sound, although the terrible majesty of God had appeared to them. Now, this was the case, because they had not rashly thrust themselves forward, but had come near at the call of God. Hence we learn that our boldness never exceeds its due bounds, nor can be condemned as presumption, when it is founded on the command of God; whilst worse than any pride or self-confidence is timidity, which, under pretense of modesty, leads us to distrust the word of God. If any one of the people had attempted to do the same as the rulers, he would have experienced in his destruction what it is to advance beyond bounds. But the reason why their free and bold access turned out successfully to the elders, was because they obeyed the command of God.

What follows, as to their eating, I interpret to mean a solemn banquet, which was a part or appendage of a sacrifice, as we have seen on Exodus 18[319] and in many other places.

12. *And the Lord said unto Moses, Come up to me.* Moses himself is now taken up higher; because it was sufficient that the elders should be admitted to that intermediate vision, from whence they might certainly know that he would not proceed further, except by God's command, in order that he might be received to familiar colloquy. Although, however, Joshua began to go on with him, it is plain that he was only his companion for six days, until Moses left him behind, and was gathered into the cloud. When God declares that He will give him "a law and commandment," this must not be understood of any new instruction, but of the authentic writing (consignatione) of the Law: for, after having spoken of the two tables, He immediately mentions, in apposition, the

Law and Commandment, by way of explanation; as if He had said that He would give the tables, which were to be a divine monument [320] of His covenant; so that a summary of doctrine should exist among the people, not written with ink, and by the hand of man, but by the secret power of the Spirit. I am afraid the speculation of Augustine is more subtle than correct, that the Law was written by the finger of God, [321] because only the Spirit of God engraves it on our hearts; for, to pass over the fact that the hardness of the stones was not changed, what will their breaking mean, which will be spoken of hereafter? Surely it does not accord that, whereas the grace of regeneration endures unto the end, the Law should be only engraven efficaciously by the Spirit upon men's hearts for a moment. What I have advanced, however, is beyond controversy, that the Law was inscribed upon these polished stones, that the perpetuity of the covenant might be testified in all ages.

14. *Tarry ye here for us, until we come again.* I do not take the words so precisely as to suppose that he commanded them to stand still in the same place; but since he was just about to be separated from intercourse with men, I suppose, that our earthly dwelling-place is indicated by the adverb, [322] since it immediately follows, that if anything should occur, Aaron and Hur were to be his substitutes for ruling the people and settling quarrels. For, since care and anxiety might beset their minds, as being deprived of their only guide in counsel, and minister of safety, he offers this consolation to relieve their despondency. Hence it follows that they were sent back to occupy their charge, which could not be the case, unless they were in communication with the people. We are not aware whether Moses was pre-informed as to the time (of his absence, [323]) although it is more probable that he was in doubt and suspense, until he penetrated into the secret counsel of God. From the last verse but one, we learn, that though the majesty of God was more clearly revealed to the elders, still it was conspicuous to all, from the least to the greatest, lest any excuse for ignorance should remain; for when the fire was seen burning for six continuous days, as if it would consume the mountain, how could they afterwards pretend that it was not fully understood from what Author the Law proceeded?

Exodus 31

Exodus 31:18

18. And he gave unto Moses, when he had made an end of communing with him upon mount Sinai, two tables of testimony, tables of stone, written with the finger of God.

18. Et dedit Deus Most, quum finem fecisset loquendi cum eo in monte Sinai, duas tabulas Testimonii, tabulas lapideas scriptas digito Dei.

18 *And he gave unto Moses.* It must be observed, that, after the voice of God had been heard from the midst of the fire, and He had delivered the Ten Commandments, and the form of the tabernacle had been described, and the work had been already finished by the artificers, though its dedication had not yet taken place, Moses was again withdrawn from the sight and intercourse of men, that he might be taught apart by himself to be a faithful interpreter of the Law. For although God had briefly comprised in the Ten Commandments the

sum of His doctrine, which might suffice for the rule of a pious and righteous life, still a clearer exposition was needed, such as Moses afterwards added. With this object he was taken up into the sanctuary (adytum) of heaven, as it were, in order that he might familiarly learn all things that concerned the full and complete understanding of the Ten Commandments, since he could never have attained their genuine meaning if God had not been his Master and Teacher. Hence we gather that he wrote his five books not only under the guidance of the Spirit of God, but as God Himself had suggested them, speaking to him out of His own mouth. Wherefore he observed silence for forty days, that he might afterwards freely speak by the authority of God. Thus ought all true pastors of the Church to be disciples, so as to teach nothing but what they have received. But although God might in a moment have fully perfected His servant, yet, in order more surely to evince that he advanced nothing which did not proceed from the school of heaven, he was separated for forty days from the human race, so that the Israelites might henceforth look up to him as to an angel sent from heaven; for there could be no savour of earth about him who had thus lived with God, without meat and drink, or any other means of nourishment, and divested of all infirmity of the flesh.

Finally, the Ten Commandments were written on two tables, so that they might never be lost. I have elsewhere stated why they were divided into two tables, viz., because they consist of two parts, the first of which is the rule of piety, whilst the second prescribes how we must live righteously, innocently, and chastely with men. Thus the worship of God comes first in order, and then the duties of charity follow. The tables were of stone, inasmuch as it is usual for enduring monuments to be engraven on brass, or stones. That they were "written with the finger of God," we must understand to mean that the characters were formed without the hand or skill of men, by the secret virtue of God; nor is it a matter of wonder that a writing should have suddenly been brought into existence at the same will (nutu) of God, whereby the waste and shapeless materials of the world, which they call chaos, were changed so as to be resplendent with astonishing elegance and beauty. This expression, however, is metaphorical, whereby what is only applicable to men is figuratively spoken of God; for God is not corporeal so as to write with His finger; and for Him to act is only to command; as it is said in the Psalms,

"He spake, and all things were made; he commanded, and they were created." (Psalm 33:9; 148:5.)

Many approve of the allegory, that the Law was written by the Spirit of God on stones, because the hardness of our heart does not receive it without the grace of regeneration; but we must rather hold to the antithesis of Paul, wherein he shews that the Gospel differs from the Law in this respect, because it is written on fleshy hearts, subdued unto obedience, (2 Corinthians 3:3;) and indeed it is by no means fitting that we should trifle in such conceits as this, when the simple intention of God is abundantly manifest, viz., that the Law was registered upon stones, in order that the perpetuity of its doctrine should be maintained in all ages.

Exodus 32

Exodus 32:1-35

1. And when the people saw that Moses delayed to come down out of the mount, the people gathered themselves together unto Aaron, and said unto him, Up, make us gods, which shall go before us; for as for this Moses, the man that brought us up out of the land of Egypt, we wot not what is become of him.

1. Videns antem populus quod moram faceret Moses ad descendendum e monte, tunc congregatus est contra Aharon, et dixerunt ei, Surge, fac nobis Deos qui praecedant nos: huic enim Mosi viro illi qui eduxit nos e terra Aegypti, nescimus quid acciderit.

2. And Aaron said unto them, Break off the golden ear-rings which are in the ears of your wives, of your sons, and of your daughters, and bring them unto me.

2. Et dixit illis Aharon, Eripite, (vel, detrahite,) inaures aureas, quae sunt in auribus uxorum vestrarum, filiorum vestrorum et filiarum vestrarum, atque afferte.

3. And all the people brake off the golden ear-rings which were in their ears, and brought them unto Aaron.

3. Eripuerunt a se igitur totus populus inaures aureas, quae erant in auribus eorum, et attulerunt ad Aharon:

4. And he received them at their hand; and fashioned it with a graving-tool, after he had made it a molten calf: and they said, These be thy gods, O Israel, which brought thee up out of the land of Egypt.

4. Quas accepit de manu eorum, formavitque illud style, et fecit ex illo vitulum fusilem: et dixerunt, Isti sunt dii tui o Israel, qui eduxerunt te e terra Aegypti.

5. And when Aaron saw it, he built an altar before it; and Aaron made proclamation, and said, Tomorrow is a feast to the Lord.

5. Quod videns Aharon, tunc aedificavit altare coram eo: et elamavit Aharon, dixitque, Solennitas Jehovae erit cras.

6. And they rose up early on the morrow, and offered burnt-offerings, and brought peace-offerings: and the people sat down to eat and to drink, and rose up to play.

6. Et summo mane surrexerunt sequenti die, atque obtulerunt holocausta, et adduxerunt hostias prosperitatum: seditque populus ut manducaret et biberet, postea surrexerunt ut luderent.

7. And the Lord said unto Moses, Go, get thee down; for thy people, which thou broughtest out of the land of Egypt, have corrupted themselves:

7. Loquutusque est Jehova ad Mosen: Vade, descende, corrupit se populus tuus quem eduxisti e terra Aegypti.

8. They have turned aside quickly out of the way which I commanded them: they have made them a molten calf, and have worshipped it, and have sacrificed thereunto, and said, These be thy gods, O Israel, which have brought thee up out of the land of Egypt.

8. Recesserunt cito de via quam praecepi eis: fecerunt sibi vitulum fusilem, adoraveruntque illum, et sacrificaverunt ei, dixeruntque, Isti dii tui, Israel, qui eduxerunt te e terra Aegypti.

9. And the Lord said unto Moses, I have seen this people, and, behold, it is a stiff-necked people:

9. Dixit praeterea Jehova ad Mosen, Vidi populum hunc: et ecce populus durae cervicis est.

10. Now therefore let me alone, that my wrath may wax hot against them, and that I may consume them; and I will make of thee a great nation.

10. Nunc igitur dimitte me, ut excandescat furor meus in eos, consumamque eos: te autem faciam in gentem magnam.

11. And Moses besought the Lord his God, and said, Lord, why doth thy wrath wax hot against thy people, which thou hast brought forth out of the land of Egypt with great power, and with a mighty hand?

11. Et precatus est Moses faciem Jehovae Dei sui, et dixit, Utquid, O Jehova, exardescet furor tuus in populum tuum quem eduxisti e terra Aegypti in fortitudine magna et manu forti?

12. Wherefore should the Egyptians speak, and say, For mischief did he bring them out, to slay them in the mountains, and to consume them from the face of the earth? Turn from thy fierce wrath, and repent of this evil against thy people.

12. Utquid dicent Aegyptii dicendo, In malum eduxit eos, ut occideret eos in montibus, utque consumeret eos e superficie terrae? convertere ab ira furoris tui, et poeniteat te super malo populi tui.

13. Remember Abraham, Isaac, and Israel, thy servants, to whom thou swarest by thine own self, and saidst unto them, I will multiply your seed as the stars of heaven; and all this land that I have spoken of will I give unto your seed, and they shall inherit it for ever.

13. Recordare Abraham, Isaac et Israel servorum tuorum, quibus jurasti per teipsum, et dixisti eis, Multiplicabo semen vestrum sicut stellas coeli, et totam terram istam quam dixi dabo semini vestro, et haereditate accipient illam in seculum.

14. And the Lord repented of the evil which he thought to do unto his people.

14. Et poenituit Jehovam super malo quod dixerat se facturum populo suo.

15. And Moses turned, and went down from the mount, and the two tables of the testimony were in his hand: the tables were written on both their sides; on the one side and on the other were they written.

15. Tunc vertit se Moses, et descendit e monte: erantque dutc tabulae testimonii in mann ejus, tabulae scriptae ab utraque super-ficie sua, hinc et inde erant scriptae.

16. And the tables were the work of God, and the writing was the writing of God, graven upon the tables.

16. Et tabulae erant opus Dei, scriptura Dei, scriptura erat sculpta in tabulis.

17. And when Joshua heard the noise of the people as they shouted, he said unto Moses, There is a noise of war in the camp.

17. Audiens autem Jehosua vocem populi in vociferatione ejus, dixit ad Mosen, Vox praelii est in castris.

18. And he said, It is not the voice of them that shout for mastery, neither is it the voice of them that cry for being overcome; but the noise of them that sing do I hear.

18. Qui respondit, Non est vex respondens fortitudini, neque vex respendens infirmitati, sed vocem cantionum ego audio.

19. And it came to pass, as soon as he came nigh unto the camp, that he saw the calf, and the dancing: and Moses' anger waxed hot, and he cast the tables out of his hands, and brake them beneath the mount.

19. Accidit quum appropinquasset ad castra, vidit vitulum et choros: et excanduit iracundia Mosis, abjecitque e manibus suis tabulas, et fregit eas sub monte.

20. And he took the calf which they had made and burnt it in the fire, and ground it to powder, and strawed it upon the water, and made the children of Israel drink of it.

20. Tulit quoque vitulum quem fecerant, et combussit igni, contrivitque donec redegit in pulverem: et sparsit in superficiem aquarum, et potavit filios Israel.

21. And Moses said unto Aaron, What did this people unto thee, that thou hast brought so great a sin upon them?

21. Et dixit Moses ad Aharon, Quid fecit tibi populus iste, quod induxisti super eum hoc peccatum grande?

22. And Aaron said, Let not the anger of my lord wax hot: thou knowest the people, that they are set on mischief.

22. Tunc dixit Aharon, Ne excandescat iracundia domini mei: tu nosti populum quod in malo sit.

23. For they said unto me, Make us gods which shall go before us: for asfor this Moses, the man that brought us up out of the land of Egypt, we wot not what is become of him.

23. Dixerunt autem mihi, Fac nobis deos qui nos praecedant: quia isti Mosi viro qui eduxit nos e terra AEgypti, nescimus quid acciderit.

24. And I said unto them, Whosoever hath any gold, let them break it off. So they gave it me: then I cast it into the fire, and there came out this calf.

24. Quibus respondi, Cui est aurum, private vos. Et dederunt mihi: et projeci in ignem, egressusque est vitulus iste.

25. And when Moses saw that the people were naked, (for Aaron had made them naked unto their shame among their enemies,)

25. Vidit autem Moses quod populus discoopertus esset: (nam discooperuerat eum Aharon ad ignominiam inter hostes eorum,)

26. Then Moses stood in the gate of the camp, and said, Who is on the Lord's side? let him come unto me. And all the sons of Levi gathered themselves together unto Him.

26. Stetit ergo Moses in porta castrorum, et dixit, Quis est Jehovae? Ad me. Et eongregati sunt ad eum omnes filii Levi.

27. And he said unto them, Thus saith the Lord God of Israel, Put every man his sword by his side, and go in and out from gate to gate throughout the camp, and slay every man his brother, and every man his companion, and every man his neighbor.

27. Quibus dixit, Sic dixit Jehova Deus Israel, Ponite quisque gladium suum super femur suum: transite et revertimini a porta ad portam in castris, et occidite quisque fratrem suum, et quisque amicum suum, et quisque propinquum suum.

28. And the children of Levi did according to the word of Moses: and there fell of the people that day about three thousand men.

28. Fecerunt ergo filii Levi secundum sermonem Mosis: et ceciderunt e populo in die ilia circiter tria millia virorum.

29. For Moses had said, Consecrate yourselves to-day to the Lord, even every man upon his son, and upon his brother; that he may bestow upon you a blessing this day.

29. Dixerat autem Moses, Consecrate manum vestram hodie Jehovae, nempe quisque in filio suo, et in fratre suo: ut detur hodie vobis benedictio.

30. And it came to pass on the morrow, that Moses said unto the people, Ye have sinned a great sin: and now I will go up unto the Lord; peradventure I shall make an atonement for your sin.

30. Fuit postridie ut diceret Moses populo, Vos peccastis peccato magno: nunc tamen ascendam ad Jehovam, si forte propitiem eum super peccato vestro.

31. And Moses returned unto the Lord, and said, Oh! this people have sinned a great sin, and have made them gods of gold!

31. Reversus est itaque Moses ad Jehovam, et dixit: Obsecro: peccavit populus hic peccato magno: feterunt enim sibi deos aureos.

32. Yet now, if thou wilt forgive their sin --: and if not, blot me, I pray thee, out of thy book which thou hast written.

32.: Nunc si remiseris peccatum eorum: quod si non, dele me agedum e libro tuo, quem scripsisti.

33. And the Lord said unto Moses, Whosoever hath sinned against me, him will I blot out of my book.

33. Et dixit Jehova ad Mosen, qui peccavit mihi, delebo eum e libro meo.

34. Therefore now go, lead the people unto the place of which I have spoken unto thee. Behold, mine Angel shall go before thee: nevertheless, in the day when I visit, I will visit their sin upon them.

34. Nunc ergo vade, duc populum ad locum de quo loquutus sum tibi. Ecce, Angelus meus ibit ante te: in die autem visitationis meae etiam visitabo in eos peccatum eorum.

35. And the Lord plagued the people, because they made the calf which Aaron made.

35. Et percussit Jehova populum, eo quod fecissent vitulum quem fecerat Aharon.

1 And when the people saw that Moses. In this narrative we perceive the detestable impiety of the people, their worse than base ingratitude, and their monstrous madness, mixed with stupidity. For their sakes Moses had been carried up above the state of terrestrial life, that he might receive the injunctions of his mission, and that his authority might be beyond the reach of controversy. They perversely declare that they know not what has become of him, nay, they speak contemptuously of him as of a person unknown to them. It is for this that Stephen severely blames them, [324] This is that Moses (he says) whom your fathers rejected, though he was the minister of their salvation. (Acts 7:35.) They confess that he had been their deliverer, yet they cannot tolerate his absence for a little time, nor are they affected with any reverence towards him,

unless they have him before their eyes. Moreover, [325] although God offered Himself as if present with them by day and by night in the pillar of fire, and in the cloud, they still despised so illustrious and lively an image of His glory and power, and desire to have Him represented to them in the shape of a dead idol. For what could they mean by saying, "make us gods which shall go before us?" Could they not see the pillar of fire and the cloud? Was not God's paternal solicitude abundantly conspicuous every day in the manna? Was he not near them in ways innumerable

Yet, accounting as nothing all these true, and sure, and manifest tokens of God's presence, they desire to have a figure which may satisfy their vanity. And this was the original source of idolatry, that men supposed that they could not otherwise possess God, unless by subjecting Him to their own imagination. Nothing, however, can be more preposterous; for since the minds of men and all their senses sink far below the loftiness of God, when they try to bring Him down to the measure of their own weak capacity, they travesty Him. In a word, whatever man's reason conceives of Him is mere falsehood; and nevertheless, this depraved longing can hardly be repressed, so fiercely does it burst out. They are also influenced by pride and presumption, when they do not hesitate to drag down His glory as it were from heaven, and to subject it to earthly elements. We now understand what motive chiefly impelled the Israelites to this madness in demanding that a figure of God should be set before them, viz., because they measured Him by their own senses. Wonderful indeed was their stupidity, to desire that a God should be made by mortal men, as if he could be a god, or could deserve to be accounted such who obtains his divinity at the caprice of men. Still, it is not probable that they were so absurd as to desire a new god to be created for them; but they call "gods" by metonymy those outward images, by looking at which the superstitious imagine that God is near them. And this is evident from the fact, that not only the noun but the verb also is in the plural number; for although they were satisfied with one God, still they in a manner cut Him to pieces by their various representations of Him. Nevertheless, however they may deceive themselves under this or that pretext, they still desire to be creators of God.

Those who suppose that confusion is implied by the word "delayed," are, in my opinion, mistaken; for, although the word בשש, boshesh, with its third radical doubled, is derived from בוש, bush, which means to be ashamed, still it is clear from Judges 5:28, that it is used simply for to delay, where it is said, in the address of the mother of Sisera, "Why [326] does his chariot delay (or defer) to come?"

Hence we may understand that hypocrites so fear God as that religion vanishes from their hearts, unless there be some task-master (exactor) standing by them to keep them in the path of duty. They duly obeyed Moses and reverenced his person; but, because they were only influenced by his presence, as soon as they were deprived of it they ceased to fear God. Thus, whilst Joshua was alive, and the other holy Judges, they seemed to be faithful in the exercise of piety, but when they were dead, they straightway relapsed into disobedience.

2. And Aaron said unto them, Break off the golden ear-rings. I doubt not but that Aaron, being overcome by the importunate clamor of the people, endeavored to escape by means of a subterfuge; still, this is no valid excuse for him, since he ought to have heartily opposed them in a direct reply, and sharply to have inveighed against their wicked renunciation of God. By commanding

them to give him gold, he might have quieted their intemperate demands through dread of the expense; but it was a remedy more likely to be successful, to snatch from them those ornaments and trinkets of which women do not willingly allow themselves to be deprived. He therefore purposely requires of them a hateful, or at any rate a by no means pleasant thing, that he might thus impede their sinful design; but without success, for the power of superstition to carry people away is not less than that of lust. Perhaps also he had the tabernacle in view, lest they should sacrilegiously proceed to lay hands on the sacred vessels; and there was a probability that, if it remained uninjured, the sight of it might at length recall them to a better mind. Besides, the recollection of their recent profuse liberality might have extinguished or cooled their ardor, from the fear of being utterly drained. He says emphatically, "Break [327] off the ear-rings from your wives and children," that they may desist from the purpose out of dread of giving offense, since women are slow to part with such objects of gratification. But it is added immediately afterwards, that they were so blinded by the fervor of their foolish zeal, that they undervalued everything in comparison with their perverse desire, and thus the ornaments were taken from their ears. The readiness with which this was done was wonderful; and not by one person, or by a few, but by the whole people, as if in rivalry of each other. Even in these days ear-rings are worn by the [328] Orientals, though it is not so common among us. Now, if unbelievers are so prodigal in their absurdities as to throw away thus carelessly and rashly whatever is precious to them, how shall their tenacity be excusable who are so niggardly in providing for the service of God? Hence let us learn to beware of foolishly squandering our possessions in unnecessary expenditure, and to be liberal where we ought; especially to be ready to spend ourselves, and what we have, when we know that our offerings are pleasing and acceptable to God.

4. And he received them at their hand. He briefly narrates this base and shameful deed; yet sufficiently shows, that whilst Aaron yielded to their madness, he still desired to cure it, though, at the same time, he was weak and frightened, so as to pretend to give his assent, because he feared the consequences of the tumult as regarded himself. For why does he not command the ear-rings to be thrown into some chest, lest he should pollute himself by the contagion of the sacrilege? Since, therefore, he received them into his own hands, it was a sign of a servile and effeminate mind; and thus he is said to have been the founder, or sculptor of the calf, when it is nevertheless probable that workmen were employed upon it. But the infamy of the crime is justly brought upon him, inasmuch as he was its main author, and by his guilt betrayed the religion and honor of God.

The Hebrew word [329] חרט, cheret, some translate a stylus or graving-tool, some a mould; the former think that the rough mass was formed by sculpture into the shape of a calf; the latter, that the calf was cast or founded; as we say, jetter en mousle, to cast in a mould. Ridiculous, however, is the fable, that when the gold was thrown into a furnace, it came forth like a calf without human workmanship; but thus licentiously do the Jews trifle with their fond inventions. The more probable conjecture is, that Aaron designedly sought a remedy for the people's folly.

It was a disgraceful thing to prostrate themselves before a calf, in which there was no connection or affinity with the glory of God; and with this the Prophet expressly reproaches them, that "they changed their glory (i.e., God, in whom alone they should have gloried) into the similitude of an ox that eateth grass." (Psalm 106:20.) For, if it be insulting to God to force Him into the likeness of men, with how much greater and more inexcusable ignominy is His majesty defiled, when He is compared to brute animals? Still it had no effect towards bringing them to repentance; and this is expressed with much force immediately afterwards, when they said to each other, "These be thy gods, O Israel." Surely the hideousness of the spectacle should have struck them with horror, so as to induce them voluntarily to condemn their own madness; but, on the contrary, they mutually exhort one another to obstinacy; for there is no doubt but that Moses indicates that they were like fans to each other, and thus that their frenzy was reciprocally excited. For, as Isaiah and Micah exhort believers, that each of them should stretch out his hand to his brother, and that they should say to each other,

"Come ye, and let us go up to the mountain of the Lord;" (Isaiah 2:3; Micah 4:2;)

thus does perverse rivalry provoke unbelievers mutually to excite each other to progress in sin. Still they neither speak ironically nor in mockery of God, nor have any intention of falling away from Him; but they cover their sin against Him under a deceitful pretext, as if they denied that by their new and unwonted mode of worship, they desired to detract from the honor of their Redeemer; but rather that it was thus magnified because they worshipped Himself under a visible image. Thus now-a-days do the Papists boldly obtrude their fictitious rites upon God; and boast that they do more for Him by their additions and inventions than as if they merely continued within the bounds prescribed by Himself. But let us learn from this passage, that whatever colouring superstition may give to its idols, and by whatever titles it may dignify them, they remain idols still; for, however those who corrupt the pure worship of God by their inventions, may pride themselves on their good intentions, they still deny the true God, and substitute devils in His place.

Their conjecture is probable who suppose that, Aaron devised the calf in accordance with Egyptian superstition; for it is well known with what senseless worship that nation honored its god [330] Anubis. It is true that they kept [331] a live bull to be consulted as the supreme god; but, inasmuch as the people were accustomed to this fictitious deity, Aaron seems in obedience to their madness to have followed that old custom, from whence they had contracted the error, which was so deeply rooted in their hearts. Thus from bad examples does contagion easily creep into the hearts of those who were else untainted; nor is it without good reason that David protests that idols should be held in such abomination by him, that he would not even "take up their names into his lips," (Psalm 16:4;) for, unless we seriously abhor the ungodly, and withdraw ourselves as far as possible from their superstitions, they straightway infect us by their pestilential influence.

5. And, when Aaron saw it, he built an altar before it. When he sees the people so infuriated, that he despairs of being able to resist their conspiracy, in perfidious cowardice he gives way to compliance. And this end awaits all those who do not dare ingenuously and firmly to maintain what is right, but who bargain, as it were, and descend to compromises; for, after they have vacillated for a while, [332] they at length succumb altogether, so as to shrink from nothing,

however unworthy and disgraceful. He seems, indeed, by his proclamation to uplift their minds to the worship of the true God; but, when he is violating the law just given, it is a wretched quibble to shield their offensive and degenerate worship under God's sacred name.

6. *And they rose up early on the morrow.* The earnestness of the people in the prosecution of their error is again set forth; for there is no doubt but that it was at their demand that Aaron proclaimed the solemn sacrifice; and now it is not only added that they were ready for it in time, but their extraordinary diligence is declared in that they appeared at the very dawn of day. Now, if, at the instigation of the devil, unbelievers are thus driven headlong to their destruction, alas for our inertness, if at least an equal alacrity does not manifest itself in our zeal! Thus it is said in the Psalm, (110:3,)

"Thy [333] *people (shall come) with voluntary offerings in the day (of the assembling) of thy army."*

What follows as to the people sitting down "to eat and to drink," many[334] ignorantly wrest to mean intemperance; as also they wrongly expound their "rising up to play," as meaning lasciviousness; whereas thus Moses rather designates the sacred banquet and sports engaged in, in honor of the idols; for, as we have seen elsewhere, the faithful feasted before God at their sacrifices, and so also heathen nations celebrated sacred feasts, whilst they worshipped their idols in games. Of this point Paul is the surest interpreter, who quotes this passage in condemnation of the idolatry of the ancient people, and ably accommodates it to the purpose he had in hand; for the Corinthians had not gone to such an excess as to bow their knees to idols, but were boon-companions of unbelievers in their polluted sacrifices. (1 Corinthians 10:20.)

7. *And the Lord said unto Moses, Go, get thee down.* This was a violent temptation to shake the faith of Moses. He thought that his own and the people's happiness was absolutely complete, when God's covenant was engraven on the tables to secure its perpetuity; whereas now he hears that this covenant was violated, and almost annihilated by the perfidy and rebellion of the people, whilst its abolition involved the loss of salvation and all other blessings. Moreover, that God might more sorely wound the mind of the holy man, He addresses him exactly as if part of the ignominy fell upon himself; for there is an indirect reproach implied in the words, "thy people, which thou broughtest out of the land of Egypt." Yet Moses had only taken this charge upon him by God's command, and, indeed, unwillingly; how, then, is this deliverance thrown in his teeth, wherein he had only obeyed God? and why is his devotedness spoken of in mockery, as if he had bestowed his labor amiss, when no part of the blame attaches to him? I have already said that God sometimes thus pierces the hearts of the godly to the quick, in order to prove their patience, as if their well-directed zeal had been the cause of the evils which occur. Some [335] give too subtle an exposition to this, viz., that they are called the people of Moses, because they had ceased to be the people of God; and suppose that there is an antithesis here, as if it were said, -- your people, and not mine; but I fear this is not well founded; for, since they had broken the covenant, they were not more alienated from God than from Moses the minister of the Law. I do not deny that it is an implied renunciation of them; but we must bear in mind that design of God, to which I have already adverted, that

Moses was in a manner implicated in their crime, in order that his patience might be tried, and also that he might be more grieved at its enormity. Meanwhile, it is obvious that God refers to His recent grace, because it was a monstrous and incredible thing that those who had been lately delivered by this amazing power, and with whom He had just renewed His covenant, should be so suddenly drawn away into rebellion. He adds also, in aggravation of their crime, that they had immediately turned aside from the way which was pointed out to them. Forty days had not yet elapsed since Moses left them, when they were impelled by their depravity to such madness as this. A little time ago they had manifested a wonderful zeal for God's service, by abundantly contributing what was required; the glory of the tabernacle was presented to their eyes to restrain them; and yet they burst through all these barriers, and rush impetuously after their own lust, when scarcely six months had passed since the promulgation of the Law. The verb שחת shicheth, being in the Pihel conjugation, is active; and yet is employed without being intensive; I have, therefore, rendered it, corrupted themselves, though it might be appropriately taken passively, viz., that the people had been corrupted.

8. They have turned aside quickly out of the way. So speedy a transgression, as I have said, aggravates their crime. God then states the nature of their corruption, that they have worshipped a molten calf, that is to say, the work of their own hands. But it is to be observed, that what they had put forward as a colouring for their ungodliness is alleged last, as the climax of their sin; for, when they said that these were their gods which had brought them up, their object was to advance a legitimate excuse, as if they were not falling away from the worship of the true God, and their Deliverer, but that rather it was an evidence of their more fervent zeal, that they should fall down as worshippers before the calf in honor of Him. But God retorts this upon them, and complains of the gross indignity which was put upon Him, when the dead image of a calf was substituted in the place of His glory.

9. I have seen this people, and behold. This was, indeed, the sharpest and sorest trial of the faith of Moses; when God seemed to contradict Himself and to depart from His covenant. If ever, after having been long oppressed by excessive calamities, we are not only wearied by the delay, but also agitated with various doubts, which at length tempt us to despair, as if God had disappointed us by deceptive promises, the contest is severe and terrible; but when God seems at first sight to throw discredit upon His own words, we have need of unusual fortitude and firmness to sustain this assault. For, since faith is founded on the Word, when that Word appears to be at issue with itself, how in such conflicting circumstances could pious minds be sustained unless they were supported by the incomparable power of the Spirit? Still in the mind of Abraham there was such strength of faith, that he came forth as a conqueror from this kind of temptation. He had heard from God's own mouth, "In Isaac shall thy seed be called;" he is afterwards commanded to slay him, and reduce his body to ashes; yet, because he is persuaded that God was able to raise him up seed even from the dead, he obeys the command. (Hebrews 11:17-19.) The same thing is here recorded of Moses, before whom God sets a kind of contradiction in His Word, when He declares that He has the intention of destroying that people, to which He had promised the land of Canaan. Nevertheless, we see how successfully he strove, since, trusting in the eternal and inviolable covenant of God, he did not cease to cherish a good hope. If any

still should ask whether it was right for him to despise or count for nothing what was said to him in the second place as to the utter destruction of the people, I reply, that the victory of his faith did not consist in subtle disquisitions, but that having embraced God's covenant with both arms, as they say, he was so fortified by his confidence that he had room for no objections; and, in point, of fact, pious minds which rest on firm assurance, although unable to free themselves from every perplexity which occurs, still do not waver, but keep a tight grasp on what the Spirit of God has once sealed to them; and, if sometimes it happens that they begin to doubt or vacillate, nevertheless they come back to their foundation and break through every obstacle, so as never to desist from calling upon God. Meanwhile, it is certain that, whilst God is trying the faith of Moses, He quickens his mind to be more earnest in prayer, even as Moses himself was led in that direction by the secret influence of the Spirit. Nor is there any reason why slanderous tongues should here impugn God, as if He pretended before men what He had not decreed in Himself; for it is no proof that He is variable or deceitful if, when speaking of men's sins, and pointing out what they deserve, He does not lay open His incomprehensible counsel. He here presents Himself in the character of Judge; He pronounces sentence of condemnation against the criminals; he postpones their pardon to a fitting season. Hence we gather that his secret judgments are a great deep; whilst, at the same time, His will is declared to us in His word as far as suffices for our edification in faith and piety. And this is more clearly expressed by the context; for He asks of Moses to let Him alone. Now, what does this mean? Is it not that, unless he should obtain a truce from a human being, He will not be able freely to execute His vengeance? -- adopting, that is to say, by this mode of expression, the character of another, He declares his high estimation of His servant, to whose prayers He pays such deference as to say that they are a hinderance to him. Thus it is said in Psalm 106:23, that Moses "stood in the breach, to turn away the wrath" of God. Hence do we plainly perceive the wonderful goodness of God, who not only hears the prayers of His people when they humbly call upon Him, but suffers them to be in a manner intercessors with Him.

He assigns as the reason why He should be implacable, that He well knew the desperate and incurable wickedness of the people; for by "stiff-necked," indomitable obstinacy is metaphorically expressed; and the similitude is taken from stubborn oxen who cannot be brought to submit to the yoke. Now, where such hardness and obstinacy exists, there is no room for pardon. It is indeed an expression which must not be taken literally, that God had learnt by experience that they were a stiff-necked people; but we know that God often assumes human feelings; for unless He should thus come down to us, our minds could never attain to His loftiness. The sum is, that the character of the people was desperate, inasmuch as they had already manifested their inflexible perverseness by many proofs. Still, lest Moses should grieve at the loss of his noble chieftainship, a compensation is promised him; by which trial it appeared that he did not regard his own private interests or advantages.

11. And Moses besought the Lord his God It is clear that this prayer sprang from faith, though in it he seems to fight against the very word of God; for God had said, Get thee down to thy people; but his answer is, Nay, it is thine. But, as I have lately stated, inasmuch as he firmly grasped the principle, that it was impossible for God's covenant to be made ineffective, he breaks through or

surmounts all obstacles with closed eyes as it were. He proves them to be God's people by the benefit they had so recently received; yet he mainly relies on the covenant; nay, he mentions their deliverance as a result of it; for he proceeds afterwards to say, "Remember Abraham, Isaac, and Israel." We see, therefore, that the first ground of his confidence is the promise, although Moses refers first of all to the fact that the people had been delivered by the hand of God. He so expressly particularizes His "mighty hand," and "great power," to signify that the more conspicuous God's miracles had been, the more was His glory exposed to the calumnies of the ungodly; and this he immediately afterwards explains, "Wherefore should the Egyptians speak," etc.

The particle, ברעה, beragnah, which the old interpreter [336] renders craftily, and others maliciously, I prefer simply to translate unto evil, (ad malum,) as denoting an unprosperous and unhappy issue. The exposition which others give, "under an unlucky star," seems to me to be too far-fetched. [337] I have no doubt, therefore, but that Moses signifies that this would be a consolation to the Egyptians in their misfortunes if the people should be destroyed, as if God had thus avenged them against their enemies; besides, by this misapprehension, the memory of God's grace, as well as of His judgment, would have been destroyed; for the Egyptians would have hardened themselves, and would have been untouched by any sense of guilt, deeming that God would shew no mercy to His elect people.

What follows, "repent of this evil," is spoken in accordance with common parlance, for the saints often stammer in their prayers, and, whilst unburdening their cares into the bosom of God, address him in their infirmity as by no means befits His nature; as, for instance, when they ask Him, How long wilt thou sleep? or be forgetful? or shut thine eyes? or hide thy face? But with God repentance is nothing but a change of dealing, wherein He seems to retrace His course, as if He had conceived some fresh design. When, therefore, it is said a little further on that "the Lord repented of the evil," it is tantamount to saying, that He was appeased; not because He retracts in Himself what He has once decreed, but because He does not execute the sentence He had pronounced. If my readers [338] desire more on this point, let them consult my Comments on Genesis and the Prophets.

13. Remember Abraham, Isaac, and Israel, thy servants He does not bring them forward as patrons, by the assistance of whose voice he might obtain what He seeks; but because the promise was lodged with them, which they transmitted as an inheritance to their descendants. We must observe, then, the quality or character with which God had invested the Patriarchs. For which reason it is said in Psalm 132:1, "Lord, remember David, and all his afflictions." And hence the ignorance and folly of the Papists are easily refuted, who imagine from these testimonies that the dead are ordained to be intercessors.

He also purposely refers to God's oath, whereby He had more solemnly bound Himself, so that His promise might be more sure and authoritative. The Apostle, in the Epistle to the Hebrews, 6:13, tells us why God swears by Himself; viz., "because he could swear by no greater;" though sometimes to the same effect He swears by His throne in heaven, or His sanctuary.

In fine, it is uncertain whether there is a ὕστερον πρότερον or not in this prayer, for we shall see as we proceed that when Moses returned a second time, he prayed for the preservation of the people, and was heard. Nor was this done in a moment; but he again occupied forty days in reconciling the people with God. To myself it seems probable that Moses, amazed at the horrible denunciation, immediately offered his prwer; and without receiving a reply promising pardon, came down in suspense to apply a remedy to the evil; for it was by no means likely that, after having heard so severe and weighty a threat, he would have interposed no supplications, when he was so deeply anxious for the safety of the people.

15. And Moses turned, and went down, from the mount Moses comes down by God's command to be a spectator of this wicked revolt, that the enormity of the act might the more arouse him both to disgust and detestation of the crime, and to the endeavor to find a remedy for it. Although, however, God had pronounced sentence of rejection against the people, He still leaves the tables that testified of the covenant untouched in the hands of Moses, not that He wished them to remain whole, as we shall soon see, but that first the sight of them, and then the breaking of them, might inspire the apostates with greater horror, whose madness had otherwise stupified them.

Why the Law was divided into two tables has been elsewhere seen, viz., because it first sets forth piety and the worship of God; and, secondly, prescribes the rule of righteous living between man and man, and instructs us in the mutual offices of charity. It was doubtless in testimony of the perfection of their doctrine that they were written on both sides. A fuller revelation was indeed afterwards added; but God would have it clearly understood that He had thus embraced all in ten commandments, so that it was not lawful to add anything; and, [339] therefore, lest men should annex anything of their own inventions, God filled both sides, so that nothing remained unwritten upon. Moreover, the tables are called "the work of God," because he had prepared them for the purpose of being written on. Thus they are distinguished from those that came afterwards, on which, although God inscribed His Law, yet He willed that the stones should be chiselled and fashioned by the hand and workmanship of men. The sum is, that not only were the ten commandments written by God on the first tables, but there was nothing human in the fashioning of the stones; and if it be inquired how the stones were engraved and the letters formed upon them, Moses indeed replies by a similitude, that it was done by the finger of God, meaning thereby His secret power; for He who created the world out of nothing by his more volition (nutu,) can by the same word convert all creatures to His own use in whatever way He pleases.

17. And when Joshua heard the noise of the people This is introduced to inform us how intemperately the people raged in their insane worship of the calf, since their shouting was heard from afar. It is thus that the devil bewitches poor miserable men, so that dissolute licentiousness with them is pious ardor. So there is nothing too disgraceful or abominable to please the Gentiles, in order that they may prove that they omit nothing which may appease their false gods. Nor can it be doubted but that, under the pretense of holy zeal, superstitious men give way to the indulgences of the flesh; and Satan baits his fictitious modes of worship with such attractions, that they are willingly and eagerly caught hold of and obstinately retained. It arises from Joshua's solicitude for the people that he deems it to be the cry of battle; whilst Moses,[340] having been informed by God, conjectures that it is not the voice of men fighting, since they utter no cry to correspond with the exhortations of the conquerors, nor is there any sound like the wailing of the conquered.

19. And it came to pass, as soon as he came nigh unto the camp He who had before humbly pleaded for the safety of the people, now, when he sees the calf, bursts forth into rage, and the hideousness of the crime awakens him to different feelings. Now, since anger is here mentioned with praise, the stoics must abandon their paradox, that all the passions (motus animi) are vicious. I allow, indeed, that whilst men are led by nature, they are never angry without vice; because they always exceed due bounds, and often also do not aim at a proper object. But it must be observed that this occurs from the corruption of nature; and, consequently, anger is not in itself or absolutely to be condemned. For the principle which the Stoics assume, that all the passions are perturbations and like diseases, is false, and has its origin in ignorance; for either to grieve, or to fear, or to rejoice, or to hope, is by no means repugnant to reason, nor does it interfere with tranquillity and moderation of mind; it is only excess or intemperance which corrupts what would else be pure. And surely grief, anger, desire, hope, fear, are affections of our unfallen [341] (integrce) nature, implanted in us by God, and such as we may not find fault with, without insulting God Himself. Moreover, the anger which is here ascribed to Moses is, in Deuteronomy 9, attributed to the person of God Himself. Whence we infer, that, since it emanated from the impulse of the Spirit, it was a virtue worthy of praise.

In breaking the tables, however, he seems to have forgotten himself; for what sort of vengeance was this, to deface the work of God? Howsoever detestable the crime of the people was, still the holy covenant of God ought to have been spared. Therefore certain Rabbins, [342] to excuse him, invent one of their customary fables, that, when the tables were brought into the polluted place, the writing became effaced. Others think that he was carried away by his wrath, and did not sufficiently consider what he was about, as he would have done had his mind been composed. I have no doubt, however, but that he broke the tables in reference to his office, as if to annul the covenant of God for a time; for we know that God commits both charges to the ministers of His word, to be the proclaimers of His vengeance, as well as the witnesses of His grace. Thus, whatever they bind on earth is bound also in heaven, and they retain sins unto condemnation, and are armed with vengeance against the unbelieving and rebellious. (Matthew 16:19; John 20:23; 2 Corinthians 13:10. [343]) Therefore God rejected the people by the hand of Moses, renouncing the covenant which He had recently established in a solemn ceremony; and this severity was more useful as an example than as if He had sent Moses back empty-handed; for else it would never have suggested itself to the Israelites of how incomparable a treasure they had been deprived. It was then necessary that the tables should be produced, as if God so presented Himself to their sight and shewed His paternal countenance; but when, on the other hand, the monstrous abomination of the calf was encountered, it behoved that these same tables should be broken, as if God turned His back upon them and retired. Meanwhile, it must be borne in mind, that the covenant of God was not altogether annulled, but only as it were interrupted, until the people had heartily repented. Still this temporary rupture, if I may so call it, did not prevent the covenant itself from remaining inviolable. In the same manner also afterwards God put away His people, as if He had utterly renounced. them, yet His grace and truth never failed; so that He at least had some hidden roots from whence the Church sprang up anew; as it is said in Psalm 102:18, "The people which shall be created shall praise the Lord."

20. And he took the calf which they had made It might seem to be a cruel and inhuman punishment that Moses should in a manner infect the bowels of the people with the corruption of the crime. They had already polluted both their bodies and souls more than enough, without the contagion entering any deeper. Besides, he was thus likely to drive them to despair, when they bore within them the ground of their condemnation, as a woman nourishes her offspring in the womb. Nevertheless, such was the remedy to be applied to their senselessness; for, however they might have been terrified for a moment, the recollection of their crime and their fear of punishment would have immediately vanished had not this brand of their defilement been thoroughly impressed upon them. This, then, was a kind of tautcry, whereby they might feel that the disgrace of such foul idolatry not only cleaved to their skin, but was fixed deep in their very bowels. For thus also was their shame enforced upon them when they admitted the substance of their god into their belly, to be soon afterwards ejected with their excrements. Therefore were they compelled to drink and to void a part of their god, in order that their superstition might be the more offensive to them. Besides, if the ashes had been scattered on the ground, there was danger lest some of the more obstinate might collect the relics; and this evil was prevented when the gold, of which the false god was molten, was mixed with ordure. Finally, Moses is said to have made them drink of the accursed water, not because he himself held out the cup to each of them, but because the dust was cast into the stream of which they all drank; as is stated in Deuteronomy 9:21

21. What did this people unto thee? He casts the blame on Aaron, inasmuch as he, who is possessed of power, seems to permit the evil which he does not prevent. We have previously seen that when Moses went up into the mount he resigned his charge to Aaron; it was therefore his duty so to preside over them as, in right of his power, to restrain the people, however perverse they might be. Consequently he is deservedly reproved with this severity, as if he had been the author of the sin which he had suffered to be committed. Hence we gather how weighty a burden is borne by all [344] who are appointed to be governors; for if any sin is committed through their negligence, or timidity, or indolence, they must themselves give account for it, as if they had given the signal for licentiousness. The reproof here is very emphatic, viz., that he was as bitter an enemy to the public welfare as if he had desired to avenge himself on his mortal enemies. Not that vengeance would be lawful, although he might have had any colorable ground for it, but Moses means that if Aaron had desired to ruin any persons, and had therefore purposely endeavored to do the worst thing he could against them, he could not have injured them more. Hence He deserves the greater reprehension for having taken such bad care of this poor people, the charge of whom he had undertaken; nay, for having, as far as in him lay, brought final destruction upon them. This, too, is worthy of observation, that when God's service is in question, Moses no more spares his own and his only brother than he would an utter stranger. If he had consulted flesh and blood, it would have been easy to invent some pretext for being more lenient towards his brother, since he had been compelled by necessity and violence to make the calf; but, inasmuch as he knew how strenuously we should contend for God's glory, he assails his brother as if he were entirely unconnected with him. This is a rare virtue; but, unless we strive to attain it, we

shall often betray God's cause by our treacherous indulgence towards our relatives.

22. And Aaron said, Let not the anger of my Lord wax hot Aaron extenuates his crime as much as He can. The sum, however is, that the people, whom Moses himself knew to be depraved and perverse, had tumultuously assailed him, and compelled him against his will. Now, although the commencement of his address has an appearance of modesty, still the excuse is frivolous. Rightly, indeed, does Aaron, though the elder, submit himself with reverence to his brother; since he acknowledges him as God's minister, and trembles at his reproof; but it would have been better ingenuously to confess his guilt, than to escape the ignominy of condemnation by subterfuge; for it was the business of the chief to guide the whole body, and to quiet the tumult by authority and firmness; and, if their extravagance had even advanced to madness, rather to die ten times over than to yield such base and servile compliance. But from the close it appears that, whilst in our anxiety for our reputation, we take pains to conceal or excuse our faults, our hypocrisy will at length appear ridiculous. It is obvious that when Aaron says he cast the gold into the fire, and the calf came out, he endeavors, at any rate, to cover the fault, which he cannot altogether efface, by this poor and flimsy tale; but by this childish trifling he only betrays his impudence, so that such stupid confidence does but complete his condemnation. This is the just reward of our ambition, when we take refuge in disguises, and set our hypocrisy against God's judgment.

25. And when Moses saw that the people were naked The vengeance is here recorded which Moses employed to expiate the sin; not that this punishment was satisfactory, as they call it, before God; but because it was useful to efface the memory of their guilt; or at any rate was profitable, as an example. For by the slaughter of three thousand of them, they were reminded that they all had deserved the same. Nor can it be doubted but that he cleansed the camp of the chief authors of the evil, in order that God might be more inclined to pardon. First, therefore, the cause is set forth, whereby he was inflamed to such severity, viz., because he saw the people in such a state of nakedness, as to be even exposed as a laughing-stock to their enemies. The exposition [345] which some give of their nakedness, i.e., that they were stripped of their ornaments, is by no means consistent; for it is immediately added, that it was "to their shame among their enemies;" and it will be seen in the next chapter that they were still splendidly ornamented; nay, that they wore the outward tokens of profane rejoicing. There is no doubt, then, but that he signifies that they were rejected of God, who was to them, as it were, their sole ornamental garment, and under whose protection they were secure. The enormity of the evil is, therefore, set forth in these words, because they were not only deprived of God's assistance, who is culled "the dwelling-place" of his people, (Psalm 90:1,) but also abandoned to ignominy, whilst they were surrounded on all sides by enemies. Hence the holy indignation of Moses, in inflicting punishment on the leaders of the rebellion. And again, it is to be noted, that Aaron is charged with the chief part of the crime, because he had not resisted the people's folly with sufficient firmness.

Herein the astonishing power of God was manifested, that when Moses had summoned the Levites, and had commanded them openly in the gate to gird themselves with their swords, the other tribes did not all of them mutiny; for it was probable that they were thus to be armed, in order to execute punishment on the criminals. How, then, came it to pass that those, who were conscious of guilt, were quiet, except because the power of God's Spirit restrained their courage and fury?

The form of the command is also worthy of observation, "Whoso is the Lord's, let him betake himself to me:" from whence we learn, that if we love religion as it deserves, we must not halt between two sides; but that an ingenuous confession is required of us, so as to range ourselves every one under the banner of God; for, by calling all God's servants to him, he condemns the cowardice, nay, the treachery, of all who shall stand in indecision.

The question, however, arises, whether the Levites were not implicated in the crime, since they step forward at once to execute his command, like sincere upholders of God's glory. I answer, that though they were not free from guilt, yet, inasmuch as they yielded to the people under the influence of fear, their sin was lighter than as if they had approved by their consent of the detestable idolatry. But here we perceive the wonderful indulgence of God, who not only pardoned them, but deigned to assert His glory by their instrumentality, and appointed them his ministers for the punishment of a crime, in the toleration of which they had been guilty of base effeminacy and cowardice. Again, it may be asked, how it occurred that of the rest of the multitude not one stirred a foot at the command of Moses? My opinion is, that they were kept back not by contempt or obstinacy, but only by shame; and that they were all inspired with so much alarm, that they waited in astonishment to see what Moses was about, and how far he would proceed. It is, however, probable that the Levites were called out by name, and this we gather from the result; because they all immediately came forwards, and not one of any other tribe.

27. *Thus saith the Lord God of Israel* He commands the Levites to gird themselves with their swords, to commit slaughter throughout the whole camp; and this may at first sight seem to be cruel and inhuman, when they are forbidden to spare their brothers, their friends, and neighbors; but it was by no means excessive, if we reflect how much more grievous it is to profane the sacred worship of God, than to inflict injury on man. Nor does he desire that all should be slain promiscuously; but only bids the Levites proceed courageously; so that, if they should chance to meet with any one worthy of death, neither relationship, nor friendship, nor familiarity, should hinder or delay the just course of severity. Nay, since it soon after follows that the Levites did as they were commanded, we gather that he was content with a moderation more akin to leniency than to rigor. If any sedition has arisen in an army, which has proceeded to violence and slaughter, the general is wont, as an ordinary rule, to decimate the offenders; how much milder here is the rate of punishment, when only three thousand perish out of six hundred millions! Although he may have, therefore, dealt harshly with a few, yet the chastisement must appear lenient which permits so many to escape, though guilty of the same crime. It is, however, asked, whether they made any, and what distinction? for it would have been an act of blind and headlong impetuosity to kill every one they might happen to meet. In order to evade this absurdity, some of the [346] Jews take refuge, as usual, in a silly fable, that the bellies of those who were polluted by the sin, swelled after drinking the water. If this is accepted, the swelling must have affected them all. But, rejecting all such inventions, it is probable that the Levites were by no means ignorant who were the chief leaders of the evil

counsel, by whose instigation the rest were drawn into rebellion. [347] Judicially, therefore, and discriminately they executed vengeance on three thousand; and hence it came to pass that the severity was endurable, and that the whole people quietly submitted, when they saw that their own welfare was consulted by the removal from amongst them of these pestilent persons. But, although Mosesrestrains himself, it must be remarked that he requires of the Levites inflexible firmness, lest any regard to intimacy should soften their hearts, because there is nothing more opposed to a sound judgment than προσωπολημψία (respect of persons.) Now, it is not without reason that the Levites are praised for obeying his command; for it demanded no common magnanimity to attack the whole twelve tribes, to whom they were not equal even by a twelfth part. We gellerally see that when many persons are concerned in a crime, the judges are alarmed by a fear of sedition, and in the end have not the courage to perform their duty. [348] It was, then, all extraordinary instance of zeal in the Levites, that setting aside all consideration of danger, they dared intrepidly to provoke so great a multitude against them. And this holy indignation was the fruit of their repentance, since they did not hesitate to attack with drawn swords those whose threatening countenances they had previously quailed at. Surely it would have been a lighter cause of offense to have prevented the idolatry of the people by bold rebuke, than to execute capital punishment on the transgressors. Their piety and fear of God, therefore, aroused their hearts to new vigor when they dreaded no peril of death.

29. For Moses had said, consecrate yourselves today It is obvious that this verse was added exegetically, to give the reason why this unintimidated ardor impelled the Levites manfully to fulfill their charge, viz., because the exhortation of Moses carried them over every obstacle. The verb, "had said," must be therefore construed in the pluperfect tense. The translation of some, [349] "ye have consecrated your hands," in the perfect tense, is very unsuitable, since the promise is immediately added as a means of stimulating them to greater alacrity; whence it appears that the command of Moses, which has been mentioned, is now repeated in different words. They are, however, increased in forciblcness, since he declares that it will be a sacrifice sweet and acceptable to God, if, in forgetfulness of flesh and blood, they avenge the polluted worship of God. The causal particle, [350] ci, is introduced, which I have rendered nempe, (namely,) as being here an intensitive, as if he had said, such submission to God must here be shewn, that they should not even restrain their hand if necessary from their very sons and brothers. What, therefore, was lately spoken as to their relatives generally, and here of their sons, must be taken as if in the potential mood; for, if all the Levites had joined themselves with Moses, what need was there of bidding them execute punishment on their brothers or sons? So that Moses only wished to condemn that absurd regard to humanity whereby judges are often blinded, and, to the detriment of religion, are cruelly merciful in tolerating and encouraging impiety. First, therefore, let us learn from this passage, that when judges overlook crimes, their hands are defiled by their very remissness, because impunity increases licentiousness in sin. Thus Solomon teaches that,

"He that justifieth the wicked, and he that condemneth the just, even they both are an abomination to the Lord." (Proverbs 17:15.)

Let us also learn that nothing is less consistent than to punish heavily the crimes whereby mortals are injured, whilst we connive at the impious errors or sacrilegious [351] modes of worship whereby the majesty of God is violated.

30. And it came to pass on the morrow, that Moses said Inasmuch as this judgment of God was terrible, lest the Israelites should altogether fall into despair, Moses addresses a consolation to them to calm their sorrow, promising that he will make entreaty to God in their behalf. Meanwhile, in order that they might betake themselves as humble suppliants to God's mercy, he reminds them of the enormity of their sin. The Hebrew words literally mean, [352] ye have sinned a great sin; there is, however, no ambiguity in the sense; for he would humble them by setting the greatness of their crime before them, in order that they may earnestly give themselves to repentance. To the same effect is [353] the particle אולי, auli, which is often used to express uncertainty, but here, as in many other places, only denotes difficulty; lest, as is frequently the case, they should think of asking pardon unconcernedly and carelessly, and not with anxious earnestness. Thus, when Peter addresses Simon Magus, he bids him pray, "if perhaps" his iniquity may be forgiven him, (Acts 8:22;) not that he should vacillate or waver in his mind like those who are in suspense or doubt, but that terrified by the fear of God's wrath, he should anxiously seek after the remedy.

31. And Moses returned unto the Lord This relation does not stand in its proper place, since, as we have already said, Moses does not exactly preserve the order of time. For we shall see in the next chapter that God refuses with respect to His angel what he here accords; since it is [354] a mere quibble to say that a mere ordinary angel is here promised, in whom God will not so manifest His presence as He has done before. Therefore now Moses briefly records what he will afterwards more fully set forth, i.e., how God was appeased and received the people back into favor, which was not the case until he was commanded to hew out or polish the new tables. And we know that it was a figure of speech in common use with the Hebrews to touch upon the chief points of a matter, and then to fill up, in the progress of the history, what had been omitted.

His prayer commences with confession; for in such a case of wicked ingratitude nothing remained but freely to acknowledge their guilt, so as to look nowhere else for safety in their state of ruin and despair but to the mercy of God; for hypocrites only inflame His wrath the more by extenuating their offenses. The particle אנא, ana, which we have followed others in translating "I beseech," (obsecro,) is sometimes expressive of exhortation, and used like Agedum, (come on;) here it only signifies what the Latins express by amabo[355] After having anticipated God's judgment by the confession of their guilt, he nevertheless implores for pardon; and this with extreme earnestness, which is the reason why his address is suddenly broken off, for the sentence is imperfect, as is often the case in pathetic appeals, "if thou wilt forgive their sin." I have no objection to make if any should construe the particle [356] אם, im, "I would," (utinam,) still in the vehemence of his feelings he seems to burst forth into an exclamation, "Oh, if thou wilt forgive;" though it may be but a modest petition, "Wilt thou forgive?" for, though the prayers of the saints flow from their confidence, still they have to struggle with doubts and questionings within themselves, whether God is willing to listen to them. Hence it arises that their prayers begin hesitatingly, until faith prevails.

What follows may in many respects appear to be absurd; for Moses both imperiously lays down the law to God, and in his eager impetuosity seeks to overthrow, as far as he can, His eternal counsel, and inconsiderately robs him of His justice. Surely all must condemn the pride of this address, Unless thou sparest the offenders, count me not as one of thy servants; nor can there seem to be less of folly in his attempt to bring to nought God's eternal predestination. Besides, when he desires that he himself should be involved in the same punishment, what is this but to destroy all distinction, that God should rashly condemn the innocent with the transgressors? Nor would I indeed deny that Moses was carried away by such vehemence, that he speaks like one possessed. Still it must be observed, that when believers unburden their cares into God's bosom, they do not always deal discreetly, nor with well-ordered language, but sometimes stammer, sometimes pour forth "groans which cannot be uttered," sometimes pass by everything else, and lay hold of and press some particular petition. Assuredly there was nothing less present to the mind of Moses than to dictate to God; nor, if he had been asked, would he have said that what God had decreed respecting His elect before the creation of the world could be overthrown. Again, he knew that nothing was more foreign to the Judge of all the world than to destroy the innocent together with the reprobate. But since his care for the people, whose welfare he knew to be consigned to him by God, had absorbed, as it were, all his senses, nothing else occupies his mind but that they may be saved, whilst he does not entertain a single thought which interferes with this his great solicitude. Hence it is, that arrogating far too much to himself, he throws himself forward as the people's surety, and forgets that he is predestined to salvation by God's immutable counsel; and, finally, does not sufficiently consider what would be becoming in God. Nor is Moses the only one who has been thus carried away; but Paul has gone even further, expressing himself thus in writing after full premeditation, "I could wish that myself were accursed from Christ for my brethren." (Romans 9:3.) The fact is, that intent on the welfare of the elect people, they neither of them examine critically into particulars, and therefore devote themselves in behalf of the whole Church; inasmuch as this general principle was deeply rooted in their minds, that if the welfare of the whole body were secured, it would be well with the individual members. Hence [357] the question arises whether it is a pious feeling to prefer the salvation of others to our own? Some being afraid lest the example of Moses and Paul should be prejudicial, have said that they were only influenced by their zeal for God's glory, when they devoted themselves to eternal destruction; and that they did not prefer the people's salvation to their own. Even, however, though this should be accepted, still their words would have been hyperbolical; for, although God's glory may well be preferred to a hundred worlds, yet He so far accommodates Himself to our ignorance, that He will not have the eternal salvation of believers brought into opposition with His glory; but has rather bound them inseparably together, as cause and effect. Moreover, it is abundantly clear that Moses and Paul did devote themselves to destruction out of regard to the general salvation. Let, therefore, that solution which I have advanced hold good, that their petition was so confused, that in the vehemence of their ardor they did not see the contradiction, like men beside themselves. Nor is it matter of surprise that they should have been in such perplexity, since they supposed that by the destruction of the elect people God's faithfulness was abandoned, and He Himself in a manner brought to nought, if the eternal adoption wherewith He had honored the children of Abraham should fail.

By "the book," in which God is said to have written His elect, must be understood, metaphorically, His decree. But the expression which Moses uses, asking to be blotted out of the number of the pious, is an incorrect one, since it cannot be that one who has been once elected should be ever reprobated; and those lunatics who, on this ground, overturn, as far as they can, that prime article of our faiith concerning God's eternal predestination, thereby demonstrate their malice no less than their ignorance. David uses two expressions in the same sense, "blotted out," and "not written:"

"Let them be blotted out of the book of the living, and not be written with the righteous." (Psalm 69:28.)

We cannot hence infer any change in the counsel of God; but this phrase is merely equivalent to saying, that God will at length make it manifest that the reprobate, who for a season are counted amongst the number of the elect, in no respect belong to the body of the Church. Thus the secret catalogue, in which the elect are written, is contrasted by Ezekiel 13:9 with that external profession, which is often deceitful. Justly, therefore, does Christ bid His disciples rejoice, "because their names are written in heaven," (Luke 10:20;) for, albeit the counsel of God, whereby we are predestinated to salvation, is incomprehensible to us,

"nevertheless (as Paul testifies) this seal standeth sure, The Lord knoweth them that are his." (2 Timothy 2:19.)

33. Whosoever hath sinned against me, him will I blot out In these words God adapts Himself to the comprehension of the human mind, when He says, "him will I blot out;" for hypocrites make such false profession of His name, that they are not accounted aliens, until God openly renounces them: and hence their manifest rejection is called erasure. Moreover, God reproves the preposterous request of Moses, inasmuch as it does not consist with His justice to reject the innocent; whence it follows, that Moses had prayed inconsiderately. The sum is, that God, whenever He punishes the ungodly and iniquitous, pays them the wages which they have earned; whereas He never punishes the just. Yet it is to be observed, that when God declares that he will be the avenger of sins, His mercy is not excluded, whereby He buries the transgressions of His people, so that they come not into mind. Thus, when Paul says, "Neither fornicators, nor adulterers, nor thieves, nor covetous, nor murderers, nor revilers, shall possess the kingdom of God," [358] (1 Corinthians 6:9, 10;) it would be incorrect to conclude that they were all shut out from the hope of salvation; since he only speaks of the reprobate, who never repent, so that being converted they may obtain grace.

34. Therefore now go, lead the people In these words God shews that He is appeased, for it was a sure sign of His reconciliation that His angel is appointed to guide them during the rest of their way. The exposition which some give, that an angel is now promised to take care of them, such as Daniel testifies to have been sometimes assigned even to heathen nations, and an instance of which we shall see in the next chapter, is but a poor conjecture; besides, God

declares that though the people have departed from the faith, still He stood firm to His agreement as to their enjoyment of the promised inheritance.

His postponement of their punishment is an indirect reproof of the people's wickedness, as though He had said that they were of so perverse a nature that they would hereafter give many fresh occasions for it. If any object that, whenever God afterwards punished other sins, He did not then take into account this act of idolatry, I reply that it is no new thing with God, when men contract again fresh guilt, to accumulate their punishments, and also to call to judgment many sins together under one general punishment. Besides, we know that God casts the iniquity of the fathers upon the children to the third and fourth generation. Lastly, there is nothing to prevent Him from visiting at another time with temporal punishments the iniquity which He has once pardoned; for wherefore did He then forgive them? Was it not lest the truth of His covenant, should perish? Those, then, whom He thus was unwilling to destroy, He might at His own time call up again for punishment, provided the chastisement were but moderate. Hence let us learn not to flatter ourselves, if ever God suspends His judgment, [359] nor to abuse His long-suffering, as if we had escaped with impunity.

35. And the Lord plagued the people Moses here briefly attributes to God what he had before related as to the slaughter of the three thousand, lest any should think that he had smitten them with immoderate severity Therefore Paul bids us consider in this history, as in a mirror, how greatly displeasing to God idolatry is; lest we should imitate those who were smitten by His hand. (1 Corinthians 10:7.) The indignation of Moses is consequently connected with the command of God. Meanwhile he commends the mercy of God in having spared Aaron, whilst he speaks of the calf as his work, as well as of the whole of the people; in a different way indeed, for Aaron formed the calf at their request; still the criminality was common to them.

Exodus 33

Exodus 33:1-23

1. And the Lord said unto Moses, Depart, and go up hence, thou and the people which thou hast brought up out of the land of Egypt, unto the land which I sware unto Abraham, to Isaac, and to Jacob, saying, Unto thy seed will I give it:

1. Loquutus autem fuerat Jehova ad Mosen: Vade, ascende hinc tu et populus quem eduxisti e terra AEgypti in terram de qua juravi ipsi Abraham, Isaac, et Jacob, dicendo, Semini tuo dabo eam.

2. And I will send an Angel before thee; and I will drive out the Canaanite, the Arnorite, and the Hittite, and the Perizzite, the Hivite, and the Jebusite;

2. Et mittam ante to Angelum, et ejiciam Chananaeum, et Amorrhaeum, et Hitthaeum, et Perizaeum, Hivaeum, et Jebusaeum.

3. Unto a land flowing with milk and honey: for I will not go up in the midst of thee; for thou art a stiff-necked people: lest I consume thee in the way.

3. Ad terram scilicet fluentem lacte et melle. Non enim ascendam in medio tui (nam populus durae cervicis es) ne forte consumam to in via.

4. And when the people heard these evil tidings, they mourned: and no man did put on him his ornaments.

4. Audiens autem populus verbum hoc malum, luxerunt: nec posuit quisquam ornamentum suum super se.

5. For the Lord had said unto Moses, Say unto the children of Israel, Ye are a stiff-necked people; I will come up into the midst of thee in a moment, and consume thee: therefore now put off thy ornaments from thee, that I may know what to do unto thee.

5. Dixerat enim Jehova ad Mosen, Die filiis Israel, Vos estis populus durae cervicis: momento uno ascendam in medium tui, et consumam te. Nunc ergo depone ornamentum tuum a te, et sciam quid faciam tibi.

6. And the children of Israel stripped themselves of their ornaments by the mount Horeb.

6. Et spoliaverunt se filii Israel ornamentis suis a monte Horeb.

7. And Moses took the tabernacle, and pitched it without the camp, afar off from the camp, and called it The Tabernacle of the Congregation. And it came to pass, that every one which sought the Lord went out unto the tabernacle of the congregation, which was without the camp.

7. Moses autem accepit tabernaculum, et extendit illud sibi extra castra, procul a castris: (vocaverat autem illud tabernaculum conventionis) et quicunque requirebat Jehovam, egrediebatur ad tabernaculum conventionis quod erat extra castra.

8. And it came to pass, when Moses went out unto the tabernacle, that all the people rose up, and stood every man at his tent-door, and looked after Moses, until he was gone into the tabernacle.

8. Praeterea quando egrediebatur Moses ad tabernaculum, assurgebat universus populus: stabantque singuli ad ostium tentorii sui, et aspiciebant post Mosen, donec ingrederetur tabernaculum.

9. And it came to pass, as Moses entered into the tabernacle, the cloudy pillar descended, and stood at the door of the tabernacle, and the Lord talked with Moses.

9. Erat autem quando egrediebatur Moses tabernaculum, descendebat columna nubis, stabatque ad ostium tabernaculi, et loquebatur eum Mose.

10. And all the people saw the cloudy pillar stand at the tabernacle-door: and all the people rose up and worshipped, every man in his tent-door.

10. Videns vero universus populus columnam nubis stantem ad ostium tabernaculi, assurgebat universus populus, et adorabat quisque ad ostium tentorii sui.

11. And the Lord spake unto Moses, face to face, as a man speaketh unto his friend. And he turned again into the camp: but his servant Joshua, the son of Nun, a young man, departed not out of the tabernacle.

11. Et loquebatur Jehova facie ad faciem, quemadmodum alloquitur quispiam amicum sumn: postea revertebatur ad castra, at minister ejus Jehosua filius Nun juvenis non recedebat e medio tabernaculi.

12. And Moses said unto the Lord, See, thou sayest unto me, Bring up this people: and thou hast not let me know whom thou wilt send with me: yet thou hast said, I know thee by name, and thou hast also found grace in my sight.

12. Et dixit Moses ad Jehovam, Vide tu dicis mihi, Educ populum hunc, et tu non indicasti mihi quem missurus sis mecum. Atqui tu dixisti, Novi te ex nomine, atque etiam invenisti gratiam in oculis meis.

13. Now therefore, I pray thee, if I have found grace in thy sight, shew me now thy way, that I may know thee, that I may find grace in thy sight; and consider that this nation is thy people.

13. Nunc ergo si modo inveni gratiam in oculis tuis, ostende quaeso mihi viam tuam et cognoscam to, atque inventare gratiam in oculis ruts, et vide quod populus tuus sit gens ista.

14. And he said, My presence shall go with thee, and I will give thee rest.

14. Et dixit, Facies mea praecedet, et requiescere faciam te.

15. And he said unto him, If thy presence go not with me, carry us not up hence.

15. Cui respondit, Nisi facies tua praecedat, ne educas nos hinc.

16. For wherein shall it be known here that I and thy people have found grace in thy sight? Is it not in that thou goest with us? so shall we be separated, I and thy people, from all the people that are upon the face of the earth.

16. Et (certe) qua in re notum erit hic quod invenerim gratiam in oculis tuis ego, et populus tuus? nonne quum ambulaveris nobiscum, et separabimur ego et populus tuus ab omni populo qui est super faciem terrae?

17. And the Lord said unto Moses, I will do this thing also that thou hast spoken; for thou hast found grace in my sight, and I know thee by name.

17. Et dixit Jehova ad Mosen, Etiam rem hanc quam dixisti faciam: quia invenisti gratiam in oculis meis, et novi te ex nomine.

18. And he said, I beseech thee, shew me thy glory.

18. Adjecitque, Ostende mihi quaso gloriam tuam.

19. And he said, I will make all my goodness pass before thee, and I will proclaim the name of the Lord before thee; and will be gracious to whom I will be gracious, and will shew mercy on whom I will shew mercy.

19. Cui respondit, Ego praeterire faciam omnem decorem meum ante faciem tuam, et vocabo ex nomine Jehovae coram te: et miserebor, cujus miserebor: et clemens ero in quem clemens ero.

20. And he said, Thou canst not my face: for there shall no man see me, and live.

20. Dixit praeterea, Non poteris videre faciem meam: quid non videbit me homo, et vivet.

21. And the Lord said,: Behold, there is a place by me, and thou shalt stand upon a rock:

21. Dixit postremo Jehova, Ecce, locus apud me, et stabis supra petram.

22. And it shall come to pass, while my glory passeth by, that I will put thee in a cleft of the rock, and will cover thee with my hand while I pass by:

22. Erit autem quum pertransibit gloria mea, ponam te in spelunca petrae, et protegam te manu mea donec transiero.

23. And I will take away mine hand, and thou shalt see my back parts; but my face shall not be seen.

23. Postea removebo manum meam, et videbis posteriors mea, facies vero non videbitur.

1. Depart, and go up hence, thou and the people I have used the pluperfect tense; [360] for the reason is here given, whereby Moses was stirred up to such vehemence in prayer, viz., because, although God had not altogether abandoned the care of the people, still He had renounced His covenant, and had proclaimed to them that, after He had once performed His engagement of giving them possession of the land, He would have no more to do with them. Wherefore, what is here related, preceded, in order of time, the prayer of Moses; for, being astonished at the sad and almost fatal message, he burst forth into that confused and wild request, that he might be blotted out of the book of life.

Let us now endeavor to elicit the true meaning of the passage. It is plain, that when God bids Moses depart with the people, He utterly renounces the charge which He Himself had hitherto sustained. He only promises that He will cause them to attain the promised inheritance, and not that He will preside over them, will there preserve them in safety, and even cherish them, as a father does his children; in fact, that he will merely fulfill the promise He had made to their fathers. And thus He anticipates their complaints; for they might reply, that consequently His promise would be rendered vain and ineffectual; but by way of anticipation, He says, that although He should renounce them, still He should maintain this truth, because He will cast out the inhabitants of the land of Canaan, so that their abode would be vacant for them. In sum, He repudiates them, that they may no longer count themselves to be His peculiar people, or expect more from Him, than as if they were strangers, He mentions His oath, lest they should accuse Him of faithlessness; as if He had said that He should be discharged from His engagement when they had obtained the land. And thus, whilst depriving them of the hope of salvation, and the grace of adoption, He still asserts the stability and stedfastness of His covenant. I, therefore, understand the word angel in a different sense from that which it has just before, and in many other passages of this book; for, when mention was before made of the angel, the familiar presence of God was denoted by it, nay, it was used interchangeably with the name of God itself. But here God is said to be so about to send the angel, as to separate Himself from the people. "I will not go up (He says) in the midst of thee;" and the reason is subjoined, viz., because it could not be that He could endure any longer their perverse spirits. Again He uses a similitude taken from refractory oxen, which cannot be broken to bear the yoke. The sum is, that because they are so intractable, God cannot perform the office of their guide without straightway destroying them.

4. And when the people heard these evil tidings Hence it more clearly appears that, as I have said, it was like a thunderbolt to them when God withdrew Himself from the people; for this divorce is more fatal than innumerable deaths. It might indeed at first sight seem delightful to be the masters of a rich and fertile land; but dull as the people generally were, God smote them suddenly, so that all its delights became insipid, and its fruitfulness like famine itself, when they perceived that they would be but fatted unto the day of slaughter. A useful piece of instruction is to be gained from hence, viz., that if we neglect God's favor and are captivated by the sweetness of His blessings, we are ensnared like fishes on a hook. God promised the Israelites what might attract them for a little season: He denied them what they should

have alone desired, that He would be their God. The evil tidings affected them with sorrow, for they felt that men cannot be happy unless God be propitious; nay, that nothing can be more wretched than to be alienated from Him. "It is good for me to draw near to God," (Psalm 73:28,) says David; and elsewhere, "Blessed is the nation whose God is the Lord," (Psalm 33:12, and Psalm 144:15;) again, "the Lord is the portion of mine inheritance, my lot is fallen in pleasant places." (Psalm 16:5, 6.) This, therefore, is the climax of all miseries to have God against us, whilst we are fed by His bounty; and consequently the Israelites began to shew some wisdom, when, awaking from their lethargy, they counted all other things as naught, unless God should pursue them with His paternal favor. We infer from the grossness of their stupidity, that it was brought to pass by a special gift of God, that they were affected with such sorrow as to conduct them to a solemn mourning. First, Moses says that they did not put on their ornaments, and then that they were commanded by God to put them off; but this will be perfectly consistent if we take the latter as explanatory, as if he had said that they did not wear their ornaments because God had forbidden it, by enjoining them to mourn.

God here assumes the character of an angry judge, preparing to inflict vengeance in His wrath, in the words, "I will come up into the midst of thee in a moment, and consume thee;" in order that their alarm may humble them the more, and stir them up to earnest prayer. It was a visible sign of mourning to He in squalidhess and uncleanness, that thus their penitence might be openly testified; for there was no efficacy in the rite and ceremony to propitiate God, except in so far as the inward affection of the mind manifested itself by a true and genuine confession. For we must bear in mind what God requires by Joel, (2:13,) that we should "rend our heart, and not our garments;" nevertheless, whilst He cares not for the outward appearance, nay, whilst He abominates hypocrisy, still, if the sinner has truly repented, it cannot be but that, humbly acknowledging his guilt, he will add the outward profession of it. For if Paul, who was guiltless of any offense, deemed that the Corinthians were to be mourned for by him when they had not "repented of their uncleanness, and fornication, and lasciviousness," because God humbled him in their sin, (2 Corinthians 12:21;) how should not those mourn publicly who are conscious of their own guilt, especially when, being convicted by the judgment of men, they are summoned to the tribunal of God? And therefore it is not without reason that he elsewhere teaches, that the sorrow which worketh repentance should also bring forth these other fruits, viz., carefulness, clearing of themselves, indignation, fear, vehement desire, zeal, revenge. (2 Corinthians 7:10, 11.) For the sake of example also, sinners should not only grieve in silence before God, but willingly undergo the penalty of ignominy before men, so as by self-condemnation to confess that God is a just Judge, to provoke others to imitate them, and, by this warning of human frailty to prevent them from a similar fall.

After, however, God has inspired them with fear, He allays His anger as it were, and declares that He will consider what He will do with them, in order that they may gather courage to ask for pardon; for, although he does not actually pardon them, He sufficiently arouses them to hope, by giving them some taste of His mercy; for, by seeming to leave them in suspense, it is not with the intention that they should approach Him hesitatingly to ask forgiveness, but that their anxiety may urge them more and more to earnest prayer, and keep them in a state of humility.

7. **And Moses took the tabernacle** This was a sign of the divorce between God and the Israelites, that the tabernacle should be removed from the camp and pitched at a distance, as if God were tired of His connection with them. He had promised as a special blessing that He would dwell in the midst of the people; and now, by departing elsewhere, He declares them to be polluted. In a word, the removal of the tabernacle was like the breaking of the tables; for, just as by the breaking of the tables Moses dissolved the covenant of God, so he thus deprived the Israelites for a time of His company and presence. [361] The explanation which some give that it was Moses' own tabernacle, is refuted by many sound arguments. First, it is not said that he took away his own tabernacle, but the word tabernacle is used simply and without any affix, κατ᾽ ἐξοχήν Secondly, he did not change his own place of habitation, but only went out thither from time to time for the purpose of worshipping, or, at any rate, of consulting God. Thirdly, it would have been by no means lawful to assign the sacred name which God had bestowed on His Sanctuary to a private tabernacle. Fourthly, God, by manifesting His glory there, testified that it was His own dwelling-place. Fifthly, it would have been absurd that the people should have sought God in that direction, unless the place had been sacred. Sixthly, the object (of its removal,) which I have above adverted to, must be taken into consideration, for Moses did not withdraw himself from the people, but rather continued, as was his custom, in the midst of the camp, and merely wished to shew that God withdrew Himself from that profane place lest He should be infected by the contagion; so that it was a kind of excommunication. It is said, indeed, that he pitched it for himself, yet not for his private use, as is plain from the context, but in accordance with the common form of expression, [362] in which לוֹ, lo, is often redundant; still properly speaking, he did pitch it for himself, for he alone, had access to it, apart from others. Those who understand it to have been his private tabernacle, suppose that their opinion is supported by what follows, viz., that he called it, the tabernacle, Moed; [363] for they thence infer that it had not before been distinguished by that honorable title. But this objection is easily got over, since it is more probable that this was inserted parenthetically in the text, and therefore may be properly rendered in the pluperfect tense. For by this clause the reason is alleged why God had betaken Himself elsewhere, viz., that the place which He had appointed for covenanting with the people should remain deserted. Nevertheless, if we should refer it to this actual time, it will not be unsuitable that the people, at the present moment, should be reminded of their sad separation, and that Moses, in order to inflict more ignominy and shame upon them, should have called it the tabernacle of convention, though it was now far distant from the camp. As to the word Moed, I will not repeat what I have elsewhere said. Let my readers, therefore, refer to it at the end of chapter 29. [364]

7 **and it came to pass that every one which sought the Lord** Some translate it, "asked counsel;" but, in my opinion, the ordinary signification is preferable. Whether, therefore, they desired to testify their piety by public worship, or to pray, or to seek counsel in doubtful matters, they went out towards that sanctuary in order that their eyes might rest upon it. Moses does not mean that they actually came to the place, from access to which they knew themselves to be prohibited on account of their pollution. But their thus going out was in token of repentance; as though they acknowledged that they were unworthy to receive an answer from God, unless they departed from that place which they

had defiled by their atrocious crime. Now, it was useful for them to be thus
humbled, in order that idolatry might be held in greater detestation. Nor is there
any contradiction in what follows, viz., that they "stood, every man at his tent-
door," whenever Moses went out; for the glory of God, which at that time was
more manifest, was such as then to inspire them with greater reverence and
terror. Whensoever, therefore, the mediator presented himself before God, they
were permitted to do no more than behold from afar the pillar of cloud which
then enveloped Moses, so as to separate him from them. Meanwhile, it must be
observed, that though God at this time departed from them, it was only so far as
to reject them from close access to Him, and not that they were altogether
alienated. For their worship was a sign of faith; they were allowed to pray to
God and implore His favor; and they knew that they were heard in the person of
Moses. Their separation, therefore, was not such as totally to cut off the hope of
pardon, but such as to quicken their anxiety, and to exercise them to
repentance. Thus God often designedly hides His face from sinners in order to
invite them to Him in true humiliation. And this we nmst carefully attend to,
lest, when He chastises us either by word or deed, terror, or a sense of our
criminality, should hinder our prayers; but rather let us seek Him from however
great a distance. The object of excommunication is nearly similar; for those
whom the Church rejects from the company of the faithful, are delivered to
Satan, but only "for the destruction of the flesh, that the spirit may be saved in
the day of the Lord;" (1 Corinthians 5:5;) and hence Paul would not have them
counted as enemies, but admonished as brethren. (2 Thessalonians 3:15.)

When it is said that "the people rose up, and stood every man at his tent-
door," some improperly, as I conceive, refer it to mere respect to him as a civil
magistrate, as if honor was thus paid to their leader; but I rather suppose that:,
when at stated hours Moses presented himself before God in the name of all,
they partook in his service and worship. Wherefore also they followed him with
their eyes, until the cloud covered him. To the same effect this rising up is
repeated immediately afterwards, where reference is made to the cloudy pillar.
Wherefore I have no question but that both verses must be expounded as
relating to spiritual worship. But we have elsewhere shewn how they testified
their piety before the visible sign, without worshipping God therein in any
gross imagination.

11. And the Lord spake unto Moses face to face Moses will hereafter be
dignified by this distinction, where God would declare the difference between
him and other Prophets. (Numbers 12:8.) Familiar intercourse is therefore
described in this phrase, as if it were said that God appeared to Moses by an
extraordinary mode of revelation. If any object that there is a contradiction
between this statement and what we shall presently see, "Thou canst not see my
face," the solution is easy, viz., that although God revealed Himself to Moses in
a peculiar manner, still He never appeared in the fullness of His glory, but only
so far as man's infirmity could endure. For this expression contains an implied
comparison, i.e., that no man was ever equal to Moses, or arrived at such a
pitch of dignity. And this tends to magnify the Law, that Moses its minister
reported what he had familiafly learnt, so that no ambiguity might be suspected.
When it is said that Joshua departed not from the tabernacle, we gather that the
dwelling-place of Moses was in the camp; and perhaps the fact of his being a
young man is mentioned, [365] in order more highly to illustrate God's grace, in
choosing that he should have the charge of the sanctuary. It is true that Joshua

at this time was of mature age; but God's special blessing was manifested in him, in that God passed over many old men, and set him who was younger to be the keeper of His tabernacle.

12. *See, thou, sayest unto me, Bring up this people* Moses is still diligently engaged in endeavoring to reconcile the people, for the fuller promise was inserted by way of anticipation. Since the revolt, however, God had promised no more than that He would give the land to the people; but although wishing only to assure them that they should possess the land, He had added that His angel should lead them, still this was but a temporary blessing, and one which He is wont to confer promiscuously on other nations also. Thus Moses saw that he and the people were deprived of a special privilege which they had previously enjoyed; for that same angel who had gone before them was frequently called the God of hosts, in order that they might perceive that God was present with them in a peculiar manner. Hence Moses complains not without cause that God had not signified whom He would send, inasmuch as, when He spoke generally of an ordinary angel, He had withdrawn that special Deliverer, the guardian of the people, and the perpetual maintainer of their safety. He does not, therefore, request that Aaron should be restored to him, or that any companion should be associated with him in his difficult and arduous task; but he desires to be assured of the continuance of God's previous favor. As the ground of his confidence in asking, he adduces nothing but the promises of God. He rests, then, on no dignity of his own, nor alleges any duties performed, whereby he had merited so great favor; but contents himself with this brief statement, Lord, cause the event to correspond with Thy words. We have already shewn [366] what it is to "know by name," viz., to choose from amongst others, or to hold in peculiar honor. After, however, Moses had made mention of what had been promised by God, he implores him by this grace, "if (says he) I have found grace in thy sight," confirm or ratify it by this proof, i.e., by again undertaking the care of us; for by the way of God he means that guidance in which He had declared that He would go before them to shew them the way. In a word, he requests that this token of favor should be given them, that God should continually guide His people. Therefore, He says, *thus shall I know thee,* and it will appear that I am acceptable to thee. Finally, he refers to the Covenant of God with the whole people; as much as to say, that although God should be unwilling to grant this to him alone individually, still there was a weightier reason, viz., because God had adopted that people; and, consequently, it was just that he should distinguish it from other nations by peculiar marks.

14. *And he said, My presence shall go with thee* We gather from this answer what the desire of Moses was, for God, in accepting his prayer, affirms in one word that He will go before them as He was wont, and this was a sure pledge of His presence in no ordinary manner. For although the whole world is governed by His providence, still His face does not therein appear so conspicuously as in His protection of the Church's welfare. And, in fact, since the same Angel, who had before presided over the camp, now undertakes the charge of guiding the people, the eternal divinity of Christ is clearly proved from hence.

This clause, "My face [367] shall go before," is equivalent to his saying, I will so go before thee, that thou shalt truly perceive that I am with thee, as if thou shouldst see my face set before thine eyes in a mirror. Now, since this was fulfilled in Christ, it follows that He is the eternal God, whose glory, power, and majesty is far above all creatures. The rest which He promises has reference to the perseverance of His grace, and its final accomplishment, [368] as if it were said, when the people shall have entered the land, they shall be under God's protection and guardianship; for what was common to the whole people is ascribed to the person of Moses.

15. And he said unto him, If thy presence go not Moses accepts what is accorded to him, whilst at the same time he signifies that it would be better and more desirable for him to perish in the desert than to go any further without the manifest token of God's presence; and this he confirms in the following verse, and therefore I have inserted the expletive particle certe (indeed,) although the copula might also be resolved into the causal particle nam (for.) For he declares that the paternal favor wherewith God had embraced the people could not be known unless He should remain with them. They are mistaken who suppose that something different is here indicated from what was said just before, for exactly in the same sense God is said to go before, and to dwell in the midst of His people; but Moses refers to the promise already given, the symbol of which was the Tabernacle of the Covenant, which just before had been removed from its proper place to punish the people's sin. What he adds at the end of the verse,[369] "and we shall be separated," may also be resolved, "that thus we may be separated," or, "because in this way we shall be separated." Whence it is abundantly clear that the favor which is mentioned refers to their election or gratuitous adoption, and is its fruit or effect. For it was the intention of Moses to restore the Covenant which had been violated by the people to its original force, as if the people were reinstated in that honorable condition from whence they had fallen. And surely this is our real happiness after all, to be separated from heathen nations as God's own property; as it is said in Psalm 106:4, "Remember me, O Lord, with the favor that thou bearest unto thy people: O visit me with thy salvation."

17. And the Lord said unto Moses, I will do this thing also He adds nothing new, but confirms by repetition what He had just said, in order to remove all doubt. Still He declares that He is induced by no other reason than by the gratuitous favor wherewith He had embraced Moses. This, therefore, is a kind of renewal of the Covenant, when the people is consecrated to God, so as to recover again the sacerdotal kingdom.

18. And he said, I beseech thee, shew me thy glory Thus far the desires of Moses had been confined within the limits of moderation and sobriety, but now he is carried beyond due bounds, and longs for more than is lawful or expedient; for it is plain from his repulse that he had inconsiderately proceeded further than He should. He desires that God should be revealed to him more closely, and in a more manifest form than before. Still it is not foolish curiosity that impels him to this, which so often tickles men's minds, so that they daringly attempt to penetrate into the deepest secrets of heaven; for he had no other design than to be animated to confidence, whereby he might more cheerfully go on with his charge. But that the desire itself was improper though its object was correct, we learn from the reply of God, wherein He shows that it would be injurious and fatal to Moses, if he should obtain that which he seeks as great privilege. [370] How, then, will it be with us, if the vanity of our nature tempts us to investigate God's glory more deeply than is right? Wherefore let this passage act as restraint upon us, to repress the speculations which are too wild and wanton in us, when we desire to know what God would have

concealed from us. This is the rule of sound and legitimate and profitable knowledge, to be content with the measure of revelation, and willingly to be ignorant of what is deeper than this. We must indeed advance in the acquisition of divine instruction, but we must so keep in the way as to follow the guidance of God.

19. And he said, I will make all my goodness pass At the outset He declares how far He has listened to Moses; but a limitation is presently added to prevent excess. Thus his prayer is not altogether rejected, but only so far as he was too eagerly set on beholding the perfection of God's glory. The passing by signifies a vision of brief duration; as if He had said, Let it suffice thee to have seen once, as for a moment, my glory, when it shall pass before thine eyes. The word טוב, tub, which I have rendered beauty, (decorem,) others translate good, (benum;) and hence, some take it to mean goodness; but the expression beauty (pulchritudinis, vel decoris) is more suitable, in which sense we find it used more than once. Hence that which is pleasing and delectable is said to be good to be looked upon.

"To call in the name of the Lord," [371] I understand thus, to declare in a clear and loud voice what it is useful for us to know respecting God Himself. It had been said before to Moses, "I am the God of Abraham, of Isaac, and of Jacob, -- but by my name, -- was I not known to them." (Exodus 6:3.) Whereas, then, Moses was already superior to the patriarchs, he is now still more highly exalted, inasmuch as God makes Himself more fully known to him, and carries His manifestation of Himself to its very utmost. First, therefore, it must be borne in mind that God was now known to Moses more familiarly than heretofore; still, at the same time, let it be observed, that although a vision was exhibited to his eyes, the main point was in the voice; because true acquaintance with God is made more by the ears than by the eyes. A promise indeed is given that he shall behold God; but the latter blessing is more excellent, that God will proclaim this name, so that Moses may know Him more by His voice than by His face; for speechless visions would be cold and altogether evanescent, did they not borrow efficacy from words. Thus, therefore, just as logicians compare a syllogism to the body, and the reasoning, which it includes, to the soul; so, properly speaking, the soul of a vision is the doctrine itself, from whence faith takes its rise.

and will be gracious to whom I will be gracious It will be well to consider how this sentence is connected with the foregoing, which has been either altogether neglected, or not sufficiently attended to. As to me, although I think that God's mercy is magnified by the fact, that He deals so indulgently to this guilty people, still I have no doubt but that He desired purposely to cut off occasion from the audacity of men, lest they should exclaim against his unwonted and as yet unheard of liberality; for, whether God executes His judgments, or mercifully pardons sins, profane men never cease to quarrel with Him; [372] thus, out of mere disputatiousness, they ask why He delayed the advent of His Son for so many ages; why He has deigned to bring forth the light of the Gospel out of darkness in our own days; nay, they take flight even to the creation of the world, inasmuch as it seems absurd to them that God should have been idle for so many ages, and therefore they inquire, in ridicule, why it at length entered His mind to make the world, which has not yet reached its sixth millennium? Especially, however, does the frowardness of many advance beyond all due bounds on this point, viz., because the reason does not appear, why God should be merciful to one nation or one age, and severe both to other ages and other nations. Hence the admirable counsel of God, whereby He has chosen some, and reprobated others, has always been exposed to the calumnies of ungodly men; for unless they see the cause of the diversity, they do not hesitate to condemn the injustice of God in making this distinction between the two. [373] God here checks this insanity, and asserts His power, which men, or rather worms of the earth, would gladly deprive Him of, viz., that according to His own will He exercises peculiar mercy towards whomsoever He pleases. When the Prophet relates how the fathers obtained possession of the land of Canaan, he assigns no other reason except that God "had a favor unto them." (Psalm 44:3.) And this doctrine, which filthy dogs endlessly assail with their barking, everywhere occurs in the Scriptures. Especially, however, do they rail when God shews Himself to be propitious, and beneficent towards the unworthy. For this reason Paul reminds believers of the incomprehensible counsel of God, because, by the preaching of the Gospel, He revealed the mystery, which was kept secret from all eternity. (Romans 16:25.) Again, because by ingrafting the Gentiles into the body of the Church, from which they had so long been aliens, He commends the depths of that mystery, which, though hidden even from angels, He made known to all men in the fullness of time. (Ephesians 3:9.) With the same intent, He here expressly declares that the cause why He manifests Himself to Moses more fully than of old to the patriarchs, is only to be sought in His own counsel or good-pleasure. Now, although this in the first place relates to Moses, still, inasmuch as he beheld the glory of God for the common good of the people, this mercy, which is referred to, extends to them all. And assuredly it was an inestimable proof of God's grace that, after this most disgraceful fall and wicked apostasy of the people, He nevertheless revealed Himself more clearly than before to Moses for their spiritual good. This, indeed, is certain, that by this reply a restraint is put upon whatever carnal feelings might allege in consideration of the novelty of the act; as if God had declared in one word that the dispensation of His grace is in His own sole power; and that men not only do amiss: but are carried away by impious and blasphemous madness when they endeavor to interfere with Him; as if it were their business to arraign that supreme Judge whose subjects they are. The mode of expression simply tends to this, that God's will is superior to all causes, so as to be the reason of all reasons, the law of laws, and the rule of rules. And surely, as long as men permit themselves to inquire into the secret counsels of God, there will be no bounds to their seditiousness. God, therefore, does not correct this insanity by disputing with it, but by the assertion of His right to be free in the dispensation of His grace; for in His sovereignty He says that He will be merciful to whomsoever He will. Let us beware, then, lest, when He is kind, our eyes should be evil.

Further, the better to convince dissatisfied men of their pride and temerity, He sets forth His mercy and compassion; as much as to say, that He is under obligation to none; and hence that it is an [374] unworthy thing in them to murmur, because He does not indiscriminately do good to them to whom He owes nothing. Hence it is clear how appropriately Paul, when treating of gratuitous election, accommodates this passage to the matter in hand, (Romans 9:15,) viz., that God must be by no means accounted unjust, because He passes by some and elects others; for the words loudly proclaim that God's grace is destined to a certain number of men, so as not to appear equally in all. The phrase itself needs no exposition, for it is common in all languages when we wish to prevent our reasons from being investigated, to repeat the point in question; thus, a person, wishing to rid himself of the censures of others, would say, I will go whither I will go, or I will do what I will do.

20. And he said, Thou canst not see my face Moses had indeed seen it, but in such a mode of revelation, as to be far inferior to its full effulgence. Long before the birth of Moses, Jacob had said, "I have seen God face to face," (Genesis 32:30;) and to Moses, as I have lately shewn, a still clearer vision was vouchsafed. Now, however, he obtains something better and more excellent; and yet not so as perfectly to see God such as He is in Himself, but so far as the human mind is capable of bearing. For, although the angels are said to see God's face in a more excellent manner than men, still they do not apprehend the immense perfection of His glory, whereby they would be absorbed. Justly, therefore, does God declare that He cannot be seen by a mortal man; for we shall not see him as He is, until we shall be like Him. (1 John 3:2.) For it must needs be that that incomprehensible brightness would bring us to nothing. God, therefore, whilst He withholds us from a complete knowledge of Him, nevertheless manifests Himself as far as is expedient; nay, attempering the amount of light to our humble capacity, He assumes the face which we are able to bear.

21. And the Lord said, Behold, there is a place by me This description may illdeed appear puerile, but it is well adapted to our imperfection; nor will any despise it who is duly conscious of his own imbecility and ignorance. There seems to be a contradiction between these two things, that the beauty of God should be shewn to Moses, and still that the sight of Him should be refused. This difficulty is here solved, for Moses was to see God only from behind. It is a similitude taken from men, whom we only partially recognise, if their face be turned away; for clear recognition is only obtained by seeing the face and countenance.

The fissure or hole in the rock was like a narrow and oblique window, which so far admits the sun's rays as that one, who is shut up in a deep and obscure place, may receive some advantage from the light, yet never see the sun itself nor enjoy its brightness. Thus we, imprisoned as it were in our bodies, cannot behold God's glory freely and directly; but He illuminates us obliquely, so that at least we see Him from behind. I do not speak of all, but of the most perfect amongst us, such as Moses was, who, although he obtained the extraordinary privilege which is here recorded, yet could not endure God's glory through the infirmity of his flesh; and therefore the hand of God was interposed, so that he should only see Him in part. By God's hand is meant the darkness wherewith He was covered, lest the eyes of Moses should be stretched in curiosity to see further than was lawful. Some [375] refer "my back parts" to the fullless of time, when Christ was manifested in the flesh, as if it were said, Thou shalt not see me until clothed in human nature; this is a subtle speculation, but by no means sound, nay, altogether wide of the genuine meaning.

Exodus 34

Exodus 34:1-10, 27-35

1. And the Lord said unto Moses, Hew thee two tables of stone like unto the first; and I will write upon these tables the words that were in the first tables, which thou brakest.

1. Et ait Jehova ad Mosen, Dola tibi duas tabulas instar priorum: et scribam in his tabulis verba quae fuerunt in tabulis prioribus quas fregisti.

2. And be ready in the morning, and come up in the morning unto mount Sinai, and present thyself there to me in the top of the mount.

2. Esto ergo paratus mane, et ascende mane montem Sinai: stesque mihi illic super verticem ipsius montis.

3. And no man shall come up with thee, neither let any man be seen throughout all the mount; neither let the flocks nor herds feed before that mount.

3. Nullus ascendat tecum, nec ullus videatur in toro monte, etiam oves ant boves non pascantur in prospectu montis hujus.

4. And he hewed two tables of stone, like unto the first: and Moses rose up early in the morning, and went up unto mount Sinai, as the Lord had commanded him, and took in his hand the two tables of stone.

4. Dolavit ergo duas tabulas lapideas instar priorum: consurgens Moses mane ascendit in montem Sinai, sicut praeceperat ei Jehova, et accepit in manu sua duas tabulas lapideas.

5. And the Lord descended in the cloud, and stood with him there, and proclaimed the name of the Lord.

5. Tunc descendit Jehova in nube, et stetit coram eo illic, et clamavit in nomine Jehova.

6. And the Lord passed by before him, and proclaimed, The Lord, The Lord God, merciful and gracious, long-suffering, and abundant in goodness and truth,

6. Transiens, inquam, Jehova ante eum, clamavit, Jehova, Jehova, Deus misericors et clemens, tardus ad iram, et multus misericordia et veritate:

7. Keeping mercy for thousands, forgiving iniquity, and transgression, and sin, and that will by no means clear the guilty; visiting the iniquity of the fathers upon the children, and upon the children's children, unto the third and to the fourth generation.

7. Servans misericordiam millibus, auferens iniquitatem, et transgressionem, et peccatum, et innocentem non faciens, visitaris iniquitatem patrum super filios filiorum in tertios et quartos.

8. And Moses made haste, and bowed his head toward the earth, and worshipped.

8. Festinans autem Moses inclinavit se ad terram, et adoravit,

9. And he said, If now I have found grace in thy sight, O Lord, let my Lord, I pray thee, go among us, (for it is a stiff-necked people,) and pardon our iniquity and our sin, and take us for thine inheritance.

9. Dixitque, Si nunc inveni gratiam in oculis tuis, Domine mi, proficiscatur agedum Dominus meus in medio nostri: et quia populus durae cervicis est, propitius sis iniquitati nostrae et peccato nostro, ut possideas nos in hereditatem.

10. And he said, Behold, I make a covenant: before all thy people I will do marvels, such as have not been done in all the earth, nor in any nation: and all the people among which thou art shall see the work of the Lord: for it is a terrible thing that I will do with thee.

10. Et dixit, Ecce, ego pereutiam foedus eoram toro populo tuo, et edam miracula quae non sunt creata in universa terra, et in cunctis nationibus: et videbit totus populus in eujus medio es, quod terribile sit opus Jehovae quod facio tecum.

27. And the Lord said unto Moses, Write thou these words: for after the tenor of these words I have made a covenant with thee and with Israel.

27. Et dixit Jehova ad Mosen, Scribe tibi verba haec: quia secundum verba haec pepigi foedus tecum, et cum Israele.

28. And he was there with the Lord forty days and forty nights; he did neither eat bread, nor drink water: and He wrote upon the tables the words of the covenant, the ten commandments.

28. Fuit autem ibi cum Jehova quadraginta dies, et quadraginta noctes: panem non edit et aquam non bibit: et scripsit in tabulis verba foederis, decem verba.

29. And it came to pass, when Moses came down from mount Sinai with the two tables of testimony in Moses' hand, (when he came down from the mount,) that Moses wist not that the skin of his face shone while he talked with Him.

29. Factum est autem quum descenderet Moses e monte Sinai, habens duas tabulas testimonii in manu sun: quum ergo descenderet e monte, nesciebat quod resplenduisset cutis faciei suae quando loquutus erat cum eo.

30. And when Aaron and all the children of Israel saw Moses, behold, the skin of his face shone: and they were afraid to come nigh him.

30. Viditque Aharon et omnes filii Israel ipsum Mosen, et ecce, splendebat cutis faciei ejus: timueruntque accedere ad eum.

31. And Moses called unto them: and Aaron and all the rulers of the congregation returned unto him: and Moses talked with them.

31. Et vocavit filius Moses: reversique sunt ad eum Aharon et omnes principes coetus. Tunc loquutus est Moses ad cos.

32. And afterward all the children of Israel came nigh: and he gave them in commandment all that the Lord had spoken with him in mount Sinai.

32. Deinde appropinquarunt omnes filii Israel, et praecepit eis cuncta quae loquutus fuerat Jehova cum eo in monte Sinai.

33. And till Moses had done speaking with them, he put a vail on his face.

33. Porro quum finem fecisset loquendi Moses cum eis, posuit velamen super faciem suam.

34. But when Moses went in before the Lord, to speak with him, he took the vail off, until he came out. And he came out, and spake unto the children of Israel that which he was commanded.

34. Quum vero ingrederetur Moses in conspectum Jehovae ad loquendum cum illo, auferebat velamen, donec egrederetur: egressus autem alloquebatur filios Israel quod jussus erat.

35. And the children of Israel saw the face of Moses, that the skin of Moses' face shone: and Moses put the vail upon his face again, until he went in to speak with Him.

35. Videbunt igitur filii Israel faciem Mosis, quod resplenderet curts faciei Mosis, et reducebat Moses velamen super factem suam, donec ingrederetur ad loquendum cum co.

1. And the Lord said unto Moses, Hew thee two tables of stone Although the renewal of the broken covenant was ratified by this pledge or visible symbol, still, lest His readiness to pardon should produce indifference, God would have some trace of their punishment remain, like a scar that continues after the wound is healed. In the first tables there had been no intervention of man's workmanship; for God had delivered them to Moses engraven by His own secret power. A part of this great dignity is now withdrawn, when Moses is commanded to bring tables polished by the hand of man, on which God might write the Ten Commandments. Thus the ignominy of their crime was not altogether effaced, whilst nothing was withheld which might be necessary or profitable for their salvation. For nothing was wanting which might be a testimony of God's grace, or a recommendation of the Law, so that they should receive it with reverence; they were only humbled by this mark, that the stones to which God entrusted His covenant were not fashioned by His hand, nor the produce of the sacred mount. The conceit by which some expound it, -- that the Jews were instructed by this sign that the Law was of no effect, unless they should offer their stony hearts to God for Him to inscribe it upon them, -- is frivolous; for the authority of Paul rather leads us the other way, where he fitly and faithfully interprets this passage, and compares the Law to a dead and deadly letter, because it was only engraven on tables of stone, whereas the doctrine of salvation requires "the fleshy tables of the heart." (2 Corinthians 3:3.)

3. And no man shall come up with thee Again men as well as beasts are prohibited from access to the mount, as had been the case at the first promulgation of the Law, in order that the people might obediently receive the Law as if come down from heaven. Why God admitted no witness, is a question the answer to which must remain with God Himself. The miracle indeed would have been illustrious if the writing had appeared in a moment on the empty tables; but God would leave some room for faith, when He employed the intermediate agency of man. But still He amply provided what was sufficient to establish the dignity of the Law, when Moses brought the Ten Commandments written upon two tables which the people had lately seen taken up void and empty, whereas He could not have found in the mount a chisel or graving-tool. For [376] God so administers the dispensation of His heavenly doctrine as to prove the obedience and teachableness of believers, whilst He leaves no room for doubting.

5. And the Lord descended in the cloud It is by no means to be doubted but that the cloud received Moses into it in the sight of the people, so that, after having been separated from the common life of men for forty days, he should again come forth like a new man. Thus did this visible demonstration of God's glory avail to awaken faith in the commandments.

The descent of God, which is here recorded, indicates no change of place, as if God, who fills heaven and earth, and whose immensity is universally diffused, altered His position, but it has reference to the perceptions of men, because under the appearance of the cloud God testified that He met Moses. Therefore, according to the usual phrase of Scripture, the sacred name of God is applied to the visible symbol; not that the empty cloud was a figure of the absent Deity, but because it testified His presence according to the comprehension of men.

At the end of the verse, "to call in the name of the Lord," is equivalent to proclaiming His name, or promulgating what God would make known to His servant. This expression, indeed, frequently occurs with reference to prayers. Some, [377] therefore, understand it of Moses, that he called on the name of the Lord. In this opinion there is no absurdity; let us be at liberty, then, to take it as applying either to Moses or to God Himself, i.e., either that God Himself proclaimed in a loud voice His power, and righteousness, and goodness, or that Moses himself professed his piety before God. But what immediately follows must necessarily be referred to God, when He passed by, to cry out and to dignify Himself with His true titles. First of all, the name of Jehovah is uttered twice by way of emphasis, in order that Moses might be rendered more attentive. The name אל el, is added, which, originally derived from strength, is often used for God, and is one of His names. By these words, therefore, His eternity and boundless power are expressed. Next, He proclaims His clemency and mercy; nor is He contented with a single word, but, after having called Himself "merciful," He claims the praise of clemency, inasmuch as He has no more peculiar attribute than His goodness and gratuitous beneficence. The nature also of His goodness and clemency is specified, viz., that He is not only placable, and ready, and disposed, to pardon, but that He patiently waits for those who have sinned, and invites them to repentance by His long-suffering. For this reason He is called "slow [378] to anger," as if He would abstain from severity did not man's wickedness compel Him to execute punishment on his sins. Afterwards He proclaims the greatness of His mercy and truth, and on these two supports the confidence of the pious is based, whilst they embrace the mercy offered to them, and securely repose on the faithfulness and certainty of the promises. Everywhere, therefore, in the Psalms, where mention is made of God's goodness, His truth is connected with it as its inseparable companion. Another reason also is because God's mercy cannot be comprehended, except upon the testimony of His word, the certainty of which must needs be well assured lest our salvation should be wavering and insecure. What follows, that God keeps mercy to a thousand generations, we have expounded in chapter 20; whilst, on the other hand, the punishments which He requires for men's sins are only extended to the third and fourth generation, because His clemency surpasses His judgment, as is said in Psalm 30:5, [379] "There is only a moment in his anger, but life in his favor;" and although this only relates properly to believers, yet it flows from a general principle. To the same effect is the next clause, "forgiving iniquity, transgression, and sin;" for thus the greatness of His clemency is set forth, inasmuch as He not only pardons light offenses, but the very grossest sins; and again, remits not only sin in one case, but is propitious to sinners by whom He has been a hundred times offended. Hence, therefore, appears the extent of His goodness, since He blots out an infinite mass of iniquities. Lest, however, this indulgence should be perverted into a license for sin, it is afterwards added, by way of correction, "with [380] cleansing He will not cleanse," which, with the Chaldee interpreter and others, I understand as applying to His severe judgment against the reprobate and obstinate; for I do not like their opinion who say that, although God indeed pardons sins, yet He still moderately chastises those who have sinned; since this is a poor conjecture, that punishment is required though the guilt is remitted; and besides, it is altogether untrue, inasmuch as it is manifest, from experience that God passes over many sins without punishment. But what I have stated is very suitable, that, lest impunity should beget audaciousness, after God has spoken of His mercy, He adds an exception, viz., that the iniquity is by no means pardoned, which is accompanied by obstinacy. And hence the Prophets seem to have quoted from this passage, [381] "Clearing should ye be cleared?" (Jeremiah 25:29; 49:12,) when they address the reprobate, to whom pardon is denied. The words, therefore, may be properly paraphrased thus: Although God is pitiful and even ready to pardon, yet He does not therefore spare the despisers, but is a severe avenger of their impiety. Nevertheless, the opposite meaning would not be inappropriate here, "With cutting off He will not cut off;" for this is sometimes the sense of the verb נקה, nakah; and it would thus be read conneetedly, that God pardons iniquities because He does not wish entirely to cut off the human race; for who shall escape if God should choose to call to judgment the sins even of believers? And perhaps Jeremiah alluded to this passage, where [382] he mitigates the severity of the vengeance of which he had been speaking by this same expression, for there it can only be translated, "With cutting off I will not cut thee off." If this be preferred, it will be the assignment of the reason why God pardons sins, viz., because He is unwilling to cut off men, which would be the case if He insisted on the utmost rigor of the Law. Some [383] thus explain it, That God pardons sins, because no one is innocent in His sight; as if it were said, that all are destitute of the glory of righteousness, and thence their only refuge is in the mercy of God. This is true indeed, but not so nmch an exposition as a plausible conceit.

8. *And Moses made haste, and bowed his head* This haste shews that Moses was astounded when he first beheld the brightness; for thus does God, when He reveals Himself, immediately ravish the godly into such admiration of Him, that there is no time for delay. [384] This prayer follows, that God would journey with His people, and bear with their frowardness; for, since God had said that He could not possibly dwell with so stiff-necked and intractable a people, Moses proposes the remedy, viz., after he has confessed that the people are of a hardened and stubborn spirit, he still expresses a hope of their safety, if God will be pitiful in sparing them. What follows is worthy of observation, "that thou mayest possess us;" [385] for the copula has the force of the causal particle, as if he had said, That God could not enjoy the inheritance He had chosen, unless by pardoning their sins. And surely so it is; for such is man's frailty, that they would straightway fall from grace were they not reconciled to God. Nor was this spoken only of this ancient people, but refers also to us; for, in order that God should possess us too, it is needful that our sins should be constantly pardoned, as this embassy, according to Paul, daily resounds in the Church. (2 Corinthians 5:20.) Consequently, not only does the origin of our salvation flow from gratuitous adoption, but its continual progress even to the end can only be accomplished by God's freely reconciling us to Himself.

10. *And he said, Behold, I make a covenant* It is not specified with whom God would make the covenant. Some interpreters, [386] therefore, supply the name of Moses, and this they seem to do on probable grounds, especially since

it is added at the end of the verse "the work [387] that I will do with thee." But, inasmuch as Moses stipulated in the name of all, the meaning comes to the same thing, if we read, I will make a covenant openly with the whole people. By this promise, then, God, as it were, entirely restored the Israelites, for He declares that He will deal so marvellously in the discomfiture of the nations, as to prove that He is the peculiar God of that people; and this was to distinguish them from other nations, according to the prayer of Moses. he says that they shall all be eye-witnesses of this, that, being thus at length convinced by their own senses, they might sincerely and faithfully submit themselves to his dominion.

28. And he was there with the Lord forty days The number of forty days is repeated, in order that the second Tables might have no less credit than the first; for we have stated that Moses was withdrawn from the common life of men, that he might bring the Law, as it were, from heaven. If he had only been kept a few days in the mount, his authority would not have been ratified by so conspicuous a miracle; but the forty days obtained full credit for his mission, so that the people might know that he was sent by God; inasmuch as the endurance of a fast for so long a period exceeded the capacity of human nature. Wherefore, in order that the majesty of the Law might be indubitable, its minister was invested with angelic glory; and hence he expressly records that "he did neither eat bread, nor drink watch" since it was requisite that he should be distinguished from other mortals, in order that his official character might be unquestionable. Now, it must be borne in mind, that this was not a mere fast of temperance or sobriety, but of special privilege, whereby exemption from the infirmity of the flesh was vouchsafed to Moses for a time, in order that his condition might be different from the rest of the human race. For neither did he feel any hunger, nor did he struggle with any longing for food, nor desire meat and drink any more than one of the angels. Therefore this instance of abstinence was never alleged as an example by the Prophets, nor did any one attempt to imitate what they all knew to be by no means accorded to them. I except Elijah, who, being sent to revive the Law, when it was almost lost, like a second Moses, abstained also from eating and drinking for forty days. The reason for the fast of Christ was similar, (Matthew 4:2;) for, in order to acquire full credit for tits Gospel, He desired to make it manifest that He was by no means inferior to Moses in this particular. Wherefore, [388] the less excusable is that error, which sprang from gross ignorance, when all, without exception, endeavored to rival the Son of God in their annual fast, as if a new promulgation of the Gospel was entrusted to them. For neither did Christ fast forty day's more than once in His life; nor during the whole of that time, as it is clearly specified, did he experience hunger; and His heavenly Father separated Him from communion with men, when He was preparing Himself to undertake the office of teacher.

29. And it came to pass when Moses came down Another remarkable honor given to the Law is here narrated, viz., that the brightness of the heavenly glory appeared in the face of Moses; for it is said that his face gave forth rays, or was irradiated. The word is derived from קרן keren, a horn; and therefore it is probable that rays shone forth from his face, which rendered it luminous; and this effulgence God shed upon him, whilst He was speaking to him in the mount. It is not certain what was the reason why Moses himself was ignorant that he was thus illumined by God, except that it seems probable that it was

concealed from him for a short time, in order that he might approach the people with more freedom, and thus that the miracle might be more evident from close inspection. When it is said afterwards, that Aaron and the children of Israel were so alarmed at the brightness, that "they were afraid to come nigh him," I do not understand it, as if they fled from him immediately; for, since they were recalled by his voice, undoubtedly they had not seen the rays from a distance, but when they were in the act of receiving him, and he, on his part, delivering to them the commands of God. Therefore, what follows soon afterwards, that, when he had done speaking, he covered his face with a vail, [389] I refer to his first address, which He was obliged to break off on account of the departure or flight of the people, so that the meaning is, when He knew the cause of their alarm, He left off speaking, and covered his face with a vail; for he could not have known the reason of their flying except by inquiry. Some, in order to avoid the difficulty, separate the second clause from the first, and transpose their order; but this exposition appears to me to be forced. It seems, however, in my opinion, to be perfectly consistent that Moses, after he saw them departing in consternation, ceased from speaking, because they did not listen to him, and, when he discovered the reason, put on the vail. Hence arises a question, viz., How Moses could have borne the brightness of God's glory, whilst the people could not bear the rays which shone from his face? But this is easily answered: that they were branded with this mark of disgrace, in order that they might confess how far by their ingratitude they had departed from God, since they were terrified at the sight of this servant. They were, therefore, humbled by this difference between them, that, whilst Moses securely advanced to them from his conference with God, although he bore upon him the indications of God's terrible power, they, in fear and astonishment, recoiled from the sight of a mortal man.

After Paul has shewn the genuine object of this brightness, viz., that the Law should be glorious, he proceeds further, and shews that it was a presage of the future blindness which awaited the Jews. (2 Corinthians 3:13.) He begins, therefore, by saying, that although the Law was only a dead letter, and the ministration of death, yet it was graced with its own peculiar glory; and then adds what is accidental, that there was a vail before the face of Moses, because it would be the case that the Jews would not be able to see what is the main thing in the Law, nor to pay attention to its true end; and so it actually is, that since the coming of Christ, their senses have been blinded, and the vail is upon them, until Moses shall be [390] turned by them to Christ, who is the soul of the Law. But, since now in the Gospel God presents Himself with open face, we must take care that the prince of this world does not darken our minds, but rather that we may be transformed from glory to glory.

Footnotes:

290. Augustin. Confess. 10. 40. "Et tota spes mea non nisi in magna valde misericordia tua. Da quod jubes, et jube quod vis." See also ibid., Section 45, 7. Edit. Bened., Tom. 1, pp. 184, 186, 191; et Tom. 10. 851 A.

291. Addition in Fr., "Laquelle estoit la premiere en dignite;" which was the highest in dignity.

292. See [32]vol. 2, p. 143, and [33]note.

293. "Every one, whom his spirit made willing." -- A.V.

294. Addition in Fr., "Pour s'en defaire;" to deprive themselves of them.

295. "To perceive." -- A.V. See ante, [34]vol. 1, p. 390, and [35]vol. 2, p. 441.

296. Added from Fr.

297. "Qui gardent leurs mains pures et nettes;" who keep their hands pure and clean -- Fr.

298. All the difficulties connected with this matter are set at rest by our increased acquaintance with Egyptian Antiquities. C., and almost all the earlier commentators, were evidently possessed with the idea that the mirrors of the women were literally looking-glasses; and hence arose the various solutions which are here given, and others which might be added. Sir G. Wilkinson, in his "Popular Account of the Ancient Egyptians," tells us; -- "One of the principal objects of the toilet was the mirror. It was of mixed metal, chiefly copper, most carefully wrought and highly polished; and so admirably did the Egyptians succeed in the composition of metals, that this substitute for our modern looking-glass was susceptible of a lustre which has even been partially revived at the present day, in some of those discovered at Thebes, though buried in the earth for many centuries. The same kind of metal-mirror was used by the Israelites, who doubtless brought them from Egypt." -- Vol. 2, p. 346.

299. "Entre les bagages superflus des femmes." -- Fr.

300. C. here affords the reader a curious proof that he composed this note with S M. under his eye, by employing Munster's word labrum for the Hebrew כיור, which he had previously rendered concha in his own text. But whilst S M had

translated צבאת אשר צבאו, (mulierum) militantium, quae militabant, C. had the sagacity to drop the metaphor, and render the words convenientium, quae conveniebant צבא, says Professor Robertson, to assemble for worship, or for war. Clav Pentat in loco. -- W

301. Numbers 4:3, "All that enter into the host." -- A.V. Numbers 8:24, "They shall go in to wait upon the service," margin, "Heb., to war the warfare of the tabernacle." -- A.V.

302. "These are the counted-things." -- Lat. So also Ainsworth.

303. "Afin que les Levites sceussent ce qu'ils devoyent avoir en garde;" in order that the Levites might know what they ought to have in charge. -- Fr.

304. See on Exodus 30:12, [36]vol. 1, p. 482.

305. "A ceux, qui desia estoyent en degre d'honneur;" to those who were already honourably distinguished. -- Fr.

306. "Septante et deux;" seventy-two. -- Fr.

307. "Ces trois estats;" these three estates. -- Fr.

308. "Had written." -- Lat.

309. "Pillars." -- A V. "Some think that this altar was set upon twelve stones, such as Elias built, 1 Kings 18:31; and Joshua 4:20; in which places, however, the word used is אבנים, (abanim,) which signifieth stones, which were gathered together to make one altar or heap; but here the word is מצבה, (matsebah,) which is a pillar, so called a stando, because it standeth alone, and is erected and set up as a monument." -- Abridged from Willet in loco. See ante, [38]vol. 2, p. 117, and [39]note

310. "Ce qui n'est attribuE qu'a ceux qui ont la charge speciale de

sacrifier;" which is only applied to those who have the special charge of sacrificing. -- Fr.

311. "Peace-offerings." -- A.V. Vide ante, [40]vol. 2, pp. 139 and [41]333.

312. "In all solemn leagues and covenants, they sacrificed to the gods by whom they swore, offering for the most part either a boar, ram, or goat; sometimes all three; sometimes bulls or lambs instead of any of them. Hence comes the phrase, ὅρκια τέμνειν; in Latin, ferire foedus, i e., to make a covenant." -- Potter's Arch. Graeca., Book 2. ch. 6. For the same custom, as existing among the Romans, see Liv. 1. 24. Virg. Aen. 8. 641.

313. "Par tel sacrement." -- Fr.

314. See C in loco. Calvin Soc. edit., p. 74, where, however, I question whether his statement on the word σπουδὰς is correct.

315. "Comme si le Loy, et les Prophetes, et l'Evangile en estoyent escrits;" as if the Law and the Prophets, and the Gospel were written with it. -- Fr.

316. "Devant que sacrifier;" before sacrificing. -- Fr.

317. Ainsworth, "A work of sapphire-brick. Heb., brick of sapphire: whereby is meant sapphire-stone, hewed like brick, wherewith the place under Him was paved. So also the Greek translateth it. Or, it may be Englished, of whiteness of sapphire, i.e., of white sapphire-stone: for brick hath the name in Hebrew of whiteness. The Chaldee translateth, under the throne of his glory was, as it were, a work of precious, stone." "The Hebrews, (says Willet, in loco,) whom Lyranus and Lippoman follow, -- in that the pavement or brick-work was like sapphire, -- understand the

happy change which was now made for Israel: their servitude in making of brick was turned into glorious liberty, as if a floor should be paved with sapphire instead of brick!"

318. So Aben-Ezra, in Willet; and Faigius and S. Munster in Poole. Boothroyal says, "This phrase evidently means, He slew them not;' compare Genesis 22:12; and 37:22; Nehemiah 12:21; Esther 2:21; Psalm 55:20."

319. See ante, [42]vol. 1, pp. 300, 301.

320. "Un document celeste et infallible;" a celestial and infallible document. -- Fr.

321. See Augustine, Serm. 155: De verbo Apost. sect. 3, tom. 5, pp. 742, 743, (Edit. Bened.) See also Serm. 8. sect. 14, ibid., p. 48. See also Quaest. in Exodus 25, tom. 3., p. 429; and Quaest. 166., ibid., pp. 471, 472. "Proinde magna oritur quaestio, quomodo illae tabulae, quas erat Moyses Deo utique praesciente fractures, non hominis opus esse dicantur, sed Dei, nec ab homine scriptae, sed digito Dei: posteriores vero tabulae tamdiu mansurae, ac in tabernaculo et templo Dei futurae, jubente quidem Deo, tamen ab homine excisae sint, ab homine scriptae. An forte in illis prioribus gratia Dei significabatur, non hominis opus, qua gratia indigni facti sunt revertentes corde in Aegyptum, et facientes idolum; unde illo beneficio privati sunt, et propterea Moyses tabulas fregit: istis vero tabulis posterioribus significati sunt qui de suis operibus gloriantur; unde dicit Apostolus (Romans 10:3) Ignorantes Dei justitiam, et suam volentes constituere, justitiae Dei non sunt subjecti; et ideo tabulae humano opere exsculptae et humano opere

conscriptae datae sunt, quae cum ipsis manerent, ad eos significandos de suis operibus gloriaturos, non de digito Dei hoc est de Spiritu Dei."

322. "Le mot d'ici;" the word here. -- Fr.

323. Added from Fr.

324. It will be seen that C. does not give the actual words, but the sense of Stephen.

325. "Mais qui pis est;" but what is worse. -- Fr.

326. "Why is his chariot so long in coming?" -- A.V.

327. Auferte. -- Lat.

328. "The ear-rings now worn in the East are various in form and size. They are generally thick, sometimes fitting close to the ear, and in other instances very large, perhaps three or four inches in diameter, and so heavy as greatly to distend the lobe of the ear, at the same time enlarging in a very disagreeable manner the orifice made for the inserting of the ring." -- Illustrated Commentary in loco. For the ear-rings worn by the Egyptian Ladies, see Sir G. Wilkinson, "Popular Account of the Ancient Egyptians," vol. 1, p. 145, where he figures a group of them from Thebes evidently talking about their ear-rings; and vol. 2, p. 335, etc.

329. Professor Robinson says a graving tool; but more properly to be rendered a bag here. C. alludes to what S.M. tells us, that the Rabbins, wishing to excuse their forefathers, said that there came forth a calf, not wrought by any workmen, but produced by the magical arts, which some of the Egyptians, mixed with the people, now employed to introduce idolatry. -- W. Lightfoot has a characteristic note on this: "Expositors cannot tell what to say of their intent, for they cannot think they were such calves, (as to turn the glory of God into a calf,) and yet what else can we say? Jonathan saith, The devil got into the metal, and fashioned it into a calf.' The devil, indeed, was too much there; but it was in their fancies more than in the metal." Explan. of divers difficult passages of Scripture. Decad, 1. 4. He elsewhere also refers to the probability, stated below by C., that the idol was made after an Egyptian pattern: "Israel cannot be so long without Moses, as Moses can be without meat. The fire still burneth on the top of Mount Sinai, out of which they had so lately received the Law; and yet so suddenly do they break the greatest commandment of that Law to extremity; -- of Egyptian jewels they make an Egyptian idol, because, thinking Moses had been lost, they intended to return for Egypt." -- A handful of gleanings out of Exod., sect. 32.

330. This appears to have been either a slip of the pen, or of the memory. It was not Anubis, but Osiris, "who was worshipped under the form of Apis, the Sacred Bull of Memphis, or as a human figure with a bull's head, accompanied by the name Apis. Osiris." -- See Sir Gardner Wilkinson's "Ancient Egyptians," vol. 4, p. 347; 3d edition.

331. It is a strange notion of R. Salomon Jarchi, that the molten calf was alive; because it is said in Psalm 106:20, that it was the "similitude of an ox that eateth grass." See also Breithaupt's note in loco.

332. Addition in Fr., "Et nage entre deux eaux;" and swam between two waters.

333. C. here quotes his own translation, see Calvin Soc. edit., [43]vol. 4. 301, with the Editor's [44]note. It will be seen that it nearly agrees with the Prayer-book version of the Church of England.

334. Willet, in loco, attributes the opinion rejected by C. as to their intemperance to Ambrose, and, after him, to Simler. The latter notion, with respect to the word play, seems to be a very common one with the Commentators. Bushe says it implies "not only such sports as singing, dancing, and merry-making in general, but in some cases also a species of conduct which the epithet wanton as correctly defines as any term which we deem it proper to employ. Compare the use of the same original word rendered mock, Genesis 39:14. Compare also Numbers 25:1, 2." Corn. A Lapide quotes a striking parallel as to the abuse of sacrifices among the heathen, from Epicharmus, ap Athenoeum, lib. 2, -- "Ex sacrificio epulum, ex epulo facta est potatio, ex potatione comus, ex como ludus, ex ludo judicium, ex judicio condemnatio, ex condemnatione compedes, sphacelus, et mulctatio;" and adds, that "drunken-bouts were called μέθας, because they were indulged in μετὰ τὸ θύειν, i e., after sacrifices." Dathe appears precisely to represent C.'s view: "Postridie igitur mane holocausta et eucharistica sacrificant, atque commessationibus et compotationibus peractis, ad saltationes solennes sese convertunt."

335. This seems to be a very general opinion of the Commentators, from Jerome downwards. "Though Calvin mislikes this sense, yet it is warranted by that place, Deuteronomy 32:5. They have corrupted themselves, not being his children." -- Junius in Willet.

336. "For mischief." -- A.V.By the old interpreter (C. means the V. which renders the word "callide," craftily. The version of LXX. is μετὰ πονηρίας, with maliciousness. "Some thus, (says Poole,) malo sidere, under an evil star; because the Egyptians attributed all things to the stars. Fagius, Vatablus."

337. Addition in Fr., "et profane."

338. See on Genesis 6:6, (Calvin Soc. Edit., [45]vol. 1, pp. 248, 249,) the latter part of which passage is quoted by Hengstenberg on the Pentat., vol. 2, p. 373, "On the repentance of God," with the following remark: "These last words show how very deeply Calvin had gained the right point of view in reference to Anthropomorphisms. In his esteem they formed a glorious ornament of holy writ. How totally different the apologists since the times of Deism! One remarks, on all occasions, how gladly they would dispense with Anthropomorphisms. They try to be satisfied only with that which they cannot alter." See also C. on Minor Prophets, vol. 1, [46]p. 402; 2, [47]p. 61; 3, pp. [48]115, [49]126, [50]408; and Institutes, Book 1, ch. 17. Section 13, vol. 1, p. 263. (Calvin Soc. editions.)

339. This sentence is omitted in Fr.

340. Ver. 18, ענות. In the first clause A. V. renders this word shout, in the second cry, in the third sing. S.M. renders it resound in the two first, and in the last singers; but observes that it is literally to answer, and C. follows his rendering. -- W

341. "Mises en nous en l'integrite, qui estoit en notre pere Adam;" implanted in us in the integrity which was in our father Adam. -- Fr.

342. C. found in S. M.'s notes the Rabbinical fancies about the vanishing of the letters, etc. -- W.

343. The reference here in the original, and in the French translation, (which always copies such errors, and, alas! they are multitudinous,) is to 2 Corinthians 11:15. I have substituted one, which appears to me more probable, and which the reader may compare with its parallel passages; but I am not so certain of my correction here, as I generally am.

344. "Tous juges, et chefs du people;" all judges and rulers of the people. -- Fr.

345. The glossa ordinaria gives the three usual opinions as to this statement, viz., either that they were stripped of the ornaments, whereof the idol was made; or that they had manifested their corrupt will, which was previously concealed; or that they had lost the help and protection of God. De Lyra adopts the first. Dathe calls it a very difficult passage; but inclines to the rendering of the LXX., διασκέδασται, were scattered, or dissipated. "The people were in a dissolute, disorderly state; and therefore in a condition to be attacked with advantage." -- Geddes.

346. "Quelques Rabins des Juifs;" some Jewish Rabbins. -- Fr. So Aben-Ezra, and R. Salomon.

347. "Qui avoyent mene la danse pour desbaucher les autres, et ausquels le mal devoit estre impute;" who had led the dance to corrupt the others, and to whom the evil must be imputed. -- Fr.

348. "Les juges sont en grand souci, par quel bout its commencerout, et qu'ils tremblent jusques a defaillir en le fin de leur office;" the judges are in great anxiety as to what end they shall begin at, and that they are so much alarmed as at length to fail in their duty. -- Fr.

349. Amongst others, of the Vulgate. Boothroyd thus defends it: "This verb may either be the second person plural of the imperative, or the third of the preterite, of both the active and passive voices. The Masorets have pointed it in the former, and are followed by our version. By this rendering, the order of the narrative is perverted; for after that command given to the Levites is stated to have been executed, and the number of the slain specified, then we have another command. Render in the preterite, and all is clear and consistent, Ye have consecrated, etc."

350. A.V., "Even," which, though different from the ordinary meanings of this particle, is sanctioned by several other texts cited in Noldii Conc. Part., whilst C.'s rendering has no such sanction, nor is it supported by S. M. -- W. "Le mot, que j'ay translate voire, signifie en Hebrieu car: mais il est ici entralasse pour plus grande vehemence;" the word, which I have translated namely, signifies in Hebrew for, but is here introduced for the sake of greater vehemence. -- Fr.

351. "Superstitions." -- Fr.

352. So A.V. It will be seen that C. renders the nouns in the ablative case, Ye have sinued by a great sin.

353. See C. on Amos 5:15. -- Minor Prophets, Cal. Soc. edit., [51]vol. 2 p. 277.

354. "R. Menacheus on this place saith, "This angel is not the Angel of the Covenant, of whom He spake in the time of favorable acceptance, My presence shall go; for now the holy blessed God had taken away His divine presence from amongst them, and would have led them by the hand of another angel. And Moses' speech in Exodus 33:12, seemeth to imply so much." -- Ainsworth in loco.

355. "Formula (says Facciolati) obsecrantis, vel obtestantis: di grazia, deh, per cortesia." Elsewhere, it would appear, our translators have always rendered אנא, "I pray thee; or I, or we, beseech thee," except at Psalm 116:16, where it is translated as here, "oh." -- Taylor's Concordance. "The Scriptures deal but sparingly in such interjectional phrases as the present, and, wherever they occur, they indicate the most profound emotion in the speaker." -- Prof. Bush.

356. A. V., "If." Noldius, obsecro; equivalent to the rendering towards which C. inclines. -- W. "Vray est que le sens est tel, O que tu leur pardonnes: mais cependant il ne parle qu'a demie bouche, comme un homme angoisse, et s'escrie que si Dieu leur pardonne, il a tout gagne;" it is true that this is the sense, O that thou wouldest pardon them! but still he speaks but half his meaning, like a man in anguish, and cries out, that if God would pardon them, he has gained all he wants. -- Fr.

357. See this difficult subject somewhat more fully discussed by C. himself on Romans 9:3, (Calvin Soc. edit., [52]pp. 335-337,) together with Mr. Owen's [53]note. If, however, the opinion of many, as stated by Prof. Bush, as to this passage be adopted, and it surely has much show of reason, it is far more easily comprehended than the expression of St. Paul: "There is no intimation in these words of any secret book of the Divine decrees, or of anything involving the question of Moses' final salvation or perdition. He simply expressed the wish rather to die than to witness the destruction of his people. The phraseology is in allusion, probably, to the custom of having the names of a community enrolled in a register, and, whenever one died, of erasing his name from the number."

358. It will be seen that C. here, as is often the case, quotes from memory.

359. "L'execution de son jugement;" the execution of His judgment. -- Fr.

360. See Lat., "Locutus autem fuerat Jehova;" but the Lord had spoken, etc. Prof. Bush says, "The right adjustment of the events of this chapter in the chronological order of the narrative, is a matter attended with some difficulty. From the rendering of our established version, it would seem that what was now said to Moses was posterior in point of time to the incidents recorded in the close of the preceding chapter; but from an attentive consideration and collation of the tenor of the whole, we are persuaded, with Calvin, and other critics of note, that the proper rendering of ver. 1 is in the pluperfect, The Lord had said,' and that the appropriate place for the interview and incidents here related is prior to the order and the promise contained in ver. 34 of chap. 32. In that verse God declares his purpose of sending his angel before the people, and we naturally inquire how it happens

that such an assurance was necessary? Was there any danger that an angel would not be sent? Had any intimation been given that his guidance and protecting presence would be withdrawn? To this the correct answer undoubtedly is, that all that is related in chap. 33 had occurred anterior to the promise made in chap. 32:34. God had threatened to send Moses and the people forward without the accompanying presence of the angel of the Shekinah, and it was only in consequence of the fervent intercession of Moses that He was induced to retract this dread determination. In the foregoing chapter, therefore, the historian merely, states in a summary way the fact of his earnest prayer, and the concession made to it; in the present, he goes back and relates minutely the train of circumstances which preceded and led to the declaration above mentioned. In doing this he virtually makes known to us one main ground of the urgency of his supplications. He was afraid that God would withdraw the tokens of his visible presence. As a punishment for the mad attempt of the people to supply themselves with a false symbol of his presence, he was apprehensive that God might be provoked to take from them the true, and hence his impassioned entreaty that He would not visit them with so sore a judgment."

361. So the LXX., Καὶ λαβὼν Μωυσῶς τὴν σκηνὴν αὐτοῦ the Syriac, Grotius, and many other commentators quoted in Poole. The greater number, however, even although disagreeing with C. in his notion that the tabernacle was already built, (see [54]vol. 2, p. 143, et seq.,) are satisfied with his

reasons why it should not be the private tent of Moses. "Wherefore, this was some peculiar tabernacle which Moses erected specially for the service of God, as it may appear by the name of it, (for) it hath the same name which the other great tabernacle was to be called by; there was the cloud, the visible sign of God's presence, and the people worshipped towards that place. Simlerus, Osiander, Tostatus," in Willet. So also Rosenmuller, "after Michaelis, and some of the Hebrews," in Brightwell; and Prof. Bush, who adopts C.'s opinion as to the clause, "he called it the Tabernacle of the Congregation." -- Vide infra.

362. לו, is properly either. for him, or, for it. -- W. Ainsworth's literal translation is, "And Moses took a tent, and pitched it for him."

363. מועד moed, or, mogned. A.V., "The tabernacle of the congregation." The noun is formed from יעד to call together, to appoint either a place, or time of meeting; and hence it means either an appointed place, or time of meeting. -- W.

364. See [55]vol. 2, p. 297, on Exodus 29:42, where C. gives his reason for translating the words, Tabernaculum conventionis.

365. "So called (says Ainsworth) in respect of his service, not of years, for he was now above fifty years old, as may be gathered by Joshua 24:29. But because ministry and service are usually by the younger sort, all servants are called young men. See Genesis 14:24." "Perhaps, (adds Adam Clarke,) נער naghar, here translated young man, means a single person, one unmarried." Others suppose that he was so called as being integer, upright,

and without guile; and De Lyra, as being young in respect to Moses.

366. See ante on Exodus 31:2, [56]p. 291.

367. "My presence shall go with thee." -- A.V.

368. "Et au but ou Moyse pretendoit;" and to the object at which Moses aimed. -- Fr.

369. "Le mot que, j'ay translate,. Afin que nous soyons glorifiez, signifie aussi estre separez;" the words which I have translated, To the end that we may be glorified, signifies also to be separated. -- Fr.

370. This interrogative sentence is entirely omitted in Fr.

371. "Proclaim the name of the Lord." -- A. V.

372. "Voyla, comme aujourd'huy beaucoup de gaudisseurs pour debatre de toutes choses;" behold, how now-a-days many jeerers, to dispute about everything. -- Fr. C. discusses the third question, as to the creation of the world, in his Inst., Book I., chap. 14, sec. 1. It is also very neatly met in Pet. Martyr. Loci. Com. C1. I., chap. 12, sec. 2. "Sunt qui quaerant, Cum potuerit Deus longe prius mundum producere, cur tam sero? Est petulans, et procax haec inquisitio, nec humanae curiositati, nisi illam retundendo, satisfieri potest: nam quoeunque puncto temporis ante ficti vel imaginati dedissem tibi factum mundum, tu adhuc conqueri posses id sero fuisse factum, si tuam cogitationem referres ad Dei aeternitatem. Igitur hic pie est agendum, non hac procaci, et temeraria, curiositate."

373. Addition in Fr., "Seulement pour son plaisir;" only for his pleasure.

374. "C'est trop grande presomption;" it is too great a presumption. -- Fr.

375. "Tertullian referreth these backer or latter parts to the latter times of the Messiah: My glory which thou desirest to see, shall be revealed in the latter times." -- Willet in loco. Owen's exposition of this passage is worthy of quotation: "The face of God, or the gracious majesty of his Being, his essential glory, is not to be seen of any in this life; we cannot see him as he is. But the glorious manifestation of himself we may behold and contemplate. This we may see as the back parts of God; that shadow of his excellencies which he casteth forth in the passing by us in his works and dispensations. This Moses shall see. And wherein did it consist? Why, in the revelation, and declaration of this name of God. Exodus 34:6, 7. To be known by this name, to be honored, feared, believed, as that declares him, is the great glory of God." -- Owen's Expos. of Psalm 130. (Edin., edit. 1851, vol. 6, p. 481.)

376. "Voyla comment Dieu dispense par bon moyen le cognoissance de sa Parole;" Behold how God dispenses in a good way the knowledge of His Word. -- Fr.

377. So the V. "Stetit Moyses eum eo, invocans nomen Domini."

378. A.V. "Long-suffering;" as also in Numbers 14:18, and Psalm 86:15. In Nehemiah 9:17, and elsewhere, "slow to anger." Heb., אפים 5 אר' long of nostrils, or anger.

379. See C.'s own translation. Calvin Soc. edit., [57]vol. 5, p. 346.

380. נקה לא ינקה A.V., "Will by no means clear;" S. M. and C., "Not making (the guilty) innocent;" or, in C.'s own comment, "He will not with

cleansing cleanse;" but C. presently acknowledges that it might be taken to mean, "He will not utterly cut off," inasmuch as the verb נקה is sometimes used for to blot out, to destroy, to exterminate; to which class of meanings more than one lexicographer has assigned its use in this text. -- W. Bush gives a very careful note on this clause, which he says is "of exceedingly difficult interpretation," and declares himself satisfied that the sense which C. condemns is the true one, viz., "who will not wholly, entirely, altogether clear,' i.e., who, although merciful and gracious in his dispositions, strongly inclined to forgive, and actually forgiving in countless cases and abundant measure, is yet not unmindful of the claims of justice. He will not always suffer even the pardoned sinner to escape with entire impunity. He will mingle so much of the penal in his dealings as to evince that his clemency is not to be presumed upon."

381. "Should ye be utterly unpunished?" "Art thou he, that shall altogether go unpunished?" -- A. V.

382. Poole on Jeremiah 49:12, after quoting C.'s translation, "impune feres?" adds, "Since, however, this phrase is explained very differently by others, both Exodus 34:7, and Jeremiah 25:29, as well as these words, may be thus rendered: Thou therefore thyself shalt be utterly cut off."

383. "The translation of V. is, "Nullusque apud to per se innocens est."

384. "Qu'ils n'ont point loisir de deliberer de ce qu'ils ont a faire, mais sont du premier coup abatus;" that they have no time to deliberate

as to what they should do, but are abashed at once. -- Fr.

385. "And take us for thine inheritance." -- A. V. "Inherit, or possess thou us." -- Heb.

386. Thus the LXX.; Καὶ εἶπε Κύριος πρὸς Μωυσῶν, ἰδοὺ ἐγὼ τίθημί σοι διαθήκην

387. "The thing." -- A.V.

388. For a fuller development of this argument, see Institutes, Book 4, chap. 12, sec. 20, 21; and Harm. of the Evangelists, [58]vol. 1, p. 208. Calvin Soc. edit.

389. "Till Moses had done speaking with them, he put," etc. -- A. V. Rosenmuller translates it with C. and the LXX., "and, when," etc. "We need not (says Willet) with Oleaster to transpose the words, he put a vail upon his face, and so finished to speak unto the people;' but either we may read with Junius,' While he had finished to speak unto the people, he put a vail:' or rather to read it in the praeter-pluperfect tense, with the Genevan version, So Moses made an end of communing with them, and he had put a covering upon his face.'"

390. So C. translates the words in his Comment. on 2 Corinthians 3:16, "and when he (i.e., Moses,) shall have turned to the Lord," and thus defends it: "This passage has hitherto been badly rendered, for both Greek and Latin writers have thought that the word Israel was to be understoon, whereas Paul is speaking of Moses. he had said that a vial is upon the hearts of the Jews when Moses is read. He immediately adds, As soon as he will have turned to the Lord, the vial will be taken away. Who does not that this is said of Moses, that is, of the Law? For as Christ is the end of it, (Romans 10:4,) to which it ought to be referred, it was

turned away in another direction, when the Jews shut out Christ from it." Calvin Society edition, [59]vol. 2, p. 183. Camerarius, in Poole, remarks on the difficulty of the passage, arising from the fact that the verb ἐπιστρέψ⁷Y may either be the third person singular subjunctive active, or the second person singular of the first future middle; but he concludes, that "it seems somewhat harsh to apply it to Moses."

A Repetition of the same History

Deuteronomy 9

Deuteronomy 9:7-21, 25-29

7. Remember, and forget not, how thou provokedst the Lord thy God to wrath in the wilderness: from the day that thou didst depart out of the land of Egypt, until ye came unto this place, ye have been rebellious against the Lord.

7. Memento, ne obliviscaris quod ad iram provocasti Jehovam Deum tuum in deserto, a die qua egressus es e terra AEgypti, donec ingressi estis ad hunc locum, rebelles fuistis Jehovae.

8. Also in Horeb ye provoked the Lord to wrath, so that the Lord was angry with you, to have destroyed you.

8. Nam in Horeb provocastis Jehovam: et excanduit Jehova in vos ad perdendum vos.

9. When I was gone up into the mount, to receive the tables of stone, even the tables of the covenant which the Lord made with you, then I abode in the mount forty days and forty nights; I neither did eat bread nor drink water:

9. Quum ascendissem in montem ut acciperem tabulas lapideas, tabulas faederis quod pepigerat Jehova vobiscum, tunc mansi in monte quadraginta noctes, ubi panem non comedi, et aquam non bibi.

10. And the Lord delivered unto me two tables of stone, written with the finger of God: and on them was written according to all the words which the Lord spake with you in the mount, out of the midst of the fire, in the day of the assembly.

10. Et dedit mihi Jehova duas tabulas lapideas scriptas digito Dei, et in ipsis erat juxta omnia verba qum loquutus fuerat Jehova in monte e medio ignis, in die conventus.

11. And it came to pass, at the end of forty days and forty nights, that the Lord gave me the two tables of stone, even the tables of the covenant.

11. Et factum est a fine quadraginta dierum et quadraginta noc tium, ut daret Jehova mihi duas tabulas lapideas, tabulas foederis.

12. And the Lord said unto me, Arise, get thee down quickly from hence; for thy people which thou hast brought forth out of Egypt have corrupted themselves; they are quickly turned aside out of the way which I commanded them; they have made them a molten image.

12. Dixit autem mihi Jehova, Surge, descende hinc celeriter: quia corrupit se populus tuus quem eduxisti ex AEgypto: recesserunt cito e via quam praeceperam illis: feterunt sibi conflatile.

13. Furthermore the Lord spake unto me, saying, I have seen this people, and, behold, it is a stiff-necked people.

13. Tunc dixit mihi Jehova, Vidi populum hunc, et ecce, populus est durae cervicis.

14. Let me alone, that I may destroy them, and blot out their name from under heaven: and I will make of thee a nation mightier and greater than they.

14. Sine me ut perdam eos, deleamque nomen eorum sub coelo, et faciam to in gentem potentiorem, et majorem illa.

15. So I turned, and came down from the mount, and the mount burned with fire; and the two tables of the covenant were in my two hands.

15. Tunc verti me, et descendi e monte (mons autem ipse ardebat igni) et duae tabulae foederis in manibus meis erant.

16. And I looked, and, behold, ye had sinned against the Lord your God, and had made you a molten calf: ye had turned aside quickly out of the way which the Lord had commanded you.

16. Et vidi, et ecce, peccaveratis in Jehovam Deum vestrum, foceratis vobis vitulum conflatilem, recesseratis cito de via quam paeceperat Jehova vobis.

17. And I took the two tables, and cast them out of my two hands, and brake them before your eyes.

17. Tunc apprehendi duas tabulas, et projeci eas e manibus meis, confregique in oculis vestris.

18. And I fell down before the Lord, as at the first, forty days and forty nights: I did neither eat bread nor drink water, because of all your sins, which ye sinned, in doing wickedly in the sight of the Lord, to provoke him to anger.

18. Et procidi coram Jehova sicut prius, quadraginta dies et quadraginta noctes: panem non comedi, et aquam non bibi, propter omne peccatum vestrum quod peccaveratis, impie agendo in oculis Jehovae ad ipsum provocandum.

19. (For I was afraid of the anger and hot displeasure wherewith the Lord was wroth against you to destroy you.) But the Lord hearkened unto me at that time also.

19. Timui enim propter excandescentiam et tram qua excanduerat Jehova contra vos ad perdendum vos: et exaudivit me Jehova etiam hac vice.

20. And the Lord was very angry with Aaron to have destroyed him: and I prayed for Aaron also the same time.

20. Contra Aharon quoque excanduit Jehova vehementer ad perdendum eum, et oravi etiam pro Aharon tempore illo.

21. And I took your sin, the calf which ye had made, and burnt it with fire, and stamped it, and ground it very small, even until it was as small as dust: and I cast the dust thereof into the brook that descended out of the mount.

21. Porro peccatum vestrum quod feceratis, nempe vitulum, accepi, et combussi ilium igni, et contrivi bene molendo, donec comminutus esset in pulverem: ae projeci pulverem ejus in torrentem qui descendebat e monte illo.

25. Thus I fell down before the Lord forty days and forty nights, as I fell down at the first; because the Lord had said he would destroy you.

25. Et procidi coram Jehova quadraginta diebus et quadraginta noctibus, quibus procidi: quia dixerat Jehova se perditurum vos.

26. I prayed therefore unto the Lord, and said, O Lord God, destroy not thy people, and thine inheritance, which thou hast redeemed through

thy greatness, which thou hast brought forth out of Egypt with a mighty hand.

26. Oravi igitur Jehovam, et dixi, Dominator Jehova, ne perdas populum tuum, et haereditatem tuam quam redemisti magnitudine tua, quem eduxisti ex AEgypto manu valida.

27. Remember thy servants, Abraham, Isaac, and Jacob; look not unto the stubbornness of this people, nor to their wickedness, nor to their sin;

27. Memento servorum tuorum, Abrahae, Isaac et Jacob, ne respicias ad duritiem populi hujus, et ad impietatem ejus et peccatum.

28. Lest the land whence thou broughtest us out say, Because the Lord was not able to bring them into the land which he promised them, and because he hated them, he hath brought them out to slay them in the wilderness.

28. Ne forte dicant in terra, unde eduxisti nos, Propterea quod non potuit Jehova introducere eos in terram quam dixerat illis, vel quia oderat filius, eduxit eos ut interficeret in deserto.

29. Yet they are thy people, and thine inheritance, which thou broughtest out by thy mighty power, and by thy stretched-out arm.

29. Ipsi autem sunt populus tuus, et haereditas tua, quam eduxisti fortitudine tua magna, et brachio tuo extento.

7. Remember, and forget not, how thou provokedst In order to reprove the ingratitude of the people, Moses here briefly refers to some of their offenses; but he principally insists on the history of their revolt, in which their extreme and most detestable impiety betrayed itself. He therefore narrates this crime in almost the identical words which he had previously used in Exodus. He begins by urging them often to reflect upon their sins, lest they should ever be forgotten; and this constant recollection of them not only tended to humiliate them, but also to teach them at length to lay aside their depraved nature, and to accustom themselves to become obedient to God. Afterwards he proceeds to the history itself, shewing that God had been provoked by their idolatry to destroy them. If a question be here put, how it was that God was prevailed upon by Moses to change His intention, our curiosity must be repressed, lest we should dispute more deeply than is fitting respecting the secret and incomprehensible decree of God. Sure it is that God did not act otherwise than He had determined; but Moses goes no deeper than the sentence that was revealed to him; just as we must assuredly conclude that destruction is prepared for us when we transgress; and that God's anger is appeased when we fly to His mercy in true faith, and with sincere affections. The rest has been already expounded.

17. And I took the two tables, and cast them out Moses here accuses himself of no transgression; he does not, therefore, give us to understand that he was urged to break the tables by the impetuosity of excessive anger; but rather he again repeats what they had deserved, and consequently that he discharged the office of a herald, [391] so as to denounce, not by word of mouth only, but by a solemn rite also, that God's Covenant was broken and made void by their perfidiousness. For which reason also he cast down and broke the tables before their eyes, in order that being alarmed by so awful a punishment, they might more earnestly betake themselves to the expiation of their sins.

18. And I fell down before the Lord The order of the narrative is confused; for this fact of which he speaks did not precede his second ascent into the mount, when he was commanded to prepare the second tables. If so, he would have fasted three times, which we gather from other passages not to have been the case; but we must not be surprised that the same thing should be often repeated, as we shall see at the beginning of chapter 10, as well as shortly afterwards. The mention of it here, however, is seasonable, because the Covenant was to be renewed, and therefore, as if nothing had been done, he again abstained from meat and drink for forty days. Yet we have elsewhere seen that there were other prayers which had intervened before He ascended the mount a second time; but He does not here distinctly record the details, nay, he mixes up the prayers, whereby he interceded with God, with the second fast, because this was the point most worthy of observation, that the first promulgation of the Law had failed of its effect, and the Covenant which they had violated was to be repeated, as it were, from its very commencement.

Although he says that "because of their sins" he had not eaten bread nor drunk water, he does not signify that this fast was a sign of grief and mourning, like as Joel invites the people to sackcloth and ashes, and urges them to weeping and fasting for the purpose of testifying their repentance. (Joel 2:12.) For abstinence, as I have already shewn, was no more difficult or grievous to Moses than to the angels. But he simply reminds them that so great a sin could not be expiated, unless he had again renounced the life of men and had been taken up to God. Meanwhile, it must be borne in mind that previously to this, he had already made entreaty for the people, and had also been accepted; inasmuch as it was a token that God was reconciled and appeased, when He called up Moses to receive the Law, and to bring it down to them a second time. To this refers what he adds in the next verse, "For I was afraid of the anger," etc., for he was still in anxiety as to the welfare of the people, since God did not cease to menace them. We see, therefore, that this fear and anxious earnestness in prayer are separated from the fast, as different things; and assuredly he had already propitiated God, when, by His command he hewed out the new tables whereon the Covenant was to be renewed. Still, I do not deny that he labored also in the mount in the cause of obtaining pardon, just as believers, by continuing the requests which have already been granted, confirm their faith more and more. I only warn my readers to observe the distinction of time which I have noticed.

20. And the Lord was very angry with Aaron It hence appears how vain are the pretexts whereby men endeavor to conceal their faults, until they are subdued by genuine fear of God to acknowledge their guilt. Although Aaron did not boast that he was altogether innocent, still he endeavored to blot out, or at any rate to extenuate the enormity of his crime by alleging that he was under compulsion. But Moses declares that God was very angry with him. Whence it follows that he was guilty of a very gross sin, which is also more certainly declared by the greatness of its punishment; for God would never have been thus moved even to destroy him, unless because he was worthy of this condemnation.

In the next verse, the word sin is not applied to the act; itself, [392] but is transferred by metonymy to the calf, as its apposition shews. Again, by saying that he had thoroughly broken the calf to pieces by grinding it till it was reduced to powder, he signifies once more how abominable this idol was, especially when he adds, that the powder was cast into the stream, lest any memorial of it should continue in existence.

25. **Thus I fell down before the Lord forty days** Again the narrative is blended together; for it is certain that this prayer was offered before he remained fasting in the mount during the second forty days. But inasmuch as then also, being still in anxiety, he continued the same prayers, it is not to be wondered at that he should include in the forty days' fast whatever had been done before. For there is no absurdity in supposing that after having obtained the safety of the people, for which he had petitioned, he should still be in trepidation. Moreover, that this fast was posterior to the prayer which he mentions at the same time, may be inferred from the beginning of the next chapter, where he records that the second tables were given to him, but says not a word of the fast. I have stated why he so often repeats his allusion to the forty days, viz., because it would not have been sufficient merely to intercede, unless this reconciliation had followed, which he obtained when he received the new covenant. The rest I have already expounded.

Deuteronomy 10

Deuteronomy 10:1-5, 10, 11

1. **At that time the Lord said unto me, Hew thee two tables of stone like unto the first, and come up unto me into the mount, and make thee an ark of wood.**

1. In tempore illo dixit mihi Jehova, Dola tibi duns tabulas lapideas similes prioribus, et ascende ad me in montem, et fac tibi arcata ligneam.

2. **And I will write on the tables the words that were in the first tables which thou brakest, and thou shalt put them in the ark.**

2. Et scribam in tabulis verba quae erant in tabulis prioribus, quas fregisti, et pones eas in arca.

3. **And I made an ark of shittim-wood, and hewed two tables of stone like unto the first, and went up into the mount, having the two tables in mine hand.**

3. Feci igitur arcata e lignis sittim, ac dolavi duas tabulas lapideas similes prioribus: ascendique in montem habens duas tabulas in manu mea.

4. **And he wrote on the tables, according to the first writing, the ten commandments, which the Lord spake unto you in the mount, out of the midst of the fire, in the day of the assembly: and the Lord gave them unto me.**

4. Tunc scripsit in tabulis juxta scripturam priorem decem verba quae loquutus fuerat Jehova vobiscum in monte, e medio ignis, in die conventus: et dedit illas mihi Jehova.

5. **And I turned myself, and came down from the mount, and put the tables in the ark which I had made; and there they be, as the Lord commanded me.**

5. Conversus autem descendi e monte: posuique tabulas in arca quam feceram: et fuerunt illic, quemadmodum praeceperat mihi Jehova.

10. **And I stayed in the mount, according to the first time, forty days and forty nights; and the Lord hearkened unto me at that time also, and the Lord would not destroy thee.**

10. Ego autem steti in monte secundum dies priores, quadraginta dies, et quadraginta noctes: et ex-audivit me Jehova etiam hac vice, nec voluit Jehova perdere te.

11. And the Lord said unto me, Arise, take thy journey before the people, that they may go in and possess the land which I sware unto their fathers to give unto them.

11. Itaque dixit mihi Jehova, Surge, vade, proficiscendo ante populum ut ingrediantur et possideant terram quam juravi patribus eorum me daturum illis.

1. At that time the Lord said unto me He had had intercourse with the people for some time, before he returned into the mount with the second tables; and therefore he now begins to relate more fully what he had already mentioned in the inverted order of time, i.e., that he stayed in the mount forty days to make entreaty for them. And this also the repetition in the 10th verse more clearly demonstrates, where he says, that he stayed in the mount "according [393] to the first days." But, although he there says that he was hearkened to when he interceded in the mount, still he includes the prayers which he had previously offered when he heard of the people's revolt, and after he had broken the tables and taken away God's tabernacle, in which he prayed apart to obtain pardon for their sin. What is also here said respecting the ark is not in its proper place; for it was a part of the tabernacle, as we have elsewhere seen. It is, therefore, exacting too much to require that the things which are related together, should be referred to the same instant of time.

Exodus 40

Exodus 40:1-35

1. And the Lord spoke unto Moses, saving,
1. Loquutus est Jehova ad Mosen, dicendo:
2. On the first day of the first month shalt thou set up the tabernacle of the tent of the congregation;
2. Die mensis primi, prima ejusdem, eriges tabernaculum, tabernaculum conventionis.
3. And thou shalt put therein the ark of the testimony, and cover the ark with the vail.
3. Et pones ibi arcam testimonii quam teges velo.
4. And thou shalt bring in the table, and set in order the things that are to be set in order upon it; and thou shalt bring in the candlestick, and light the lamps thereof.
4. Introducesque mensam, et ordinationem ejus: introduces insuper candelabrum, et accendes luernas ejus.
5. And thou shalt set the altar of gold for the incense before the ark of the testimony, and put the hanging of the door to the tabernacle.
5. Pones praeterea altare aureum ad suffimentum e regione arcae testimonii: et pones aulaeum ostii tabernaculi.
6. And thou shalt set the altar of the burnt-offering before the door of the tabernacle of the tent of the congregation.
6. Dein pones altare holocausti coram ostio tabernaculi conventionis:

7. And thou shalt set the laver between the tent of the congregation and the altar, and shalt put water therein.

7. Postea pones concham inter tabernaculum conventionis et altare, in qua pones aquam.

8. And thou shalt set up the court round about, and hang up the hanging at the court-gate.

8. Postremo pones atrium in circuitu, et aulueum portae atrii.

9. And thou shalt take the anointing oil, and anoint the tabernacle, and all that is therein, and shalt hallow it, and all the vessels thereof: and it shall be holy.

9. Tunc accipies oleum unctionis, et unges tabernaculum atque omnia vasa qum sunt in eo: sanctificabisque illud et omnia vasa ejus, et erit sanctum.

10. And thou shalt anoint the altar of the burnt-offering, and all his vessels, and sanctify the altar: and it shall be an altar most holy.

10. Unges et altare holocausti, atque onmia vasa ejus: sanctificabisque altare, et erit altare sacrosanctum.

11. And thou shalt anoint the laver and his foot, and sanctify it.

11. Unges etiam concham et basira ejus, sanctificabisque illam.

12. And thou shalt bring Aaron and his sons unto the door of the tabernacle of the congregation, and wash them with water.

12. Tunc appropinquare facies Aharon et filius ejus ad ostium tabernaculi conventionis, lavabisque cos aqua.

13. And thou shalt put upon Aaron the holy garments, and anoint him, and sanctify him; that he may minister unto me in the priest's office.

13. Et induere facies Aharon vestes sanctas, ungesque eum, et sanctificabis eum, ut sacerdotio fungatur mihi.

14. And thou shalt bring his sons, and clothe them with coats:

14. Filios quoque ejus appropinquare facies, et indues eos tunicis.

15. And thou shalt anoint them, as thou didst anoint their father, that they may minister unto me in the priest's office: for their anointing shall surely be an everlasting priesthood throughout their generations.

15. Ungesque filius, quemadmodum unxeris patrem eorum: et sacerdotio fungentur mihi, eritque unctio eorum ut sit els in sacerdotium perpetuum per generationes suas.

16. Thus did Moses: according to all that the Lord commanded him, so did he.

16. Fecit ergo Moses juxta omnia quae illi praeceperat Jehova, sic fecit.

17. And it came to pass in the first month, in the second year, on the first day of the month, that the tabernacle was reared up.

17. Et factum est mense primo, anno secundo, prima mensis, erectum filit tabernaculum.

18. And Moses reared up the tabernacle, and fastened his sockets, and set up the hoards thereof, and put in the bars thereof, and reared up his pillars.

18. Erexit igitur Moses tabernaculum, posuitque bases ejus, et tabulas ejus, et vectes ejus, atque erexit columnas ejus.

19. And he spread abroad the tent over the tabernacle, and put the covering of the tent above upon it; as the Lord commanded Moses.

19. Extendit praeterea tentorium super tabernaculum, et posuit operimentum tentorii super idud superne, quemadmodum praeceperat Jehova, Mosi.

20. And he took and put the testimony into the ark, and set the staves on the ark, and put the mercy-seat above upon the ark.

20. Tulitque et posuit testimonium in arca ipsa, posuit quoque vectes super arcata, et propitiatorium super arcata superne.

21. And he brought the ark into the tabernacle, and set up the vail of the covering, and covered the ark of the testimony; as the Lord commanded Moses.

21. Induxitque aream in tabernaculum, posuitque velum tentorii, et texit arcata testimonii, quemadmodum praeceperat Jehova ipsi Mosi.

22. And he put the table in the tent of the congregation, upon the side of the tabernacle northward, without the vail.

22. Posuit et mensam in tabernaculo conventionis ad latus tabernaculi ad aquilonem extra velum.

23. And he set the bread in order upon it before the Lord; as the Lord had commanded Moses.

23. Et ordinavit super eam ordinationem panum coram Jehova, quemadmodum praeceperat Jehova ipsi Mosi.

24. And he put the candlestick in the tent of the congregation, over against the table, on the side of the tabernacle southward.

24. Posuitque candelabrum in tabernaculo conventionis ex adverso in latere tabernaculi ad meridiem.

25. And he lighted the lamps before the Lord; as the Lord commanded Moses.

25. Et accendit lucernas coram Jehova, quemadmodum praeceperat Jehova ipsi Mosi.

26. And he put the golden altar in the tent of the congregation before the vail:

26. Posuit etiam altare aureum in tabernaculo conventionis coram velo:

27. And he burned sweet incense thereon; as the Lord commanded Moses.

27. Et incendit super illud suffimentum aromaticum, quemadmodum praeceperat Jehova ipsi Mosi.

28. And he set up the hanging at the door of the tabernacle.

28. Posuit praeterea aulaeum ostii tabernaculi.

29. And he put the altar of burnt-offering by the door of the tabernacle of the tent of the congregation, and offered upon it the burnt-offering, and the meat-offering; as the Lord commanded Moses.

29. Et altare holocausti posuit ad ostium tabernaculi, tabernaculi conventionis: et obtulit super illo holocaustum, et minham, quemadmodum praeceperat Jehova ipsi Mosi.

30. And he set the laver between the tent of the congregation and the altar, and put water there, to wash withal.

30. Et posuit concham inter tabernaculum conventionis et altare, in qua posuit aquam ad lavandum.

31. And Moses, and Aaron, and his sons, washed their hands and their feet thereat.

31. Et lavabant ex ea Moses et Aharon et filii ejus marius suas et pedes suos.

32. When they went into the tent of the congregation, and when they came near unto the altar, they washed; as the Lord commanded Moses.

32. Quando ingrediebantur tabernaculum conventionis, et quando accedebant ad altare, lavabant se, sicut praeceperat Jehova ipsi Mosi.

33. And he reared up the court round about the tabernacle and the altar, and set up the hanging of the court-gate: so Moses finished the work.

33. Postremo erexit atrium in circuitu tabernaculi et altaris, posuitque aulaeum portae atrii. Itaque, absolvit Moses opus ipsum.

34. Then a cloud covered the tent of the congregation, and the glory of the Lord filled the tabernacle.

34. Et operuit nubes tabernaculum conventionis, gloriaque Jehovae replevit tabernaculum.

35. And Moses was not able to enter into the tent of the congregation, because the cloud abode thereon, and the glory of the Lord filled the tabernacle.

35. Neque poterat Moses ingredi tabernaculum conventionis, quia habitabat super illud nubes, et gloria Jehovae replebat tabernaculum.

Numbers 9

Numbers 9:15, 16

15. And on the day that the tabernacle was reared up, the cloud covered the tabernacle, namely, the tent of the testimony; and at even there was upon the tabernacle as it were the appearance of fire, until the morning.

15. Quo die erectum fuit tabernaculum, operuit nubes tabernaculum supra rectum testimonii: vespere autem erat super tabernaculum tanquam species ignis usque mane.

16. So it was alway: the cloud covered it by day, and the appearance of fire by night.

16. Sic erat jugiter: nubes operiebat ilud, et species ignis noctu.

Exodus 40:2. On the first day of the first month I cannot at all approve of the opinion of those commentators who think that the tabernacle was only now set up. That it was already complete in all its parts before Moses went the second time into the Mount, we infer from the fact that the ark was then prepared in which the tables were deposited, as we shall see from the context. Besides, it has elsewhere [394] been shewn by sound arguments, as I think, that it was pitched without the camp in token of divorce, from the time that the people had made the calf. What, then, is the meaning of the setting-up which is now spoken of? I reply, that it is said to have been set up, when [395] it was brought back from its strange to its proper place. For then it was both anointed and honored by sacred oblations, whilst Aaron and his sons were consecrated to the performance of the priestly office. Since, therefore, it had not yet been duly placed in the middle of the camp, nay, rather had been removed from the people lest they should enjoy that pledge of God's presence, its solemn dcdication is justly celebrated after the renewal of the covenant. This passage also confirms what I have said elsewhere, [396] that this was the tabernacle which Moses pitched at a distance from the camp; for, by the addition of its title, he speaks as of something well known, "Thou shalt set up (He says) the tabernacle, viz., the tabernacle of convention." Now Moses himself had already stated that this name had been given it by the mouth of God. He repeats, however, the same injunctions, not that He distrusted the memory of His servant, but that it might be more fully apparent that He was Himself the sole Author of the whole work, and also that it nlight obtain more reverence, since He had so often deigned to give initructions as concerning things of very great importance.

9. And thou shalt take the anointing oil There was by no means any virtue or efficacy for sanctification in the oil, except in so far as it was a type of the Spirit, from whom as its only source all holiness emanates. Assuredly the oil, as being a corruptible fluid, neither penetrates into the soul, nor would by itself at all avail unto spiritual service. It appears, however, from many pnssages of Scripture, that it was a symbol of all the gifts of the Holy Spirit. This figure, therefore, clearly shews that nothing pleases God, that nothing is pure or holy in His sight, except what has been purged, and duly consecrated by the influence and grace of the Holy Spirit. Moreover, God would have all the vessels of the sanctuary set apart by this sacred anointing from common use, in order that the Israelites might distinguish between things sacred and profane, and thus that God's service might receive its due reverence, so that none should intrude the pollutions of the flesh into that place, the purity of which had been signalized by that sacred symbol. A question, however, here arises why he dignifies the altar of burnt-offering with a more exalted title; for, after having called the tabernacle itself with its vessels simply holy, He calls the altar "holy of holies," which I have rendered sacrosanctum. I doubt not but that it acquired this name from the sacrifices, which are also so called on account of the expiation made by them, [397] as we have seen elsewhere. The children of Israel, therefore, were instructed that God is truly reconciled by holocausts and burnt-offerings, since "the holiness of holinesses" resided on the altar itself.

12. And thou shalt bring Aaron and his sons I have already expounded all that might seem to be profitable with respect to the garments and the mode of anointing; only let; my readers remember that the priest, [398] who had been before appointed, is now at length inaugurated, in order that he may begin the discharge of his office. At the same time, let them also bear in mind that this oil was consecrated by God. Hence it appears how foolishly the Popish bishops, as it were, ape Moses, when, in imitation of him, they sprinkle their priests and altars and other rubbish with stinking oil, since it is abundantly clear that this ceremony of anointing, belonging as it did to the ancient shadows of the Law, ceased at the coming of Christ. What Augustine [399] reminds us of is also worthy of observation, that Moses, who is commissioned to anoint the others, was never consecrated himself by any visible symbol, in order that we may understand that outward signs are not to be estimated by the dignity of the minister, but only by the ordinance of God; and again, that invisible grace has profited some without visible sacraments, whilst visible sanctification may be imparted, but cannot profit, without invisible.

17. And it came to pass in the first month In all the arrangements, which are here described, it must be especially noted, that Moses obeyed God in such a manner as not to vary in the most trifling point from the form prescribed to

him. He therefore so frequently enforces the fact, that he did as God had commanded him; and not without reason, for there is nothing to which men are more prone than to mix up their inventions with God's commands, as if they would be wiser than He is. In order then that the people might know that there was nothing of human invention in all the legal service, Moses so carefully insists on this point, and so often testifes to his obedience. But if so great the Prophet dared to attempt nothing of himself in trifling matters, how great is the audacity and arrogance of those men who arbitrarily invent innumerable figments, whereby God may be worshipped! Let us, however, learn from this passage to embrace with reverence whatever has proceeded from God, whilst we reject whatever men advance of themselves.

34. Then a cloud covered the tent The holiness of the tabernacle was proved by this signal or pledge, for the people assuredly knew that it had not been set up in vain, but that the promise given before was actually fulfilled, and that it was chosen to be the dwelling-place of God, who would be the Leader and Keeper of His people. For it was not a natural thing that the cloud should settle over the sanctuary in which the Ark of the Covenant was deposited; and much less so that by day a cloud should be seen and a fire by night, especially when this did not occur once only, but when they succeeded each other in perpetual alternation. It is fitly said, that when the tabernacle was covered by the cloud, it was at, the same time filled with the glory of God; for this was a magnificent distinction, that an earthly edifice should be rendered illustrious by a more than heavenly ornament, as if God's majesty were visibly presented to them.

Whereas before Moses had been concealed and separated from the people by the cloud, its density is now said to have prevented even him from entering; thus, then, ought their reverence and admiration of the place to have been increased, when the greatness of its glory was a hinderance to their holy Prophet. It is probable that by his example not only the rest of the multitude, but all the Levites also, were admonished that they should not endeavor to penetrate further than they were allowed. For, after the possession of the priesthood was transmitted to his brother, he, as well as his descendants, was excluded from that sacred dignity.

Numbers 7

Numbers 7:1-89

1. And it came to pass on the day that Moses had fully set up the tabernacle, and had anointed it, and sanctified it, and all the instruments thereof, both the altar, and all the vessels thereof, and had anointed them, and sanctified them,

1. Et fuit quo die finivit Moses erigere tabernaculum, unxit illud et sanctificavit, omniaque utensilia ejus, altare quoque et omnia utensilia ejus, ex quo unxit ca et sanctificavit.

2. That the princes of Israel, heads of the house of their fathers, (who were the princes of the tribes, and were over them that were numbered,) offered.

2. Tunc obtulerunt principes Israelis, capita domuum patrum suorum, principes tribuum, hi erant praefecti numeratis.

3. And they brought their offering before the Lord, six covered waggons, and twelve oxen; a waggon for two of the princes, and for each one an ox: and they brought them before the tabernacle.

3. Et attulerunt oblationem suam coram Jehova, sex plaustra operta, et duodecim boves, plaustrum pro binis principibus, et bovem in singulos obtulerunt coram tabernaculo.

4. And the Lord spake unto Moses, saying,

4. Dixerat autem Jehova ad Mosen, dicendo:

5. Take it of them, that they may be to do the service of the tabernacle of the congregation; and thou shalt give them unto the Levites, to every man according to his service.

5. Accipe ab els, et servient in ministerio tabernaculi conventionis: et dabis ea Levitis, cuique secundun, rationem sui ministerii.

6. And Moses took the waggons and the oxen, and gave them unto the Levites.

6. Accepit itaque Moses plaustra et boves, et dedit Levitis:

7. Two waggons and four oxen he gave unto the sons of Gershon, according to their service:

7. Duo plaustra, et quatuor boves dedit filiis Gerson secundum rationem ministerii ipsorum.

8. And four waggons and eight oxen he gave unto the sons of Merari, according unto their service, under the hand of Ithamar the son of Aaron the priest.

8. Et quatuor plaustra et octo boves tradidit filiis Merari secundum rationem ministerii ipsorum sub manu Ithamar filii Aharon sacerdotis.

9. But unto the sons of Kohath he gave none; because the service of the sanctuary belonging un to them was, that they should bear upon their shoulders.

9. Filiis veto Cehath nihil dedit: quia ministerium sanctuarii quod illis injunctum erat, humero ferebant.

10. And the princes offered for dedicating of the altar, in the day that it was anointed, even the princes offered their offering before the altar.

10. Obtulerunt autem principes pro dedicatione altaris die quo unctum fuit: obtulerunt, inquam, principes oblationem suam coram altari.

11. And the Lord said unto Moses, They shall offer their offering, each prince on his day, for the dedicating of the altar.

11. Et dixit Jehova ad Mosen, Singuli principes singulis diebus offerent oblationem suam ad dedicationem altaris.

12. And he that offered his offering the first day was Nahshon the son of Amminadab, of the tribe of Judah.

12. Obtulit itaque primo die oblationem suam Nahason filius Amminadab de tribu Jehudah.

13. And his offering was one silver charger, the weight whereof was an hundred and thirty shekels, one silver bowl of seventy shekels, after the shekel of the sanctuary, both of them were full of fine flour mingled with oil, for a meat-offering:

13. Fuit autem oblatio ejus patina argentea, centum triginta siclorum pondus ejus: phiala una argentia, septuaginta siclorum, secundum siclum sanctuarii: ambae plenae similaconspersa oleo in minha:

14. One spoon of ten shekels of gold, full of incense:

14. Cochlear unum aureum decent siclorum, plenum suffitu:

15. One young bullock, one ram, one lamb of the first year, for a burnt-offering:

15. Juvencus unus, filius armenti, aries unus, agnus unus anniculus in holocaustum:

16. One kid of the goats for a sin-offering:

16. Hircus caprarum unus pro peccato:

17. And for a sacrifice of peace-offerings, two oxen, five rams, five he-goats, five lambs of the first year. This was the offering of Nahshon the son of Amminadab.

17. Pro sacrificio autem prosperitatum, boves duo, arietes quinque, hirci quinque, agni anniculi qumque. Haec fuit oblatio Nahason filii Amminadab.

18. On the second day Nethaneel the son of Zuar, prince of Issachar, did offer.

18. Die autem secundo obtulit Nethanel filius Suar princeps Issachar.

19. He offered for his offering one silver charger, the weight whereof was an hundred and thirty shekels, one silver bowl of seventy shekels, after the shekel of the sanctuary, both of them full of fine flour mingld with oil, for a meat-offering:

19. Obtulit oblationem suam, patinam argenteam unam, centum triginta siclorum pondus ejus: phialam unam argenteam, septuaginta siclorum, secundum siclum sanctuarii, arebas ipsas plenas simila conspersa oleo in minham:

20. One spoon of gold of ten shekels, full of incense:

20. Cochlear unum decem siclorum, aureum, plenum suffitu:

21. One young bullock, one ram, one lamb of the first year, for a burnt-offering:

21. Juvencum unum, fillum armenti, arietem unum, agnum anniculum in holocaustum:

22. One kid of the goats for a sin-offering:

22. Et hircum caprarum unum pro peccato:

23. And for a sacrifice of peace-offerings, two oxen, five rams, five he-goats, five lambs of the first year. This was the offering of Nethaneel the son of Zuar.

23. Et pro sacrificio prosperitatum, boves duos, arietes quinque, hircos quinque, agnos anniculos qninque. Haec est oblatio Nethanel filii Suar.

24. On the third day Eliab the son of Helon, prince of the children of Zebulun, did offer.

24. Die tertio princeps filiorum Zebulon, Eliab filius Helon.

25. His offering was one silver charger, the weight whereof was an hundred and thirty shekels, one silver bowl of seventy shekels, after the shekel of the sanctuary, both of them full of fine flour mingled with oil, for a meat-offering:

25. Oblatio autem ejus fuit patina argentea una, centum triginta siclorum pondus ejus: phiala una argentea, septuaginta siclorum, secundum siclum sanctuarii: ambae ipsae plenae simila conspersa oleo in minham:

26. One golden spoon of ten shekels,full of incense:

26. Cochlear unum decem siclorum, auremn, plenum suffitu:

27. One young bullock, one ram, one lamb of the first year, for a burnt-offering:

27. Juvencus unus, filius armenti, aries unus, agnus unus anniculus in holocaustum:

28. One kid of the goats for a sin-offering:

28. Hircus caprarum unus pro peccato:

29. And for a sacrifice of peace-offerings, two oxen, five rams, five he-goats, five lambs of the first year. This was the offering of Eliab the son of Helon.

29. Et pro sacrificio prosperitatum boves duo, arides quinque, hirci quinque, agni quinque anniculi. Haec fuit oblatio Eliab filii Helon.

30. On the fourth day Elizur the son of Shedeur, prince of the children of Reuben, did offer.

30. Die quarto princeps filiorum Ruben, Elisur filius Sedeur.

31. His offering was one silver charger, of the weight of an hundred and thirty shekels, one silver bowl of seventy shekels, after the shekel of the sanctuary, both of them full of fine flour mingled with oil, for a meat-offering:

31. Oblatio ejus fuit patina argentea una, centum triginta siclorum pontius ejus: phiala una argentea, septuaginta siclorum, secundum siclum sanctuarii, ambae ipsae plenae simila conspersa oleo in minham:

32. One golden spoon often shekels, full of incense:

32. Cochlear unum decem siclorum, aureum, plenum suffitu:

33. One young bullock, one ram, one lamb of the first year, for a burnt-offering:

33. Juvencus unus, illius armenti, aries unus, agnus unus anniculus in holocaustum:

34. One kid of the goats for a sin-offering:

34. Hircus caprarum unus pro peccato:

35. And for a sacrifice of peace-offerings, two oxen, five rams, five he-goats, five lambs of the first year. This was the offering of Elizur the son of Shedeur.

35. Et pro sacrificio prosperitatum boves duo, arietes quinque, hirci quinque, agni anniculi quinque. Haec fuit oblatio Elisur filii Sedeur.

36. On the fifth day Shelumiel the son of Zurishaddai, prince of the children of Simeon, did offer.

36. Die quinto princeps filiorum Simeon, Selumiel, filius Surisaddai.

37. His offering was one silver charger, the weight whereof was an hundred and thirty shekels, one silver

37. Oblatio ejus fuit patina argentia una, centum triginta siclorum pondus ejus: phiala una argentea,

38. One golden spoon of ten shekels, full of incense:

38. Cochlear unum decem siclorum, aureum plenum suffitu:

39. One young bullock, one ram, one lamb of the first year, for a burnt-offering:

39. Juvencus unus filius armenti, aries unus, agnus unus anniculus in holocaustum:

40. One kid of the goats for a sin-offering:

40. Hircus caprarum unus pro peccato:

41. And for a sacrifice of peace-offerings, two oxen, five rams, five he-goats, five lambs of the first year. This was the offering of Shelumiel the son of Zurishaddai.

41. Et pro sacrificio prosperitatum boves duo, arietes quinque, hirci quinque, agni anniculi quinque. Haec fuit oblatio Selumiel filii Surisaddai.

42. On the sixth day Eliasaph the son of Deuel, prince of the children of Gad, offered.

42. Die sexto princeps filiorum Gad, Eliasaph filius Deuel.

43. His offering was one silver charger, of the weight of an hundred and thirty shekels, a silver bowl of seventy shekels, after the shekel of the sanctuary, both of them full of fine flour mingled with oil, for a meat-offering:

43. Oblatio ejus fuit patina argentea una, centum triginta siclorum pondus ejus, phiala una argentea, septuaginta siclorum, secundum siclum sanctuarii, ambae ipsae plenae simila conspersa oleo in minham:

44. One golden spoon of ten slhekels, full of incense:

44. Cochlear unum decem siclorum, aureum, plenum suffitu:

45. One young bullock, one ram, one lamb of the first year, for a burnt-offering:

45. Juvencus unus, filius armenti, aries nuns anniculus in holocaustum:

46. One kid of the goats for a sin-offering:

46. Hircus caprarum unus pro peccato:

47. And for a sacrifice of peace-offerings, two oxen, five rams, five he-goats, five lambs of the first year. This was the offering of Eliasaph the son of Deuel.

47. Et pro sacrificio prosperitatum, boves duo, ariet es quinque, hirci quinque, agni anniculi quinque. Haec fuit oblatio Eliasaph filii Deuel.

48. On the seventh day Elishama the son of Ammihud, prince of the children of Ephraim, offered.

48. Die septimo, princeps filiorum Ephraim, Elisarea filius Ammihud.

49. His offering was one silver charger, the weight whereof was an hundred and thirty shekels, one silver bowl of seventy shekels, after the shekel of the sanctuary, both of them full of fine flour mingled with oil, for a meat-offering:

49. Oblatio ejus fuit patina argentea una, centum triginta siclorum pondus ejus: phiala una argentea, septuaginta siclorum, secundum siclum sanctuarii: ambae ipsae plenae simila conspersa oleo in minham:

50. One golden spoonoften shekels, full of incense:

50. Cochlear unum decem siclorum, aureum, plenum suffitu:

51. One young bullock, one ram, one lamb of the first year, for a burnt-offering:

51. Juvencus unus, filius armenti, aries unus, agnus unus anniculus in holocaustum:

52. One kid of the goats for a sin-offering:

52. Hircus caprarum unus pro peccato.

53. And for a sacrifice of peace-offerings, two oxen, five rams, five he-goats, five lambs of the first year. This was the offering of Elisharod the son of Ammihud.

53. Et pro sacrificio prosperitatum, boves duo, arietes quinque, hirci quinque, agni anniculi quinque. Haec fuit oblatio Elisama filii Ammihud.

54. On the eighth day offered Gamaliel the son of Pedahzur, prince of the children of Manasseh.

54. Die octavo princeps filiorum Manasse, Gamliel filius Padahsur.

55. His offering was one silver charger, of the weight of an hundred and thirty shekels, one silver bowl of seventy shekels, after the shekel of the sanctuary, both of them full of fine flour mingled with oil, for a meat-offering:

55. Oblatio ejus fuit patina argentea una, centum triginta siclorum pontius ejus, phiala una argentea, septuaginta siclorum, secundum siclum sanctuarii: ambae ipsae plenae simila conspersa oleo in minham:

56. One golden spoon often shekels, full of incense:

56. Cochlear unum decem siclorum, aureum, plenum suffitu:

57. One young bullock, one ram, one lamb of the first year, for a burnt-offering:

57. Juvencus unus, filius armenti, aries unus, agnus unus anniculus in holocaustum:

58. One kid of the goats for a sin-offering:

58. Hircus caprarum unus pro peccato:

59. And for a sacrifice of peace-offerings, two oxen, five rams, five he-goats, five lambs of the first year. This was the offering of Gamaliel the son of Pedahzur.

59. Et pro sacrificio prosperitatum, boves duo, arietes quinque, hirci quinque, agni anniculi quinque. Haec fuit oblatio Gamliel filii Pedahsur.

60. On the ninth day Abidan the son of Gideoni, prince of the children of Benjamin, offered.

60. Die nono princeps filiorum Benjamin, Abidan filius Gidoni.

61. His offering was one silver charger, the weight whereof was an hundred and thirty shekels, one silver bowl of seventy shekels, after the shekel of the sanctuary, both of them full of fine flour mingled with oil, for a meat-offering:

61. Oblatio ejus fuit patina argentea una, centum triginta siclorum pondus: phiala una argentea, septuaginta siclorum, secundum siclum sanctuarii: amble ipsae plenae simila conspersa oleo in minham:

62. One golden spoon of ten shekels, full of incense:

62. Cochlear unum decem siclorum, plenum suffitu:

63. One young bullock, one ram, one lamb of the first year, for a burnt-offering:

63. Juvencus unus, filius armenti, aries unus anniculus in holocaustum:

64. One kid of the goats for a sin-offering:

64. Hircus caprarum unus pro peccato:

65. And for a sacrifice of peace-offerings, two oxen, five rams, five he-goats, five lambs of the first year. This was the offering of Abidan the son of Gideoni.

65. Et pro sacrificio prosperitatum, boves duo, arietes quinque, hirci quinque, agni anniculiquinque. Haec fuit oblatio Abidan filii Gidoni.

66. On the tenth day Ahiezer the son of Ammishaddai, prince of the children of Dan, offered.

66. Die decimo princeps filiorum Dan, Ahiezer filius Ammisaddai.

67. His offering was one silver charger, the weight whereof was an hundred and thirty shekels, one silver bowl of seventy shekels, after the shekel of the sanctuary, both of them full of fine flour mingled with oil, for meat-offering:

67. Oblatio ejus fuit patina argentea una, centum triginta siclorum pontius ejus: phiala una argentea, septuaginta siclorum, secundum siclum sanctuarii: ambae ipsae plenae simila conspersa oleo in minham:

68. One golden spoon of ten shekels, full of incense:

68. Cochlear unum decem siclorum, argenteum, plenum suffitu:

69. One young bullock, one ram, one lamb of the first year, for a burnt-offering:

69. Juvencus unus, filius armenti, aries unus, agnus unus anniculus in holocaustum:

70. One kid of the goats for a sin-offering:

70. Hircus caprarum unus pro peccato:

71. And for a sacrifice of peace-offerings, two oxen, five rams, five he-goats, five lambs of the first year. This was the offering of Ahiezer the son of Ammishaddai.

71. Et pro sacrificio prosperitatum boves duo, arietes quinque, hirci quinque, agni anniculi quinque. Haec fuit oblatio Ahiezer filii Ammisaddai.

72. On the eleventh day Pagiel the son of Ocran, prince of the children of Asher, offered.

72. Die undecimo princeps filiorum Aser, Pagiel filius Ochran.

73. His offering was one silver charger, the weight whereof was an hundred and thirty shekels, one silver bowl of seventy shekels, after the shekel of the sanctuary, both of them full of fine flour mingled with oil, for a meat-offering:

73. Oblatio ejus fuit patina argentea una, centum triginta siclorum pondus ejus, phiala una argentea, septnaginta siclorum, secundum siclum sanctuarii, ambae ipsae plenae simila conspersa oleo in minham:

74. One golden spoon of ten shekels, full of incense:

74. Cochlear unum decem siclorum, auremn, plenum suffitu:

75. One young bullock, one ram, one lamb of the first year, for a burnt-offering:

75. Juvencus unus, filius armenti, aries unus, anniculus in holocaustum:

76. One kid of the goats for a sin-offering:

76. Hircus caprarum unus pro peccato:

77. And for a sacrifice of peace-offerings, two oxen, five rains, five he-goats, five lambs of the first year. This was the offering of Pagiel the son of Ocram

77. Et pro sacrificio prosperitatum, boves duo, arietes quinque, hirci quinque, agni anniculi quinque. Haec fuit oblatio Pagiel filii Ochran.

78. On the twelfth day Ahira the son of Enan, prince of the children of Naphtali, offered.

78. Die duodecimo, princeps filiorum Nephthali, Ahira filius Enan:

79. His offering was one silver charger, the weight whereof was an hundred and thirty shekels, one silver bowl of seventy shekels, after the shekel of the sanctuary, both of them full of fine flour mingled with oil, for a meat-offering:

79. Oblatio ejus fuit patina argentea una, centum triginta siclorum pondus ejus, phiala una argentea, septuaginta siclorum, secundum siclum sanctuarii: ambae ipsae plenaee simila conspersa oleo in minham:

80. One golden spoon of ten shekels, full of incense:

80. Cochlear unum decem siclorum, argenteum, plenum suffitu:

81. One young bullock, one ram, one lamb of the first year, for a burnt-offering:

81. Juvencus unus, filius armenti, aries unus, agnus unus anniculus in holocaustum:

82. One kid of the goats for a sin-offering:

82. Hircus caprarum unus pro peccato:

83. And for a sacrifice of peace-offerings, two oxen, five rams, five he-goats, five lambs of the first year. This was the offering of Ahira the son of Enan.

83. Et pro sacrificio prosperitatum, boves duo, arietes quinque, hirci quinque, agni anniculi quinque, Haec fuit oblatio Allira filii Enan.

84. This was the dedication of the altar (in the day when it was anointed) by the princes of Israel: twelve chargers of silver, twelve silver bowls, twelve spoons of gold:

84. Haec fuit dedicatio altaris, die quo unctum fuit a principibus Israel: patrum argentine duodecim, phiale argenteae duodecim, cochlearia aurea duodecim.

85. Each charger of silver weighing an hundred and thirty shekels, each bowl seventy: all the silver vessels weighed two thousand and four hundred shekels, after the shekel of the sanctuary.

85. Centum triginta siclorum erat patina una argentea, et septuaginta phiala una: omne argentum vasorum, duo millia, et quadringenti sicli, secundum siclure sanctuarii.

86. The golden spoons were twelve, full of incense, weighing ten shekels apiece, after the shekel of the sanctuary: all the gold of the spoons was an hundred and twenty shekels.

86. Cochlearia aurea duodecim plena suffitu: decem siclorum erant cochlearia secundum pondus sanctuarii: omne aurum cochlearium, centurm viginti siclorum.

87. All the oxen for the burnt-offering were twelve bullocks, the rains twelve, the lambs of the first year twelve, with their meat-offering; and the kids of the goats for sin-offering twelve.

87. Omnes boves in holocaustum, duodecim juvenci, arietes duodecim, agni anniculi duodecim, cum minha; ipsorum: et hirci caprarum duodecim pro peccato.

88. And all the oxen, for the sacrifice of the peace-offerings, were twenty and four bullocks, the rams sixty, the he-goats sixty, the lambs of the first year sixty. This was the dedication of the altar, after that it was anointed.

88. Orenos autem boves sacrificii prosperitatum viginti quatuor, juvenci arietes sexaginta, hirci sexaginta, agni anniculi sexaginta. Haec fuit dedicatio altaris postquam unctum fuit.

89. And when Moses was gone into the tabernacle of the congregation to speak with him, then he heard the voice of one speaking unto him from off the mercy-seat that was upon the ark of testimony, from between the two cherubims: and he spake unto him.

89. Quum autem ingrediebatur Moses tabernaculum conventionis, ut loqueretur cum eo, audiebat vocem loquentis ad se e propitiatorio, quod erat super arcam testimonii inter duos Cherubim, et loquebatur ei.

1. And it came to pass on the day that Moses This was the second contribution of the people, after the completion of the Tabernacle; for although mention is only made of the princes, it is probable that each of them presented what the whole tribe had subscribed, since there was no private person at that time wealthy enough to give so much gold and silver of his own. Let it be understood, then, that they brought in the name, and at the desire of all, what they had received from the members of their respective tribes. Before, however, I proceed any further, it must be remarked that the sacrifices were not killed, before the sanctuary was anointed. Moses himself is said to have anointed it, as he had his brother Aaron; for the exposition of some, that what properly applies to Aaron is attributed to his brother, does not appear to be sound. We have said elsewhere that God thus freely used the visible signs, in order that He might by no means bind the grace of the Spirit to particular persons. When Moses, therefore, who was not anointed himself, anointed both the sanctuary and the priest, it was manifestly shewn that the efficacy of consecration did not emanate from himself, inasmuch as He could not give of his own that which he did not possess. Consequently the entire virtue and utility of signs depend on the command of God. We have elsewhere seen why it was necessary to consecrate the tabernacle, the altar, and all the vessels by a sacred anointing. Here let us only observe, that the connection of the two words anointing and sanctifying is not superfluous: that we may understand that the symbol of the oil was not vain and inefficacious, but that true spiritual sanctity was annexed to it; for God institutes nothing in vain, but, by filling what He typifies with the secret influence of the Spirit, He effectually proves Himself to be true. It is said that the princes were set "over them that were numbered," i.e., after the people were numbered, and separated into their several divisions, these were chosen as the chiefs of the tribes. The exposition which some give, that they assisted when the people were numbered, in my opinion, is far-fetched.

3. And they brought their offering before the Lord, six covered waggons These waggons were dedicated for the conveyance of the tabernacle: for its pillars and many other parts of it could not be carried on men's shoulders; and therefore they are said to have been covered, lest the things which were deposited in them should be exposed to the rain. For it is by no means suitable to suppose that they were litters; [400] and, in fact, a pair of oxen is assigned to every waggon. It is pretty clear, then, that the materials of the tabernacle were placed in them when they were travelling from one place to another.

This oblation is stated to have been made "before the Lord," and then "before the tabernacle," but the meaning is precisely the same; for God had, as it were, put on that face in which he might be beheld by believers. What follows, "But the Lord had spoken to Moses," etc., I thus interpret, That God had required this tribute of the people: I have thought it well, therefore, to render it in the pluperfect tense, whereas others translate it, "The Lord said unto Moses," as if Moses had not been ordered to receive it, before it was actually presented by the princes and the people. Indeed, it is probable that the number of the waggons was not accidentally determined, but by a just calculation of the things which they were to carry.

10. And the princes offered for dedicating of the altar Here is another kind of offering, viz., a silver dish and bowl from every tribe, besides a golden spoon, [401] which properly means a censer. Their use was as follows, -- that the sacred cakes should be received in the dishes, the wine of libation in the bowls,

and the frankincense in the censers. But God would have each tribe contribute their respective vessels, in order that the common interest of the whole people in the sacrifices might be the better testified. Although the word shekel [402] is derived front its being weighed, still it is almost everywhere used for a coined piece of money, which, as we have seen at Exodus 30, was of the value of twenty oboli. Josephus estimates it at an Attic tetradrachm. But Ezekiel, when he is inveighing against their fraud in having diminished its weight, settles its value at twenty oboli, and adds that it is the third part of a pound or mina. (Ezekiel 45:12.) But it must be borne in remembrance, as we have also seen elsewhere, that the shekel of the sanctuary was double the ordinary one, for it was worth four drachmas, whereas the common shekel was only worth two drachmas, or a stater. Now, if we calculate, we shall find that the value of each dish amounted to nearly a hundred French livres; and that of each bowl to forty-four. If we take the shekel in the same sense with reference to the censers, or spoons, they must have been very small, only being about seven livres in value: whereas a gold vessel of this size would scarcely hold three grains of frankincense. Wherefore, I doubt whether they had not also gold shekels; but I leave it undecided as a point on which we have no knowledge.

Lastly, follow the animals offered as victims, a young bullock, a ram, and a lamb for a burnt-offering; a kid for a sin-offering; two oxen, five rams, five he-goats, and five lambs for a sacrifice of thanksgiving. It would, however, have been difficult for each prince to present so many out of his own folds or stalls; whence it is probable that they were aided by a general contribution. God chose that each tribe should have its peculiar day appointed for it in order, not only that there might be no confusion or disturbance, but; also that by this lengthened exercise the hearts even of the careless might be stirred up to zealous devotion.

12. And he that offered his offering the first day The oracular declaration which God made by the mouth of Jacob is well known. "The scepter shall not depart from Judah," etc. (Genesis 49:10.) Non, although the time had not yet arrived when the truth of this prophecy should be manifested by its fulfillment, still it was brought to pass by the admirable counsel of God that certain marks of supremacy should exist in the tribe of Judah; and, by general consent, if not dominion, at least the chief dignity, was always lodged in it. The assignment of the first day to Nahshon was, therefore, a presage of that future kingdom which was at length set up in the person of David. If any should allege the absurdity that the tribe of Reuben, who was the first-born, should be kept back till the fourth day, I reply that the tribes of Zebulun and Issachar were ranked under the banner of Judah; since it will appear in chapter 10. [403] that the twelve tribes were divided into four divisions of three. Thus it was more honorable for the tribe of Reuben to have the fourth day, so as to have the two tribes over which it presided attached to it. But the fathers of the two tribes, which God placed under the banner of Judah, were the two youngest sons of Leah, who followed next after Judah, her fourth son. We see, therefore, that the kingdom was thus obscurely shadowed forth, from which salvation was to be hoped for by the whole people: in order that they might be the more attentive to the promise given them; although this indication of it had but little effect on their sluggish minds.

89. And when Moses was gone into the tabernacle There seems at first sight to be a kind of contradiction between this passage and the other, in which

we saw that a thick cloud stood in the door of the tabernacle, so that Moses could not enter it. It might, indeed, be answered that this only occurred once; but to me it appears more probable that, Moses sought the replies of God at the mercy-seat, until Aaron began to exercise the priesthood, and then abandoned his dignity, which was only temporary, as far as regarded the entering of the sanctuary. For we know that by the established Law of God the priesthood was distinct from the civil government; and therefore that he could not, except by special privilege, be at the same time the leader and the priest. [404] If this exposition be accepted, he does not here record in its proper place that answers were given to him by God from the mercy-seat; since it is by no means unusual that what has preceded in order of time should be annexed at the end of a narrative. His intention, indeed, was to declare to posterity that God had not promised in vain that the Israelites should experience the presence of His favor; because He had chosen His dwelling-place in the sanctuary, to sit between the cherubim. By this testimony, therefore, of God's grace, the external anointing was ratified and confirmed, inasmuch as God appeared to Moses upon the Ark of the Covenant.

A fuller Explication of the same thing - Leviticus 8

Leviticus 8:4-36

4. And Moses did as the Lord commanded him; and the assembly was gathered together unto the door of the tabernacle of the congregation.

4. Et fecit Moses quemadmodum praecperat ei Jehova. Et congregatus est coetus ad ostium tabernaculi conventionis.

5. And Moses said unto the congregation, This is the thing which the Lord commanded to be done.

5. Tunc dixit Moses ad congregaionem, Hoc est verbum quod praecepit Jehova facere.

6. And Moses brought Aaron and his sons, and washed them with water.

6. Et accedere fecit Moses Aharon et filios ejus, quos lavit aqua.

7. And he put upon him the coat, and girded him with the girdle, and clothed him with the robe, and put the ephod upon him, and he girded him with the curious girdle of the ephod, and bound it unto him therewith.

7. Postea induit eum tunica, et cinxit baltheo, et pallio induit eum, et superimposuit ephod, et cinxit eum cingulo ephod: cinxit inquam illo.

8. And he put the breastplate upon him: also he put in the breastplate the Urim and the Thummim.

8. Et superimposuit ei pectorale, et reposuit in pectorali Urim et Thummim.

9. And he put the mitre upon his head; also upon the mitre, even upon his fore-front, did he put the golden plate, the holy crown; as the Lord commanded Moses.

9. Deinde cidarim imposuit capiti ejus, ponens super cidarim ante faciem ejus laminam auream, coronam sanetam, sicut praceperat Jehova Mosi.

10. And Moses took the anointing oil, and anointed the tabernacle, and all that was therein, and sanctified them.

10. Accepit quoque Moses oleum unctionis, et unxit tabernaculum, et quaecunque erant in eo: et consecravit illa.

11. And he sprinkled thereof upon the altar seven times, and anointed the altar, and all his vessels, both the laver and his foot, to sanctify them.

11. Et aspersit ex eo super altare septem vicibus, unxitque altare atque omnis vasa ejus, et concham et basim ejus, ut consecraret ea.

12. And he poured of the anoint oil upon Aaron's head, and anointed him, to sanctify him.

12. Fudit etiam ex oleo unctionis super caput Aharon, unxitque eum ut consecraret eum.

13. And Moses brought Aaron's sons, and put coats upon them, and girded them with girdles, and put bonnets upon them; as the Lord commanded Moses.

13. Fecit praeterea Moses accedere filios Aharon, induitque filius tunicis, et cinxit filius baltheo, atque alligavit eis mitras, quemadmodum praeceperat Jehova ipsi Mosi.

14. And he brought the bullock for the sin-offering: and Aaron and his sons laid their hands upon the head of the bullock for the sin-offering.

14. Adduxit quoque juvencum in hostium pro peccato, imposuitque Aharon et filii ejus manus suas super caput juvenci hostiae pro peccato.

15. And he slew it; and Moses took the blood, and put it upon the horns of the altar round about with his finger, and purified the altar, and poured the blood at the bottom of the altar, and sanctified it, to make reconciliation upon it.

15. Et mactavit, tulitque Moses sanguinem, posuitque super cornua altaris per circuitum digito suo, et expiavit altare: reliquum vero sanguinem fudit ad basim altaris, et sanctificavit illud ad expiandum illud.

16. And he took all the fat that was upon the inwards, and the caul above the liver, and the two kidneys, and their fat, and Moses burned it upon the altar.

16. Tulit praeterea totum adipem qui erat super intestina, et fibram jecoris et duos renes, adipemque eorum, adolevitque ea Moses super altare.

17. But the bullock and his hide, his flesh and his dung, he burnt with fire without the camp; as the Lord commanded Moses.

17. Juvencum vero et pellem ejus, et carnero ejus, et fimum ejus combussit igni extra castra, quemadmodum praeceperat Jehova ipsi Mosi.

18. And he brought the ram for the burnt-offering: and Aaron and his sons laid their hands upon the head of the ram.

18. Post haec adduxit arietem holocausti, et admoverunt Aharon et filii ejus marius suas super caput arietis.

19. And he killed it; and Moses sprinkled the blood upon the altar round about.

19. Et mactavit, sparsitque Moses sanguinem super altare per circuitum.

20. And he cut the ram into pieces; and Moses burnt the head, and the pieces, and the fat.

20. Arietem quoque concidit in frusta sua, adolevitque Moses caput, et frusta et adipem.

21. And he washed the inwards and the legs in water; and Moses burnt the whole ram upon the altar: it was a burnt sacrifice for a sweet savor,

and an offering made by fire unto the Lord; as the Lord commanded Moses.

21. Intestina vero et crura lavit aqua, et adolevit Moses totum arietem super altare: holocaustum est in odorem quietis: oblatio est ignita Jehova, quemadmodum praeceperat Jehova Mosi.

22. And he brought the other ram, the ram of consecration: and Aaron and his sons laid their hands upon the head of the ram.

22. Accedere fecit et arietem secundum, arietem consecrationum: posueruntque Ahaxon et filii ejus marius super caput arietis.

23. And he slew it; and Moses took of the blood of it, and put it upon the tip of Aaron's right ear, and upon the thumb of his right hand, and upon the great toe of his right foot.

23. Et mactavit, tulitque Moses de sanguine ejus, et posuit super tenerum auris Aharon dextrae, et super pollicem manus ejus dextrae et super pollicem petits ejus dextri.

24. And he brought Aaron's sons, and Moses put of the blood upon the tip of their right ear, and upon the thumbs of their right hands, and upon the great toes of their right feet; and Moses sprinkled the blood upon the altar round about.

24. Adduxit et filius Aharon, posuitque Moses de sanguine super tenerum auris eorum dextrae, et super pollicem marius eorum dextrae, et super pollicem pedis eorum dextri: sparsitque Moses sanguinem super altare per circuitum.

25. And he took the fat, and the rump, and all the fat that was upon the inwards, and the caul above the liver, and the two kidneys, and their fat, and the right shoulder:

25. Tulit deinde adipem, et caudam: totumque adipem qui erat super intestina, et fibram jecoris, duosque renes, et adipem eorum, et armum dextrum.

26. And out of the basket of unleavened bread that was before the Lord he took one unleavened cake, and a cake of oiled bread, and one wafer, and put them on the fat, and upon the right shoulder:

26. De canistro quoque infermentatorum quae erant coram Jehova, tulit tortam infermentatam unam, et tortam panis oleati unam, et laganum unum, posuitque cum adipe et cum armo dextro.

27. And he put all upon Aaron's hands, and upon his sons' hands, and waved them. for a wave-offering before the Lord.

27. Et posuit omnia haec in manibus Aharon, et in manibus filiorum ejus, et ea agitate fecit agitatione coram Jehova.

28. And Moses took them from off their hands, and burnt them on the altar upon the burnt-offering: they were consecrations for a sweet savor; it is an offering made by fire unto the Lord.

28. Dein accepit Moses ilia ex manibus eorum, adolevitque super altare in holocaustum, consecrationes enim sunt in odorem quietis, oblatio ignita est Jehovae.

29. And Moses took the breast, and waved it for a wave-offering before the Lord: for of the ram of consecration it was Moses' part; as the Lord commanded Moses.

29. Tulitque Moses pectus, et agitavit illud agitatione coram Jehova: et ex ariete consecrationum ipsi Most fuit in partera, quemadmodum praeceperat Jehova ipsi Most.

30. And Moses took of the anointing oil, and of the blood which was upon the altar, and sprinkled it upon Aaron, and upon his garments, and upon his sons, and upon his sons' garments with him; and sanctified Aaron, and his garments, and his sons, and his sons' garments with him.

30. Tulit etiam Moses ex oleo unctionis, et de sanguine qui erat super altare, aspersitque super Aharon, super vestes ejus, et super filios ejus, et super vestes filiorum ejus cum eo: consecravitque Aharonem, et vestes ejus, et filios ejus, et vestes filiorum ejus cum eo.

31. And Moses said unto Aaron and to his sons, Boil the flesh at the door of the tabernacle of the congregation; and there eat it with the bread that is in the basket of consecrations, as I commanded, saying, Aaron and his sons shall eat it.

31. Et dixit Moses ad Aharon et ad filios ejus, Coquite carnes ad ostium tabernaculi conventionis, ibi deniqne comedite eam, et panem qui est in canistro consecrationum, quemadmodum praecepi, dicendo, Aharon et filii ejus comedent eam.

32. And that which remaineth of the flesh and of the bread shall ye burn with fire.

32. Quod vero superfuerit de carne et pane, igni comburetis.

33. And ye shall not go out of the door of the tabernacle of the congregation in seven days, until the days of your consecration be at an end: for seven days shall he consecrate you.

33. Et ex ostio tabernaculi conventionis non egrediemini septem diebus, usque ad diem qua completi fuerint dies consecrationum vestrarum: septem enim diebus consecrabit manum vestram.

34. As he hath done this day, so the Lord hath commanded to do, to make an atonement for you.

34. quemadmodum fecit in die hac, praecepit Jehova facere ad expiandum vos.

35. Therefore shall ye abide at the door of the tabernacle of the congregation day and night seven days, and keep the charge of the Lord, that ye die not: for so I am commanded.

35. Et ad ostium tabernaculi conventionis manebitis die et nocte, septem diebus, observabitisque observationem eoram Jehova, et non moriemini: sic enim jussus sum.

36. So Aaron and his sons did all things which the Lord commanded by the hand of Moses.

36. Fecit itaque Aharon et filii eius omnia verba quae praeceperat Jehova per manum Mosis.

4. **And Moses did as the Lord commanded him** Although these things relate to the priesthood, the authority and nature of which I expounded under the Second Commandment, yet, inasmuch as they are historical, it is not without reason that I have thought fit to defer them till this place: for, if I had referred to them in connection with the Commandment, unpractised readers would not have easily taken notice of their time. This distinction, however, will be of great assistance to them, that after the doctrine which was properly contained in the Decalogue has been set forth, they will now see how faithfully Moses fulfilled whatever he was commanded, and will be able to compare his obedience with the injunction, as they have done in the whole of the making

and dedication of the tabernacle. Besides, there is no question but that the narrative must be thus connected; for it may be readily inferred from many passages, that the priests were anointed on the same day that the tabernacle was consecrated. I will now hastily run through the words. Moses says that he brought near Aaron and his sons, i.e., to set them before God and the people; and then that he "washed them with water," to make it manifest that they did not bring from their homes the purity which befitted the sanctity of their office, and, inasmuch as they were men, that they could not be clean before God, unless their impurity was washed off. A description of their apparel afterwards follows, which I pass over, lest I should weary my readers by twice repeating the same thing.

10. And Moses took the anointing oil I have stated why God commanded that the priest himself, as well as all the vessels, should be consecrated with oil, viz., because, without the influence of the Spirit, all the sacrifices would be unsavory. And it is by the operation of the same Spirit that Christ was made the peace-maker between God and men; because this dignity would not otherwise belong to flesh and human nature. Aaron was therefore anointed, together with his sons, before he was admitted to the priestly office; for it is afterwards added, that "the bullock for sin" [405] was brought, upon which Aaron laid his hands. Now, although even then he began to discharge his office, yet Moses still occupied the first place, and performed, as it were, the final act. Hence it was that he sprinkled the horns of the altar with the blood; poured the residue at its base for expiation; and burned the sacrifice upon the altar. Now, the imposition of hands in the sacrifices was not only a symbol of presentation, but also a testimony of guilt transferred to the victim. Since, however, this last statement may be obscure on account of its brevity, I will explain it a little more clearly. If any private person offered a victim, the imposition of hands signified that he cast the guilt of his sin upon the victim. Hence the name of piaculum; [406] because it sustained the curse of God, and was substituted in the sinner's stead, who disburdens himself upon it of whatever exposed him to the judgment of God. But, inasmuch as common hands were unworthy to consecrate a victim to God, the sacerdotal office interposed. This is the reason why Aaron and his sons put their hands on each of the sacrifices, in order that this kind of atonement (piaculi) might be the beginning of their consecration, which was completed in the second ram, with the blood of which Moses stained their right ears, the thumbs of their right hands, and the great toes of their right feet. A multitude of questions here arises: Why only one side of the priests was consecrated, as if their left side remained polluted? Why consecration was not also imparted to their eyes, and especially to their mouth, which was to be the organ of the Holy Spirit? But this warning must be always borne in mind, that we should be soberly wise in those points, the certain knowledge of which cannot be elicited from Scripture; for our curiosity is not only frivolous, but also perverse and injurious, when we desire to know more than God has revealed. The conjecture, however, is probable, that the whole body was consecrated in the right side. We have already seen elsewhere, [407] that by the hands and feet the whole life and actions of men are designated. In which view the cleanness of the heart and the purity of the hands comprehend all that is internal and external in man, as the root and the fruit. As to the feet, the metaphor of walking is notorious; and the feet are said to run to evil, and to be swift to shed blood, when the wicked and the despisers of God betake

themselves to evil deeds. Besides, since this consecration was not to the office of teaching, but to that of intercession, the ear rather than the tongue is stained with blood; because the chief virtue, which obtains grace in the sacrifices, is obedience. To this the passage in Psalm 40:6, refers, "Sacrifice and offering thou didst not desire; mine ears hast thou bored:" [408] to which the words of Jeremiah correspond,

> *"Did I command anything respecting sacrifices, and not rather that your fathers should obey my voice?"* [409] (Jeremiah 7:22, 23.)

And hence Moses commenced the consecration at the ear, in order to devote the priest to God unto obedience. Paul shews how this was fulfilled in Christ, where he celebrates His obedience in the sacrifice of His death, in order to reconcile His Father to us. (Romans 5:19.) I have spoken elsewhere of the kind of wave-offering which they called tnupha. [410]

31. And Moses said unto Aaron and his sons, Boil the flesh This is the universal rule, as we have seen elsewhere. [411] One thing only is special, that God kept them in the tabernacle seven days, that they might learn to subordinate all their domestic cares and worldly business to their sacred duties. It has been elsewhere said, also, [412] that perfection is denoted by the number seven, which this passage confirms, for by the seven days they were reminded that they were no longer their own masters for the rest of their life.

Leviticus 9

Leviticus 9:1-24

1. And it came to pass on the eighth day, that Moses called Aaron and his sons, and the elders of Israel;

1. Factum est die octavo, ut vocaret Moses Aharon, et filius ejus, et seniores Israel.

2. And he said unto Aaron, Take thee a young calf for a sin-offering, and a ram for a burnt-offering, without blemish, and offer them before the Lord.

2. Dixitque ad Aharon, Tolle tibi vitulum filium bovis in sacrificium pro peccato, et arietem in holocaustum, integros, et offer coram Jehova.

3. And unto the children of Israel thou shalt speak, saying, Take ye a kid of the goats for a sin-offering; and a calf and a lamb, both of the first year, without blemish, for a burnt-offering;

3. Ad filius vero Israel loqueris, dicendo, Tollite hircum caprarum in sacrificium pro peccato, et vitulum, et agnum, anniculos immaculatos in holocaustum.

4. Also a bullock and a ram for peace-offerings, to sacrifice before the Lord; and a meat-offering mingled with oil: for to-day the Lord will appear unto you.

4. Bovem quoque et arietem pro sacrificio prosperitatum, ut sacrificetis coram Jehova, ct minham conspersam oleo: quia hodie Jehova apparebit vobis.

5. And they brought that which Moses commanded before the tabernacle of the congregation; and all the congregation drew near, and stood before the Lord.

5. Tulerunt ergo qum praeceperat Moses coram tabernaculo conventionis, et accessit totus coetus, et steterunt coram Jehova.

6. And Moses said, This is the thing which the Lord commanded that ye should do: and the glory of the Lord shall appear unto you.

6. Tunc dixit Moses, Hoc est verbum quod praecepit Jehova, facite, et apparebit vobis gloria Jehovae.

7. And Moses said unto Aaron, Go unto the altar, and offer thy sin-offering, and thy burnt-offering, and make an atonement for thyself, and the people: and offer the offering of the people, and make an atonement for them; as the Lord commanded.

7. Ad Aharon vero dixit Moses, Accede ad altare, et fac oblationem pro peccato tuo, et holocaustum tuum, et expiationem fac pro te et pro populo: fac etiam oblationem populi, ire expiationem pro eis, quemadmodum praecepit Jehova.

8. Aaron therefore went unto the altar, and slew the calf of the sin-offering which was for himself.

8. Accessit itaque Aharon ad altare, et mactavit vitulum suum, oblationem pro peccato.

9. And the sons of Aaron brought the blood unto him; and he dipped his finger in the blood, and put it upon the horns of the altar, and poured out the blood at the bottom of the altar:

9. Et obtulerunt filii Aharon ei sanguinere, qui tinxit digitum suum in sanguine, et posuit super cornua altaris, residuum veto sanguinem fudit ad basira altaris.

10. But the fat, and the kidneys, and the caul above the liver of the sin-offering, he burnt upon the altar; as the Lord commanded Moses.

10. Adipem autem et renes, et fibram jecoris hostiae pro peccato, adolevit super altare, quemadmodum praeceperat Jehova Mosi.

11. And the flesh and the hide he burnt with fire without the camp.

11. Camera vero et pellem igni combussit extra castra.

12. And he slew the burnt-offering; and Aaron's sons presented unto him the blood, which he sprinkled round about upon the altar.

12. Mactavit et hostiam pro holocausto, et obtulernnt filii Aharon ei sanguinem, quem sparsit super altare per circuitum:

13. And they presented the burnt-offering unto him, with the pieces thereof, and the head; and he burnt them upon the altar.

13. Holocaustum quoque ei obtulerunt in frustis suis, et caput: et adolevit super altare.

14. And he did wash the inwards and the legs, and burnt them upon the burnt-offering on the altar.

14. Deinde layit intestina et erura, ei adolevit cum holocausto super altare.

15. And he brought the people's offering, and took the goat, which was the sin-offering for the people, and slew it, and offered it for sin, as the first.

15. Obtulit et oblationem populi, tulitque hircum oblationis pro peccato qui erat populi: mactavitque eum, et pro peccato obtulit ipsum sicut primum.

16. And he brought the burnt-offering, and offered it according to the manner.

16. Obtulit quoque holocaustum, et apparavit illud secundum praescripture.

17. And he brought the meat-offering, and took an handful thereof, and burnt it upon the altar, beside the burnt-sacrifice of the morning.

17. Obtulit et minham, implevitque manum suam ex ipsa, et adolevit super altare, praeter holocaustum matutinum.

18. He slew also the bullock and the ram for a sacrifice of peace-offerings which was for the people: and Aaron's sons presented unto him the blood, which he sprinkled upon the altar round about,

18. Mactavit insuper bovera et arietem in sacrificium pacificorum quod erat populi: et obtulerunt filii Aharon sanguinem, quem sparsit super altare per circuitum.

19. And the fat of the bullock and of the ram, the rump, and that which covereth the inwards, and the kidneys, and the caul above the liver:

19. Et adipes bovis et arietis, caudam et adipem qui operit intestina et renes, et fibram jecoris.

20. And they put the fat upon the breasts, and he burnt the fat upon the altar:

20. Posueruntque adipes super pectuscula, et adolevit adipes super altare.

21. And the breasts and the right shoulder Aaron waved for a wave-offering before the Lord; as Moses commanded.

21. Pectuscula vero et armum dextrum agitavit Aharon agitatione coram Jehova, quemadmodum praeceperat Jehova Mosi.

22. And Aaron lifted up his hand toward the people, and blessed them; and came down from offering of the sin-offering, and the burnt-offering, and peace-offerings.

22. Posthaec elevavit Aharon ma-num suam ad populum, benedixitque eis, et descendit a faciendo oblationem pro peccato, et holocaustum, et sacrificium prosperitatum.

23. And Moses and Aaron went into the tabernacle of the congregation, and came out, and blessed the people: and the glory of the Lord appeared unto all the people.

23. Et venit Moses et Aharon ad tabernaculum conventionis, et egressi sunt, et benedixerunt populo: et apparuit gloria Jehovae toti populo.

24. And there came a fire out from before the Lord, and consumed upon the altar the burnt-offering and the fat: which when all the people saw, they shouted, and fell on their faces.

24. Egressusque est ignis a facie Jehovae, et consumpsit super altare holocaustum et adipes: quod videns universus populus, laudaverunt, et ceciderunt super facies suas.

1. And it came to pass on the eighth day We have here related how Aaron and his sons, after the time of their consecration was fulfilled, began to execute their office. It was necessary that He should be his brother's disciple, in order to follow the pattern laid down by God. And we must bear in mind that Moses, who was not appointed priest by a solemn rite, sanctified the others, in order that the authority and the efficacy of the outward sign should rest in God alone. This, therefore, is contained in the earlier portion of the chapter, how, after Aaron had been initiated in the priest's office for seven days, He commenced the work entrusted to him by God's command: the second part shews how the sacrifices were approved by a divine miracle, in ratification of the priesthood which God had instituted. But, first of all, He enumerates the ordinary kinds of

sacrifice, viz., for sin, the burnt-offering; and for thanksgiving, the sacrifice with the meat-offering (minha) and the sprinkling: that in every respect Aaron might be accounted the lawful priest of God.

6. And Moses said, This is the thing which the Lord commanded He seems, indeed, to address himself to the whole people, to whom also the promise belonged; but in the word "do ye," [413] He specially speaks to the sons of Aaron; and he promises what, at the end of the chapter, he will state to have been fulfilled, that the glory of God should be manifested in approbation of the priesthood, in order that they may set about their duties more cheerfully. For this was no common aid to their faith and assurance, that their office should be thus, as it were, sealed by God.

7. And Moses said unto Aaron, Go unto the altar Here is repeated what was stated elsewhere, that the priest, as being himself a sinner, must first make entreaty for himself, before he propitiates God towards others. Hence the Apostle justly infers that the legal priesthood was weak and merely typical. (Hebrews 5:1.) For none can be a true peace-maker, except he, who, in reliance on his perfect innocence, presents himself before God to obtain pardon for others, and, being pure from every blemish, requires no expiation for himself. All else to the end of the chapter I pass over, because Moses only records how Aaron sacrificed according to God's command and the legal ritual.

22. And Aaron lifted up his hand toward the people This was a kind of application of the sacrifice, in order that the people might know that God was reconciled to them through the priest as their mediator and surety. The form of benediction [414] has been already expoundled; at present let this one point suffice, that, when by the lifting up of their hands the priests testified of God's paternal favor to the people, their commission was ratified and efficacious. Of this the sacred history presents to us a memorable instance, where it records, that

"the priests and Levites blessed the people, and their voice was heard, and their prayer came up to his holy dwelling-place, even unto heaven." (2 Chronicles 30:27.)

The fulfilment of this type was at length manifested in Christ, who is not only the source and cause of blessing, but publishes it by the Gospel with effectual results; for He came to "preach peace to them which were afar off, and to them that were nigh," (Ephesians 2:17;) and although He does not appear or speak in a visible form, yet we know what He says, viz., that

"whatsoever His disciples shall bind on earth shall be bound in heaven; and whatsoever they shall loose on earth shall be loosed in heaven." (Matthew 18:18.)

23. And Moses and Aaron went into the tabernacle This is a repetition of the same statement, except that what had been said of Aaron only is now also ascribed to Moses, i.e., that he blessed the people, but for a different reason, for although he was God's prophet, yet Aaron, in right of his office, was the only mediator. What follows, "the glory of the Lord appeared," may be read separately, viz., that the majesty of God was manifested in some conspicuous sign; or else it is connected with the concluding verse, where it is said, that

"there came a fire out from before the Lord, etc." If we prefer the latter, the account of the consuming of the sacrifice was added expositively, as if it were said that God appeared when He sent forth the fire to consume the sacrifice. By this auspice, or rather miracle, God manifested that He was the Author of the legal priesthood, so that it should be held in reverence for ever. The same thing sometimes occurred afterwards, when in troubled circumstances, it had need of extraordinary confirmation: thus fire consumed the sacrifice of Manoah, (Judges 13:20;) or, when God's service and pure religion required to be vindicated in opposition to superstitious counterfeits; thus the sacrifice of Elijah was utterly consumed and reduced to ashes without the application of fire. (1 Kings 18:38.) Or, lastly, when God would shew that He delighted in Mount Sion, which He had chosen for His resting-place and home: for which reason, the first sacrifice of Solomon was consumed by fire from heaven. (2 Chronicles 7:1.)

Lest posterity should doubt of this matter, as if it were not thoroughly certain, Moses says that the whole people was stirred up by the sight to praise God, "and fell on their faces."

Numbers 8

Numbers 8:20-22

20. And Moses, and Aaron, and all the congregation of the children of Israel, did to the Levites according unto all that the Lord commanded Moses concerning the Levites, so did the children of Israel unto them.

20. Fecit itaque Moses et Aharon, et omnis congregatio filiorum Israel, de Levitis: secundum crania quae praeceperat Jehova Mosi de Levitis, sic feterunt illis filii Israel

21. And the Levites were purified, and they washed their clothes; and Aaron offered them as an offering before the Lord; and Aaron made an atonement for them to cleanse them.

21. Et purificaverunt sese Levitae, laveruntque vestimenta sua et obtulit Aharon filius oblationem coram Jehova, et expiavit eos Aharon, ut purificaret eos.

22. And after that went the Levites in to do their service in the tabernacle of the congregation before Aaron, and before his sons: as the Lord had commanded Moses concerning the Levites, so did they unto them.

22. His peractis aggressi sunt Levitae fungi ministerio suo in tabernaculo conventionis coram Abaton, et coram filiis ejus: quemadmodum praeceperat Jehova Mosi de Levitis, sic fecerunt illis.

20. And Moses, and Aaron, and all the congregation The Levites also are now inaugurated for the performance of their duties, but in their proper order, because their condition was inferior. Here it must be noted that the sons of Moses and their descendants were placed in this lower rank, and excluded from all expectation of the priesthood. Hence the ingratitude of the whole people, and especially of the tribe of Levi, was all the more base, when they presumptuously sought the honor from which Moses had shut out his children for ever. It was then no ordinary act of obedience in him to execute what God

had appointed respecting the Levites. Aaron is here mentioned, because he consecrated the Levites in right of his priesthood. As regards the people, their consent is merely commended, because they agreed to what was the pleasure of God. But this virtue in them only increased their ignominy afterwards, when they sought to overthrow that divine decree of which they had approved.

21. And the Levites were purified, and they washed their clothes We have already spoken of the washing, for since it was required of all private individuals, much less would it be allowable for the Levites to handle the sacred things, unless they were first purified. But what follows as to their presentation by the hands of Aaron, was a shadowing forth by symbol of the truth, which at length shone out at the coming of Christ; for it had been of old predicted by the Prophets, that, in the renovation of the Church, those who had hitherto been but of the multitude should become Levites. Therefore, by this figure, God would declare that none even of His elect servants would be approved of and accepted by Him, unless sanctified by the one Priest. [415] And thence an atonement is joined with their offering, in order that the Levites might be pure.

22. And after that went the Levites in to do their service In these words Moses signifies that, in the type, nothing was omitted relative to the ancient priesthood which pertains to the legitimate service of God, the main point in which is obedience, and thence the purity which flows from it. The Levites are said to have done their service before Aaron, because they humbly submitted themselves to the yoke, and allowed themselves to be controlled by the will of the priest, since God had so enjoined. But the progress of the history will presently shew how prone man's nature is to rebellion. Hence it arises that the end does not always correspond with the beginning, but that sad and unhappy conclusions sometimes follow successful commencements.

Leviticus 10

Leviticus 10:1-7, 12-20

1. And Nadab and Abihu, the sons of Aaron, took either of them his censer, and put fire therein, and put incense thereon, and offered strange fire before the Lord, which he commanded them not.

1. Acceperunt autem filii Aharon:, Nadab et Abihu quisque acerram sham, et posuerunt in ipsis ignem, et supposuerunt suffimentum, obtuleruntque eoram Jebova ignem alienum secus quam praeceperat eis.

2. And there went out fire from the Lord, and devoured them; and they died before the Lord.

2. Tunc egressus est ignis a facie Jehova, et mortui sunt coram Jehova.

3. Then Moses said unto Aaron, This is it that the Lord spake, saying, I will be sanctified in them that come nigh me, and before all the people I will be glorified. And Aaron held his peace.

3. Et dixit Moses ad Aharon, Hoc est quod dixit Jehova, dicendo, In propinquis meis sanctificabor, et in conspectu totius populi glorificabor, et siluit Aharon.

4. And Moses called Mishael and Elzaphan, the sons of Uzziel, the uncle of Aaron, and said unto them, Come near, carry your brethren from before the sanctuary out of the camp.

4. Et vocavit Moses, Misael et Elsapham filios Uziel patrut Aharon, et dixit illis, Accedite, exportate fratres vestros a conspectu sanctuarii extra castra.

5. So they went near, and carried them in their coats out of the camp; as Moses had said.

5. Accesserunt ergo, et exportaverunt eos cum suis tunicis extra castra, quemadmodum praeceperat Moses.

6. And Moses said unto Aaron, and unto Eleazar and unto Ithamar, his sons, Uncover not your heads, neither rend your clothes, lest ye die, and lest wrath come upon all the people: but let your brethren, the whole house of Israel, bewail the burning which the Lord hath kindled.

6. Dixit etiam Moses ad Aharon, et Eleazar, et Ithamar, filios ejus, Capita vestra ne nudetis, et vestes vestras ne scindatis, ut non moriamini, ac me in totam congregationem irascatur: fratres autem vestri, tota domus Israel, flebunt incendium qued incendit Jehova.

7. And ye shall not go out from the door of the tabernacle of the congregation, lest ye die: for the anointing oil of the Lord is upon you. And they did according to the word of Moses.

7. Neque ab ostio tabernaculi conventionis egrediemini: ne moriamini: quia oleum unctionis Jehovae est super vos. Et fecerunt secundum verbum Mosis.

12. And Moses spake unto Aaron, and unto Eleazar and unto Ithamar, his sons that were left, Take the meat-offering that remaineth of the offerings of the Lord made by fire, and eat it without leaven beside the altar: for it is most holy.

12. Loquutus est autem Moses ad Aharon, et Eleazar et Ithamar filios ejus, qui reliqui erant, Tollite minha quae remansit ex oblationibus ignitis Jehovae et comedite illam cum azymis juxta altare: qnia sanctitas sanctitatum est.

13. And ye shall eat it in the holy place, because it is thy due, and thy sons' due, of the sacrifices of the Lord made by fire: for so I am commanded.

13. Comedetis, inquam, illam in loco sancto: quia in statutum tibi et in statutum iiliis tuis est de oblationibus ignitis Jehovae: quia sic jussus sum.

14. And the wave-breast and heave-shoulder shall ye eat in a clean place; thou, and thy sons, and thy daughters with thee: for they be thy due, and thy sons' due, which are given out of the sacrifices of peace-offerings of the children of Israel.

14. Et pectusculum agitationis, et armum elevationis comedetis in loco mundo, tu et filii tui, et filiae tuae tecum: quia in statutum tibi et in statutum filiis tuis data sunt de sacrificiis prosperitatum filiorum Israel.

15. The heave-shoulder and the wave-breast shall they bring, with the offerings made by fire of the fat, to wave it for a wave-offering before the Lord; and it shall be thine, and thy sons with thee, by a statute for ever; as the Lord hath commanded.

15. Armurn elevationis, et pectusculum agitationis cure oblationibus ignitis adipum afferent, ut agites agitatione coram Jehova: et hoc erit tibi et filiis tuis tecum in statutum perpetuum, quemadmodum princepit Jehova.

16. And Moses diligently sought the goat of the sin-offering, and, behold, it was burnt: and he was angry with Eleazar and Ithamar, the sons of Aaron which were left alive, saying,

16. Et hircum oblatum pro peccato requirendo requisivit Moses, et ecce, combustus erat: tum iratus est contra Eleazar et Ithamar filius Aharon relictos, dicendo:

17. Wherefore have ye not eaten the sin-offering in the holy place, seeing it is most holy, and God hath given it you to bear the iniquity of the congregation, to make atonement for them before the Lord?

17. Cur non comedistis oblationem pro peccato in loco sanctitatis? est enim sanctitas sanctitatum, quum illam dederit vobis ad portandum iniquitatem congregationis, et ad expiandum cos eoram Jehova.

18. Behold, the blood of it was not brought in within the holy place: ye should indeed have eaten in the holy place, as I commanded.

18. Ecce, nequaquam illatus est sanguis ejus in sanctitatem intrinsecus: comedendo comedere debueraris illam in sanctuario, quemadmodum praecepi.

19. And Aaron said unto Moses, Behold, this day have they offered their sin-offering and their burnt-offering before the Lord; and such things have befallen me: and if I had eaten the sin-offering to-day, should it have been accepted in the sight of the Lord?

19. Loquutus est autem Aharon ad Mosen, Ecce, hodie obtulerunt oblationem suam pro peccato, et holocaustum suum coram Jehova: et evenerunt mihi talia, et, si comedissem oblationem pro peccato bodie, nunquid placuisset in oculis Jehovae?

20. And when Moses heard that, he was content.

20. Postquam id audivit Moses: placuit ei.

1. And Nadab and Abihu, the sons of Aaron A memorable circumstance is here recorded, from whence it appears how greatly God abominates all the sins whereby the purity of religion is corrupted. Apparently it was a light transgression to use strange fire for burning incense; and again their thoughtlessness would seem excusable, for certainly Nadab and Abihu did not wantonly or intentionally desire to pollute the sacred things, but, as is often the case in matters of novelty, when they were setting about them too eagerly, their precipitancy led them into error. The severity of the punishment, therefore, would not please those arrogant people, who do not hesitate superciliously to criticise God's judgments; but if we reflect how holy a thing God's worship is, the enormity of the punishment will by no means offend us. Besides, it was necessary that their religion should be sanctioned at its very commencement; for if God had suffered the sons of Aaron to transgress with impunity, they would have afterwards carelessly neglected the whole Law. This, therefore, was the reason of such great severity, that the priests should anxiously watch against all profanation. Their crime is specified, viz., that they offered incense in a different way from that which God had prescribed, and consequently, although they may have erred from ignorance, still they were convicted by God's commandment of having negligently set about what was worthy of greater attention. The "strange fire" is distinguished from the sacred fire which was always burning upon the altar: not miraculously, as some pretend, but by the constant watchfulness of the priests. Now, God had forbidden any other fire to be used in the ordinances, in order to exclude all extraneous rites, and to shew His detestation of whatever might be derived from elsewhere. Let us learn, therefore, so to attend to God's command as not to corrupt His worship by any strange inventions. But if He so severely avenged this error, how horrible a

punishment awaits the Papists, who are not ashamed obstinately to defend so many gross corruptions!

3. Then Moses said unto Aaron, This is it that the Lord spake Moses restrains his brother from giving way to excessive grief; for this was a very bitter stroke after their recent joy to see himself at once deprived of two sons on the same day, and at the same moment, he might, too, have been disposed to murmur against God for the cause of their death. Lest, therefore, He should give way to such want of self-control, Moses reminds him that he must submit to the just judgment of God. We shall, however, seek in vain for what is here referred to, [416] "I will be glorified in them that come nigh me." He had often threatened the priests witlt death if they departed in the least degree from the prescribed rule: He had often set before them the sacredness of their office, lest they should defile themselves by any sacrilegious act; in a word, He had chosen them to be His ministers in holy things, on the condition that they should know themselves to be subject to greater guilt and punishment than the rest of the people. By this consolation, then, Aaron's grief is quieted, that God had not dealt cruelly with his sons, but had shewn forth in them a just and profitable example, in order that their successors might be more attentive in their duties; for thus should the sentence be paraphrased: In order that I may be glorified before the whole people, I must be sanctified by those of the highest degree and consequence; or, When I shall have been sanctified by the priests themselves, whose dignity is the highest, my glory will shine forth before the whole people. And, in point of fact, although God may punish whole bodies of obscure persons, such lessons have but little effect; but the punishment of men of more noble and illustrious condition draws almost all eyes to the judgments of God. For God is said to be sanctified in us in many ways, whether He shews Himself to be a pitiful or a severe Judge. This declaration, then, is an exhortation to those whom he has dignified with peculiar honor, to walk in fear and trembling; for, since "judgment begins at the house of God," the greater are the gifts and the higher the pre-eminence is with which any one is blessed, the greater is his obligation to God, and his ingratitude worthy of severer punishment.

3. And Aaron held his peace Much is this silence of Aaron to be applauded, whereby he confessed that his sons were slain by the just judgment of God; for Moses indicates that he yielded to his admonition, and was thus restrained from complaining against. God. Thus Paul teaches us that Scripture is given to teach us patience. (Romans 15:4.) Wherefore, whenever our passions are too much excited, let us learn that this is the best remedy for quieting and repressing them, to submit ourselves to God, and to humble ourselves beneath his mighty hand. David invites us to this by his own example when he says,

"I was dumb, I opened not my mouth; because thou didst it." (Psalm 39:9.)

4. And Moses called Mishael and Elzaphan Lest Eleazar and Ithamar should carry [417] forth the corpses, Moses commanded these others to anticipate them. It may also have been the case that all were stupified by terror. He forbids the father and brothers to mourn their death, not so much in accordance with the law, whereby all except the high priest were permitted to mourn for their own brother, as to prevent this memorable lesson from being obscured by their grief, since thus was the sanctity of their religion magnificently asserted.

Nevertheless, God allowed the dead men to be bewailed by the people, lest the recollection of their punishment should too soon be lost.

When he forbids (Aaron [418] and his sons) to go out from the door of the tabernacle, he does not mean so to fix them to that place as to banish them from their own private tents, but he withholds them from all pollution which might have compelled them to desert or interrupt their duty.

12. And Moses spake unto Aaron, and unto Eleazar Lest hereafter the priests should transgress through ignorance, Moses admonishes them of their duty; and perhaps he was moved by some immediate reason to give these particular injunctions rather than any others. As yet they were but little practiced in the observance of the rites; and what had happened to their brethren must have rendered them anxious. Now, this consternation at the death of their brethren might have so confounded their senses, that they could not apply themselves with so much composure as they ought to the service of God; and thus the offering would have been improperly made. Lest, therefore, their grief should so disturb them as to prevent the due performance of their office, he commands them to eat what remained of the meat-offering with the burnt-sacrifices. Whence we gather that he endeavored to prevent them from transgressing on that day in consequence of their minds being occupied by their recent grief. And in order to induce them to obedience, he sets before them the authority of God, to which it was fitting that the priesthood should be subject, as being founded upon it.

16. And Moses diligently sought the goat of the sin-offering Moses had not omitted to tell them what was to be done with the goat; and the sacrifice which he had himself performed, was a visible instruction to them. He had set before them what they should imitate, and this would have been enough even for children. But, as I have said, in such serious matters Moses had not spared labor and care, whereas the sons of Aaron, as if they had neither heard nor seen anything of the sort, pervert the whole order of them, although they had been just before reminded that they had been appointed to keep the charge of God. Perhaps they were impelled to this error by the trouble arising from their grief; but we gather from hence that however exquisite may be the ability of masters and teachers, it may be often fruitless unless they have obedient scholars with retentive memories. And hence also we learn that when God often inculcates the same thing, His labor is not superfluous, because we do not understand what we seem to understand; or what has been clearly shewn to us soon afterwards escapes.

Further from the anger of Moses, which is mentioned in his praise, we may infer that the transgression was no light one, although it was not so severely punished as the presumption of Nadab and Abihu. The excuse which some make for them, or allege in extenuation of their crime, that they thought they were deprived of the right before accorded to them, and therefore abstained through modesty, is refuted by the answer of Aaron himself. It was, therefore, grief alone which impelled them to this error. But the reason why God was more merciful to them than to their brethren, is only known to Himself. Conjectures may, indeed, be advanced; but at last we must come to this, that because God's judgments are hidden, they are not therefore unjust; but that we must humbly adore their depth into which the minds of men cannot penetrate.

19. And Aaron said unto Moses, Behold, this day Aaron replies that it arose from pious fear that they had not feasted before God, because they would

in a manner have defiled the sanctuary by their tears and melancholy, as if he had said, Part indeed of the sin-offering was reserved for our food, but we could not properly partake of it except in cheerfulness and with thanksgiving. The grief arising from his sudden bereavement did not allow of this; but it was not a just defense; for he ought rather to have striven against the feelings of the flesh, so that his domestic calamity should not withhold him from the service of God. But, inasmuch as in his perplexity his fear was deserving of pity, Moses forgives him; and it is said that he was appeased, because he finds less of evil than he supposed.

Numbers 1

Numbers 1:1-54

1. And the Lord spake unto Moses in the wilderness of Sinai, in the tabernacle of the congregation, on the first day of the second month, in the second year after they were come out of the land of Egypt, saying,

1. Loquutus est autem Jehova ad Mosen in deserto Sinai, in tabernaculo conventionis, in primo mensis secundi, anno secundo ex quo egressi sunt e terra AEgypti, dicendo:

2. Take ye the sum of all the congregation of the children of Israel, after their families, by the house of their fathers, with the number of their names, every male by their polls;

2. Capite summam totius coetus filiorum Israel per familias eorum, per domos patrum eorum, juxta numerum nominum, onmem masculum per capita eorum.

3. From twenty years old and upward, all that are able to go forth to war in Israel: thou and Aaron shall number them by their armies.

3. A filio viginti armorum et supra, Omnem egredientem ad bellum in Israele numerabitis eos per excreitus suos tu et Aharon.

4. And with you there shall be a man of every tribe; every one head of the house of his fathers.

4. Sintque vobiseum viri de singulis tribubus, quorum quilibet caput domus sit patrum suorum.

5. And these are the names of the men that shall stand with you: Of the tribe of Reuben; Elizur the son of Shedeur.

5. Haec sunt autem nomima virorum qui stabunt vobiscum: de Ruben, Elisur, filius Sedeur.

6. Of Simeon; Shehmiel the son of Zurishaddai.

6. De Simeon, Selumiel filius Surisaddai.

7. Of Judah; Nahshon the son of Amminadab.

7. De Jehudah, Nahason filius Amminadab.

8. Of Issachar; Nethaneel the son of Zuar.

8. De Issachar, Nethanel filius Suar.

9. Of Zebulun; Eliab the son of Helon.

9. De Zebulon, Eliab filius Helon.

10. Of the children of Joseph: of Ephraim; Elishame the son of Ammihud: of Manasseh; Gamaliel the son of Pedabzur.

10. De filiis Joseph, de Ephraim, Elisamama filius Ammihud: de Manasses, Gamliel illius Pedahsur.

11. Of Benjamin; Abidan the son of Gideoni.

11. De Benjamin, Abidan filius Gidoni.

12. Of Dan; Ahiezer the son of Ammishaddai.

12. De Dan, Ahiezer filius Ammisaddai.

13. Of Asher; Pagiel the son of Ocran.

13. De Aser, Pagiel filius Ochran.

14. Of Gad; Eliasaph the son of Deuel.

14. De Gad, Eliasaph filius Deuel.

15. Of Naphtali; Ahira the son of Enan.

15. De Nephthali, Ahira filius Ellan.

16. These were the renowned of the congregation, princes of the tribes of their fathers, heads of thousands in Israel.

16. Hi sunt nobilissimi synagogae, principes tribuum patrum suorum: capita millium Israelis erant.

17. And Moses and Aaron took these men which are expressed by their names:

17. Accepit igitur Moses et Aharon viros istos qui expositi sunt per nomina.

18. And they assembled all the congregation together on the first day of the second month; and they declared their pedigrees after their fanlilies, by the house of their fathers, according to the number of the names, from twenty years old and upward, by their polls.

18. Et universam synagogam congregaverunt primo mensis secundi, et secundum genealogiam recensiti sunt per familias suas: per domos patrum suorum, juxta numerum numerum per capita sua, omnis masculus a filio viginti armorum et supra, onmis egrediens ad pugnam.

19. As the Lord commanded Moses, so he numbered them in the wilderness of Sinai.

19. Quemadmodum praeceperat Jehova ipsi Mosi, numeravit eos in deserto Sinai.

20. And the children of Reuben, Israel's eldest son, by their generations, after their families, by the house of their fathers, according to the number of the names, by their polls, every male from twenty years old and upward, all that were able to go forth to war;

20. Fuerunt itaque filii Ruben primogeniti lsrael per generationes suas, per familias suas, per domes patrum suorum, juxta numerura nominum per capita sua, omnis masculus a filio viginti annorum et supra, omnis egrediens ad pugham,

21. Those that were numbered of them, even of the tribe of Reuben, were forty and six thousand and five hundred.

21. Numerati eorum de tribu Ruben, sex et quadraginta millia, atque quingenti.

22. Of the children of Simeon, by their generations, after their families, by the house of their fathers, those that were numbered of them, according to the number of the names, by their polls, every male from twenty years old and upward, all that were able to go forth to war;

22. De filiis Simeon per generationes suas, per familias suas, per domos patrum suorum, munerati ejus, juxta humerum niminum, per capita sua, omnis masculus a filio viginti armorum et supra, omnis; egrediens ad pugnam:

23. Those that were numbered of them, even of the tribe of Simeon, were fifty and nine thousand and three hundred.

23. Numerati inquam eorum de tribu Simeon, novera et quinquaginta millia, atque trecenti.

24. Of the children of Gad, by their generations, after their families, by the house of their fathers, according to the number of the names, from twenty years old and upward, all that were able to go forth to war;

24. De filiis Gad per generationes suas, per familias suas, per domus patrum suorum, juxta numerum nominum, a filio viginti annorum et supra, omnis egrediens ad pugnam.

25. Those that were numbered of them, even of the tribe of Gad, were forty and five thousand six hundred and fifty.

25. Numerati eorum de tribu Gad, quinque et quadraginta milliae, atque sexcenti et quinquaginta.

26. Of the children of Judah, by their generations, after their families, by the house of their fathers, according to the number of the names, from twenty years old and upward, all that were able to go forth to war;

26. De filiis Jehudah per generationes suas, per familias suas, per domus patrum suorum, juxta numerum nominum, a filio viginti annorum et supra, omnis egrediens ad pugnam:

27. Those that were numbered of them, even of the tribe of Judah, were threescore and fourteen thousand and six hundred.

27. Numerati eorum de tribu Jehudah, quatuor et septuaginta millia, atque sexcenti.

28. Of the children of Issachar, by their generations, after their families, by the house of their fathers, according to the number of the names, from twenty years old and upward, all that were able to go forth to war;

28. De filiis Issachar per generationes suas, per familias suas, per domum patrum suorum, juxta nuroerum nominum, a filio viginti annorum et supra, omnis egrediens ad putnam:

29. Those that were numbered of them, even of the tribe of Issachar, were fifty and four thousand and four hundred.

29. Numerati eorum de tribu Issachar, quatuor et quinquaginta millia, atque quadringenti.

30. Of the children of Zebulun, by their generations, after their families, by the house of their fathers, according to the number of the names, from twenty years old and upward, all that were able to go forth to war;

30. De filiis Zebulon, per generationes sues, per familias suas, per domos patrum suorum, juxta numerum niminum a filio Viginti annorum et supra, omnis egrediens ad pugnam:

31. Those that were numbered of them, even of the tribe of Zebulun, were fifty and seven thousand and four hundred.

31. Numerati corum de tribu Zebulon, septem et quinquaginta millia, atque quadringenti.

32. Of the children of Joseph, namely, of the children of Ephraim, by their generations, after their families, by the house of their fathers, according to the number of the names, from twenty years old and upward, all that were able to go forth to war;

32. De filiis Joseph, de filiis Ephraim, per generationes suas, per familias suas, per domos patrum suorum, juxta numerum nominum, a filio viginti annorum et supra, omnis egrediens ad pugnam:

33. Those that were numbered of them, even of the tribe of Ephraim, were forty thousand and five hundred.

33. Numerati eorum de tribu Ephraim, quadraginta millius atque quingenti.

34. Of the children of Manasseh, by their generations, after their families, by the house of their fathers, according to the number of the names, from twenty years old and upward, all that were able to go forth to war;

34. De filiis Manasse, per generationes suas, per domos patrum suorum, juxta numerum nominum, a filio viginti annorum et supra, omnis egrediens ad pugnam:

35. Those that were numbered of them, even of the tribe of Manasseh, were thirty and two thousand and two hundred.

35. Numerati corum de tribu Manasse, duo et triginta raillid, atque ducenti.

36. Of the children of Benjamin, by their generations, after their families, by the house of their fathers, according to the number of the names, from twenty years old and upward, all that were able to go forth to war;

36. De filiis Benjamin, per generationes suas, per familias suam, per domum patrum suorum, juxta numerum nominum, a filio viginti annorum et supra, omnis egrediens ad pugnam:

37. Those that were numbered of them, even of the tribe of Benamin, were thirty and five thousand and four hundred.

37. Numerati eorum de tribu Benjamin, quinque et triginta millie, et quadringenti.

38. Of the children of Dan, by their generations, after their families, by the house of their fathers, according to the number of the names, from twenty years old and upward, all that were able to go forth to war;

38. De filiis Dan, per generationes suas, per familias suas, per domos patrum suorum, juxta numerum nominum, a filio viginti annorum et supra, omnis egrediens ad pugnam:

39. Those that were numbered of them, even of the tribe of Dan, were threescore and two thousand and seven hundred.

39. Numerati eorum de tribu Dan, duo et sexaginta millia, atque septingenti.

40. Of the children of Asher, by their generations, after their families, by the house of their fathers, according to the number of the names, from twenty years old and upward, all that were able to go forth to war;

40. De filiis Aser per generationes suas, per familias suas, per domos patrum suorum, juxta humerum nominum, a filio viginti armorum et supra, omnis egrediens ad pugnam:

41. Those that were numbered of them, even of the tribe of Asher, were forty and one thousand and five hundred.

41. Numerati eorum de tribu Aser, unum et quadraginta millia, atque quingenti.

42. Of the children of Naphtali, throughout their generations, after their families, by the house of their fathers, according to the number of the names, from twenty years old and upward, all that were able to go forth to war;

42. De filiis Nephthali, per generationes suds, per familias suas, per domus patrum suorum, juxta numerum nominum a filio viginti annorum et supra, omnis egrediens ad pugnam:

43. Those that were numbered of them, even of the tribe of Naphtali, were fifty and three thousand and four hundred.

43. Numerati eorum de tribu Nephthali, tria et quinquaginta millia, atque quadringenti.

44. These are those that were numbered, which Moses and Aaron numbered, and the princes of Israel, being twelve men: each one was for the house of his fathers.

44. Isti sunt numerati illi quos numeravit Moses et Aharon atque principes Israelis, duodecim viri: singuli per domos patrum suorum erant.

45. So were all those that were numbered of the children of Israel, by the house of their fathers, from twenty years old and upward, all that were able to go forth to war in Israel;

45. Fueruntque omnes numerati filiorum Israel per domos patrum suorum, a filio viginti annorum et supra, omnis egrediens ad pugnam in Israele.

46. Even all they that were numbered, were six hundred thousand, and three thousand, and five hundred and fifty.

46. Fuerunt inquam omnes numerati, sexcenta tria millia, et quingenti quinquaginta.

47. But the Levites, after the tribe of their fathers, were not numbered among them.

47. At Levitin per tribum patrum suorum non fuerunt numerati in medio eorum.

48. For the Lord had spoken unto Moses, saying,

48. Loquutus enim erat Jehova, ad Mosen dicendo:

49. Only thou shalt not number the tribe of Levi, neither take the sum of them among the children of Israel:

49. Veruntamen (vel, utique, vel, tantummodo) tribum Levi non numerabis, neque summam eorum capies in medio filiorum Israel.

50. But thou shalt appoint the Levites over the tabernacle of testimony, and over all the vessels thereof, and over all things that belong to it: they shall bear the tabernacle, and all the vessels thereof: and they shall minister unto it, and shall encamp round about the tabernacle.

50. Sed tu praefice Levitas tabernaculo testimonii, et onmibus vasis ejus, et omnibus qum ad illud pertinent: ipsi portabunt tabernaculum, et omnia vasa ejus, et ipsi ministrabunt illi, et in circuitu tabernaculi castrametabuntur.

5l. And when the tabernacle setteth forward, the Levites shall take it down; and when the tabernacle is to be pitched, the Levites shall set it up: and the stranger that cometh nigh shall be put to death.

51. Quando autem proficiscetur tabernaculum, deponent illud Levitie: quum consistet tabernaculum, erigent illud Levitae et extraneus qui accesserit, morietur.

52. And the children of Israel shall pitch their tents, every man by his own camp, and every man by his own standard, throughout their hosts.

52. Et castrametabuntur filil Israel quisque in castris suis, et quisque juxta vexillum suum, et per exercitus suos.

53. But the Levites shall pitch round about the tabernacle of testimony, that there be no wrath upon the congregation of the children of Israel: and the Levites shall keep the charge of the tabernacle of testimony.

53. Levitae vero castrametabuntur in circuitu tabernaculi testimoni et non erit ira super coetum filliorum Israel: custodientque Levitiae custodiam tabernaculi testimonii.

54. And the children of Israel did according to all that the Lord commanded Moses, so did they.

54. Fecerunt ergo filii Israel juxta omnia quae praeceperat Jehova Most, sic fecerunt.

1. And the Lord spake unto Moses in the wilderness of Sinai Although this is the first numbering of the people, of which we have an account, still, inasmuch as God had already imposed a tax upon every person, the amount of which has been recorded, we infer that it was in fact the second. But the reason for thus numbering the people a second time was, because they were very soon about to remove their camp from the wilderness of Sinai to take posession of the promised land. Since, however, their impiety withheld them from doing so, there was a third census taken just before their actual entrance into the land, and with this object, that it might be obvious, on comparison, how marvellously the people had been preserved by the springing up of a new generation, in spite of so many plagues and so much slaughter; for although a great proportion of them had been cut off, almost as many persons were found as before.

Further, it must be observed, that the people were not numbered except at God's command, in order that He might thus assert His supreme dominion over them; and also, that the mode of taking the census was so arranged, that there should be no confusion of ranks either through fraud or irregularity; for this was the reason why each tribe had its superintendents, lest any one should slip into a tribe to which he did not belong; and this is expressly mentioned by way of assurance, since otherwise many might suspect that so great a multitude could hardly be distinguished into classes with certainty, so that the whole sum should be calculated without mistake.

20. And the children of Reuben, Israel's eldest son If any disputatious person should contend that one family could not increase in 250 years to so great an amount, and thus should reject as nebulous what surpasses the ordinary rule of nature, we must bear in mind what I have already stated, that, inasmuch as this increase depended on the power of God, nothing is more absurd than to measure it by ordinary rules. For the intention of the Spirit is to represent to our eyes the incredible power of God in a conspicuous and signal miracle. Meanwhile, if you compared the tribe of Reuben with some of the others, it presents in its numbers some marks of the curse, so that we may gather that Reuben was degraded from the honors of his primogeniture; for the tribes of Simeon, Issachar, Zebulun, Dan, and Naphtali were more numerous, whilst from Joseph alone, who was one of the youngest, a posterity descended which almost doubled it in numbers. God's blessing, however, is most conspicuous in the tribe of Judah, in correspondence with the prophecy of Jacob; for by this prerogative, as it were, it was already called to the right of primogeniture and to supremacy, inasmuch as it surpassed all the principal ones.

47. But the Levites, after the tribe of their fathers We shall indeed hereafter see that they also were numbered, but Moses means that they were not included in the general census of the people, because God had chosen them to be His own property, and thus had severed them from the rest of the people. He writes, therefore, that they "were not numbered in the midst of the others," [419] i.e., so as promiscuously to form a part of the multitude. Now, lest any one should object that Moses acted ambitiously in thus bestowing on his own tribe extraordinary distinction, he declares that he did not do this spontaneously, but that it was at God's bidding that the Levites had a separate class assigned to them; for translators render this passage amiss, "And God said to Moses," [420] as if he stated that the tribe of Levi was then first set apart when the sum of the people was taken, since it would have been absurd to omit a part, unless God's will had been already declared. Moses, therefore, shews why he passed over his own tribe, via, because God had consecrated the Levites for the keeping and service of the tabernacle. Now, if it was not lawful for the tabernacle to be carried or set up by all persons indiscriminately, its sanctity was enforced by this symbol; for religion would not have been held in so much reverence, if it had been allowable for all without distinction to meddle with the sacred things. Meanwhile, the Israelites were reminded that all without exception were unworthy to present themselves before God, when they were forbidden from access to the sanctuary; whereas the dignity which was conferred upon a single tribe was no ground for boasting, since it depended merely on the good pleasure of God. God, then, gave the Levites access to His tabernacle, not because they had deserved that honor by any virtue of their own, but in order to afford a testimony of His gratuitous favor. At the same time, under this image He represented the future priesthood of Christ, in order that believers might be assured that the Mediator, by whom others might have access to God, was to be of the human race; and therefore God declares by Isaiah that He would take the Levites under the kingdom of Christ from the general and dispersed body of the people. (Isaiah 66:21.) As to what relates to their office, let it be sought in its proper place.

Deuteronomy 10

Deuteronomy 10:8, 9

8. At that time the Lord separated the tribe of Levi, to bear the ark of the covenant of the Lord, to stand before the Lord to minister unto him, and to bless in his name, unto this day.

8. In tempore illo separavit Jehova tribum Levi: ut gestaret Arcam foederis Jehovae, ut staret coram Jehova ad ministrandum ei, et ad benediecudum in nomine ipsius usqae ad diem hanc.

9. Wherefore Levi hath no part nor inheritance with his brethren; the Lord is his inheritance, according as the Lord thy God promised him.

9. Idcirco non fuit ipsi Levi portio et haereditas cum fratribus suis: Jehova est haereditas ejus, quemadmodumdixit ei Jehova Deus tuus.

8. At that time the Lord separated the tribe of Levi Moses does not exactly observe the order of time in the chapter from which this passage is taken, since he deemed it sufficient to collect here and there what was required to complete

his general exhortation. The object indeed of the recital of this history was, lest any should attempt to overthrow God's invioable decree in their pride and audacity; and therefore, in order that the dignity of the tribe of Levi may not beget envy, he testifies that God is its author. The clause, "unto this day," seems to refer to those instances in which God had manifested His favor towards the Levites, lest any similar rivalry should hereafter arise. The rest has been expounded elsewhere.

Numbers 2

Numbers 2:1-34

1. And the Lord spake unto Moses and unto Aaron, saying,

1. Et loquutus est Jehova Mosi et Aharon, dicendo:

2. Every man of the children of Israel shall pitch by his own standard, with the ensign of their father's house: far off about the tabernacle of the congregation shall they pitch.

2. Singuli juxta vexillum suum, juxta signa domus patrum suorum, castrametabuntur filii Israel: procul, circum tabernaculum conventionis castrametabuntur.

3. And on the east side, toward the rising of the sun, shall they of the standard of the camp of Judah pitch, throughout their armies: and Nahshon the son of Amminadab shall be captain of the children of Judah.

3. Hi autem castrametabuntur ad orientem, a d exortum vexillum exercitus Juda per turmas suas: et princeps filiorum Juda erit SaMson filius Amminadab.

4. And his host, and those that were numbered of them, were threescore and fourteen thousand and six hundred.

4. Et exercitus ejus, numeratique eorum, quatuor et septuaginta millia, atque sexcenti.

5. And those that do pitch next unto him shall be the tribe of Issachar: and Nethaneel the son of Zuar shall be captain of the children of Issachar.

5. Castrametabuntur vero juxta eum tribus Issachar: et princeps filiorum Issachar erit Nethanel filius Suar.

6. And his host, and those that were numbered thereof, were fifty and four thousand and four hundred.

6. Et exercitus ejus numeratique ejus, quatuor et quinquaginta millia atque quadringenti.

7. Then the tribe of Zebulun: and Eliab the son of Helon shall be captain of the children of Zebulun.

7. Tribus Zebulon, et princeps filiorum Zebulon, Eliab illius Helon.

8. And his host, and those that were numbered thereof, were fifty and seven thousand and four hundred.

8. Et exercitus ejus, numeratique ejus, septem et quinquaginta millia atque quadringenti.

9. All that were numbered in the camp of Judah were an hundred thousand, and fourscore thousand, and six thousand and four hundred, throughout their armies: these shall first set forth.

9. Omnes numerati in exercitu Juda, centum octoginta sex millia atque quadringenti, per exercitus suos: primum proficiscentur.

10. On the south side shall be the standard of the camp of Reuben, according to their armies: and the captain of the children of Reuben shall be Elizur the son of Shedeur.

10. Vexillum exercitus Reuben erit ad meridiem per turmas suas: et princeps filiorum Reuben erit Elisur filius Sedeur.

11. And his host, and those that were numbered thereof, were forty and six thousand and five hundred.

11. Exercitus ejus, numeratique ejus, sex et quadraginta millla atque quingenti.

12. And those which pitch by him shall be the tribe of Simeon: and the captain of the children of Simeon shall be Shelumiel the son of Zurishaddai.

12. Castrametabuntar autem juxta enm tribus Simeon: et princeps filiorum Simeon, Selumiel, fillus Surisaddai.

13. And his host, and those that were numbered of them, were fifty and nine thousand and three hundred.

13. Et exercitus ejus, numeratique eorum, novem et quinquaginta millia atque trecenti.

14. Then the tribe of Gad: and the captain of the sons of Gad shall be Eliasaph the son of Reuel.

14. Tribus item Gad: et princeps filiorum Gad, Eliasaph filius Reuel:

15. And his host, and those that were numbered of them, were forty five thousand and six hundred and fifty.

15. Et exercitus ejus, numeratique eorum, quinqne et quadraginta millia atque sexcenti et quinquaginta.

16. All that were numbered in the camp of Reuben were an hundred thousand, and fifty and one thousand, and four hundred and fifty, throughout their armies: and they shall set forth in the second rank.

16. Omnes numerati in excreitu Reuben, centum quinquaginta millia, mille et quadringenti quinquaginta, per exercitus suos: et secundi proficiscentur.

17. Then the tabernacle of the congregation shall set forward, with the camp of the Levites in the midst of the camp: as they encamp, so shall they set forward, every man in his place, by their standards.

17. Turn proficiscetur tabernaculum conventionis in castris Levitarum, in medio castrorum: quemadmodum castrametabuntur, sic proficiscetur quisque in loco suo, juxta vexilia sua.

18. On the west side shall be the standard of the camp of Ephraim, according to their armies: and the captain of the sons of Ephraim shall be Elishama the son of Ammihud.

18. Vexilium excreitus Ephraim per turmas suas erit ad occidentem: et princeps filiorum Ephraim erit Elisarea filius Ammihud.

19. And his host, and those that were numbered of them, were forty thousand and five hundred.

19. Et excreitus ejus, numeratique eorum, quadraginta millia et quingenti.

20. And by him shall be the tribe of Manasseh: and the captain of the children of Manasseh shall be Gamaliel the son of Pedahzur.

20. Et juxta eum erit tribus Manasse: et princeps filiorum Manasse erit Gamliel filius Pedahsur.

21. And his host, and those that were numbered of them, were thirty and two thousand and two hundred.

21. Et exercitus ejus, numeratique eorum, duo et triginta millia atque ducenti.

22. Then the tribe of Benjamin: and the captain of the sons of Benjamin shall be Abidan the son of Gideoni.

22. Tribus item Benjamin, et princeps filiorum Benjamin erit Abidan filius Gidoni.

23. And his host, and those that were numbered of them, were thirty and five thousand and four hundred.

23. Et exercitus ejus, numeratique, eorum, quinque et triginta millia atque quadringenti.

24. All that were numbered of the camp of Ephraim were an hundred thousand, and eight thousand and an hundred, throughout their armies: and they shall go forward in the third rank.

24. Omnes numerati in excreitu Ephraim, centum et octo millia atque centum, per excreitus suos: et tertii proficiscentur.

25. The standard of the camp of Dan shall be on the north side by their armies: and the captain of the children of Dan shall be Ahiezer the son of Ammishaddai.

25. Vexilium castrorum Dan erit ad Aquilonem, per exercitus suos: et princeps filiorum Dan, Ahiezer filius Ammisaddai.

26. And his host, and those that were numbered of them, were threescore and two thousand and seven hundred.

26. Et exercitus ejus, numeratique eorum, duo et sexaginta millia atque septingenti.

27. And those that encamp by him shall be the tribe of Asher: and the captain of the children of Asher shall be Pagiel the son of Ocran.

27. Castrametabuntur autem juxta eum tribus Aser; et princeps filiorum Aser erit Pagiel filius Ochran.

28. And his host, and those that were numbered of them, were forty and one thousand and five hundred.

28. Et exercitus ejus, numeratique eorum, unum et quadraginta millia et quingenti.

29. Then the tribe of Naphtali: and the captain of the children of Naphtali shall be Ahira the son of Enan.

29. Tribus item Nephthali: et princeps filiorum Nephthali, Ahira filius Enan.

30. And his host, and those that were numbered of them, were fifty and three thousand and four hundred.

30. Et exercitus ejus numeratique eorum, tria et quinquaginta millia atque quadringenti.

31. All they that were numbered in the camp of Dan were an hundred thousand, and fifty and seven thousand, and six hundred: they shall go hindmost with their standards.

31. Omnes numerati in exercitu Dan, centum millia et quinquaginta septem millia, atque sexcenti: postremi proficiscentur per vexilla.

32. These are those which were numbered of the children of Israel, by the house of their fathers: all those that were numbered of the camps, throughout their hosts, were six hundred thousand, and three thousand, and five hundred and fifty.

32. Isti sunt numerati filiorum Israel per domos patrum suorum, omnes numerati qui erant in castris per turmas suas, sexcenta tria millia atque quingenti quinquaginta.

33. But the Levites were not numbered among the children of Israel; as the Lord commanded Moses.

33. Craterum Levite non fuerunt numerati inter filius Israel quemadmodum praeceperat Jehova Mosi.

34. And the children of Israel did according to all that the Lord commanded Moses: so they pitched by their standards, and so they set forward, every one after their families, according to the house of their fathers.

34. Et fecerunt filii Israel juxta omnia qum praecepit Jehova Mosi: sic castrametati sunt per vexilia sua, sicque profecti sunt quisque per familias suas, per domum patrum suorum.

1. And the Lord spake unto Moses, and unto Aaron This distribution into separate bands must have served to prevent contention; for, had not God thus assigned to each their proper position, so natural is ambition to man, that they would have quarrelled for the place of honor. It would have been grievous to the family of Reuben, the first-born, to resign his dignity; and, even if they had patiently submitted to the punishment inflicted upon them, they would have been made to take the lowest place, as being condemned to ignominy. Disputes would also have arisen respecting the children of the concubines, for they would not have thought it consistent that; those who sprang from Leah and Rachel should yield them the superior place. Besides, in proportion as they severally had the advantage in numbers, they would have thought themselves injured unless they preceded others.

Thus the children of Simeon would never have suffered themselves to be ranged under the standard of Reuben. Again, dispute would also have arisen between the children of Ephraim and Manasseh. God, therefore, at once put a stop to all these disturbances by so arranging their ranks that each one knew his own band. Consequently, Judah, although the fourth son of Leah, received the first standard as an honorable distinction, that he might thus in a manner begin to fulfill the prophecy of Jacob by anticipation; and two tribes were united with him which would willingly submit to his rule, Issachar and Zebuhm; because they derived their origin from the children of the [421] handmaid whom Leah had substituted in her own place.

Although Reuben had been deprived of his primogeniture, still, that some consolation might remain for his posterity, he was set over the second standard; two tribes were associated with him, which on account of their connection would not be aggrieved at fighting under his command, the tribe of Simeon his uterine brother, and the tribe of Gad, which also sprang from the handmaid of Leah.

It was necessary that God should interpose His authorify, in order that two tribes should be formed of a single head, Joseph; otherwise the fact would have led to contention, because the inequality was odious in itself, and that family might appear to be elevated not without disgrace to the others. Besides, the children of Manasseh, who were superior by the law of nature, would never have been induced to obey, unless a divine decree had interposed. But thtat division could not have been better formed than of the sons of Rachel, because their consanguinity was closer; for a sharp contest might also have arisen for the leadership of the fourth band, because it was unjust that the son of a handmaid should have been placed at its head, and thus preferred to a legitimate son of Leah, and to the other son of Rachel, especially when Benjamin was so singularly beloved by Jacob, the common father of them all.[422] The sole will of God, indeed, was sufficient, and more than sufficient to prevent all quarrels; but, inasmuch as He chose rather to rule over them generously and paternally, than in a despotic manner, He rather conformed Himself to their wishes than drove them by compulsion. Still, however, because their contentions could not be prevented by mere human decisions, it is again said at the end of the chapter that Moses did nothing except by God's command. At the same time the obedience of the people is noticed in that they peaceably obeyed Moses, since thus they ratified their acknowledgment of Moses as a true and faithful minister of God; for this submissiveness is the inseparable companion of sincere piety towards God, that whatever is proposed by His approved ministers the people should reverently accept.

Numbers 3

Numbers 3:1-51

1. These also are the generations of Aaron and Moses, in the day that the Lord spake with Moses in mount Sinai.

1. Hae sunt generationes Aharon et Mosis ex quo loquutus est Jehova ad Mosen in monte Sinai.

2. And these are the names of the sons of Aaron; Nadab the first-born, and Abihu, Eleazar, and Ithamar.

2. Hac autem sunt nomina filiorum Aharon: primogenitus Nadab, et Ahihu, Eleazar et Ithamar.

3. These are the names of the sons of Aaron, the priests which were anointed, whom he consecrated to minister in the priest's office.

3. Ista sunt nomina filiorum Aharon sacerdotum unctorum, quorum consecraverat manum ut sacerdotio fungerentur.

4. And Nadab and Abihu died before the Lord, when they offered fire before the Lord, in the wilderness of Sinai, and they had no children: and Eleazar and Ithamar ministered in the priest's office in the sight of Aaron their father.

4. Mortuus est autem Nadab et Abihu eoram Jehova, quando obtulerunt ignem externum coram Jehova in deserto Sinai: et filii non fuerunt eis, ae sacerdotio functus est Eleazar et Ithamar coram Aharone patre suo.

5. And the Lord spake unto Moses, saying,

5. Loquutus est autem Jehova ad Mosen, dicendo:

6. Bring the tribe of Levi near, and present them before Aaron the priest, that they may minister unto him.

6. Appropinquare fac tribum Levi, et stare facias eam coram Aharone sacerdote, ut ministrent ei,

7. And they shall keep his charge, and the charge of the whole congregation, before the tabernacle of the congregation, to do the service of the tabernacle.

7. Et custodiant custodiam ejus, et custodiam universi coetus coram tabernaculo ecelesiae, ut exequantur cultum tabernaculi.

8. And they shall keep all the instruments of the tabernacle of the congregation, and the charge of the children of Israel, to do the service of the tabernacle.

8. Custodiant quoque omnia utensilia tabernaculi ecclesiae, custodiamque filiorum Israel, et exequantur cultum tabernaculi.

9. And thou shalt give the Levites unto Aaron, and to his sons: they are wholly given unto him out of the children of Israel.

9. Da inquam Levitas ipsi Aharon et illils ejus: dati, daft namque aunt illi a filiis Israel.

10. And thou shalt appoint Aaron and his sons, and they shall wait on their priest's office; and the stranger that cometh nigh shall be put to death.

10. Aharon autem et filios ejus praeticies, custodientque sacerdotium suum: externus sane qui accesserit, morietur.

11. And the Lord spake unto Moses, saying,

11. Loquutus est praeterea Jehova ad Mosen, dicendo:

12. And I, behold, I have taken the Levites from among the children of Israel instead of all the first-born that openeth the matrix among the children of Israel: therefore the Levites shall be mine;

12. Ego quidera tuli Levitas e medio filiorum Israel loco omnis primogeniti quod aperit vulvam a filiis Israel: eruntque mei Levitae.

13. Because all the first-born are mine: for on the day that I smote all the first-born in the land of Egypt, I hallowed unto me all the first-born in Israel, both man and beast; mine they shall be: I am the Lord.

13. Meum namque est omne primogenitum: a die quo percussi omne primogenitum in terra AEgypti, sanctificavi mihi omne primogenitum in Israel: tam ex hominibus quam ex animalibus: mea erunt: ego Jehova.

14. And the Lord spake unto Moses in the wilderness of Sinai, saying,

14. Loquutus est insuper Jehova ad Mosen, dicendo:

15. Number the children of Levi, after the house of their fathers, by their families: every male from a month old and upward shalt thou number them.

15. Numera filius Levi per domos patrum suorum, per familias suas: omnem masculum ab uno meuse et supra, numerabis.

16. And Moses numbered them, according to the word of the Lord, as he was commanded.

16. Numeravit itaque eos Moses juxta sermonem Jehovae, quemadmodum jussus fuerat.

17. And these were the sons of Levi, by their names; Gershon, and Kohath, and Merari.

17. Et fuermir isti filii Levi per nomina sua, Gerson, Cehath et Merari.

18. And these are the names of the sons of Gershon, by their families; Libni, and Shimei.

18. Haec autem sunt nomina filiorum Gerson per familias suas, Libni et Semei.

19. And the sons of Kohath, by their families; Amram, and Izhar, Hebron, and Uzziel.

19. Porro filii Cehath per familias suas, Amram, et Jehor, Hebron et Uzziel.

20. And the sons of Merari, by their families; Mahli, and Mushi: these are the families of the Levites, according to the house of their fathers.

20. Filii vero Merari per familias suas, Mahali, et Muzi. Istae sunt familiae Levi per domos patrum suorum.

21. Of Gershon was the family of the Libnities, and the family of the Shimites: these are the families of the Gershonites,

21. De Gerson, familia Libnitica, et familia Simitica: istte sunt familiae Gersoniticae.

22. Those that were numbered of them, according to the number of all the males, from a month old and upward, even those that were numbered of them, were seven thousand and five hundred.

22. Numerati eorum secundmu numerum onmis masculi, a filio mensis et supra, numerati eormn, septem millia et quingenti.

23. The families of the Gershonites shall pitch behind the tabernacle westward.

23. Familiae Gersonitiem post tabernaculum castrametabuntur ad occidentem.

24. And the chief of the house of the father of the Gershonites shall be Eliasaph the son of Lad.

24. Et princeps domus patris Gersonitarum erit Eliasaph filius Lael.

25. And the charge of the sons of Gershon, in the tabernacle of the congregation, shall be the tabernacle, and the tent, the covering thereof, and the hanging for the door of the tabernacle of the congregation,

25. Custodia autem filiorum Gerson in tabernaculo conventionis erit tabernaculum, et tentorium, operimentum ejus, aulaeum ostii tabernaculi conventionis.

26. And the hangings of the court, and the curtain for the door of the court, which is by the tabernacle, and by the altar round about, and the cords of it, for all the service thereof.

26. Cortinae item atrii, et aulaeum ostii atrii quod erat juxta tabernaculum, et juxta altare per circuitum, funes quoque ejus pro omni ministerio ejus.

27. And of Kohath was the family of the Amramites, and the family of the Izharites, and the family of the Hebronites, and the family of the Uzzielites: these are the families of the Kohathites.

27. Et ipsius Cehath erit familiae Amramitica, et familia Isharitica, et familia Hebronitica, et familia Uzzielitica: istae sunt familiae Cehathiticae.

28. In the number of all the males, from a month old and upward, were eight thousand and six hundred, keeping the charge of the sanctuary.

28. Secundum numerum omn masculi a filio mensis et supra, fuerunt octo millia sexcenti, custodiente custodiam sanctuarii.

29. The families of the sons of Kohath shall pitch on the side of the tabernacle southward.

29. Familiae filiorum Cehath castrametabuntur ad latus tabernaculi ad meridiem.

30. And the chief of the house of father of the families of the Kohathites shall be Elizaphan the son of Uzziel.

30. Et princeps domus patris familiarum Cehathitarum erit Elisaphan filius Uzziel.

31. And their charge shall be the ark, and the table, and the candlestick, and the altars, and the vessels of the sanctuary wherewith they minister, and the hanging, and all the service thereof.

31. Custodia autem eorum erit arca, et mensa, et candelabrum, et altaria, et vasa sanctitatis in quibus ministrabunt, et aulaeum, et universum opus ejus.

32. And Eleazar the son of Aaron the priest shall be chief over the chief of the Levites, and have the oversight of them that keep the charge of the sanctuary.

32. Porro princeps principum Levitarum erit Eleazar filius Aharon sacerdotis: praefectura custodientium custodiam sanctitatis erit el.

33. Of Merari was the family of the Mahlites, and the family of the Mushites: these are the families of Merari.

33. Ipsius Merari erit familia Mahalitica, et familia Musitica. Istae sunt familiae Merari.

34. And those that were numbered of them, according to the number of all the males, from a month old and upward, were six thousand and two hundred.

34. Numerati autem eorum secundum numerum ordinis masculi, ab uno mense et supra, sex millia et ducenti.

35. And the chief of the house of the father of the families of Merari was Zuriel the son of Abihael: these shall pitch on the side of the tabernacle northward.

35. Et princeps domus patris familiarum Merari erit Suriel filius Abihael: atque hi ad latus tabernaculi castrametabuntur ad Aquilonem.

36. And under the custody and charge of the sons of Merari shall be the boards of the tabernacle, and the bars thereof, and the pillars thereof, and the sockets thereof, and all the vessels thereof, and all that serveth thereto,

36. Praefectura autem custodia filiorum Merari, tabulum tabernaculi, et vectes ejus, et columnae ejus, et bases qius, omniaque vasa ejus, et universum opus ejus.

37. And the pillars of the court round about, and their sockets, and their pins, and their cords.

37. Columnae quoque atrii per circuitum, et bases earum, et clavi earum, et funes earum.

38. But those that encamp before the tabernacle toward the east, even before the tabernacle of the congregation eastward, shall be Moses, and Aaron and his sons, keeping the charge of the sanctuary for the charge of the children of Israel; and the stranger that cometh nigh shall be put to death.

38. Qui vero castrametabuntur ante tabernaculuun, ad Orientem, in parte anteriore tabernaculi conventionis, ad orientem erunt Moses et Aharon, filiique ejus custodientes custodiam sanctuarii, pro custodia filiorum Israel: externus certe qui accesserit morietur.

39. All that were numbered of the Levites, which Moses and Aaron numbered at the commandment of the Lord, throughout their families, all the males, from a month old and upward, were twenty and two thousand.

39. Omnes numerati Levitarum, quos numeravit Moses et Aharon juxta sermonem Jehovae per familias eorum, omnes mares ab uno mense et supra, duo et viginti millia.

40 And the Lord said unto Moses, Number all the first-born of the males of the children of Israel, from a month old and upward, and take the number of their names.

40. Et dixit Jehova ad Mosen, Numera omne primogeniture masculmn filiorum Israel ab uno meuse et supra, et accipe humerum nominum eorum.

41. And thou shalt take the Levites for me, (I am the Lord,) instead of all the first-born among the children of Israel; and the cattle of the Levites instead of all the firstlings among the cattle of the children of Israel.

41. Capiesque Levitas mihi (ego Jehova) loco omnium primogenitorumn filiorum Israel, et bestias Levitatum loeo omnium primogenitorum ex bestits filiorum Israel.

42. And Moses numbered, as the Lord commanded him, all the first-born among the children of Israel.

42. Numeravit itaque Moses quemadmodum ei paeceperat Jehova, omnem primogeniture in filiis Israel.

43. And all the first-born males, by the number of names, from a month old and upward, of those that were numbered of them, were twenty and two thousand two hundred and threescore and thirteen.

43. Fueruntque omnia primogenita mascula, secundum numerum nominum, ab uno filio mensis, et supra, per numeratos eorum, duo et viginti millia, et ducenti septuaginta tres.

44. And the Lord spake unto Moses, saying,

44. Loquutusque est Jehova ad Mosen, dicendo:

45. Take the Levites instead of all the first-born among the children of Israel, and the cattle of the Levites instead of their cattle; and the Levites shall be mine: I am the Lord.

45. Cape Levitas loco omnium primogenitorum in filiis Israel, et bestias Levitatum pro bestiis eorum, eruntque mei Levitae: ego Jehova.

46. And for those that are to be redeemed of the two hundred and threescore and thirteen of the first-born of the children of Israel, which are more than the Levites;

46. Porro redemptiones ducentorum septuaginta trium redundant ultra Levitas, a primogenitis filiorum Israel.

47. Thou shalt even take five shekels apiece by the poll; after the shekel of the sanctuary shalt thou take them: (the shekel is twenty gerahs:)

47. Capies quinos siclos in singuls; capita, secundum siculum sanctuarii capies: viginti obolorum est siclus.

48. And thou shalt give the money, wherewith the odd number of them is to be redeemed, unto Aaron, and to his sons.

48. Dabisque pecuniam illam Aharoni et filiis ejus, redemptiones eorum qui exuperant in illis.

49. And Moses took the redemption-money of them that were over and above them that were redeemed by the Levites.

49. Accepit ergo Moses pecuniam redemptionis ab its qui superabant ultra redemptos Levitarum:

50. Of the first-born of the children of Israel took he the money; a thousand three hundred and three score and five shekels, after the shekel of the sanctuary:

50. A primogenitis filiorum Israel accepit pecuniam mille trecentos sexaginta quinque siclos, secundum siclum sanctuarii.

51. And Moses gave the money of them that were redeemed unto Aaron, and to his sons, according to the word of the Lord, as the Lord commanded Moses.

51. Deditque Moses pecuniam redemptionum Aharoni et filiis ejus, juxta sermonem Jehovae, quemadmodum praeceperat illi Jehova.

1. These also are the generations of Aaron and Moses He now separately enumerates the Levites; but, before he proceeds to state their number, he first shortly refers to what he had just before more fully narrated, that of the four sons of Aaron only two survived their father, inasmuch as Nadab and Abihu had suffered the penalty of their negligence in their defilement of the sacrifice. The six verses [423] which Moses inserts respecting the office of the priests have been expounded in their proper place. The dignity of the tribe of Levi is here exalted, when God compares the Levites to the first-born; the distribution of their charges is also touched upon, [424] but, since these things are connected with the census of the people, and the mode of pitching the camp, I have thought it best to annex them to what has just preceded, inasmuch as otherwise the history would be interrupted. And, in fact, in the order that I have followed, the office of each family is only incidentally treated of, so that all might know their proper station.

12. And I, behold, I have taken the Levites A little further on we shall see more clearly why God claims one tribe for Himself; He now only shews that the Levites rightfully belong to Him, because by special privilege the first-born of the people were preserved in the destruction of the Egyptians. God, therefore, declares that those, whose lives were thus gratuitously spared, were purchased to Himself. Since, then, He had the free option of devoting to Himself the first-born of every tribe, He was no less at liberty to take [425] only the twelfth part of the people from one tribe. Thus He cuts off all handle for complaint, inasmuch as it would have been intolerable ingratitude to withdraw from His control those whom He had miraculously redeemed; therefore He says that they did not perish in the general slaughter, in order that tie might subject them to ttimself.

15. Number the children of Levi after the house of their fathers The enumeration of the tribe now follows, commencing with the three sons of Levi, Kohath, Gershon, and Merari, from whom many families afterwards descended. It must, however, be observed, that all were numbered down to the youngest infants, whereas of the rest of the people only those who had passed their twentieth year were taken into account; whence it appeared that this was the smallest tribe; but by causing the infants to be reckoned, God intended to maintain a just proportion, as we shall see; for, if He had only taken them above their twentieth year, it would not have been known how many first-born there were, and thus the compensation to be made for them would have been uncertain. By this indulgence the people should have been induced to pay the tribute for the surplus with more readiness; for since, after the computation was made, it appeared how much their number came short of the required amount,

God justly willed that those should be redeemed for money, who would else have been transferred to that tribe which represented the first-born, and it would have been an act of malignity to refuse God what he demanded, when He had spontaneously condescended to so just a compact. There was also another reason why the Levites were included in the census from their earliest childhood, rather than the others, viz., because it was not necessary that they should be fit for war, when God enrolled from the rest of the people soldiers for Himself who might afterwards bear arms.

17. And these were the sons of Levi by their names Hence it appears that the tribe of Levi, like the others, had made an astonishing progress from a small and contemptible beginning; for whereas he himself had only begotten three sons, Gershon and Merari only two each, and Kohath four; who would have expected such an increase, that twelve men in so short a time should have grown into so many thousands? But thus powerfully does God work under the semblance of weakness, that thus His glory may be the more conspicuous. But that He promoted the family of Kohath above the others, not only in the priesthood of Aaron, but also in their common ministry, proceeded from the same source of His gratuitous good pleasure, as the calling of Moses. He then, who had dignified also by so honorable an office, was, for his sake, gracious also to the family of Kohath. Neverthless, lost he should be suspected of ambition, or lest occasion of calumny should be given to the ungodly, God chose that the sons of Moses should remain in the ordinary station of the Levites.

45. Take the Levites instead of all the first-born The compensation of which I have spoken follows; for, since the complete portion of God was not found in the tribe of Levi, it must needs be supplied from elsewhere. Since, then, the Levites, infants as well as men, were less by two hundred and seventy-three than the first-born of the twelve tribes of Israel, God required that five shekels of the sanctuary should be paid for every head. We have elsewhere seen that the shekel of the sanctuary was double, amounting to two ordinary ones.

Numbers 4

Numbers 4:1-3, 21-23, 29, 30, 34-49

1. And the Lord spake unto Moses and unto Aaron, saying,

1. Loquutus est Jehova ad Mosen et Aharon, dicendo:

2. Take the sum of the sons of Kohath from among the sons of Levi, after their families, by the house of their fathers,

2. Tolle summam filiorum Cehath e medio filiorum Levi, per familias suas, per domos patrum suorum.

3. From thirty years old and upward, even until fifty years old, all that enter into the host, to do the work in the tabernacle of the congregation.

3. Ab eo qui natus est triginta annos et supra, usque ad eum qui natus est quinquaginta annos, quotquot ingrediuntur congregationem, ut faciant opus in tabernaculo conventionis.

21. And the Lord spake unto Moses, saying,

21. Loquutus est Jehova ad Mosen, et Aharon dicendo:

22. Take also the sum of the sons of Gershon, throughout the houses of their fathers, by their families:

22. Tolle summam filiorum Gerson, ipsos quoque per domos patrum suormn, et per familias suas:

23. From thirty years old and upward, until fifty years old, shalt thou number them; all that enter in to perform the service, to do the work in the tabernacle of the congregation.

23. Ab eo qui natus est triginta annos et supra, usque ad eum qui est quinquaginta annorum, numerabis eos: quotquot ingrediuntur congregationem, ut faciant opus in tabernaculo conventionis.

29. As for the sons of Merari, thou shalt number them after their families, by the house of their fathers:

29. Filios Merari, per familias suas, per domos patrum suorum nu merabis:

30. From thirty years old and upward, even unto fifty years old, shalt thou number them, every one that entereth into the service, to do the work of the tabernacle of the congregation.

30. Ab eo qui natus est triginta annos et supra, usque ad eum qui natus est quinquaginta annos, numerabis eos: quotquot ingrediuntur congregationem, ut faciant opus in tabernaculo conventionis.

34. And Moses and Aaron, and the chief of the congregation, numbered the sons of the Kohathites, after their families, and after the house of their fathers,

34. Numeravit ergo Moses et Aharon et princeps congregationis filios Cehath, per familias suas, domos patrum suorum.

35. From thirty years old and upward, even unto fifty years old, every one that entereth into the service, for the work in the tabernacle of the congregation:

35. Ab eo qui natus erat triginta annos, et supra, usque ad eum qui natus erat quinquaginta annos: quotquot ingrediuntur in congregationem illam ad ministerium peragendum in tabernaculo conventionis.

36. And those that were numbered of them, by their families, were two thousand seven hundred and fifty.

36. Fueruntque numerati eorum per familias, duo millia septingenti quinquaginta.

37. These were they that were numbered of the families of the Kohathites, all that might do service in the tabernacle of the congregation, which Moses and Aaron did number, according to the commandment of the Lord, by the hand of Moses.

37. Isti sunt numerati familiarum Cehath, omnes ministrantes in tabernaculo conventionis, quos numeravit Moses et Aharon juxta imperium Jehovae per manum Mosis.

38. And those that were numbered of the sons of Gershon, throughout their families, and by the house of their fathers,

38. Numerati filiorum Gerson per familias suas, et per domum patrum suorum.

39. From thirty years old and upward, even unto fifty years old, every one that entereth into the service, for the work in the tabernacle of the congregation;

39. Ab eo qui natus erat triginta annos et supra, usque ad eum qui natus erat quinquaginta annos: quotquot ingrediuntur in congregationem illam ad ministerium peragendum in tabernaculo conventionis.

40. Even those that were numbered of them, throughout their families, by the house of their fathers, were two thousand and six hundred and thirty.

40. Numerati inquam eorum per familias suas, per domum patrum suorum, duo millia et sexcenti triginta.

41. These are they that were numbered of the families of the sons of Gershon, of all that might do service in the tabernacle of the congregation, whom Moses and Aaron did number, according to the commandment of the Lord.

41. Isti sunt numerati familiarum filiorum Gerson, omnes ministrantes in tabernaculo conventionis: quos numeravit Moses et Aharon juxta sermonem Jehovae.

42. And those that were numbered of the families of the sons of Merari, throughout their fanlilies, by the house of their fathers,

42. Numerati autem familiarum filiorum Merari per familias suas, per domos patrunt suorum.

43. From thirty years old and upward, even unto fifty years old, every one that entereth into the service, for the work in the tabernacle of the congregation;

43. Ab co qui natus erat triginta annos et supra, usque ad eum qui natus erat quinquaginta annos: quotquot ingrediebantur in congregationem illam ad ministerium peragendum in tabernaculo conventionis.

44. Even those that were numbered of them, after their families, were three thousand and two hundred.

44. Numerati inquam eorum per familias suas, tria millia et ducenti.

45. These be those that were numbered of the families of the sons of Merari, whom Moses and Aaron numbered, according to the word of the Lord by the hand of Moses.

45. Isti aunt numerati familiarum filiorum Merari, quos numeravit Moses et Aharon juxta sermonem Jehovae per manum Mosis.

46. All those that were numbered of the Levites, whom Moses and Aaron, and the chief of Israel, numbered, after their families, and after the house of their fathers,

46. Omnes numerati quos numeravit Moses et Aharon, et principes Israel, de Levitis per familias suas, et per domos patrunt suorum:

47. From thirty years old and upward, even unto fifty years old, every one that came to do the service of the ministry, and the service of the burden in the tabernacle of the congregation;

47. Ab eo qui natus erat triginta annos et supra, usque ad eum qui natus erat quinquaginta annos: quotquot ingrediebantur ad peragendum ministerium cultus, et ad peragendum oneris in tabernaculo conventionis.

48. Even those that were numbered of them, were eight thousand and five hundred and fourscore.

48.: Numerati, inquam, erarum ruerunt otto nilIlia et quingenti octoginta.

49. According to the commandment of the Lord they were numbered by the hand of Moses, every one according to his service, and according to his burden: thus were they numbered of him, as the Lord commanded Moses.

49. Juxta sermonem Jehovae numeravit eos per manum Mosis, singulos secundum ministerium suum, et secundum onus suum: numerati autem ejus fuerunt hi quos ipsi praeceperat.

1. **And the Lord spake unto Moses and unto Aaron** This census had a different object from the former one, which we have just been considering, viz., that an equal distribution of the charges should be made in proportion to the number of the individuals. First, as regarded age, a distinction must be observed between this tribe and the others; for we have already seen that all the Israelites above twenty years of age were numbered, because they were then fit to bear arms. But it was not without reason that a more mature age was required in the case of the Levites, so that they should not begin to discharge their ministry before their thirtieth year. For not only is strength and rigor of body requisite for spiritual warfare, but seriousness and gravity also. If they had been admitted in their youth, their levity might have detracted from the reverence due to sacred things, since the young are often led to act intemperately by their fervor and licentiousness. Access to the sanctuary, therefore, was not permitted them till they had grown up to be men; for by their thirtieth year men ought to have become so staid, as that it shall be base and inexcusable for them to give way to the wantonness of youth.

From their fiftieth year they were released from their duties; since sloth and inactivity generally accompany old age. The case is different as to war, because we find many who are vigorous after their fiftieth year. Furthermore, since religion is more precious than all earthly affairs, diligent care was to be taken lest it should fall into disesteem on account of the idleness and somnolency of its ministers.

34. **And Moses and Aaron and the chief of the congregation** Another exception is subjoined, viz., that none should be received unless they were free from all defect and blemish; for we have seen elsewhere that those, who were blind and lame, or defective in any part of their body, were excluded from the tabernacle, lest their disfigurement should produce contempt; and also that they might be admonished by this external sign, to preserve themselves more diligently from all spiritual defilement. Therefore, those are said to enter into the sanctuary who are fit to exercise the priesthood; and hence the expression, "for the service," [426] is added.

Inasmuch as the inequality (of their charges) might have been the source of envy, God's authority is asserted at the end of the chapter, where Moses records that he was only acting ministerially, and that he distributed the offices among them according to God's command.

Numbers 10

Numbers 10:11-28

11. **And it came to pass on the twentieth day of the second month, in the second year, that the cloud was taken up from off the tabernacle of the testimony.**

11. Fuit autem anno secundo, mense secundo, vicesima mensis, ascendit nubes a tabernaculo testimonii.

12. And the children of Israel took their journeys out of the wilderness of Sinai; and the cloud rested in the wilderness of Paran.

12. Tunc profecti sunt filii Israel per profectiones suas e deserto Sinai, substititque nubes in deserto Paran.

13. And they first took their journey, according to the commandment of the Lord by the hand of Moses.

13. Profecti itaque sunt primum ad os Jehovae per manum Mosis.

14. In the first place went the standard of the camp of the children of Judah, according to their armies: and over his host was Nahshon the son of Amminadab.

14. Et profectum est vexilium castrorum filiorum Jehuda primo loco per exercitus suos: et super exercitum ejus erat Nahason filius Amminadab.

15. And over the host of the tribe of the children of Issachar was Nethaneel the son of Zuar.

15. Super exercitum autem tribus filiorum Issachar erat Nethanel filius Suar.

16. And over the host of the tribe of the children of Zebuluu was Eliab the son of Helon.

16. Et super exercitum tribus filiorum Zabulon erat Eliab filius Helon.

17. And the tabernacle was taken down; and the sons of Gershon and the sons of Merari set forward, bearing the tabernacle.

17. Depositum autem fuerat tabernaculum: et profecti sunt filii Gerson et filii Merari portantes illum.

18. And the standard of the camp of Reuben set forward, according to their armies: and over his host was Elizur the son of Shedeur.

18. Deinde profectum est vexillum castrorum Ruben per exercitus suos: et super exercitum ejus erat Elisur filius Sedeur.

19. And over the host of the tribe of the children of Simeon, was Shelumiel the son of Zurishaddai.

19. Super exercitum vero tribus filiorum Simeon erat Selumiel filius Surisaddai.

20. And over the host of the tribe of the children of Gad was Eliasaph the son of Denel.

20. Et super exercitum tribus filiorum Gad erat Eliasaph filius Deuel.

21. And the Kohathites set forward, bearing the sanctuary; and the other did set up the tabernacle against they came.

21. Et progredi eccperunt Cehathitae portantes sanctuarium: erexerunt autem tabernaculum donec venerint ipsi.

22. And the standard of the camp of the children of Ephraim set forward, according to their armies: and over his host was Elishmna the son of Ammihud.

22. Postea profectum est vexilium castrorum filiorum Ephraim per exercitus suos: et super exercitum ejus erat Elisama filius Ammihud.

23. And over the host of the tribe of the children of Manasseh was Gamaliel the son of Pedahzur.

23. Super exercitum vero tribus filiorum Manasse erat Gamliel filius Pedahsur.

24. And over the host of the tribe the children of Benjamin was Abidan the son of Gideoni.

24. Et super exercitum tribus filiorum Benjamin erat Abidan filius Gidoni.

25. And the standard of the camp of the children of Dan set forward, which was the rere-ward of all the camps throughout their hosts: and over his host was Ahiezer the son of Ammishaddai.

25. Profectum est insuper vexillum castrorum filiorum Dan, recolligens onmia castra per exercitus suos: et, super exercitum ejus erat Ahiezer filius Ammisaddai.

26. And over the host of the tribe of the children of Asher was Pagiel the son of Ocran.

26. Super exercitum tribus filiorum Aser erat Pagiel filius Ochran.

27. And over the host of the tribe of the children of Naphtali was Ahira the son of Enan.

27. Et super exercitum tribus filiorum Nephthali erat Ahira filius Enan.

28. Thus were the journeyings of the children of Israel, according to their armies, when they set forward.

28. Istm sunt profectiones filiorum Israel per exercitus suos: ac ita profecti sunt.

11. And it came to pass on the twentieth day Moses records that after leaving Mount Sinai, the camp was first pitched in the wilderness of Paran; and although the distance was not great, -- being, as we shall soon see, a three days' journey, -- still the fatigue was sufficient to harass and weary the people. It is mentioned in praise of their obedience that they were expeditious in setting forth "according to the commandment of God;" but presently, through failure of the spirit of perseverance, their levity and inconstancy betrayed itself.

When it is said that "they journeyed by their journeyings," (profectos esse per suas profectiones,) it refers to their whole progress through the desert. As to the word, I know not why Jerome translated it turmas, (troops,) for its root; is the verb נסע nasang, which is used with it; and according to its constant use in Scripture, it plainly means stations, [427] or halting-places. We say in Frealch journees, or gistes.

14. In the first place went the standard of the camp The actual order of march is here described. The whole people, with the exception of the Levites, is divided into four hosts, or parts, since four of the tribes were set over the others, so as to have two under the command of each. And this was the mode of proceeding, that whenever they halted anywhere, the four standards encompassed the sanctuary and the Ark of the Covenant from the four quarters of the world; whilst on the march, the Levites carrying the tabernacle, according to the burdens respectively imposed upon them, were mixed with the several bands. The Ark, borne upon the shoulders of the Levites, preceded the whole army, in order that all might more confidently follow, God thus manifestly shewing them the way. Nahshon, of the tribe of Judah, led the first host; Elizur, of the tribe of Reuben, the second; Elishama, of the tribe of Ephraim, the third; and Ahiezer, of the tribe of Dan, the fourth. It is obvious that in the precedency given to the tribe of Judah, God in some degree afforded an anticipation of the prophecy of Jacob; for the Reubenites, being descended from the first-born, would not have willingly abandoned their position, unless that right had been transferred to the tribe of Judah by God's decree, pronounced through the mouth of Jacob. Not that the sovereignty and royal power was actually his before the time of David, but because God would have a single spark to shine in the midst of the thick darkness, whereby He might

cherish the hope of the promised salvation in every heart; and that thus the dignity of this tribe might at length more readily reduce all to obedience. Herein, however, it appeared how perverse and intractable was the spirit of that greater portion of them who strove against the divine decree in their rejection of David.

Reuben occupied the second place, as an alleviation of his disgrace. Again, by the subjection of the tribe of Manasseh to the posterity of Ephraim, in this respect, too, the prophecy of the same patriarch was fulfilled. Nor does there seem to be any other reason why the fourth standard should have been given to the tribe of Dan, except because Jacob had declared, "Dan shall judge his people." (Genesis 49:16,) by which expression his pre-eminence was denoted.

Although it may be that the four standard-bearing tribes were chosen from their strength and the numbers of their people, still, unless the children of Reuben and Manasseh had been thoroughly persuaded that their degradation was in accordance with the command of God, their jealousy would never have suffered them calmly to submit themselves to others, whose superiors they were by the ordinary rules of nature. Their self-restraint, therefore, was praiseworthy, in that voluntary subjection kept them within bounds, without the application of any power of compulsion; and at the end, Moses records that it was not once only that they thus advanced, but that they observed the same order and regulations during the whole course of their travel, and that their camp was always so arranged that no contention arose to disturb them.

Footnotes:

391. Lat. "Fecialis munere;" alluding doubtless to the custom of the Roman Feciales, in throwing a bloody spear into the territories of others as a declaration of war. See Liv. 1:32.

392. "Il appelle le veau Peche du peuple, pource qu'il avoit este la matiere et object de leur idolatrie;" he calls the calf the Sin of the people, because it had been the matter and object of their idolatry. -- Fr.

393. See Margin, A.V.

394. See [60]ante.

395. "Lors qu'il a este assis en son droit lieu, et legitime, assavoir au milieu du peuple duquel il avoit este comme estranger;" when it was fixed in its right and legitimate place, that is to say, in the midst of the people, to whom it had been, as it were, a stranger. -- Fr.

396. See [61]ante.

397. See on Leviticus 6:25, ante, [62]vol. 2, p. 366.

398. "Aaron, ayant este cree auparavant Sacrificateur." -- Fr.

399. Quaest. in Leviticus 84. Edit. Bened. tom. 3, p. 524.

400. So Vatablus, quoted in Poole. "In Leviticus 11:29, (says Ainsworth,) צב (tsab) is a tortoise, so called from the shell that covereth it: accordingly here they may be called עגלת צב, (gnegeloth tsab,) waggons of the tortoise, (or of covering,) because they were like to a tortoise, covered above."

401. V., mortariolum. LXX.,: θυΐσκη Ainsworth, cup. Heb., כן from whence probably our English word cup.

402. שקל shekel, from שקל, shakal, to weigh. C. follows LXX. in renderining גרה gerah, -- the twentieth part of a shekel, -- by the word obolus, ὀβολός The general opinion of modern commentators

is, that the shekel, throughout the Old Testament, expressed not a coin, but a weight of about half an ounce Troy, which would bring its value in silver, at a rough calculation, to 2s. 6d., and in gold to 2 Pounds sterling: though indeed it appears impossible to ascertain either the intrinsic or relative value of the precious metals at so early a period with anything like accuracy. The Rabbins (see Ainsworth) consider the estimate of the golden vessels to have been made by the shekel of silver.

403. "Que la compagnie a suyvi son chef: car les douze lignees," etc.; that the company followed its chief; for the twelve tribes, etc.-- Fr.

404. This sentence is omitted in Fr.

405. "For the sin-offering." -- A. V.

406. "Et voyla pourquoy les bestes ont porte le nom d'offense;" and behold wherefore the beasts bore the name of offence. -- Fr. "Piaculum; sacrum piaculare, et quicquid ad piandum et purgandum pertinet. Metonymice, ipsa res, qum piaculi causa adhibetur; sic AEn. 6:153. Duc nigos pecudes: ea prima piacula sunto." -- Facciolati.

407. See ante, [63]vol. 2, p. 211.

408. A. V., "Mine ears hast thou opened." Margin, "Heb., digged." See C.'s translation and note. Cal. Soc. edit., [64]vol. 2, p. 99.

409. This quotation is much abbreviated. C.'s exposition of the passage, (Cal. Soc. edit., [65]vol. 1, p. 393,) and Mr. Owen's [66]note, are worthy of consultation.

410. Heb., תנופה, thenuphah. See ante, [67]vol. 2, p. 132, and [68]note

411. See ante, [69]vol. 2, p. 133.

412. Ibid., [70]p.26.

413. "That ye should do." -- A. V.

414. See ante on Numbers 6:22-27, [71]vol. 2, p. 245 et seq.

415. Addition in Fr., "Auquel ceste dignita a este commise;" to whom this dignity has been entrusted.

416. A. V., "I will be sanctified;" and so also C.'s own version; but he embodies the two clauses. Some, as De Lyra, refer this to Exodus 19:22; Others to Exodus 29:43. "Some think it was spoken, but not written, as many things beside. Oleaster, Lorinus, Caietan; but," adds Willet, "they are of this mind, that they may have here some show for their unwritten traditions. Therefore," he concludes, "without any more circumstance, we find this to have been spoken, Leviticus 8:35, Keep ye the Lord's charge, that ye die not;' there they are commanded to observe the Lord's ordinances, which he gave them, (Junius;) and because Nadab and Abihu did not so, they are punished with death."

417. "Se polluassent en portant les corps morts de leurs freres;" should pollute themselves by carrying the dead bodies of their brothers. -- Fr. Blunt has a very ingenious conjecture that Mishael and Elzaphan were the very persons "defiled by the dead body of a man," mentioned in Numbers 9:6, 7, and who therefore could not keep the Passover. "The Veracity of the Five Books of Moses." Art. 14. But surely, out of such a large body of persons, there must have been many deaths daily, and consequently others would have been defiled besides Mishael and Elzaphan.

418. Added from Fr.

419. Among them. -- A. V.

420. So the Vulgate, v. 48.

421. This is a singular oversight of C., which is also copied in the French; "Pource qu'elles estoyent descendues de la chambriere de Lea;" because they were descended from the handmaid of Leah. It is perhaps still more strange that Attersoll in his Commentary on the Book of Numbers should have adopted it, evidently following C.; "He (Judah) was the fourth son of Jacob by Leah, with whom he associateth such two tribes as were in reason most likely to submit themselves to him, inasmuch as Zebulun and Issachar were the sons of Zilpah, Leah's maid, whom she gave to her husband, and set in her own place." I need scarcely remind my readers that Gad and Asher were the sons of Zilpah, and Zebulun and Issachar of Leah herself.

422. Attersoll seems to have correctly, though somewhat quaintly, interpreted here the meaning of C., which else perhaps may not be quite clear; "from hence might hurly-burlies and heart-burnings arise, which are all pacified and compounded by the express commandment of God, who joineth to Dan, Naphtali his mother's son, (for both of them were the sons of Bilhah, Rachel's maid,) and Asher, the son of Zilpah, Leah's maid." -- Commentary on numbers in loco.

423. Viz., verses 5-10. See ante, [72]vol. 2, p. 220.

424. "Quant a ce que Moyse touche ici des charges particulieres de chacune famille, combien que cela concerne le service duquel il a este traitte sur le Seconde Precepte, toutefois je n'ay peu aucunement faire, que de la mettre ici, afin que le fil de l'histoire ne fust point rompu;" with respect to the reference here made by Moses to the peculiar charge of each family, although it relates to the service which has been treated of under the Second Commandment, nevertheless I could not do otherwise than introduce it here, in order that the thread of the history might not be interrupted. -- Fr.

425. "Moins que la douzieme partie;" less than the twelfth part. -- Fr.

426. "For the work." -- A. V. Ver. 35.

427. "Stationibus, vel auspiciis;" the latter being evidently a misprint for hospitiis. -- Lat. "Gistum, hospitium, susceptio; Gall, giste; jus, quod dominis feudalibus competebat in vassallorum suorum praediis, qui staffs ae condietis vicibus eos in domibus suis hospitio, et conviviis excipere tenebantur. Quod quidem jus Mansionaticum sub prima et secunda Regum Francorum stirpe, sub tertia vero Gistum, Procuratio, Coenaticum, Comestio, Pastus, Prandium dictum suis locis observamus." -- Adelung's Du Cange.

www.ingramcontent.com/pod-product-compliance
Lightning Source LLC
Chambersburg PA
CBHW060325100426
42812CB00003B/885